# THE CALLING OF AN EVANGELIST

# THE CALLING OF AN EVANGELIST

*The Second International Congress*
*for Itinerant Evangelists*
*Amsterdam, The Netherlands*

*Edited by J.D. Douglas*

WORLD WIDE PUBLICATIONS
1303 Hennepin Avenue
Minneapolis, Minnesota 55403
U.S.A.

41-43

PUBLISHER'S NOTE

All the Plenary Sessions and Seminars at Amsterdam 86 have been included in this volume. However, only a few of the many workshops have been included. This is no reflection on the content of the many excellent workshops but a necessity of putting the conference into one published volume.

Many of the talks were transcribed from tape and it is our hope that each session included remains faithful to the speaker's intent. And because there is such a diversity of views expressed in this collection it is necessary to point out that these views do not necessarily reflect in every instance the views of the leadership of the International Conference for Itinerant Evangelists of the Billy Graham Evangelistic Association.

*The Calling of an Evangelist.* ©1987 World Wide Publications; All Rights Reserved.
Published by World Wide Publications.
1303 Hennepin Avenue,
Minneapolis, Minnesota 55403, U.S.A.

Library of Congress Catalog
Card Number: 87-050275
ISBN 0-89066-087-5

Printed in the U.S.A.

# EDITORIAL PREFACE

Our previous volume, *The Work of An Evangelist*, contained a selection of addresses given at Amsterdam 83. The message has not changed, so why another book for Amsterdam 86 that goes over the same ground? Because there is much new material here, spoken to a new (and larger) audience by many speakers who did not appear on the platform three years ago—and even those who did were now three years wiser!

There are some differences in this second volume. It is rather smaller, so that many more copies of a convenient size can be made available for distribution worldwide. While the plenary addresses are given more or less in full, workshop material has been reduced by tighter editing and by avoiding more obvious duplication. Some workshop leaders, moreover, worked only with an outline, others used videos and other forms of illustration not easily translatable into cold print. And it was not practicable to reproduce the lively discussions that followed many such sessions.

It is a sign of health in a conference that speakers reflect a wide variety of approach and content, even if now and then these are not necessarily the views of the Conference organizers.

The task of preparing this book has been lightened by many colleagues and encouragers, notably Dr. John Corts and Carol Mellott of the ICIE Program Department; and Dr. George M. Wilson, DeWayne Herbrandson, and Kathy Ganz TerMeer of World Wide Publications. And, of course, by the ready cooperation of speakers who told so vividly of laboring in very different fields toward the same Great Harvest.

—J.D. Douglas

# CONTENTS

## III.   Various Methods of Evangelism

*Plenary Sessions

# OPENING WORDS
*Billy Graham*

What a marvelous sight it has been to see these banners representing 174 countries of the world! We've been told by the United Nations that this conference of evangelists in Amsterdam may be the most representative conference ever held, secular or religious, in the history of the world.

I heard about a preacher who dreamed that he was preaching—and he awoke, and he discovered that he was!

This is like the way I feel tonight, and many of you also are suffering from jet lag and are tired from long travel, and getting adjusted to Amsterdam.

No one knows better than I the price you pay to be evangelists in times like these. Some of you come with scars, physical signs of suffering for Christ's sake. Among you, there are some who have been beaten, stoned, imprisoned, slapped, punched, kicked, even shot and left for dead.

Some of you come weary, burned out, close to tears—emotional signs of suffering for Christ's sake. Some of you have been rejected, scorned, ridiculed, mocked, ignored, harassed, hounded, overworked, underpaid, misunderstood, even despised by family, friends, neighbors, leaders in the towns and villages, states and nations where you minister.

Others of you suffer from psychological scars. Many of you have problems that you seemingly cannot overcome. Personal problems, marriage problems, financial problems, problems of doubt.

But there are many of you who come from thrilling evangelistic efforts where you have seen many people come to Christ. There are others of you who have come from countries where a spiritual revival and renewal is under way. You have seen great and powerful movements of the Holy Spirit.

With our different backgrounds, we have come to share with each other our victories, our problems, and our defeats.

We have been warmly welcomed by the people of the Netherlands. Their culture is totally different from the culture from which many of you come. There will be things that you will see and hear that will excite you, thrill you, and shock you. There are tens of thousands of true believers in this country. They love Christ, and they are praying for the success of this conference.

Therefore, I want to take this opportunity to thank the people of the Netherlands, and especially Amsterdam, for the wonderful hospitality and cooperation that we have received from the churches, from the government, from the airlines (particularly KLM), and especially the RAI Center, which is one of the most beautiful and extensive conference centers in the world. I am certain that those of you who have been here even for a few hours recognize that this is one of the most beautiful and historic cities in all of Europe, and we are deeply grateful for the privilege of meeting here.

Also, from the very beginning, I want to take this opportunity to thank Dr. Walter Smyth and the Reverend Werner Burklin, Bob Williams, John Corts, and others who have been here for many months with a large staff of over one hundred working in preparation for this conference. Their task has been tremendous, handling many thousands of inquiries, finding beds for each of you, arranging for your travel from so many different parts of the world, arranging for food, and the millions of other details to try to make your stay here as comfortable as possible. Many of them have been working extremely long hours with very little sleep so that we could be here at this hour today.

Why have we come together? What is God's agenda for this gathering? I am sure we do not know all that God will do through our time together, because He "is able to do immeasurably more than all we ask or imagine" (Ephesians 3:20). But it has been my prayer, and the prayer of all who have had a part in planning this conference, that at least three things would be accomplished in our lives. I am praying that God will do these things in my life, and that He will do them in the life of every one of you who have come to Amsterdam 86.

When many of us left here three years ago, we were sad to learn that there were thousands of other qualified evangelists who had to be turned away because of lack of finances, lack of room, etc. When we started out to plan Amsterdam 83 we did not know how many evangelists there were in the world. We thought there might be five hundred or a thousand—it turned out to be nearly 50,000. Unfortunately, we have had to turn away thousands of requests to come to Amsterdam 86. Thus, each of us has a tremendous responsibility while we are here to get all that we can in our hearts and in our notebooks and from our Bibles, to take back and share with our brothers and sisters in the places from which we come.

First, let us pray that we will be renewed spiritually in our personal lives. I have come here spiritually depleted. I have a longing to rededicate myself to Christ in a deeper way than ever before. I have a longing to be overflowing with the presence and power of the Holy Spirit when I leave here. I am looking to our fellowship and the messages we hear and the prayer meetings to which we go to re-equip me for the task that I have even during the rest of this year in the proclamation of the Gospel. I am sure that Cliff Barrows and other members of my Team share this same sense of spiritual need.

Second, let us pray that God will give to each of us new tools to help us be more effective witnesses for Christ in our ministry. I do not mean technological tools. I mean spiritual tools. Perhaps a greater knowledge of the Bible. Perhaps a clearer understanding of the Gospel. Perhaps a new motive for giving our time and effort.

In addition, God may show us some new tools of presenting the Gospel through films, television, radio, and many of the other things that you are going to see demonstrated here. That is why there will be addresses and workshops on various topics— such as the content of the Gospel, every facet of our personal lives, sermon preparation, finances, working with churches, and setting up city- or village-wide evangelistic efforts, or single churches, or street ministry. We represent many cultures and ethnic groups. Our backgrounds are different, and our needs are different. But I believe God wants to equip us during this conference to be better and more effective instruments in His hands.

Third, let us pray that God will give each of us a fresh vision of our task. We live in a time which is without parallel in the history of the human race. It is a time of world revolution and change. History cannot repeat itself. We are the first generation that has the awesome capacity to destroy mankind from the face of this planet, because of the development of incredible weapons of mass destruction. But we also have within our hands technological breakthroughs in communication which make it possible to reach every corner of the earth with the Gospel in this decade of the eighties. Let us therefore ask God to give us a fresh vision, a vision of the world that is outside Christ, a world for which Christ died, a world which is filled with fear, guilt, chaos, and spiritual emptiness. Let us pray that God will give us a fresh vision of our calling as evangelists.

The gift of the evangelist is as valid today as it was in the first century. May each of us go from Amsterdam with a new commitment to "do the work of an evangelist" (2 Timothy 4:5).

I do not believe any of us are here by chance. God has brought each one of us here for a purpose. May God set us ablaze with fire from off the altar. May the Holy Spirit descend on us in mighty pentecostal power. This is the word of the Lord: "Not by might, nor by power, but by my Spirit, saith the Lord of hosts" (Zechariah 4:6).

Let us all say it together: "NOT BY MIGHT, NOR BY POWER, BUT BY MY SPIRIT, SAITH THE LORD OF HOSTS."

# I

# THE EVANGELIST
# AS A PERSON

# THE EVANGELIST AND THE PERSONAL LIFE OF HOLINESS
*Stephen F. Olford*

*Reading: 1 Timothy 6:11-16*

*Text: "But thou, O man of God, flee these things; and follow after righteousness, godliness, faith, love, patience, meekness. Fight the good fight of faith, lay hold on eternal life . . ." (6:11,12).*

Paul wrote two letters to Timothy, his son in the faith. In the first, the apostle calls him a "man of God" (6:11); and, in the second, he exhorts him to "preach the word . . . and . . . do the work of an evangelist" (4:2,5). The order here is significant. It implies that before we can discharge our task as preachers of the Gospel we must be known as men of God. What we are is far more important than what we do. Indeed, if what we are does not satisfy the demands of God, then what we do is virtually worthless. Let us then consider these solemn words to young Timothy as a preacher and evangelist. Observe three imperatives that must be fleshed out in our lives, if we are going to be used as men of God in the ministry of the Gospel:

1. *The evangelist must flee the vices of the ministry*
    ". . . O man of God, flee these things . . ." (1 Timothy 6:11). As we study the immediate context, we find that it is divided into two main parts; the first has to do with false teachers, while the other has to do with wrong values. As Paul reflects upon what he has written on these two matters he pleads, "O man of God, flee these things . . ." (6:11). There are two vices that have to be shunned:
    a. *There is the vice of Liberalism*—"If any man teach otherwise, and consent not to [the] wholesome words, even the words of our Lord Jesus Christ, and to the doctrine which is according to godliness . . . from such withdraw thyself" (6:3-5). In Paul's day, there were liberal teachers and evangelists—just as we have them in our time—and Paul was most concerned that young Timothy not be caught up in the "battle of words" which characterized their ministry.
    William Barclay reminds us: "The circumstances of life, in the ancient world, presented the false teacher with an opportunity which he was not slow to take. On the Christian side, the church was full of wandering prophets, whose very way of life gave them a certain prestige. Christian [worship] was much more informal than it is now. Anyone who felt he had a message was free to give it; and the door was wide open to men who were out to propagate a false and misleading message. On the pagan side, the ancient world knew all about the wandering [itinerant], the so-called philosopher who was out for gain. There were men who were called Sophists, which means 'wise men.' These men made it their business, so to speak, to sell philosophy. They had two lines. For a fee they claimed to be able to teach men to speak well and to argue cleverly; they were men who with their smooth tongue and their adroit minds were skilled in 'making the worst appear the better reason.' They had turned philosophy into a way of becoming rich and well-to-do. Their other line was to give demonstrations of public speaking. The Greeks have always been fascinated by the spoken word; they loved an orator; and these itinerant Sophists went from town to town giving their oratorical demonstrations. They went in for advertising on an intensive

scale. They even went the length of delivering by hand personal invitations to their displays. The most famous of them drew people literally by the thousands to their lectures; they were in their day the equivalent of the modern film stars" (*The Letters to Timothy, Titus and Philemon*, 1960, p. 143).

This, then, was the climate and context in which Paul was warning Timothy. It is a fact that when an evangelist, a preacher, or a pastor rejects the sound or healthy words of the Gospel he succumbs to a spiritual sickness which manifests itself in a subversive liberalism. And I might add that this is happening right now among well-known names in our evangelical world. Were it not for the keeping power of the grace of God, I would be scared to death! When this liberalism begins to influence our preaching four things happen:

(i)    *Our message becomes corrupted.* We no longer ". . . consent . . . to [the] wholesome words . . . of our Lord Jesus Christ . . ." (6:3). The verb "consent" suggests the act of one who accepts another's offer. The liberal refuses to accept the simple words of the Gospel and settles for "another gospel" (Galatians 1:6,9). Instead of being determined, like the apostle Paul, to know nothing but ". . . Jesus Christ, and him crucified" (1 Corinthians 2:2), he tends to focus on national politics, social concerns, liberation theology, and other attractive subjects. I know evangelists who were once flaming prophets of the Gospel who are now so sidetracked with their own hobbyhorses that the message of the Gospel no longer comes through with searching clarity and saving power. I am not suggesting that some of the above-mentioned issues should not be addressed in our contemporary times; but when they take precedence over the centrality of Christ and the simplicity of the Gospel, the divine power of preaching is annulled and the glory departs. No wonder Paul warns: ". . . though we, or an angel from heaven, preach any other gospel unto you than that which we have preached unto you, let him be accursed" (Galatians 1:8).

(ii)    *Our mindset becomes conceited*—"If any man teach otherwise . . . he is proud, knowing nothing" (6:3,4). In pronouncing this verdict, Paul uses strong language. He tells us that a preacher like this is blinded by conceit. Williams renders it, "he is a conceited ignoramus." It is impossible to reason with anyone thus minded.

I have spent unnumbered hours trying to straighten out men who are too proud to listen to words of caution or counsel. Such evangelists strut about like peacocks, call the shots wherever they go, and make unreasonable demands. These men do more harm than can be estimated this side of eternity; yet tens of thousands of people watch them on television or crusade platforms, because of their natural charisma and attractive oratory.

(iii)    Our manner becomes contentious—"If any man teach otherwise . . . he [becomes obsessed with questions and disputes] of words, [of which come] envy, strife, railings, evil [suspicions], perverse disputings of men of corrupt minds, and destitute of the truth . . ." (6:3-5). Paul enumerates five social consequences which flow from this mentally-deceived condition. Worse still is the spiritual character of the men who are occupied with such teaching. They are described as ". . . men of corrupt minds, and destitute of the truth."

I have lived long enough to know of organizations that were allegedly committed to evangelism that have been torn apart because of contentiousness. Millions of dollars have been expended in charges and countercharges in an attempt to justify their own point of view; and this goes on continually in our Christian world—to the delight of the devil and to the disgrace of our Lord.

(iv)    *Our motive becomes commercial*—". . . supposing that gain is godliness" (6:5). When an evangelist departs from the truth he soon finds himself involved in commercialism. He makes himself believe that a show of godliness is a profitable investment, a lucrative business, advancing one's worldly interests. I shall return to this matter of covetousness in a moment; but suffice it to say here that the love of gain is a deadly vice, when it grips a man in the ministry—especially an evangelist! We should shun it like the plague!

Even though some manuscripts omit the words at the end of verse 5, the warning still stands; for with the vice of liberalism in mind Paul cautions: ". . . from such withdraw thyself" (6:5). It is the popular thing today to be liberal in doctrine and, therefore, loose in behavior. With eroding standards in the pulpit and in the pew, we are thought naive and outdated when we conform to the wholesome words of our Lord Jesus Christ. God make you and me faithful to the Gospel—cost what it may!

So there is the vice of liberalism. But Paul speaks of another vice:

b.   *There is the vice of Mammonism*—". . . they that will be rich fall into temptation and a snare, and into many foolish and hurtful lusts, which drown men in destruction and perdition. For the love of money is the root of all evil: which while some coveted after, they have erred from the faith, and pierced themselves through with many sorrows" (6:9,10). Jesus warned us that we ". . . cannot serve God and mammon" (Matthew 6:24). Mammon is the worship of wealth or riches. There is nothing wrong with money, in and of itself. It is the *love* of money that poses the problem. The apostle is here quoting a secular proverb which reads, ". . . the love of money is the metropolis [or world] of every evil . . ." (William Hendriksen, *Commentary on 1 and 2 Timothy*, 1957, p. 200). While there is some difference of opinion as to whether or not the verse should read "a root" or "the root of all kinds of evil" is immaterial. While there are other roots or sources of evil besides the love of money, such as bitterness (see Hebrews 12:15), and unforgivingness (see Ephesians 4:30-32), the love of money is indeed a root of all kinds of evil (6:10).

You will remember that it caused the man with many flocks and herds, in Nathan's parable, to steal the poor man's lamb (see 2 Samuel 12:1-7). It caused the handsome young ruler to turn away from Christ (see Luke 18:23). It caused the rich fool to deceive himself into thinking all was well when, indeed, he was on the brink of hell (see Luke 12:16-20). And perhaps saddest of all, it caused Ananias and Sapphira to lie to the Holy Spirit and bring great distress upon the early church at Jerusalem (see Acts 5:1-11). The desire for money has been the cause of innumerable frauds, dollar-sign marriages, shameful divorces, and ruined ministries.

One of the papers I had to prepare in my college days concerned the failure of men of the pulpit throughout the centuries. I must confess I was greatly shocked to discover that if such men did not go astray theologically or morally, they inevitably wrecked their ministries on the rock of material gain. It is sad to have to state it—and yet it is unquestionably true—that our religious world is just full of pastors and evangelists who are nothing more than financial rapists. Whether permanent or itinerant in their ministries, they are forever after money, and are not only destroying the work of the Lord, but also dishonoring His name.

It is important to notice how this vice of mammonism develops:

(i)   *Mammonism starts with a lure*—". . . they that will be rich fall into temptation and a snare . . ." (6:9). There is something very attractive about being rich, and evangelists are not immune. In fact, many of them preach a "health and wealth gospel" for this very reason.

I remember being in the Philippines for a series of meetings. After having visited some of the poverty-stricken areas of one of the islands, I was taken to a hotel to stay. I felt embarrassed to be in the relative comfort of a room that had a television set. I was even more shocked when I turned the TV on and heard an evangelist from the United States telling his viewers of the Cadillacs he possessed, and how the Lord had provided them all. There he was, with a psychedelic suit, shiny shoes, and a red flower attached to his lapel, telling poverty-stricken people that if they would only trust God they could be as rich as he. Later that day I was interviewed by the press. The first question I was asked was whether I preached the "health and wealth gospel." My reply was a resounding "No!" And then I went on to state that I followed a Christ who was born in a stable, had nowhere to lay His head during His itinerant ministry, was nailed to a cross, and laid to rest in a borrowed tomb—a Christ who challenged His followers to deny themselves, take up the cross, and follow Him.

Fellow evangelists, I warn you: Beware of the lure of mammon!

(ii)    *Mammonism leads to a lust.* The Word says, ". . . they that will be rich fall into . . . many foolish and hurtful lusts . . ." (6:9). That word "lust" suggests an insatiable passion which stops at nothing. It affects not only individuals, but also religious organizations.

Jeffrey K. Hadden, a University of Virginia sociologist, notes that churches, synagogues, and their charities take in 25 billion dollars a year—more than the sales of all but eleven of the largest U.S. corporations. "It's a serious matter," he says, "when donors can no longer be sure that their money is being spent honestly and well." Many church historians relate the surge in financial scandals to the growth of ministries operating outside the financial control of major denominations (James Mann, "Why Churches Get Into Money Muddles," *U.S. News & World Report*, August 16, 1982, p. 36).

*The Wall Street Journal* in an article on "The Electric Church" (June, 1979) reported that astronomical sums of money pass through the hands of TV preachers—as much as a quarter-of-a-billion dollars. Yet it is a well-known fact that financial statements that account for the donations are scarcer than hen's teeth. Most of the giving is done by born-again people who were saved in local churches. Such people generously support TV preachers and programs that give them practically no accounting of funds and are unable to furnish vital personal service when needed, while they sit idly by, watching their own church struggle and die for lack of tithes and offerings ("Big, Big Business," Editorial, *Florida Baptist Witness*, August 3, 1978, p. 4). You know as well as I do that this passion for wealth comes through most of the appeals you hear on the radio broadcasts, or you see on the telecasts, or you read in the newsletters. Nothing could be more hurtful or harmful to the evangelist and his ministry.

But it goes even further than this:

(iii)    *Mammonism ends with a lostness*—". . . they that will be rich [are drowned] in destruction and perdition" (6:9). The term "destruction" relates to the ruin of body and soul, while "perdition" warns of the loss of the soul for all eternity. Indeed, Paul employs the word "drowned" to give the picture of a man sinking in the turbulent waves of a materialistic world. This whole matter of mammonism raises the question of our responsibility and accountability as men who handle money in the very cause of the Gospel. It is true that those who ". . . preach the gospel should live of the gospel" (1 Corinthians 9:14); and that ". . . the laborer is worthy of his hire . . ." (Luke 10:7). But how careful we should be that we are never caught up in the lure, lust, and lostness of mammonism.

Dr. G. Campbell Morgan recalls that when the Salvation Army started its work General William Booth was charged with dishonesty. People said that all the property was in his name and that he, at any time, might have converted that property into money and appropriated it for himself. That was the criticism of the work. However, from the very first, he was careful to publish his accounts, and in the process of the years that criticism ceased entirely. God make us men of integrity and honesty, when it comes to the question of money!

So we have seen what the evangelist has to flee. There is the vice of liberalism and mammonism. Paul says, ". . . flee these things . . ." (6:11). It is important to observe that the tense here stresses the continuing duty; so the word to you and me is: Be ever fleeing. We must never let these things catch up with us. The devil is subtle; therefore, we must maintain a margin of safety by walking in the light, knowing that ". . . the blood of Jesus Christ [God's] Son [goes on cleansing and protecting] us from all sin" (1 John 1:7).

This brings us to our second consideration:

2. *The evangelist must follow the virtues of the ministry*

"O man of God . . . follow after righteousness, godliness, faith, love, patience, meekness" (6:11). It goes without saying that, under the inspiration of the Holy Spirit, Paul has chosen these words carefully. I agree with most expositors of God's Word that these virtues go in couplets and represent three important aspects of the evangelist as a man of God.

a. *He must be a holy man*—". . . follow after righteousness [and] godliness . . ." (6:11). There is a sense in which "righteousness" and "godliness" are the two sides of the coin of holiness. "Righteousness" is our relation to God, whereas "godliness" is our reflection of God. In this context, righteousness means *maturity in the Word of God*, for we are reminded that ". . . every one that useth milk is unskillful in the word of righteousness: for he is a babe" (Hebrews 5:13). What a challenge this brings to you and me! Are we men of the Word? What about our devotional life? Is it disciplined and consistent? We are only as tall in the pulpit as we are on our knees in the study; or as Donald Grey Barnhouse put it: "The man who is to thunder in the court of Pharaoh with an imperious 'Thus saith the Lord' must first stand barefooted before the burning bush" (*We Prepare and Preach*, p. 30).

Before I leave this matter of maturity in the Word of God, I want to make a plea for expository preaching in our evangelistic message. I have never used any other method, and I believe God has honored this with solid results in reaching saints and sinners alike. Anointed expository preaching need never be heavy, complicated, or lacking in evangelistic fervor. On the contrary, it brings people back to the Bible, back to the reality of God, back to the power of the Gospel.

A well-known businessman said: "Like most laymen, I go to church to hear the mind of Christ, not the mind of man. I want to hear expounded the timeless truths contained in the Scriptures, the kind of preaching that gets its power from 'Thus saith the Lord.'" Such preaching is hard to find these days. We must remember that the Holy Spirit only answers to the Word; souls are ". . . born again, not of corruptible seed, but of incorruptible, by the word of God, which liveth and abideth for ever" (1 Peter 1:23). Paul urges Timothy to "preach the word; . . . [and] . . . do the work of an evangelist" (2 Timothy 4:2,5).

But we must go on to note that righteousness means *conformity to the will of God*—". . . every one that doeth righteousness is born of him" (1 John 2:29). Holiness of life is not an option, but rather an outcome and obligation of a man who is truly born of God. If such holiness is not apparent, then our testimony is worthless.

After the death of the saintly Robert Murray McCheyne, a letter addressed to him was found locked in his desk, a letter which he had never shown to anyone. The writer said that McCheyne had been the means of leading him to Christ, and it concluded, "It was nothing you said that made me wish to be a Christian; it was rather the beauty of holiness which I saw in your face!'' (Henry G. Bosch, ''The Beauty of Holiness,'' *Our Daily Bread*, Radio Bible Class, July 29, 1972). Can that be said of you or of me?

Righteousness means *activity in the work of God.* John speaks of ''. . . the righteousness of saints'' (Revelation 19:8). All we do and say should be characterized by moral rectitude and ministerial integrity which result from a right relationship to God. Our preaching, like our living, should be a righteous activity.

Dr. A. W. Tozer once said, ''I've heard all kinds of preachers. I've heard the ignorant boasters; I've heard the dull, dry ones; I've heard the eloquent ones; but the ones who have helped me most were the ones who were awestruck in the presence of the God about whom they spoke. They might have a sense of humor, they might be jovial; but when they talked about God another tone came into their voice altogether; this was something else, something wonderful. I believe we ought to have again the old biblical concept of God which makes God awful and makes men lie face down and cry, 'Holy, Holy, Holy, Lord God Almighty.' That would do more for the church than . . . anything else . . .'' (quoted by A.L. Sorenson, *Pulpit Helps*, April 1979, p. 1).

But then there is ''godliness'' which is a reflection of God. As I think of this aspect of holiness, I am reminded of the Shunamite woman who entertained Elisha in her home. After some days she said to her husband, ''I perceive that this is a holy man of God, which passeth by us continually'' (2 Kings 4:9). As people observe us in the home, on the crusade platform, and over the meal table, can they truly call us holy men of God? After all, this is what really matters!

Alexander Maclaren once told a group of ministers: ''The first, second, and third requisite for our work is personal godliness; without that, though [we] have tongues of men and angels, [we are] harsh and discordant as sounding brass, monstrous and unmusical as tinkling cymbals . . . It takes a crucified man to preach a crucified Savior'' (quoted by A.L. Sorenson, *Pulpit Helps*, March 1979).

As evangelists we must be holy, even as God is holy (see 1 Peter 1:16). Holiness must permeate and activate every area of our lives. Without holiness we shall never see God, leave alone serve Him (see Hebrews 12:14).

But there is another couplet of virtue:

b. *He must be a happy man*—''. . . follow after . . . faith [and] love . . .'' (6:11). Paul's favorite words are ''faith,'' ''hope,'' and ''love'' (see 1 Corinthians 13:13). These have been described as ''the summation of Christian doctrine and duty'' (W. Griffiths Thomas). But here the apostle employs just the two—''faith'' and ''love.'' ''The one may be termed the hand that lays hold of God's mercy; and the other, the mainspring of the Christian life'' (Spence). In practical terms, they are ''trust'' and ''obedience.'' Faith is trusting Christ, and love is obeying Christ. How true are those familiar words:

> Trust and obey,
> For there's no other way
> To be *happy* in Jesus,
> But to trust and obey.

It follows, therefore, that:

(i) *Happiness is a life of faith*—''. . . follow after . . . faith . . .'' (6:11). ''. . . without faith it is impossible to please [God] . . .'' (Hebrews 11:6). We live by faith (see Romans 1:17), we pray by faith (see Matthew 21:22), we fight by faith (see Ephesians 6:16), we win by faith (see 1 John 5:4), we die by faith (see Hebrews 11:13). No wonder the Bible says, ''. . . whoso trusteth in the Lord, happy is he''

(Proverbs 16:20). There is no greater ambition that you and I can have than to *please the Lord.* And as we have observed already, we do this by faith, and faith grows and glows as we look off to ". . . Jesus the author and finisher of . . . faith" (Hebrews 12:2). Faith grows and glows as we live in the Word of God, for ". . . faith cometh by hearing, and hearing by the word of God" (Romans 10:17); faith grows and glows as we lean on the Spirit, for ". . . the fruit of the Spirit is . . . faith" (Galatians 5:22). Faith is

> Simply trusting every day,
> Trusting through a stormy way;
> Even when my faith is small,
> Trusting Jesus, that is all.

Happy is the evangelist whose trust is in the Lord!

(ii) *Happiness is a life of love*—". . . follow after . . . love . . ." (6:11). The Bible teaches that ". . . the fruit of the Spirit is love" (Galatians 5:22); and again: ". . . the love of God has been poured out . . . by the Holy Spirit who [has been] given to us" (Romans 5:5). From heaven's standpoint, love is three-dimensional here on earth: it is spiritual, social, and personal.

*If we would know spiritual happiness,* each of us must love the Lord our God with all our heart, soul, mind, and strength (see Mark 12:30). One of the old Roman coins was printed with a figure of an ox standing between an altar and a plow, along with the inscription READY FOR EITHER. That spirit typifies true Christianity—ready for service or sacrifice—whatever the Lord may require. Having been bought with a great price, even the precious blood of our Lord Jesus Christ, we belong to Him—spirit, soul, and body. Therefore, out of love it is our reasonable service that we should dedicate our all to Him. This is the only response we can make to God.

*If we would know social happiness,* we must love our neighbor as ourselves (see Mark 12:31). Whether it be friend or foe, saint or sinner, we must love our neighbor (see Mark 12:31); we must ". . . love the brotherhood . . ." (1 Peter 2:17); and we must love our enemies (see Matthew 5:44). This includes a passion for souls.

In the old days of slavery, a missionary to the West Indies was employed to reach the people he desired to influence for Christ. They had to work long hours each day, and at night they were too exhausted to listen to his preaching. He tried every means to bring them the good news of Christ, but all without success. Finally, he decided to take a drastic step. *He sold himself as a slave* to one of the plantation owners and was driven with the others to work, where he had occasional opportunities to talk to them. Although he lost his life of freedom for the Gospel's sake, he found it again in the hearts of the many he was able to lead to Christ. This is true *agapē* love for the souls of men (Henry G. Bosch, "The Sacrifice of Self," *Our Daily Bread,* Radio Bible Class, June 18, 1980).

*If we would know personal happiness,* we must love our wives as our own bodies, for ". . . he that loveth his wife loveth himself" (Ephesians 5:28). Alas, this is where there is unprecedented breakdown in the lives of evangelists, pastors, and teachers, in these challenging days in which we live.

I was speaking at a preachers' conference some while ago on marital faithfulness in the ministry. The spirit of conviction fell upon that meeting with such power and penetration that hundreds of men came forward and wept at the altar. Among these were six ministers who resigned their pastorates, there and then. One man was having an affair with his secretary. Another was involved with several women in the choir. Still another was attending a massage parlor at the expense of the church—and I could go on! God's Word teaches that if a leader—be he an evangelist or pastor—does not know how to rule his own house well, and have his children in submission with all reverence, he disqualifies himself from taking care of the church of God (see 1 Timothy 3:4,5).

As husbands, we should love our wives with a *sacrificial* love, even as the Lord ". . . loved the church, and gave himself for [her]" (Ephesians 5:25). We should love our wives with a *spiritual* love, that He might ". . . sanctify and cleanse [them] with the washing of water by the word" (Ephesians 5:26). We should love our wives with a *sympathetic* love, even as we love our own bodies and take care of them in every respect (see Ephesians 5:28). Only then shall we know personal happiness and freedom in our ministry.

But Paul goes further:

c.  *He must be a humble man*—". . . follow after . . . patience [and] meekness" (6:11). Humility is both a discipline and a devotion, and no man can be used by God who does not seek and show humility. "God resisteth the proud, but giveth grace unto the humble" (James 4:6).

(i)  *Humility is a Christ-ordered discipline*—". . . follow after . . . patience . . ." (6:11). Humility is implied in this word "patience." The term means "steadfastness," or more literally, "bearing all the way, carrying through and never sagging." This calls for strong discipline under the Lordship of Christ.

One of the greatest sins in the ministry today is indiscipline—indiscipline in our quiet time, indiscipline in our sermon preparation, indiscipline in our family prayers, indiscipline at meal times, indiscipline in physical exercise, indiscipline in listening to others, indiscipline in planning for relaxation times with the wife and family; and on and on I could go. Only such discipline produces the humility which Andrew Murray calls "the beauty of holiness."

John Wesley had rules for his preachers which help to illustrate what we have been saying about the virtues of humility. Only a humble man would bow to his instructions for preachers. Consider them carefully:

*Be diligent.* Never be unemployed. . . . Never [waste] time, nor spend more time at any place than is strictly necessary.

*Be serious.* Let your motto be "Holiness to the Lord." Avoid all lightness, jesting and foolish talking.

*Be careful* not to condemn until proven guilty. Put the best construction on everything. You know the judge is always supposed to be on the prisoner's side. Speak evil of no one. Keep your thoughts within your own [heart] till you come to the person concerned.

*Be ashamed of nothing but sin.*

*Be punctual.* Do everything exactly [on time] and do not [amend] our rules but keep them, and that for conscience' sake.

*Be a gentleman.* A preacher of the Gospel is the servant of all.

*Be a soul-winner.* Spend and be spent in this [holy] work.

(ii)  *Humility is a Christ-offered disposition*—"follow after . . . meekness" (6:11). The word could be interpreted as "gentleness," but I define it as Christlikeness. After all, the Lord Jesus said, "Learn of me; for I am meek and lowly in heart: and ye shall find rest unto your souls" (Matthew 11:29). While the word "meek" in this verse is not the same as the one above, it underscores the meekness and gentleness of our Lord. Meekness is not weakness, but strength under control. This was the supreme virtue which took the Lord Jesus to the humiliating crucifixion on the cross, and to the exalting coronation on the throne. It was the supreme virtue which set the Savior above men. Like David of old, He could look up to heaven and say, "Thy gentleness hath made me great" (Psalm 18:35).

I believe one of the main reasons why Billy Graham has been so used of God throughout the years of his evangelistic ministry is because of this virtue of humility—both as a discipline and as a disposition. No one in our time has been subjected to more praise, on the one hand, or criticism, on the other, and yet has maintained that sweet spirit of meekness and teachability. God has set him forth as an example for us to follow. So let us imitate him, even as he has followed Christ in the virtues of holiness, happiness, and humility.

This brings us to our third consideration of the evangelist as a man of God:

**3.** *The evangelist must fight the variables of the ministry*

"Fight the good fight of faith, lay hold on eternal life, whereunto thou art also called, and hast professed a good profession before many witnesses. I give thee charge in the sight of God, who quickeneth all things, and before Christ Jesus, who before Pontius Pilate witnessed a good confession; that thou keep this commandment without spot, unrebukeable, until the appearing of our Lord Jesus Christ" (6:12-14).

Paul always had a healthy fear about finishing the course God had mapped out for him. He could say, "I therefore so run, not as uncertainly; so fight I, not as one that beateth the air: but I keep under my body, and bring it into subjection: *lest that by any means, when I have preached to others, I myself should be a castaway*" (1 Corinthians 9:26,27). Now he is handing over the torch of responsibility to Timothy. He exhorts him to fight the variables of the ministry. As we examine the words before us, it seems that there are two variables that should challenge every preacher and evangelist:

a. *There is the temptation to vary our Christian confession*—"Fight the good fight of faith . . ." (6:12). The verb here is in the present tense. Literally, it reads, "Go on agonizing, or contesting, for the faith." The word implies a disciplined struggle (see Colossians 1:29). The question is: What faith is Paul referring to here? The answer, of course, is personal faith in the Lord Jesus Christ, based upon the body of faith which is objective truth. Indeed, the text goes on to read, "Lay hold on eternal life, whereunto thou art also called, and hast professed a good profession before many witnesses" (6:12). The apostle is saying: Just as you first trusted Christ and declared your faith at your baptism and ordination, so fight to the very end.

Now sad and strange as it may appear, this Christian confession is what constitutes one of the variables of our Christian ministry. We all know men who had a radiant testimony when they were converted, and even when they entered the ministry, but now they have lost the glow and glory of it all. Paul is so concerned about this that he encourages his son in the faith to recall the stand which the Lord Jesus took when He witnessed a good confession before Pontius Pilate (see 6:13). To Timothy, this would conjure up immediately those tragic, yet triumphant, hours before the crucifixion when our blessed Lord stood before Pilate, under every conceivable pressure, and yet He never varied His confession of faith. As the Son of man, He was hungry, He was bleeding and exhausted; but notwithstanding this He could affirm: "Thou sayest that I am a king. To this end was I born, and for this cause came I into the world, that I should bear witness unto the truth. Every one that is of the truth heareth my voice" (John 18:37).

Oh, that God would enable us to live out this "unflinching steadfastness" of our blessed Savior, by the power of the indwelling Spirit! It is one thing to start the race, and even to continue it, but quite another matter to be able to say at the end, "I have fought a good fight, I have finished my course, I have kept the faith: henceforth there is laid up for me a crown of righteousness, which the Lord, the righteous judge, shall give me at that day: and not to me only, but unto all them also that love his appearing" (2 Timothy 4:7,8).

During the terrible Boxer Rebellion in China the insurgents captured a mission station, blocked all the gates but one, and in this opening placed a cross flat on the ground. Then the word was passed to those inside that anyone who trampled the cross under foot would be permitted their freedom and life; but that any refusing would be shot to death. Terribly frightened, the first seven people trampled the cross under their feet and were allowed to go free. But the eighth student, a young girl, refused to commit the sacrilegious act. Kneeling beside the cross in prayer for strength, she arose, and moved carefully around the cross and went out to face the firing squad. Strengthened by her example, every one of the remaining 92 students followed her to death (Peter Lee Tau, *Encyclopedia of 7700 Illustrations*, p. 787).

The second variable is just as perilous. There is not only the temptation to vary our Christian confession, but:

b. *There is the temptation to vary our Christian commission*—"I give thee charge in the sight of God . . . that thou keep this commandment without spot, unrebukeable, until the appearing of our Lord Jesus Christ" (6:13,14). William Hendriksen, in his commentary, points out that this is a mandate to keep the *commission of the ministry* without spot, so that here on earth, or later at the judgment seat of Christ, we might be able to present our certificate of ordination without a stain.

With regret we have to admit that in every country of our modern world there are pastors, evangelists, and missionaries who have not only varied in their Christian confession but have varied in their Christian commission. When Jesus challenged His disciples to serve Him to the end, He said, "No man, having put his hand to the plow, and looking back, is fit for the kingdom of God" (Luke 9:62). Our religious world is littered with one-time leaders who have varied, either in their confession to trust Christ, or their commission to serve Christ. This explains the tragedy of vacated pulpits or, even worse, evangelists who have made shipwreck of their ministry.

I have seldom been so moved as when I heard Dr. E.V. Hill of the Mount Zion Missionary Baptist Church in Los Angeles, California, share with pastors the temptation he had to vary his Christian commission. He had been invited by the President of the United States—Ronald Reagan—to accept a position of responsibility which, to say the least, was most enviable. He would report to the President himself and exercise considerable influence over the Black community of America. In his inimitable way, he pictured the chauffeur-driven limousines, first-class hotels, satin sheets, sumptuous meals, and the applause of men.

While he was weighing up his response, he was invited to speak for a soul brother in a small church in Albany, New York. He flew to Albany and was met by a humble pastor. On the way home, they had endless car trouble. Later that night, when nature called, he had to go outside in lashing rain to relieve himself. As he returned to his bedroom he pictured again those satin sheets, the comfortable surroundings of a hotel, and wondered what his decision should be! Then the Holy Spirit fell upon him in deep conviction, and a voice from heaven seemed to say: "E.V. Hill, you wouldn't step down from the high calling of a preacher to be a mere servant to the President, would you?" Such was the inner working of the Spirit that he wept in repentance, reaffirmed his vows to the Great Commission to serve Christ to the end; and the next day, after consulting with his wife, phoned the President and declined the offer. This is faithfulness to the call of God; and we have to fight this "fight of faith" every day of our lives until we see Jesus face to face.

As I speak, some of you may have failed in one or the other of those three areas we have been talking about—the vices of the ministry, the virtues of the ministry, and the variables of the ministry—and the Spirit of God has been convicting you. You sense that you have failed.

I have a word for you. Failure is not final. If you have fallen, God can lift you up. George Whitefield put it perfectly when he said concerning those who had sinned, "Do they profess repentance towards God, and faith in our Lord Jesus Christ, and holiness after conversion? If so, they are my brethren" (Al Bryant, *1000 New Illustrations*, p. 139).

The ultimate word comes to us from John's epistle, where he declares: "If we confess our sins, he is faithful and just to forgive us our sins, and to cleanse us from all unrighteousness" (1 John 1:9). Three steps are clearly implied here: first, we must *tell God* about our sins. That is the meaning of confession. We must agree with God that sin is sin. Observe, carefully, that we are to name them as sins; yes, and nail them. So often this is where we make the big mistake. Second, we must *trust God* about our sins. Because of the faithfulness of His word in Christ, and the righteousness of His work in Christ, He is ready to forgive and to cleanse us from all unrighteousness. Third, we must *thank God* about our sins. If God is God, then what He promises to do He will never fail to do; therefore, we must thank Him. If we do not thank Him it is because we have not trusted Him, and if we have not trusted Him it is because we have not told Him.

This, then, is the way of restoration for those of us who have failed in our personal lives, or in our public ministries. Let us not rest until we have cried with David, "Restore unto me the joy of thy salvation" (Psalm 51:12).

We see, then, that this matter of being a man of God is intensely serious. It is one thing to be ordained to the ministry, but it is quite another matter to fulfill that ministry to the very end. The apostle's words come to us afresh: "O man of God, flee these things; and follow after righteousness, godliness, faith, love, patience, meekness. Fight the good fight of faith, lay hold on eternal life, whereunto thou art also called, and hast professed a good profession before many witnesses" (6:11,12). As we have seen, this means that we are to flee the vices of the ministry, follow the virtues of the ministry, and fight the variables of the ministry. Only *then* can we join in the doxology with which the apostle concludes this paragraph and say, "Our Lord Jesus Christ . . . is the blessed and only Potentate, the King of kings, and Lord of lords; who only hath immortality, dwelling in the light which no man can approach unto; whom no man hath seen, nor can see: to whom be honor and power everlasting. Amen" (6:14-16). Quite obviously, the secret of our ministry and the solution to our mistakes is *the surrender of our lives to Jesus Christ as King of kings and Lord of lords.* Only when He is the undisputed Sovereign will the precious blood cleanse our lives, and the Spirit of God fill our lives. Jesus Christ is either Lord of all, or not Lord at all. Let us see to it that every area of our personal lives and public ministry is under His sway. With the hymn writer let us sing, and mean:

> Have Thine own way, Lord! Have Thine own way!
> Hold o'er my being absolute sway!
> Fill with Thy Spirit till all shall see
> Christ only, always, living in me!

# THE GIFT AND CALLING OF THE EVANGELIST
*Billy Graham*

*Why are we here at Amsterdam 1986?*

You are here tonight because God has gifted you and called you to be an evangelist. Some of you come from hard places that are unreceptive to the Gospel, and perhaps you are discouraged because there seem to be so few results and you wonder if it is worth it to continue preaching. Some of you come with family problems. Some with personal, overwhelming temptations and trials.

On the other hand, some of you have seen hundreds, and even thousands, come to Christ through the preaching of the Gospel. Whether you have seen many or few respond to the Gospel, you are an evangelist and God has called you to this ministry of evangelism.

But if God has given you the gift of an evangelist and called you to proclaim the Gospel, your goal must be to be faithful to that gift and that call. We are here in Amsterdam to affirm that gift and that calling, and to rededicate ourselves to the task God Himself has given each of us.

We are here also because of the urgency of the hour. The evangelistic harvest is always urgent. We do not always know when there will be a great harvest. But it is not the *size* of the harvest that is important—it is the *fact* of the harvest that is crucial. We must prepare the ground, sow the seed of God's Word, and water it. Paul declared to the Corinthians, "I have planted, Apollos watered; but God gave the increase" (1 Corinthians 3:6).

At the same time, I am convinced we are facing a period of unprecedented harvest for the Gospel. For one thing, many people are disillusioned because secular answers have failed them. They have tried everything in their desperate search for peace and security—materialism, politics, drugs and alcohol, sex, money, false philosophies and religions, and all of them have failed. Millions are open to the message of hope and new life in Christ. There is a gigantic spiritual vacuum in our age, and this could lead to the greatest harvest for the Gospel our world has ever seen. Could it be the last great harvest before Christ returns?

It also is harvest time because of world events. Almost every newspaper and book screams from its pages, "The harvest is ripe."

Jesus spoke of a time when there would be "upon the earth distress of nations, with perplexity; the sea and the waves roaring; men's hearts failing them for fear, and for looking after those things which are coming on the earth" (Luke 21:25-26). He could well have been describing our generation. Seldom has the soil of the human heart and mind been better prepared. The words of Jesus challenge me as never before: "Behold, I say unto you, Lift up your eyes, and look on the fields; for they are white already to harvest" (John 4:35).

There is nothing more urgent than a field which is ripe for harvest. Those of you who have grown crops know that harvest lasts only a short time. If there is no harvest, then ripeness soon turns to rottenness and the crop is lost. Proverbs 10:5 says: "He that gathereth in summer is a wise son: but he that sleepeth in harvest is a son that causeth shame."

## 1. The gift and call of the evangelist

Today, the world church is not sure what evangelism is, and often the gift of the evangelist is neglected—evangelism is not taught in many of our Bible schools and seminaries. Today we have scores of definitions of what evangelism is, and what an evangelist is. Some think of evangelism simply in terms of getting more people to join the church. Others define evangelism as attempting to change the structures of society.

Unless we believe in a future judgment, or that people are lost without Christ, then the cutting edge of evangelism is blunted.

That brings us to a very crucial question: What is an evangelist? *An evangelist is a person with a special gift and a special calling from the Holy Spirit to announce the good news of the Gospel.* It is a gift of God. It cannot be manufactured, organized or manipulated. It is a calling from God.

God has given us a gift—and He has called us to use it for His glory. When we understand this, it will save us from two dangerous temptations.

First, it will save us from pride, because we know that whatever gift we have and whatever opportunities may open up to us, are from God. We cannot take any credit or glory for ourselves. And second, it will save us from discouragement and the temptation to give up, because we know our calling is not from man but from God. As Paul said, "For though I preach the gospel, I have nothing to glory of: for necessity is laid upon me; yea, woe is unto me, if I preach not the gospel!" (1 Corinthians 9:16).

The Greek word for "evangelist" means "one who announces the good news." It is listed as one of the gifts God has given to the Church in Ephesians 4:11, "He gave some apostles; and some, prophets; and some, evangelists; and some, pastors and teachers." Philip is termed an evangelist (Acts 21:8); and Timothy is charged by Paul to "do the work of an evangelist" (2 Timothy 4:5).

In other words, the gift of the evangelist is one of God's great gifts to His Church, as outlined in Ephesians 4. It is just as important as a teacher or a pastor and is just as valid a gift today as it was in the early decades of the Christian Church. An evangelist is called in Scripture: an ambassador, a proclaimer, an advocate, an announcer of good news. One of the greatest needs today is for the Church throughout the world to recognize and recover the legitimacy and importance of the gift and calling of the evangelist.

The term "evangelism" encompasses every effort to declare the Good News of Jesus Christ, to the end that people may understand God's offer of salvation and respond in repentance, faith and discipleship. We must always make it clear that there is a "cost" to following Christ. There is the denial of self, and the taking up of a cross. Christ never offers cheap grace. He never lowers His standard for entrance to the kingdom of God.

2. *The motives of the evangelist*

That brings us to a basic question: What is our motive in evangelism? What is the motive behind our evangelism? Why did the Apostle Paul go from place to place, suffering as few men have suffered?

The first motive is found in Paul's words in 1 Corinthians 5:14, "The love of Christ constraineth us." I am convinced the greatest act of love we can ever perform for another person is to tell him about God's love for him in Christ.

Our love for others is not just an emotional feeling—it is a compassionate concern for them in their spiritual need, a concern which leads us to action.

Where missionaries went around the world carrying the message of Christ's redeeming love, hospitals were built. Schools, orphanages, leprosariums, and hundreds of other good works followed. Many missiologists will admit the mistakes some missionaries made in various parts of the world, yet it is quite easy to criticize them in hindsight!

Hundreds of them were separated from loved ones for years on end. Hundreds suffered martyrdom in order to bring the light of the Gospel to various parts of the world. It was those early missionaries who brought the message of the Gospel to the United States.

Another motive for our evangelism is the approaching Judgment. Paul said, "Knowing therefore the terror of the Lord, we persuade men" (2 Corinthians 5:11). When Paul preached his great sermon at Mars Hill in Athens, he said, "God . . . commandeth all men everywhere to repent: because he hath appointed a day, in which he will judge the world in righteousness by that man whom he ordained" (Acts 17:30,31). There is a Judgment Day approaching. The secular world is talking more and more about Armageddon and the end of the world.

In recent years, many have rejected the biblical doctrine that men are individually sinners before God and will be held responsible to Him at the Judgment. Instead, they believe in a doctrine of collective sinfulness and of the corporate guilt of society. I accept the fact that sin affects society as a whole, and we must take that seriously. But we are in danger of neglecting the need for personal repentance of sin, and faith in the Lord Jesus Christ. We are forgetting the "you" and the "must" in "*you* (individually) *must* be born again"—which is where the New Testament places its emphasis.

But our primary motive, in my view, is the command of our Commander-in-chief, the Lord Jesus Christ. We engage in evangelism today not because we want to, or because we choose to, or because we like to, but because *we have been told to*. We are under orders. Our Lord has commanded us to go, to preach, to make disciples—and that should be enough for us. Evangelistic inactivity is disobedience.

The so-called Great Commission occurs *five times* in our Bibles—at the end of each of the four Gospels, and once at the beginning of Acts. I am sure that He repeated these commands many times. When Paul stood on trial before King Agrippa he recounted God's call to him on the Damascus road, and his response. He told the king, "I was not disobedient unto the heavenly vision" (Acts 26:19). May we have the same kind of obedience. If there are no visible results—it would still be enough. It is not optional. We have no choice. We are ambassadors under authority.

### 3. *The message of the evangelist*

Let us be clear and simple in our proclamation of the Gospel—I will say more about this when I speak tomorrow morning.

A few years ago I listened to one of the greatest challenges to me that I have ever had, from an unexpected source. We were just beginning our Crusade in Osaka, Japan. At a wonderful reception for us with hundreds of leaders of Osaka and Kyoto, the Governor of Osaka in his brief address of welcome turned to me and asked: "Dr. Graham, why is it that the church in Japan is about the same as it was in the 17th century?" He said, "I believe it is because the Gospel has not been made clear to the Japanese people. I hope that you will make it clear."

There are millions in Europe for whom the Gospel has not been made clear. We have failed in our communication, so that people have only a hazy idea of what it means to be a true follower of Jesus Christ.

Several months ago, a friend of mine sat in a hut in a Masai village in East Africa talking with an evangelist who had just completed a walking trip of 110 miles among many remote villages of his people. My friend asked the evangelist, "How do you explain to the Masai how much God really loves them?"

Through an interpreter the evangelist replied, "My people love their animals, especially their cattle, very much. If one of their cows becomes lost, they will not rest until it is found and brought back safely with the others. I tell them the story that

Jesus told about the shepherd who had 99 sheep safe in the fold and went out to look for the one that was lost. Then they understand how much God loves them and what Jesus did for them when He died on the Cross.''

The evangelist knew how to make the message clear so that the Masai could understand.

Jesus used simple, everyday stories to make the Gospel clear and plain. What is our basic message? While the evangelist always emphasizes service, fellowship and worship, the message of the evangelist is primarily the kerygma which Paul summarized in 1 Corinthians 15, ''Moreover, brethren, I declare unto you the gospel which I preached unto you, which also ye have received . . . that Christ died for our sins according to the scriptures; and that he was buried, and that he rose again the third day according to the scriptures'' (1 Corinthians 15:1, 3-4).

What is our message? First, biblical evangelism is committed to the full and final authority of Scripture alone. Our authority is not based upon our experiences, or upon our traditions, or upon the latest ideas of philosophers or politicians. Our authority and our message are solely based on what God has revealed to us in His Word, the Bible. In boldness we can proclaim, ''Thus saith the Lord.''

Second, biblical evangelism preaches Christ alone as the Savior of men. Paul told the Corinthians, ''For I determined not to know anything among you, save Jesus Christ, and him crucified'' (1 Corinthians 2:2). He alone is the way to God. Apart from Him, we are spiritually dead and lost.

Jesus Christ by His death and resurrection *became* the Gospel. Jesus Christ *is* the Gospel! As Dr. Ed Hill emphasized over and over in '83: ''Preach Jesus! Preach Jesus!''

It is not just a new set of morals, or a guide for happy living. It is the solemn message that we are alienated from God, and only Christ by His death and resurrection can save us. Any message other than the Gospel of Jesus Christ is not evangelism. If you preach any other message, you are not an evangelist.

I do not have time for my next point on the methods of the evangelist, but it will be discussed in seminars, workshops, and by other speakers in plenary sessions.

I, along with my associates, am praying that God will send us back to our various places of service singing a new song that we will someday sing as recorded in the fifth chapter of Revelation: ''And they sang a new song, saying, Thou art worthy . . . for thou wast slain, and hast redeemed us to God by thy blood out of every kindred, and tongue, and people, and nation; and hast made us unto our God kings and priests: and we shall reign on the earth'' (Revelation 5:9,10).

Tonight we say with John on Patmos, ''Worthy is the Lamb that was slain to receive power, and riches, and wisdom, and strength, and honor, and glory, and blessing'' (Revelation 5:12).

# THE PRAYER TIME OF THE EVANGELIST
*Richard Kriese*

In the Amsterdam Affirmations of 1983 we read: "A life of regular and faithful prayer and Bible study is essential to our personal spiritual growth and to our power for ministry."

This is a tremendous prospect. In our quiet time we can step on holy ground with our Bibles and in prayer, where we are recharged in the light of eternity with the powers of the world to come. Dynamic changes take place, which enable us to proclaim the Gospel as a message of victory.

The classical herald is described as follows: "The messenger appears, lifts his right hand in greeting and calls with a loud voice: 'All hail! Rejoice! We have won the battle.' Even his outward appearance demonstrates that he is carrying good news. His face beams, the top of his spear is decorated with laurel, his head adorned, he waves a palm branch. There is exultation and rejoicing in the city."

Symbolically this can be applied to the evangelistic ministry. The messenger and the message blend into one transparent unity. Satan wants to prevent this with innumerable tricks. We will be the more aware of this the more we realize that we are moving with accelerating speed into an era which the last book of the Bible calls repeatedly "Babylon." A Babylonian secular spirit under religious disguise wants to destroy our quiet time. It does not come to this, though, when we let God's Spirit work. We should consider five viewpoints.

1. *In listening and obedient adoration we avoid self-destructive egotistic activism*

"Let us build us a city and a tower, whose top may reach unto heaven; and let us make us a name . . ." (Genesis 11:4). This was the slogan of Babylonian activists. With newly discovered techniques they wanted to bring paradise down from heaven to earth. This materialistic striving for progress found its visible expression in the worship of a golden Marduk statue on the highest step of the temple tower. The secular spirit of the late 20th century manifests itself in a similar way.

Daniel separated himself in prayer from this activism. Three times a day he knelt in prayer at his open window with his face towards Jerusalem. It is noteworthy that he "gave thanks." If appointments and responsibilities drive us from one task to the next we should do likewise. There is no substitute for prayer. Martin Luther used to say: "I have lots of work to do; that is why I have to pray a lot."

Certainly, we will not always immediately attain this worship of praise and thanksgiving like Daniel. We would rather complain about the pressure which we hope is not the result of our own fault. Of course, we are allowed this too, we may vent our heart's feelings through prayer. In the New Testament the word used for prayer encompasses a wide range of concepts. It starts with calling, groaning, lamenting and crying; then goes on to asking, entreating, imploring and desiring; ending with thanksgiving, praising, glorifying, rejoicing and even exulting—comparable to a scale on which our lamentations turn to songs of praise. So, do not always only complain about appointments and schedules, but also give a little bit of thanks! After all, it is a privilege to serve our Lord. If we pray through to praising—and you have to take time for that—we come to the point where we can say: in waiting upon God my soul is still. He is my defense (Psalm 62:1,2).

When we come to rest in prayer, God opens our ears; He enables us to listen to Him in such a way that we recognize His plan for this specific situation. Our Lord does not expect us to do everything ourselves. He wants to complement our service through others, who relieve us and perform better than we ourselves.

We should make it a habit to wait in our quiet time for a special promise regarding our scheduled responsibilities. In this manner, our amount of work would shrink to normal. It is simply not true that we must enter all "open doors." In adorational listening we recognize clearly the *one* door, the *prepared* situation, the work, which our Lord already *began* (John 5:19,20). He who works incessantly and does nothing else is going in circles in his ministry. The one who only prays and leaves the work to others is similar. If we use both oars, "prayer" and "work" at the same time, we are getting ahead.

Our quiet time is holy ground, on which with heaven-turned eyes we receive the right view of the world; and then look up again in adoration to our risen Lord—from adoration to adoration. A basic attitude is essential, however. When a slave in old times prostrated himself before his master and kissed his master's feet, he wanted to express: "Master, 24 hours a day you can do with me whatever you like." In the language of the New Testament this was called *proskynesis*, which is equal to adoration. This type of adoration we only achieve as we abandon Babylonian activism and detach ourselves from the misconception that we can—through secular actions and programs—save our world, that is ready for judgment, from apocalyptic events.

2.  *In the quietness of prayer we are motivated to strive for spiritual unity, which differs totally from a syncretistic centralization movement*

Different nations with diverse cultures built the Babylonian tower—by the way, a symbol of a self-glorifying uniform religion. It is approaching us with accelerating speed as a global centralization movement. It unites on the one hand all present elements of truth, but on the other hand systematically undermines biblical standards by humanistic tolerance. Through it, man hopes to achieve a "knotting together" and a "netting together" of group consciousness with the goal of tapping cosmic energies. What a tremendous challenge, which we can only confront with spiritual prayer cells.

Daniel did not only pray alone, but in critical situations he also prayed with others. He formed a prayer fellowship with Hananiah, Mishael and Azariah, which God confirmed by His approval (Daniel 2:17,18). Evangelists who stand alone are a good target for Satan. He who does not want to be shot at must not remain alone; he must look for the supplementation, correction and encouragement of a prayer fellowship. David was spiritually encouraged through Jonathan, and Paul through Ananias. If you have a prayer partner, thank God; if you have none—pray for one. He will be given to us, if we, according to Isaiah 58, do away "with the pointing finger and malicious talk." God's adversary has started to split up and push evangelical groups into extreme positions. We have to deal with this danger, walk towards each other and meet in the center. The closer we are to the Cross, the closer we are standing with each other. We are united, and experience the sending power of the Holy Spirit. That is why it is so important to put aside tensions and discord in our interpersonal relationships. The revival in Canada in 1972 started when two elders were reconciled publicly. The spiritual awakening in Sierra Leone began when the leaders of the Evangelical Alliance there approached each other again.

3.  *The quietness of prayer trains us for a disciplined life-style and offers joy and peace in the Holy Spirit instead of mind-expanding euphoria*

Babylon is depicted in the last book of the Bible as a drunken prostitute. In a sensual orgy which grew into ecstasy, people wanted to cross the "gate of God" on the top of the temple tower, while remembering that "Babylon" also meant "gate of

God." From chemical intoxication to religious ecstasy, people today also want to cross the border to a super world. In the paradise of drugs, of whatever kind, people try to reach that alteration of consciousness through mind-expansion which links up the supposedly unused divine potential in man with cosmic forces.

Daniel is again a guiding example. Even as a young man he had decided not to adapt to the eating habits of his chief of government because he knew part of the food was offered to idols. He lived a disciplined life and practiced prayer and fasting. He knew only too well that at the peak of Babylonian towers people worshiped different idols in ecstatic experiences. Today, as in those days, and also in apocalyptic prospectives tomorrow: sensuous pleasures at any cost! The religion of our time, which is called by some groups "the age of Aquarius," wants "high life," euphoria, ecstasy.

This eschatological perspective challenges us to discover anew fasting prayer. In the New Testament it is mentioned twenty times. In fasting and prayer, with the Bible in our hands, we can critically ask ourselves: Am I disciplined in my eating and drinking habits? Is there a balance between work and rest? Am I keeping my vows? Do I give ten percent of my income for the kingdom of God? Am I exaggerating in my preaching, which some call "lying to the honor of God"? Has my ministry still the right motivation? Let us thank God if we can still cry over such and similar failures.

Torrey, an evangelist blessed the world over at the beginning of the 20th century, tells in his book *The Power of Prayer*, how he had to break with a sin that he tolerated first of all with an "if." He prayed: "O God, if this thing is wrong in your eyes, I want to give it up." There was no answer. But when he said: "O God, this thing is wrong, it is sin, I give it up now," he received an answer. Healing began. The ministry progressed.

An eagle, according to a Polish preacher, rejuvenates himself by sharpening his beak in a quiet place at a rocky ridge, and by rubbing his wings at a boulder until all old scales and feathers are shed. Then comes a time of waiting during which a new layer of horn forms on his beak and also new feathers grow. During moult the eagle rejuvenates himself. So does the evangelist in fasting and prayer. When we fast and pray the vertical dimension obtains the absolute priority over the horizontal dimension. The powers of eternity are able to detoxicate our souls; renewal begins, old things are put away and our ministry can start with new vigor. Joy overflows. Andrew Murray said: "Fasting strengthens and deepens the decision to sacrifice all, yes even ourselves, in order to attain that which we want to reach for the kingdom of God."

4. *In the quietness of prayer we are led to identification with the crucified One and can conquer the egotistic self-realization through self-denial*

Nebuchadnezzar made a huge human image of gold in Babylon that people had to worship while music played in the background. Today in the same way the Babylonian secular spirit puts man into the very center and makes him the measure of all things. Lately there has been optimistic talk of a "great leap forward in evolution of the divine potentials in man." As a member of a new world fellowship, man could reach "a state of a god-son"—at least this is being claimed.

The human self is considered the divine spark of "truth, beauty and goodness," which will eventually blaze up into a bright flame by self-knowledge, self-development, and self-realization. A humanistic care for our fellowman is equated with divine love, *agapē*. But still, despite all these self-redemptive attempts, there always remains the longing to be delivered from the restraints of a self-reflecting ego-isolation.

This freedom is given to us when we identify with Jesus Christ in the way Paul described it in his letter to the Galatians. "And they that are Christ's have crucified the flesh with the affections and lusts'' (Galatians 5:24). And in chapter 6:14 he continues: "But God forbid that I should glory, save in the cross of our Lord Jesus Christ, by whom the world is crucified unto me, and I unto the world."

This central biblical truth was revealed to the Chinese martyr Watchman Nee in his quiet time. He identified himself anew with Christ. Beside himself with joy he ran to his brothers and shouted over and over again: "I am crucified with Christ!"

This is the crucial point of the initial ignition of divine love. "Crucified with Christ, dead with Christ, buried with Christ, risen with Christ, in heavenly places with Christ." We can practically express all of the Pauline theology in these five statements. It climaxes in the liberating confession: "Nevertheless I live; yet not I, but Christ liveth in me: and the life which I now live in the flesh I live by the faith of the Son of God, who loved me, and gave himself for me" (Galatians 2:20). That is the deep dimension of the message of the Cross. Are not evangelists always in danger of worshiping statistics, just as they are in danger of being career-minded? Often, successful evangelists are being imitated so much that it virtually becomes a "life-lie" to the imitator. Often, there is religious show with sensationalism, even at evangelistic crusades. Often, there is spiritual covetousness which goes hand in hand with false ambition and ungodly jealousy. Often, there is self-realization camouflaged in a Christian way, in which even the evangelistic charisma makes itself suddenly independent.

The proclamation of the "I-am-awareness," which maintains that the good in man is identical with Christ, clashes head on with the message of the Cross. At this point there can be no compromise. It is impossible to bridge the contrast between the flesh and the spirit, egocentric piousness and self-denying discipleship. However, he who takes a stand, proclaims the "whole counsel" of God and evangelizes aggressively, must count on being ill-reputed. The approaching world religion understands itself as the "soft conspiration." It is challenging the Gospel. Since neo-humanistic thought even undermines evangelical churches, Bible-believing proclaimers of the Gospel must count on losing popularity. But they also experience how people pass from egocentric oppression into the glorious freedom of the children of God with the jubilation: "I thank God through Jesus Christ our Lord."

In the quiet time with our Bibles and in prayer, our risen Lord wants to enable us to proclaim the message of the Cross in its deepest dimensions. However, this can only happen if we don't see ourselves as heroes and stop working "to make a name" for ourselves. The Holy Spirit cannot tolerate the cultivation of a pious image.

5. *In the quietness of prayer we are enabled to preach eschatologically, which focuses on a new heaven and earth instead of an occult world view*

On the top of the Babylonian towers, people did not only discover the conformity of planetary star constellation, but created at the same time the often quoted Babylonian world view which was made up by astrological statements. Today, parallel to this, the "age of Aquarius" is being proclaimed with a new world view. Time and eternity, as well as matter and spirit, merge into one another without distinction and form a universe, which regenerates itself evolutionally "in the cosmic dance." By this process, occultism—as has been justly stated—becomes increasingly scientific and physics increasingly occult. In this world picture the supernatural becomes the natural, and earth and heaven can no longer be distinguished. If we neglect in our quiet time the perspective of God's new world in lieu of an optimistic view of our present life, is not the decisive direction of God missing?

Daniel prays fervently, persistently, trustingly (Daniel 9:3) and receives a prophetical overview reaching up to the time of the Antichrist. Major lines become visible. In the prophetic realm single events appear, which point into the future, but also throw light on the situation of the Israel of the Old Testament in Babylonian captivity. With this background he interprets prophetically the *mene tekel*. All this was in stark contrast to the world view of the temple tower. There, astrology and astronomy blended into the Babylonian world view. It was believed that cosmic energies ruled in a godlike fashion all happenings in the microcosmos and macrocosmos. And again occultism plays a role with its astrologically based announcement of the "age of the sun." Certainly a challenge at the time, as it is today!

And so as the 20th century draws to a close we cannot leave out evangelism which has a prophetic perspective, and should associate world events with the returning Lord. Therefore, a two-fold emphasis is important. On the one hand, we have to clearly express the *mene tekel* which hovers over our civilization, pointing out the command: "Go ye forth of Babylon with a voice of singing"; on the other hand, we may encourage each other with "maranatha" and "lift up your heads for your salvation draweth nigh."

During the European Congress for Evangelism in Amsterdam, the brethren from Eastern Europe told me: "When you preach over the radio, preach about heaven—that is our only hope." The Rumanian revival, which is the largest in Europe, is dominated by the expectation of the returning Lord. If our praying and preaching are dominated by this aim, a specific word is given to us. In the language of the New Testament the Greek word *rhema* stands for "message," "command," "resolution," and means a specific news. We should pray until we receive it.

Before the revival in Nepal, a villager came to my friend who is a Wycliffe Bible translator. Until that time this man had never held a Bible in his hands. He told my friend about a vision, in which he saw a Scripture scroll. When my friend asked him about the contents, he was totally surprised to find out that the wording was identical to the sermon on the Mount of Olives in Matthew 24 where the signs of the returning Christ are given.

That is our hope. In the power of the Holy Spirit, we can relate this hope prophecy gives us to the happenings of our present time.

Our Lord does not leave us helplessly exposed to the onslaughts of a Babylonian secular spirit, which with accelerating speed aims at the world religion of the Antichrist. He wants to recharge us again and again with His Holy Spirit, as He did in the Acts of the Apostles.

This is no progressing materialism with lots of action, but a concrete service in the power of praise and thanksgiving; no egocentric self-idolizing, trying to build a name for oneself, but selfless love, which strives to glorify only the name of Jesus. It is no crossing of a Babylonian-perceived entrance to God with ecstatic euphoria, but instead the powerful joy of the Holy Spirit under an open heaven. It is no centralization bringing uniformity, but rather a spiritual unity created by the Holy Spirit; and no Babylonian confusion of tongues, but a spiritual communication of the language of love. It is no worldly oriented world view with political actions, but rather the goal-oriented expectation of a new heaven and a new earth.

The crucial point of our quiet time with our Bibles and in prayer also becomes visible through George Müller, the father of the orphans of Bristol. Asked about the secret of his ministry, he answered: "There came a day in my life when I died. I died to the self of George Müller, my opinions, my preferences, my will. I died also to the world. I died to the praise and the accusation and the criticism of friends. Since then I have tried nothing else than to please God."

At this point, we can proclaim with Paul: "For God, who commanded the light to shine out of darkness, hath shined in our hearts, to give the light of the knowledge of the glory of God in the face of Jesus Christ" (2 Corinthians 4:6). This is what the devotions of the evangelist finally aim at.

# THE EVANGELIST'S PERSONAL WITNESS
*Bill Bright*

I greet you in the name of our risen Lord. He is here with us today in all of His resurrection power. The living Christ dwells within each one of us who has received Him as our Savior and Lord. The Bible says that Jesus is the visible expression of the invisible God (Colossians 1:15). In Him dwells all the fullness of the Godhead bodily (Colossians 2:9). To Him, God has given all authority in heaven and on earth (Matthew 28:18). This same incomparable, peerless Savior, the Lord Jesus Christ, came to this world for one purpose. He came to seek and to save the lost. And He has commanded each one of us to join with Him in this, the greatest of all challenges. Jesus said, "Follow me, and I will make you fishers of men" (Matthew 4:19).

Since Jesus indwells each one of us, and since He has commanded us to follow Him with the promise that He would make us fishers of men, there is absolutely no more important subject that we could possibly consider at this great International Conference for Itinerant Evangelists than the subject, "The Evangelist's Personal Witness."

As one who serves our Lord along with a staff of more than 16,000 in 151 countries, I spend much of my time in group meetings, evangelistic gatherings and in crowds—large and small. I speak to groups of all sizes—to a dozen people here, a few hundred there, sometimes a few thousand.

But I have found that most of my messages are to Christians, challenging them to personal evangelism and helping them to fulfill the Great Commission of our Lord. These messages are greatly enhanced by my own *personal* witness and involvement in helping to fulfill the Great Commission.

Without a willingness to speak to *individuals* about the love and forgiveness of our wonderful Savior, I would have very little credibility in speaking to the crowds. You see, to me, there is something more exciting in the Christian life than preaching a sermon, though I love to preach. I have found that the most exciting experience of life is the joy of introducing a single individual to Christ.

My friends, are *you* regularly introducing others to our Savior and Lord? Is your concern for the souls of men burning within you so that it carries over into your daily life, compelling you not only to reach out to the masses but to talk with individuals whom you meet each day? The apostle Paul was so constrained by the love of Christ that he proclaimed, "Everywhere we go, we talk about Christ to all who will listen" (Colossians 1:28).

Would you be surprised to learn that many of your non-Christian friends and those whom you meet casually are ready to receive Christ? I am convinced as a result of millions of surveys which we have taken in 151 countries, that at least one billion people would receive Christ today if they were properly and prayerfully approached by a trained, Spirit-filled Christian.

I was in a largely Roman Catholic country recently where there is little freedom to witness publicly. In order to get from meeting to meeting, I rode with at least twenty taxi drivers during the few days that I was there. In every case, I got in the taxi and announced through an interpreter, "I am here in the city to meet with a number of Christian friends. We are convinced that Jesus Christ is the Prince of Peace, the Savior of man and the hope of the world. Do you know Jesus personally?" All of the twenty cases to which I refer responded positively that, yes, they believed in God and, yes, they knew that Jesus Christ was the Son of God, and yes, they believed that He died for their sins. But in all but a couple of cases, they did not know Him personally. They did not have assurance of their salvation.

So through the interpreter, I explained God's love and forgiveness to them by using a simple little booklet called the Four Spiritual Laws, which explains in their language the distilled essence of the Gospel. I encouraged them to take the booklet and study it and, when they came to the prayer on page 16 in the booklet, to get on their knees and invite Jesus Christ to come into their lives and determine to follow Him. In all of the twenty cases, there was a very positive, affirmative indication that they would, when they got home, read the little booklet that I gave them, and they would get on their knees and invite our Lord into their lives. On this same trip, approximately half of the people who heard the Good News of Christ expressed their desire to receive Him. What a privilege it is to introduce another person to our wonderful Savior!

1. *Why it is so important to witness personally of our Lord and Savior regularly as a way of life*

a. *We witness personally because our Lord commands us to witness.* Every believer, including evangelists, is commanded to witness. Jesus commands us, "Follow me and I will make you fishers of men" (Matthew 4:19). It is our responsibility to follow Jesus, and His responsibility to make us fishers of men. Jesus also commands us, "Go into all the world and preach the Good News to everyone everywhere" (Mark 16:15). "Go and make disciples in all the nations . . ." (Matthew 28:19). "When the Holy Spirit has come upon you, you will receive power to testify about me with great effect to the people in Jerusalem, throughout Judea, in Samaria and to the ends of the earth about my death and resurrection" (Acts 1:8).

Not to witness is to disobey our Lord who so loved us that He died for us. To disobey our Lord robs us of His mighty power in our lives and witness.

b. *We witness personally out of gratitude for all that Christ has done, and is doing, for us.* Jesus has liberated us out of the darkness and gloom of Satan's kingdom and brought us into His kingdom of love and of God (John 1:12). Jesus forgives our sins (Ephesians 1:7). By receiving Jesus, we have become new creatures in Christ (2 Corinthians 5:17). Through what Jesus has done for us, we have peace with God (Romans 5:1). And finally, though He does a thousand other things and more for us, Jesus gives us the assurance of eternal life (1 John 5:11-13). As we meditate on all Jesus has done for us and daily does for us, how can we remain silent in our personal witness for Him, when we are surrounded by others who do not know Him?

c. *We witness personally for our Lord because men, women, children—all people—are lost without Christ.* God's Word reminds us, "There is no other name under heaven that has been given among men, by which we must be saved" (Acts 4:12).

If we had a cure for cancer, we would want to share it with everyone who has cancer. All men and women without Christ are dying of the "cancer" of sin, and unless introduced to Christ, will be forever separated from God in hell. We must tell everyone everywhere the Good News of God's love and forgiveness in Christ.

d. *We witness personally because of the great spiritual hunger all around us.* The greatest spiritual harvest of all time is taking place today in most parts of the world. As Augustine said centuries ago, "Thou hast made us for thyself, O God, and our hearts are restless until they find their rest in Thee."

e. *We witness personally because every individual is important to God.* "He so loved the world that He gave His only begotten Son, that whosoever believeth in Him should not perish but have everlasting life." (John 3:16).

f. *We must witness personally because of the urgency of the harvest.* Every harvest comes to an end, whether it be a harvest of grain or fruit or vegetables. So it is with spiritual harvest.

A careful study of Christianity confirms that, throughout the centuries, there have been times of great spiritual harvest, followed by times of spiritual drought. The greatest spiritual harvest of 2,000 years is taking place today, and we do not know how long it will last. We must not miss this.

g. *We witness personally because it will enhance and strengthen our public ministry.* As you will see, your personal witness will not only enrich your life and the lives of others whom you influence, but will also enrich your public ministry. No one can experience a vital, dynamic, Spirit-filled ministry in the pulpit who is not witnessing regularly for our Lord. The reason is obvious: disobedient Christians cannot be filled and empowered by the Holy Spirit. Not to witness personally and regularly is to disobey God.

It is a sad fact that a large percentage of pastors and evangelists do *not* witness personally. As a result, they lose not only power with God and man, but they fail to model for other Christians who are looking to them for an example of a Christ-like witness. A very famous evangelist in America called me long distance late one night. He explained to me that his daughter had participated in a Campus Crusade for Christ Lay Training Institute for Evangelism, where she had learned how to share her faith in Christ with others by using the Four Spiritual Laws booklet. Afterward, she went home and taught her father how to use this means of witnessing to introduce an individual to Christ. Not long afterward, a man approached him after one of his messages. The man was ready to receive the Lord, so this famous pastor/evangelist introduced him to Christ, using the simple format of the Four Spiritual Laws. He was so very excited that he telephoned me long distance.

"Bill," he said, "I believe that I have led thousands of people to Christ through my sermons, in my churches, on television and on radio, and through my books and other writings. But this is the first person I have ever led to Christ personally, and I used the Four Spiritual Laws which you wrote. I want you to know how thrilled I am and that I want to make this a regular practice."

Frankly, it was a credit to his humility that he would acknowledge that he had never led anyone to Christ personally, since he is one of the most famous pastors and evangelists in America. But this was a momentous occasion for him. He had made a great discovery. He discovered how easy it is to introduce others to Christ when you are filled with the Holy Spirit, and when you know what to say and how to say it.

There are many well-known Christian leaders, evangelists and preachers who, from their own admission, seldom if ever lead others to Christ personally. There are many reasons for this. Even though they have been trained to preach, they all too often have not been trained to share the life-changing message of our Lord with individuals. Many have been intimidated by Satan to believe that it is difficult to talk to a person individually about Christ. Some believe that they don't have the gift of personal, one-to-one evangelism. Or they prefer to speak to the masses, and let the layman speak to the individuals. Others are convinced by Satan that individuals are not interested in the Gospel and would not speak with them if approached. As a result, they keep silent.

Still others rationalize that they are doing their part in reaching others for Christ through their evangelistic preaching. So they are really too busy and important, they think, to take their valuable time to witness to one person when they can preach to hundreds and thousands.

Some reason: "I live a good, moral life. That is my witness for Christ." Of course, our lives must demonstrate what we proclaim. We must lead holy, godly lives to deserve a hearing. But it has been argued by writer Mark McCloskey in his book, *Tell It Often, Tell It Well,* that the rationale of "I don't speak, I let my life do the talking," forces us to ask: Whose life is good enough for such an assignment? Our wonderful Lord and Savior lived the perfect life, but even He was misunderstood and crucified.

A dear friend in Singapore emphasized this point. His story illustrates the fruitlessness of silent witnessing, of simply living a good life. He shared with me the story of how for years he "witnessed" by his godly life, and how he prayed daily that God would use his life to be a model to those with whom he worked, so that they would take the initiative and ask him what made him different. Then, as a result, he would have the opportunity to be a witness of Christ to them.

The weeks and the months passed. A couple of years later, he was still praying, "Lord help me to be such a model of you in my life that this man will want to know you, too."

One day, the man said to him, "Fred, I've been watching you."

My friend said, "Oh Lord, thank you. At last, you have answered my prayer."

"I have observed that your life is different."

"Thank you, Lord, he sees the difference in my life."

"I want to ask you a personal question."

"Thank you, Lord, now this is the moment that I have been praying for."

His friend asked, "Fred, are you a vegetarian?"

At that moment, my friend said he realized that he needed to do more than to live a good moral life. He needed to be a vocal witness for Christ.

There is no doubt that we must take the initiative to verbalize our faith in Christ to others.

One morning on my way to the airport after a conference in the United States, I said to the young woman who was driving the motel bus, "Isn't this a beautiful day that the Lord has made?" She nodded in the affirmative. "Do you know the Lord?" I asked. "No," she replied, "but I am very interested." She explained that her fiancé was a very dedicated Christian and that she had been seeking to become a Christian, too, but didn't know how. I shared my personal testimony briefly. Then I showed her a Four Spiritual Laws booklet and proceeded to explain to her how she could know God in a personal way by receiving Jesus Christ as her Savior. When we turned to the prayer, she said she would like to pray. Within a few moments after arriving at the airport, we bowed together in prayer as she received Christ. What a joyful and exciting experience for both of us.

The Bible is filled with examples of godly evangelists of their day who took time apart from their evangelistic meetings to witness to individuals. On many, many occasions, even our Lord paused from His busy public ministry to touch the lives of individuals.

John 4:5-42 records the conversation Jesus struck up with the woman at the well. He could have rationalized that He was tired from traveling, or that custom frowned on His speaking with a woman, and a Samaritan woman especially. But, instead, He asked her for a drink of water and began to speak to her about living water, which He could give. They talked at such length that when the disciples saw them they were greatly surprised. But, by that time, the Samaritan woman was convinced that there was something special about this Man.

Jesus enjoyed conversations with rich men, poor men, the diseased, and the spiritually blinded. His witness to Nicodemus of the need to ''be born again'' provides an example for each one of us in our preaching and personal witness. Even as Jesus was dying on the cross, He turned to the thief on one side of Him to speak with him about his salvation.

Acts chapter 8 records the story of Philip, the deacon, who was holding a successful city-wide evangelistic campaign in Samaria. Through his inspired preaching and the miracles which he performed, many believed in Christ, and there was much joy in the city. But, by a special revelation, God gave him another assignment. Philip was led by the Holy Spirit to *leave* his very successful, city-wide evangelistic campaign to witness to *one* Ethiopian eunuch.

God had prepared the heart of the Ethiopian eunuch, and when Philip approached him he was ready to receive Christ. According to tradition, God used the Ethiopian eunuch to take the message of our living Lord to his own country.

The Bible contains many other examples that underline the importance of speaking to individuals about our Savior. We should never be so busy with our evangelistic campaigns and our big crusades that we cannot talk to an individual about Christ. Whether he is a shop keeper, a farmer, a businessman, a newspaper reporter or a janitor in the auditorium where we are speaking, every person is of equal worth in God's sight, and no one soul is more important than any other.

My reference to the Ethiopian eunuch whom Philip introduced to Christ reminds me of another Ethiopian whom I met recently while in Washington, D.C. On this particular trip, person after person had received Christ with me while in flight, or in the airports. I had spent the morning meeting with senators and congressmen on Capitol Hill in Washington, several of whom had received Christ through my personal witness. On the way back to the airport, I began to talk to the taxi driver. When I discovered that he was an Ethiopian, I reminded him of the Ethiopian eunuch mentioned in Acts 8. I asked him if he remembered that story, and he did. He said that he was very active in his church and had a knowledge of the Scripture. But when I asked him if he knew Jesus Christ personally, he said that he did not. He knew Him only as a religious leader whom he admired and respected.

I explained to him the importance of faith in receiving Christ, and, with great joy and rejoicing, he responded. He pulled the taxicab over to the side of the road, and we had prayer together. He prayed and received Christ, and then I prayed for him. He went on his way rejoicing, even as the eunuch of old.

2.   *Witnessing opportunities benefit the evangelist and his ministry as well as the individual who has the privilege of hearing about our Lord Jesus*

a.   *It gives you an idea of questions being asked by your listeners.* Knowing these questions, you will understand more intimately how to tailor your messages to your audience's needs. I have found that some of the best illustrations which I use in my public messages to explain God and the supernatural Christian life came to me when I was witnessing to an individual and trying to explain the Gospel in a fresh and meaningful way.

b.   *Our availability to witness to others can be a gauge to measure our obedience to Christ.* If you feel no desire to witness for our Savior, the reason could be that you have neglected the most important part of sharing your faith—that of being filled with the Holy Spirit and maintaining your first love for our Savior.

Before you speak to others, make sure there is no unconfessed sin in your life. If God brings to mind any sin, confess it to Him. Thank Him that He has already forgiven you. Then invite the Holy Spirit to fill and empower you. Only as we are filled with the Spirit will we have the desire and the power to be fruitful witnesses for Him.

Never hesitate to tell others about our Lord. He has commanded us to tell the Good News to all men, and we are disobedient if we keep silent.

3. *How can we begin to share our faith with individuals encountered during the day?*

a. *Begin with prayer.* When I awaken for the day, I get on my knees and worship and praise the living Lord who dwells within me. I acknowledge His Lordship, I invite Him to walk around in my body, think with my mind, love with my heart, and speak with my lips. And since He came to this world 2,000 years ago to seek and save the lost, I ask Him to lead me to those whom He has already prepared for my witness.

b. *Look for God's divine appointments.* As I begin the day, I go about with an expectant attitude, looking for people with whom He might want me to speak. I am always asking, "Lord, is it he? Is it she? What about this person? What about that person?" If I am on a plane or a train or a bus, or if I am meeting on the college campus or in an executive office, I am always asking the question, "Is this person one with whom you would have me share your love and forgiveness?"

c. *Initiate the conversation.* This can be done in different ways, depending on the country and the culture. There are some countries where there is such an understanding and knowledge of God that you do not have to spend much time establishing rapport, nor do you have to prove the existence of God.

I often initiate a witness with stewardesses on planes by announcing, "I have something very exciting I want to share with you. I would like to give you this little booklet called the Four Spiritual Laws, which I encourage you to read. After you have finished reading it and are no longer busy caring for the other passengers, come back to see me, and we will talk." There have been many, many stewardesses who have read the Four Laws, returned to talk with me, and have received Christ.

d. *Consciously leave the results to God.* Successful witnessing is simply taking the initiative to share Christ in the power of the Holy Spirit and leaving the results to God. This is tremendously liberating to me, because not every unbeliever with whom I share Christ responds positively. In fact, at least 25 percent, and in some situations as many as 50 percent, do not respond positively.

Sometimes people tell me that they don't believe in God, or they don't believe in the Bible, or they don't believe in Jesus Christ. They offer all kinds of arguments, none of them original. Most of these objections have been offered for approximately 2,000 years. Most people are not rejecting Christ. For the most part, they are rejecting a false impression of Christianity. Oftentimes, they have had some kind of unfortunate emotional experience with their parents, a pastor, or some other Christian who has disappointed them. I find that very few people who have seriously considered the facts concerning Jesus Christ have said "No" to Him.

Recently I was talking with a brilliant young Nobel laureate, a professor on a university campus, who proclaimed himself an atheist. He was so adamant about it that I chided him a bit in a conversation following his address. "You know," I said, "it is not possible to be an atheist. It's not intellectually tenable, because, in order to be an atheist (one who claims that God does not exist except in our minds), you would have to know everything about everything, because God could exist in that realm of which you have no knowledge."

He exploded in anger. "Oh, you Christians make me sick!" he said, and he went on to explain his dim view of Christians. I put my hand on his arm and apologized. "Look," I said, "please forgive me. I'm your friend, not your critic. But it occurs to me that you are angry because of some unfortunate experience which has turned you away from a belief in God." He exploded again. "I'm married to a born-again Christian," he said, "and we're fighting this battle of Christianity daily. And have for three years!" As you can see, he had not rejected Christ but was reacting to an emotionally-charged marriage relationship.

e. *Seek to follow up each person you talk to about Christ.* I copy down their names and addresses and make a point of sending them literature or recorded messages which will help explain the importance of their decision for Christ and how they can begin to grow spiritually.

4. *The problem of fear which keeps us from witnessing personally*

Perhaps you would like to tell others about Christ, but when you try it, you find that you are fearful of speaking one-to-one with others. I have found that many eloquent, gifted evangelists and preachers who enjoy speaking to large crowds have a fear of talking to individuals. I have had those experiences myself. Paul encourages Timothy, his son in the faith: "God has not given us the spirit of fear, but of power and of love and of a sound mind" (2 Timothy 1:7). It is reasonable to believe that even Timothy was shy and reserved, and probably had a fear of witnessing. This is not unusual.

The fear exists because we do not wrestle against flesh and blood, but against the rulers of darkness in this world. Whenever we witness to nonbelievers, we are invading enemy territory. Paul says in Colossians 1:13, 14, "For he (God) delivered us out of the darkness and gloom of Satan's kingdom and brought us into the kingdom of his beloved Son, who bought our freedom with his blood and forgave us all our sins."

Every nonbeliever is a member of Satan's kingdom. I was once a member of that kingdom, and so were you. So we can expect Satan to do everything he can to keep us from witnessing. One of his favorite tricks is to try to convince me that the man with whom I am speaking is not interested in the Gospel. "Don't waste your time talking to him," the devil says. "He won't respond anyway."

It is a battle that never ceases. For forty years that small voice of the enemy has been trying to convince me that nobody wants to know about Jesus, that I have no right to "impose my views" on other people, that they have a right to their own religion, and other such arguments.

But God honors faith and obedience. Since the steps of a righteous person are directed by the Lord, expect that God has already prepared the hearts of those with whom you share the Good News, provided you are filled with the Holy Spirit. Expect God to use you. As Christ said, "Be it done to you according to your faith."

All around you, people are ready to receive Christ. I would like to encourage you while you are here in Amsterdam to take the materials "Peace With God" (or whatever materials are available) and approach individuals on the street, in the restaurants, in the markets, and share with them in their own language the message of Jesus Christ. If you need an interpreter, ask someone to go with you. Don't wait until you get home. Start here. Begin to share Christ as a way of life, and do it joyfully, with as much regularity as eating and sleeping. There is nothing more important that you can ever do than to lead others to the Savior.

Jesus took the time to express His love and concern for individuals wherever He went. He never hesitated to meet the needs of individuals whom He encountered during the course of His days. Philip obeyed God by leaving a successful evangelistic campaign to give the good news of the Gospel to one individual. Many other Scripture references emphasize the importance God places on the individual.

Frequent witnessing also benefits your ministry. It helps you maintain your first love for Christ. It keeps you in tune with your audiences. It keeps your illustrations fresh, alive, and meaningful to your audience. And it keeps you trusting our Savior, obedient to Him, allowing Him to seek and save the lost through you.

Simply pray before you begin each day. Make sure that you are filled with the Holy Spirit by faith, and that there is no unconfessed sin in your life. Then look for opportunities. Every day is filled with potential divine appointments. Initiate conversations with those to whom God leads you, and talk about Jesus. Explain the Gospel simply and clearly, perhaps using an aid such as The Four Spiritual Laws booklet to help you. Leave the results to God. Follow up those who respond so they can learn more about our wonderful Savior and the new life they have begun. Wherever possible, help those who are still seeking through further counsel, prayer, and by giving them appropriate literature.

We are all rightly concerned about the poor, the orphans, the widows, especially the millions of people who are dying because of lack of food in famine-stricken parts of the world. We should be concerned, and we should do everything within our power to help alleviate suffering in the name of Christ, wherever we find it. But all around us there is a greater tragedy. There are people who are well-fed and properly groomed who live lives of desperation, who are members of Satan's kingdom. They are lost, and they will soon leave this world and go to a Christless eternity—to hell, separated from God forever. I submit to you that their plight is far worse than that of those who are dying of starvation, unless they, too, are lost without Christ.

In closing, let me tell you of an influential woman in America who is at the helm of many endeavors designed to help people grow in their Christian faith. In her monthly magazine column, she has often admitted to a kind of skepticism about such a personal thing as talking about her personal relationship with God to strangers. She admits that she shares her faith only when she feels that she knows a person well.

Recently, in one of her columns, she wrote how she had gotten to know Roger, her hairdresser, during the many visits she paid to him over a period of several years. She learned how he'd grown up in Morocco and worked his way into a partnership in a successful salon. Eventually, they talked about more personal topics—his children from a previous marriage, his dream of producing a record album, his hopes of becoming a millionaire. One day he wore an ornate cross around his neck, and she asked him about it. It was just for decoration, he said. "Religion was part of my life when I was a child," he said. "But it just doesn't fit in now."

Though they discussed God and religion at times, there was never a time that this influential Christian businesswoman simply explained the Gospel to him. In fact, she wrote in her column that often she was rather proud that she was a "sophisticated" Christian, one who did not stuff tracts in people's faces or open a conversation with the Four Spiritual Laws. "I like the idea of life-style evangelism and sharing my faith," she said, "only after I'm sure the other person wants to hear about it."

Months passed before her next appointment with Roger. When she finally called the beauty salon and asked to speak to Roger, there was only silence. Finally, the woman on the other end of the line choked out, "Roger passed away three months ago. He had a heart attack."

Now this same Christian businesswoman writes in her column that she often thinks of Roger. She wishes she hadn't been so proud or so concerned about seeming naive that she didn't bring the simple fact of Jesus into Roger's sophisticated, but empty, life.

For Roger, it is too late.

But for millions in this city and around the world, it is *not* too late to communicate the love and forgiveness of our living Lord. There is nothing more important that you and I can do for them than to introduce them to Christ—to liberate them out of the darkness and gloom of Satan's kingdom. Begin today, and make it your daily practice, no matter how large the great evangelistic crowd you address, no matter how many opportunities you have to speak. Each day make it your God-given responsibility to take advantage of every opportunity to talk to individuals, as well as to the multitudes. Tell them about the Greatest Person who ever lived, the One who loves them unconditionally, who died for them that they may live for Him.

God's Word reminds us, "Anyone who calls upon the name of the Lord will be saved. But how shall they ask Him to save them unless they believe in Him? And how can they believe in Him if they have never heard about Him? And how can they hear about Him unless someone tells them? And how will anyone go and tell them unless someone sends him?" That is what the Scriptures are talking about when they say, "How beautiful are the feet of those who preach the gospel of peace with God and bring glad tidings of good things."

In other words, how welcome are those who come preaching the Good News!

# THE EVANGELIST'S PASSION FOR THE LOST
*George Sweeting*

May 10, 1940, fear swept the streets of Europe. On that day, the armies of Hitler invaded Holland, Belgium, and Luxembourg. Europe was in the midst of World War II. Three days later, May 21st, Winston Churchill spoke to the House of Commons: I have nothing to offer but blood, toil, tears, and sweat . . . You ask, "What is our policy?" I will say: It is to wage war—by sea, by land, and air, with all our might and with all the strength that God can give me.

Winston Churchill had a passion for justice and victory!

Tonight, a far greater battle is raging. It is a battle fought for the souls of men and women. It is a battle between the forces of light and darkness. It is a battle between the armies of Christ and Satan. It is a battle that will result in eternal life to those who receive Jesus Christ, and eternal death to those who reject Him.

First, I want to define two words: Consider the word, "soul." *What is the soul?* The soul is *the real you*! Genesis 2:7 reads, "God breathed into man the breath of life, and man became a living soul."

Jesus placed the highest possible value on the soul. Matthew 16:26 reads, "For what is a man profited if he gains the whole world and loses his own soul? Or what will a man give in exchange for his soul?" The soul is eternal and it will never die.

As evangelists we must remember that *God* has a passion for souls. John 3:16 reads, "For God so loved the world, that He gave His only begotten Son, that whoever believes in Him should not perish, but have eternal life."

*Jesus* has a passion for souls. Because of His passion, Jesus obeyed the Father and "became obedient to death, even the death of the cross" (Philippians 2:8).

The *apostles* had a passion for souls. They accepted the commission of Jesus to go into all the world and preach the Gospel. No trip was too far if, by taking that trip, a soul could be won. No expense was too great if, by making that expenditure, a soul could be won. No suffering was too intense if, by suffering, a soul could be won. No sacrifice was too deep if, by sacrificing, a soul could be won.

The soul is of *infinite value*!

Second, What do we mean by the word, "passion"? It means "to suffer." Often we speak of the saving work of Jesus on the Cross as "His passion." Jesus was completely committed to giving His life for lost sinners. Matthew 16:25 reads, "Whoever desires to save his life will lose it, and whoever loses his life for my sake will find it." Jesus plainly said, "If you hold onto your life, you will lose it; but if you lose it for my sake, you will save it."

I want you to consider three areas: a *single* passion; a *heart* passion; and a *life* passion.

## 1. We need a single passion

I was the proud owner of an attractive pocket knife when I was a boy. The knife had three blades, plus a can opener, a screw driver, a nail file, and a miniature pair of scissors. The whole thing cost only a dollar, but it wasn't worth a dime. The knife was so versatile that it was ineffective.

I have a sign on my desk that reads, "Keep off the detours."

The Moody Bible Institute, in many ways, is a conglomerate. Often, I remind our people, "The main thing is to keep the main thing the main thing."

—Matthew 6:22—Jesus said, "If thine eye be *single*, your whole body will be full of light."

—Psalm 27:4—David prayed, "*One thing* have I desired of the Lord."

—James 1:8 reminds us "a double-minded man is unstable in all his ways."

*The life of Jesus illustrates a single passion.* Jesus was fully yielded to the Father's will. His single passion is expressed in Luke 19:10: "For the Son of Man has come to seek and save that which was lost." Satan repeatedly tried to stop Jesus from His single passion of dying for a lost world. In the wilderness temptation, Satan offered an alternative to the Cross. He said, in effect, "You don't have to die for sinners. I'll give you the kingdoms of this world if you fall down and worship me." Again, when Jesus spoke to Peter about His death on the Cross, Peter rebuked Jesus and said, "Be it far from you." When Jesus was dying on the Cross, Satan spoke through the mocking crowd, saying, "Come down from the Cross and save thyself . . ."

*Jesus had a single passion*—to give Himself a ransom for many.

*John the Baptist had a single passion.* The crowds from Jerusalem came to him and asked, "Are you the Messiah?" John answered, "No. I'm just a voice crying in the wilderness. I am not the way, I'm only the way-shower."

*Peter and Andrew had a single passion.* Jesus called them to stop catching fish, and to start catching men, and that became their all-consuming passion (Matthew 4).

*Paul the Apostle had a single passion.* "Necessity is laid upon me; yea, woe is unto me, if I preach not the gospel" (1 Corinthians 9:16).

Paul's single passion is seen in his letters. He knew who he was and what he was to do.

—He begins Romans 1: "Paul, a bond servant of Christ Jesus, called as an apostle, set apart for the gospel of God."

—He begins 1 Corinthians 1: "Paul, called as an apostle of Jesus Christ by the will of God."

—He begins Galatians 1: "Paul, an apostle, not sent from men, nor through the agency of man, but through Jesus Christ, and God the Father."

—He begins 1 Timothy 1: "Paul, an apostle of Christ Jesus according to the command of God our Savior, and of Christ Jesus, who is our hope."

—He begins 2 Timothy 1: "Paul, an apostle of Christ Jesus by the will of God, according to the promise of life in Christ Jesus."

—He begins Titus 1: "Paul, a bond-servant of God, and an apostle of Jesus Christ for the faith of those chosen of God."

Philippians 3:13,14 express Paul's single passion—"This one thing I do: forgetting what lies behind and reaching forward to what lies ahead, I press on toward the goal for the prize of the upward call of God in Christ Jesus."

After graduating from Moody, I attended the Art Institute of Chicago. I remember the famous paintings of the Dutch artist Vincent Van Gogh. Van Gogh lived an unhappy life that ended in insanity and suicide. His father was a pastor. At one time in his life, Vincent felt called to be an evangelist.

At the age of 25 (1878), Van Gogh enrolled in short term training as an evangelist in Brussels. After graduation, during his first mission in South Brussels, he became *overwhelmed*. He took his eyes off of his *single passion* . . . quit preaching . . . and launched into another career.

The apostle Paul urged Timothy to "stir up the gift of God that was in him." May God help each of us to be controlled *by a single passion.*

2. *We need a heart passion*

John Henry Jowett has written some powerful words for us: "The gospel of *a broken heart* demands the ministry of bleeding hearts . . . As soon as we cease to bleed, we cease to bless . . . We can never heal the needs we do not feel. Tearless hearts can never be the *heralds of His passion*."

Abraham of the Old Testament had a heart of passion (Genesis 18). As he saw the condition of the people of Sodom, he was moved for the sake of the righteous. Abraham felt something of the compassion of God. "Abraham . . . said, 'Will you also destroy the righteous with the wicked? Possibly there are fifty righteous within the city: will you also destroy the place for the fifty righteous that are therein?'" (Genesis 18:23,24).

Because Abraham could not find 50 righteous souls, he asked the Lord to withhold judgment for the sake of 45, then 40, then 30, then 20; and finally he pleaded for the sake of 10 souls. Abraham had a heart passion.

*Moses had a heart passion.* While Moses was on Mt. Sinai, the children of Israel made a golden calf and worshiped it. Exodus 32:31,32 shows the heart of Moses: "This people have sinned a great sin, and have made them gods of gold. Yet now, will you forgive their sin—and if not, blot me, I pray, out of your book which you have written."

Moses so completely identified with his people that he was willing to be blotted out of God's book forever. Moses had a *heart passion*.

*Jesus Christ had a heart passion.* Once Jesus looked over the city of Jerusalem *and wept* (Matthew 23:37): "O Jerusalem, Jerusalem . . . how often I wanted to gather you . . . (as a hen gathers her chicks) and you were not willing."

Have you ever wept over your town?

Matthew chapter 9, verse 36, says of Jesus: "When he saw the multitudes, he was moved with compassion for them, because they were weary and scattered, like sheep having no shepherd."

God loves people—all people—and so must we.

D. L. Moody, the founder of the Moody Bible Institute, preached a sermon of compassion. Journalists asked him, "How did you prepare that sermon?" Mr. Moody told them that while on his knees he read several passages of Scripture about the compassion of Jesus. As he read, he was overcome with a burden for the lost. Mr. Moody said, "I laid on the floor of my bedroom and prayed, and read, and wept. As I did, I wrote down the thoughts that came to my mind and heart."

D. L. Moody had a *heart passion*.

E. G., a young Salvation Army officer, wrote to General Booth: I'm ready to quit! I've tried everything! General Booth wired back, *"Try tears."*

Paul the Apostle had a heart passion. The depth of Paul's passion is felt in Romans 9:1,2: "I say the truth in Christ, I lie not, my conscience also bearing me witness in the Holy Ghost, that I have great heaviness and continual sorrow in my heart."

Dr. C. E. Autrey, former chairman of evangelism at Southwestern Seminary, has an important comment for us: "The keen observer can detect the difference between the mighty currents of passion for souls and foamy emotions. When the waves come in, there will always be some foam . . . Some emotion may be expected. We should wisely guard against the excesses. But let us not forget that spiritual deadness and moral indifference are to be feared far more than emotion. Our danger today doesn't lie in the direction of uncontrolled emotionalism; it is in the realm of a cold, passionless Christianity."

May each of us ask the Lord for *a heart passion.*

3.    *We must have a life passion*

A single passion . . . A heart passion . . . *A life passion*

The apostle Paul had a *life passion.* Geographically, Paul shares the extent of his passion in Romans 9:2,3: "I have great heaviness and continual sorrow in my heart. For I could wish that I myself were accursed from Christ for my brethren, my kinsmen according to the flesh."

Paul is saying, "I am willing to go to hell, if by going to hell my relatives and countrymen will be saved." Paul possessed an all-consuming, all-directing passion.

Recently, I've seen several articles about burn-out due to stress and overwork, and I want to go on record saying I understand that—that is very possible and we must be careful. And yet, there is such a thing as "burning out for God." Moody did! George Whitefield did!

Hebrews 12:3,4 speaks of serving, even to the shedding of blood! "Consider Jesus, who has endured such hostility by sinners against Himself, so that you may not grow weary and lose heart." Now listen. . . . "You have not yet resisted to the point of shedding blood."

This is speaking of *a life passion.*

Henry Martyn, missionary to India, prayed, "Let me *burn out* for God." Henry Martyn had a *life passion.* In 1793, William Carey, age 32, offered his life to serve India. For 44 years, he laid down his life. *Carey had a life passion.* When George Whitefield was 20, he sensed God's call to evangelize North America. He crossed the Atlantic Ocean 13 times. At age 56 he died. Whitefield had a *life passion.* He burned out for souls. John Wesley began preaching in 1739 and continued for 50 years until he died. He traveled 225,000 miles, mostly on horseback, and preached 40,000 times—until he died. My friends, Wesley had a *life passion.*

A *life passion* for God—Do you have that?

There is an interesting verse in Genesis chapter 30, verse 1. It is the heart cry of Rachel for a child. Listen to it: "Now when Rachel saw that she bore Jacob no children, Rachel envied her sister, and said to Jacob, 'Give me children, or else I die!'" Rachel was concerned, ashamed, and desperate.

John Knox prayed a similar prayer for the souls of Scotland: "Oh God, give me Scotland, or else I die!" John Knox had a *life passion.*

This spring, several young Americans were lost in a sudden snowstorm while climbing Mt. Hood. As the rescue teams searched day after day, they grew weary, and wanted to quit. Many did quit. Some would not quit as they worked against unsurmountable odds. Eventually, they found two still alive.

The Bible commands us to go as long as there are lost sheep. As the Apostle Paul was stirred by the cries of the man from Macedonia—and the cries from Athens, Corinth, and Rome—may we hear the cries of our people, our towns, and our churches.

Listen to a short, potent paragraph by John Henry Jowett: "To be . . . in the sacrificial succession, our sympathy must be a passion, our intercession must be a groaning . . . and our service must be a martyrdom. In everything, there must be a shedding of blood!"

Have we served to the shedding of blood? The call, my evangelist friend, is not to silver, satin, silk, or precious stones, but to blood, toil, tears, and sweat.

And may we so live and preach, that when we stand on the shores of eternity, it will be said of you and me: "Never in the field of human conflict was so much owed . . . by so many . . . to so few!"

# THE EVANGELIST'S FAITHFULNESS
*Anne Graham Lotz*

Would you turn please to the book of Jeremiah, chapter one? As you locate it in the Old Testament, I would like to describe Jeremiah to you. Jeremiah was an evangelist, sent by God to his own people, to his own country. He preached for about 65 years without ever receiving one positive response. No one ever made a commitment when he gave an invitation; he never led anyone to salvation. Yet his ministry was so outstanding from God's perspective that 52 chapters of the Bible are devoted to recording it for eternity. And 600 years later, when people were trying to give an account for who Jesus of Nazareth was, some said He was Jeremiah come back from the dead.

You are an evangelist. To whom has God sent you? To your own people? To your own country? How long have you been preaching? What kind of response have you received? How many people have you led to salvation in Jesus Christ? Are you discouraged this morning because the response has not been what you think it should be? What actually determines a successful evangelistic ministry from God's perspective?

Would you listen to the personal testimony of a man who was a successful evangelist from God's perspective? Listen to Jeremiah's personal testimony. It includes three main points:

1. I was called to be an evangelist
2. I was commanded to be an evangelist
3. I was committed to be an evangelist

Let's look first at Jeremiah's calling to be an evangelist which gave him two things. It gave him, first, confidence in his ministry. Read 1:5. Jeremiah was called by God to be an evangelist. Why are you in the ministry? Examine your reasons. Do you know in the very depth of your heart and soul that God has called you? The only valid reason for being an evangelist is that God has called you to be one. And if God has called you to be an evangelist, nothing should shake your confidence. However, Jeremiah testifies that when he was first called, he was afraid. Which of his fears is yours? Read 1:6. I don't know how to speak—I don't know all the native dialects in my country—I am not eloquent—I don't have all the answers to people's questions about God; I am just a child—I am not educated—I am weak—I am poor—I don't have much Bible knowledge—I am inadequate to be an evangelist. How did God answer Jeremiah's fears? Read 1:7,8. "Jeremiah, I have called you to be an evangelist. Your fears are valid if your confidence is in yourself. Place your confidence in me—I am adequate—I will do this through you if you will make yourself totally available to me—just answer my call." Is your confidence in yourself, or in God?

The calling of God gave Jeremiah confidence, not in himself, but in his ministry. Second, the calling of God to be an evangelist gave Jeremiah clarity to his message. A preacher or Bible teacher speaks on many subjects. But an evangelist specializes in one. It is one message that has two basic elements, and at the beginning of his ministry Jeremiah was told by God what they were, as represented in two visions. Read 1:11. When you see the bud, you know the flower and fruit will follow. Therefore the first vision contains the element of hope and promise. Read 1:13. The Babylonians were gathering to invade Israel from the north, and would be used as God's instruments of judgment. Therefore, this second vision contains the element of judgment. These two elements make up the one message of the evangelist. It is the message of the Cross. The Cross stands as a symbol of man's hope and God's promise of forgiveness, of a right relationship with Himself, of eternal life, for those who receive Jesus Christ by faith as Savior and Lord. However, the Cross also stands as a symbol of judgment for those who reject Jesus Christ. Jeremiah preached hundreds of sermons which all contained these two basic elements because the calling of God brought clarity to his message. How clear is your message? Are you in danger of being diverted from the basic elements symbolized by the Cross? Preach—and when you preach, preach the Cross, again and again and again. Jeremiah personally testifies that he was called to be an evangelist. And that calling gave confidence to his ministry, and clarity to his message.

Then, too, he was not only called, he was commanded to be an evangelist (1:7, 17-18). Of whom are you afraid? Tribal leaders? Government Officials? Priests in other religions? Your own family? God said, "Don't be afraid of them, be afraid of me—if you disobey my command—I am the One to whom you are accountable." God has not only called you to be an evangelist, He commands you to be an evangelist (cf. Matthew 28:19,20). God did two things so that Jeremiah could obey His command. First, God equipped Jeremiah. Read 1:9. Jesus said in Mark 13:11, "Take no thought—don't worry about what you shall speak . . . it is not you that speaks, it is the Holy Spirit."

Part of God's equipping you to obey His command to be an evangelist is this conference. How many workshops, how many plenary sessions, how many opportunities to talk with someone one-on-one, have you missed? God has supplied the equipment—you must take advantage of it. God not only equipped Jeremiah, He also enabled Jeremiah to be obedient (1:8,18,19). Who is fighting against your ministry? God told Jeremiah that he would be opposed but the opposition would not overcome him for two reasons: God was with him enabling Jeremiah by His Presence; and God would rescue him enabling Jeremiah by His Power. What reason do you have for not obeying God's command to be an evangelist? There is no reason to disobey—only excuses. Jeremiah's personal testimony was that he was called to be an evangelist; he was commanded to be an evangelist; therefore he had no alternative but to commit himself to be an evangelist.

Jeremiah accepted the call, obeyed the command, made the commitment to be an evangelist who was powerful. He was powerful for two reasons. First because of his communication with God that involved two things. One, it involved time spent alone in God's Word. Read 1:2,4. Again and again in the Book of Jeremiah there is the phrase "Jeremiah stood in the counsel of the Lord." In other words, he made time to take in God's Word so that he could give it out. When do you make time to read and study God's Word—not books about God's Word? Do you make time for this every day? Jeremiah did. Read 15:16. He spent time alone in God's Word because he loved it and because there is no shortcut to a powerful ministry—it requires time spent alone in God's Word. That was half of his communication with God.

The other half involved time spent alone in prayer. Someone has said that what you do in private determines who you are in public. What do you do in private? When no one is around? When no one is looking? When you have some time to yourself? Jeremiah had a private life—it was a life of prayer. Read 12:1,3a. Then God speaks. Read 12:5. "I am conditioning you for what lies ahead." Read 15:15. Then God speaks (15:19). "Stop feeling sorry for yourself." When do you pour out your heart to the Lord in open, honest, reverent prayer? When you do, do you pick up your Bible and read so that God can speak to you in response? There is no shortcut to a powerful ministry. It requires not only time spent alone in God's Word, but time spent alone in prayer. Jeremiah was powerful because of his communication with God; and, second, because of his identification with the people. Read 8:21-9:1. He identified with them because he cared for them. What is your attitude toward the people to whom God has sent you? Do you care enough to pray for them? Do you care enough to weep for them? Do you care enough to ask God to break your heart for that which breaks His? Stephen Olford has said that the keys to effective evangelism are "wet eyes, bent knees, and a broken heart." Jeremiah, when faced with the sin of his people, so identified with them that instead of being critical, judgmental, self-righteous, he wept, he prayed, and he allowed God to break his heart. Jeremiah identified not only with the people to whom he was sent, but with the message that he gave.

Chapter 13 tells how he bought a linen belt, wore it, buried it, dug it up rotten, demonstrating Israel's uselessness to God. In chapter 19 he bought a clay pot, smashed it before the people, demonstrating that God would smash Israel in judgment if she did not repent. In chapter 27 he put a yoke on his neck, walked around Jerusalem, demonstrating Israel's coming oppression by Babylon. Again and again he lived out his message before the people; he didn't just preach it in words. His life was a demonstration of his message. How clearly does your life demonstrate your message? Someone has said that you can't teach your children to enjoy eating their food if every time they see you eating yours, you gag. You won't get others to love Jesus, to accept His forgiveness, to live lives pleasing to Him, if they don't see those things in you.

Jeremiah committed himself to be an evangelist—powerful because of his communication with God and his identification with the people and the message. Because he was powerful, he was also persecuted by those in authority. In chapter 20 he was beaten and placed in stocks, in chapter 37 he was imprisoned in a dungeon, in chapter 38 he was thrown into an empty, muddy cistern, and left to die. When have you experienced persecution? How has it affected your commitment to be an evangelist? Jeremiah was humiliated again and again, but never intimidated. The persecution did not weaken his commitment, it strengthened it. He was also persecuted by the people themselves in that they totally rejected him and his message (36:23,32; 37:1,2; 44:16).

What kind of response have you received to your ministry? Has it been less than you have prayed for? Less than you have expected? Less than you have desired? How has the rejection, the lack of response, affected your ministry? Are you discouraged and disheartened? Even beginning to doubt your call to be an evangelist? In chapter 25, Jeremiah said that every morning for 23 years he got up early to make time for prayer and to receive God's Word. Every day for 23 years he preached to the people; and every day for 23 years they rejected him and the message. Yet, Eugene Peterson has said, every day Jeremiah got up as though he was responding to an encore. Matthew 5:11, Jesus said, "Blessed are you *when* men shall persecute you"—not *if*. And in John 15:20 Jesus said, "Remember the word that I said unto you, the servant is not greater than his Lord—if they have persecuted me, they will also persecute you." If your ministry lacks power, people will leave you alone, or just ignore you. One evidence of Jeremiah's power was that he was persecuted.

Jeremiah was powerful, persecuted, and persevering. He persevered because he was personally fulfilled by his ministry. To what are you looking for satisfaction and fulfillment in your ministry? Jeremiah's satisfaction and fulfillment did not come from the praise, encouragement, or response that he received—he received none. His fulfillment and satisfaction came from being committed to what God had called and commanded him to do. Read Jeremiah 20:8b,9. Read Lamentations 3:19-24. Jeremiah's joy, satisfaction, and fulfillment were independent of the people's response to his ministry—it was centered in his commitment to God Himself.

In his perseverance, Jeremiah was fulfilled and also faithful to the end. The last scene of Jeremiah's life in chapter 44 shows him preaching to a people who continued to reject him. Jewish history tells us that Jeremiah—after pouring out his life for 65 years in commitment to what God had called and commanded him to do—was stoned to death by the very people to whom he had been sent. How faithful are you to your commitment to be an evangelist? Especially when it involves personal sacrifice and even danger?

God calculates your success as an evangelist, not by the number of people who hear your message and respond, but by your faithfulness to give it out. Would you choose to commit yourself to do what God has called and commanded you to do, regardless of the response you receive?

What is your personal testimony? Would you choose to say with Jeremiah: I am called to be an evangelist, I am commanded to be an evangelist, I am committed to be an evangelist?

# THE EVANGELIST'S FAMILY LIFE
*Cliff Barrows*

Some time ago, my Billie and I were eating in a restaurant. Sitting close by was a couple, each with a touch of silver in their hair, who were very happy together and enjoying their evening out. There was a look of contentment and peace on their faces. They talked quietly and pleasantly to each other. As we observed them from time to time throughout the course of the meal, there was such a serenity and grace about this couple—quite a contrast to some of the others sitting close by—that we couldn't help but notice. I remarked to my Billie, "You know they have got a good thing going!" We asked each other: "If they were observing us, would they be inclined to say the same thing about us?"

I am very much aware that we come from different parts of the world, different backgrounds, different cultures, each with its own traditions and life-styles, but perhaps it would be a fair question to ask—when seen together in public, with our wife, our family—would people be inclined to say, "That family, that couple has a good thing going"?

Good family relationships are increasingly hard to come by these days. The problems we face, the pressures of society, the social and economic pressures, the demands of a particular life-style or just the burden of everyday living can be overwhelming. Yet I am absolutely convinced that in spite of the difficulties, the pressures, and the problems, we can as Christian believers, and particularly as Christian workers, experience a meaningful and joyous family relationship that will be a blessing and benediction to our families, and to those we come in contact with day by day.

As Christians, we have the responsibility and privilege of reflecting the joy and presence of Christ in our lives.

I am excited about this time together and about the privilege I have of sharing some of the problems, burdens, lessons, and observations that my Billie and I have made over forty years of ministry as traveling evangelists and in over forty-one years of our married life together.

Looking back, there are many things we wish we had done differently. We have made many mistakes, but we are so grateful for God's mercy and His faithfulness to us. Our five children are all serving the Lord and are very busy and committed in raising their families. Having five children and now 12 grandchildren, my Billie and I are very grateful for every lesson we have learned and the experiences which God has taken us through. Our "family nest" at home is now empty, and that has presented a new development and understanding in our relationship together for which we are very grateful. One thing we have found is that our marriage relationship with all its demands, responsibilities, problems, and rewards does not remain static.

Through the years, however, my Billie has had much of the responsibility of being both mother and father to the children, and she has done a marvelous job in God's strength and by His grace. She has never complained about the added responsibility and load that she has had to carry. And she has always been my most faithful supporter and encourager, my most valued and trusted critic, and my dearest friend. Today, I along with all of our children "rise up and call her blessed."

In discussing "The Evangelist's Family Life" it was suggested that attention be given to certain questions which would enable us as evangelists to understand not only what our relationship and responsibilities to the family are from a biblical perspective, but also how better we might fulfill them through guidelines and practical suggestions that might be of help and encouragement.

I approach this subject with a great sense of personal need and dependence upon the Holy Spirit and the understanding that He can give through the Word of God. There is no subject of greater interest and concern to most of us here, since it applies directly to the area of our personal life and ministry, and because of its impact upon the effectiveness of our ministry.

The Scriptures have much to say about our family relationship; but they require our meditation, our study and understanding, and our obedience in submission and application. "This book of the law shall not depart from your mouth; but you shall meditate on it day and night, that you may observe to do according to all that is written in it. For then you will make your way prosperous and then you will have good understanding " (Joshua 1:8).

Let me say that I am aware that many here in this conference are single. You do not have a family relationship as a married person. Some of you are single by choice. The "right one" has not been revealed to you as yet. Others have taken the vow of celibacy either for life, or for a given period of time. Some are single because of death of a beloved partner. Some are single because of separation or a divorce that has taken place. Whatever the case, I want to affirm you in your ministry as a single person today and assure you that in speaking of the family life in evangelism we are in no way implying that your situation or status in life is of less importance. In fact, it is just the contrary. You are able to give your undivided attention to your ministry as an evangelist. It is my hope and prayer, however, that as we discuss this area of the family together it will be of mutual benefit and blessing to you.

It is interesting to note that some of the clearest teaching on the subject of marriage came from the lips and pen of the Apostle Paul who was single! (At least at the time of his writing!) And our greatest example of all is Jesus Christ who was not married. But the important thing for us all to remember is that the fulfillment of life and fulfillment in our God-called ministry is not dependent upon whether we are single or married, but in knowing that we are in the center of God's will and that we are trying faithfully to do it.

Now to the questions suggested by our topic:

1. *What are the biblical responsibilities for the evangelist to his spouse and to his children?*

This prompts further questions. Is it possible to be a dedicated and committed evangelist and at the same time be an effective, exemplary husband or father? Does my calling as an evangelist take precedence over my family? Does my family take precedence over my calling as an evangelist?

I believe the evangelist's faithfulness at home and his commitment to the home, his spouse and his family, is directly reflected in his public ministry. No evangelist can be described as "successful" if his home is in shambles because of his commitment to his calling as an evangelist. Perhaps we have opted for difficulty, tensions, stress and misunderstanding in our marriage and family relationships as part of "our cross or burden" we must bear in fulfilling our calling as an evangelist. God never intended this to be so. He holds us responsible and accountable for changing this situation through His grace and by His power.

The Scriptures have much to say about our marriage and family relationship and responsibilities.

Ephesians 5:22-25: "Wives submit yourselves to your own husbands as to the Lord. For the husband is head of the wife, as also Christ is head of the church; and

He is the Savior of the body. Therefore, just as the church is subject to Christ, so should the wives be to their own husbands in everything. Husbands love your wives just as Christ also loved the church and gave Himself for it.''

The second Scripture is 1 Peter 3:7: "Likewise you husbands, dwell with them with understanding, giving honor to the wife, as to the weaker vessel, and as being heirs together of the grace of life that your prayer not be hindered.''

The third Scripture is Ephesians 6:4: "And you fathers, do not provoke your children to wrath, but bring them up in the training and admonition of the Lord.''

In these Scriptures and several others which could be referred to, we as husbands are to be the spiritual head and leader of the home, and this includes our wife and our children. This is not a particularly popular teaching in many circles today. But we need to underscore this truth and be willing to face the responsibility of it squarely and honestly. As the head of our wife we are to be her protector, her provider, her partner, and her spiritual counselor. We are to protect her not only physically but, even more important, mentally and emotionally from the pressure of people and society around her. From the pressure and abuse, sometimes, from the children in the family itself. From the unique pressure of our ministry as evangelist. The loneliness, the isolation, the lack of communication, resentment, jealousy and envy, worry and fear are all very real problems that she has to cope with, particularly because as traveling evangelists we are gone so much of the time. It is our responsibility to recognize the special problems that she faces, and do all in our power to help her cope with them.

The Living Bible gives additional insight to 1 Peter 3:7 when it says: "You husbands must be careful of your wives, be thoughtful of their needs and honoring them as the weaker sex. Remember that you and your wife are partners in receiving God's blessings, and if you don't treat her as you should, your prayers will not get ready answers.''

This is not just a suggestion for us to consider but a positive statement as to our responsibility to her.

We are to dwell—to live with our wife—with understanding. She is an equal partner in this relationship. But if the truth were known, often she has not been treated as such. We have given her the full responsibility of the family while we have been away. We have left her to struggle with the running and management of the household. We have often let her assume the problems of the home and the discipline of the children while we have immersed ourselves completely in our work, with little thought about what she is going through at home. This is not "dwelling with her in understanding.''

With regard to our leadership role as head of the wife, the Apostle Paul clearly gives us an example of Christ Himself. Ephesians 5:23: "We are the head of our wife, even as Christ is the head of the church and He is the Savior of the body.'' We as husbands accept this quite readily perhaps, but we fail to recognize another significant characteristic of the life of Christ, and that was His "servant attitude.'' He came not to be ministered unto but to minister. He was constantly seeking His Father's will, not His own; and His living demonstration of humble service in the washing of His disciples' feet was climaxed with His words, "You also should wash each other's feet!'' His attitude is a constant reminder to us that this should also be our attitude, one of service to our wives and our families.

We are to work to develop spiritual oneness with our wives. A phrase in 1 Peter 3:7, *"heirs together,"* speaks volumes to us at this point; and the word "together,'' I believe, is one of the key words of this verse. It is also a key word in our relationship.

We are to "dwell *together*." This means that we are to walk together in harmony and fellowship. We are to talk together, read together, pray together, grow together, and share together. And, brothers and sisters, this puts a double responsibility upon us as evangelists who are gone a great deal of the time. We must make up for lost time when we are at home. Tragically, this is not done in so many cases. Joseph Bayly has noted: "It almost seems as if alienation from wife and children is a badge; one to prove devotion to the Lord's work."

Here are some practical suggestions that may be of help to you, as they have been to me, in working at developing this spiritual oneness:
- —keep short accounts with each other and with God
- —pray together with her and with the children
- —keep in close contact by letter, by phone (if possible) when you are away (more about this later)
- —set goals in Scripture reading and memorization
- —set a specific time, if possible, for your personal devotions even while you are apart. As you think of each other studying the same truths, God will use this to bring you together mentally and spiritually even though you are miles apart physically.

Here is a special word for you to share with your wife. She must develop and cultivate her own spiritual life. This is a necessary "survival factor" not only for her marriage and home but for your ministry as well.

Our attitude in this regard is so important. And these words from the Apostle Paul in Romans 15:5 are helpful: "May God who gives patience, steadfastness and encouragement help you to live in complete harmony with each other, each with the attitude of Christ towards the other."

As we look again at Ephesians 5:25: "Husbands love your wives just as Christ also loved the church and gave Himself for it," we are reminded that our love relationship with our wife should be of such quality that it can be likened to the love that Christ had for the Church. Christ's love for the Church was a sacrificing love. He gave His life for the Church. Our love for our wife should be a sacrificing love. There should be no thing, including my own life, that is so dear that I would not be willing to give it for her. We are commanded to love our wives—as Christ loved the Church. This implies that I must seek for ways in which I could give myself, my time and energy, my thoughts and concern, to her.

Christ's love was a serving love. We are commanded to serve one another in love and, this surely means our wife! We serve her in kindness, serve her in doing things for her. We put our creative sources to work to see in what ways we can exemplify the servant attitude in our relationship to our wife. We did it when we were courting her!

Christ's love was a sanctifying love. He set His bride, the Church apart—dedicated to the worship and praise and glory of God the Father alone. What can I do to set my wife apart so that she may be encouraged, strengthened, better prepared in time, in training, in devotion to God to be the fulfilled person that God intended her to be—as an heir together with us of the grace of Life?

May God give each of us a greater understanding, day by day, of what it means to love our wives as Christ loved the Church.

I want to mention one other dimension in this regard. Some have asked, what place or part does romantic love play in the Christian marriage? More specifically: what part does it play in the life of a Christian worker, of an evangelist? Can it be developed if it presently does not exist? Do our children know that we really love each other by our attitude and our actions in the home?

It is a sad commentary that so often our Christian young people are learning more about love from the world and its cheap portrayal of it than they are from the Bible and the example that they see from their mother and father in the home. On the other hand, how marvelous it is to see the sparkle, the glow, the kind attention and the consideration in the life and manner of a couple who are truly in love with God and with each other. Do we as evangelists portray this kind of an exciting relationship with our spouse that speaks volumes to her, and to our family as well? We should.

Maybe your love has grown cold, and there is no romance in your marriage. I believe it can be restored.

We have all witnessed the reconciling power of the Gospel of Christ in the lives of men and women who have responded to the preaching of the message in our meetings. Husband and wife out of fellowship, out of touch with God—and certainly with each other—have attended the meetings unknown to one another. Both have responded to the invitation—have seen each other in the counseling area and have literally fallen into each other's arms to begin a new relationship all over. But this time with the new Life of Christ within to help them.

The principle that we can "love by faith" is the key. It has been rightly said that "we cannot feel our way into acting," but we can "act our way into feeling." We can "love by faith, doing those things that we would normally do if we really did feel love for our spouse."

Do you remember the New Testament story of the wedding in Cana? A Toronto pastor has written, "In a sense the wine of marriage may run out sometime. There are days of emptiness when the early wine of rapture runs dry and we are disappointed in love. But, the point that saves the story and gives us hope is that Jesus was there to supply what was lacking." It is wonderful to know that when Jesus comes into our marriage He can replenish what has been used up and exhausted. There is a new quality, "a royal wine" which He makes to flow freely for us.

Howard Hendricks has suggested, "If you really want to gauge the quality of your spiritual life, check your love dimensions. Not how often you read your Bible, or how much Scripture you have memorized—but whether the people with whom you are living regard you as a lover—a person reflecting the Love of Christ which He sheds into your heart."

This brings us to our relationship and responsibilities with our families. As we talk about this area we realize that we seldom "get it all together." How true it is, as someone has said, "About the time you gain enough experience to be a good parent, you find yourself out of a job."

In Ephesians 6:4 we are told: "Fathers, do not exasperate your children; instead, bring them up in the training and instruction of the Lord." There are other Scriptures that we could turn to (Proverbs 22:6; Deuteronomy 6:6-9; Psalm 78:1-9; Proverbs 23:26).

We are to be *spiritual leaders* of our home and family, as well as the physical father to our children. We are to assume responsibility with our children in the home by example (1 Timothy 4:12); in teaching and training (Proverbs 22:6); in provision (1 Timothy 5:8); in discipline (Ephesians 6:4). These responsibilities are not always easy to carry out as evangelists, especially when we are away from home so much of the time. This does not absolve us from our responsibility to do so, even if it is difficult.

We are to exercise loving discipline. We should be an example to our children in our homes. In the Old Testament we have the illustration of Eli and Samuel. The result with their children was tragic.

If my Billie and I could do it over again we would spend more time with our children. Is it not true that we are often so busy with other people's children that we don't have time for our own?

*2.    What are the guidelines for an evangelist to determine when he is giving enough attention to his family?*

This question brings into focus the whole area of priorities in our family relationships and in our ministry as an evangelist (how to establish what they are and how to carry them out). How can this be done? Is there a formula that will help me? What order should my priorities take?

Some have suggested this order: God first, family second, work third, then leisure. Even this however, has been difficult. Because no matter how hard I try, it is hard at times to be consistent even with the best of intentions to do so.

Here is another concept with regard to establishing priorities that I have been working through in recent years, and that has been a help to me. Let's take the familiar wheel illustration developed and used so effectively by the Navigators organization, and apply it to our family responsibility and ministry as an evangelist. I have drawn the wheel for you: let's fill it in together.

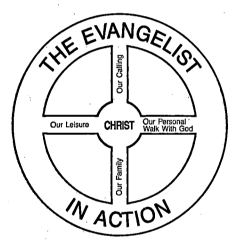

Put Christ in the center—He is the hub of this wheel.

In the upper spoke let's write "OUR CALLING," in the spoke to the right "OUR PERSONAL WALK WITH GOD," the bottom spoke "OUR FAMILY," and the left spoke "OUR LEISURE." You may have an additional spoke or two. I think the principle can still be applied. There are times when the "ministry spoke" meets the road. All of my interest, attention, and concentration must be given to this. But in the forward motion and progress of my life, and of our lives together as a family, another spoke moves into that position, and attention and concentration are given. Perhaps it is only for a shorter time—or maybe longer—but in either event, with Christ as the hub and each spoke anchored in Him, there is no conflict. And we find mutual encouragement, effectiveness, and progress in our family relationships and in our ministry. Admittedly, we will question at times the decisions we have to make, and we will wonder where the emphasis should be. But, in this connection Psalm 25:12,13, has been a tremendous help and encouragement to me. "Who then, is the man that fears the Lord? God will teach him how to choose the best. He shall live within God's circle of blessing and his children shall inherit the earth.''

How do I know that I have a proper balance and am giving enough attention to my wife and family? I have to give it all to the Lord, knowing and believing that He is in control and will enable me to keep the wheel of our life and ministry in balance.

3. *How can we, as evangelists, make the time spent with our families more effective quality time?*

It takes planning and scheduling. We need to write ''HOME'' on our appointment calendar just as we would the dates of our next meeting. We have to ''make time.'' It is never available.

I'd like to suggest that we schedule a special day or a half-day for the family and do what *they* would like to do. We should also set aside a specific day or evening for our wives (at least once a week, if possible). Not only will this strengthen our relationship, but our children will see how important we are to each other. We will be establishing role models for them which will give them a sense of security. Nothing makes the children feel more secure than to see that their mother and dad really do love each other, and care enough to take time to be with each other.

a. Give the children the best part of their available day.

b. Plan your schedule to fit theirs.

c. Have devotions with them at night. Put the younger ones to bed.

d. Take time to chat with them. This is when they like to talk.

e. Spend time alone with each child and give each one your undivided attention when you do. This will make each one feel important! When they are old enough, take them ''one child at a time'' on one of your trips or crusade meetings. Perhaps you could arrange to take your whole family at a certain time—if resources would permit. I wish we had done more of this.

f. Study the particular interests and talents of each child and cultivate them. Become involved with them in their school interests and activities. Attend their functions, special events, sporting events, etc., when possible.

g. Show an interest in your children's friends and help them develop right relationships.

h. The greatest gift we could give them, and probably the most costly, is the gift of ourselves—the gift of time. So let's be sure that we give them this gift.

I am sure that many here today could suggest other things that could be done which you found to be most helpful. These are just a few that I wish I had applied more diligently.

Above everything, we should show appreciation and kindness to our wives and to our family. Appreciation for the things they do and for the persons they are. Kindness, Christ-likeness, should characterize our life and relationship with them—not rudeness, meanness, impatience, harsh and bitter attitudes. Remember Ephesians 4:32 applies just as much to our family relationship as in any other relationship, ''Be kind one to another, tenderhearted, forgiving one another just as God in Christ also has forgiven you.''

4. *How can we maintain family worship in the home while absent?*

It is surprising how many leave this responsibility to their wives even when they are home. It would also be surprising to know how many don't even participate in them at home, excusing themselves from the family worship. This is hard to believe, but it is true. Remember we are to assume a spiritual leadership in the home. Of course, this responsibility falls heavily upon the wife when we are gone, but the pattern and example that we set will enable her to be more effective in carrying out the responsibility for us in those times we are away.

a.  We should plan before we leave home the Scripture lessons and devotionals to use and the Scriptures that we would memorize together. Remember it is better to work on just one or two verses, learn them well, and repeat them often, than to take on a much larger assignment.

b.  If it is possible, make a tape for them with two or three brief devotionals and prayers before you leave home. Your children and family know your voice. May it remind them more and more of a father who knows God and communicates with God. This is best done in our warm and personal devotions together.

c.  Call each child by name on occasion in your devotionals, thereby letting them know how important each one is.

d.  Assign some of the older children on occasion to lead the devotionals while you are away. Teach them all the joy of praying and talking to their heavenly Father in "conversational prayer."

e.  Affirm your wife's leadership in this area of responsibility before your children. She is the key in developing and maintaining a devotional time with your family while you are away.

f.  Make a frequent report on tape for them while you are away for a long time. Perhaps in your part of the world this is impossible, but for others it could easily be done.

g.  Write to each child separately from time to time even if it is only a postcard; it lets them know that they are special and daddy is thinking about them.

One other thought that would apply both in response to this question concerning the devotional time with the children, and the previous question about making our time more effective when we are at home. We should endeavor to involve the children in our work as much as possible. Particularly the older children. We could have them do special projects *with* us when we are home with them, and *for* us when we are away. I wish I had done more of this when our children were growing up. Psalm 90:16: "Let your work appear to your servants and your glory to their children."

This, of course, is speaking of God's work and God's glory. We are God's servants doing God's work, and our prayer should be that our children will see His glory in His work which we are privileged to do. So often they see the other side: our tiredness, our discouragement, our impatience, our trials, or our problems. We are the key to fulfilling the Psalmist's request: "Let us see your miracles again, let our children see glorious things, the kind you used to do and let the Lord our God favor us and give us success." We need to share in our concerns and burdens for the work of God to which we have been called and also for the responsibility within the family. But they should also witness and share in our "enthusiasms" and "joyous" commitment to the family and to our work. They need to be able to say, "My dad is doing the most important work in all the world!"

5.  *What are the evangelist's responsibilities and opportunities to witness to his neighbors?*

First of all we should realize that we do have a very definite responsibility to witness to them. I know this is difficult. It is relatively easy to preach from a platform in a community where we are not known, but where there is the support and interest of people surrounding us. It is quite a different matter to witness on a personal level to those who live nearby and with whom we come in contact day by day. If we are concerned about winning them for Christ, and we should be, then we will look for ways to communicate our love and interest in them. We, of course, know that we are to let our light shine before others that they may see our good works and glorify our Father who is in heaven. This certainly means our neighbor next door.

We should endeavor to build bridges of friendship to them. This would include doing something for them. Helping them in their garden, helping to hoe their weeds, helping to plant their corn, helping to carry water for them, showing an interest in them. Be watchful when they are sick and show special interest. Look for ways to exhibit the love of Christ. Perhaps your wife can cook a meal for them. Invite them over to your place, even if it is only for a cup of coffee or tea. Let them get to know you. Get to know them. I know how difficult this is, since we are gone so much of the time.

Perhaps you could plan a neighborhood party or fellowship time. Show them what a Christian party can be. Food, fellowship, and wholesome fun. Then take a few moments; don't preach but in a very casual, warm and friendly way, share your faith and your personal experience with Christ. Remember this: "The light that shines the farthest shines the brightest at home." The greatest witness to your neighbor will be the love and harmony and joy that you and your family demonstrate. Remember: They are watching when you aren't.

Francis of Assisi commented to his students one day, "Let's go into the town and preach." They walked together to the city and then came back to their quarters again without stopping to preach. The students said, "I thought we were going to town to preach." Francis said, "We did! We preached as we walked about the town and people observed us."

Our responsibility is to love them even when it is difficult to show an interest in them. To befriend them when possible. To help them in their times of troubles and sickness. To pray for them. Pray for them with your family. Let your family know your concern for them. Encourage your family to look for ways to help your neighbors, to be kind and helpful to them. Invite your friends and neighbors to go with you to certain functions, especially to church. We sometimes sing a little chorus that says: "Lord, lay some soul upon my heart and love that soul through me; and may I humbly do my part to win that soul for Thee." That soul should be our neighbor, and even as I have shared this with you today, I realize how far short I have fallen in reaching out and being the witness that I should to my neighbors. May the Lord help us especially in this area.

In summary, may I offer a few practical suggestions which have been a help and encouragement to me.

   a.  Carry the picture of your wife and family with you and put it on the table or dresser in the room where you are staying.

   b.  Put your Bible and notebook out.

   c.  Dedicate that room to God and ask Him to make it His place of refuge and refreshment for you. Bathe that room with your prayers.

   d.  Practice the presence of Jesus in that room. Talk with Him openly and frequently. There is a motto we see displayed often in Christian homes which says: "Christ is the unseen guest at every meal, the silent listener to every conversation." We are not alone. Jesus Christ is with us wherever we go. Let us never forget that fact.

   e.  Exercise the discipline of self-control over the thoughts that you think, the books and magazines that you read, the television programs that you watch. I do not know the situation in the country from which you come, but in North America and in parts of Europe one of the greatest hindrances to a personal walk with God and spiritual power in our life can be the TV set and the time spent watching it.

f.   Keep in touch with your family as frequently as possible, by writing or by the telephone. I realize this is not possible in many countries, but for others it is.

g.   Build a spiritual network, beginning with your family. Some are blessed to have extended family members nearby to help them. Aunts, uncles, grandparents, etc. Others are less fortunate, but we can develop an extended family of loving, caring people who can become in a sense aunts, uncles, grandparents to our children, and sources of encouragement and strength to our wives, especially when we are away. These extended or adopted family members can be anchors to the wife and children when you are away.

The family itself can also be of mutual strength and encouragement to each other and to you. The more you involve them in your own life and work—and the more you become involved in theirs—the stronger that union will be, and the greater support and encouragement you will be to each other.

Our families, with our leadership and support, can be this kind of encouragement and blessing to each other. But it is up to us to take the initiative. How many times in my earlier years have I boarded a plane for some distant city, waved goodbye to a family of six, knowing as I left that they were supporting me and praying for me as I was for them. As the years passed and one by one they left the nest, until now it is just my Billie who sees me off at the airport, I have been nonetheless encouraged by the fact that not only is she praying daily and constantly for me, but also the children, wherever they are.

I remember our youngest son Bill saying his prayers one night when he was only five years old: "Dear Jesus, please save everybody in the world real quick so Daddy can stay home." At least he had some idea why I was gone so much of the time! But just a few days ago in talking with him on the phone he said, "Dad, I'll be praying for you and mother as you go to Amsterdam." Most of us here today know what it means to have our children praying for us daily, and how grateful we are for them.

In addition to the family network, develop a friendship with a friend, a buddy, a pastor, a fellow evangelist, or someone in the community in whom you can confide. Talk with him, have fellowship with him, and pray with him. There is a spiritual principle involved in this kind of a relationship which God will honor and which will be of tremendous encouragement and support to you. You can also be this same kind of encouragement and blessing to him. This will also help build your spiritual network.

h.   Remember, the more you pray for your family and commit them to God, the closer you are in heart and spirit to them. Before you leave home, prepare them for your leaving. Share your prayer burdens and concerns. Have them share theirs with you. Tell them about where you are going and something about the people there.

i.   Be sure to report the blessing and answers to prayer when you return. That will let them know how much you cared.

6.   *Conclusion*

There is no area of life that is more important than your family. Successful meetings, large crowds, popular appeal, or response to the invitation, whatever barometer of success one may use, will never compensate for failure in our homes.

The divine resources are at our disposal to use. The resources of God's Word, the person of the Lord Jesus Christ, the presence of the Holy Spirit, the power of prayer and the family network to encourage and strengthen us. The responsibility lies with us in appropriating these through personal discipline and commitment.

The rewards, I believe, will be manifold. Many of us are already experiencing some of them. There will be a new togetherness in our relationship with our spouse that will bring a new dimension to that relationship and understanding in communication, in appreciation, in expression that we haven't experienced before. There will be a growing sense of partnership and togetherness in our role as parents that will give stability, direction and purpose for our children. And there will be a new deepening of our personal walk with God. This in turn will bring new effectiveness, new challenge, and new excitement in our calling as evangelists and in our role as parents.

There is no one sitting here today, including the speaker, who doesn't realize that we have failed in some area of our family relationship in one way or another. Some of us have failed so miserably that we despair of trying again, or we wonder if there is any hope for a new relationship to begin. The good news is that there is forgiveness with God. He *is* the God of the second and third and fourth chance. We can begin again. Even as we preach to others, let us apply it to ourselves. But we must take that first step.

We stand today on the threshold of a new beginning in our family relationship. For some, it will be a fulfilling continuation of what we have been experiencing in the past. For others, it will mean a return to biblical patterns and standards. It will mean a humbling of ourselves before God and our loved ones—asking forgiveness, and claiming together His grace for cleansing and for courage to begin again. For all of us, it will require a new surrender to His will and the dedication to the task ahead. This will be costly but will pay with dividends.

Perhaps many of us here today have not taken our responsibilities and relationship to the family as seriously as we should; but through the Holy Spirit we have been made to see where we have failed and what our response should be.

May God speak to our hearts and lead us to a full and complete surrender.

*Prayer of St. Francis of Assisi*
It is a good prayer for us as evangelists to pray today as we dedicate ourselves and our families and ministry to God.

> Lord, make me an instrument of your peace;
> Where there is hatred, let me sow love;
> Where there is injury, pardon;
> Where there is doubt, faith;
> Where there is despair, hope;
> Where there is darkness, light;
> And where there is sadness, joy.
>
> O Divine Master, grant that I may not so much seek to be
> consoled as to console;
> To be understood as to understand;
> To be loved as to love;
> For it is in giving that we receive,
> It is in pardoning that we are pardoned,
> And it is in dying that we are born to eternal life.
> AMEN!

# THE EVANGELIST'S STRENGTH IN WEAKNESS
# (What Are You Doing Here, Elijah?)
## Leighton Ford

"Elijah was a man just like us" (James 5:17).
"Elijah was afraid and ran for his life . . ." (1 Kings 19:3).
"What are you doing here, Elijah?" (1 Kings 19:9).

God asked His prophet, "What are you doing here, Elijah?" It is the question for each one of us as we begin Amsterdam 86. "What are you doing here, evangelist?"

We have all been invited here by Billy Graham to learn, to fellowship with each other, to receive inspiration and to be better evangelists and ministers. But all of us—and some of us especially—have come to Amsterdam in great need of being restored.

What evangelist from the past do you most admire? I am sure there is one who has been a great inspiration to you because of his or her boldness, zeal, courage, and the blessing of God on his ministry. You would like to be like him or her, but if you could see that person from the inside, as God sees him and as he sees himself, you might be very surprised. You think of him as always strong, but he probably sees himself as often weak.

The Scripture always shows us the heroes of the faith as both strong and weak. This is for our comfort and for our warning.

Take Elijah. He is certainly a heroic figure. When King Herod heard of Jesus' miracles, he said, "John the Baptist, or Elijah, has come back." Elijah and Moses were the two Old Testament leaders who spoke with Jesus on the Mount of Transfiguration. Think of Elijah confronting the wicked King Ahab and saying, "As the Lord God lives, there will be no rain in the next few years except at my word." I picture him praying and there was no rain. I see him on Mount Carmel, taunting the prophets of Baal, calling down fire from God to consume the sacrifice. Who would not like to be like Elijah?

Yet James writes, "Elijah was man just like us. He prayed earnestly that it would not rain, and it did not rain on the land for three and a half years. Again he prayed, and the heavens gave rain, and the earth produced its crops" (James 5:17,18). But also the Scripture tells us, "Elijah was afraid and ran for his life" (1 Kings 19:3).

*"What are you doing here, Elijah?"*

Is this the same Elijah we've read about? Is this the prophet who is fresh from the most dramatic scene of a generation? Is this the man of God who was used to expose the false prophets and who could pray and call down fire? Is this the great intercessor who prayed for rain and saw a cloud as small as a man's hand grow into a tremendous rainstorm? Is this the same man of whom we read, "The power of the Lord came upon Elijah and, tucking his cloak into his belt, he ran ahead of Ahab all the way to Jezreel"—nearly the length of a marathon?

Now the Scripture shows him going out into the desert. He comes to a broom tree, sits down under it and prays that he might die. "I have had enough, Lord," he says, "take my life; I am not better than my ancestors." And all because a wicked woman had said, "Boo. I'm going to get you." King Ahab had told his wife Jezebel how Elijah had killed the false prophets and Jezebel sent to say, "May the gods deal with me, . . . if by this time tomorrow I do not make your life like that of one of them." Elijah was afraid and ran for his life.

Have you ever felt like that? Despair and discouragement can lay hold of us at the most unexpected times. Elijah had more reason to be elated than to be depressed. We never know when the enemy will launch his guided missile of discouragement.

Our Lord Jesus went into the wilderness and was tempted by the devil immediately *after* He was baptized by John and the Spirit came upon Him. So often the devil attacks when we are depleted after a crusade, after a tremendous victory—perhaps even during or after Amsterdam 86.

All of us spend some time under the broom tree. Our bodies and minds get weary. Our hopes are frustrated and disappointed. We may feel we have failed. We lose a loved one or a friend, and are in grief. Or perhaps in a time of discouragement and temptation we have sinned.

Some of us may even be surprised that Amsterdam 86 is not the mountaintop experience of Mount Carmel that we had expected, but a time of sitting under the broom tree and praying that we might die.

"What are *you* doing here, Elijah?"—the Lord's question came a little later. And not just Elijah. But Leighton Ford. And you. And your most admired evangelist. The preacher of the Gospel is especially subject to such moods. The devil comes and says, "Who are you, a man or woman of God to be so weak? You've worked so hard and seen such small response. Your family and friends don't appreciate you. Why not just give up?" Remember, like Elijah, Moses also asked God to take his life. Remember the great apostle Paul wrote that in Asia, "We were under great pressure, far beyond our ability to endure, so that we despaired even of life. Indeed, in our hearts we felt the sentence of death" (2 Corinthians 1:8,9).

"What are *you* doing here, Elijah?" Don't be surprised that it happened to Elijah. It happens to you and to me.

What were the *causes* of Elijah's condition? I think I can see three causes which help us to understand how Elijah was a man just like us.

Physically, he was totally exhausted. He had survived the three-year famine. He had spent tremendous nervous energy on the top of Mount Carmel where he challenged the false prophets. He had poured himself into his prayers and then—by the power of the Lord and the inspiration of that high moment—he had run for perhaps twenty miles ahead of Ahab's chariot. He had given all that he had.

I have read what some of the commentators have to say about Elijah, and several take him to task for his fear and for his lack of faith. I think they are partly right, but they overlook the physical facts. No one can put tremendous physical and emotional energy into his work without having a reaction. A "low" always follows a "high." Elijah had a "mountaintop" experience and then he had an anti-climax. He was experiencing what one psychologist calls the "post-adrenalin blues."

You and I need to understand that we are men and women just like Elijah. We can pray and be tremendously high. Then we can run and be terribly low. For me, it often happens after a big meeting or a major project I have been working on for weeks and months. I have learned to expect a feeling of being let down. Sometimes this happens to me on a vacation after a busy year. I expect a vacation to be a wonderful time and instead I feel blue and down.

We need to understand that there is a rhythm God has built in to us. After we have had a high and a great flow of adrenalin and are physically tired, we need to feel let down. Our emotions are a gift from God. And when we are down it's because we need a time of recovery and refreshing—and that's what God gave Elijah.

Closely tied to Elijah's physical fatigue was his emotional sense of loneliness and perhaps of anger.

I look at Elijah standing in front of the false prophets, no flinching, no fear, all alone, and I think, "Here is a man who is strong. Elijah needs no companion to encourage him. I wish I were like him."

But such a man never existed. Recently a pastor told me of another pastor friend of his who is constantly whipping and exhorting his congregation. "You're mad at your people," he said. "You say they are up and down and on and off. Well, you must have different people than I know about. The *only* people I know are up and down and on and off."

Just because we are evangelists does not mean we are not emotional creatures. When we were preparing for the Amsterdam conference, I asked some evangelists what their needs were. One said, "How can I stay motivated day after day especially when I am away from home?" Another said, "Many evangelists I know have a sense of inferiority and a poor self-image. That may be what drives us. How do we deal with that?" Some of you at Amsterdam 86 come from areas where Christians are persecuted and evangelists are despised, and you are a minority of a minority.

The cost of often traveling away from home alone is high on our emotional life. When I was younger, I often found that we would open a campaign on Sunday and on the Monday I would feel very low. I didn't understand why. I thought it was just a spiritual battle. Now I understand that it was because I had to be away from my family. I could be up for the first night, but the next day the emotional change of leaving home affected me. Once I understood that, I began to deal with it better.

As God's messengers, we are not immune to the blows of life. A great disappointment or loss may bring us to the place of saying, "Lord, take me home. I have had enough." Our older son Sandy died during heart surgery four and a half years ago. We were very close and loved each other dearly. He was a strong Christian and was headed for the ministry. For many months afterward I had very little strength. I felt as if everything inside me had been sucked out. I didn't want to leave home. Every time I stood to speak there was a terrible sense of weakness. Like Elijah, I just wanted to go home and be with the Lord. Heaven was very appealing and it still is. Yet, I found that God's strength was made perfect in my weakness. I didn't have strength to stand and speak, but when I did, somehow the Lord was always there to give that extra strength that was needed. Some asked, "How did you call down God's power?" My answer, "I didn't. It was just there."

But like Elijah, I felt I was under a broom tree.

Elijah's emotions were assaulted by loneliness, by disappointment, and by anger. When the Lord said, "What are you doing here?" he replied, "I have been zealous for the Lord God Almighty. The Israelites have rejected your covenant, broken down your altars, put your prophets to death. I am the only one left, and now they are trying to kill me, too." Feel the loneliness—"I am the only one left." Sense the anger—"the Israelites have rejected your covenant." Hear the self-pity—"I've been very zealous . . . now they are trying to kill me."

Loneliness, self-pity, and anger—these are some of the most common emotional temptations and trials for God's servants. Often we do have to travel and perhaps stand alone. Frequently our word is not received. Often we may be misunderstood. Some of you work in countries which are very cold to the Gospel. Others of you are part of a minority where Christians are persecuted. Evangelists are sometimes looked down upon and despised even, sadly, by church leaders. Before we know it, we are given to self-pity, which is pride turned upside down. Or anger becomes our vice. We get angry at our leaders for not leading and our followers for not following—anger at our families who make us feel guilty, anger at ourselves for not being all we want to be. "It is a frozen anger, an anger which settles into a biting resentment and slowly paralyzes a generous heart," writes Henri Nouwen. "If there is anything that makes the ministry look grim and dull, it is this dark, insidious anger in the servants of Christ." Anger, when we turn it in upon ourselves, becomes depression.

Underlying the physical exhaustion and the emotional weakness there is a spiritual cause for Elijah's condition. In a word, he was disappointed. He had worked so hard. He had prayed so fervently. He had tried to be so faithful. He had zealously preached the Word of the Lord. He had given all that he had and what was the result? "They have rejected your covenant, broken down your altars, put your prophets to death and now they are trying to kill me." All his great effort had gone for nothing.

Where was God? Elijah faced the crisis of faith. Again, you and I are men and women just like Elijah. Even our Lord Jesus faced this trial. "My God, my God, why have you forsaken me?" Don't you think Jesus our Savior must have been tempted to feel that, as He hung on the Cross, opposed by His foes, deserted by His friends?

Our Lord trusted His Father, even on that dark night of His soul. And Elijah needed to learn to trust God. He thought he had accomplished nothing and he was wrong, but he didn't know it. There were still 7,000 in Israel whose knees had not bowed to Baal. Elijah did not realize that the best results of his work were still unseen.

When I was a 14-year-old boy, my family was being torn apart. I knew Christ as my Savior, but had no fellowship with Him as my friend. I went to a summer youth conference and was touched by the enthusiasm and reality of the other young people. Dr. Oswald Smith of Toronto was the speaker, the great missionary statesman and pastor who died earlier this year. His talks on the morning watch and the quiet time had a profound effect on my life. For the first time I began to have a daily time of Bible reading and prayer. The overflow of this experience was great, and we began to have evangelistic youth rallies in my part of Canada. It was through them I met Billy Graham and was called into the work of evangelism. Later, when I was in college, Dr. Smith came to speak in our chapel. I reminded him of that conference several years before and told him what had happened in my life. "You mean the Bluewater Conference?" he said in amazement. "Why, I thought that was a wasted week. I didn't think anything happened to anyone that week."

So some of us here are being tempted to give in to disappointment, to wonder if our work is worthwhile, and to ask where God is.

"*What* are you doing here, Elijah?" Elijah wasn't really doing anything. He was being ministered to. Thank God that He didn't take Elijah's mood of the moment for the man he had been and could be. God overlooked Elijah's momentary despair and restored him to new strength. Let's look at how God cured the prophet's condition.

Elijah said, "I have had enough. Take my life." Then he lay down under the tree and fell asleep. All at once an angel touched him and said, "Get up and eat." He looked around and there by his head was a cake of bread baked over hot coals and a jar of water. He ate and drank and lay down again.

The angel of the Lord came back a second time and touched him and said, "Get up and eat, for the journey is too much for you." So he got up and ate and drank. Strengthened by that food, he traveled forty days and forty nights until he reached Horeb, the mountain of God (1 Kings 19:5-8).

See how realistically, how practically, how physically God worked. "Elijah was a man just like we are." He had a body, not just a spirit. You and I, evangelists, are whole people—we are bodies, affected by our emotions and made for a spiritual relationship with God. So God dealt with Elijah.

God's treatment was a quiet place, two long sleeps, two meals of bread made in the angel's kitchen, and two long drinks of water.

None of us is so spiritual that we don't need sleep, food, quietness, relaxation, and an affectionate touch. This is especially true when our work demands a high level of energy and adrenalin. The more we live on high adrenalin and energy levels, the less we will feel the need for sleep. When our adrenalin level goes up, our sleep needs come down.

Perhaps you are under the broom tree, brother, because you are just tired. Have you planned for proper relaxation and sleep? It used to make me feel very guilty when I read that John Wesley got up at 4 o'clock in the morning to read and pray. Then I found out what time Wesley went to bed—about 8 o'clock at night, because they didn't have lights back in those days! That made me feel better. Some of us are tempted to laziness and sleeping-in too long, and we need to set the alarm clock and get up and pray and read and go to work. But many doctors believe that the average adult needs eight to nine hours of sleep each night. "I have so much to do that I must go to bed," said a French philosopher.

The Scripture says, "He gives his beloved sleep." Sleep is a gift from God as much as work and prayer. There are some very good reasons why we need to work time into our schedule for proper relaxation and sleep. Those of you who are younger may have tremendous levels of energy. You can get your adrenalin level up and keep going, going and going. You can even get to the place where you manipulate people and dominate people out of your sheer drive. If you are not careful, you will mistake energy and adrenalin for the work of the Holy Spirit. You need to let yourself down physically in order to find out whether you are really operating in the Spirit rather than in the flesh. Those of us who are older will find that our adrenalin level does not drop as easily. We get used to living on a high output, but that inevitably affects our heart and the rest of our physical system. If we don't get the proper rest, we will be wearing out this wonderful body that God has given us as His instrument.

If God calls you to unusual demands which wear you out physically, then accept it gladly and offer yourself up as a living sacrifice. But don't let your own ego, the feeling that you are irreplaceable or super-spiritual, drive you to burn yourself out before it's God's time.

Are you and I "called people" or "driven people"? If we are driven by our own needs, we will never be able to stop and relax without feeling guilty. If we are called by God to meet others' needs we will know that we must stop. Jesus had a tremendous sense of urgency. But He knew also there were times to withdraw and be quiet, to sleep (even in a storm) and to pray. He was not driven by the "tyranny of the urgent." He didn't heal every sick person—He didn't feed every hungry person—He didn't personally forgive every sinner. But at the end of three years of ministry, He could say, "Father, I have finished the work you gave me."

Let's learn to pace ourselves. I am trying to take a five-minute break in the midst of a heavy schedule—to walk, to listen to the birds, to send up a quiet prayer. In the middle of a busy campaign schedule, I work from early morning to mid-afternoon and I work hard—writing, preparing, speaking, counseling. Then if possible, at mid-afternoon I take a break and a long walk. Usually I will lie down for twenty to thirty minutes and don't go to sleep, but let my mind and body come down and relax. After a light meal I am ready to get up my mind and heart, and to preach with renewed vigor that night.

The past few months have been very busy ones as we prepare to launch a new ministry. I was caught up short recently when my wife Jeanie said lovingly, "When is your Sabbath?'' I realized that I was gone days at a time traveling and speaking. Then I would come home to a desk full of work and correspondence and plow right into it. I, who told other people to take a day off, wasn't taking one myself. For the past three months I have been making a day for Sabbath rest each week and what a difference it has made!

Are you and I better than Jesus who needed to rest? Are we different from Elijah who crashed when he didn't? No. So let us allow God to restore us physically as He did the prophet.

Elijah was also restored emotionally. This happened in three ways:

An angel *touched* him and told him to get up and eat. This was a touch of a spiritual being, but how much also the touch of a friend or loved one can do when we are feeling down. I remember once years ago when I was very discouraged. A major campaign we were planning was not going well. I really felt for some time as if God had just disappeared. I was filled with a sense of worthlessness. All one long night my wife Jeanie stayed up with me. In the early hours of the morning she took my face in her hands. Looking directly in my eyes, she said, ''Leighton, I love you, I love you, I love you.'' And she kept saying that until it got through to me. Blessed is the evangelist who has a spouse or a close friend or an angel who will touch in time of need.

God also gave Elijah a helper and companion. ''Anoint Elisha to succeed you as prophet,'' the Lord told him (1 Kings 19:16). Elijah found Elisha, threw his cloak around him, and Elisha set out to follow Elijah and become his attendant. Elijah was not so strong and independent that he didn't need a brother to be with him. Is that not one of the reasons the Lord sent His disciples out two by two? If you don't have an Elisha to be a companion, a helper and partner, pray that God will supply that need. When David was being hunted by Saul in the desert, and was feeling very threatened, Jonathan, the king's son, went out and found him and the Scripture says, ''Jonathan helped David to find strength in God.''

Look at the brother or sister sitting to your left and to your right. That person may be carrying the soul of Elijah right now. There may be hundreds of us in this conference who have come and are sitting under the broom tree. Be an Elisha to that Elijah. Be a Jonathan to that David. Be alert to the lonely and discouraged person who is here. Let them talk out their burdens and discouragement. Pray through it with them. You and I have not been sent here only for what we can get from this conference and just to build up our own ministry. We are part of the body of Christ to supply what the other is needing, not to think just about our own concerns, but to think of others with the mind of Christ.

Remember that after a spiritual high and a great victory you need to allow for an emotional letdown. Don't be surprised. Don't fight it. Thank God for it. Allow time to let your soul, as well as your body, recover.

Most crucial of all, the Lord restored Elijah spiritually. ''What are *you* doing here, Elijah?'' he asked (1 Kings 19:9). Perhaps the emphasis is on you, Elijah. Of all people, what are *you* doing here? Did I not call *you* years ago? Did I not answer *your* prayer for no rain, and for it to rain again? Did I not feed *you* when there was a famine, by the ravens and the widow? Did I not send down fire when *you* prayed? ''What are *you* doing here, Elijah?'' Elijah, whose very name means: The Lord is my God.

Elijah answered, ''I have been very zealous . . . I am the only one left . . . now they are trying to kill me.''

The Lord said, ''Go out and stand on the mountain in the presence of the Lord, for the Lord is about to pass by.

"Then a great and powerful wind tore the mountains apart and shattered the rocks before the Lord, but the Lord was not in the wind. After the wind there was an earthquake, but the Lord was not in the earthquake. After the earthquake came a fire, but the Lord was not in the fire. After the fire came a gentle whisper. When Elijah heard it, he pulled his cloak over his face and went out and stood at the mouth of the cave" (1 Kings 19:11-13). He knew he had heard God. Now he was ready to listen.

Why was God not in the wind, the earthquake, the fire? At other times He was. God was in the wind when He blew back the Red Sea for Moses. God was in the wind when the Holy Spirit came at Pentecost. God was in the earthquake when Moses was at Sinai, and when Paul was in the Philippian jail. God had been in the fire when Elijah prayed and the fire came down and consumed the sacrifice. There are clearly times when God is in earthquake, wind and fire. Why then, did He speak to Elijah only in the gentle whisper?

I think perhaps God was saying, "Elijah, sometimes I work in a big and a great and a grand way. But just as often I work in the gentle and quiet way. I want you to learn that it is not by might or by power, not by earthquake, wind and fire, but by my Spirit."

I wonder if Elijah was getting to the place where earthquake, wind and fire were too important. Did he think God could work no other way? Or, was it that Elijah was getting built up so that the Lord was not being seen? Perhaps we get a hint of this in his self-pity. "I have been very zealous, now they are trying to kill me." Perhaps Elijah needed to be reminded of the point of his ministry—not that Elijah should be seen as a great prophet, but that Jehovah should be seen as a great God.

"What are you doing here, Elijah?" Let's you and I ask that question of ourselves at Amsterdam 86. Perhaps we are not here to learn ways of producing more earthquakes and wind and fire. Perhaps God has called us to stand in His presence and hear that gentle whisper, to bring us back to size and back to ourselves.

We can't always get rest and food when we are hungry and tired. We won't always have an Elisha by our side, as we may have to travel away from friends and family and be alone. But always we can stand in God's presence and listen for His gentle whisper. Listen to God speak in the messages of these days. Take time, read His Word, and pray. Take a solitary walk, if you need to, with Him.

Then the Lord asks the second time. "What are you doing *here*, Elijah?" Why here? You needed some time in the desert. But now He says, "Go back the way you came . . . anoint Hazael king . . . anoint Elisha to succeed you . . . and yet I reserve 7,000 in Israel—all whose knees have not bowed down to Baal and all whose mouths have not kissed him" (1 Kings 19:15-18). And so Elijah went.

Restored spiritually, God recommissioned him to his task. Instead of letting him die, He gave him new heart. Now he had a helper and successor in Elisha. There was a future and a hope. Far from being left alone, God gave him 7,000 who would stand with him.

Several weeks ago in Calcutta we had the privilege of visiting Mother Teresa, that little Albanian lady who has poured out her life for the dying poor in the streets of Calcutta. She is a little lady, four feet eleven, with deep wrinkles, big glasses, dressed in a blue and white habit. She was barefoot and wearing a bunion.

I asked her what we could pray for her. I thought she might need money or staff. She said, "Pray that I may be humble like Mary and holy like Jesus." I asked her what she would tell you, the evangelists at Amsterdam 86 if she could speak here. She said, "Tell them to be holy and love one another. We need holy pastors and holy preachers."

Then I said, "Mother Teresa, how do you keep hope and joy in the midst of all the poverty and death and destitution?" She answered, "We do our work for Christ, with Christ, to Christ, and that's what keeps it simple." *For* Christ, *with* Christ, *to* Christ—are you working that way?

"*What* are you doing here, evangelist?" Are you on the mountain or under the broom tree?

"What are you *doing* here, evangelist?" Are you here to be restored in body, mind, and spirit?

"What are *you* doing here, evangelist?" You, who have been called by God and seen His blessing. Are you here to see the glory of the Lord whether in earthquake, wind, fire, or gentle whisper?

"What are you doing *here*, evangelist?" Are you here to stand in God's presence and to be sent forth renewed to His work? Then do your work *for* Christ, *with* Christ and *to* Christ. Then, in all our weakness—though we are women and men just like Elijah—Christ will make us strong.

# APPROACHING THE END OF THE AGE
*Billy Graham*

*Texts: Matthew 24:3*
*Acts 1:9-11*

Most church creeds that I have ever read, teach the coming again of Jesus Christ.

The secular world is talking about the end of the world and Armageddon.

According to *Time* magazine, most Americans' "number one" concern in life is how they can deal with "the coming apocalypse."

Other religions are also looking for a leader that will come and deliver them from the bondage of this world.

In the Jewish creed drawn up by Maimonides, it states: "I believe with perfect belief in the coming of the Messiah, and though he tarry I will wait daily for his coming."

Hindus generally believe in ten reincarnations of the god Vishnu, of which nine have already taken place; and the tenth is expected to appear at the end of the age. He will be a conquering hero mounted on a white horse bearing a blazing sword—a universal ruler.

Buddhism expects a future incarnation of Buddha, an incarnation represented as a fat and laughing Buddha welcoming all comers.

Both Shiite and Sunni Muslims look forward to the coming of a ruler appearing the last days upon earth. Shiites believe he has already appeared, and is concealed in some secret place until the day of his manifestation before the end of the world. The Sunnis believe he has not yet appeared in the history of Islam.

Where have these universal ideas come from? The disciples asked two questions: What will be the signal for your coming? When will the end of the age come?

Jesus warned against speculating on a date, but He did give us signs that we are to watch for. There are many signs. Some theologians say 21. Here are at least 5 of them:

1. *The moral state of the world.* It will be as in the days of Noah (Matthew 24:37-39).

2. *An increase in lawlessness.* Jesus said, "As lawlessness spreads, men's love for one another will grow cold" (Matthew 24:12).

Jesus said that just before the end, lawlessness would be worldwide. He said: "Ye shall hear of . . . commotions" (Luke 21:9). This word "commotions" carries with it the idea of rebellion, revolution, terrorism, and lawlessness—indicating that this was a sign of the approaching end of the age.

3. *Wars.* "And ye shall hear of wars and rumours of wars" (Matthew 24:6). The Bible indicates that toward the end, wars will become more widespread, more devastating, and more frequent.

4. *Knowledge and travel.* "At the time of the end: many shall run to and fro, and knowledge shall be increased" (Daniel 12:4). The meaning of Daniel's words could not possibly have been understood until the last 150 years. Today we know what Daniel meant. Most of you came here by airplane. Just 50 years ago, it would have been impossible to have a conference like this. Until 1830, a man could travel no faster than a horse could run. And man's knowledge is now tripling every 15 years.

**5.** *Deceivers and scoffers.* Jesus said, "And many false prophets shall rise, and shall deceive many" (Matthew 24:11). "Now the Spirit speaketh expressly, that in the latter times some shall depart from the faith, giving heed to seducing spirits and doctrines of devils" (1 Timothy 4:1).

Cults will grow. Witchcraft will flourish. False teachers will even infiltrate the church. The Bible will be under severe attack. There are wolves in sheep's clothing, about which Jesus warned His followers. They are leaders of the "falling away," which is to characterize the church at the end of the age.

Our world is waiting with urgency for leadership. Who is going to stop the evil? Who is going to bring peace to the world? The world is waiting for a messiah, a leader.

A little girl was listening to a grandfather clock that was supposed to strike 12 times, and through a malfunction struck 13 times. She ran to her mother and cried, "Mother, it's later than it ever was before!" It's never been this late before.

But God has a plan. Secular thinkers are asking, "What is history all about?" "Why is man on this earth?" "Where is he going?"

Some say that history is like a drunken fly with feet wet with ink, staggering across a piece of white paper—the tracks lead nowhere and reflect no pattern or meaning.

Modern philosophy is described as being like a blind man in a room with no windows looking for a black cat that isn't there!

The great teaching of the Bible is that God has not abandoned this world. God has a plan. His plan is that Jesus will return and bring peace and justice to our world. Until then we have a job to do!

Our Lord said, "Occupy [or, be faithful] till I come" (Luke 19:13). He further states, "This gospel of the kingdom shall be preached in all the world for a witness unto all nations; and then shall the end come" (Matthew 24:14).

In a hopeless world, we are to leave Amsterdam with a message of hope. "We are saved by hope" (Romans 8:24). "Ye may abound in hope" (Romans 15:13). "Hope maketh not ashamed" (Romans 5:5).

The Scripture teaches He will come with clouds (angels), "and every eye shall see him" (Revelation 1:7). To those of us who know Christ as Savior, it will be a glorious and thrilling moment. For those who have rejected Him, there will be wailing and gnashing of teeth.

We are to help the poor, the needy, the oppressed. We are to work for social justice. But primarily our task is to proclaim the Gospel of redemption centered in the Cross and the Resurrection.

For the first time in history, we have the possibility of reaching all nations in our generation. While one part of technology is setting about to destroy the world, another part of the technology is being used to carry the Gospel to the ends of the earth. There is hardly a place in the world today that you cannot get the Gospel by radio. Dr. Paul Freed, founder and head of Trans World Radio, indicates that there is not a place in the world that is not reached by Christian radio. Soon we will get it by satellite on television screens, in every country of the world.

We live between the times of Christ's first and second coming—and His Second Coming draws near.

It is a staggering fact that God has entrusted to people like us, redeemed sinners, the responsibility of carrying out the divine purpose. Why did God not do it Himself? Why did He not use the angels? Why did He commit it to us?

While we do our job, we will suffer. There will be opposition. "For we wrestle not against flesh and blood, but against principalities, against powers, against the rulers of the darkness of this world, against spiritual wickedness in high places" (Ephesians 6:12).

Why did He commit the job of evangelization to us? We do not know. This is deep in the mysteries of the sovereignty of God.

The Apostle Paul has warned us in 1 Corinthians 1:26-31, "For ye see your calling, brethren, how that not many wise men after the flesh, not many mighty, not many noble, are called. But God hath chosen the foolish things of the world to confound the wise; and God hath chosen the weak things of the world to confound the things which are mighty; and base things of the world, and things which are despised, hath God chosen, yea, and things which are not, to bring to nought things that are: that no flesh should glory in his presence. . . . He that glorieth, let him glory in the Lord."

He wants us to proclaim His message of the Gospel of the kingdom. This means that what we have been doing here in Amsterdam is more important than a meeting of the United Nations. What the church does with the Gospel has greater significance than any decisions made at the Kremlin or at the White House.

After this Gospel of the Kingdom has been preached to the world, Scripture says, "Then shall the end come." We cannot set dates, yet I believe when we have finished the task of evangelizing (not Christianizing) the world, it has something to do with when He comes back. This staggers us, it is hard for us to believe that God has committed such responsibility to us. We are now closer to finishing this mission than any previous generation.

But you say, "There are many closed doors around the world." While I am concerned about the closed doors, I am more concerned about the ones that are open, that we do not enter. Many times we only enter them superficially and not in depth, so that people are uncertain what it means to both accept and follow Christ. To the church at Philadelphia, Jesus said, "I know thy works: behold I have set before thee an open door, and no man can shut it: for thou hast a little strength, and hast kept my word, and hast not denied my name" (Revelation 3:7,8). The Word of God is not bound.

This evil world stands on the threshold of judgment. God has given us good news to spread throughout the world for these last days. He has given a spiritual power and the tools to take that Gospel to all the world.

If you have not rededicated your life and ministry to Christ during these days at Amsterdam, I pray that you will do it tonight. "Seeing then that all these things shall be dissolved, what manner of persons ought ye to be in all holy [living] and godliness" (2 Peter 3:11).

For the evangelist, it will be a dangerous life. It will often be a lonely life. It will be a burdened life. It may be that you will live in weakness, as many evangelists do. But if you are filled with the Holy Spirit, the Holy Spirit is producing fruit in your life—such as love, joy, peace, longsuffering, gentleness, goodness, faith, meekness, temperance—and also power!

I believe we could be living in the last period of world history. The next phase of history will be the phase of the Kingdom of God. God can reign in our hearts now, and His Kingdom will be within us. But there is coming a time when He will reign throughout the whole world. Every time you win a soul to Christ, I believe you are helping to bring back the King!

Some day we will "see the Son of man coming in the clouds of heaven with power and great glory" (Matthew 24:30).

In 1743, King George II was in Covent Garden Theater the first time "THE

MESSIAH" by Handel was ever played. The king heard the "Hallelujah Chorus" and the words:

> "King of kings,
> Lord of lords,
> Hallelujah, Hallelujah.
> And He shall reign for ever and ever."

At once the king rose to his feet, and the whole audience stood also. The king said: "How could I sit in the presence of One who is the King of kings!" And from that moment to this, it has been customary for people to stand whenever the "Hallelujah Chorus" is sung.

What a day! "When Christ, who is our life, shall appear, then shall ye also appear with him in glory" (Colossians 3:4).

But doesn't that make us complacent? Critics of those that believe in the Second Coming say they lose incentive to work. It has been my experience that those who believe it are the hardest workers, the most zealous, and the most dedicated. Dr. Gallup pointed out in his address to the press here that evangelicals do far more about social problems than non-evangelicals.

It has been pointed out that there are 22 quotations in the Epistles alone that call for purity, patience, service, and good works in the light of Christ's return. The King is coming!

During this conference we have heard the groan of the world. Ours is a world that groans—groans for freedom, groans for wholeness, groans for liberation. Joel said multitudes are in the valley of decision, for the day of the Lord is near (Joel 3:14).

Till Christ comes, we have a great commission to obey. Jesus said, "The harvest truly is plenteous, but the laborers are few; pray ye therefore the Lord of the harvest, that he will send forth laborers into his harvest" (Matthew 9:37,38). "And it shall come to pass, that whosoever shall call on the name of the Lord shall be delivered" (Joel 2:32).

Some of you have sat through this conference and may not know Christ. What if you knew Christ would return in one minute—would you fall on your knees and cry out for mercy—and realize you had never been converted yourself? Suppose it was 45 seconds—and there are many people you have neglected to witness to. Their blood will be on your hands.

Suppose you were the only one that knew Christ would return in 30 seconds. Would you run out into the street and scream at the top of your voice, "Jesus is coming, repent and be saved!"?

—20 seconds. . . . you realize you have not lived a holy life, you are not ready to see Christ. You are now desperate. Ten seconds, 9, 8, 7, 6, 5, 4, 3, 2, 1 . . . and you are not prepared spiritually or morally to see Christ.

There is coming a day when all our hopes and dreams will be fulfilled. "And God shall wipe away all tears from their eyes; and there shall be no more death, neither sorrow, nor crying, neither shall there be any more pain: for the former things are passed away" (Revelation 21:4).

I'll see you in the sky: I'll see you in heaven!

Two young men at university had as neighbor in the next room a man who was always talking on his ham radio. These boys rigged the wires into the next room. The next night they announced with professional sounding voices that America was under attack, and the whole country would likely be destroyed in less than an hour. The ham radio fellow believed it! He jumped up and shouted at the top of his lungs, "Get ready! We are going to be destroyed in the next hour!''

Without shoes on, dressed only in his shorts, he ran to the girls' dormitory. It was locked and he couldn't get in. He shouted at the windows and one of the girls leaned out. He told her. She believed it and she rang the fire alarm. Then they told the dean of the university, and he believed it. It came down to 20 minutes to the deadline and the people were desperate. They began to pray before they found out that it was a hoax.

This one man, who had heard this message, was willing to make a fool of himself. Because one man had believed, he had made a believer out of many other intelligent people.

Do you believe the Gospel of Jesus Christ and the fact that He is coming again, and that one of these days you are going to die and this world is going to end? And do you believe it enough to go and witness and preach and make a fool of yourself, if necessary?

You face your journey back home. The first step back home should be rededication and recommitment. Ten thousand men and women totally committed!

When D. L. Moody first visited England, he met Henry Varley, a converted butcher. One day Varley told him, ''Moody, the world has yet to see what God could do with the man who would totally yield himself to Christ.'' Moody reflected on a park bench. He got up and said, ''By the grace of God, I will be that man!''

You could start tonight.

# BY FAITH
*E.V. Hill*

My brothers and sisters, through our Lord Jesus Christ.

I have been led to preach from 1 Peter, the fifth chapter. Here Peter gives to us several exhortations worthy of note at this conference.

In verse 2, he says, "Feed the flock."

In these days, when there are so many that are offering lethal, deadly, poisonous food to people, it is important that we be reminded to feed the flock—the solid Word of God.

Farmers know that the reason for the restlessness and breaking out on the part of animals in the morning is due to the fact that they have not been fed. So it is with mankind; the search for inner peace, the use of deadly substitutes are signs of not having received solid food. So take your Bible and feed the flock—feed them willingly. With joy, enjoy watching them eat. Feed them not in exchange for filthy lucre but feed them as a result of your anxiety to fulfill God's call of you to such a high and noble responsibility.

In verse 3 we are reminded that our ambition is not that of being lord over God's heritage but rather being examples to the flock.

It is true that we are not to preach ourselves. It is also true that we are to point men and women to Jesus as the great example, our great perfect example.

However, it is equally true that men and women look to us as examples, and what they see in us is often what they remember about us more than what we say and preach. Thus, be thou an example. Not as superstars but as ordinary believers, who stumble but rise, who sin but repent, and constantly move with humility toward the likeness of Jesus our Christ.

Verse 5 exhorts us to also remember that God resisteth the proud but giveth grace to the humble.

In verse 8 with great alarm he cries out to us to be sober, not so much from alcohol—and that, too—but try always to be alert, awake, watchful at all times, because the Gospel has an enemy. The devil himself walketh to and fro like a roaring lion. A lion who walketh to and fro is hungry, and he is not walking for exercise but rather seeking whom he may destroy.

Just because you preach, just because you are an evangelist, just because you seek to turn men and women to the marvelous light in Jesus Christ, you are subject to satanic attacks—physically, emotionally, and through greed and pride.

Thus, the most important factor in your life and mine is our faith. You and I have in us the capacity to have faith—to believe, to have confidence. We can, at will, transfer this capacity or element to whomever we will; or we can put it all in ourselves—our ability, our wealth, etc. We can place this capacity in statues, ideologies, men, or fame, but history has proven over and over that these are poor places to put your faith.

Thus, let us look again to 1 Peter 5, for it is not only filled with exhortations but it has nuggets of encouragement. Verse 1 says, He, Jesus, shall come—and this time His glory shall be revealed.

When He was here before, for our sakes He became poor, with His glory in somewhat obscurity—born lowly, reared in poverty, abused and crucified. Only now and then did glimpses of His glory appear. Peter, James and John experienced it on the day of Pentecost.

But this time His glory shall be revealed. He shall come riding—King of kings, Lord of lords. When He shall come every knee shall bow and every tongue shall confess that He is Lord. The whole earth shall behold Him, and not only Him but all of those who have put their trust in Him. Therefore, my brethren, preach—for we shall share in His glory.

Right now, where you may have been called to serve there may be very little glitter and glory. But cast not away, therefore, your confidence. For yet a little while and He that shall come—He that promised to come—He for whom my mama sought— and for whom I seek to see will come.

Preach on, preacher, for Jesus is coming in His glory. And look again at the promise in verse 4. When the Chief Shepherd shall come He will bring with Him for us a crown of glory that fadeth not away. These little earthly crowns so quickly fade but, preach on, preacher, for the crown that fadeth not away.

Not only is this chapter filled with exhortations, warnings and expectations, but it is loaded with many "in the meantime" promises of God. I know He will come, but in the *meantime* I must preach to an unbelieving, stiffnecked generation. I know I shall share His glory, but in the *meantime* I must suffer afflictions.

But thank God for God's promises to those who have put their faith in Jesus. Look at verse 5: He "giveth grace to the humble." Thank God for whatever betide, preacher; God giveth us grace.

God giveth us unmerited favors. Grace in health. Grace to endure. Praise God for God's grace—by the grace of God we made it to Amsterdam. His grace has brought us safe thus far and His grace will lead us on.

Look at verse 6: it says God will exalt us in due time—it may be a long time—but in due time God will bring us forth. In due time all things will work together for good to them that love God. In due time that which should be will be. In due time all prayers will be answered.

But, in the meantime look at verse 7: cast all your cares upon Him. Put all your faith in Him. Put all your trust in Him. Put all of your confidence in Him.

Have faith in God. He's on His throne. Have faith in God, for He watches over His own. He cannot fail. He must prevail. Have faith, preacher. Have faith in God.

Faith is believing when there is no encouraging evidence. Faith is substance when there is nothing seen. Faith is climbing without a ladder. Faith is going forth when reason and logic advise us to stay put.

By faith we are saved (Ephesians 2:8).

By faith we live (Romans 1:17)

By faith we are justified (Galatians 2:16).

By faith we are sanctified (Acts 26:18).

By faith we are counted as righteous (Romans 4:5,9).

By faith we have access and peace with God (Romans 5:2).

By faith we walk (2 Corinthians 5:7).

By faith we are protected (Ephesians 6:16).

Finally, my brethren, look at verse 10. "The God of all grace who hath called us unto His eternal glory by Christ Jesus, after that ye have suffered awhile" will "make you perfect, stablish, strengthen, [and] settle you."

Will faith work? What testimonies do we have?

By faith Abel brought a pleasing offering to God (Hebrews 11:4).

By faith Enoch did not see death; God took him (Hebrews 11:5).

By faith Noah believed God, prepared for the flood and was saved from the flood (Hebrews 11:7).

By faith Abraham went out looking for a city whose builder and maker was God (Hebrews 11:8,9) and offered up Isaac (Hebrews 11:17).

By faith Sarah conceived and gave birth to a child while old enough to be his grandmother (Hebrews 11:11).

By faith Moses refused to stay in Pharaoh's house in favor of being with the people of God (Hebrews 11:23,24,27).

By faith the Red Sea was crossed (Hebrews 11:29).

By faith the walls of Jericho fell (Hebrews 11:30).

By faith the harlot was saved (Hebrews 11:31).

By faith lions were slept with (Hebrews 11:33).

By faith fiery furnaces were walked in (Hebrews 11:34).

By faith women received their loved ones back from the dead (Hebrews 11:35).

By faith I was born almost hopeless and homeless. Poor, ragged and tattered, I lived in a log cabin, finished a sub-standard school, subjected to segregation, discrimination, racism, and rejection. But I can testify to verse 7 that God will take care of those who cast all of their cares upon Him—for He careth for us.

Preach, brother, God cares for you. Preach, brother, God sees and knows you. Preach, my brother, not out of your strength, knowledge, or power, but out of the riches of His grace.

# THE EVANGELIST AS A PERSONAL SOUL-WINNER
## T.W. Wilson

1. *The necessity of doing personal evangelism*
   —because *all* men everywhere are lost until they accept Christ
   —in Acts 8, 9, 10, we see four predominate truths:

   a. *Universal problem.* . . . the eunuch, Saul and Cornelius. The eunuch was an Ethiopian, Saul a Jew, Cornelius a Roman. Three different races, yet the problem with all these races was *sin*. Romans 3:23—"all have sinned."

   b. *Universal hunger.* It was racial, social and geographic. The Ethiopian had a *money* background, Saul a *mental* (intellectual) background, Cornelius a *military* background. And yet all three had a hunger for something that their assets didn't offer. The Ethiopian came from Egypt, Saul from Tarsus, Cornelius from Rome, and yet their hunger was the same.

   c. *Universal Savior.* Acts 8:35— ". . . Philip opened his mouth and preached unto him Jesus"—to the wealthy Ethiopian.

   Acts 9:17—Ananias spoke to Saul and preached unto him Jesus — to the intellectual Jew.

   Acts 10:33-36—Peter spoke to Cornelius and preached unto him Jesus—to the military leader.

   *Jesus* is our message.

   *Philip* was a man of *availability*.

   *Ananias* was a man of *expendability*. He was afraid of Saul but he said, "Jesus sent me."

   *Peter* was a man of *adaptability*.

   Jesus Christ, the Son of God, became the Son of Man; so that the sons of men might become the sons of God. So He truly is a *universal Savior*.

   d. *Universal command.*

   Jesus said, "Go."
   Acts 8:26—"Arise and go."
   Acts 8:27—"*Philip* arose and went."
   Acts 9:11—"Arise and go."
   Acts 9:17—"*Ananias* went."
   Acts 10:20—"The Spirit said arise and go."
   Acts 10:21—"Then *Peter* went."

   The reason we do what we do, and witness, is because *Jesus said to do it.*

   "Go ye therefore, and teach all nations, baptizing them in the name of the Father, and of the Son, and of the Holy Ghost: teaching them to observe all things whatsoever I have commanded you: and, lo, I am with you alway, even unto the end of the world. Amen" (Matthew 28:19,20).

   The last command Jesus gave the Church just before His ascension was for them to be witnesses.

   "But ye shall receive power, after that the Holy Ghost is come upon you; and ye shall be witnesses unto me both in Jerusalem, and in all Judaea, and in Samaria, and unto the uttermost part of the earth" (Acts 1:8).

   We talk about mass evangelism. Anything more than one is *mass*. Mass evangelism is just a group of personal evangelists. We still must have that one-on-one basis.

"There's joy in the presence of the angels of God over one sinner that repenteth" (Luke 15:10).

Many people that we witness to have already been witnessed to by someone else, and we may just be able to be on hand when they say "yes" to Jesus.

Now, an evangelist who limits his witnessing to the pulpit is a *backslider*. This is God's *Universal Command* — "Go!"

2.  *The value of doing personal evangelism*

"He that winneth souls is wise" (Proverbs 11:30). Wonder why?

a.  *We are all in the soul-winning business.* This is the main business of a Christian.

*George Williams started the YMCA as a means to an end:* to give young men the Gospel through athletics.

*Crittenden Homes* are for unwed mothers.

*General William Booth* founded the Salvation Army to give the Gospel by means of food.

Orphanages, hospitals, mental institutions and others—were founded for one purpose only.

b.  *Most of Jesus' miracles were with one individual*

He cleansed the leper.

He healed the centurion's servant.

He healed Peter's mother-in-law.

He cast out the devil from the man of Gadara.

He healed the daughter of the ruler of the synagogue.

He healed the woman with an issue of blood.

He cleansed the man who was born blind and dumb.

He healed the Syrophenician woman who was so poor and needy.

He gave sight to the blind man at the pool of Bethesda.

He witnessed to the rich young ruler and told him there was none good, no not one. The young man went away sorrowfully because he had great possessions, the Scripture says.

He gave sight to blind Bartimaeus.

He healed the man sick of palsy.

He raised Lazarus from the dead

Most of His miracles were on a one-to-one basis.

3.  *Methods of doing personal evangelism*

a.  We should be much in *prayer* and show forth the spirit of love. Billy Graham says the way to have genuine revival has a three-fold ingredient: pray, pray, and pray. Someone said, "Pray when you feel like it, pray when you don't feel like it, pray until you do feel like it, but pray."

b.  Do not argue—*talk positively.*

(i)    A good salesman does not knock his competitor's product. If anything, he will brag on it, then tell why his product is better. We Christians should not tell sinners that they are not having a good time living for the devil. The Bible says, "There are pleasures in sin" but it also says "only for a season" (Hebrews 11:25). The good salesman knows what the manual teaches about the product. We Christians need to know what the Bible teaches about our "product." A good salesman should be sold on his own product. He should try to clinch the deal or make a sale. A real witness for Christ should try to get a decision immediately.

(ii)    Be a good fisherman. Jesus said, "I will make you to become fishers of men'' (Mark 1:17). To be a good fisherman, you need to go where the fish are, use the right kind of bait, and be patient.

c. Keep trying to settle the issue—while the Lord is working, the devil is also working. Don't give up!

4. *Examples and illustrations of personal evangelism*

a. A great scientist in California responded to the invitation to receive Christ. Then he began to argue with the counselor. They sent for me. He did not need an argument, he needed Christ.

b. A young soldier in the Midwest wanted to argue about hell. He didn't need an argument, he needed Christ.

c. A wealthy well-known attorney in Hollywood, California, wanted to argue about the Bible being God's Word, life after death, etc. He didn't need an argument, he needed Christ.

d. Glenn Wilcox, a travel agent in North Carolina, was concerned about his relationship to Christ. God met his need beside the road in an automobile. His son, Wallace, was in the back seat and he made his decision for Christ as well.

e. An alcoholic, Alan Phillips, accepted Christ.

Many of you have had similar experiences. Every case is different. One was a soldier, one a scientist, one an attorney, one a travel agent, and one an alcoholic. All their situations were different, yet each had the same basic need.

5. *Jesus in personal evangelism*

John 4—with the woman at the well

a. *He established a mutual interest.* v. 7—the Samaritan woman came to draw water, and Jesus asked her for a drink.

b. *He overcame tradition.* v. 9—''How is it that you, a Jew, ask a drink of me, a woman of Samaria?'' He was a Jew, she a Samaritan. Jesus dealt with all classes and colors. And then there was the woman/man relationship. Jewish men did not speak to women in public.

c. *He overcame her preoccupation with the physical instead of the spiritual.* v. 11—the woman said, ''You have nothing to draw with and how are you going to get this water?''

d. *He overcame her mockery and ridicule.* v. 12—''Are you greater than our father Jacob?'' Who do you think you are, etc.? Jacob gave us this well. Do you think you are better than he?

e. *He overcame her sarcasm.* v. 15—''Sir, give me this water that I thirst not, neither come hither to draw.'' This wasn't a statement, this was sarcasm. Give this to me and I'll never have any worries again.

f. *He overcame her evasiveness.* v. 17—She said, ''I have no husband.'' He said, ''It's true, but you've had five husbands; and the man that you are now living with is not your husband.''

g. *He overcame her flattery.* v. 19—She said, ''I perceive that you are a prophet.''

h. *He overcame her religiosity.* v. 20—She said, ''Our fathers worshipped in this mountain. You say that in Jerusalem is the place where men ought to worship.'' Often people will try to talk about religion instead of their personal relationship to Christ.

i. *He came to the very point of the Gospel.* v. 26 — Jesus said, ''I that speak unto thee am He.''

j. *The result.* v. 39—''And many of the Samaritans of that city believed on him for the saying of the woman which testified, he told me all things that ever I did."

Here we see the multiplication of faithful witnessing. Take three people who are willing to fervently, faithfully witness. You can multiply yourselves four times a year. Now look at this. This means four times each year three individuals would be faithfully trying to multiply themselves. In the first year, if you witness to three, and they witness to three, at the end of the second quarter there would be 9 people. In the third quarter 9 people times three people is 27. In the fourth quarter you would have 81. The second yeaar you would have 243 in the first quarter, 729 in the second, 2,187 in the third, and 6,561 in the last quarter. Now if you multiply this on your calculator you will find that at the end of the fourth year, with three people trying to multiply themselves in their witnessing, there would be 43,046,721.

Lack of witnessing and fervent testimony is certainly reflected among today's Christians. We evangelists should set the good example.

6. *The call to personal work*
    a.  Christ commands it
Acts 1:8—"And you shall be witnesses unto me"
    b.  Gratitude demands it
"Jesus said, . . . Go home to thy friends and tell them how great things the Lord hath done for thee and hath had compassion on thee" (Mark 5:19,20). "Freely you have received, freely give" (Matthew 10:8).
    c.  The world sorely needs it   (John 3:16)
"I in them, and thou in me, that they may be made perfect in one; and that the world may know that thou hast sent me, and hast loved them, as thou hast loved me" (John 17:23). "But even the Son of man came not to be ministered unto, but to minister, and to give his life a ransom for many" (Mark 10:45).
    d.  The Church needs it
"And upon the rock of testimony I will build my church and the gates of hell shall not prevail against it" (Matthew 16:18).
    e.  The Christian grows by it
"And he gave some, apostles; and some, prophets; and some, evangelists; and some, pastors and teachers; for the perfecting of the saints, for the work of the ministry, for the edifying of the body of Christ" (Ephesians 4:11,12).
    f.  Experience abundantly warrants it
Someone has said that 85 percent of commercial business is put through by personal solicitation. Modern inventions and machinery have tremendously increased production in the industrial world. The machine now does the work of 100 men in some lines. At the same time, the demand for individual salesmanship is greater than ever in the world's history.

Personal work is the means God uses to extend and expand His kingdom.

If we would think daily of what Jesus did for us on the Cross, we would not get too busy to witness.

If we would think daily of what Jesus did for us—died for us, shed His blood for us on the Cross—we would not be too timid.

If we get a fresh glimpse every day of what Jesus did for us on that Cross, we will try to win somebody to Christ.
*EVERY EVANGELIST SHOULD BE A PERSONAL SOUL-WINNER!*

# YOUR INNER LIFE AS AN EVANGELIST
*Stephan Tchividjian*

Our key verse is found in Ephesians 3:16, "I pray that out of his glorious riches he may strengthen you with power through his Spirit in your inner being."

The Bible tells us that it is necessary to be strong in the inner man. In order to have a strong ministry, we need to be strong in the inner man. In many of our cultures, in different countries, in different continents, there is a lot of emphasis put on the external life. This is probably more true in some of our western countries than it is in the eastern countries. And yet all over the world there is a lot of emphasis on the external life. A lot of the education our children get is focused on things to achieve, on things to acquire, and there is little that is taught about cultivating your inner life.

By profession, I am a clinical psychologist which means in the course of days and weeks I see people from all walks of life that for one reason or another have come to a crisis point in their lives and they don't know how to deal with it. They can't deal with it because they have never cultivated their inner life. As Christians they have not cultivated and learned to draw on the God-given resources that are available. So as long as things go well—no problems and no crises—people just go along. But when the "evil day," as the Bible says, comes upon us and we are faced with a problem, we don't know where to turn. This comes from the fact that too many of us do not place enough emphasis on our inner life. Placing the emphasis on your inner life has to be balanced with the external life. I am not advocating that we only look inward. Also, I want to make it clear that when we talk about inner life and looking at ourselves we are talking about doing so in the light of the Scriptures and in the light of the Holy Spirit. The Bible says, "In your life, Lord, we see light." So the light we use to look at ourselves, inside of ourselves, is not our own light; it is the light of the Holy Spirit and it is the teaching of Scripture.

In order to have a strong ministry, it is necessary to be strong in the inner man. But what is a strong ministry? A strong ministry is: (1) A ministry that has integrity—integrity, and I'll come back to that. (2) A ministry that has responsibility or accountability. (3) A ministry of consistency.

Now when you have integrity, accountability, and consistency in your ministry you have a strong and a credible ministry.

Integrity has to do with honesty before God. One of the most comforting things in all of Scripture is the honesty of David in the Psalms. David wasn't always up; he wasn't always down. David didn't always understand, didn't always agree; but David had integrity. And because of that, the Bible says he had "a heart after God's own heart." Integrity is measurable. I can spend the day helping people and helping them to find deliverance, to find peace of mind, to find a healing for their emotions, and that's good. But you see, God is also going to look at me when I get home. He is watching how I deal with my seven children. And God is watching when I come home and deal with my wife. Because I cannot have integrity in my ministry if I get home and I don't give my wife and don't give my children the same kind of love, attention, and even more so, that I do my patients. I'd have every reason and every excuse to do it. I'm tired, I've worked all day; and, granted, I have to take time to rest. But God is watching me there at least as much as He is watching me in my office.

God may be watching you in your ministry on the street, or in the hall, or in a church, or one-on-one, and you may have full integrity as you relate to that person.

But God is watching you in what *we* call (He doesn't call) what we call the little things in life. That's what I mean by integrity. I firmly believe that we will never have a ministry that has power even one inch beyond the level of our integrity. In other words, if we have a little bit of integrity, we will have a little bit of a ministry. If we have a great deal of integrity we will have a great ministry.

When I was growing up my father kept short accounts. When he gave me money, he wanted me to write down what I spent it on. I thought it was very difficult to do. Every time I spent something I had to take out my little notebook and write down what I spent. And I didn't understand why he did that and then when I wanted to show it to him he said, "I don't need to see it." I said, "Why did you ask me to do all this?" He said, "Because I want you to learn to keep short accounts." God keeps short accounts.

Accountability is the second characteristic of a strong ministry, and I find that it is all too easy for us not to be accountable to any one. And you know the Bible says the human heart "is desperately wicked." A lot of my patients have gotten to the point where they are because they have rationalized the truth. They have lied to themselves a little bit at a time. And the reason they were able to go on doing that is that they were not accountable to anyone. They didn't allow themselves to be accountable. So there was no one there who could say, "Wait a minute, you are getting off track here. Brother, sister, what are you doing?" Accountability. You will not have a strong ministry unless you have accountability.

Third, a strong ministry has to have consistency. The world has to see that when we meet adversities and difficulties as well as when we meet success we're the same. Not that we're superhuman. Not that we don't get hurt, or weep, or get discouraged. We're human, we experience everything as everybody else does but we have the peace of God in our hearts; and people sense that. It is amazing how unbelievers can sense the peace of God. I've had unbelievers come to my office—not knowing I was a Christian—and after a while say, "I don't even know why I am coming back but there is something here; I can't quite put my finger on it." So I want them to come back, so I don't tell them. I say, "Just keep coming back, maybe one day you'll find out." Consistency. Let's always remember before we go any further that your ministry is you as a person. It's not your church, your organization; it's not your methods; it's not your finances; it's not even your gifts and your talents. You don't have to go out there and minister; you *are* a minister. The man is the ministry. And if the man is going in the wrong direction, the ministry will not go in the right direction.

How do we become strong and how do we remain strong? The basic principle of inner growth and inner strength deals with three things. These are simple things, but things we most easily forget. I think Satan has the ability to make us forget the simple things and the true things, so we need to repeat them. I said the basic principle of inner growth and strength deals with three things, or you and I are the product of three things: (1) Our relationship with God. (2) Our relationship with ourselves. (3) Our relationship with other people. Now this is not psychological mumble jumble. This is a reality. This is the way God has set it up that we are the product of our relationship with God, our relationship with ourselves, and our relationship with others. It's as if those three things are three legs on a stool, and all three are important. They have to be equally developed. They have to be equally strong. They have to have the same length, and all three have to be there for the stool to be level. We need to learn the discipline of keeping those three things in balance.

Let's look at some practical applications in our own lives of these three basic elements of a strong inner self. Because in this, as in many other things—and this is the value of workshops—it's not so much how much we know that is important, but how we much we live what we know. This is what the Bible says. The Bible says that we are responsible to live up to the light we have received. So it is not how much you've heard here during these days and how much more you will hear. That is not how God is going to judge you. He is not going to say, "That is wonderful that you've had all the opportunity to hear, to learn, to listen, to take notes, etc." It is wonderful but what really makes a difference is how much of it do we live.

First, let's talk about our relationship with God. The first point I want to empha-size is that after we have become a new creation in Christ—I don't care if it's one minute after, or ten years after—we have to learn and remember that we live in a state of reconciliation with God. You know, one of the most difficult things to learn as a new Christian is that we live in a state of reconciliation with God. The way I under-stand it is that for so many years we have lived in a state of alienation from God. We have lived separated from God. We have developed feelings and thoughts that God was against us, and He *was* in the sense that He was against our sin; not against us but against our sin. But it has marred our thinking and even our emotional life. So we still after we become Christians tend to feel God is there, "Now you are in the family. But I am going to watch you every step of the way, because you better walk straight." And God becomes more of a General or an Accountant, someone who is respectfully said to be "on the other side of the fence." I always have to watch. But that reminds us, doesn't it, of our great-grandparents—in the Garden of Eden, I mean. They were afraid of God all of a sudden, you see. They were uncomfortable. God might come around and ask an explanation.

We have learned to think of God as being an adversary, and Christ came to die on the Cross, as we know, to reconcile us. And we know this in our heads, but in our emotions and our thoughts we still tend to think of God as an adversary. That's why I am saying after our salvation, we live, we have to remember and relearn our relation-ship with God. We are not in a state of reconciliation. The Bible says we are "ac-cepted in the beloved." God sees you and God sees me through Christ. And because H sees me and He sees you through Christ, He is pleased with us. Now there is no way He could be pleased with me on my own, or with you on your own, because we sin and make mistakes every day. But you see God doesn't see us like this anymore. God sees us through Christ. It is like Christ and the work of the Cross become a filter, and through that filter God sees us perfect and it is a very serious issue. It is not just so that we feel better.

The reason it is very serious is because we neglect to learn to live as being recon-ciled to God. What we in fact do is, we neglect the work of the Cross. We're believ-ing and thinking and feeling as though the Cross had never happened. After our salvation we live in a state of reconciliation. God is with us. That doesn't mean that God overlooks our sin. His Holy Spirit is there to convict us of sin, to restore us. The blood of Christ is available to cleanse us. We live in the state of reconciliation. Sec-ond, in our relationship with God we need to learn again to practice living at peace with God.

You know on this continent—I'm from Switzerland—many countries have had to learn and are learning—relearning to live at peace with one another. Because not so long ago they were at war with one another, and they hated one another, and they tried to destroy one another. And now they have to learn to live at peace with one another. See the practice of living at peace with God comes from the fact that we honor God, number one. And because we honor God, what do we practice? We wor-ship Him. So the practice of living at peace with God means we worship Him.

Second, we are grateful for Christ, we're grateful for answered prayer, we're grateful for needs that are being met. And the practice of that is that we praise God. How much praise do we offer God compared to our petitions? I find myself so often crying out to God at a time of need, and when He answers the need I barely remember to say thank you. The practice of living at peace with God is because we honor Him, we worship Him. Because we are grateful we praise Him. Those are actions, things we do—not things we talk about or listen to. Because we trust God we make petitions to Him. Because we trust God we go to Him with our needs. That's a practical thing. So we worship God, we praise Him and we petition Him. And last, the practice of living at peace with God is because we believe in the truth. We act.

I do not believe that it is possible to believe, really believe, in the truth and not act upon it. The practice. God's Word tells us who God is. That's why we have to stay in the Word. Because all of what I've said right now depends on things that are revealed in the Word. God's Word tells us who He is, and because God's Word tells us who God is we honor Him. Because we honor Him, we worship. God's Word tells us what God gave us; that's why we praise Him. God's Word tells us what He will do for us; that's why we petition Him. And God's Word tells us what reality is; and that's why we can act. Because we are a strange bunch of people in this world. In a sense, we don't live in reality, because the reality we have around us is not reality. It's very temporary.

What is reality is the truth of God's Word. And that's why people think we are crazy, and in a sense they're right. The Bible tells us what reality is, not the psychologist, not the scientist, not the businessman, not the politician. Reality, brothers and sisters, is what God tells us is reality. It is so easy to be deceived. It is too easy to be carried away with things that seem to be legitimate and good, but they are not part of God's reality, as God's reality is presented in His Word.

We're talking about basically two things, prayer in which we worship, we praise, we petition, we plan our action. And being in the Word, that's the basis for our prayer. And then we count on the Holy Spirit—not our own minds, not our own education, not our own culture—to make the truth real to us. Because when you open His Book, when you read it, it becomes truth to you. When you read it, something jumps out at you. It is all truth; it is all the inspired Word of God but the Holy Spirit activates it so we have to allow the Holy Spirit free access, free control over our minds and our emotion and the rest of our lives.

Second, our relationship with ourselves. We cannot have a relationship with ourselves unless we have a relationship with God first. You see, the world speaks of self-worth or positive self-image which means you think well of yourself, but how can you think well of yourself unless you have a relationship with God? God is the one who makes you at peace with yourself. And this is where an unbeliever is in trouble. Because if I think poorly of myself—and all of us have plenty of reason to think poorly of ourselves—and I say to myself, "You're a fine person," why should I believe myself if I thought I was not much of a person to begin with? We need God to say, "You're okay." It is not enough to say, "I'm okay." It just won't do. And believe me, in the laboratory of a practice such as mine, I see it; it doesn't work. It sounds good, and people wish it would work. But it doesn't work because God—nobody else will do—has to say, "You're okay." That's why I am saying a relationship with God is first. Only after our relationship with God is established can I now have peace with myself and have a good relationship with myself.

We are talking about a positive self-image. That's a term that is used too often but I can't come up with a better one because it is still true. A positive self-image is when you think that you are okay. Except the difference is that now, as a Christian, you can truly accept the positive self-image because it is a Christ-given self-image. It's nothing to be proud about; it's nothing to be arrogant about because it has been given to you. You haven't done anything to earn it; you haven't done anything to develop it. You've received it as a gift. But you see Christ gave you a new person. Would Christ give you a person that was in bad need of repairs? No. Christ has given you a new person and you can think well of yourself because Christ has given you yourself. That's what a positive self-image is. So as Christians we are not to go around feeling bad about ourselves and how sinful and short we come of the goals, and how much of a discredit we are to God.

When we talk about a positive self-image as a Christian this is important not just for you, but it is important for your ministry. Because that is the kind of message you have to bring to the world, that Christ came to make us new. And we can proudly praise God for the new person, because it has nothing to do with us. He paid for it and we received it as a gift. Because all too often we go around, and we present forgiveness and salvation; but after that it is even worse, in a certain sense, because now we know the truth. Now we have light, so when you have light you see many more of the spots, and the imperfections, and the dirt. That's why Christ came to give us a whole new person; that positive self-image. So it's not just nice to have a good self-image as a Christian, it's a responsibility. It's not just to make us feel better for the few years we are in this world. It's a responsibility, something that Christ Himself paid for.

The second is growth from confronting your fears. Now that sounds very general. What it really means is that basically in life—and I have thought about this for a long, long time, and I've seen it in other people's lives—we are controlled by one of two things. What you do is controlled by one of two things. Either it is controlled by faith, or it's controlled by fear. Think about it as long as you want, and there is no other power at work in your life and my life but faith or fear. And it is so easy—whether it be in everyday life, in little things or in bigger things—to allow fear to control us. Now there are many problems with that. Obviously the first one is that it is very, very uncomfortable. You've seen people that are totally controlled by fear, and they are the most miserable people you have ever seen. But that is not the most important. What is more important than that for the Christian is that it paralyzes us. God cannot use us if we are controlled by fear. Now, how do we get rid of it?

There are two ways to get rid of fear, and it's really two sides of the same thing. You confront it. You don't negotiate with it; you don't avoid it; you don't rationalize it; you confront it. You confront it based on obedience. The Lord says, "Do this, this is the right thing. This is the right thing to do, this is the right thing to say." But I'm afraid. But God says, "This is the right thing to do." The first part is *doing* it, because what happens all too often, we try to confront. And this is where Satan gets us—we try to confront the fear by quoting Scripture. And we quote Scripture and we quote Scripture, and the fear doesn't go away. I say, "What's the matter? It's the Word of God, it's the all-powerful Word of God and I believe in it but it doesn't work." The reason is that quoting Scripture is only half of the answer. Acting upon it is the second half. That's what I mean by confronting the fear.

Let me take a simple example in everyday life that doesn't seem like much, but it is a whole lot bigger than you think. The example is that when among Christians there's been an offense. That is, somebody has offended you. And I don't mean somebody has irritated you, somebody has just made you nervous or been rude to you—I mean offended you, really offended you. Now as a Christian you have one of two reactions. Sometimes you may want to immediately react, maybe get angry, punish them or you say, "No, as a Christian, I'm not supposed to do this; I'm supposed to forgive." And you go to your room to pray and then you see this person, and you keep praying and something is not right. Somewhere, you feel before the Lord, I should go to this brother or this sister and say, "You have offended me." Speaking the truth in love as the Bible says. You see, strangely enough, we are afraid to do that.

We are so afraid as Christians to confront one another, not judgmentally—in love, in humility confront one another as members of the same body. Those of you that have children, when your children do something wrong, do you just not tell them, or do you confront them? Why do you confront them? Because you want them to learn. You want them to be purified. You want them to understand. You want them to grow. You confront them out of love, but we're afraid. The Bible says clearly that we should go to our brother and tell him or tell her, but we're afraid. So in a small every-day example—purposely, I did not choose a dramatic example—in a small way we are controlled by fear. And remember that fear, if it wins this much today is going to control more tomorrow, and still more the day after. Fear never stands still, so growth comes from confronting your fears and living by faith and not by fear.

Just as our self-image is related to our relationship with God, our relationship with other people is based upon our self-image. In other words, I will relate to you in a certain way depending upon how I see myself. You know if I see myself as being very inferior and ignorant, and I see you as being very educated and intelligent, I will relate to you in such a way. Or vice versa, if I feel superior to you. You understand how my self-image is going to affect how I relate to you. So it is all tied in together. So the way I see myself depends on the way I relate to God. The way I relate to you depends on the way I relate to myself. They are all interconnected. The point I want to make here is this: The key principle when you talk about relationships with others, the principle that covers everything, is that the basis of our relationship with others is (1) to speak the truth in love. And think about all of your relationships in your family, with your friends, with your co-workers, with church members. There is not one relationship that has gone wrong that cannot experience healing if we simply obey the biblical command to speak the truth in love. But many times, we speak the truth—it's absolutely the truth—but there is no love. Or we have this love, but we are so afraid if we speak the truth, it will destroy the relationship. We have the love, but we don't speak the truth. This is why our relationships are so weak a lot of the times. That's the basic principle. We have to: (2) be available in our relationship with others; we have to be available to serve others. We know that. It has been explained many, many times and we know it.

I would like to emphasize that (3) we have to learn to be served by others. You can't really have one without the other. It's a strange thing. I don't understand it alto-gether, but you can't really have a deep growing relationship with someone else un-less you serve them, and you allow them to serve you. It is very difficult for me to receive. I love to give, and by the grace of God, I have no problems with giving. Sometimes, I promise, I give too much. I get in trouble. I love to give but it is very difficult to give me something.

When somebody wants to give me something, I say, "No, let me give you some-thing." Now this sounds very wonderful, but it is not so wonderful; it's imbalanced. We need to learn to receive. Remember when Jesus washed the disciples' feet and some of them said, "No, not me, Lord, don't do this for me." They couldn't let Him serve them. And, third, we have to learn in our relationship with others, we have to be available to serve them; we have to be available to let them serve us. And fourth, we have to work together in unity.

There is nothing that is accomplished in the kingdom of God—I didn't say in *this* kingdom, I am saying in the kingdom of God—when we act on our own. This particular meeting could never have taken place if people had not realized that they had to work in the unity of Christ. We have to learn to work together in unity. And if we can't work because we don't have unity, let's get on our knees and get unity; let's not go to work until we get unity. This is the basis of our relationship with others as Christians and as ministers. Serve them and allow them to serve us, and learn to work together in unity.

# THE ROLE OF THE EVANGELIST IN PRAYING FOR SPIRITUAL AWAKENING

*Glenn L. Sheppard*

From every corner of the world, people are crying for answers regarding how to live their lives and find meaning and peace in a time that is marked by evil and instability. The country of Judea also knew what it was like to be in the midst of turbulence. Their history is marred by their wicked deeds that eventually brought upon them the just retribution for their sins. Under David, because of his relationship with God, the country prospered. Under his son Solomon, they built a temple to honor God. Solomon knew no temple could contain God, yet he prayed for His presence. God answered with His promise of redemption, forgiveness, and healing which He still offers to us today. This promise is 2 Chronicles 7:14, "If my people which are called by my name, shall humble themselves, and pray, and seek my face, and turn from their wicked ways; then will I hear from heaven, and will forgive their sin, and will heal their land."

During the time of Christ, the first disciples began to see the power of prayer in Christ's life and the priority He placed upon it, often rising before day to pray and withdrawing from them at times to be alone with God in prayer. They asked, "Lord, teach us to pray" (Luke 11:1).

## 1. Terms defined

Prayer, divine communication with God, is a prerequisite to His fellowship. In His fellowship is every good thing. Christ urged His disciples, and present-day disciples in turn, to pray. "Men ought always to pray and not to faint" (Luke 18:1). In preparation for revival and spiritual awakening, there is no substitute for prayer. The history of spiritual awakenings, historical and present-day, points to prayer, in humility and in faith, as being the call that God hears and responds to even as He did in years past. The broken, humble cry of man who agonizes for God's reviving presence will be heard.

According to E.M. Bounds in *The Necessity of Prayer*, "Prayer is the contact of a living soul with God. In prayer, God stoops to kiss man, to bless man, and to aid in everything that God can devise or man can need." Charles H. Spurgeon, writing on the subject of prayer in his sermon series titled *Twelve Sermons on Prayer*, says that "prayer is the slender nerve that moveth the muscles of omnipotence." In *The Hour That Changes the World*, Dick Eastman says, "Prayer is divine communion with our heavenly Father. Prayer does not require advance education. Knowledge is not a prerequisite, only an act of the will is required to pray."

Revival is God moving among His people bringing them to abundant life from spiritual coldness, carnality, powerlessness, and lack of spiritual understanding. Dr. J. Edwin Orr, in *The Re-study of Revival and Revivalism*, defines revival as "times of refreshing from the hand of God." He says that revival occurs among those who already possess eternal life. The term "awakening" is the sudden coming into life of a corporate interest in spiritual things. The Oxford Association for Research in Revival has adopted "revival" for believers and "awakening" for the community.

Spiritual awakening, then, is the result of revival. It is usually experienced when God's people in a given area have been so revived in a life-changing way that the secular world is profoundly affected and "awakened" to spiritual matters.

Evangelism is when the revived church goes into the sin-filled secular world and, in divine power (Acts 1:8), communicates (Acts 2:37-41; Acts 4:31-33) the Gospel of Jesus Christ with supernatural anointing (Acts 2:1-4) and effectively leads individuals to a saving knowledge of Jesus Christ.

Effective prayer is the means by which we not only communicate with the One we love and serve, but it is also the means by which we are equipped and anointed to reach the lost.

## 2.   *Present day illustrations of spiritual awakening*

In Korea, where God has been moving in a mighty way, the Christian population has grown from less than two percent to approximately 32 percent of the entire population of South Korea in the last three decades. The key to this amazing growth is the early morning prayer meetings and the prayer and fasting retreat centers located throughout that nation. The churches in South Korea have made prayer a priority. Many of their prayer meetings begin as early as 4:30 a.m. and last several hours. The effectiveness of the Korean churches is directly related to the intercessory prayer life of the people.

Prayer is the power behind the church in China, also. Having just returned from China, I have seen firsthand the freshness of anointing on the churches there. During the past decades as the people experienced repression and persecution, it was not possible to have open churches except in a few cities. However, the church continued to grow, often times winning its oppressors. Dr. Thomas Wang, founder and director of the Chinese Coordination Center of World Evangelism in Hong Kong, reported to the Lausanne Committee over two years ago that the church in China today numbers somewhere between 50 and 100 million. This is 60 times larger than the church was in 1949. Chinese Christians tell us today that the key is the prayers of the Christians.

Some of you have probably thought of another country where God is moving in a mighty way: Nagaland. In 1981, when Dr. J. Edwin Orr had recently returned from a visit to Nagaland, an autonomous state to the northeast of India and below Tibet, he told me that in the past decade Christianity had grown to such an extent that 80 percent of the population of 3/4 million people had come to Christ. Last year, Dr. Ben Waddie, Nagalander by birth and a Christian missionary, told me that now the Christian population may be as high as 87% of the population.

In response to my asking why and how this phenomenal growth occurred, both Dr. Orr and Dr. Waddie gave me the same answer: There was a call to prayer preceding the visit of Dr. Billy Graham some twelve years ago. They prayed a year in preparation for his planned one-day visit to their country. There was a great outpouring of the Spirit and converts were swept into the Kingdom at an amazing rate. They did not stop praying. They continued, and Christianity is still spreading. How can we separate prayer from evangelism?

In my country, America, in 1970 in a small college town, Wilmore, Kentucky, a revival began among the Christian students and in a few days spread to the town and to many other states. It began as the result of a small group of college students spending many hours over a period of five months praying for an outpouring of the Spirit of God. This revival, now known as the Asbury Revival, swept across many other campuses and touched the lives of countless young people. Today, many Christian leaders trace their own revival experience back to the Asbury Revival, and to the small group of students who prayed. Dr. Robert Coleman, in his book *One Divine Moment*, shares the experiences of these days and their direct correlation to prayer.

No doubt many of you could relate other exciting stories about how God has moved to honor His Word in 2 Chronicles 7:14. You, too, have seen Him do the miraculous in response to the humbled praying Christian. Do we dare neglect prayer in such a time as this?

**3.  *What happens when believers pray***

In Acts 4 when the disciples were released, they returned to their people and began to praise God for His mighty acts on their behalf. With one accord, in agreement, they asked for boldness, for signs and wonders in the name of Jesus, and for God, their Deliverer, to notice how they were being threatened. The Scriptures say that "when they had prayed, the place was shaken and they were filled with the Holy Spirit." They were now equipped to speak the Word with boldness.

By verse 32, "the multitude of them that believed were of one heart and of one soul." The result of one powerful prayer was experiencing the presence of God in an extraordinary way, being filled with His Holy Spirit, being equipped to speak with boldness and power, and a multitude snatched away from the devil. Not bad results for one prayer! They had experienced the presence of God, received the power of God and achieved the purpose of God.

Prayer has always been, and continues to be, the means by which God and His people unite to change the world. Andrew Murray recognized this awesome power. In his book, *With Christ in the School of Prayer*, he says, "The man who mobilizes the Christian church to pray, will make the greatest contribution in history to world evangelization."

**4.  *Conclusion***

As world evangelizers, the one thing that we cannot neglect is prayer. God can still use us if we're lacking in education, if we're lacking in ability, if we're lacking in years or even good health, but our harvests will be meager and rootless if we neglect prayer in our personal lives.

We do the new converts a great disservice, as well as those more mature Christians we encounter, if we do not teach and insist that they learn the practice of prayer. A new, prayerless Christian is tasty bait for the enemy who prowls around seeking whom he may devour.

World evangelizers, we must realize our responsibility to change the course of human history by growing praying Christians wherever we go. We have opportunity to start millions of tiny networks of prayer all over the world. It only takes two or three to form a prayer cell. As we plant these small groups to pray, we must encourage them to spend specific times daily or weekly in prayer and realize they will hasten the cause of the Kingdom in a way that we will never do with our messages alone. When these prayer groups are established, urge them to begin more. They will multiply.

Together, with hearts united in prayer the world over, we can raise up the standard of the Lord, defeat Satan's influence, and see captives of sin set free. I believe we can cause the soil to be made ready to receive the precious seed of the Master. Our united praying can prepare the way for the glory of the Lord to be revealed, and we can watch spiritual awakening begin in the hearts of mankind as we pray. Would you join with the disciples and ask, "Lord, teach us to pray" so that we might see spiritual awakening and world evangelization in our generation?

# HOW TO HOLD A CONFERENCE FOR EVANGELISTS
*Robert L. Williams*

I'm not going to attempt to motivate you—I'm not going to attempt to encourage you to have a conference for evangelists in your country. My assumption, which I hope is right, is that you are already interested in having a conference for evangelists in your country, or else you wouldn't be in this workshop; you would be in some other workshop. Many of you have asked the question, "How can we do it?"

So let's try here for the next few moments to share a little bit about what a conference for evangelists in your country should be; and then, second, a little bit about how to do it; and then, third, some of the major mistakes which you need to avoid. Hopefully there will be some time for questions and answers, so that you can share some of those pressing questions which you have. And perhaps we can answer them, or perhaps some of your colleagues there can answer them.

Second Timothy 2:2 gives us the biblical injunction to take the things which we have seen and heard and commit those things to faithful men, so that those men can also teach others. And this really is the method that the church should be using. I use the "church" talking about not only the local church but you as an evangelist, who should be arms and legs of the church. But we need to take the things which we've heard and seen here, and in other training opportunities which we have, and commit those things to faithful people. So that they can take those things which you've learned and commit those to others, so that the church can grow not by addition but by multiplication. That's the way we are going to win the world to Christ. Second Timothy 2:2—Paul gave that example and that biblical admonition to Timothy. He said, "Timothy, take the things which you've seen and heard and watched me do; you followed me for several years. Commit those things to faithful people, so that they can grow and commit those things to others."

## The Objectives of Amsterdam 86

We have attempted to apply 2 Timothy 2:2 to Amsterdam 86. Let me share three basic objectives of our program. We decided that everything we wanted to do for the evangelists fit into one of three categories. You know how we decided this: We went out and interviewed evangelists just like you. We said, "What are your needs? What are your problems? What are your concerns? What makes you discouraged? What kind of questions do you need answered?" And every one of the thousands of answers fit into these three categories:

1. *The evangelist as a man or as a woman.* The evangelist is a human being. Believe it or not, you as an evangelist are a human being! Now some of the people you minister to don't think you are. They think you walk on water; they think that you have the answers to everything; they think that you are always smiling; they think that you never have any spiritual problems. Now I know that you know better than that, but you know a lot of people in the Christian church say that pastors and evangelists just don't have problems.

You know as well as I do, that the thing which drives evangelists and pastors and Christian ministers out of the ministry more than anything else is our own personal lives. You're giving and giving, and preaching and preaching and preaching, and going and going and going, until you become dry. And you'll find a great emphasis on the evangelist as a human being, a spiritual being who needs not only to be responsible for studying Scripture for the purpose of communicating to others but studying Scripture for the purpose of feeding his soul and allowing the Holy Spirit to speak. The evangelist is traveling away from his family and there are temptations and struggles. There are problems with his own family. The evangelist is always giving. The evangelist who travels often doesn't have the support group that a person who is in a ministry locally has. And so think in terms of what the evangelist as a human being in your part of the world needs for encouragement.

A lot of what we are doing in this conference has nothing to do with education. It has to do with inspiration and encouragement. We want to send evangelists home inspired and encouraged as well as being trained, and they need encouragement. You know that. Don't pass that up. Don't get so educationally minded that you fail to remember the human being who is behind the evangelist.

2.   *The evangelist's message.* We find that the average—not the good but the average—evangelist has two temptations with the message. One is to *add* something to the Gospel message, or perhaps the temptation is to take something *away* from the Gospel message. And you need to speak to that in your conference for evangelists.

Why do evangelists get tempted to add to the message? You want to know why? Because the evangelist begins to get off and away from his objective.

If God has called you to do evangelism, then recognize what evangelism is and do it. And leave the expounding of all the other doctrines to the church and to the pastor and to the teachers, and to those who have been given that gift, or perhaps to the segment of your ministry when you have time to deal with those issues. But when you are doing evangelism, get the message simple, get it pure, get it powerful, get it authoritative. Get it simple enough so a five-year-old can understand it, and yet challenging and authoritative enough that a university professor will be challenged by it. So often we add things to it trying to create interest, trying to speak to all of the issues of today—and we may need to try and speak to those issues that are confronting us in this confused and chaotic world—but stay with the Gospel.

I have attended evangelistic meetings in different parts of the world. And I know evangelists who preach and preach and preach, and give an invitation, and no one comes forward. No one accepts Christ. You want to know why? I've heard over and over and over all kinds of other subjects, but I didn't hear the Gospel clearly presented. And if I couldn't hear it clearly presented after all these years of working in evangelism, how can the person who is blind spiritually understand and accept the Gospel? The evangelist needs to understand the message very clearly, and understand how to communicate it very clearly.

Why does the evangelist take things away from the Gospel message? Several years ago we were preparing for a crusade in a country, in fact for six crusades in that country. And the local committee came to us and said, "When Billy Graham comes and preaches, please tell Billy Graham, 'Do not say that Jesus Christ is the only way.'" I said, "What do you mean?" They said, "Please tell Billy Graham that in this culture it would be inappropriate to say 'Jesus Christ is the only way.'" I said, "I'm sorry. In John 14:6, Jesus Christ said in His own words, 'I am the way, the truth, and the life: no man cometh unto the Father, but by me.' And that has been our theme for forty-four years. I can't go to Billy Graham and tell him not to preach that." Well, to make a long story short, he preached it and he preached it harder than he has ever preached it before. And we had the largest percentage of people come forward in that country than in any other country we have ever been in the world, even though the committee said, "Don't preach it, you'll offend people."

The power of the Gospel cuts through a culture, and it cuts through backgrounds. In this particular country they said 2,000 years of experience and culture says that there are many good ways. I said, "I'm sorry, the Bible says there is only one way." And Mr. Graham stayed true to that. In fact, he preached it so much and preached repentance so hard that he was almost getting ready to preach salvation by works—not intentionally. You know salvation is free, it's by grace. but he was preaching so hard that you have to turn away from every other god and put aside all other things and follow Jesus Christ. And many evangelists are tempted as they travel from place to place to avoid offending people, and we need to do as much as we can to adapt and adjust to the culture, but let me tell you something. Jesus Christ Himself said, "The Gospel is an offense." So help your evangelist understand what the Gospel is, and their responsibility and their authority to preach it.

3. *Various methods of evangelism.* How to prepare an evangelistic sermon, how to give an invitation without using gimmicks, how to train counselors, how to train follow-up workers, how to work *with* the local church instead of against it, or instead of in spite of it. Even though the local church may not be what it ought to be, it is God's institution on this earth. You want to know one of the secrets why Billy Graham has been as successful as he has been for the last forty-four years? He will not go around the local church. We only go where we are invited by the local church; we will not go around it. All of our work, as you heard Mr. Graham say, is working with the local church. We don't bring a large team of people into a community. We go in and we motivate and mobilize the local church. We let them do the work. An evangelist needs to recognize that.

Find the methods that are germain—how to work with youth, how to work with children, how to use music in evangelism, how to use film and drama, how to work with certain groups in certain cultures—to your part of the world. Find the methods that you think will work in your culture and speak to those issues. Don't assume that because you know how to use those methods the average evangelist in your country will.

*Holding A Conference in Your Own Country*
"Why would you want to have a conference in your country?" Now, I can't answer that question. Only you can answer that question. What is it that you want to accomplish before beginning a conference in your country? Before beginning any task, actually, you need to ask yourself, "Why do we want to do it? What do we want to accomplish?" You need to answer those questions very specifically. Don't answer by saying, "We want to have a good time." Don't answer by saying, "Well, we want to have more evangelism in our country." Don't answer by saying things that are general in nature but be very specific. For every conference, for every event of this nature there ought to be a key, pivotal question that's burning in your heart, a vision that God has given you, an overwhelming vision, a key problem that needs to be resolved. And you believe that that conference, that event, or that process is the answer to that burning question, is the answer to that overwhelming reason, that burning problem.

Set an objective. Write out on paper what you want to accomplish with a conference in your country. Set an objective. Set a goal. Clarify that objective. Clarify that goal. Make it very clear. Don't take the Amsterdam 86 objective and simply repeat it, unless it is what God tells you to do. But pray with other leaders in your country, "What does God want us to do here in Zambia, Tanzania, or Columbia, or North America, or Australia?" Set that objective and pray that is an objective that God has given you—not just one that has come from your head, or from watching or copying other people. And then, with other leaders in your country, agree on that objective. Make sure that everyone agrees that this is God's objective, God's goal for God's time in your part of the world. If you don't have an objective, it would be like gathering a group of mechanics together and simply saying, "Build." One mechanic would build a bicycle, another mechanic would built a boat, one mechanic would build an elevator or a lift, one would build a jet plane, and one would build an automobile. Set a very specific objective and pull the leadership together and say, "Is this what God wants us to do?"

One of the biggest reasons for failure in any event such as a conference or an evangelistic crusade is attempting to do everything, instead of attempting to do an objective that God called you to do. It's really one of the problems in the church. You're filled with vision, you're filled with zeal, you're filled with compassion, you're filled with concern about the people in your part of the world. So you go out and try to do everything—and you end up quite often, doing very little because you try to do everything. Ask God what it is He wants you to do, and let God speak to others about some of those other things. Set a very clear objective or purpose. Clarify it. Get the people that are with you to agree on it and stay with it.

Don't get sidetracked into other issues. One of our biggest burdens as we've been preparing for Amsterdam 86 is that people all over the world—good people, qualified people, competent people, intellectual people from many different cultures—have said, "Speak about this subject, and deal with this issue and speak to this problem, and deal with this concern." And we can't do everything. And quite a few people are not very happy because we have said, "This is the objective that God laid on Billy Graham's heart—to have a training school for itinerant evangelists or traveling evangelists, to meet their needs and their concerns." This is an important issue. Yes, over here, this other issue. But it's an issue that some other conference needs to speak to. God has given us this issue. Here's another subject over here. It's an important subject, but it's not the subject God called us to for this moment. It's very important—and maybe later or maybe someone else—but for this time, Amsterdam 86, we've set our goals on one particular issue, concern, burning question, burning need, pivotal concern, and that is to train fellow evangelists in such a way that they can go home and do a better job. So whatever the objective is given to you by the Lord, clarify it, make it very specific, and then stay with it.

Very closely connected with your objective is what we call the "target audience." You'll have everyone who has any concern about evangelism wanting to come to your conference, and that on one hand is very good. I hope and pray that there are thousands and hundreds of thousands of people in your part of the world that are interested in evangelism. But if you bring everyone in you begin to create confusion, and you begin to get away from your objective, and you get off on other issues.

Let's suppose that I was responsible, or that you were responsible, for conducting a conference in your country for heart surgeons—for people whose job and responsibility and expertise and calling in life is to perform heart surgery. If we invited into that conference all people involved in the medical world, podiatrists who work on feet, dentists who work on teeth, ear surgeons who work with ears, dermatologists who work with skin, kidney specialists, etc., they are going to become upset because your agenda, your program, your objective is to speak to the issues, concerns, and needs of heart surgeons.

If you take your program and spread it out to the point where it speaks to all of these different people and has something for the dentists and something for the dermatologists who deal with skin problems and something for the ophthalmologists who deal with the eyes and something for the kidney specialists, then the heart specialists are not going to get what they need. Let the kidney specialists have their conference. Let the dentists have their conference. Let the podiatrists who deal with foot problems have their conference. And you have a conference for heart specialists, or else you dilute yourself, you water down to the point where you are saying a little bit about everything, but not enough about anything.

We have struggled with that, and it is one of the biggest problems in church conferences around the world. We struggle with that ourselves. We say a little bit about everything, and end up not saying enough about anything. So stay with your objective and get a target audience. Don't try to speak to all the issues. Don't try to meet the needs of all religious workers in your country. You will not meet the needs. You'll speak to some of the subjects, but you will not speak to the subjects sufficiently. So maybe you ought to have several conferences in your country. Maybe you ought to have one for pastors and pastor-evangelists. Maybe you ought to have one for those working with children. Maybe you ought to have one for the laymen. You ask God to help you clarify your objective and then clarify your target audience; because if you try to please everyone you end up pleasing no one. Whom do you want to reach? You need to be very specific about that. Whom do you want and need present in your meeting in order to achieve your purpose? What is the profile of the average person in your target audience?

Also, do not develop and direct your program to speak to the concerns of the good evangelist in your country. When you develop a topic at school, to teach at school—those of you who are involved in education—you do not develop your content and curriculum for those who know everything about that topic. You develop it for those who know nothing about that topic, or relatively little. Perhaps they took course number one last year and you're teaching course number two. If so, you develop your curriculum and content for those who took course number one. But develop your content and curriculum for—forgive me for saying this—for the poor, not poor economically but for the not-so-good, not-so-effective evangelist. Don't assume things; don't assume that they understand. Develop your training school—because that's really what a conference for evangelists is—for those who need the training, not for those who don't need the training.

Paul Little, who is with the Lord today, a professor of evangelism for many years said, "If you want to reach people, you need to learn to scratch them where they itch." To scratch people where they itch, to meet their needs, find out what their needs are, their problems are, their concerns are. Many of you over the last 18 months have received correspondence from us—and perhaps personal visits from Werner Burklin—asking you what the problems are that you have in your work. And those kinds of evaluations and interviews and questions helped us to develop the program for you. You need to do that with your target audience. You need to ask what is the profile, what is the educational level? Are they part-time pastor, part-time evangelists? How much experience have they had in evangelism? How much training have they had in evangelism? What are their needs? What are their problems? What are their concerns? So if, in summary, you set a very clear objective, you clarify a very clear target audience and study that target audience. Because that will help you to speak to their needs, instead of just speaking about whatever kind of subject happens to sound good.

You can talk about what a conference ought to be, and there's much more that can be said there. And we are going to come back and touch on what needs to be in the program of a conference in a few moments. But the big question is, "Who's going to do the work?" It's surprising to most people how much work it takes to do God's work. It *is* God's work. But for some reason which I don't understand, God has chosen to use people like you and like me. We don't happen to be supernatural and perfect like He is. We have supranatural power available to us. But God for some reason, and we can explain it theologically but I'm still going to discuss it with Him when I see Him face to face, has chosen to rely upon you and me to receive the power of the Holy Spirit in our lives; and to go out and apply the power of the Holy Spirit to the work that He has called us to. And there is no way to get around it, if you are going to have a conference or any kind of event in your part of the world, prepare for a good large amount of hard work. There is no way to get around it.

Nothing, absolutely nothing in the Christian world or in the secular world, happens without a lot of hard work. You know that, and I know that. In order to get a plane in the air, it requires a lot of hard work for hours and hours before you ever show up to board that plane. It requires a lot of hard work to make the clothes you are wearing. You know that. Expect a lot of hard work if you are going to have a conference in your country. Who will do the work? Many more people than most people realize.

I would suggest that if God is giving you a burden for a conference in your country, that you start thinking now. And start writing down names of others who you think might join you with this burden, with this concern, and in this project. People who perhaps do not have full time available, but who will add to their busy schedule some additional time to give to this project. Share your burden with them, and ask them if they would pray before the Lord. Don't convince them; let the Holy Spirit do the convincing. Because if you bring people into the work who are convinced by you, then you'll be convincing them from now until the day the conference is over with. Let them be convinced by God. Share the vision, and ask them to pray and see whether or not God gives them the vision as well. If they receive the vision and burden from the Lord, then join together. But think now about others, from your denomination, from your geographical region as well as from others.

I believe that there are two levels of leadership necessary in order to have an effective evangelistic conference for other evangelists in your country. And I am not saying that one particular group needs to be spiritual and one needs to be administrative. But I do believe you need a group of leaders in an advisory capacity to give leadership; some of the older people in your country who have some years of wisdom, some years of experience, a cross section geographically, a cross section in the evangelical churches in your community—and ask them to join with you. Two reasons: there's wisdom in good counsel. Scripture teaches there is wisdom in seeking the counsel and advice of the elders. So get a group of elders around you to give you spiritual leadership. But a second reason, and it is a little more political. If you want to get evangelists from denomination "A," and evangelists from denomination "B," and the evangelists and pastor-evangelists from denomination "C," then you had better get leadership from those denominations to be involved in the conference you are planning. Because people follow their leaders, and if the leadership of your conference, let's say, is all Assembly of God then you are basically going to get Assembly of God people.

If that is what God's burden is, then stay with that. But if God has given you the burden to reach your country, then reach out to the other denominations outside your normal walk of life. Seek for leadership out there, and try to impress on them the burden God has given you. And pray that God will give it to them as well, because people respond to something they feel they are a part of, not something they have been invited in on. So from the very beginning, get others involved.

There may be in your part of the world some religious denominations that are Protestant, or perhaps they call themselves evangelical, but they are not really committed to evangelism as much as your church group. If that is the case, then God will help you find at least a few people within that particular group. While the hierarchy of the church and leadership of that particular church or denomination may not be excited about evangelism, there is probably someone in that group that could be, and is already, excited about evangelism. Because they are the ones who need it the most. Whom do you send to school—the people who are already educated or the ones who need the education? Whom do you send to the doctor—the people who are ill, or the people who don't need a doctor? So go after those groups in your particular part of the world who need more training in evangelism, and the obvious need is that they are not doing very much. It is very tempting for us, all of us, myself included, to gather around us those people who are of like mind. But I think you can find people in some of those denominations, and use your conference as a bit of a mission endeavor to some of those groups and church groups and denominations who are perhaps not that evangelistic.

The second level of leadership is the administrative leadership, those who actually do the work, not just those who are giving counsel. And let me clarify very quickly and tell you that those who are involved in the administrative side of the work had better be spiritually minded and spiritually mature persons or the work won't get done. So let's not leave the spiritual responsibility to one group of leadership, and the work responsibility to another. Those who are involved in administrative work will not make it, unless they also have spiritual maturity, and unless their roots are also in Jesus Christ. But I have listed six key areas of administrative leadership. I have found this very, very difficult to do. Because in certain parts of the world, I would suggest maybe fifteen areas of leadership; and in other parts of the world I would suggest less. And so some of you may decide in your part of the world to adjust this. This is not some secret formula, but six basic areas of preparation where leadership needs to give attention.

1.   First of all, I would suggest that you find an administrative chairman, the number one leader, the person who is going to let most of the responsibility fall on his or her shoulders. This is a person who would select the other personnel, following the advice and counsel of your spiritual and advisory leadership. This is the one who gives overall coordination, who would be responsible for communication between departments, who would be responsible as a bit of a referee, like in a football game to settle disputes and disagreements between departments. And you know, we still have disagreements in the church, don't we? This one needs to be a strong leader spiritually, able to take criticism, but also a strong leader administratively, someone who has some background in leading people. Not only leading them—don't find the one who is a great preacher, that's not the qualification for this person. He may happen to be a great preacher as well.

Find someone who is spiritually mature, not only one capable of communicating, but one who is capable of leading people in work. Not the general who says, "Go get 'em," but the general who says, "Follow me, I will work with you." That's the kind of administrator/leader you need.

2.   You need a program chairman and perhaps a committee to work with the program chairman, one who will study the target audience, who will develop the content of the

program, who will choose the topics that need to be spoken to, the issues that need to be discussed, who will choose speakers and workshop leaders, giving attention to their qualifications, giving attention to their representation, who will prepare materials and the myriads of details involved in the program. His orientation really should be that he has an educational background, someone who has some training in communicating and teaching, a program chairman. And he needs to gather around him some people who can assist in developing the program. I would suggest very strongly that the people this program chairman gathers around him be evangelists, be the very people to whom you are trying to minister.

Don't gather great theologians. It may be good to have a good theologian on this committee to make sure we don't get off base theologically, but if you want to develop a program for evangelists, let the evangelists help you develop that program. That's the best way to get it.

3.   You need an arrangements chairman, a committee to arrange for the location of the meetings, the workshops, the equipment, for the physical needs such as tables and chairs and sound. And this person's orientation ought to be one that has a background that is good on detail, and faithful to do the work himself or herself. One who understands some of the needs in terms of physical arrangement and equipment, one who has a background, perhaps, in construction—or in the business world and who understands these needs.

4.   You need what we call a hospitality chairperson or hospitality committee. All of these people ought to have committees working with them. Use the principle of delegation. Use the principle of the more people you get involved in it, the more successful it is going to be—as long as you have good leadership to coordinate the people. You need to be concerned about living accommodations, you need to be concerned about means, travel arrangements, etc. And this needs to be a person whose background and orientation is one that has a thorough understanding of the local situation.

Don't get a person—let's suppose you are working on a conference in Nigeria, and you are planning to have a conference in Lagos. Don't get a person who lives in Kano who knows nothing about Lagos and nothing about the churches in Lagos. Don't get a person who knows nothing about the local situation. Get a person who has local business contacts, who has an understanding of the churches, and who has an understanding of whom to see to get assistance concerning housing, preparation of meals, and that type of thing.

And let me say something also about accommodations, meals, and travel arrangements. Napoleon, the great French general of many years ago, great perhaps in some ways and not-so-great in others, once said that an army marches on its stomach. And you've attended the different meal sessions here either in living accommodations, at the coffee breaks, the evening meals here; and I know we've had some people who didn't like the food and some people who thought it was too much, and some who thought it was too spicy. We could have saved literally hundreds of thousands of dollars by making our meals cheaper, by making less food, less quality, but we decided that if you were going to come to this conference, number one—we wanted to keep you healthy. We had a conference about twelve years ago in another part of Europe. About 4,000 people were invited. We put 4,000 seats in the auditorium. We always had about 1,500 seats empty. We thought maybe they were out sightseeing. We found out they were back in the hotels sick, because the food we were serving them was very economical; but they were getting sick from the food. So we worked hard to make sure that the quality of our food is sufficient, so that you will not become ill.

Most of our complaints about the living accommodations here have been that they are too luxurious. We had several people just this morning say, "Why didn't you save money? You don't need this, and you don't need that. Many of my friends could have come if you had saved money and not had all these living accommodations; and just given us mats on the floor. Some of my other friends could have come from the money that you saved." Well, you know no matter what you do, somebody doesn't like it. But our objective is to make sure that our living accommodations do not drain you physically to the point where you are so tired when you arrive in the morning that you're ill. And you don't get anything out of the sessions and out of the workshops. There's no use bringing people halfway across your country—much less halfway around the world—just to become ill, and so tired they fall asleep in the sessions. But give attention to not only doing enough to get by, but do enough to make sure the living accommodations and the meals and those types of things do not detract from your objective and take so much energy from your people that they get nothing out of the sessions.

5.   A promotion person is needed. I do not recommend that you put advertisements in your newspapers, billboards on your streets, speakers on top of your cars, and go up and down the streets and announce that you are having a conference for evangelists, if that is what God has called you to do. Because, when you do, you'll get everyone else paying attention and wanting to attend, and you get away from your target audience. But you do need some promotion and communication to the target audience. The very people who need your conference the most are the ones who are not that interested in it. They think they know it all. They think they have all the answers. They don't think they need help, and so you've got to convince them. You've got to talk to them, you've got to let them know through a promotional department, through a communications department that communicates to the leadership of various groups; and says look, here's our objective, here is our target audience, these are the kinds of people we think will benefit the most, here are some of the subjects we are speaking to, some of the issues that we are dealing with. You've got to communicate with those people.

I would also suggest that your promotional chairperson and committee promote within the church, not attendance because that is something that should be promoted only to your target audience, but promote within the church, prayer. We touch on this just for a few moments in this workshop. But if it weren't for the fact that literally thousands and thousands and thousands, and perhaps hundreds of thousands, maybe even millions of people around the world have been praying for Amsterdam 86, it would not have taken place. I will not give you illustrations; trust me on that. It has been a battle for the last twenty months. Physically, emotionally, spiritually, socially, it has been a battle. Any time you attempt to do anything for God, any time you attempt to fulfill the burden, the vision that God has given you, Satan knows about it and he will try to stop you. You know that in your own ministry.

Mr. Graham has often quoted an old evangelist from years ago. When asked, "What is the secret to your evangelism?" he said, "The most important ingredient is prayer. And the second most important ingredient is prayer, and the third most important ingredient is prayer." If you are not willing to get on your knees and pray, perhaps even tonight, about whether or not you ought to have a conference to train other evangelists in your country; if the leadership is not on their knees praying, not just at the appointed time once a week, but praying in your planning meetings and praying through your planning meetings, praying in the midst of a heated discussion in order to ask God to give patience, and praying when you don't know an answer to a problem, praying constantly, your conference will fail. Get the church in your country, in your part of the world, to pray—to help you decide whether or not you ought to have a conference, to begin with, and then pray all the way through that conference. All through the preparations, pray for the evangelists who don't want to come. Pray God will give them the conviction they ought to come. Pray that God will prepare their hearts, prepare the speakers, for everything, saturate it with prayer. Don't fight the battle physically and socially and intellectually and emotionally. Fight it all spiritually, because believe me, Satan fights on that spiritual battlefield.

This promotional chairman should have the ability to communicate verbally and also in writing. This needs to be someone who knows something about communicating to other people—maybe an editor of a local newspaper, maybe an editor of a Christian journal in your country who would help to communicate effectively to the people in your part of the world.

6. The last person, the last worker, the last department, the last committee you need would be administration. That is the person, the department, which handles the files, the registration, the finances, the budget, the fund raising and the records, etc. And this needs to be an administrator who has the ability to handle the details of office management. Now you may or may not have the finances to pay all of these people.

We have seen over the last three years about 22- or 23-some conferences done around the world in such a way that not one single person was full-time. But volunteers in addition to their work, in addition to their vocation, in addition to their ministry, said, "Yes, I will be responsible for leading a committee handling hospitality, or I will be responsible for a committee doing the work of promotion, or I will be responsible for a committee doing the work of administration." Don't look for those people who have nothing to do, because there's probably a reason for their having nothing to do. They probably don't want to do anything. You know the old story, go to those people who are already busy. They are usually the ones who will get your job done.

*Implementing the Work*

A lot of failure happens if in a particular task or particular job work needs to be done by two or three departments in order to get that job done; and department number one and department number two gets it done, but department number three hasn't heard anything about it yet. So you need a master schedule—when to do what, and when it should be completed. I'm sure you can find materials in the bookstores in your country about scheduling, and about organization and coordination of various departments. And then constantly review, constantly take a look at what you are doing. Are you staying with your objective? Is your target audience the same as nine months ago when you studied it? And then be sure you have coordination between committees. Be sure the right hand knows what the left hand is doing.

There is much more that could be said, but let me touch on another important point. Seek counsel. I have a big ego. You have a big ego. Most Christian leaders have a strong personality. Most of us feel that we are right. You know, I have an opinion about everything, and I'm right about it. I know better than that, and you know better than that. And one of the things I am slowly learning is that I don't know everything. There is wisdom in seeking counsel and advice from others from the very beginning—even about whether or not you ought to have a conference, about what the objective ought to be, about what the target audience ought to be, about what kind of personnel you ought to have, etc. Seek advice—advice concerning spiritual matters of the conference, concerning the educational matters of the conference, concerning the business matters of the conference, concerning the administrative matters of the conference. Seek advice and counsel.

In conclusion, there are several major errors you should attempt to avoid in preparing for a conference in your country:

1. Don't move away from your objective. Don't move away from the objective and purpose that God called you to, simply because someone is putting pressure on you to cover other subjects and other issues. Stay with your objective. Don't try to solve all the problems. Find out what the burning question is, what that burning topic is, what that real need is in your community. Ask God if a conference of this nature will solve that problem, will answer those questions, and then stay with the objective.

2. Don't move away from the target audience. Don't invite foot doctors to a conference for heart surgeons. They would get nothing out of it; they would simply be critical, they would be disappointed, they would be upset, and create a spirit of dissension, a spirit of turmoil. One of the reasons why there is so much unity in this conference is that you all came with the same background, the same vision, the same desire, the same needs, the same concerns. Stay with your target audience. Let other conferences and other people—or perhaps you at another time—deal with the other issues and the other needs.

3. Don't try to do it by yourself. Don't try to plan a conference by yourself. Seek the leadership of other people. Seek the leadership of people from other church groups and evangelistic groups in your country, your community. Don't try to conduct a conference for evangelists, a training school for evangelists by yourself. Seek counsel, seek advice. There is good wisdom in that.

4. Get God in on it from the very beginning, and make sure that it is His program, His burden, His conference. If it's not, it will fail. You want to know why? Because if you don't have the spiritual power that comes from God's presence and God's involvement, and God's being the one who lays the vision and the burden and the desire upon your heart—God in the midst of all the organization, God in the midst of the selection process of speakers and the program content, etc.—you are going to fail miserably because Satan is there. You can know that he is there.

Satan will try to stop you. If you try to do it by yourself and don't recognize the absolute necessity, irrefutable necessity, for its being God's conference that He has asked you to do, you'll fail miserably. It is not simply an educational process. It is not simply a group of people coming together and having good fellowship. It is a time when God's Holy Spirit convicts and God's Holy Spirit takes from speakers what you need; and takes something else from that speaker that someone else needs, and works to meet our needs and our problems.

I spoke to a radio reporter yesterday. She's not a Christian. She'd blind spiritually, she doesn't understand the things you and I understand about spiritual matters. She said, "How in the world can a speaker stand in front of 10,000 people and speak for 30 minutes and expect anyone to get anything out of it?" And I said, "Ma'am, the speaker may be speaking to 10,000 people, but the Holy Spirit is speaking to individuals."

There's a spiritual dimension in the work. When God is involved in what is happening from the very beginning—and it is His plan, His program and His speaker, His process, His conference—He will take even the horribly communicated words of a speaker, and His Holy Spirit will drive that into this evangelist and that evangelist, and that pastor and meet needs. Don't forget the spiritual dimension of what you are doing. The organizational dimension is not enough; the spiritual dimension is more important.

If you really have a burning desire, and you believe that God is calling you and other leaders within your country to have a conference for evangelists—to train the evangelists who couldn't come and perhaps to amplify it for those evangelists who did come—then you need to write to the Amsterdam 86 Follow-up Department, P.O. Box 9313, Minneapolis, Minnesota 55440, U.S.A.

When you write, you've got to convince us that this is a burden from the Lord. Is there a broad cross section of people in your particular part of the world who really want this? These things must be answered. There is help available through the Follow-up Department. We're not going to send a team of 150 people to your country to do the work. We're not going to send hundreds of thousands of dollars to help you, but there is help available.

# TESTIMONY
*Joanne Shetler*

I grew up on an American farm. When I was twelve years old, I heard verses from the Bible like "*Go* into all the world and *preach* the Gospel . . . *make disciples . . . teach* people." I was only twelve; I thought you *had* to obey God. I wondered what I'd gotten myself into, this becoming a Christian—it cost so much! But still, it made such good sense. After all, look at what God had done for me! I indeed owed Him my whole life.

About that same time I also heard that most of those who go, preach, and make disciples, were doing it to only a very few of the world's population. That was like nine people carrying one end of a burden while only one person struggled to carry the other end! So it was only logical to go help where there were so few working. What drove me on is what drives *you* on . . . *how* can I enjoy this salvation and not share it with others?! So, God's call to me to missions was really just logical common sense.

But I felt so inadequate. I don't know how! I'm only a woman! I only grew up on a farm! I am not skilled! I am ashamed to talk in public! I never even saw the big city until I went away to college! But God would never accept my excuses of inadequacy. Of course, I was inadequate. In fact, I found out that God delights in inadequate people—that just proves that the honor all goes to Him.

But besides feeling inadequate, I was afraid. What if all a person ever knew about God was what I told them? How would I have money to live?

I did logical things: I went to a Christian school, for that seemed like a logical thing to do if one is going to be a missionary. I took a one-year nursing course—that seemed like a logical thing to do if I were going to a remote area as a missionary. Since most of us Americans aren't good at learning a foreign language, I took a course that would help me learn a foreign language. It seemed like a very logical thing for me to do. But it seemed that I was always doing "just what seemed logical." Is *this* really how God leads people? I would have preferred some special dreams or voices or something wonderful, but all I had were the "facts" of the need and the "logic" of meeting those needs.

But what exactly did God want me to do? I didn't know and I was afraid; I felt inadequate. What could I do that would last? Or that would really help people? It was at the end of that language course when God caused me to understand about Bible translation! Why, I could give people *God's* Word in their language! God Himself could speak to them, just as He had spoken to me through His Word. Then they would also respond to God as missionaries and evangelists! I was excited!

There are about 3,000 languages in the world that are not written, with no Scriptures translated into them. God speaks only a foreign language to them—one with no "teeth" in it. One of these languages was Balangao. Those people were ex-headhunters and lived in the mountains of northern Philippines. Anne Fetzer and I were assigned to go live with them, learn their language, and translate the Scriptures for them, so they could also believe and then reach others. It was hard to get there. We rode a bus for three days and then climbed through rugged mountains for two more days before we got to Balangao. We arrived exhausted, rain-soaked, muddy, and bleeding from leech bites; and the people were shocked, for they had never seen white women before. Balangao is not only five days north of Manila, it was also centuries back from the modern world. But the people were amazing; they had carved rice terraces out of the side of the mountains, and all they had to eat was what they grew.

They'd not seen much of the outside world when we got there. One day we were listening to the news on a short-wave radio. A lady walked in and stared in wide-eyed amazement. She didn't know what that radio was, but she knew that was a person's voice talking. Finally she couldn't stand it any longer. She asked, "How big are the people you keep in that little box?"

The man who agreed with our leaders to have foreigners come live with them and learn their language was upset when he saw Anne and me. "*Not* women!" he cried out. "Don't you know it's not safe for women to be here? Don't you know we're headhunters? You will need someone to take care of you . . . I'll be your father."

Where did he get that idea? This man didn't know the Word of God! He didn't know it said, "If any man leave father and mother, sister and brother for my sake and the Gospel, I'll give him more fathers and mothers, sisters and brothers than he left." Ever since I was young I'd been praying for the people I'd go to someday, that God would make them ready for the Gospel. This was part of God's preparation, and it encouraged us and humbled us. Here God was taking care of us, His children, in a beautiful way, before we even started doing any missionary work!

No one could figure out why we'd really come to Balangao, even though we tried to explain. They finally decided among themselves that we were either looking for husbands, or else we were going to sell their language in America. We set about to learn to speak Balangao. We'd climb up the bamboo ladders into their dark, smoky little one-room houses on stilts, sit by their open fires, eat rice and snails with our fingers, and learn about why they had to sacrifice pigs and chickens to the evil spirits. Their life was hard, and they were always afraid. For if a spirit wanted to increase his chickens or pigs, he'd just make a child sick, then they would have to exchange a pig or chicken for the life of that child by sacrificing it to the spirits. Or if someone was getting wood in the forest, and accidentally stepped on the house of an evil spirit—or even worse, on the child of an evil spirit—he'd have to sacrifice, or someone would die. They were always afraid. The spirits were never merciful to them.

Well, *we* had the answer to their problems! We explained to our Balangao family daily about God and how to believe. But no one really listened to us; we were too young and we were foreigners. And we didn't realize that it wasn't proper for children to teach parents, for parents are the ones to teach children. We didn't even know that we weren't going about it right! However, God was still at work in our Balangao father; God even gave him a dream to think about. In his dream, our Balangao daddy saw a strange man, a man he'd never seen before in Balangao. He asked him, "Just *why* have those American children come here, anyway?" And the man in his dream said, "They have come to tell you something that is more solid than a mighty rock; you *believe* what they tell you." We go at God's bidding, but *He* is the one to prepare people to believe.

But in my first five years, only two had believed. I went back to America for furlough very frustrated. Why won't those Balangaos believe? I knew they were ready to believe, but they just wouldn't! One man told me, "Yeah, we'd stop sacrificing pigs and chickens to the spirits if we just had protection, but what are we going to do when our children are sick . . . let them die?"

What do you do when the situation looks impossible? Well, you must get your home churches to pray for you! I shared with them and that was the time those people at home *really* started to pray for us. I found out that it doesn't work when we try to do God's work without enough prayer support. I was trained; I knew the answers; I did all the right things, but it is only God who can make people believe. So my friends at home started to earnestly pray for me and the Balangaos, and then things changed.

When I returned to the Philippines, I still wasn't aware of the problem: that my Balangao father couldn't listen to me because children don't teach their fathers. In desperation I gave him a typed copy of the book of 1 John that I had translated, and asked him if he'd please "correct" the Balangao grammar. He started to read it. He was amazed! Before he was half finished, he said, "My child, this stuff is good! Why, people would believe this if they could just hear it." I was amazed. This was what I'd been trying to tell him for six years! But all I said was, "What are we going to do so they can hear?"

I didn't know it, but that was the wisest thing I said in Balangao. You see, that was me asking him for help. He went out into the village, and brought a whole bunch of people to my house, sat them down, and then he said to me, "Here we are, teach us." This was God answering people's prayers at home. For God was helping me, the evangelist, follow the proper custom. Because when the father asks the daughter to teach, that's when she has the right to speak and people will listen. But she doesn't have the right to teach before he asks! "What do you want me to teach you?" I asked.

And then they started asking me the questions that all Balangaos must have answered before they can believe. "Where did people come from? Where did sin come from? Where did Satan come from? Why do we sacrifice to evil spirits instead of God?" I told them about the liar and the great deceiver, and then about how God Himself became a man to reach men, and redeem them . . . in some sense they themselves were trying to redeem the lives of their children from the evil spirits. Along with all their other questions they also started to ask, "Now what is that I tell God when I want to become one of His children?" I'd give them a simple prayer to pray, and they'd become children of God. One man prayed right there, in the middle of our Bible study. After he finished he lifted his head and asked, "Is it OK if we tell this to other people?" The spirit of the evangelist!

Soon after that we had a real "power confrontation"—it was God against the evil spirits. In the end, the people saw God actually defeat the evil spirits right before their very eyes when these spirits tried to kill two spirit mediums who believed, but they couldn't. Then people flooded into the village from miles around, wanting to know just *who* this God was who had more power than the evil spirits. The church was born when God showed His power.

Then people from all the villages were begging for someone to come and teach them too. But who would go? I was the Bible translator . . . I couldn't hike all over as they could; I couldn't sleep just anywhere; I was a woman, and I was a foreigner. I could never do that job as well as they could. It had to be the men who were believing. I tried to persuade them to go teach others; I would beg and plead and reason with them . . . but they absolutely refused. They said they couldn't understand people's questions. And there was another problem, too—the Balangaos wouldn't pray out loud. They liked me to pray, but they were ashamed. They needed to learn how to pray, but they just wouldn't!

What does a Bible translator do when she has a new church on her hands? I knew I was responsible for the growth of the new believers, even though they wouldn't pray out loud. I started to translate the Pastoral Epistles with my Balangao father.

While translating, we came to the verse in Timothy where Paul says to Timothy, "I will that men everywhere pray." I didn't know it, but God spoke to my Balangao father there, through His Word. And that night at supper, as I was about to pray, my daddy cleared his throat and announced, "I will be the one to pray tonight." And that began their praying out loud.

Even though they only had a few books of the New Testament in their language at this time, I longed for them to pray about everything in their lives and not just for food. I'd hint, and then describe how we did it in America. I'd explain and give examples, but all my attempts to convince them were futile. Finally in desperation I told God, "I don't care what you need to do, please teach these people how to pray in depth!"

That prayer nearly cost me my own life—literally—because it wasn't long after this prayer that Balangaos pulled me from a helicopter crash with many badly broken bones and much bleeding. They thought I wouldn't live through the night, so they crowded all around me and this time they prayed on their own, "God, don't let her die—the book isn't finished yet!" That was the beginning of the Balangaos' praying about many things: for the sick, about their problems, and for others.

Our Sunday Bible studies in Balangao were hours of questions and answers as people explored the Scriptures. People came from all over to study. But some Sundays I was away from Balangao, and to my dismay, there would not be a Sunday study. I couldn't bear that, so I tried to get the men to teach. I told them I'd go over the lesson with them first. But they still wouldn't do it! My reasoning, begging, and pleading were without avail. They just would not teach. "We just don't know enough about all this," they insisted. I was frustrated again.

I continued to translate in Timothy with my daddy. Then we came to the verse where Paul says to Timothy, "I don't allow women to teach men." My Balangao father didn't make even one comment. But that afternoon after we'd finished our work, he asked what we were studying on Sunday. I thought he was just curious, so I told him. Then on Sunday morning, before I could stand and teach, he stood and said, "My daughter here knows more about this than I do, but we found in the Bible where it says women aren't supposed to teach men, so I guess I have to be the one." That's when the men started to teach in Balangao! What I could not do by reasoning power, God did by using His Holy Word.

By now I realized more than ever that I had to get the written Word of God into believers' hands as quickly as possible. Of course, this was my job—I was already committed to getting the Scriptures into the hands of the people, and in their own language. But it was as if I wasn't really fully aware of how *powerful* it was. Truly God's Word was more powerful than my ability to teach or explain.

After translating the book of James I handed out a dozen typed copies to different ones. A few days after Fanganan had gotten his, he came running, shouting, "Come quick! My boys are dying!" They'd been off to the forest and had eaten poison berries and they *were* dying! I froze. "Bu . . . bu . . . but I don't know what to do!" I insisted. His frustration was mounting. At last he nearly shouted at me, "But can't you at least come and *pray*? That's what that letter of James says you're supposed to do, that you gave me to read!"

I gulped. Somehow I guess I hadn't grappled with the fact I'd really have to *do* what the Scriptures said. Nevertheless, even though I was afraid, I went with him and prayed. And immediately the boys were both well. I was surprised! But Fanganan wasn't. "That's what it said, wasn't it?" You see, I *knew* things of God's Word by my studying. But I had to learn the *reality* of God's Word by experience. God wants us both to give His Word to people, and to obey it ourselves in front of them.

The church in Balangao has grown; and that church has given birth to many other churches. They are having their problems, and Satan tries to stop their outreach. But the Word of God is alive and powerful among them. They have evangelists among them and their impact as evangelists far surpasses that of the Westerners, because they are living proof of the power of God in a relevant setting.

The work God has given to us is hard. It's not easy for me. It's not easy for you, either. But God didn't call us to a life of ease. But it is worth everything. I cannot tell you how much I love my Balangao daddy; and I will never forget the tears in his eyes as we were parting after the New Testament dedication. He shook my hand, thanking me over and over again, saying, "We would *never* have known this if you hadn't come and told us . . . *thank you—thank you* for coming. And please tell your parents thank you too, for letting you come." The world is full of people who will also shake *your* hand and thank you, with tears, for your sacrifice for them. Don't ever give up!

# TESTIMONY
*Tokunboh Adeyemo*

My life is very similar to the life of the Apostle Paul recorded in Philippians 3. His life can be divided into three segments: before he met Jesus Christ, at the time he met Him, and after he met Him.

My life before I met Jesus Christ in 1966 was one of prosperity. I was born into one of the wealthiest families in the city of Ibadan. It happened to be a royal family. So I was born with a silver spoon in my mouth! I had the best education available at the time. I was born into a religion and, for an African, there is no dichotomy between religion and secular life. They go together. Mine was a Muslim home and, when I was young, I was sent to the Arabic or Koranic school. I was made to memorize the Koran. I was very religious. I observed five hours of daily prayer. I would fast during the month of Ramadan. I was good at giving alms to the poor because it was a religious duty. I never failed in reciting the creed: *"There is no God but Allah, and Mohammed is his Prophet."*

As far as the five pillars of faith were concerned, the only thing I did not do was make a Holy Pilgrimage to Mecca. But before the people, I was a very good boy. By the time I left college, I made a ten-year development program—what I would like to become ten years from then. It was my desire to become President of my country. I had a precedent. My uncle was a parliamentarian. And I took time to involve myself in politics as well. I was secretary to one of the local parties in my city. At the same time, I was working as headmaster of an elementary school with twelve teachers. I had everything going for me.

Among my friends, I was known as "All Wool," because I was always wearing velvet or wool. Wealth and fame were there. But I was miserable. There was an emptiness within me. One day, I sat down to assess my life, and there were two questions I asked. First, "What is life?" This is an important question we should all ask. Somebody said that the unexamined life is not worth living. What is life? Is it just going through the motions, vicious circles, and routines? You wake up in the morning and eat, work, play, and go back to bed at night. There must be something more important to life than just going through the motions. I wanted to know.

My second question was, "Where do men go from this world?" What is man's hope? Does anything lie beyond the grave? Or is that the end of life? So I was bogged down with these two questions—the purpose of life and its objective or goal. These questions led me into research. I got involved in many things including a "Free Thinkers Group." They did not believe in anything. The leader of this group was educated in Moscow. But soon I realized it was just a mad attempt to manipulate and use others. So I left. Then one of the teachers in my school invited me to his church to talk with the pastor. For a Muslim, church is a forbidden place. But he said I could stand afar off and just watch what was going on. Being open-minded, I said that I would listen to him, so I went. When I got to the church, I was impressed with what I saw. What did I see? I saw beautiful people in the church singing joyously. What was the difference in their lives? Why were they happy? I had a car! These people did not have a car! I had money! These people had hardly anything. What did they have that made them happy? I had to find out!

I kept going to church. But alas, as I got involved I was sidetracked from my search for reality. I saw all the beautiful ladies and I was carried away. There are many people like that in the church today. They go to church, go through all the worship services and activities, they attend all the conferences, but they are doing it only because of those who are there. So I was in church Sunday after Sunday for four years without Jesus Christ in my life. Then, I got frustrated with myself. I looked into my ten-year development program and discovered I was not developing at all. Most of my colleagues were taking their university degrees; I was just teaching. So I left. It got so bad and I was so depressed that I was going to commit suicide. Many would ask me what was wrong. They said that I showed promise, I had money, everything I could want—so what was my problem? My problem was greater than just material things. An African philosopher said, "God has created us for His own purpose, and the soul of man will be restless until it finds its rest in his Creator." I was doing everything of my own volition, but God was kept outside.

In 1966, there was a revival tent meeting in a small church. The speaker was from South Africa. He came for a week. It was at the meeting on Wednesday, September 13th, that I was confronted with the claims of Jesus Christ. The speaker preached from John 10:10, where Jesus tells of His purpose for coming into this world; *"I have come that you may have life and have it more abundantly."* This man went on to explain why many people are not experiencing God's purpose of abundant life. It was then that I was brought face to face, for the first time, with the question of sin in my life. After his message, he gave an invitation to surrender to Christ, to let Jesus take control of my life. I went forward that night to accept Jesus Christ by faith as my Lord and Savior.

I could go on all night, but do not have the time. All I need to say is, *"If any man is in Christ, he is a new creation. Old things have passed away. All things have become new."* Since Jesus Christ entered my life, I have never been the same. I placed my life in His hands and, since then, He has led me from victory to victory. Today I am general secretary of a Christian organization for the whole of Africa, serving in over 32 countries with about 35 million believers on our membership roll. My goal is to know Christ, and to make Him known. Having decided to follow Jesus, there is no turning back. Closing on a glorious note: five other members of my Muslim family (including my mother who opposed the Gospel and rejected me) have been converted. Today, we are all rejoicing in the Lord. What a difference it makes!

# II

# THE EVANGELIST'S MESSAGE

# THE EVANGELIST'S AUTHORITY: THE WORD AND THE SPIRIT
*Samuel O. Libert*

When I was young, I used to prepare my talks amid a mountain of books. Religious books and secular books. Books on archeology and books on theology. Sermon books and picture books. Dictionaries and commentaries. Big books and small books. My table would be filled with them. Sometimes I would put some of them on the floor. Some were mine, others I had borrowed, others belonged to some library. And I also had a Bible. Generally my messages were very much like my table: they were full of books! When I was in the pulpit, I would speak of trends in psychology, philosophy, and theology. Books were my favorite authority.

And in the pews in my church there were people who didn't understand me; others were bored; some admired me; and perhaps many of them pitied me. My congregation grew and diminished; diminished and grew, alternatively, like tides in the ocean. Some days I felt flattered. Other days I felt frustrated. Once a lady told me: "Pastor, every time I heard you preach, I went away *empty*." Empty! Why? It hurt me. I spent hours studying. My messages were full of quotations from great scholars. I used the best techniques for convincing people. I tried to serve God in the best possible way. This lady's criticism seemed unfair to me.

I still was under this emotional impact when I heard Billy Graham saying: "Preach the Bible!" It was at the Baptist Alliance World Congress in 1960 in Rio de Janeiro, Brazil. "Preach the Bible!" Of course, Billy said some other things, but "Preach the Bible" remained in my heart. I thought I had preached the Bible. Yes, but frequently I had mixed it with strange elements until it was left in a secondary place. Many times my messages were blurred. There were "decisions," but I wasn't sure they were decisions for Christ. There were emotions, but I didn't know if they were produced by the Holy Spirit. There were people attending, but I doubted whether they came to hear God's Word or if they came simply because they were used to listening to me.

That day the Lord touched me. I repented. Yes, I repented and decided to accept the authority of the Bible, and preach the Bible, only the Bible, and nothing more than the Bible. Other books, research books, other materials, technical resources for preaching, all—absolutely all—were put from then on entirely under the authority of the Scriptures.

## 1. The biblical foundation of our evangelistic message

These days the authority of the Bible is broadly questioned. The Scriptures are being attacked from several directions that doubt its integrity, its purity, its infallibility, and even its divine origin. Let me remind you of five of these areas. First, religions affirming that their sacred books are God's word. For instance, Muslims sincerely believe that the Koran is truly God's word. The so-called "Saints of the Last Days" say that the Book of Mormon is also God's word. Members of the Baha'i sect declare that the Book of Certainty (El Kitab-i-Iqan), is God's word. We could go on naming sacred books of cults that give their own scriptures the authority of God's word.

Second, political ideologies that corrupt the Bible text, using it wrongly, in favor of their own objectives. Scriptures are quoted with doubtful intentions—their meaning mutilated or deliberately twisted. These weak "second readings" of the Bible confuse many Christians who, even if they believe they are yielding to the authority of the Scriptures, are in reality yielding to the designs of interests and powers alien to the Word of God.

Third, the "sacred cow" of higher criticism and those who want to put the Bible under their own human academic authority. Fourth, atheism, nihilism, skepticism, materialism and unbelief in general. And fifth, without going into detail, those who, perhaps unconsciously, trust the authority of their mystical experiences more than the authority of the Holy Scripture.

Of course, these attacks—and others—shouldn't surprise us. The authority of the Bible as God's Word is a *supernatural fact.* In 1 Corinthians 2:14 we read that "the natural man receiveth not the things of the Spirit of God, for they are foolishness unto him, neither can he know them, because they are spiritually discerned." What is at stake in these attacks is not the integrity of the Scriptures, but the integrity of our message and our own integrity as evangelists, without allowing these aggressions to intimidate us. We don't present excuses to skeptics for not thinking as they do. Neither do we get defensive or need to ask forgiveness for having strong convictions. We don't have inferiority complexes. We are not to yield because of these attacks. We don't kneel in front of the "sacred cow" of higher criticism, nor feel shamed or humbled because of the characteristic pride of some of this world's wise people. We declare that the authority of the Bible as God's Word is a matter of *faith,* and not of mere apologetics.

The authority of the Bible is one of the great principles ruling the history of the true Church of God. The leaders of the Reformation in the 16th century accepted without hesitation the authority of the Bible, and decided to yield their lives and their convictions to the final judgment of the Holy Scriptures, and not to any other authority. We maintain the same position, not allowing political ideologies, philosophic trends, academic influences, government or "power-that-be" pressures, natural thinking or our own emotions to change in any way this unquestionable authority.

That's why the evangelistic message has a scriptural basis. If it doesn't, it's neither evangelistic nor the message of the Lord. We have been called to preach the Word of God. According to Chapter 13 of the book of Acts, when Paul and Barnabas preached in Antioch in Pisidia, they didn't preach their own ideas, but "the Word of God" (44-46). "The Word of the Lord was published throughout all the region" (49). We preach what the Bible says, what the Bible tells, what the Bible teaches, what the Bible reveals. The world must see in us the evidence of full certainty in our convictions regarding the Scriptures. We will inspire trust as we live out our principles. People who are bewildered, confused by the labyrinth of ideas, afraid and anxious because of today's events, will be more willing to hear those who *know what they believe and believe what they know*; those who not only affirm the authority of God's Word, but also yield to it.

Regardless of the outcome, the world must hear a message that starts with the affirmation: "Thus says the Lord." If we do this, even if there are not visible results, we will be able to say with Paul: "Thanks be unto God, which always causeth us to triumph in Christ, and maketh manifest the savor of his knowledge by us in every place. For we are unto God a sweet savor of Christ, in them that are saved, and in them that perish: to the one we are the savor of death unto death; and to the other the savor of life unto life" (2 Corinthians 2:14-16).

This doesn't mean that we reject the healthy contribution that other helps can give, provided that the Bible is not given a second place. Let's speak of the danger there is when the church claims the same authority as Scripture, or even higher authority. In some Catholic circles, the Roman church is called "The Holy Mother." We evangelicals sometimes do the opposite, and act as if the church is "our daughter," as if we had given birth to it! In this way the church—as it were a mere human creation—becomes a civil institution, an instrument of our own planning, a field of action for other institutions, a common structure in the social life of our community. And then, when the church becomes "our daughter," it starts to discover many parents, or many parental counselors that in other circumstances could be very useful: denominational, interdenominational and non-denominational bodies; native and foreign experts; manifold advisers.

If the church is "our daughter," many of them will feel they have a right to give instructions to it, make plans, teach new theories; have it form a mosaic of strange structures. Thus the church, "our daughter," will be like a good computer, programmed by tactical erudites and strategy experts. It will have systems, projects, and goals orientated by specialized technicians, It may become a new church, but never a renewed church. The Bible will be left in a second place, due to the presence of so many human authorities. The church—"our daughter"—will inherit our nature, and with it, our ills. If we make it, it will be like us. Its machinery will lack Bible foundation and authority in its evangelistic message.

That's why we must be careful in this area, in order to avoid the substitution of the Word of God by the word of the church or the word of the technicians. The Bible is not the voice of the Church. The Bible is the voice of God: He is its Author. The Church doesn't live by listening to itself, but by listening to the Lord through the written Word. Christ's true Church is not "our daughter." It is a Church of divine origin, born in the heart of God. It is a Church built on the Eternal Rock—Jesus Christ—made and protected by Him, who, at the same time, is its Founder and Foundation. As children of God we are in it, members of the Body of Christ, a chosen generation, a royal priesthood, an holy nation, God's own people, to declare the wonderful deeds of Him that called us out of darkness into His marvelous light (cf. 1 Peter 2:9).

## 2. The inspiration and infallibility of the Bible

Some years ago I was invited to preach the Gospel for a few evenings in a theater in Buenos Aires. In the middle of the campaign I had a surprise. Several members of the organizing committee were waiting for me at the door before the service one evening, and told me: "Samuel, we have a problem. Three scientists have come to hear the message." I replied: "It seems to me that it is good news. I don't see where the problem lies." Their answer was: "They are not believers. We think they are professors at the university. One of them is a specialist in nuclear physics and, apparently, the other two teach philosophy. We are concerned with your topic for your talk." I told them: "I'm going to preach on Noah's ark." But I didn't feel sure.

Then we went to pray in a small room of the theater, to ask God to confirm my topic. After praying we had no more doubts. That evening's message was "Noah's Ark," literally following the biblical narration. When I finished, several people came forward to publicly acknowledge their desire to accept Christ. Among them were two of the three scientists. The third one said he wanted to learn more about God. The authority of the Bible had been greater than the authority of scientific skepticism.

We have already repeated several times the sentence: "The authority of the Bible," but we must more clearly define this concept. What does it mean for us to say "the authority of the Bible"? In what sense do we believe that the Bible has authority? What kind of authority? What is its scope? What are its limitations? We could, for instance, say that the Bible has a "moral authority," because of its ethical teachings. Or that the Bible has "the authority of a document," because of its reliable historic narrations. Or that the Bible has "the authority of a sacred book," because it affirms that it is the Word of God. And so on.

But such answers aren't enough. Of course the Bible is much more than a treatise on ethics; much more than an historic document; much more than a religious book. That's why there are other opinions saying that "the authority of the Bible is the authority it receives from the church." And yet, as history shows, church institutions are fallible. Opinions of the church depend in a great measure on human origins, on the thinking of its theologians, on the criteria of its scholars, and on other instruments equally frail. It is not the Church that gives authority to the Bible, but the Church accepts the authority the Bible has of *its own*.

For us, the term "the authority of the Bible" is exactly the same as saying "the authority of the Word of God," because we firmly declare that *all* the Holy Scripture *is* the Word of God, as the Holy Spirit is *its Author*. And let's not forget that the words "author" and "authority" have the same root! The God that speaks and works through the times is the One that confronts us with the authority of its written Word. I insist: the Bible is the written Word of God. There is no mixture of the word of man with the Word of God. Being the Word of God it is divinely inspired, sufficient, perfect, infallible, inerrant, absolutely trustworthy, full of authority.

The Holy Spirit led writers of the sacred text so that they wrote exactly what God wanted to reveal to men. Each writer left in the Bible some clues to his personality. That is evident. But God inspired each word, each expression, each thought, so that there was not the slightest deviation. "All Scripture is given by inspiration of God," says Paul (2 Timothy 3:16). The evangelist must believe it, and must remember that God has promised to prosper His Word; only His Word and not one human word. "So shall my word be that goes forth from my mouth; it shall not return to me empty, but it shall accomplish that which I purpose, and prosper in the thing for which I sent it" (Isaiah 55:11, RSV).

Peter says in his second epistle, 1:20,21, that the prophecies of Scripture were never a product of human will, "But holy men of God spake as they were moved by the Holy Ghost." Also, Paul declares in 1 Corinthians 14:37: "If any man think himself to be a prophet, or spiritual, let him acknowledge that the things that I write unto you are the commandments of the Lord." Both of them emphatically affirm the divine origin of the Holy Scriptures. Both of them emphasize its inspiration and authority. Both of them know that the Bible, in all and every one of its parts, is the inerrant written Word of God, directed to man. They didn't worry or tremble because of the fate of the Holy Scripture. Brothers, God doesn't need us to protect Him or His Word. The Lord continues to reign, and will reign for ever and ever.

3. *The Word and the Spirit*

In these times of confusion there exists in some Christian groups the tendency to make a separation between the Word and the Spirit. The mistake consists in emphasizing some experiences and teachings ascribed to the Spirit which aren't founded in the Scripture. When the Spirit doesn't clearly agree with the Scripture, we should suppose that, in reality, the Spirit isn't involved. Everyone knows that the Holy Spirit is the author of the Holy Scriptures. Therefore, the Word is inseparable from the Spirit, as shown, for instance, in Isaiah 59:21: "My spirit which is upon you, and my words which I have put in your mouth, shall not depart out of your mouth, or out of the mouth of your children, or out of the mouth of your children's children, says the Lord, from this time forth and for evermore." The Spirit and the Word are inseparable. When the Holy Spirit shines, the Holy Scripture shines at the same time. This happened at Pentecost. In the same way, when the Word of God is faithfully preached, the Holy Spirit manifests Himself with power. This also happened at Pentecost. I repeat—the Word and the Spirit are inseparable.

The Holy Spirit always accompanies Scripture and confirms it in the mind and heart of every true Christian. We know that the Holy Spirit persuades the believer to accept the authority that the Bible has *for itself*, and applies it to every aspect of everyday life. That's why we don't agree with people who say that the Scripture "comes to," or "becomes" the Word of God. We affirm the intrinsic authority of the Holy Scriptures, without ambiguities. John Calvin said that the final authority of the Holy Scripture resides in *itself*, because it is inspired by God. The innermost witness of the Holy Spirit in our hearts is important, because the Spirit bears witness that this Scripture is, by itself, the Word of God. Thus both powers, the power of the Word and the power of the Spirit, live and are manifested in our lives.

In true evangelistic preaching, the Word and the Spirit are inseparable. The authority of the Word of God must be preached in the power of the Holy Spirit. Let me tell you about a young Argentine named Daniel. I met him in 1977, a few minutes before an evangelistic service. Some Christian young men had found him in the street, high on drugs and almost unconscious. He was untidy and dirty. Due to the effect of the drugs, he remained quiet, with fixed eyes, alien to reality. I tried to speak with him, but it was useless. I couldn't learn his name. Our young people took him to our church. When I started preaching, I saw him in the audience, seated, absent-minded. How could I reach the heart of this boy, who seemed to be a tree, an indifferent vegetable? I preached the Word of God, as I thought of those vacant eyes. I kept trusting in the power of the Spirit. During the invitation, Daniel remained motionless. The same thing happened several times. Daniel came in with his unseeing eyes and went out in silence.

But one day the Word and the Spirit touched Daniel instantly and in an unexpected way. He came forward to receive Christ. He was baptized in January 1978. After that he faced great struggles. He had great conflicts and serious falls. He had problems with other drug addicts. He had difficulties with the police. He had times of rebelliousness and depression. But the Word and the Spirit kept working amid adversity. Today Daniel is married, has two children, and is a preacher of the Gospel. Yes, my brethren, the Word of God is like a fire and as a hammer that breaks the rock in pieces (Jeremiah 23:29). "The word of God is living and active, sharper than any two-edged sword" (Hebrews 4:12). Let's preach the Word, in the power of the Spirit!

I think of the great prophet John the Baptist, who was faithful to the Word and full of the Spirit. When Jesus spoke about him, He said, "He was a burning and shining lamp, and you were willing to rejoice for a while in his light" (John 5:35). The Bible says that multitudes went out to see him. They wanted to see him burning. They wanted to see his light. The union of the Word and the Spirit lighted a fire in his heart. Day after day people came to hear his voice. John the Baptist had authority: the authority of the Word; the authority of the Spirit; "And there went out to him all the country of Judea, and all the people of Jerusalem" (Mark 1:5). If our life and our message are under the authority of the Spirit and of the Word, we too shall be torches. We shall burn and will be light, as the fire of the Spirit and of the Word is lit in our hearts. People will come to see the light. And many will yield to Christ, also becoming inflamed by the same fire.

My brethren, never doubt the power of the Spirit and of the Word. Never light strange fires. Never accept other "powers." Never believe false teachers. Preach the Bible, only the Bible, in the power of the Spirit.

### 4.  *Spiritual warfare*

Many years ago an experienced pastor told me: "Samuel, never forget that each time you preach the Gospel you have three classes of listeners. Some of them make up the congregation, the people who come to hear the Word of God, and must not be disappointed. Others are the Lord's angels, because the Bible says that the manifold wisdom of God is now 'made known to the principalities and powers in the heavenly places' (Ephesians 3:10), and that into those things 'angels long to look' (1 Peter 1:12). And yet some others are the fallen angels, the principalities, the powers, the world rulers of this present darkness, the spiritual hosts of wickedness in the heavenly places" (cf. Ephesians 6:12). And he added: "Human beings come to listen to the message of salvation; angels attend to get a better comprehension of God's grace; and demons come because they try to hinder your preaching, and to make difficult or impossible the work of grace."

In his *Word Studies from the Greek New Testament,* Kenneth S. Wuest says that "the Church has become an university for angels, and each saint is a professor." I felt deeply moved remembering that each time I go into the pulpit, God's angels will be listening to my evangelistic preaching. But, as I thought there would also be satanic forces trying to oppose the ministry of the Word and hinder the decisions of the listeners, I understood that each proclaiming of the Gospel is a new battle in spiritual warfare. By God's grace and our Lord Jesus Christ's victory, we are on the victorious side, but we must resist the attacks of the enemy.

These battles can start *before* the evangelistic proclamation, as happened to Paul and Silas in Philippi, when a satanic spirit spoke through a possessed girl that followed them. It can happen *during* a crusade, as happened to Philip in Samaria, when he faced Simon the magician; or *during* a sermon, as happened at Paphos, when Barnabas and Saul preached the Gospel to the proconsul Sergius Paulus, and Elymas the magician opposed them. It can happen *after* a victorious experience, as in Jerusalem, after Pentecost, when Satan filled Ananias' heart, and made him and his wife Sapphira lie to the Holy Spirit. Jesus had to battle the devil at *the very beginning of His ministry!* Yes, my brethren—we are in a spiritual warfare!

The book of Revelation teaches us that in Smyrna and Philadelphia there were synagogues of Satan; that in Pergamum was Satan's throne; that in Thyatira there was a diabolic prophetess called Jezebel, who taught the doctrine of the deep things of Satan. Spiritual warfare was evident then, and it still is made evident and intensified in the churches of the Lord, in all the earth.

You are an evangelist. When you enter the pulpit, don't enter to show off your abilities, your capabilities as a preacher. You should enter as a fighter, as a faithful soldier of Jesus Christ, to go on fighting the good fight of faith, as you do every day, against the attacks of the enemy. The Bible says that your fight is not against flesh and blood, but against Satan's armies.

What weapons will you use in this spiritual warfare? Philosophy? Psychology? Logical thinking? Some prestigious theological trend? Eloquent speech? Your titles, if you have any? Your dress and the way you perform? With the proselytizing techniques of political parties? No. A thousand times no! Satan is a great expert in these specialties. He is a great theologian, a persuasive preacher, a lawyer, a prosecutor, a scholar. He pretends to be a judge. He presents himself as an angel of light. He inspires many brilliant thoughts. He has thousands of years of experience. Your emotional appeals and your convicting methods will be useless. As you face him it will do you no good to trust in your own personality, your capabilities, your fame, your prestige, and any promotion. Satan has his own champions in all these areas. That's why the Bible says that "the weapons of our warfare are not worldly but have divine power to destroy strongholds. We destroy arguments and every proud obstacle to the knowledge of God, and take every thought captive to obey Christ" (2 Corinthians 10:4,5, RSV).

When Jesus Christ faced the devil in the temptation in the desert place, He used only one weapon: the Scripture. The phrase "it is written" made Satan flee. The Lord knew that "the sword of the Spirit is the Word of God" (cf. Ephesians 6:17). As evangelists, our weapon is the Word of God, in our personal lives and in our pulpits. It is "the sword of the Spirit" because the Holy Spirit is its author, its inspirer. In this spiritual warfare, no weapon can be compared with the Word of God preached in the power of the Holy Spirit, when we have yielded to the authority of the Word and of the Spirit.

We read in the Bible that "the Spirit expressly says that in latter times some will depart from the faith by giving heed to deceitful spirits and doctrines of demons." These days have arrived; we are in the last times. The spirit of the Antichrist that John mentions in his first epistle exerts its malignant influence. We see the growing activity of the spirit of error, of the spirit of lies, of the spirit of deceit. This International Conference for Itinerant Evangelists will be attacked; its conclusions will be contradicted, its messages may be ridiculed. It will be scoffed at and criticized groundlessly in many magazines and in many places.

Brethren, have no doubt that we are protagonists of the last battles in spiritual warfare! That's why, beloved, we must not be confused. False wisdom, of diabolic origin, must not be faced with our human answers. This is not an ideological warfare. We have identified the true enemy, and that enemy is called Satan. Our Lord Jesus Christ defeated him on the Cross. Our Lord Jesus Christ defeated him in the Resurrection. The devil can debate our reasonings, but he cannot defeat the evangelist working under the authority of the Spirit and the Word—he who in every battle of spiritual warfare uses the Holy Scriptures as the invincible sword provided by the Holy Spirit.

*Conclusion*

Brethren, the Bible is a Living Book. It's not a science-fiction book. It's not a book of fanciful stories about gods, nor a compendium of mythologically-based beliefs. It wasn't written to amuse us, but to inspire and guide us with all authority. When, because of our responsibility and historical situation, we feel fearful, we remember that the Bible is the Word of God amid the crisis of history. The Holy Spirit inspired it in a real world, as real as our present world. It was the world of Hosea and Amos, of David and Caiaphas, of Abraham and Pontius Pilate, of Peter and Moses, with true—not fanciful—protagonists. It was a world with concrete places, with Egypt, Goshen and the Sinai Desert, with Jerusalem and Antioch, with baptisms in the Jordan River and fishing in the Sea of Galilee, with riots in Ephesus and prisons in Rome. It was a world with the histories of Noah and the Flood, Jonah and the big fish, Daniel and the lions' den, or Paul and Silas in the prison of Philippi. It was a world with a manger and a Calvary, with an empty tomb and a Pentecost Sunday.

So the Bible came down to us. It is not a mere volume of secret divinations, nor a collection of oracles and mysterious riddles, but the *Word of God*, inspired by the Holy Spirit, whose riches are revealed to all who want to scrutinize it. The Jesus of the Bible is the Jesus of history. The Bible is the Word of God revealed from inside man's history, from inside *our* history. Because it is *in* our history where the teachings, the promises and the prophecies of the Scripture have a real fulfillment. That's why its authority is not an abstract concept; it's an authority exercised every day in concrete acts. We don't adore it. We aren't "Bible worshipers." We don't reckon it to be a magic book. But we recognize in it the authority of its inspirer, the Holy Spirit, its supreme author.

Therefore, with it in hand, we preach the redeeming works of Christ. With it we say to the world: "Christ is coming again!" Yes! The King is coming! All men, all angels, and all demons may hear us say that *Jesus Christ reigns*, that "man will not live by bread alone, but by every word that proceeds from the mouth of God."

# THE LOSTNESS OF MAN
*Ravi K. Zacharias*

The story is an old one, but thankfully there is always somebody in every audience who has not heard it. There was a rather well-built, able-bodied man out of work. He was sure that after all of his attempts at body-building some suitable form of employment could be found. Utterly desperate, he saw an advertisement for an unspecified job at the zoo. Arriving for the interview, he was rudely shocked to find out that the zoo had been spending vast sums of money looking for a gorilla but could not find one. Their next option was to hire a human being, dress him up in a perfectly duplicated gorilla costume, and no one would know the difference. The manager appealed to the applicant, reminding him that his muscles that bulged like watermelons made him an ideal candidate. Money can buy anything—and the man had himself a job.

For a few days it was thoroughly enjoyable. All he had to do was pensively pace the floor, swing from a few branches, and recline and eat at the appropriate times. All went well until a contingent of school children arrived and insisted on feeding him more bananas and nuts in one hour than one should eat in a lifetime. Nauseated, he thought he would break away and entertain them by swinging from one branch to another. In his overstuffed and dizzy condition, he swung too far, slipped and fell into the lions' den. Instantly and impulsively he let out a scream, "Help! Help!" The lion scampered over to him and whispered, "If you don't shut up, we'll both lose our jobs." The show was over! The masks were off—it was now closing time.

Man's attempt at playing games and flying in the face of reality is not restricted to building a zoo when he has no animals. That, unfortunately, is only a humorous story. Unfortunately, man's farcical attempts come into play in every dimension of his existence as he tries to build a civilization without knowing who he is. He is designing a building, but does not know the master designer. He is philosophizing about life, but he does not know the master philosopher. He artistically portrays his perceptions, but he does not know the master artist. He pontificates on life, but he does not understand what it truly means to live.

One scrutinizing glance at this world reveals to us that there is something twisted and almost demonic within the very heart of man. At this very moment there are forty wars raging in this world. More blood has been spilled in this century than the previous nineteen put together. We continue to live under the illusion of progress but reality screams back at us. What is the problem? G.K. Chesterton, in his cynical but effective way, deals with this. Somebody once wrote to him and asked him what he thought of civilization. He said, "I think it is a wonderful idea—why doesn't somebody start one?" When a magazine ran an article, "What's Wrong With the World," Chesterton sent back the shortest letter to the editor. He said, "Dear Sir, regarding your article, "What's Wrong With the World," I AM. Yours truly, G.K. Chesterton."

That sums it up. I am wrong with the world. The Bible diagnoses man's dilemma as the problem of sin. To put it differently, he is lost in a world whose Creator he does not know, and rather than seeking the Creator, he busily attempts to play God himself. Time and again, he sees the collapse of his ideals, makes a havoc of his dreams, and brings his pathetic optimism crashing in disaster. All he does then is scream, "Help"—only to find that the one he screams out to is playing the same game as he. No doctor can prescribe a cure until he diagnoses the "disease." No solution can be found for man until he understands the problem.

The Bible makes it explicit and persuasive—man's dilemma is sin. He is lost in his sin, and desperately needs the rescuing attempts of a Savior. Not only does the Bible identify the problem as sin, but it states the problem as being universal in extent. All of us have sinned. John R.W. Stott expresses it in the following words:

"The universal extent of human sin is, however, not a truth which can be known only by revelation. It is a fact of our own everyday experience. We see it as we travel abroad or mix with our fellowmen. We see it in our own home. We see it in our own lives. Nearly all our legislation, whether in law or by-law, has grown up because human beings cannot be trusted to settle their disputes with honesty and without self-interest. Many of the happenings of civilized society would not exist if it were not for human sin. A promise is not enough, we need a contract. Doors are not enough, we have to lock and bolt them. The payment of fares is not enough, we have to be issued tickets which are punched, inspected, and collected. Law and order are not enough, we need the police to enforce them. All these things and many others, to which we have grown so accustomed that we take them for granted, are due to our sin. We cannot trust each other. We need protection against one another. It is a sorry state of affairs."

The undeniability of the above statement is certain. Our human experience universally sustains this. There is no culture, race, or government, that has escaped the blight of sin. The only difference is the degree of sophistication with which we manifest this condition. What then is sin? The Bible goes about teaching this in different ways. It teaches us of sin by the very choice of words. The two main words used are stated negatively and positively. Negatively, the word may be translated as a "shortcoming," failing to make the mark. Positively, it is stated as "the violation of a boundary." If that boundary can be seen as the law of God which emerges from His Person, setting the parameters of our thought and conduct, then any sidestepping of that would be a violation. Both of these concepts are absolutely pivotal. Some, in self-justification, may deny the latter, but they cannot deny the former. We just don't measure up to the glory and standard of God. Without an understanding of this, we cannot understand what grace and mercy really mean. Man is in an impossible position to rescue himself, for the very attempt at self-rescue is an intensification of the sin dilemma. The harder he tries, the more he proves his lostness.

In the Bible, beyond the use of particular words, is a descriptive treatment of man's sinfulness. In 1 John 2:16, we read, "For all that is in the world, the lust of the flesh, and the lust of the eyes, and the pride of life, is not of the Father, but is of the world." This presents sin in three main manifestations: sensuality, greed (or materialism), and pride. These are not of God but of a "worldly" mindset. If this is man's condition, as stated by the revealed Word of God and experienced by the expressed will of man, then an incisive analysis and a decisive prognosis are needed for man to understand who he is and who he was meant to be.

Romans, chapter one, may well be one of the most definitive treatments of the subject. Paul is, of course, writing to the people of the capital city of a powerful empire. It was the city to which all roads led. It was the throbbing heartbeat of a civilization that esteemed itself as the measure of all things. It was the utopia for pleasure-seekers, and the ultimate expression in some of man's gallant endeavors and self-perception. Everybody wanted to go to Rome. It was to the materialist what Mecca is to the Muslim and the river Ganges is to the Hindu.

Paul wastes no time in getting to the heart of the matter. He begins with a minimum of pleasantries and then immediately launches into a penetrating analysis of man's present condition. He portrays man's slide into utter lostness in four stages. Four words capture the predicament: rejection, separation, domination and condemnation.

1. *The rejection of God.* While the Bible is far more detailed in dealing with the fallenness of man than with the fall itself, it certainly does not ignore the latter. The book of Genesis makes it clear right from the beginning that one could not live in the Garden of Eden without respect for its moral parameters as set by God. There was a clearly stated invitation, "Thou shalt," and an equally clear prohibition, "Thou shalt not." The choice facing Adam and Eve was either to allow God to be God, or to usurp His authority and attempt to be His equal—in effect, to become the god of God. Humanism is really the second oldest religion in the world—an attempt to live in Eden without the acknowledgment of God. Their choice of doubt and disobedience was thus a doubting of His Word and a rejection of His Person. The calamity that was brought by that choice defies imagination.

The same attitude of rejection surfaces again and is manifested in Cain. "Faith cometh by hearing and hearing by the Word of God." Cain must have had some idea of what God expected of him. But in his offering, Cain revealed a character that was in rebellion against God, and when he had that pointed out to him, his answer was in anger that led to murder. At a museum in Denmark there is a marvelous sculpture of Adam carrying the bloodied body of Abel to his grave. It is captioned "The First Funeral." It is not accidental that the first book of the Bible, that which portrays our roots, begins with "In the beginning God," and ends with "So Joseph died—and was placed in a coffin." We start out with God and end up in the loneliest of all experiences—death. In that first book alone we see that sin came through Adam's transgression, that death came by sin, that Adam's sin involved the whole race, that this racial guilt did not destroy any man's personal responsibility, and that sin and death obtained universal dominion. Man had fallen and was in need of redemption.

It is important, though, at this juncture, to point out some key thoughts. For man in his fallen state, sin is not just an act, it is an attitude. Man is not a sinner because he is a transgressor; he is a transgressor because he is already a sinner. The offense is not only in the transgression but in the intention, not merely in the violation of law but in the disposition of the heart. The Sermon on the Mount explicitly states this. Lust is adultery though it never passes beyond the look of desire. Hateful anger is murder even if blood is never spilled. Materialism is lust of the eyes even if one is not rich. This is so because the seat of sin is in the heart and the will. Some manifest it overtly and some passively.

As a further understanding, it is interesting to notice that while the same man may not break all the Commandments, he is generally very proud of those he keeps, and has no sympathy with men who are violators in areas where he himself is virtuous. The drunkard will often boast of his charity. The immoral man is thankful that he is not a thief, and the profane swearer flatters himself that he never lies. It is a profound statement of our condition, therefore, when the Bible tells us, "How deceitful and desperately wicked the heart is—we cannot fully understand it." It is describing our root problem when it tells us that out of the heart are the issues of life. From the deviousness of Saul, claiming that he brought the animals to sacrifice to God (in violation of God's command regarding those animals), to the dastardly lie of the woman in Solomon's day who was willing to witness the cleaving of the baby in two, claiming it as her own while it was not, it is the darkness of sin in the heart of every man and every woman. It is the wretched condition of self-will in rejection of God's will.

In a book entitled *The Stranger*, the Algerian philosopher Albert Camus describes a man who is living completely disjointed from reality. He is equally distanced in passion from one who owns a brothel and one who beats his dog. He has systematically destroyed his emotions, and in this desensitized state does not care about anyone or anything. Finally charged with murder, he finds himself in a prison being spoken to by a chaplain. The stranger rejects all of the chaplain's allusions to God saying, "Look, I really don't believe God exists." The chaplain says, "How do you know that?" The stranger replies, "Whether God exists or not, I don't know—what I'm really trying to tell you is, that I don't care whether He exists or not." That attitude of disinterest and rejection of God makes him "the stranger" for he is now an alien in God's world. From rejection he moves to the next step, "separation."

2.   *Separation.* Romans 1 describes the slippery slope onto which man has set his foot. It tells us that what may be known about God is plain to him, both His power and His deity. Instead of heeding that, he suppressed the truth with his life-style of unrighteous choices. God, therefore, describes his spiritual condition as resultantly being darkened, and inheriting a mind that has become foolish. He has rejected God's wisdom and has traded away the glory or beauty of the immortal God for the crass images of mortal man, birds, animals, and creatures. There is now a darkness and a foolishness that is the opposite of God's light and wisdom. In replacing God he has lowered himself to worship the created instead of the Creator.

The prophet Habakkuk deals with the predicament of such a man and the sorry state he comes to when the perils of warfare and suffering close in on him. He distinguishes the lifelessness of these man-created gods in stark contrast to the living and the true God, the Author of life. He says in chapter 2:18-20: "Of what value is an idol, since a man has carved it? Or an image that teaches lies? For he who makes it trusts in his own creation; he makes idols that cannot speak. Woe to him who says to wood, 'Come to life.' Or, 'Lifeless stone, wake up.' Can it give guidance? But the Lord is in his holy temple; let all the earth be silent before him."

The prophet Isaiah in 29:8, has a striking analogy for those who live under the illusion of strength, and their dismay when the harshness of reality puts them in peril. He says they are "as a hungry man who dreams that he is eating, but he awakens and his hunger remains; as when a thirsty man dreams that he is drinking, but he awakens faint, with his thirst unquenched."

In His Sermon on the Mount, talking about laying up treasures in heaven and having spiritual sensitivity, Jesus uses the physical body as an illustration. He says, "The eye is the lamp of the body. If your eyes are good, your whole body will be full of light. But if your eyes are bad, your whole body will be full of darkness! If then, the light within you is darkness, how great is that darkness!" Habakkuk captures the lifelessness of idolatrous pursuits as destitute of truth; Isaiah catches it as an illusory dream that leaves one hungry, and Jesus in biting words describes the separation from God as a shroud of darkness.

This separation from God is, therefore, a separation from wisdom in his choices, a separation from light in his pathway, a separation from direction in his journey, and the absence of purpose in his entire life. He is now as a drunken man reeling from one wall to another, knocking himself senseless with every hit. Man is now a stranger in a land where he thinks he speaks the language, but he does not really understand.

The book of Hosea graphically portrays one of the sternest judgments of God and how He works from the simple to the complex in reaching them. He says to the Northern Kingdom of Israel, "I will be to you as a moth; I will be to you as a lion; I will remove my presence and depart from you." A moth weakens the fabric. A lion tears its victim apart. God is basically saying, "I will try to force you to listen to me by weakening you. If you still don't listen, I will tear you apart as a nation. If you still don't listen, I have no other option but to remove my presence and depart from you." The ultimate desolation is to be destitute of God's wisdom. The road map is lost; the road is narrowing. There is no one to seek help from and darkness is closing in.

G.K. Chesterton captures the pathos of a world without God as waking up some morning and looking into a mirror and seeing nothing. Indeed, man's alienation is showing itself in the absence of all moral perspectives, till this technological age will bring about monstrous abilities with no moral limitations. Knowledge becomes a deadly friend when no one knows the rules. It is not that he may end up believing in nothing. It is much worse; he will end up believing anything.

C.S. Lewis, in an allegorical story of his conversion, captures this alienation in a most graphic way. He pictures himself in a mountain called The Spirit of the Age. All expressions around him are grim. He himself has his hands bound behind his back. (This is an interesting way of describing the Spirit of the Age because the world advertises its exploits as the source of freedom and laughter.) All those who surround him are not perceived as people but as parts of bodies—lungs, kidneys, ribs, etc. After some time, he is served his breakfast. He comments on the tastiness of the milk and how nutritious it is. To this, the waiter mockingly responds by saying, "You only call it nutritious and refreshing milk. All it is, is . . ." and the waiter gives it a crude and derogatory description. He struggles at the waiter's description but does not know how to respond to it. A few moments go by and he comments on the tasty nourishing eggs. The waiter really laughs out aloud and derisively gives a nauseating, even more crude, description of what eggs are. Now he is really stunned, but silenced by both shock and nausea. Then comes this classic line. He says that some time goes by and "Reason alone" comes riding on a horse and rescues him, and as they ride off, Reason turns to the waiter and says, "You lie! You do not know the difference between what nature has meant for nourishment and what nature has meant for garbage."

This illustration so poignantly captures the alienation. Man has lost the very wisdom and sensitivity to differentiate between that which is for his good and that which brings about his destruction. Ironically, in pursuing reason, he has become irrational. In pursuing the deification of self he has brought about his own defacement. He has come adrift from his moorings and remains at the mercy of the waves. It is at this point that the loneliness of existence becomes overbearing, if not oppressive, for having rejected the One who created him. In his separation he feels the alienation from truth itself. Augustine's famous statement expresses this dilemma: "You have made us for yourself, and our hearts are restless until they find their rest in thee." In attempting to be free, man has made himself a slave. This leads into the next posture. He has moved from rejection to separation to domination.

3. *Domination.* The servitude that he has brought upon himself is a tyranny beyond any of his wildest dreams. In surveying the state of modern man, what do we see? Indeed he has pursued freedom with an intensity that is staggering.

Professor Hoon of New York Union Theological Seminary, in expounding on man's tension between freedom and bondage, says:

"Technology has freed him from the confines of space to travel at 25,000 miles an hour. Industrialization frees him to move to a new job or a new home, or from a lower to a higher income tax bracket. Electronics frees him to turn a dial and enter into a multitude of life-experiences other than his own. Education frees his mind—and in many respects his conscience. Medicine frees him from disease; psychiatry and chemistry free his emotions. Music and art free his imagination. Government—at least in theory—frees him for political decision. A thousand tyrannies in both his inward and outward life have been broken, and man today has rightly been called 'homo per-tubatus,' restless man, intoxicated with such freedom as he has never known before. Yet, mingled with his freedom is a sense of being bound, even at times of imprisonment. The man who travels at 25,000 miles an hour has a nervous breakdown. Affluence and poverty, each in its own way, lock him in. Television captures his sensibilities and homogenizes his tastes. Education becomes a 'treadmill.' Vogues in art fasten on the public consciousness, and three million people buy the same novel. Drugs 'enslave'; wars become 'stalemated'; diplomatic negotiations become 'dead-locked.' The 'system' or 'establishment' constricts; anarchy erupts and law answers with repression. 'Determinism' is still a reality-term in psychologists' lexicons, and death still lies at the end of life. Fate seems to ride into history on the back of human freedom as easily as it did on that of ancient authorities.''

Prince Philip, speaking to a university audience that was heckling him, stopped and said, ''Shut up—freedom can be destroyed as easily by making a mockery of it, as it can by its retraction.'' Man made a mockery of the freedom that God gave him and destroyed it. Now in his enslavement he tries to solve it by dealing with surface issues rather than the cause of all his malady. He enacts laws and studies sociology only to trap himself more and more. He fails to see that the process of breaking this domination can only begin by changing his master. Like Alexander the Great, he has conquered the world but cannot conquer his inner man. While electronics gives more visual glimpses of reality, he is still a slave to his lust. The domination of lust, greed, and pride continues to bind him, so that what is sometimes dismissed as religious passivity is just the scream of a trapped animal.

D.L. Moody, the American evangelist whose work was done in the latter part of the 19th century, was not a very educated man, but his perceptions of the nature of man and his exploits have turned out to be very true. Moody said that if a man is stealing nuts and bolts from a railway track, and in order to change him you send him to college, at the end of his education he will steal the whole railway track.

A contemporary of Moody was German philosopher Nietzsche, who popularized the phrase ''God is dead.'' He predicted that since God has died, at least two things were going to happen in the 20th century; that universal madness would break out, and that the 20th century would become the bloodiest century in history. Moody, a relatively uneducated preacher, and Nietzsche, an educated philosopher, both saw a causal connection between belief in God and the state of man. The ultimate tragedy seems to be that man still has not learned that while his imagination continues to probe the outer limits of pleasure, his utopia has hitherto eluded him and seems to constantly outrun him. Yet, he deceives himself, thinking it is always around the corner.

One famous writer has captured the ruthless deception under which man lives. She says, ''Nothing is so beautiful, nothing is so continually fresh and surprising, so full of sweet and perpetual ecstasy as the good; no desert is so dreary, monotonous and boring as evil. But with fantasy it's the other way round. Fictional good is boring and flat, while fictional evil is varied, intriguing, attractive and full of charm.''

This is truly a graphic description of reality and the human mind. Having rejected God and being separated from Him, we have allowed our minds to run wild. In those wild pursuits of fantasy, we have stirred our imagination in evil so deliriously that we believe its lies, and systematically erode sensitivity to truth. Thus, while nothing is so lovely as the truth and nothing so boring and monotonous as evil, we have fantasized ourselves into believing the opposite till we have plunged this world into a kind of lunacy.

Nowhere is this more visible than in the Western world's inability to cope with the process of aging and, ultimately, death. The cosmetic industry has exploded into a multi-billion dollar business, churning out products to make us look better, smell better, or feel younger, and a dozen other innocent forms of disfigurement. Creams are invented to smooth the wrinkles and patch up the cracks. Colors and dyes are created to reverse the gray in our hair. Oils are massaged into our skin to make it feel softer. And advertisements with their blatant "bunkum," scream out at us that we can knock off ten years of our apparent age if we eat, drink, sniff, or rub their product into our systems. Then, what cosmetics cannot do, surgeons say they can. They stretch our skins to make us look more youthful, implant hair to make us look more bushy-headed, graft on skin in plastic surgery to put the dimples in the right places, and narrow the nose and chin down to look like what we wished we did. But alas! The surgeon can only transplant so much. Finally, it is cancer or a heart attack that lands us in the coffin. So what do we do? We make a final outlandish effort to slap enough cream on and dip into the mortician's cosmetic bag to make one last-ditch attempt at denying death itself, till everyone files past the coffin to pay the ultimate death-denying compliment—"He looks just like himself, doesn't he?" What masters of deceit we have become. Denying the Author of life, bankrupt of morality, we then make a feeble attempt at immortality by cosmetically escaping the inescapable.

This tragedy may be considered laughable if it were an innocent sideshow. However, it is symptomatic for many who have carried such intense denial into their spiritual malady. It has been rightly stated that: "The worst effect of sin is manifest not in war or pain or bodily defacement; but in the discrowned faculties, the unworthy loves, the low ideals, the brutalized and enslaved spirit."

In Romans 1:29-32, Paul delineates for us the long list of enslavements: "They have become filled with every kind of wickedness, evil, greed and depravity. They are full of envy, murder, strife, deceit and malice. They are gossips, slanderers, God-haters, insolent, arrogant and boastful; they invent ways of doing evil; they disobey their parents; they are senseless, faithless, heartless, ruthless. Although they know God's righteous decree that those who do such things deserve death, they not only continue to do these very things but also approve of those who practice them."

The reprobate mind is given over to all sorts of iniquity. G.K. Chesterton rightly said, "There are many, many angles at which one might fall, but only one angle at which he can stand straight." Is it any wonder that one who was in the torment of such bondage cried out, "Intense is the agony, when the eye begins to see; the ear begins to hear, the pulse begins to throb; and the heart begins to pound, when the soul feels its flesh; and the flesh its chains."

The enslavement in sin is as deep a bondage as one could imagine. That is why Paul cried out, "Oh, wretched man that I am; who shall deliver me from this body of death?" Yet, the immensity of man's lostness is only deepened by the fact that he does not know that fact. From rejection he moves to separation, domination, and finally to condemnation.

4. *Condemnation.* Paul talks about the wrath of God and the judgment of God upon such. This judgment of God that they have brought upon themselves, at death becomes final and eternal, conscious and painful. Some choose to interpret it as temporal, but the Scripture makes it plain that the judgment after death is final and eternal. The word eternal is used many times in the Bible (Matthew 18:8, 25:41, 46; Mark 3:29; 2 Thessalonians 1:9; Hebrews 6:2; Jude 7; etc.) It is translated as "forever and ever." Some venture to say that it does not teach a finality and eternality. However, a study of the usage makes it explicitly clear that those are the very ideas contained.

A.A. Hodge, in his *Outlines of Theology*, says, "The Greek word possesses no more emphatic terms with which to express the idea of endless duration than these." "The word 'aion,'" says Leon Morris, "got the significance of 'eternal' because it was applied to the never-ending 'age to come.'"

Ajith Fernando, in his book, *A Universal Homecoming?* says, "The word 'eternal' is applied sixty-four times to the divine and blessed realities of the other world . . . and in these cases it is beyond all doubt a question of a duration without end . . . would it not be logical to conclude that in seven occurrences of 'eternal' to describe the antithesis of these blessings (eternal punishment) the idea is that of duration without end?"

Other passages that give credence to the eternal state of punishment are Mark 9:43, 48 describing hell as "the unquenchable fire . . . where the worm does not die." This irreversibility is also stated in Luke 16:19-31, in the story of Lazarus and the rich man. Another strong statement supporting this is in Matthew 26:24, where Jesus says of Judas, "It would have been better for that man if he had not been born." It is inconceivable that a statement like that would be valid if eternal damnation were reversible.

It is most sobering to look at these passages. I am always reminded of what the British preacher, Robert W. Dale, said in the preaching of hell. "The only man I can listen to preaching on hell is D.L. Moody, because I have never heard him talk about it without breaking down and weeping." Charlie Peace, the criminal in England who was condemned to die, in effect expressed the same need for intense pathos when dealing with the concept of hell. On that fatal morning in the Armley Jail, in Leeds, England, after he received a dispassionate sermon on hell, Peace delivered one of his own that the chaplain would never forget. "Sir," said Peace, "If I believed what you and the Church of God say that you believe, even if England were covered with broken glass from coast to coast, I would walk over it, if need be, on hands and knees and think it worthwhile living, just to save one soul from an eternal hell like that."

We, as evangelists, would do well to remind ourselves that there is no joy in preaching on hell. The joy is to proclaim redemption from a destiny such as that. The good news is that Christ has paid the price and our destiny may now be altered. Gethsemane and Golgotha should be etched into our minds so that we may fully understand the marvel of the empty tomb. Just as Dostoevsky's character in *The Brothers Karamazov* turned his attention to God because he got a glimpse of the devil, let us understand the condemnation of man so we might better proclaim our Savior. It is understandable why Paul said, "Necessity is laid upon me; woe is me, if I preach not the Gospel!" Elsewhere, he said, to the Galatians, "My little children, of whom I travail in birth again until Christ be formed in you." His ministry was not a career but a commission and a call. Before closing this section, though, we shall also remind our audience that hell is not the choice of God, it is the choice of man. We are not consigned there, but by rejecting Him we have entered the pathway of destruction. It is a choice with a damnable destiny.

A simple yet meaningful parable well portrays the end result. The story is told of a builder who was given a contract to build the best house he could build for a rich man. The wealthy man said, "Money is no restriction, just build me the best house you can." The builder thought to himself, "Here is my opportunity to really make an awful lot of money. The rich man travels so much he will not come by and inspect all the hidden parts of the house." So the builder skimped on the quality of material for the foundation and the timber, etc. He bought the cheapest and the worst and on the exterior made it look like the most expensive and the best. All in all, it was a weak and a dangerous house but only the builder knew how treacherous was the whole endeavor. The house was now readied and the builder invited the wealthy man to close the transaction and take possession. The man came to see it and after walking through said, "I really have a wonderful surprise for you. I have watched you and your family and felt sorry for you. I know your business has not done very well, so I wanted to do something for you. I wanted you to have the best house you could build. I knew how awkward it was to just give you a house, so I had you build one of your best and now it is my privilege to present this house to you. I would like you to have it for you and your family." There was only one deceiver in this story—the builder. There was only one who would live with constant remorse—the builder. Galatians 6:7,8 makes it plain: "Do not be deceived: God cannot be mocked. A man reaps what he sows. The one who sows to please his sinful nature, from that nature will reap destruction; the one who sows to please the Spirit, from the Spirit will reap eternal life."

All of this is so morbid and depressing, but just as the greatest darkness is just before dawn, so the good news of the Gospel is not only that the problem is diagnosed, but also that the solution is on hand. Jesus Christ came into the world to seek and to save that which was lost. He came to offer redemption to mankind, bankrupt in his own sin. That is why the privilege of the evangelist is so great. It is interesting that both Matthew and Luke, in their first usage of the word "darkness," place it alongside the light of Jesus. Matthew, in 4:16, describes the preaching ministry of Jesus and refers to Him as the fulfillment of the prophecy of Isaiah: "The people living in darkness have seen a great light; on those living in the land of the shadow of death, a light has dawned."

Luke, in giving us the song of Zechariah, to whom the mission of his son, John, had just been revealed, tells us how Zechariah was filled with the Holy Spirit and uttered prophetic words, describing the person of Christ as the "Horn of Salvation, the prophet of the most High God, the rising sun will come to us from heaven." He culminates that by calling the coming of Christ a light "to shine on those living in darkness and in the shadow of death, to guide our feet into the path of peace." It is this Christ, the light of the world, the way to God, the truth of God, who comes to give us life. Like the donkey who bore Him on Palm Sunday, we as evangelists carry Him to the uttermost parts of the earth. Let me close this sermon by bringing one illustration from the East and one from the West to highlight the blight of sin, the beauty of our Savior, and the universal need of this message.

I was preaching in Cambodia in 1974, just a few months before the country fell. On the last night, I went to see a play with a couple of friends and their Cambodian language teacher. It was a magnificently portrayed drama culturally presented with the beauty and creativity of those fine people. The story in the play was about a poor peasant who had just married a lovely girl from his village and was walking through the field enjoying her company. The dark clouds of abused power were suddenly going to descend upon their enchantment. The prince, riding by, asked his soldiers to bring that girl over to the palace, as he was going to keep her as his mistress. The poor peasant pleaded and begged, but to no avail; she was snatched away from him.

Wearily and dejectedly he made his way to the palace to ask the king's intervention. The king was angry that a commoner would dare to make this accusation against the prince, so the girl was brought to the king's court to deny that she had been dragged away. Under threat of her husband's life, she lied, and said she had left him voluntarily.

The man did not know what to do. And utterly helpless, he turned to walk away when the priest rose up in the court and said, "Your Majesty—something is wrong here. I do not believe a man would walk in and lie to you like this." Then he went on to say that he had a magical liquid that would bring out the truth. He said that both the prince and this peasant would have to drink it, and that within ten minutes both would speak the truth whether they wanted to or not. He also suggested that each of the men should be given five minutes alone with the woman, but there should be no contact.

So a huge barrel was brought in with two rings on the side and a pole through those rings. This barrel was to be borne by both of them and was to serve as a barrier between them. Then the peasant and the girl carried the barrel away to spend five minutes together. She told him of her love in her heart and why she had lied—only to protect him. They returned and the prince and girl carried the barrel away and they spent the five minutes together. He continued to threaten her and her husband if she told the truth.

They returned to the court. The priest stood up and said, "Now we will know the truth for sure." Suddenly the barrel split open and a little boy jumped out. He had been hiding there all along and had made a note of both conversations. The priest looked at it and said, "Your Majesty, that peasant is the actual husband. Your son is a liar." The king was livid at this accusation. Bedlam broke loose, he ordered his soldiers to kill the priest, the husband, and the little boy. The woman, overwhelmed with anguish, took a long hairpin from her head and took her own life. It was a horrible, morbid scene. A play that began with the innocent gaiety and laughter of a village wedding, ended with anguish and death all around.

As we walked away I complained to the translator and said, "I did not like the ending." One of our group said to him, "What was missing in the play?" This non-Christian man paused for a moment, and with a deep sense of pathos said, "A savior, somebody to take up the cause of the needy." That is so cogently presented from the East. With all the philosophy, passion, culture and skill, the one element missing was the presence of a savior. Shakespeare said, "All the world's a stage." Sometimes I believe the reverse is true, too—all the stage has become the world. In drama and music, man has begun to expose the deepest longings of his soul. He seems to accept his vulnerability and despair when he is playing the part.

Here is a brief and equally powerful illustration from the West, showing the same vacuum. It is a play by Ingmar Bergman called *Wild Strawberries*. The scene again is a courtroom. A professor is standing before the judge, and the judge says, "I find you guilty." The professor says, "What am I guilty of?" The judge replies, "You are guilty of guilt." "Is that serious?" asks the man. "Very serious," thunders the judge. Imagine yourself trying to counsel a very needy person and all he keeps talking about is guilt, guilt, guilt. If that is all he admits, there is very little you can do for him without playing God. Guilt, as many a secular counselor sees it, has only horizontal or societal ramifications. It is a dead-end street. It is then your responsibility enabled by the Holy Spirit to help him see that it is not guilt! guilt! guilt! but sin! sin! sin! Once he says, "I have sinned," then you can triumphantly say "Ah, friend, I have a Savior for you." Man is not just unethical; he is lost and dead. If man is only lost in guilt, it is all bad news. But he is lost in sin and our great privilege is to tell him, "We have a Savior for you." The biggest difference between Jesus and ethical and moral teachers who have been deified by man is that they came to make bad people good. Jesus came to make dead people live.

East or west, north or south, ancient or modern, the problem is the same, and the solution is the same. Once they understand the heinousness of sin they will gain a deep and lasting gratitude for God's forgiveness. In a sense, only a forgiven man comprehends the dastardliness of his condition. It was a famous German theologian who said, "Sin scorches us most when it comes under the scrutinizing light of God's forgiveness . . . not before."

One can now fully appreciate the frame of mind in which Isaac Watts penned his words,

Alas, and did my Savior bleed?
And did my Sovereign die?
Would He devote that sacred head
For such a worm as I?
Was it for crimes that I have done
He groaned upon the tree?
Amazing pity! grace unknown!
And love beyond degree!

The same sense of deliverance was captured by the converted slave trader, John Newton.

Amazing grace! how sweet the sound,
That saved a wretch like me!
I once was lost but now am found,
Was blind, but now I see.

The lostness of man is portrayed by Paul in Romans 1. From rejection he moves to separation; from separation to domination; from domination, to condemnation.

"How beautiful on the mountains are the
feet of those who bring good news, who
proclaim salvation."
Isaiah 52:7

# PREACHING THE WORD—
# REACHING THE WORLD
*Billy Graham*

*Text: Mark 1:14,15*

This is the first sermon Jesus ever preached as far as we know. Preaching is the art of exhorting, teaching, making announcements from God to the people, calling people to repent and believe.

1. *Introduction*

The basic question we are dealing with today is this: How do we communicate the Gospel in the modern world, with its different cultures, ethnic backgrounds, nationalities, and languages? Christ has commanded us: "Go ye into all the world, and preach the gospel to every creature" (Mark 16:15). But how do we obey that command? How do we preach?

In your workshops and in your personal conversations, I know that you will be dealing with many of the practical questions of preparation and preaching, and we need to learn from each other. However, I want to speak about some of the principles that must guide us if we are to be effective preachers of the Gospel.

When Paul came to the city of Corinth he said, "For I determined not to know anything among you, save Jesus Christ, and him crucified" (1 Corinthians 2:2). If you had asked Paul, "Paul, how do you communicate the Gospel? What is your secret?" he would have replied, "I preach Christ! He is the key which unlocks the door of the human heart, and He must be the center of our message."

Paul knew there was a "built-in" power in the message of the Gospel. Paul knew that the Holy Spirit takes the simple message of the Cross—the message of God's redemptive love and grace—and brings conviction, repentance, and faith. Human logic alone will not do it. Human eloquence alone will not do it. Organizing large campaigns or crusades alone will not do it.

The Spirit's work is vital, for as Paul says in 1 Corinthians 2:14, "The natural man receiveth not the things of the Spirit of God: for they are foolishness unto him: neither can he know them, because they are spiritually discerned." When we preach the Gospel of Christ, there is a divine power at work. The Holy Spirit takes the message and communicates it with power to the heart and mind, and breaks down every barrier.

No evangelist can ever have God's blessing on his ministry until he realizes his total dependence on the Holy Spirit. That means we need to prepare by prayer.

I have often been asked the secret of evangelistic crusades, and I have said there are three secrets:

     1. Prayer
     2. Prayer
     3. Prayer

In the very beginning of our Crusade ministry, we were fortunate to have a man of God who went ahead of us to coordinate the meetings and give advice to the local committee. His name was Willis Haymaker. He was a great man of prayer. He told us to put all the emphasis on prayer in everything we did in evangelism.

In the early part of our ministry, a woman in Los Angeles by the name of Mrs.

Pearl Goode would take a bus or coach to every Crusade we held, just to pray. Several nights a week she would pray all night. When she died and went to Heaven, I could almost sense it in my preaching.

In addition to prayer, we need to be sure our message is always biblical, no matter what culture or ethnic group we come from.

### 2.   *The universal needs of the human heart*

One of the most important truths I have learned as an evangelist preaching in over 60 countries is that the Gospel cuts across every cultural and social barrier.

We never change the message of the Gospel, but we try to preach it in the context of the group to whom we are talking. For example, some illustrations I use in America would not be understood in India.

The Gospel speaks to all kinds of people in all kinds of situations—whether it is at a university in America, on a street corner in Singapore, in a tribal village in Uganda, in a large stadium in England, in a cathedral in the Soviet Union, or anywhere else.

Why is this true? It is true because the basic needs of the human heart are the same around the world. No matter where I preach, I know there are certain things that are true of all people—certain psychological and spiritual factors that exist in everyone. When I face an audience I know certain factors are already present. Certain preparations of the heart have already been made.

First, I know there is a *sense of emptiness* in every life without Christ. All humanity keeps crying for something, searching for a way to fill the empty place in their hearts.

Second, when we proclaim the Gospel we can assume there is *loneliness* in our hearers. In every person there is a yearning for a relationship with someone who will love him just as he is. Most of all, it is a loneliness for God, who created us to have fellowship with Him.

Then third, we are speaking to people who have a sense of *guilt*. Although it is often not recognized, this is perhaps the most universal of all human experiences, and the most devastating. Fourth, we are speaking to people who have a *fear of death*. One of my associates was passing outside a bar in an airport when the television inside announced that the American space shuttle had blown up and killed seven astronauts. Normally that bar was filled with laughter—but suddenly it became very quiet. People had been confronted with the stark reality of death.

### 3.   *How do we communicate the Gospel?*

First, we communicate the Gospel with *authority*. Preach the Gospel with conviction and assurance, knowing that "Faith cometh by hearing, and hearing by the word of God" (Romans 10:17). Preach with the certainty that the Gospel "is the power of God unto salvation to every one that believeth."

One reason the people listened to Jesus was that He spoke as one having authority. Make the Bible your source and your authority. Quote it frequently. Let its message be your message. Study it, meditate upon it, memorize it, trust its promises, and preach it. The Word of God has its own power.

I don't understand that completely—but I have seen it time after time. Sometimes I have been preaching and suddenly a verse of Scripture would come into my mind—although it was not in my sermon notes. And later I would hear that someone had come to Christ because the Holy Spirit had used that verse to bring conviction to his heart.

Psalm 19:7 says, "The law of the Lord is perfect, converting the soul."

Perhaps some of you have been so busy you have been neglecting your study of God's Word—and slowly the fire within you has begun to die. May we be like Jeremiah: "But his word was in mine heart as a burning fire shut up in my bones" (Jeremiah 20:9). Only then, will there be authority and power in our preaching.

I learned long ago that authority in preaching comes only when we preach the Word of God in the power of the Holy Spirit.

Second, preach the Gospel with *simplicity*. The Gospel is profound—so profound the human intellect can never fully probe its depths. But the Gospel is also simple—so simple a child can understand it.

We must communicate so people understand. We need to avoid the temptation to impress people with our learning, or our travels, or our intellectual abilities, or our eloquence.

I am sure that was one of the secrets of the ministry of our Lord. The Bible says, "The common people heard him gladly" (Mark 12:37). Why? Because they understood Him. He spoke their language.

Part of preaching with simplicity means to preach with illustrations people can understand. Use common everyday stories and metaphors to illustrate the Gospel. For example, Jesus said: "I am the bread"; "I am the good shepherd"; "I am the water of life"; "I am the bread of life." Or on another occasion He might tell a farming story about wheat and tares—which everybody understood.

Preaching simply also means we should preach with repetition. Professor James Denney of Scotland once said that Jesus probably repeated Himself more than 500 times. Don't assume a truth has stuck with your listeners just because you have mentioned it once; hammer home the basic points of the Gospel repeatedly.

The Gospel may at times seem old to us. But repeat it and repeat it, for the Holy Spirit will make it new to your hearers. Never tire or be embarrassed to share the basic points of the Gospel over and over again.

Sometimes it may be hard on your pride! When I first started out, I only had seven evangelistic sermons.

Third, preach the Gospel with *urgency* and preach it for *decision*. People are dying and entering eternity without Christ. The Gospel carries with it its own sense of urgency; for "behold, now is the accepted time; behold, now is the day of salvation" (2 Corinthians 6:2).

You may be speaking to some who will never hear the Gospel again. And you do not know if *you* will ever have another chance to preach the Gospel again.

Fourth, preach the Gospel with *love* and *compassion*. Even when your message includes the fact of judgment and hell, your hearers should realize that both God and His messenger speak from a broken heart. When you speak or preach to people about Christ, do they sense your love and compassion? Do they realize God loves them because they see His love reflected in you?

We need to realize that communicating the Gospel with compassion also means we have compassion for the whole world. God so loved the whole world that He gave His only begotten Son—and as Jesus had compassion over Jerusalem and wept over it, we need to have compassion for our hurting world, especially those of the household of faith. We have a responsibility to the poor, the sick, the oppressed, the hungry, the outcast, those torn by terrorism and war—especially the believers. Remember the apostles in Antioch helped the suffering believers in Jerusalem, whom they had never seen or met.

Millions of people in our world live on the knife-edge of starvation, or in fear. Do we care? Are we doing anything? Yes, we are to love people and we are to do all we can to demonstrate that love—just as Christ demonstrated His love by meeting the physical needs of many He met. We give because God gave.

Finally, we are to communicate the Gospel in the *power of the Spirit.* I have already said this by pointing out that we are totally dependent on the Spirit of God to bring conviction to the hearts of people as we preach.

As soon as we think it is up to us, or think we do not need God's power, or we try to manipulate or manufacture success, or we try to take credit for what God is doing—then we will be set aside by God. God has declared, "I am the Lord: that is my name: and my glory will I not give to another" (Isaiah 42:8).

But preaching in the power of the Spirit means we must be living in the power of the Spirit. We must be men and women who are pure vessels for God's message. The most important preparation for our preaching is the preparation of our lives. That is why it was so important for us to hear Dr. Olford speaking yesterday morning on "The Life of Personal Holiness". It is why Luis Palau will be speaking tonight on "The Spirit-filled Life."

We must remember that we communicate the Gospel by our lives as well as our lips. We live before a watching world, a world that is waiting to see if what we say is lived out in our lives.

Is there a lack of power in your ministry? Perhaps you have neglected the preparation of your life. You have gotten too busy, and you have neglected prayer, you have neglected God's Word and the feeding of your own soul, you have neglected fellowship with other believers who can minister to you, and even correct you when necessary.

Or perhaps you have allowed some particular sin to gain a foothold in your life, and it is robbing you of your effectiveness for God—whether you admit it or not. It may be a sin of the flesh, or something like bitterness, or jealousy of another man's ministry, or pride, or covetousness, or anger, or neglect of your family.

Whatever it is, confess it, repent of it, and then walk in the power of the Spirit to gain victory over it. Only then can you discover the joy of preaching in the power of the Spirit. The devil will do all he can to blunt the effectiveness of those who have been called of God to preach the Gospel. We must take that seriously.

I have found the devil most often attacks evangelists along one of three lines: money, morals and pride. Paul warned, "Let him that thinketh he standeth take heed lest he fall" (1 Corinthians 10:12). The devil will set traps for you constantly. He can be very subtle and persuasive. "Just this one time," he whispers. "Just a little bit. No one will know." But God will know, and your effectiveness will be diminished.

May God lift our vision, and may the power of the Gospel break upon our world with fresh force, as we are obedient to Christ's call to preach the Gospel.

# THE EVANGELIST AND THE MINISTRY OF THE HOLY SPIRIT

*Luis Palau*

## Burning Heart, Flaming Message

We all want to be remembered for something. Deep down, nobody wants to waste his life, though many people end up doing just that.

Some waste their lives amassing wealth and material goods. Some desire fame, power, and the praise of men. Others spend a lifetime in fearful worship of false gods, somehow hoping to appease their wrath. Still others abandon any hope of an afterlife, and live solely for whatever pleasure this world can offer them today.

Of course, all of these people die, and what do they leave behind? Nothing. Nothing, that is, of lasting impact—only the fading memory of a life spent on themselves.

If I'm remembered for anything when I die, I want it to be this: that I had a heart and life which burned with the love and power of the Holy Spirit. A heart afire with love for God and for people. A message aflame with power to convict the souls of men and win them to Christ. That is my reason for living. That is my purpose in being an evangelist. And that, more than anything, is what I wish to communicate to you, my fellow evangelists.

The Bible pictures the Holy Spirit in various forms: oil, water, wind, and a dove, to name a few. But the picture I want God to indelibly impress on our hearts is that of the Holy Spirit as fire.

John the Baptist declared that the Lord Jesus would baptize, not with water, but with the Holy Spirit and fire (Matthew 3:11). Later, on the day of Pentecost, Christ's Holy Spirit came in mighty power, appearing as tongues of fire above each believer's head.

Fire is an apt picture for the Spirit of God. Why? Because fire is a necessary element of life. We depend on it far more than we realize. Fire cleanses and purifies. It radiates warmth and light. At high intensity it can melt the hardest steel. And its power, properly channeled, does everything from cooking an African villager's meal to mobilizing the most powerful machinery on earth.

Luke 24 tells the familiar story of two disciples on the road to Emmaus. Trudging along, they were no doubt physically and emotionally exhausted. Jesus approached and began walking and talking with them. They had no idea who this man was, but His very presence seemed to revive their lagging spirits. Not until they sat down to a meal together did they recognize Him as Jesus. Then instantly He vanished from their sight. Astonished, they asked each other, "Were not our hearts burning within us while He talked with us on the road and opened the Scriptures to us?" (Luke 24:32).

Their hearts were set ablaze with the propelling truth, hope, and purpose that come from a vital encounter with the living Christ. As believers, we have that vital encounter with Christ continuously through the Holy Spirit. And the fire of His Spirit in our lives should produce in each of us, as in those disciples, a heart that never stops burning.

1. *A heart that burns with purity*

If there's anything the Church of Jesus Christ needs today, it's purity—a willingness to take a stand for righteousness regardless of the cost. In response to Israel's unfaithfulness, the Lord said: "If you repent, then I will restore you—before me you will stand; and if you extract the precious from the worthless, you will become my spokesman'' (Jeremiah 15:19).

I see in this verse two principles regarding purity. The first is that where sin exists, genuine repentance always precedes genuine restoration to God.

In much of Christianity today, repentance is practically a dirty word. So many believers—some of them pastors, teachers, and evangelists—ignore or excuse the sin in their own lives while continuing to perform their ministry. That is a sad contradiction of what it means to minister in the power of the Holy Spirit.

God says, ''If you repent, I will restore you, that you may stand before me.'' Inherent in the concept of standing before God is that of serving God, somewhat like a steward standing before his master the king. He is ready and waiting to do whatever the king desires, whenever he desires it. It's intended to be a position of honor and confidence, not one of shame and humiliation. Sin must be dealt with honestly and painfully, if necessary. Otherwise we are unfit to stand before our Master in service for Him.

The second principle regarding purity is the necessity of separation. ''If you separate the precious from the vile, you will become my spokesman.'' What an incredible promise!

When I was just a teenager, the force of that truth struck me as on my knees I read this verse from Jeremiah. Recently it has returned to me with equal force. God commands each of us to separate the precious from the vile—to distinguish between what is valuable and what is worthless in our lives.

I cannot maintain a burning heart—and neither can you—without dealing ruthlessly with sin. That means developing a keen sensitivity to what grieves and quenches the fire of the Holy Spirit. It means listening to Him and responding to the slightest prompting of any inclination toward evil. Sin must never, ever, be covered over. It must be confessed honestly and cleansed by the blood of Christ. Both you and I know that countless ministers of the Gospel have destroyed their ministries and damaged Christ's reputation through unforsaken sin in their lives.

Do you want to be a spokesman for the living God? Your responsibility is to stand before Him with a pure, clean heart and life. Then when you speak, or write, or even when you look at a person, you will be an accurate representation of God. You can be yourself and yet display confident authority as His servant.

## 2.   *A heart that burns with passion*

God has given His Church a job—to impact the whole world for Jesus Christ. But if the task is to be accomplished, we must eliminate apathy and passivity from our lives. As the Body of Christ, both individually and collectively, we must cultivate not passivity, but passion—passion for the Lord Jesus Christ, and passion for the lost multitudes.

One day when the Lord's disciples were worrying about food, He told them, ''My food is to do the will of him who sent me and finish his work'' (John 4:34). Because of His love for the Father, Jesus had a passion to do His will and His work. Nothing else mattered by comparison. Practically speaking, Christ's passion for His Father's will translated into compassion for the multitudes. Matthew 9:36 says that when Jesus saw the multitudes, ''He had compassion on them, because they were harassed and helpless, like sheep without a shepherd.''

The Lord has given me a burning heart for the confused, lost masses of this world. Just look at the universal pain and suffering of human beings. It's easy to see why the Lord Jesus likened them to sheep without a shepherd.

Our world has so many leaders, yet so few elevate Christ as the one true leader.

Even in Christian circles, apologies are made for the Lordship of Christ. Sarcastic remarks and parenthetical comments indicate how Jesus Christ's authority and person are often watered down in our own pulpits.

If you say, "Jesus is the answer," someone inevitably replies, "Yeah, but what is the question?" No wonder the world is confused!

Think of all the trouble people get themselves into. Isn't it true that a large percentage of that trouble is self-made? It's true in my own life. Very seldom have my really big problems been produced by somebody else. With good reason the Scripture says, "We all, like sheep, have gone astray, each of us has turned to his own way" (Isaiah 53:6).

Of course, other people and difficult circumstances do create problems for us, but whatever our situation, it is still possible to live in a way that pleases God.

The evangelist must first know and love God with all his heart, soul, mind, and strength. Then he must channel that love into a passion for people—a passion which, through the Holy Spirit, will bring lost sheep to the Great Shepherd.

### 3. *A heart that burns with purpose*

Once you've heard the command of God to preach the Gospel, your life can never again be without purpose. I think back to when I was a teenager, first sensing the call of God on my life. I was just starting out, completely unknown, just a kid dreaming that the Lord would use me. In boarding school we used to sing an old hymn which said, "O Jesus, I have promised to serve Thee to the end, and hope to follow duly my Master and my Friend." The Holy Spirit drove that hymn into my heart, and I sang it so sincerely that to this day I can hardly quote it without coming close to tears.

My life has one purpose: I am committed to fulfilling that promise to serve Jesus to the very end. The dream that the Lord laid on my heart as a teenager is a dream that has never died. Who would have thought that God would take a scruffy little Argentine boy like me and put a desire in his heart to preach to multitudes? Yet that is exactly what God did in my life.

You may look at your own ministry and say, "I'll never get beyond the borders of my own village, town, or country." That may be true, if that is God's place for you. But never limit God, and never be afraid to dream great dreams. You can be certain that God's purpose for you is to glorify Himself through winning hungry souls to Jesus Christ.

### 4. *An obedient vision*

The fire of the Holy Spirit in our lives will produce a burning heart, yes. But in addition to that it will produce in us a vision to fulfill Christ's command and to do His will.

And what is Christ's command? It is to preach the Gospel to every creature and to make disciples of all nations. Often we Christians look at the world as a big pie cut into tiny slices. "I'll eat my sliver of pie," we say. "I'll do my little part and others must take care of the rest."

It's true that no one evangelistic team or missionary organization can single-handedly evangelize the whole world. But why not utilize all that's available to us, to reach as many as possible?

Christ commanded us to reach the whole world, not sixty or seventy percent of it. We all must join hands with other believers to get the job done in our generation. Don't be satisfied with one little sliver—go for the whole pie!

And in the process, make no apologies. Sure, others will criticize. "You're too much of a dreamer," they'll say; or, "Do you really expect to see lasting results from all of your evangelistic efforts?"

Answering honest questions is important. But we cannot afford to waste precious time on critics who have no desire or concern to see the world won to Christ. A journalist recently asked me, "Why do you do it? What keeps you going for crusade after crusade?" The honest answer is that I love to do it, I have to do it, and I wouldn't have it any other way. Since I was a teenager the Lord has given me a passion that burns in my heart for the lost.

Yes, I long to see the world won to Christ. But I'm also keenly aware of how much I depend on a godly team of workers to support and assist me in that endeavor. Sometimes financial or personnel problems tempt me to think, "I could do this on my own with far less stress." But the truth is, I need the wisdom, strength, and encouragement that come from a united team effort.

An important part of accomplishing the will of God in evangelism is catching the vision for ministering as a team. I have tremendous respect for my team members. Godly, hardworking individuals, they often get little recognition for their vital role in the ministry. We share the same vision, however, and apart from them my ministry as an evangelist would not be what God has made it today.

Ask God to give you a godly team. It may not be a very big team—you may not need a very big team. But as an evangelist, you need others to share your vision, your love for the lost and, quite frankly, your work load.

Men, allow your wife to share your vision and to participate in it whenever possible. Let your fire be her fire too. Pray together often concerning your evangelistic efforts. Remember that she is your closest team member and confidante. Don't allow anything to destroy the harmony of your relationship. I can't thank God enough for my wife Pat, and the ministry we have shared together these many years.

Another significant aspect of teamwork is found in joining hands with churches and sister organizations. As the Church universal we all are called to cooperate in evangelizing the world. How sad that denominational differences and petty grievances often prevent Christians from joining forces to get the job done. We need the fire of the Spirit to purge us of critical, judgmental attitudes towards fellow workers for Christ. Other evangelists don't need our criticism—they need our encouragement!

Often their effectiveness is paralyzed through lack of vision. Oh, they have plenty of missionaries on the foreign field. But too often the energy of those missionaries is not utilized for its greatest ministry potential. They go shopping, they visit other missionaries, they interact occasionally with the nationals. And they write prayer letters in which they struggle to share one new bit of encouraging news, because they're not seeing any fruit from their work. Some of them are plainly discouraged, and not without good reason.

Recently it has occurred to me often that we as evangelists, along with our teams, could be greatly used of God to mobilize existing forces. Unfortunately, many missionaries, like the American troops in Europe, are sitting around marking time. They may have mock wars, but the real thing isn't happening to them. Of the Americans who joined the armed forces after World War II, some now are retiring without ever having fought a war. While that's good for the soldiers, God forbid that our missionaries should share the same fate!

We must pray that our evangelistic teams can be used of God to help motivate missionary troops. They're fully trained, fully supported, and fully uniformed. Now they must be activated to be fully used of God.

Through the power of the Spirit, we must fulfill Christ's command; we must do His will; we must finish His work. It's one thing to start His work and another thing to finish it.

I may be getting older, but so help me, God, by the Holy Spirit, I'm not going to end with a whimper. I've been around long enough to see an unbelievable number of people fail to finish their work for Christ. I'd need a computer to keep track of all the people I've encountered who have started with a shout and ended with a whisper. And for what reason?

Maybe a little opposition. Maybe a lot of opposition. Or maybe their preconceived plans never worked out. Whatever the reason—and it could be any one of a thousand—they looked back. They gave up. They quit.

In Revelation 2:10 the risen, exalted Lord Jesus says, "Be faithful, even to the point of death, and I will give you the crown of life." Stewards must be actively faithful to the vision and call of obedience.

I love Paul's words to Archippus in Colossians 4:17: "See to it that you complete the work you have received in the Lord." That is an exhortation to which each one of us needs to be committed.

When I was a boy in boarding school, like all the other kids, I had an autograph book. When singers or speakers came to our school, I asked them to sign my book. A missionary, Mrs. Rogers, had helped lead my family to Christ. When I was eleven or twelve I asked her to sign my autograph book. She could have written any trite little saying in it, but instead she drew a picture which I treasure to this day. In it is a house with a path to its doorway. Outside it is dark, but from the window of the house a lamp shines onto the path, lighting the way. Beneath it she wrote, "So let your light shine before men, that they may see your good works and glorify your Father."

To me as a boy, it was a word from God that I have never forgotten. To this day I can hardly quote it without getting shivers down my spine. Through the years it has helped keep me faithful to the call of God in my life.

Someone else signed my autograph book with a Spanish paraphrase of Luke 9:62: "You have put your hand to the plow; never turn your head to look back." That verse comes to me less frequently, but when it does come, it bears a sense of urgency. The Holy Spirit is reminding me, "Your hand's on the plow. Don't look back, Palau, because if you look back, you're not worthy of the kingdom of heaven."

We must never regret the unique call of God on our lives as evangelists. Sure, sacrifices have to be made. We're traveling constantly, and we don't get nearly the time we'd like with our families. But we have the unmatched joy of seeing hundreds—perhaps thousands, or even millions—come to Christ.

If the work of God is to be finished, the embers of the Holy Spirit in our lives must be continually fanned into a white-hot blaze. Then we will burn so brightly that others cannot help but see our works and give all the glory to God.

## 5. *A global outreach*

God's glory—the full weight of who He is—must be displayed to every nation and people group of the world. I enjoy answering the kinds of interview questions which have been asked of me recently: "Spiritually speaking, how do you compare various parts of the world?" Or, "Why do you go to Europe when Latin America is so responsive to the Gospel?"

Part of our responsibility as evangelists is to be aware of spiritual trends in nations around the world. You may not be called of God to preach internationally, but having a concern and compassion for global evangelism can fire your own ministry with even greater purpose. Read the news publications. Be informed about world events, and on how the Holy Spirit is working through the Church around the world. If you do preach internationally, that will help you to lay strategies and to key in on target areas.

When it comes to the Gospel, Europe is hard and cynical. To me, that's all the more reason to preach there frequently and fervently. Nothing will give me greater joy than to see that hard shell of a continent cracked wide open for Jesus Christ. I hope to see millions of the younger generation truly humble themselves before God so that the Holy Spirit can move with power in Europe.

In Latin America, people are begging to hear the Gospel. A spiritual hunger and openness exist that are giving an unprecedented place for preaching God's Word.

Africa quickly is becoming a Christianized continent. But rapid growth breeds the danger of widespread heresies. Many teachings wear the banner of Christianity but distort the true Gospel of Christ. Steeped in Islam, Northern Africa—once the very center of Christian orthodoxy—now epitomizes the tragedy of sound doctrine gone sour. It's happened before in Africa and easily could happen again in the wake of phenomenal church growth.

Asia is like a virgin that must be wooed purely and brought to Jesus Christ. For the most part, it is fresh territory, untarnished by heretical, washed-out, tired forms of Christianity. The cynicism of phony Christianity is virtually nonexistent in Asia, and I find it an increasing pleasure to preach the Gospel there.

When I look at the United States, I am appalled by the spiritual confusion and sectarianism I see. I may be an Argentine by birth, but I'm an American by citizenship. And while I hate to say it, it's true that if you could scratch beneath all the plastic smiles and positive thinking for which Americans are known worldwide, you'd often find arrogance, self-righteousness and divisiveness. If there is one country that has spread sectarian denominationalism in the world, it is the United States of America.

I fear that such sectarianism is going to throw American Christianity into crisis during the next twenty years. Too many of our so-called "personal convictions" are merely self-righteous put-downs of those with whom we disagree. We need God's grace and the power of His Spirit to break down barriers and unite the Church of Jesus Christ in America today.

Pray for the nations and for a mighty working of God's Spirit in and through the Church. Pray that we may reach the world for Christ as effectively and as efficiently as possible.

Mass media can be a mighty tool for reaching multitudes for Christ. Some of you never will have access to that type of exposure. Don't let that concern you. What really counts is preaching the true Gospel of Christ through whatever means are available. But don't be afraid to ask God to open doors to mass media opportunities.

I remember, years ago, trying to relax at a missionary retreat in Mexico. I and the two fellows with me were feeling frustrated. We were exhausted from conducting fourteen campaigns that year in Mexico. Somehow we knew that campaigns alone just weren't going to fulfill the vision God had given us for the lost. And suddenly the answer seemed obvious: Mass media!

Utilizing mass media is certainly not an option for every evangelist. But for some of us it's territory we need to claim for God and possess for His glory and for the spreading of His kingdom. Our duty, through the Holy Spirit and through every available earthly resource, is to preach the Gospel faithfully.

6. *A powerful ministry*

A burning heart ultimately results in a powerful ministry. As an evangelist, you must ask yourself, "Is my preaching anointed? Is it authoritative? Is it authentic?" If the answer to any of these is "no," then the power of the Holy Spirit is missing in your ministry.

Any ministry that is not anointed by God's Spirit is not really ministry, but manipulation. The power of persuasion never must be confused with or substituted for the power of the Holy Spirit Himself. Only He can gift and anoint a believer for ministry, whether that be as a pastor, teacher, prophet, evangelist, or other servant of Christ.

Evangelists who evidence the anointing of the Spirit are those who remain perpetually fresh in their message and outlook. I thank God for the model we evangelists have in Billy Graham. He may be turning 68 this year, but he never has lost his vision or his enthusiasm for preaching the Gospel. Whenever I see him, he's always on fire with the challenge of God's latest working among the nations. That the Holy Spirit is on him is obvious in the way he has stuck with evangelism these many years. By God's grace, I plan to do the same.

If the evangelist's message is anointed by the Spirit, it will be delivered with authority. All the physical and mental energy in the world, combined with all the witty, persuasive speech imaginable, cannot manufacture the Spirit's power. Too many evangelists miss the obvious: Only the Holy Spirit can produce Holy Spirit authority. He must speak for Himself. He must have the last word if people are to repent and give their lives to Christ.

Of course, sound doctrine is an integral part of that authority. So is the integrity of the evangelist himself. Preaching must be anointed and authoritative, but it also must be authentic.

Many people will accept the teaching of anyone who is prestigious. The real question should not be, "How well known is he?" or, "How much money does he make?" or, "How many countries has he spoken in?" The real question is, "Does he live according to God's Word, privately as well as publicly?"

We must have enough spiritual discernment to realize that any evangelist who does not manifest personal integrity is simply not of God, no matter what image he portrays. Jesus said, "I have come in my Father's name, and you do not accept me; but if someone else comes in his own name, you will accept him" (John 5:43). It seems that many people are more willing to accept someone who comes in his own name, bragging about his own deeds rather than exalting Jesus Christ.

For the evangelist, a truly Spirit-empowered ministry manifests itself in the hearts of the audience. The fire of the conviction of sin is the work of the Holy Spirit. He alone can convict the world of sin and righteousness and judgment. No one can experience regeneration apart from His intervention.

The Holy Spirit is working on His people. Follow-up and discipleship on our part are vitally important, but we must remember God's part too. Those whom the Lord calls, He justifies. And those He justifies, He also sanctifies and ultimately glorifies. Nobody follows up better than the Holy Spirit Himself. "He who has begun a good work in you will complete it until the day of Jesus Christ," Paul wrote in Philippians 1:6. God finishes what He starts. The Holy Spirit keeps those He calls.

When the Holy Spirit has all there is to have of an evangelist's life, that evangelist will have all there is to have of the Holy Spirit. His conduct will be pure. His witness will be persistent. And, like that of Billy Graham, his vision will persevere. If anything, it will increase with the years. The result? He'll have both a burning heart and a flaming message—necessary ingredients to set the world on fire for Jesus Christ.

I joke about living to be 92, and I hope I do. If so, I still have 41 years to preach the Gospel with all my heart. But regardless of how long any of us lives, the night is coming when no one can work. We must push ourselves to keep the fire burning. Not to the point of wrecking normalcy or of breaking up families. But we must push our-selves to the limits without ruining the fabric of life. For the world, time is running out.

I don't believe in "burning out for God," as spiritual as that sounds. I do believe in burning *on* for Him with all of my heart, soul, mind, and strength.

I'd love to live till I'm 92, but who knows? I could be dead in three years, three months, or three days. Life is nothing we can count on. You can plan as though you are going to work for 41 years, but you have to work as though this is your last day on earth.

No one wants to waste his life. Thank God, we don't have to. Let other people do what they must do. Let other people do whatever God has called them to do. But we, brother evangelists, must do what God has called *us* to do. And we've been called to win souls to God's eternal kingdom through preaching the Gospel of our Lord Jesus Christ.

Remember this: Without the Holy Spirit, your ministry is nothing. But through the Holy Spirit, your life will ignite the world for Jesus Christ.

# THE EVANGELIST'S MESSAGE:
# THE WORK OF CHRIST
*Michael A. Baughen*

"Jesus . . . died . . . for you." These words sum up the Gospel we are called to preach. But to most people in the world they are meaningless words. "Jesus"—"who was He?" "Why should I bother about Him?" "We are sorry He died but what is that to me?"

"Died"—"so does everybody and often with cruel injustice." "Why should a death nearly 2,000 years ago mean anything in the 20th century?"

"For you"—"so what? I was not even born when it happened. How can someone dying so long ago be relevant to me?"

The evangelist is called to communicate this essential Gospel to men and women who are spiritually blind and spiritually dead. It would be an impossible task if we were not workers together with Christ and the Holy Spirit. Nobody can hope to bring people to a saving knowledge of Jesus Christ without a deep dependence on God in prayer. In the area where I work, no minister, no evangelist, and no church is making headway with the Gospel except where they really pray and look to God. I wonder whether this was why the Lord sent out the seventy (Luke, chapter 10) two by two— so that one could pray as the other spoke. When I am seeking to share the Gospel with someone, I try to split my mind into two halves—one half listening and speaking, the other half praying. Without the Lord, we can do nothing. With Him we can bear fruit. So it is with acknowledgment of our constant need to depend on the Lord of the Gospel message that we now look at that message itself.

## 1. *Jesus*

First, we present *Jesus.* The work of Christ cannot be separated from Christ Himself. We are not presenting a method or a formula but a person and what was achieved for mankind by that person.

Who a person is makes a difference to the way in which we respond. I have vivid memories of the day I casually opened a letter and found that it was from the Prime Minister on behalf of Her Majesty the Queen, inviting me to become a bishop. I certainly replied to that letter with great care because of who had written it. But if I had not respected the authority of the Prime Minister or the Queen, I might just have ignored the letter.

It is because most people have no respect for the Lord of the Gospel that they are not interested in the Gospel. They feel they can ignore it. "There is no fear of God before their eyes" (Romans 3:18). Some treat Jesus Christ as a joke or as a name for blasphemous expression. Even when they regard Him as a good man or a good teacher, there is still no fear of God, no sense of wonder or worship, and no readiness to hear or respond. So we must first present Jesus as the Son of God and as Lord.

Think through the pattern of the New Testament gospels with their account of our Lord's ministry. The first half of the gospels is when Jesus is showing the disciples who He is—by word, by signs, and by His life. Eventually, at Caesarea Philippi the great breakthrough comes: "You are the Christ, the Son of the Living God," says Peter (Matthew 16:16). Immediately Jesus then begins to teach them about the Cross and the resurrection. In Mark's gospel there are three occasions, all in the next few verses, when we are told He taught them about the passion ahead. His work was first to show them *who* He was, and *then* what He had come to do.

Think of the first preaching of the Gospel in the Acts of the Apostles. Peter begins (in Acts 2:22): "Jesus of Nazareth, a man attested to you by God with mighty works and wonders and signs which God did through him in your midst as you yourselves know—this Jesus . . ." *Then* he goes on to speak of the Cross and resurrection. But see that he begins by speaking of Jesus. Later, Peter says of Jesus in Acts 4:12: "There is salvation in no one else, for there is no other name under heaven given among men by which we must be saved," but immediately before he says this he speaks of Jesus in verse 11 as "the stone which has become the head of the corner."

Jesus Himself spoke of His being the Light, the Good Shepherd, the Way, the Truth, the Life, the Door,—the "I AM"—God among us. The Letter to the Hebrews, which so wonderfully sets out the meaning of the Cross and of the sacrifice for the sins of the whole world, begins with a magnificent statement of who Jesus is. It speaks of Him as Creator and as Sustainer of the world. It speaks of Him as the exact image of God—as exact and detailed as an imprint in wax—so that we can see God when we see Christ. It speaks of Him as the outshining of God—being light from light—but enabling us to see God in that light rather than being dazzled by looking into the light. Thus, before the writer expounds the Gospel, he uplifts Jesus.

So, the evangelist's first task is to present Jesus as the Son of God, the One at whose name every knee shall bow, the One who is Lord of lords and King of kings—supreme in all creation and eternity. Christianity is Christ!

One of the illustrations I use is from the musical play "Godspell." I describe how, at the start of this, people dressed in grey come on to the stage one by one. Round their necks is the name of a famous person in world history—Plato, Aristotle, Confucius, and so on. Each says his or her piece. Then they all talk together. The program note calls it the "tower of babble." Suddenly they all move to the side of the stage and there, alone, is the person representing Jesus. It is dramatic in its impact. It says, in effect: "You name the greatest people who have ever walked this earth and none of them can compare with Jesus Christ, for He alone is God—sharing our manhood." As He is God, all the others, who are only human beings, move to the side of the stage. Jesus is Lord.

The vital importance of presenting Jesus Christ as the Son of God is so that people will listen to what He says about their need and the way they can be helped. Imagine someone coming up to you and saying: "You are seriously ill and you will die unless you receive treatment." How you respond depends on who has said it. If it is a bus driver, a bank clerk, or a flower seller you are unlikely to take any notice. If it is an insurance salesman you will be suspicious. However, if it is a top-rank medical specialist (and especially if he treats people without charge) you will listen. So it is with the Gospel we preach. Telling people that they are sinners and that they face eternal separation from God, and telling them that you have the truth by which they can be saved and restored is likely to fall on deaf ears, for it will seem to be just one philosophy among others. But if people come to realize that what you say is with the authority of the Son of God, the Lord of all, and thus entirely different from other merely human philosophies or religions, then they are more likely to listen. When God speaks, mankind needs to listen. We bring the message of God, in the name of God, through the revealed Word of God, by the power of God, as if Christ was appealing through us. We present the credentials of the Lord of whom we are ambassadors. *Then* we present His message.

2.   *"Died"*

*Jesus . . . died.* How do we express this wonderful truth? The death of Christ is central for us but seems irrelevant to the non-Christian.

It is a little like the cartoon where a man is holding a banner which says, "Christ is the answer" and behind him is someone else with a banner that says, "What is the question?" People do not know *what* the death of Christ is dealing with in human life. So they do not see its relevance to them.

The Cross is the center of the Gospel message. It is essential to preach the Cross. Evangelistic messages that do not speak of the Cross are inadequate. All of us will know how the Holy Spirit touches people when we preach the Cross. But very often today we have a pseudo-gospel—an offer of life, of peace, of prosperity, of freedom from illness and trouble, of making us happy, that sounds more like a television commercial for a medicine or drug. Some have even spoken of being "high" on Jesus. Of course, the benefits of being in Christ are glorious, and we shall think of them later in this address under the heading *"You."* But the Christian life can often be dangerous, sacrificial, and costly—and the way in which we enter into it is through the Cross of Jesus, where God dealt with sin and judgment and separation from Himself. The message we preach is judgment and salvation; dark and light; death and life. There is no other way into life in Christ. We do not have life pumped into us like a commodity or like a wonder-drug. The new life only comes through sharing in Christ's death; resurrection life follows identifying with the crucifixion of Christ; being restored by the Holy Spirit follows being forgiven and cleansed of sin through the saving act of Jesus on the Cross. We preach a Cross-and-resurrection Christianity.

There are those who call themselves Christian teachers or theologians who say that Jesus' dying on the Cross was just an example of what happens to a good man at the hands of evil men. They then teach that we are "justified"—made right—with God by the way we live, not by His death. When we challenge them, they point to Romans 4:25. In the English translations it says this: "Jesus was put to death for our trespasses and raised for our justification." Of course, I do not know how this is translated in your Bibles, if you use a language other than English. My explanation has to be about the English translations. These "other" teachers say that the words "raised for our justification" mean that we are justified by sharing the risen life of Jesus. But there are two halves to this important verse. They match each other. The little word "for" is in each half. If it is supposed to mean "He was raised in order that we might be justified," the first half would have to read "He was put to death in order that we might be trespassed!" That makes nonsense of the verse. It is extremely important that we all understand the true meaning of this verse. The only possible translation that makes sense and which is correct from the Greek is this: "Jesus was put to death *because of* our trespasses and raised again *because of* our justification."

Thus we see that Jesus went to the Cross because of our sins and was raised because the work of justifying—by the sacrifice for our sins—was completed. So death could not hold Him. He said in His last moments on the Cross, "It is finished," and His rising again proved that the sacrifice was complete. The hallelujahs of the Gospel are at 3 p.m. on Good Friday and then are reinforced on Easter Day. We are not justified by His resurrection life but by His death. So Paul says in 1 Corinthians 15:17: "If Christ has not been raised, your faith is futile; and you are still in your sins." But, in fact, Christ has been raised! Our sins were dealt with once and for all. We rejoice in all the power and blessing of the resurrection of our Lord; we rejoice in the indwelling presence of our risen Lord; but we have been justified by His death.

That we have to live out our salvation is true; that God expects our lives to be lived by His resurrection power is true; that Jesus is alive today is true. But our salvation does not depend on the way we live; it depends on our faith in His death for our sins on the Cross. That is the faith that saves. That is the faith that enables us to say that we are justified.

It is vital to use the Bible in preaching and teaching—and never more so than in presenting the Cross and the way of salvation. We find a deep seriousness about sin and the Cross in the Bible, and this is itself a way of preaching the need for forgiveness. Most people in the world do not have a great sense of sin against God. They may feel strongly about weaknesses and wrongs in society or even in their own lives, but they do not associate that with sin against God.

A powerful tool in this aspect of our evangelism is to show how seriously God takes sin. We need to show that this is why God sent His Son into the world; that the events of Jesus' life led towards the Cross; that He *deliberately* went to Jerusalem knowing what would happen; that He carried an enormous burden on His heart as He prayed in Gethsemane and as He hung on the Cross; that the darkness over the land and that cry, "My God, My God, why have you forsaken me," was the awful separation He endured for us—the separation from God caused by sin—the sin which He, whom even His closest friends and enemies knew to be sinless, carried for the world. We need to emphasize that if sin did not matter, or if sin could be overlooked, God would not have gone to these great lengths in sending His Son to die for us. The fact that He did shows the seriousness of sin and of its penalty in the eyes of God. If salvation could be received simply by trying to live a good life, by doing good works, or by trying to be better, there would have been no need for God to send His Son to die on the Cross for us.

Whenever we can, we will want to show this from Scripture, and especially in the awesome words of 2 Corinthians 5:21: "For our sake he *made* him to be sin who knew no sin, so that in him we might become the righteousness of God." This is the most profound verse in the whole Bible. Or I would show Galatians, chapter 3:13: "Christ redeemed us from the curse of the law, having been *made* a curse for us." He was *made* sin; He was *made* a curse—not just bearing it.

People often make light of sin. They do so because they do not see its consequences. We need to show the consequences. It is similar in other spheres of human life. Take smoking for instance. Smokers make light of its threat to health. They tend to ignore literature giving warnings. The most effective way I have seen to stop someone smoking was the display in a glass case of the lung of a deceased smoker put alongside a display of the lung of a deceased non-smoker. It had a shock-effect! Similarly, we need to show people the consequences of sin, and the Cross is the greatest visual aid to show the consequences of judgment, darkness, separation, and death.

Another essential in the preaching of the Gospel is to communicate the fact that "*all* have sinned and come short of the glory of God" (Romans 3:23), that no one is excluded from this—presidents, kings and queens, sports stars, business executives, shop assistants, road sweepers, bishops or evangelists—no one! We have to make it clear that there is no distinction made by God; that we are all under the judgment of God; that we all deserve separation from a holy God; that without the saving death of Jesus Christ we are without hope.

Spiritual blindness is at its worst regarding this truth of man's sinfulness. Human beings have an inborn self-opinion that whatever anyone else is like, they themselves are really good. They assure themselves with ideas of man's being basically good and that, as long as you give man sufficient food and clothing and good living conditions, he will live happily and without war or evil. It is a nonsense for all to see. But man persists in this inward conviction about himself. He believes he is basically good. Nevertheless, in spite of this blindness the evangelist must press this truth home. There have been many people who have turned to Christ when they have realized that man actually has a bias to evil and that all the ideas of mankind's living in peace and harmony come to nothing because of man! The only philosophy or religion in the world that actually assesses man as a sinner and deals with that sin is Christianity. The truth that mankind has a basic sinfulness makes sense of why where are terrible wars, oppressions and hatreds in the world. It is because this truth alone explains man and the world that the evangelist should have confidence and persistence in explaining it and illustrating it and arguing it.

A lady in my congregation, when I worked in Manchester, had a husband who would have nothing at all to do with the church. One day I met him, by accident, face to face. I invited him to church. He said, "If you had seen the terrible suffering in the trenches during the First World War you would not believe in God either." I replied, "The sufferings were certainly terrible but surely what happened should have made you cease to believe in man, not cease to believe in God." For over 40 years he had held that accusation against God; now suddenly he understood that it was man who sinned, not God. He came back to Christ and the church.

Another way of presenting the truth that all have sinned is by demonstrating the second part of the text "and come short of the glory of God." Television advertisements for soap powders usually try to demonstrate that their powder will wash whiter than the powder of their competitors. They show a shirt washed in their powder as glistening white and one washed in another powder as gray. The actor wearing the gray shirt looks with amazement at the whiteness of his friend's shirt. Contrast is an effective way of demonstrating a product—but it is also effective in presenting the Gospel. In preaching the holiness of God, the perfection of the life of our Lord Jesus, the fruit of the Spirit intended as the character of human beings can be effective by contrast. In preaching to some congregations where most are not converted but think they are Christian, I have found that it is more effective not to tell them they are sinners but to say, "We as Christians think and act like this, don't we?" The result has been not offense but quiet self-examination. Similarly it is true that time and time again, people begin to see their need of forgiveness and transformation by seeing the lovely life of Christians. They are challenged by what they see, and they recognize that these people have something they do not have. They see the contrast.

In my student days I went on a mission with sixteen students, led by a very effective evangelist. Each night we would have a testimony. On the night the speaker was to speak on sin, he asked which of us had been drawn to the Christian faith by conviction of sin. No one responded. He said he found it regularly so. Most people are drawn to Christ first—often by what they see in Christians; they sense something of their own need and of falling short of what they see, but the full conviction of sin only comes when they have actually turned to Christ and the Holy Spirit shows them what they are really like. C.S. Lewis, that powerful Christian writer who came to Christ out of deep atheism, spoke of this being his experience and how, when he turned to Christ, he then saw himself for the first time as "a zoo of lusts, a bedlam of ambitions, a nursery of fears, a harem of fondled hatreds."

In a similar way we may show the contrast through the biblical teaching about man. Most people in the world are infected by the idea that we are all animals and nothing more. As such, our behavior may be excused. It is "being what we are"— animals! We can blame the influence of the animal society in which we live and not feel any sense of responsibility at all for what we do. But God teaches us in His Word that we are "a little less than God" (Psalm 8)—not a little above the animals. He teaches us that we are made in the image of God and that whatever bodily functions we share with the animal kingdom we are unique in God's creation—given the capacity to worship, to love, to create, and to be His children for ever. Seeing ourselves in that way, as the God-created beings we are, brings home to our hearts that we are responsible—to God—and that the sins and wrongs of our lives are in fact a falling short of being the sort of people God the Creator intended us to be.

The Cross was God's plan to deal with man's sin. We believe that, but how do we express it in our evangelism? Some modern theologians dismiss the truth of "substitutionary atonement," of Jesus bearing the penalty of our sins in our place, as "barbaric." But it would only be barbaric if God had laid the penalty of sins on someone else. It is not barbaric that He laid the penalty of sins on Himself. Instead, it is the most amazing and wonderful love the world has ever seen and will ever see. The scriptural evidence for this wonderful truth is clear and cannot be denied. First Peter 3:18: "For Christ also died for sins once for all, the righteous for the unrighteous." First Peter 2:24: "He himself bore our sins in his body on the tree."

We need in our preaching to illustrate the way in which justice and love meet in the Cross. Many of you may use a version of the story of the two boys who grew up together and who in later life found themselves facing each other as judge and as accused, in a court of law. One had followed the legal profession, the other a business venture which became illegal. There are varieties of this story, but basically it raises the question of whether for friendship's sake the judge will give a lenient sentence. Then it quotes the judge as saying that he would not be a just judge if he did not give the maximum penalty because the offense is serious. The judge then takes off his wig and robes; he descends into the well of the courtroom; he takes out his checkbook and he pays the full fine so that the accused can be acquitted and go free.

The story is extremely effective because it shows how true justice or judgment can be met by sacrificial love. The world vaguely feels that if there is a God and He is love, then He must let us all off lightly. "How can a loving God condemn anyone?" people say. But that would make nonsense of right and wrong in the universe. God must exercise true justice and that means the penalty of death for sin; but God took off the robes of His heavenly majesty and stepped down into the world; He bore the penalty; He paid the price in His own blood; He died for sin. He made it possible for accused sinners to be acquitted. Justice and love met each other in the Cross.

We recall the atonement whenever we break bread and drink wine in the Communion. We share in the symbols of our Lord's death, His broken body and His shed blood. His was the supreme sacrifice. We were ransomed, says Peter in 1 Peter 1:18, with the precious blood of Christ." He adds: "like that of a lamb without blemish or spot." This gives us another approach to understanding the Atonement. The Old Testament sacrifice of "the lamb without spot" for atonement is a vivid biblical illustration that we can effectively use. I have often described the ceremony in an evangelistic address. I have spoken of the identifying with the lamb or goat by laying sins on its head, and of its death in place of the sinners who knew they deserved that death themselves. The New Testament speaks often of our Lord as the Lamb of God, and we know that Jewish hearers would have known at once what was signified. But I have found that people who have never seen a sheep and who know nothing about the Jewish ritual can take hold of the picture of the lamb being sacrificed for sin, and then begin to understand the meaning of the Cross and how their sins can be taken by Jesus.

There was another interesting and memorable interpretation in the musical "Godspell," in the scene depicting the Last Supper. All the actors in the musical are clowns. The clown idea is, of course, depicting the falsity of humanity in its sin. In the Last Supper scene, Jesus goes to each disciple and wipes off the clown paint from his face—and goes to the crucifixion as a clown. He bore our sins in His body on the tree—our sins can be transferred on to Him.

Any preaching of the Atonement must be richly textured with the joy of God's amazing love. There can be a tendency in evangelism to be heavy on sin and light on love. Let your own wonder and thrill at God's love permeate your speaking. "God so loved that he gave . . ." "God shows his love for us in that while we were yet sinners Christ died for us" (Romans 5:8). "In this is love, not that we loved God, but that he loved us, and sent his Son as an atoning sacrifice for our sins" (1 John 4:10).

Be messengers of that love; be demonstrators of that love; be those who, by God's grace, can love even enemies of the Gospel! A few years ago there was a "Festival of Light" rally in London with a massive gathering of Christians. Many atheists came to mock the Christians. One very intelligent atheist came to demonstrate against the Christians. But he was conquered by love. His fellow atheists were hurling vile blasphemous abuse at the Christians, and the Christians responded by saying, "We love you." Christ's amazing love shone through the Christians, broke through that atheist's defenses, and he came himself to the Cross of Christ—conquered, forgiven, saved, and restored to a wonderful Christian life. Christ's love conquers. We are messengers of that amazing love!

3. *"For you"*

Jesus . . . died . . . for you. The first few verses of Romans, chapter 5, are the basis of this section of our thinking. In verse 1 there is the clear statement that we *are* justified by faith—not "hope to be," not "may be," but *"are"!*

Justification does not come by believing in one's mind alone—it has to be a belief that actually trusts Jesus Christ and what He has done. Only then do we know the liberty of forgiven sinners. Faith is a "throwing of oneself on Christ," a definite action of trust in Him and His Atonement. In John Bunyan's "Pilgrim's Progress" the burden of Pilgrim's sin rolls away at the Cross. It disappears into the sepulcher. "And I saw it no more," he says. Then, as he cries with joy and gratitude, three angels come to him to assure him of God's peace, of his sins being forgiven and of his being a member of God's redeemed family forever. Assurance was possible because he had fully trusted in the death of Christ for his sins.

It is a terrible tragedy that large numbers of people who call themselves Christian have never come to this point of assurance. And the reason is that though they believe Jesus died for them, they do not *trust* Him and they do not *trust* in His atoning death. They still carry the burden of their sin. A friend of mine was driving into an African township one day when he saw two women carrying heavy loads to the market. He just had enough room to take their loads but not the women themselves. He stopped and invited them to throw their loads in to his vehicle and said he would take the loads to the market for them. One woman gladly threw her burden into the car and stepped forward freely without it; the other woman kept the burden and struggled along the road.

The human spirit does not want to feel it can do nothing about the forgiveness of sin. It wants to *earn* forgiveness, or *achieve* it, or gain credit for it. The truth of free grace and of salvation by faith is against the self-sufficiency a human being wants to feel. In a world where commerce is constantly trying to attract people by "free offers," it seems surprising that the human being reacts against the greatest free offer to mankind—the offer of salvation and eternal life. It was so even in the Old Testament, in Isaiah, chapter 55, where people were invited to come "without money and without price." But there, as in the New Testament, though the offer is free, the requirement is repentance for sin—and proud mankind finds repentance humbling and against his human pride.

So we have to work at this truth as evangelists. We will think out ways of illustrating it. One vivid demonstration of it is in the Holy Communion service. When I am evangelizing in a church context, I will sometimes say to a younger person that he would not think of going to the communion table and saying, "Here I am, God; I have lived a fairly good life this week; give me a blessing." Instead, he will go with an empty hand to receive the symbols of the death of Christ. He will not take up anything in his hand ("Nothing in my hand I bring," as the hymn says) but in opening up an empty hand he is saying loud and clear that his trust is in what Jesus Christ has done for him and not in himself. This illustration can be effective outside church circles, but it is particularly effective in church circles where people have not trusted Christ as Savior.

In my home church when I was young, the clergyman suddenly said in the middle of his sermon one day, "Stand up, all of you who know you are saved." Some stood; some sat. Afterwards there was a colossal furor! Our family was in the middle of it. We took the line that those who stood up were self-opinionated and proud, but those who did not stand up were humble and knew that they could not say they were saved until they reached the judgment seat of God. It was only slowly that I began to see that the opposite was true. I was shown the Scriptures and began to see for the first time that those who stood up were no longer trusting themselves but were trusting Christ. It was those of us who remained seated who were self-opinionated enough to think we would be good enough for God. Those who stood were humble enough to know they would never be good enough for God, and had put their trust in Christ and His atoning sacrifice for their sins.

Another way of presenting the same truth is to demonstrate what heaven would be like if everyone arrived there by their own good deeds. It would be a self-congratulatory assembly, "I'm glad you achieved it—like me!" Instead, we shall sing together, "Worthy is the Lamb who died for us." It will be an assembly of all who have trusted Christ for salvation. Those who trusted in themselves will not be there.

To many people, Christianity is trying to be good—to have more faith, hope, and love—to live caring lives and to hope expectantly for eternal life at the end. It is a confusion of ideas that we need to sort out in our preaching. I sometimes use the illustration of when I was conscripted into the army at the age of 18. I traveled overnight by train and arrived at the army camp early in the morning. After breakfast we were signed on, we took the promises, we had our hair cut (necessary for me in those days!), we were issued with uniform, and then our civilian clothes were sent off home in the post. At the lunch table there were others who had just arrived, still in civilian clothes. They looked at us in uniform and said, "What is it like in the army?" We replied, "When you have been in it as long as us, you'll get used to it!" But, in fact, we *were* soldiers and they were not. They had not taken the promises and had not signed on. Of course, we were useless as soldiers and needed training, but we had the *status* of soldiers—we had passed from civilian state into army service. We did not try to act like soldiers in order that we might be called soldiers at the end. You see the point. Justification by faith—receiving the free gift of salvation—makes us Christ's forever. We may not be much use as a Christian but we *are* a Christian if we have trusted in Jesus and His death for our sins. We have the status of the children of God—we are His forever, even if we have only trusted Jesus that very day. We have passed from death to life. The New Testament letters are addressed to Christians—to those who are justified by faith—calling them to live out what they are, to be more like Christ, to be more effective as servants of Christ to a needy world, and so on—not in order to achieve God's justification, but to live out the justification they have received already.

We might use the illustration of marriage. Boy meets girl. They become good friends. Then they start courting, and then comes the marriage. At that point of making the promises and of sealing with a ring, the two become man and wife. There is a whole lifetime to work out their new status (and it should get better all the time!)—but on that wedding day they changed status. They became a married couple. So on the day we receive the promises of Christ and trust in His saving grace and in His sacrifice for our sins, our status is altered. We become part of the body of Christ; in His family forever!

In his letter to Ephesus, Paul uses that superb sentence in chapter 2, verse 8: "By grace you have been saved through faith; and this is not your own doing, it is the gift of God." The phrase "the gift of God" has been much used by the Holy Spirit as a meaningful description of how we receive salvation. Grace is God's giving of Himself and of His love. It is the generous love of God towards us; it is the flowing of His mercy; it is the recognition of our inability to save ourselves; it is the self-giving of God. The gift of our salvation is to be received—after repentance for sin—by faith alone, not by works. Faith reaches out and receives.

Grace is also all that God goes on giving to us in His love for eternity. In Romans, chapter 5, there are three glorious expressions of this, resulting from justification. It is important that our presentation of the Gospel embraces a view of what God has prepared for those who love Him, as well as the *way* of entering the family of His love.

*"Peace with God"* is the first result. Later on in this chapter, verse 10, Paul writes: "While we were yet enemies we were reconciled to God by the death of his Son." Enemies! It is startling! Yet before we are redeemed, we stand in the territory of the enemy of God. One of the great words of the New Testament is "reconciliation." In 2 Corinthians 5:18-20 we read, "Through Christ, God reconciled us to himself." "In Christ, God was reconciling the world to himself, not counting their trespasses against them." To preach this and teach it is part of the evangelist's message. As it says in 2 Corinthians chapter 5, God "gave us the ministry of reconciliation," or, again, that "we are ambassadors for Christ, God making his appeal through us. We beseech on behalf of Christ, be reconciled to God." It is not reconciliation between man and man, but reconciliation between man and God. And God has trusted *us* to preach it!

This peace with God should also be a peace enfolding our hearts. There should be a quiet peace about our salvation and being justified. "There is no condemnation for those who are in Christ Jesus," Paul argues in Romans 8. Later in that chapter he spells out the fact that no one can accuse us in the Judgment Day, because the only person with authority to accuse or judge is the One who died for us that we might be saved! How often does the believer's heart glow with wonder, joy, and praise that we have this peace with God, forever!

Then, in Romans 5, we have the second result: *"access into this grace in which we stand."* It is a wonderful picture of a door flung open and our entering into the light, and finding a great palace where God's grace flows. In verse 3, Paul speaks of the way in which we are carried through sufferings and are given endurance. Grace is the way by which Christians endure pain, persecution, and suffering. It is the great assuring word of 2 Corinthians chapter 12 that God's grace is sufficient for us even in our weakness. The Gospel preacher cannot avoid telling people of the cost of following the Lord Jesus in a world that is against Him, but at the same time he can assure people that God's grace is sufficient for any experience of life. We have had access into this grace in which we stand. It is marvelous and all-sufficient. It is the active presence of the Lord by His Spirit in our lives and in the circumstances we have to face.

Grace is also a word describing the unlimited blessings of the Lord to all within His family. We may use illustrations of a cup overflowing, or an unquenchable spring of water, of an inexhaustible banquet, of a glorious inheritance. We may try to show how access into this grace is like seeing life in full color instead of in black and white, of its bringing a new dimension to living, of a satisfying of the heart, of joy and love. All our descriptions fall short of what happens when we taste and see how gracious the Lord is, and so we have to encourage people to taste and see for themselves!

This grace should show in our lives as it has in the lives of so many Christians through the centuries in serving, witnessing, tackling social problems, pioneering with the Gospel, and even giving their lives for their Lord—His hands and feet and heart to a needy world. The history of Christianity is a history of grace abounding!

Lastly, in Romans chapter 5, *"we rejoice in hope of sharing the glory of God."* Do not be afraid of preaching a Gospel that offers people life after death! Do not be afraid of cynical comments about "pie in the sky when you die" or "you are only interested in the next world." Remember the words of C.S. Lewis: "Because we love something else more than this world, we love even this world better than those who know no other. Aim at heaven and you will get the earth 'thrown in'; aim at earth and you will get neither."

Do not be afraid to preach the hope of glory, because most people in the world are afraid of death! They do not like to speak about it. The subject is "the great unmentionable." They try to avoid its reality. They speak brave words about being "snuffed out like a candle" and of that being the end. But, underneath, they are frightened of death and of what lies beyond.

A clergyman I know was friendly with the leading humanist of an English city. The wife of the humanist was herself also a leading humanist. She contracted cancer. Before she died she called my clergyman friend to her bedside and asked for a Christian funeral. She said, "Humanism has no answer to death; only Christ has." She died in Christ.

We have a glorious hope. Every time I conduct the funeral of a believing Christian the triumph of the Cross overwhelms me. The sting of death is removed! The Lord receives us to Himself! The life ahead will be in the presence of the Lord with all who love Him. We only glimpse a little now of what lies ahead but it will be life eternal, without pain or death. In Christ the clouds are parted with resurrection joy. Our Lord, risen from the dead, has gone before. He is the leading runner who has crossed the line! Because He is risen, we are risen. Eternal life is already ours, in Him.

I am very excited about the Christian Gospel. It is the greatest "good news" in the world. It is wonderful to be justified by faith, to know Christ Jesus as Savior and Lord, to know peace with God, access into His flowing grace and the certain hope of glory with Him. Like all of us here, I share the task of evangelism. There is no greater privilege or more awesome responsibility for any human being than to preach Jesus Christ, to explain the Gospel, to show what it means to be justified by faith, and to tell of the grace of God and the overwhelming love of God in Christ and the Cross. We are called to go to this needy and lost world with that glorious message and to do so with prayer, communication, love, sacrifice, work, and courage. And our message of the work of Christ can be summarized in one simple but eternally profound statement: "Jesus . . . died . . . for you."

# THE EVANGELIST AND THE REVIVAL WE NEED
*Billy Kim*

*"O Lord, revive thy work in the midst of the years,
in the midst of the years make [it] known; in wrath
remember mercy"* (Habakkuk 3:2).

Many people ask me why the Korean Church is experiencing revival today. In the last decade, hundreds of thousands of people are coming to Christ. What is the explanation? Every Christian wants to know!

In 1955, there were only 4,000 churches in Korea, and only one million Christians.

In 1965, the number of churches and Christians had doubled to 8,000 churches and two million Christians.

In 1975, there were 16,000 churches with 4.3 million Christians.

Last year, the census showed that Korea had 32,000 churches, with nearly ten million Christians. The population of South Korea is only forty million people!

The number of Christians has increased so rapidly that many churches, including the one I pastor, have three morning services every Sunday morning. The Christian population is growing four times faster than the regular population! We are building fifteen new churches every day in Korea!

Scotland is the birthplace of the Presbyterian denomination, but today, the largest Presbyterian church in the world is located, not in Europe, but in Seoul, Korea!

The Methodist church began in England, but the largest Methodist church in the world is also located in Seoul, Korea. The Assemblies of God began in the U.S.A.; however, the biggest church in the world is the Seoul Full Gospel Church, with a membership of nearly half a million very aggressive and witnessing believers!

I have pondered the possible reasons for this present-day revival among the people of my country. And I believe that the principles for the revival we are experiencing in Korea can be applied to any individual Christian or any Christian ministry in any part of the world.

1. *Prayer is the premise to revival*

"If my people, which are called by my name, shall humble themselves, and pray, and seek my face, and turn from their wicked ways; then will I hear from heaven, and will forgive their sin, and will heal their land" (2 Chronicles 7:14).

   a. *Prayer prepares for revival.* "Or what man is there of you, whom if his son ask bread, will he give him a stone? Or if he ask a fish, will he give him a serpent? If ye then, being evil, know how to give good gifts unto your children, how much more shall your Father which is in heaven give good things to them that ask Him?" (Matthew 7:9-11).

   (i)   Martin Luther was not satisfied with the religious world in which he was born. His deep need for personal piety caused him to spend much time in prayer while he was professor of theology at the University of Wittenberg. During the winter of 1512, he locked himself in a room and, within the tower of the black monastery at Wittenberg, he prayed over what he was discovering in the Scriptures. The Reformation was born after that season of prayer and study. The Reformation gives us the biblical truth of Justification by Faith. Man can not work for his salvation, but salvation is the gift of God through faith. That was a result of MUCH agonizing in prayer!

(ii)    John Wesley, the son of an Anglican clergyman from Epworth, England, was dissatisfied with the state of the Church of England. He was deeply moved by the great need of the poor who had flocked to the city where they lived in terrible conditions. On the evening of May 24, 1738, at a quarter-of-nine, as he was listening to the reading of Luther's "Preface to the Epistle to the Romans," John Wesley experienced a genuine conversion. He was born again, and this led to much prayer and fasting for John and Charles, his brother, and George Whitefield. As the Church of England closed its doors to their ministry, they began ministering to large crowds—not only in Great Britain, but also in America. Thousands gathered to hear the freshly-anointed preaching of the Word of God. As a result, the worldwide Methodist Revival was born. This, too, was the result of laboring in prayer.

(iii)    Toward the end of the 19th century, God raised up evangelists like Charles Finney, Dwight L. Moody and R.A. Torrey. These men preached under the anointing of the Holy Spirit, motivated by continual prayer and fasting. Just as the preaching of the Wesleys kept Britain from following France in the Revolution of the 18th century, so, too, a new outbreak of revival can bring about the social and political changes necessary to keep us from international destruction and calamity.

b.    *Prevailing prayer brings perpetual power.* James 5:16 says that the "effectual fervent prayer of a righteous man availeth much."

(i)    Moses prayed and the sea opened up and became a super-highway for the children of Israel.

(ii)    Abraham prayed and God gave him a son, when humanly speaking, it was an impossibility!

(iii)    Joshua prayed and mighty cities fell under his leadership.

(iv)    David prayed and God helped him slay the giant, Goliath.

(v)    Elijah prayed and called down fire from heaven.

(vi)    Daniel prayed and was saved from the lions.

(vii)    Paul prayed and the prison doors were shaken right off their hinges!

(viii)    Knox prayed and Queen Mary trembled.

(ix)    Müller prayed and great orphanages were built and maintained.

(x)    Roberts prayed and a Pentecost swept Wales.

Prayer does not need proof—it needs practice. Today we *organize* instead of *agonize* on our knees before God! The purpose of prayer should not be to try to change God but to change *me!*

Jesus spent much time in prayer before He entered His public ministry. Frequently, He went off to pray long hours—sometimes all night.

You will find more prayer meetings in the Korean church than (pardon my expression) a dog has fleas! We start at 4:30 every morning—not only in our church, but in *all* the churches! At 4:30 every morning, there is a prayer meeting . . . winter, summer, rain or shine! I don't know who started it, but I would like to meet him.

Sometimes I have wondered why God called me back to Korea to be a pastor. It's hard to get up at 4:00 o'clock in the morning! But, I wish you could see some of those early morning prayer meetings—they pray for hours! They pound on the floor, crying out to God! No wonder God is blessing the Korean church today!

Every Friday night there is an all-night prayer meeting. They have prayer and fasting meetings; they have mountain prayer meetings; they have prayer retreat centers everywhere; they have seven-day prayer meetings; they have 30-day prayer and fasting meetings; they have 40-day prayer meetings; they have 100-day prayer meetings. They have more titles for prayer meetings than anything in the church program. I don't know why they have so much to pray about!

One day I was praying with some of the Christians and just wanted to hear what they prayed about. Man, I wish you could hear some of their prayers! They pray for the unification of Korea so their families can be reunited; they pray for their pastors, they pray for their church to have a revival; they pray for world revival and they pray for you evangelists and I know that God answers their prayers!

At the outset of the Korean War, we came so close to being swallowed up by Communism. The North Korean Communists controlled all but the very southern tip of Korea! When hope was almost gone, the United States and sixteen United Nations came to our rescue. They pushed the Communists back and forth, back and forth, across the 38th Parallel. During the three years of intense fighting, Seoul was nearly demolished.

At the 38th Parallel there is place nicknamed, "Heartbreak Ridge." An American newspaper reporter found the spot during his journeyings and named it "Heartbreak Ridge" because of the innumerable men who gave their lives on that one lonely ridge. He was told the story of a terrible battle that took place there just before he arrived. The United Nations and the Communist soldiers dug their foxholes on either side of that ridge. As the bullets were flying back and forth, an American soldier was hit and wounded so badly he could not crawl back to safety. He could be heard crying for help. However, no one dared to go rescue him from the safety of their foxholes until one young man was seen checking his watch time and again. At the very stroke of nine he crawled cautiously, but safely, out into the line of the enemy bullets, and brought the dying young wounded soldier back to the foxhole. After applying first-aid, the sergeant asked him, "Why on earth did you wait until nine o'clock?" His reply was brief. He said, "When I left home, my mother promised me that she would pray for me every morning at nine o'clock."

What we need today is a generation of God-fearing evangelists, with simple faith like this young soldier's mother, who are willing to kneel by their beds and pray all night for God to bring a heaven-sent revival to our world!

The Bible commands us to *pray without ceasing!*

**2. *Preaching is the plan for revival***

On November 22, 1963, a man was shot to death on the streets of Dallas, Texas, U.S.A. Within two hours the entire world knew about the tragic death of President John F. Kennedy. The whole world followed every detail.

Some 2,000 years ago a man by the name of Jesus Christ was crucified outside the walls of Jerusalem at a place called "Calvary." And yet, today, half of the world has not heard the news of that man's death. This is a paradox!

From the launching pad of Cape Kennedy, America sent the first man to the moon. The Korean government graciously prepared a forty-foot screen on Namsan Mountain near downtown Seoul. They declared a semi-national holiday so that the school children could watch the historic moment when the first man in history would walk on the moon. You can ask any person on the streets of Seoul today who that man was. They can tell you, without hesitation, that it was Neil Armstrong from the U.S.A. But ask the same person if he knows the name of the man that God took to heaven in a chariot, he probably cannot tell you that it was the great prophet Elijah—because he has never heard that story!

When Mohammed Ali and Joe Frazer had their first fight, it came "live" via satellite to Korea. That evening, I was speaking to a group of high school students. I asked them if they knew who won the boxing match. They all knew that Frazer won! Then I asked these Korean students who won the great match between the shepherd boy David and the giant Goliath. They shook their heads. They could not answer.

This, too, is a paradox!

But there is one paradox I can not understand! In the Western world there are great beautiful cathedrals and enormous church buildings, Christian centers, and Christian campuses. Many of them are nearly empty. They speak of a time past, somehow. In many parts of the world we have to make do with improvised store buildings or hastily and very cheaply built churches. These inadequate facilities are packed with hungry people wanting to know God's Word and searching for the answers to the problems of life and the future. Why does part of the world have so much and another part so little? We need revival today—it matters not whether it be a small church, big church, poor nation, rich nation, first world or third world. We need revival! Unless we plead for revival, pray for revival, seek genuine revival, this old world will soon face total chaos. "Preach the word, be instant in season, out of season; reprove, rebuke, exhort with all longsuffering and doctrine" (2 Timothy 4:2).

God has promised that His Word would be blessed. God did not promise to bless the preaching of philosophy, psychology, or any other subject. The Bible tells us that heaven and earth shall pass away, but God's Word shall not pass away. "The word of God is . . . sharper than any twoedged sword" (Hebrews 4:12).

It was the powerful preaching of the Word by Jonathan Edwards that brought a sweeping revival to New England in the early history of the U.S.A.

It was Peter's preaching of the Word that brought 3,000 souls to their knees repenting and believing.

The Psalmist tells us in Chapter 119 verses 103 and 105: "How sweet are thy words unto my taste! Yea, sweeter than honey to my mouth!" and "Thy word is a lamp unto my feet, and a light unto my path."

We must preach the Word if we are to see a real revival sweep our world!

Paul said, "We preach Christ crucified, to the Jews a stumbling-block, and to the Greeks foolishness; but to those who are called, both Jews and Greeks, it is Christ, the power of God and the wisdom of God."

> The doctrines of the Bible are holy;
> The precepts of the Bible are binding;
> The history of the Bible is true;
> Its decisions are immutable;
> Christ is its grand subject and theme;
> Our *good* is its design;
> The *glory* of God its end;
> Read it to be *wise*;
> Believe it to be *safe*;
> Practice it to be *holy*.

3. *Purity is the path to revival*

Holiness is often eclipsed by Christian activity. "Be ye holy, for I am holy" (1 Peter 1:16). Busyness for God or activity for God is a good thing, but not the best thing. The holiness or the purity of our lives is so important for revival. Activity never brought a soul-searching revival, but holiness and right living brought great, great awakening, down through the ages.

a. *We must be pure from idolatry.* "Thou shalt have no other gods before me" (Exodus 20:3). We are surrounded by all kinds of idol worship, sorcery, and compromise. We compromise our convictions for convenience' sake. Our cultural habits and practices have overtaken the Scripture's mandate for holy living.

b. *We must be pure from immorality.* "The body is not for fornication, but for the Lord: and the Lord for the body" (1 Corinthians 6:13). "Know ye not that your bodies are the members of Christ?'' (1 Corinthians 6:15).

c. *We must be pure from worldliness.* "Love not the world, neither the things that are in the world. If any man love the world, the love of the Father is not in him" (1 John 2:15). "What? Know ye not that your body is the temple of the Holy Ghost which is in you, which ye have of God, and ye are not your own? For ye are bought with a price; therefore glorify God in your body, and in your spirit, which are God's" (1 Corinthians 6:19,20).

Dr. R. W. De Haan, in one of his excellent daily readings, gives some impressive statistics demonstrating the truth of Galatians 6:7, "Be not deceived; God is not mocked; for whatsoever a man soweth, that shall he also reap." Dr. De Haan speaks of sowing and reaping in the families of two men, Jonathan Edwards and Max Jukes.

Jonathan Edwards was a man of high culture, refinement and Christian character. Out of his 1,394 descendants, 13 were college presidents, 65 were professors, 60 were prominent lawyers, 32 were noted authors, 90 were physicians, 200 were ministers of the Gospel and 300 were good farmers.

Max Jukes, on the other hand, was a notorious man. The life histories of 903 of his descendants have been recorded. Of these, 300 were delinquents, 145 were confirmed drunkards, 90 were prostitutes, 285 had "evil diseases," and over 100 spent an average of 13 years in prison.

A holy and sanctified life is essential if our ministry is to be blessed.

4. *Praise is a priority to revival*

"O praise the Lord, all ye nations: praise him, all ye people, for his merciful kindness is great toward us: and the truth of the Lord endureth forever. Praise ye the Lord" (Psalm 117:1,2). The word "praise" or "hallelujah" appears over 600 times in the Bible. "And my tongue shall speak of thy righteousness and of thy praise all the day long. O Lord, open thou my lips; and my mouth shall show forth thy praise" (Psalm 35:28 and 51:15).

"Hallelujah" and "praise the Lord" are synonymous. I have a friend for whom we coined the name of "Hallelujah Choi." He didn't get his name just because the word "Hallelujah" is an attractive name. He built and owns the tallest building in the city of Seoul—63 stories. He founded the first professional soccer team in Korea and named it "Hallelujah." Not "Raiders" or "Redskins" or "Wildcats"—but "Hallelujah." That team played in Hong Kong against the People's Republic of China; can't you just hear the television commentator saying, "Hallelujah's driving that ball into left field . . . left center . . ." Then, "Hallelujah scored a goal!" And the commentator keeps saying, "Hallelujah scored a goal! Hallelujah, Hallelujah, Hallelujah!" Over and over, "Hallelujah!" He named the soccer team specifically to be a witness for Jesus Christ and called it "Hallelujah." The Korean people love to praise the Lord!

We like that word, "hallelujah," so much that not only is there a professional soccer team, but one man built a church and called it "The Hallelujah Church"—not "First Baptist," not "First Presbyterian," but "Hallelujah Church." I have seen a beauty shop called, "The Hallelujah Beauty Shop!" I have seen a supermarket that is called the "Hallelujah Super-Market!" When I saw "Hallelujah Restaurant," I went in to see what they sold. They sold the same thing as any other restaurant, but they called it, "The Hallelujah Restaurant." I asked the manager, "Are you a Christian?" He said, "Sure, hallelujah!"

God has blessed the Korean church today, I believe, because the Korean Christians love to praise the Lord. Oh, how they love to praise the Lord! For Korea, 1983 was a year of tragedy. A 747 jumbo passenger jet was shot out of the sky by a Russian

MIG, and 269 innocent people died. One month later, in Burma, a Communist-inspired explosion took place at the National Cemetery in Rangoon. Seventeen of our cabinet members were killed.

Yet, in spite of these tragedies, the Korean church sold more hymnbooks that year than in any previous year. One million hymnbooks were published and sold. "*Praise* ye the Lord. *Praise* ye the Lord from the heavens . . . *Praise* ye him, all his angels: *PRAISE* ye him, all his hosts" (Psalm 148:1,2).

5.   *Persecution is a prerequisite to revival*

In Acts, chapter 8, we find that Saul was consenting to the death of Stephen. At that time there was great persecution against the church in Jerusalem. They were scattered abroad, and went everywhere preaching the Word. "As for Saul, he made havoc of the church, entering into every house, and haling men and women committed them to prison. Therefore they that were scattered abroad, went everywhere preaching the word " (Acts 8:3,4).

When the persecution started in the early church, they were scattered and began to preach. They went to every house and began to proclaim the unsearchable riches of Jesus Christ. I believe the Korean churches are overflowing today because the Korean church has experienced persecution. That is another reason God is sending blessing. The very first missionaries to Korea were Catholic missionaries who came 200 years ago. One hundred years ago, a Methodist missionary and a Presbyterian missionary arrived and faced grave dangers.

Korea was a hermit nation, and did not welcome foreigners to her shores. These men stepped bravely onto unfriendly territory at the port of Inchon. I wonder if they ever dreamed that just 100 years later, their efforts would result in ten million souls for Christ!

The Korean War brought persecution of Christians in the North, forcing them to move to the South. Much of the fruit in recent years and the cause for the great revival and evangelism in the southern part of Korea is the result of the North Korean Christians who fled South and shared their faith with their new neighbors. The capital city of North Korea used to be known as the Jerusalem of Asia. God used the wrath of men to praise His Name and spread His Word to us in the South! Bless His Holy Name!

In 1910, there was severe persecution of the Korean church. The churches were closed, and missionaries were all driven out of Korea. There was a small Methodist church tucked away between the hills and the rice paddies. The Japanese police told the pastor that they could not hold services there any more. It was closed for some time. But one day the police told the pastor he could gather the people for a worship service. They were very happy. Some of the people walked twelve miles to attend the service.

The Korean people love to sing heartily. As they were singing one of their favorite hymns, "Nearer, my God, to Thee," the policemen locked the doors from the outside and threw on gallons of kerosene and set the church on fire. When the church began to burn, naturally the men broke the windows and tried to escape; but policemen were standing all around the church, ready to shoot any who tried to leave. As the church began to burn, the pastor asked the congregation to join him in singing that great hymn of the faith:

> "Alas, and did my Saviour bleed?
> And did my Sovereign die?
> Would He devote that sacred head
> For such a worm as I?"

Just before the roof caved in, they could feel the intensity of the heat, and smoke began to fill their eyes. They sang the final stanza,

"But drops of grief can n'er repay
The debt of love I owe;
Here, Lord, I give myself away;
'Tis all that I can do.

At the cross, at the cross,
Where I first saw the light,
And the burden of my heart rolled away . . ."

Everyone in the church died that Sunday morning. But that is not the end of the story. . . .

In 1971 a group of Japanese pastors came to Korea. When they heard the story of the church-burning and saw a small monument erected in memory of those who gave their lives that Sunday morning, they were brokenhearted. They went home and raised money to build a church on the spot where the other one had been. They dedicated the new country church in September 1971.

It was my privilege to attend the dedication. The message was delivered, a prayer was offered, and citations given. Just before the benediction, the pastor asked us all to sing as the final song:

"Alas, and did my Saviour bleed?
And did my Sovereign die?
Would He devote that sacred head
For such a worm as I?"

The Japanese delegates stood up and walked over to the Korean delegation. They embraced each other and wept together. They forgave and promised to forget. That is the power of the Gospel of Jesus Christ!

I once heard the late Dr. Oswald J. Smith tell the following story of the Second World War. France had fallen and the United States had not yet agreed to come to the aid of Great Britain, standing alone with her back against the wall, so to speak. Winston Churchill made an urgent plea by radio.

Dr. Smith said he was driving along the highway with his wife in the seat beside him. When he heard the voice of Churchill, he quickly pulled his car to the side of the road and turned off the engine so he could catch every word of the broadcast. The Prime Minister spoke only a minute or two; but he said something Dr. Smith would never forget the rest of his life. Winston Churchill pled with the American people, saying, "Give us the tools, and we will finish the job!"

Gathered here today are 8,000 evangelists, crying out to the Christian world, "Give us the tools and we will finish the job!" The job of evangelizing this world with the Gospel of Jesus Christ!

# THE EVANGELIST'S MESSAGE:
# THE RESPONSE OF FAITH
*Stephen Mung'oma*

Dr. Billy Graham in his address "The Evangelist and a Torn World" during Amsterdam 83 said these words: "We are living in the most revolutionary period of history. In the distance, I can hear the sound of hoofbeats. The four horsemen of the Apocalypse of Revelation are even now riding this way. A mighty, terrible judgment is approaching. Man's sinfulness has the world on a self-destruct course. And you and I, God's ambassadors, are called to sound the warning to make judgment clear, to call sinners to repentance, to announce God's grace, to point to the Cross and the God-man on the Cross, to point to the empty tomb, to shout the Good News from the housetops, to point the way to peace with God and peace between nations" *(The Work of an Evangelist p. 3).*

Brothers and sisters, it is now three years since these words were uttered and I dare say that those "four horsemen of the Apocalypse" are nearer. Man's sinfulness has not diminished and God's judgment is sure to come unless there is a re-direction. We who have been privileged to gather here have a divine mandate to preach the Gospel, which is the power of God for salvation, with clarity, urgency, and expectation. Our message can and will make a difference in the eternal destiny of thousands in our time.

We have already heard brother Ravi Zacharias show us the lostness of man, and brother Michael Baughen has ably presented the work of Christ. Today, let's think together about "The Response of Faith." The evangelist's message must have a goal: to bring people to a saving faith in Jesus Christ. But when we talk about saving faith, and that people need to be converted, what do we mean? What is the relationship between saving faith and repentance? And how do we appeal to the hearers to respond without manipulating them? How do we effectively proclaim Jesus as both "Lord" and "Savior"? Finally, what is the relationship between the sovereign work of the Spirit in regeneration and the evangelist's call for a response? If God is the one who saves, is there any point in calling people to respond? We shall endeavor in these few minutes to answer these questions.

## 1. Saving faith and repentance

Our Lord Jesus after His resurrection commanded His disciples to go and preach the Gospel to all peoples. In Mark's gospel we read, "He that *believeth* and is baptized shall be saved; but he that believeth not shall be damned" (Mark 16:16). He clearly pointed out that there can be no salvation without faith. In Acts 16:30 the question is asked by the Philippian jailer: "What must I do to be saved?" And the answer is given "*Believe* on the Lord Jesus Christ, and thou shalt be saved, and thy house," (Acts 16:31).

Believing on Jesus Christ is paramount to salvation. But it is not only believing that is stressed in the preaching of the early Church. Repentance too is central. Peter on the day of Pentecost challenged his listeners, "*Repent,* and be baptized everyone of you in the name of Jesus Christ for the remission of sins, and ye shall receive the gift of the Holy Ghost" (Acts 2:38). Paul, addressing the Athenians on Mars Hill says, "And the times of this ignorance God winked at; but now commandeth all men everywhere to *repent.*" (Acts 17:30). And before King Agrippa, Paul confesses,

"Whereupon, O King Agrippa, I was not disobedient to the heavenly vision: but showed first unto them of Damascus, and at Jerusalem, and throughout all the coasts of Judea, and then to the Gentiles, that they should *repent* and turn to God, and do works meet for repentance." These few Scriptures show us that both faith and repentance are essential to salvation, and must be demanded by the evangelist.

a. *Saving faith.* In our evangelistic preaching, therefore, we need to call for a response of faith. But what is this saving faith? The New Bible Dictionary defines it as: "The attitude whereby a man abandons all reliance on his own efforts to obtain salvation, be they deeds of piety, of ethical goodness or anything else. It is the attitude of complete trust in Christ, of reliance on Him alone for all that salvation means."

First, it is a recognition that man cannot save himself. He is a lost sinner incapable of understanding or even receiving spiritual matters on his own. The Apostle Paul writing to the Romans makes this clear. He says all have gone astray; none is righteous or understands, for all indeed have sinned and come short of the glory of God (Romans 3:23). Because of this depraved state of mankind one cannot obtain salvation through his own deeds of righteousness. The inherent sinfulness of mankind renders this impossible, and this is why Paul concludes by saying that "a man is justified by faith without the deeds of the law" (Romans 3:28).

Saving faith, therefore, is this abandonment of all our human efforts at saving ourselves or guiding our own lives and destiny, and relying completely on the finished work of Jesus Christ.

This brings me to the second point. How is it that Jesus is the one qualified to save humankind? I do not need to repeat what brother Baughen has said about the work of Christ. However, I wish to stress that this Jesus of Nazareth, who 2,000 years ago was on this earth as a Palestinian first-century Jew, was none other than the God-man.

He was (and still is) God's revelation to humanity. Paul calls Him "the image of the invisible God," the perfect manifestation of God, born of a woman, lived, suffered and died like us, but unlike human beings, He rose from the dead. Though He was God, He took upon Himself the human flesh without ceasing to be God and was obedient to the Father even unto death. Being the only one perfectly obedient to the Father, He is both the propitiation and expiation for the sins of the world. In other words, He satisfied God's wrath and also was a substitute for our sins. Jesus, therefore, qualifies to be the true "High Priest" who intercedes on behalf of humanity. The writer to the Hebrews says: "Though He were a son, yet learned he obedience by the things which he suffered. And being made perfect, he became the author of eternal salvation unto all them that obey him; called of God a high priest after the order of Melchizedek" (Hebrews 5:9,10).

Faith in Jesus as "the author of eternal salvation" must be based on the facts about Jesus and conviction that He was indeed who He claimed to be. It is imperative that people know who Jesus is. Either Jesus was false and knew it—in which case He was a stupid liar who ended up on the Cross for His lies—or He was false but did not know it, in which case He was a mental case, a self-deluded megalomaniac.

But facts speak to the contrary. Of all people who have ever lived, Jesus was the most balanced. He lived for others and His whole life on earth demonstrated neither lunacy nor deception, but showed a man with the full faculties of reason and with a deep knowledge of spiritual matters that indicate a man of authority. Indeed His miracles and teaching on the Kingdom life portrayed the God-man. They demonstrated that here, in this first-century Jew was God among men, Creator and sustainer of life.

Jesus was true. He was the "Way, the Truth and the Life" without whom none can reach the Father.

If He was what he claimed to be, that is, "the personal revelation of God to man," then the only and proper response to Him is that of faith—total, unconditional submission to Him. It is a total dependence, a complete reliance on Him and Him alone for salvation. This is the saving faith that we call the hearers to respond with.

b. *Repentance.* As we saw earlier on in the Gospels and in the Book of Acts, the injunction itself is not enough. But what is repentance, and how is it related to saving faith?

There are two aspects of repentance: *turning from* and *turning towards.*

First, it is turning *from* sin. By turning from sin, we don't only mean ceasing to do overt sins, but we mean a complete turn from a self-centeredness, from a self-guidance. It is a change of mind, a change of direction and a change of life-style. Sin is a nature that is alien to God, that is hostile to God and His ways; it is being independent of God. Repentance, then, is turning from your own ways that are by nature at enmity with God. First, there is a feeling of sorrow for sin and for being rebellious against God. Then this sorrow leads to a change of mind and direction. This is what happens to the Prodigal Son we read of in Luke 15. When in the far country, hungry and wishing to feed on the pigs' food, he comes to himself, he has a change of mind which leads to a change of direction. He says, "I will arise and go to my father . . ." He turns from his own way, his own wisdom, and from his waywardness. This is the first aspect of repentance.

The second aspect of repentance is turning *towards* God through Jesus Christ. The Prodigal Son does not simply feel sorry for being such a bad child who has squandered his father's wealth; no, he makes a definite decision to return to the father. It is in this turning towards God that repentance is related to saving faith. As one turns to God, it is in total dependence on His mercy and grace that he does so, for he does not deserve the father's love or forgiveness. The Prodigal Son thinks that he can still earn something from his father by being a slave, and so in his mind he formulates what he will say to his father: "I am not worthy . . . make me as one of your hired servants . . ." But when he reaches home, he finds the waiting, loving arms of his father. He is accepted, and he too has to accept the forgiveness that is offered to him. Repentance, then, is only possible because of the mercy of God as shown in the finished work of Jesus Christ; and hence it is by faith that one turns towards God.

It is important, therefore, that we stress the importance of both saving faith and repentance; for without faith and repentance there can be no conversion or regeneration. If we only stress believing, we get "converts" whose lives do not show fruits or deeds of repentance. Many times we evangelists have called people to "only believe." We say, "All you have to do is believe. Come as you are and when you believe, Jesus will give you peace and eternal life." Indeed, people come and believe, but there is no sorrow for sin or their self-centered living, and the end result is a people whose mouths confess Jesus but whose lives do not at all manifest Him. On the other hand, a stress on repentance alone can create very unhappy Christians always mourning over their sins and their unworthiness. They do not enjoy the fruits of believing in Jesus. Some may feel guilty at the beginning but they do not know what positive step to take, i.e., trust in the finished work of Christ and appropriate the fruits of saving faith. Sometimes, when they no longer feel guilty, they resort to the old life.

We are, therefore, to present both aspects in order to get truly converted individuals whose transformed lives are a letter to be read by all who see them.

## 2.   *The appeal*

Having presented the Good News, and knowing that the hearers have understood you, how do you make the appeal clearly, directly, persuasively, and with a sense of urgency, yet without manipulation and coercion?

As I said at the beginning, the time is drawing nearer and nearer for the return of the Lord Jesus and hence we need to have a sense of urgency. Paul writing to Timothy almost 2,000 years ago exhorts him to "preach the Word in season and out of season" or as the Amplified Bible puts it, "Keep your sense of urgency (stand by, be at hand and ready, whether the opportunity seems to be favorable or unfavorable, whether it is convenient or inconvenient, whether it be welcome or unwelcome, you as preacher of the Word are to show people in what way their lives are wrong) and convince them, rebuking and correcting, warning and urging and encouraging them, being unflagging and inexhaustible in patience and teaching" (2 Timothy 4:2).

Urgency is the word which we should always keep before us. We should preach like dying preachers to dying people, for we can't guarantee them another day nor can we guarantee ourselves another opportunity. We are to be urgent in our preaching because the Lord can come anytime, and if the people do not believe in Him, they will go to hell. Paul says that the love of Christ "constraineth" us and so we persuade men and women everywhere to be reconciled to God.

We should therefore not shy away from persuasion, as it is legitimate. We believe that Jesus is the Way, the Truth and the Life; and without Him, no one can go to the Father. Since many are blind to this fact, we, as evangelists whose eyes have been opened to the truth about Jesus, must persuade them to turn away from their own ways to God's. Let's not be fearful of persuading people because we fear manipulating them. Dr. McGavran says in *Understanding Church Growth* (p. 35): "If there are many paths to God, then for Christians to induce others to follow their path may indeed be self-aggrandizement. But if Christ is the only real Savior, despite all the richness of other faiths in many respects, then persuading men to accept Him is not really open to the charge of selfishness, whatever the imperfections of the human agents of God's love."

Since we are convinced that Jesus is God's final revelation to mankind, we should not be ashamed of persuading men and urging them to accept Him as their Lord and Savior. We should use every argument, reason, and entreaty in persuading them to receive Jesus without any fear of being accused of manipulation.

But then, how should our appeal be? There are many ways of making the appeal. However, you should have in mind the customs of the church and/or the culture. You should also stick as closely as possible to a simple, clearly understood method. Some evangelists call people to the front who desire to be prayed for; others pray for those who want to receive Christ where they are. Other evangelists ask the inquirers to raise their hands. Many others do not ask them to do anything but remain in the room, or to go to a designated place after closure of the meeting. Whichever method you choose to use or are using, be clear in what you are asking them to do. Repeat the appeal a number of times in different ways to make sure they understand. For example, we were preaching in a predominantly Roman Catholic area, and after preaching we asked people if they would like to receive Christ. Many responded, but later when we inquired further we discovered that, to many of them, receiving Christ meant taking Holy Communion or going to Mass. Many had not been to Mass for a long time but after the preaching they felt convicted and wanted to start going to Mass regularly.

Here we found out that they had misunderstood us, or rather we had not made the call clearly. Use the terms that convey the intended meaning clearly. Avoid the overused words and phrases like "receive Christ," "accept Jesus," "believe in Jesus," "be born again," "be saved" unless you have explained them clearly and the audience has understood what you mean.

In your enthusiasm or excitement, you can easily manipulate the audience, so be conscious that it is God the Holy Spirit who alone will bring about conviction. Haven't you heard this kind of appeal? "Everyone close your eyes, no one looking. You keep your eyes shut and mind your own business. Now, you know that you are not saved and you are on your way to hell tonight unless you repent. I can see you there, young girl. I see you, young man, are debating within yourself—*Obey the voice of God.* Now, eyes closed, you who want to receive Jesus (and all of you unsaved people should) raise your hands. Right away . . . come on . . . you over there, you over here, raise your hands. Yes, that's right . . . thank you, thank you, thank you. I can see that hand (even if there is no hand going up). Who will join him/her? Yes, thank you, young man—that was courageous. Thank you . . . Now the next step, stand up. *Quick*, stand up. Let not the devil keep you on that seat. I saw your hand, so stand up and shame the devil. Good, now, come to the front. Stand right here before me . . . ''

Well, brethren, I must confess that I have done this before, so don't think I am picking on anybody. Ten years ago, this was part of my evangelistic appeal. I did not deliberately want to manipulate people. I believed it was right, since I had seen another older evangelist using this method. There are dangers inherent in this kind of appeal. It is manipulative and you end up with "converts" who really come forward either through fear or intimidation. I think if we have presented the Gospel clearly and have trusted the Holy Spirit to convict the people, we should not be fearful or feel failures if no one raises his/her hand or comes forward. Let the appeal be urgent, clear, and direct, but non-manipulative.

Another example I wish to share with you happened to me without my knowing. Some 12 years ago when I was pastoring a small church in Kampala, Uganda, a young man came to church at the invitation of his brother. Somehow that Sunday there was tremendous manifestation of God's power, and demons were manifested and cast out.

A girl sitting next to this young man fell down and demons began crying out of her and we cast them out. Now, I cannot remember what happened but I suppose I must have said something like, "You see the power of God being manifested and now how can you resist God? If you are not saved, come forward and be saved. You never know—demons that we have cast out might enter you, so you should surrender to Jesus. Quickly, run to the front and get saved."

I do not know the exact words used, but it could have been similar words. So this young man came forward and "got saved." Well, I never saw him again for twelve years. Last April he came to me and (of course, I could not remember him—he's grown older) told me the story. He said he had been so scared that he had gone to the front to be saved, but actually he had not been genuine. After that church service, he had decided never to enter a church, and for ten years he did not go to church. However, two years ago, he came to the Lord and now he is seeking to go into full-time ministry.

Well, I got shocked when he told me the story, for I had never imagined that I had ever manipulated people into "accepting Jesus." But it is true that sometimes we use the supernatural happenings to urge people to be saved. This can be another way of manipulating people into receiving Jesus Christ. Miracles do not necessarily lead to faith, nor do the people who see miracles necessarily become strong Christians. So those of us whose evangelistic ministry is characterized by the supernatural should be extra careful, otherwise we end up manipulating people in order to give impressive results.

Another way of manipulating people is when we give half-truths in order to get "results." For example, "Come to Jesus and all your problems will be solved." This is a half-truth and we should beware of this kind of appeal. Sometimes we play on people's emotions due to some misfortune or incident in their lives. We move them emotionally in order to get positive responses, but again such responses do not bear lasting fruit. Those of us preaching in war situations or among refugees or where the economic and social conditions have reduced people to abject poverty, should be on the lookout. It is easy to get "decisions" which are not well-founded. The appeal should not play too much on their conditions, though obviously one will refer to the situation in the preaching.

As you offer the invitation, therefore, be conscious of these points. Be relevant, clear, and urgent in the appeal; but in your persuasion, avoid manipulative techniques.

**3.   *The Holy Spirit's work and call for a response***

Perhaps this is a good place to stop and ask: how can we call for a response and yet depend upon the Holy Spirit's sovereign work in regeneration?

First of all, let's be clear about this one fact: God is always the initiator from beginning to end. Regeneration is not the work of human beings or preachers. Jesus Himself said to His disciples, "You did not choose me, but I chose you." We are saved by grace through faith, and this is not our own work. It is all by His mercy. The Holy Spirit brings conviction of sin in the heart of the sinner which leads to salvation.

But God has also chosen to save mankind through the "foolishness" of preaching the Cross, as Paul puts it. Humankind, being free moral agents, are expected to exercise this gift to respond to the preaching—which is done by other human beings—either negatively or positively. The evangelist's call to a response of faith is used by the Holy Spirit to arouse the listener to the challenges of the Gospel. His response is both an act of the will and also a work of the Holy Spirit in his heart. The mind is convinced of the facts about Jesus, the heart is touched to yield to the control of the Holy Spirit, and the will consents and this leads to an action—a positive response of faith.

As evangelists, we should constantly rely on God for wisdom as we make the appeal, for we know that ultimately it is God who brings about regeneration. And yet we have a responsibility of sowing the seed and expecting the seed to germinate and grow. Just as a farmer has to trust God to bring about the germination and growth of the seed, so the evangelist trusts God to bring about regeneration. But the farmer must plant the seed in good soil, water it and expect growth. An evangelist, too, cannot remain indifferent to the "seed" sown. He preaches with expectation and so calls for a response in full confidence that the Holy Spirit who alone brings about the growth of the seed will touch and move hearers to a positive response. It would be a foolish and irresponsible farmer who would simply "throw" seeds into the soil and never bother whether they grow or not. It would be the same with an evangelist who does not call for a response "supposedly" trusting the Holy Spirit to bring about regeneration. Actually every act of God involves the human participation, for thus He has chosen to act. He acts in mercy and grace, and man responds in faith and so a "miracle" happens. We should therefore not fear preaching and expecting conversions, for God has promised that when we trust Him as we preach, He will in His mercy and grace, bring about regeneration.

4. *Proclaim Jesus as Lord and Savior*

Finally, in our preaching and call for a response of faith, we should proclaim Jesus as both ''Savior'' and ''Lord.'' The object of faith is not just a set of doctrines or faith itself. It is Jesus who is both Savior and Lord.

In many evangelistic meetings people are called upon to receive Jesus as their personal Savior so that they receive peace, joy, satisfaction, prosperity, and even healing. Jesus becomes simply a Giver or Provider of good things in this world—and, of course, of eternal life after death. We have proclaimed Jesus as Savior only.

Brothers and sisters, I do not dispute that we should proclaim Jesus as Savior, but I feel that in many of our meetings, we have given half the picture. Jesus is not Savior before He is Lord. The New Testament preaching concentrated on declaring that Jesus was LORD. On the day of Pentecost, Peter declared clearly: ''Therefore let all the house of Israel know assuredly, that God hath made that same Jesus, whom you crucified, both Lord and Christ'' (Acts 2:36).

The resurrection was a seal of the Father, endorsing that Jesus was Lord of earth and heaven. The Apostle Paul thus is able to boldly claim that Jesus who was raised from the dead is seated at the right hand of the Father ''far above all rule and authority and power and dominion, and every name that is named, not only in this age, but also in the one to come. And He has put all things in subjection under His feet, and gave Him as head over all things to the church, which is His body, the fullness of Him who fills all in all'' (Ephesians 1:21-23).

Indeed, the Lordship of Jesus is central to the New Testament. Jesus Himself after the resurrection told His disciples, ''All authority has been given to Me in heaven and on earth'' (Matt 28:18). He is Lord of all things, seeing that all things were created by Him and for Him (Colossians 1:16).

Being Lord, He has every right over all and, therefore, the call is to respond to Him in complete submission as Lord. It is a call to a change of allegiance. Paul writes to the Colossians that we have been delivered from the ''domain of darkness, and transferred us to the kingdom of His beloved Son'' (Colossians 1:13). We have now changed allegiance from the master Satan to the Lord Jesus Christ, who now demands of us to relinquish all rights to Him and allow Him to take the reins of our lives and lead us.

We have to effectively proclaim this in order for the would-be disciples to count the cost of complete dedication to Him as Master. Attitudes, motives and life-styles are now to find a new center and that is the Master, Jesus Christ, who becomes the Lord of all aspects of your life.

Since Jesus rose from the dead, He is able to save all those who come to Him in faith. But He is able to do so because He is Lord. Hence, when He is received as Lord, obviously He is Savior too, for He will save those who accept Him as Lord. It is therefore meaningless to speak of receiving Jesus as Savior but not Lord. He could not save without being Lord, and therefore He cannot be received as Savior only. Let's go and proclaim Jesus as Lord. And because He is Lord, He is able to save, to heal the sick, to deliver the demon possessed, and to baptize believers in the Holy Spirit.

Brethren, we have a clear divine mandate to warn humanity of the coming judgment. Let us do it in love as we proclaim Jesus as Lord and Savior, and as we call men and women to repentance and faith. Do not fear to persuade them as you see the day drawing near. In your appeal, be direct, clear yet without manipulation, knowing that the Holy Spirit is at work convicting sinners and bringing them to salvation. *May the Lord bless you all.*

# THE EVANGELIST'S APPEAL FOR DECISION
*Billy Graham*

This morning I want to speak briefly about giving the invitation, and the place of decision in our ministry as evangelists. Following our break, you will have an opportunity to explore this subject in more detail; so what I want to say today will be by way of background.

1. *Validity of the evangelistic invitation*
   a. Preceding any valid commitment is personal decision. This is true:
   —at the marriage altar . . .
   "Do you take this woman . . .?" and the "I do." The minister makes the appeal and the positive response works a magic change in two lives.
   —in court . . .
   The bailiff says to the plaintiff and defendant, "Do you swear to tell the whole truth and nothing but the truth, so help me God?" The "I do" is the response which validates the legality of the proceedings.
   —in a democracy . . .
   At the ballot box you must decide which candidate . . . you are given a choice and a decision must be made.
   b. In fact, we are faced with decisions every hour of the day . . . What shall I wear? Shall I shave? What shall I eat for breakfast? How shall I go to work? What is my plan for the day? Every hour we make decisions. Most are not life and death decisions, but personal decision is required.
   I heard of a man who got a job sorting potatoes—culling the small ones out and packing the larger. But the problem was, there were too many middle-sized ones. After three weeks he said to his boss, "I quit!" "Why?" said the boss, "We pay you well." "I know," said the man. "It's those infernal *decisions*."
   Some churchmen ask, is it valid or legitimate to extend an invitation for people to come to Christ? The biblical answer is: Yes!
   But methods may vary. When a man senses the spiritual emptiness of his life, he is like a man pursued by his enemies, who comes to a raging river. He must decide if he will stay where he is and face certain death, or cross over and be safe. His life from that moment on will be determined by the choice he makes. But when the man chooses to cross over to safety, he discovers the river is too swift and wide to cross and there is no bridge. How can he cross over and be safe?
   Our great privilege as evangelists is to call on men and women to cross the river to find life, and tell them the good news of the bridge God has built for them in the Person of His Son Jesus Christ.
   The evangelistic invitation is valid for at least two reasons. First, it is valid because the Gospel demands decision; and second, it is valid because it is illustrated repeatedly in the Bible.
   As Stephen Mung'oma just reminded us, the Gospel of Jesus Christ demands decision. It is not merely a set of facts to which a person can give intellectual assent—it is a call for an individual to turn in repentance from his sin and his neglect of God and to turn to Christ in faith, accepting Him as Lord and Savior.
   God is at work in conversion. The Bible says, "Salvation is of the Lord." It is the Holy Spirit who brings conviction of sin. He applies the truth of the Gospel.

Jesus said, "When he is come, he will *reprove* the world of *sin*, and of *righteous-ness*, and of *judgment*" (John 16:8).

First Thessalonians 1:5, "For our gospel came not unto you in word only, but also in power, and in the Holy Ghost, and in much assurance; as ye know what manner of men we were among you for your sake." It is the Holy Spirit who brings new birth and new life. Jesus told Nicodemus that unless a man is born "from above," he "cannot enter into the kingdom of God" (John 3:5). This great truth should make us more dependent on God in our evangelism, knowing that ultimately it is God who changes lives and that we are helpless apart from Him.

But we also need to remember that the Bible underlines the necessity of man's response to the Gospel. Jesus said, "No man, having put his hand to the plough, and looking back, is fit for the kingdom of God" (Luke 9:62). This brings up a valid point in an invitation—don't tell people it's easy to follow Christ—make it tough and challenging. Jesus did. "Straight is the gate, and narrow is the way, which leadeth unto life, and few there be which go in thereat" (Matthew 7:14). "If any man will come after me, let him deny himself, and take up his cross, and follow me" (Matthew 16:24).

When Shackleton, the explorer, ran an ad in a New York paper to recruit men for his venture, the ad said: "Wanted, men to spend several months in the Arctic—long hours, low pay, meager food, and poor accommodations." That ad broke all the newspaper records in response to a "Help Wanted" ad!

Conversion is more than a psychological phenomenon—it is the turning of the whole man to God. It is a conscious commitment to Christ, involving repentance and faith. In the Gospel, men and women are called to make Christ Lord of every aspect of life. He is to be your life's priority! We are to follow Jesus Christ in discipleship.

Such discipleship is not only an emotional appeal to feel sorry for sins and to turn to righteousness. It is not only an intellectual appeal to accept the teaching of Jesus and imitate His example. It is not only a religious appeal to submit to certain ritual acts. The invitation is essentially a personal appeal of unqualified self-commitment to the person of Jesus Christ.

That is why throughout the Bible we repeatedly find the call to decision, and that is why the call to decision is an important part of our evangelistic preaching.

From Adam, "Where art thou?" in Genesis 3, to the final appeal of the Spirit and the Bride in Revelation 22, the Bible is one re-echoing invitation to lost humanity to turn to God.

  Moses (Exodus 32:26);
  Joshua (Joshua 24:15);
  Elijah (1 Kings 18:30, 39);
  John the Baptist (Mark 1:5);
  Jesus (Matthew 4:19);

and many more, are recorded as having given public invitations.

All persons that Jesus ever called (with the possible exception of Nicodemus), He either called them to declare publicly for Him, or He spoke to them in front of others. That is one of the reasons I ask people to make a public decision.

When Jesus was walking from Jericho to Jerusalem, a blind man named Bartimaeus cried out to Him. We read, "Jesus stood still and commanded him to be brought to him" (Luke 18:40). Jesus could have quietly gone to the man on the sidelines, but instead He called him forward publicly. In front of a vast throng of people, Jesus looked up in a tree and called Zacchaeus to come down publicly (Luke 19:5).

The apostles followed the same pattern. On the day of Pentecost, Peter urged people to repent and believe in Jesus, and 3,000 came to Christ (somebody counted them).

The call for decision—the invitation—is therefore not something just added to the end of an evangelistic sermon as an afterthought. Instead, the whole sermon leads toward it. May God help us to make that call to decision clearly, effectively, and boldly.

**2.** *Preparation for the invitation*

Every time I give an invitation, I am in an attitude of prayer inwardly, because I know I am totally dependent on God. Incidentally, this is the moment that I feel emotionally, physically, and spiritually drained. This is the part of the evangelistic service that often exhausts me physically. I think one of the reasons may be the terrible spiritual battle going on in the hearts of so many people. With me, it becomes a spiritual battle of such proportions that sometimes I feel almost faint. There is an inward groaning and agonizing in prayer that I cannot possibly put into words. I am sure every true evangelist senses this.

But I want to speak briefly about the *purposes* and *methods* of an evangelistic invitation.

a. *We make it clear to our listeners that the Gospel demands decision.* They cannot remain neutral about Christ. Not to decide is to decide not to.

b. *The method of invitation may vary.* In some places where evangelism must be done quietly, it could be a handshake, or a nodding of a head. In other situations, it could be the signing of a card, the raising of a hand, or better yet (if the situation allows it), asking them to come forward to the front of the auditorium or to a side room for a brief after-meeting of instruction. I have used all these methods of invitation.

I have known some places where all I could do is to ask them to bow their heads for a few moments of silence, and make the commitment in their hearts.

c. *It helps us to identify and help conserve the results of the preaching of the Gospel.* That is why, in our Crusades, whenever possible a counselor obtains the name and address of the person who has come forward. Then there can be follow-up so that an inquirer will be put in touch with other believers.

d. *An invitation can be a means of assurance to a person.* In later years, that person can look back to a decisive moment when he or she made a public decision for Christ. Some years ago, the great German theologian Helmut Thielicke attended one of our Crusades. He wrote me the most magnificent letter on how the invitation had affected him, and how I should never preach without giving one. And he used almost the same words that I am using now—the memory of that moment will always remind them of their vow to follow Christ, and of His promise of forgiveness.

e. *People may respond to the call for decision for various reasons.* I did a great deal of my early preaching on street corners, where I asked people to lift their hand, and after the closing prayer to see me personally.

Also, as all of us have experiences, there are constant one-to-one evangelistic encounters. Often, this is the most difficult of all—to ask for a decision from just one person. But it is extremely important that we have the boldness and courage if we are led by the Holy Spirit to do so, and if the circumstances permit.

A few minutes ago I said that the whole sermon should be directed toward the invitation. Everything we say in our sermon should, directly or indirectly, point toward the call for decision we will make. I believe it is biblical and appropriate to ask people to give an outward sign of the inward contract they have made with the Lord Jesus Christ.

I have often found it helpful to confront people with the call to decision throughout the sermon. By this I don't mean that I call them forward several times, but perhaps I will ask questions throughout the sermons and not just at the end—such as, "Have you ever really trusted Christ?" or, "Do you know that if you died right now you would go to heaven?"

Or perhaps I will make statements that make it clear that the Gospel demands decision, such as: "You can't remain neutral about Christ," or, "Let Christ come into your life right now and cleanse you from your sins and give you a new purpose for living." Throughout the sermon, therefore, I often try to make it clear that the Gospel demands decision involving intellect, emotion, but primarily the will. The whole sermon should reinforce that fact and point toward the invitation.

We may also want to speak—at least within limits—to people who need to respond to an invitation, not for first-time commitment but for recommitment, or assurance, or some other reason.

## 3.   *Method of the invitation*

There are a number of guidelines that I have learned about the call to decision which we extend at the conclusion of an evangelistic message that are very important. However, for the sake of time, I will only mention two.

*First*, make it clear what you are asking people *to believe.*

*Second*, make it clear what people *are to actually do*—and repeat it several times. Make it clear what they are to do in terms of coming forward, lifting their hand, going to a separate room (or whatever method is being used), or going home and making their commitment. We need to make it clear that we are inviting people to commit their lives to Christ as His disciples. And the cost is high. I've seen some invitations lower the cost of discipleship.

An important element might not be, strictly speaking, part of the invitation—although it should be closely related to it—and that is the words of *follow-up* you may speak to those who have responded. Often this can be important and is actually an invitation; because in it you outline the Gospel clearly and simply, perhaps lead them in a prayer of commitment, and explain to them what has happened to them and how they can grow spiritually.

If possible, those who respond also should talk individually with someone who can help them. For many years we have had a program of training counselors before a Crusade. Many people have told us it was the most important result of the Crusade—because a large number of soul-winners had been trained to bring people to Christ—not only during the Crusade, but for years to come. It is a great privilege to be used of God to point people to Jesus Christ and invite men and women to commit their lives to Him.

Part of the gift of an evangelist is the gift of giving the invitation with directness and yet sensitivity. But like any other gift which God may give us, it must be sharpened and used for His glory.

D. L. Moody never told people to go home and think about it and come back except once—and that was the night of the Chicago fire!

God bless you and make you even more effective as you call sinners "out of darkness into his marvelous light" (1 Peter 2:9).

# PREPARING AND DELIVERING AN EVANGELISTIC MESSAGE
*Robert E. Coleman*

Evangelistic preaching is the proclamation of the Gospel in the power of the Holy Spirit with the aim of making disciples for Christ. To be sure, all Christian preaching should expect a response in both faith and action, whether the sermon be a declaration of the facts of personal redemption or the teaching of some great moral truth. But in the more specialized sense, evangelistic preaching concerns the immediate message of salvation, a message that carries with it the imperative that all persons must repent and believe the Gospel. Such preaching is not necessarily any special type of sermon or homiletical method; rather, it is preaching distinguished by the call for commitment to the Son of God who loved us and gave Himself for us.

Preparing and delivering such a message is a holy task, and calls forth every resource of mind and spirit that God has given. Though the provisions for fulfilling the work are all of grace, this does not take away the responsibility of the preacher for observing basic rules of effective sermon building. With this in mind, the following nine principles appear to me most crucial.

1. *Pray it through*

The place to begin in sermon preparation is on our knees. Here, in renewal of our faith and our calling, totally submitted to the Lordship of Christ, we are in a position to receive strength and wisdom for the message. It may be that before we can get direction in what to tell others, we will have to hear what God has to say about correcting some deficiencies in our own lives, and confess the sin. Only when our vessel is clean are we fit for the Master's true use (2 Timothy 2:21).

With a heart in tune with the will of God, we can then project our thoughts to the persons to whom we will be speaking, trying to be sensitive to their needs. A message that hits home must meet people where they are, both in their interests and attitudes concerning the subject of the sermon, as well as in their feelings toward the preacher. By knowing the nature of the audience, understanding where they are coming from, the evangelist can make the appeal more direct and meaningful in their situation.

As the burden of the message and its structure takes form, it is prayed over and presented unto God as on offering of devotion. There is a sense in which it is preached to God before anyone else. Only after the sermon has His approval can the evangelist be confident in proclaiming it to the people.

The spirit of prayer continues on through delivery. It is this communication with heaven that makes the sermon "mighty through God to the pulling down of strong holds" (2 Corinthians 10:4). As Sidlow Baxter has put it, "Men may spurn our appeals, reject our message, oppose our arguments, despise our persons—but they are helpless against our prayers" (quoted by C.V. Thompson, *Master Secrets of Prayer*, p. 4). Here is evangelism in its most basic expression. To paraphrase the words of Dr. Lewis Sperry Chafer, "Winning souls is more a work of pleading for them than a service of pleading with them" (*True Evangelism*, 1919, p. 93).

2. *Lift up Jesus*

The evangelistic message itself, whatever its style, will center in Jesus Christ (1 Corinthians 1:23; 2 Corinthians 4:5; Acts 5:42), "the fullness of the Godhead bodily" (Colossians 2:9). He is the Evangel "the Good News" incarnate, "the Lamb of God which taketh away the sin of the world'' (John 1:29). In Him every redemptive truth begins and ends. "There is no other name under heaven given among men, whereby we must be saved'' (Acts 4:12). Unless people see Him, regardless of what else impresses them, they will not be drawn to God.

The Revelation reaches its climax at the blood-red hill of Calvary. There nearly 2,000 years ago Jesus bore our sins in His own body on the Cross, suffering in our stead, "the just for the unjust, that He might bring us to God'' (1 Peter 3:18). Though any interpretation of His sacrifice falls short of its full meaning, it is clear that Christ, by offering Himself, once and for all, made a perfect and complete atonement for the sins of the world.

Herein is the wonder of the Gospel. "God commendeth his love toward us, in that, while we were yet sinners, Christ died for us'' (Romans 5:8). Jesus paid it all. Nothing deserved! Nothing earned! In our complete helplessness, bankrupt of all natural goodness, He did for us what we could never do for ourselves.

His bodily resurrection and ascension into heaven brings the Cross forcibly to attention. For when one dies, who has the power to rise from the grave? In all honesty we must ask why He ever died in the first place. To this penetrating question, the evangelist declares: He died for you, and was raised for your salvation (Romans 4:24,25).

The whole message, then, turns on what is done with Jesus (Acts 17:30,31). Keenly aware of this, the evangelist must seek to bring into focus the person and work of the Savior. It matters little what the people think of the preacher; everything depends upon what they believe about Christ. That is why the measure of a sermon's power is the degree to which it exalts the Lord and makes the audience aware of His claims upon their lives. With this in mind, listening to the remarks of people after a preaching service is very interesting. If they talk more about the preacher than about Jesus, it may be that the sermon missed the mark.

### 3. *Use the Scripture*

Preaching that brings 'persons to the Savior answers to the spirit and letter of God-breathed Scripture. The word written in the Book discloses Christ the Living Word (John 20:31). It is the means by which the mind is illuminated (2 Timothy 3:16), faith is kindled (Romans 10:17), and the heart is recreated according to the purpose of God (1 Peter 1:23, 2 Peter 1:4; John 17:17). For this reason, the redemptive power of any sermon relates directly to the way one uses the immutable, inerrant, and life-changing Word of God.

This Book is the "Sword of the Spirit" in the preacher's hand (Ephesians 6:17). It gives authority to the message. Without its sure testimony, the sermon would be little more than a statement of human experience. Of course, the preacher must support the message by clear personal witness; but the ultimate authority for what is preached must be the written Word. Experience can be trusted only when it accords with the inspired Scriptures.

Thus the evangelist is commissioned simply to "preach the Word" (2 Timothy 4:2). As an ambassador of the King of heaven, he is not called to validate the message, nor to speculate or argue about conflicting opinions on the subject. God has spoken and the message imbued with this conviction is an inexorable declaration: "Thus saith the Lord!" Such preaching needs neither defense nor explanation. The Spirit of God who gave the Word will bear witness to its truthfulness (1 John 5:6; 2 Peter 1:21), and He will not let it return unto Him void (Isaiah 55:11).

This is exemplified in the preaching of Billy Graham. However, there was a time in his early ministry when this confidence was missing, and he had to duel with doubts about the Bible's integrity. The struggle came to a head one evening in 1949, when alone in the mountains of California, he knelt before the open Bible, and said: "Here and now, by faith, I accept the Bible as Thy Word. I take it all. I take it without reservations. Where there are things I cannot understand, I will reserve judgment until I receive more light. If this pleases Thee, give me authority as I proclaim Thy Word, and through that authority convict me of sin and turn sinners to their Savior" Billy Graham, "Biblical Authority in Evangelism," *Christianity Today*, October 15, 1956, p. 6).

Within weeks, the Los Angeles Crusade started. There his preaching began to manifest a new power, as he quit trying to prove the Scripture, and simply declared the truth. Over and over again, he heard himself saying, "The Bible says . . ." To use his words, "I felt as though I were merely a voice through which the Holy Spirit was speaking."

It was a new discovery for the young evangelist. He found that people were not especially interested in his ideas, nor were they drawn to moving oratory. They were hungry, "to hear what God had to say through His Holy Word."

This is a lesson every preacher must learn. And until it is reflected in our sermons, not much that we say is likely to generate faith in the hearts of hearers.

4.  *Dig out sin*

Under the refining light of the Word of God, the evangelist's message makes people face themselves before the Cross. The cloak of self-righteousness is pulled away (John 15:22), showing the deceitfulness of sin. The pretense of living independently from God is seen for what it is, the creature actually holding the will of the Creator with contempt, worshiping his own works as a false god (Romans 1:25). Its ultimate expression comes in the defiant rejection of Jesus Christ, the promised Messiah. "He came unto his own, and his own received him not" (John 1:11).

Such blasphemy cannot be ignored by a just God, since it is an affront to His holiness and justice. Inevitably, then, the profane must be separated from Him. Furthermore, His wrath upon iniquity cannot be annulled as long as the cause of evil remains. Since life is unending, all the spiritual consequences of sin continue on forever in hell.

Knowing, therefore, the terror of the Lord, the evangelist strikes at the heart of sin. Urging at one time the greatness of the rebel's guilt and at another the imminence of his doom, he seeks to awaken the human conscience. The awfulness of sin becomes vivid. Although all the diverse kinds of sin cannot be treated in one sermon, at least the basic issue of unbelief and disobedience can be disclosed, with perhaps a few specific applications to the local situation.

There should never be any confusion about whom the evangelist is addressing. It is not sin in theory but the sinner in practice that he is talking about. Indeed, it might well seem to the sinner that the preacher has been following him around all week, noting every wrong deed and thought. While, of course, considerations of propriety and good sense must be kept in mind, a sermon still must get under a person's skin and make him squirm under conviction of sin. A message that does not deal with this cause of all human woe, individually and collectively, is irrelevant to human need. Though the tragedy of rebellion and its result may be bad news, still the Gospel shines through, for God judges that He might save. One thing is certain: if people do not recognize their problem, they will not want the remedy.

5.  *Keep to the point*

The evangelistic sermon is based on a convincing course of reason. Notwithstanding the fad of irrational thinking among some existentialist ministers, consistency is still a mark of truth, and a Gospel sermon should reflect this character.

For this to happen, the objective of the message must be perfectly clear. The preacher should ask himself, "What is it that I want to get across?" Then he should try to visualize the response expected. Unless the evangelist knows what he is aiming for, almost certainly no one else will catch on. As an exercise, it may be helpful to write out the objective in a sentence, then see if that is what you want to accomplish. With the goal in mind, then the evangelist can plan how to get there.

Whatever the structure of the message, a good, balanced outline will go a long way in keeping it on course. The points should flow effortlessly out of the passage. Moreover, they should be arranged in such a way that each builds upon the other, creating a progression of thought leading up to the appeal for decision. When this is done well, the invitation seems as natural as it is necessary.

Brevity is important. The rule is to include nothing in the sermon that can be excluded. Wise counsel was given by John Wesley when he told his preachers: "Take care not to ramble, but keep to the text, and make out what you take in hand" (*Methodist Discipline*, 1784, p. 19).

Illustrations and human interest stories can be used as needed to clarify or to make more impressive an idea. Yet one should keep in mind that the strength of the sermon does not rest in the illustrative material. People like stories, and interest in the sermon must be sustained; but more important is the logic of the truth presented.

## 6.  *Make it simple*

A well-prepared sermon will be uncomplicated in its basic organization and language (2 Corinthians 11:3). Truth when reduced to its highest expression is always simple. Anybody can make the Gospel difficult to comprehend, but the person of wisdom says it so that a child can understand. Some preachers feign intellectual superiority by sermonizing in high-sounding philosophic terms, as if the message needed to be sophisticated in order to appeal to the well-educated. That some clerics labor under this illusion may partially explain why so many people, including university students, scorn the church. Whenever a theological discourse gets so complicated that only a college man can understand it, then something is wrong, either with the theology or with its presentation.

The admonition is to speak "in simplicity and godly sincerity, not with fleshly wisdom, but by the grace of God" (2 Corinthians 1:12). Paul, probably the most astute theologian of the church, expressed the ideal when he wrote: "My speech and my preaching were not with enticing words of man's wisdom, but in demonstration of the Spirit and of power; that your faith should not stand in the wisdom of men but in the power of God" (1 Corinthians 2:4,5).

Plain language and familiar terms will help accomplish this. Not that everything in the message can be given in an easy explanation; much that is revealed by God remains a mystery, such as the nature of the Trinity, the Incarnation, or the miraculous work of the Holy Spirit. But when the Gospel of salvation is stated plainly as a fact, it makes sense to the honest soul seeking after God.

This is what counts. The evangelist does not need to answer all the curious problems of theology, but he must have an unequivocal answer to the fundamental question of perishing men and women: what must I do to be saved? One way to practice this counsel is to preach the sermon first to some ordinary wayfarers on a street corner. If they can understand it, then you can be reasonably sure that persons settled in a comfortable pew will get the point.

## 7.  *Plead for souls*

The evangelist is not content merely to state the Gospel; he expects people to be changed by it. The sermon thus becomes a plea in the name of Christ that persons be "reconciled to God" (2 Corinthians 5:20). A living, personal, certain experience of saving grace is the aim of the message. Definitions of that experience are not nearly so important as its reality. Without quibbling over terms, the preacher directs the sinner to the mercy seat, where by faith redemption can be found in the precious blood of the Lamb.

This keeps the sermon from becoming merely a pious statement of orthodoxy. To be sure, the message must be unapologetically sound in doctrine. But its orthodoxy must be clothed with the brokenness of a preacher who knows that except for the grace of God he would be as those who have no hope. Humbled by this knowledge, the evangelist cannot be judgmental and brazen in pronouncements against others. Rather he enters into their sorrows with compassion wrung from his own deep experience with God, and the sermon reflects this in a tenderness that the hearer is quick to recognize.

There is a vicariousness about preaching, expressing itself supremely in the yearning that all people might come and drink freely from the same fountain of living water that has satisfied the evangelist's own soul. This passion for persons of every race and culture to partake of divine grace, and experience for themselves a new life in Christ, is what makes an evangelistic sermon consistent with its mission.

A few years after the death of the famous preacher, Robert Murray McCheyne, a young minister visited his church to discover, as he explained, the secret of the man's amazing influence. The beadle (sexton), who had served under Mr. McCheyne, took the youthful inquirer into the vestry, and asked him to sit in the chair used by the young preacher.

"Now put your elbows on the table," he said,

"Now put your face in your hands." The visitor obeyed.

"Now let the tears flow! That was the way Mr. McCheyne used to do!"

The man then led the minister to the pulpit and gave him a fresh series of instructions.

"Put your elbows down on the pulpit!" He put his elbows down.

"Now put your face in your hands!" He did as he was told.

"Now let the tears flow! That was the way Mr. McCheyne used to do!" (F.W. Boreham, *A Late Lark Singing*, 1945, p. 66).

Yes, that is the way to do it. Not that physical tears must fall, but that the compassion which they represent should characterize every preacher feeling the weight of lost souls, knowing that their destiny may hang upon his sermon.

8. *Call for a verdict*

The decision is what makes the difference. If the will is not moved to action, there can be no salvation (Romans 10:13). The truth of the message, thus, is saved from degenerating into mere rationalism on the one hand and mere emotionalism on the other by linking it with a personal response. To stir people to great aspirations without also giving them something that they can do about it leaves them worse off than they were before. They will likely become either more confused in their thinking, or more indifferent in their will. Consequently, once the Gospel is made clear, the evangelist must call to account each person who hears the message. So far as he knows, this may be their last opportunity to respond.

With this burden, the evangelist cries out almost with a sense of desperation. Tremendous issues are at stake. Immortal souls are perishing in sin. Judgment is certain. God offers mercy through the blood of His Son. All must repent and believe the Gospel. Heaven and Hell are in the balance. Time is running out. "Behold, now is the day of salvation'' (2 Corinthians 6:2).

Preaching that is dilatory about this fact lacks evangelistic relevance. The Gospel does not permit people the luxury of indecision. In the presence of the crucified and living King of kings, one cannot be neutral. To deliberately ignore Christ is to live in a state of blasphemy, refusing forgiveness; it is to close the door to the only way of life, and life abundant.

To some persons, this assertion seems arrogant. A man once said to Dr. R. A. Torrey, ''I'm not a Christian, but I am moral and upright. I would like to know what you have against me.'' Torrey looked the man in the eye, and replied: ''I charge you, sir, with treason against heaven's King'' (*Great Gospel Sermons*, I, p. 19 & 9, p. 138).

That is the issue which must be faced. It is not finally our Gospel, but His. And because Jesus Christ is Lord, before Him every knee must bow.

In this obeisance, therefore, the evangelist seeks to ''persuade men'' (2 Corinthians 5:11). ''Whosoever will'' may come (Revelation 22:17). He cannot make the decision for anyone, but as God leads, he is responsible for doing what he can to make the issues clear. Eternal destinies are at stake.

## 9.   *Depend on the Holy Spirit*

This final ingredient must be understood about evangelistic preaching, apart from which everything said thus far would be as a sounding brass and tinkling cymbal. The Spirit of God must have control. Throughout the sermon presentation, delivery, and invitation, He is the divine enabler. Preaching the Gospel, as any Christian work, is not contrived by human ingenuity. All we can do is to make ourselves available for the Spirit to use. Failure to appreciate this truth, I suspect, is the reason so many sermons fall flat.

The third Person of the Trinity effects in and through us what Christ has done for us. It is the Spirit who gives life; the flesh profits nothing (John 6:63). He initiates and guides prayer. He lifts up the Son, thereby drawing persons to the Father. He makes the inspired Scripture come alive. He convicts of sin, of righteousness, and of judgment. He guides the obedient servant into truth, making the message clear to seeking hearts. He recreates and sanctifies through the Word. And He extends the call for weary and heavy laden souls to come to Jesus. From beginning to end, the whole enterprise of evangelism is in the authority and demonstration of God's Spirit.

We can understand, then, why the glorified Savior told His disciples to tarry until they be filled with His Spirit (Luke 24:49; Acts 1:4,5,8). How else could they fulfill their mission? The Word and work of their Lord had to become a burning compulsion within them. The superhuman ministry to which they were called required supernatural help—an enduement of power from on high.

This is nowhere more necessary than with Gospel preachers. Any sermon that circumvents this provision will be as lifeless as it is barren. So let us trust Him. As God has called us into His harvest, He will provide what is needed to do the work. The secret of evangelism, finally, is to let the Holy Spirit have His way.

This then is the task of preparing and delivering an evangelistic message: Pray the sermon through; lift up Jesus and His saving work; use the authority of Scripture; come to grips with sin; keep the logic of the message clear; make the presentation simple; plead with compassion for persons to experience the Savior; call for a decision; and wait upon the Holy Spirit of God. Such preaching will shake the gates of hell, and make the courts of Heaven reverberate with shouts of glory.

One January day in 1930, Walter Vivian of CBS was checking the equipment which had been installed to carry the message of King George V to the British navy around the world. In a last-minute inspection, Vivian discovered a break in the wires. There was no time for it to be repaired. So grasping the two segments of the wire— each with a hand—he became the conductor through which 250 volts of electricity passed. He came out of the experience with burned hands, but the King's message was transmitted to the ends of the earth (Lloyd Merle Perry, ''Preaching for Decision,'' *Evangelism on the Cutting Edge*, (ed. Robert Coleman), 1986, p. 124). So may it be with us in transmitting the message of the King of Heaven. Whatever it takes, wherever we may be placed in His service, let us become a conductor through which the Spirit of God can bring the Good News of Jesus Christ to every creature.

# EXTENDING THE EVANGELISTIC INVITATION
*Ralph Bell*

An English theological student was sent by a professor to hear a noted preacher. He came back with the sophisticated disgust that some young seminarians possess and said, "Why, that man did not do anything but say, 'Come to Jesus.'" "And did they come?" his professor gently asked. "Well, yes they did," the student grudgingly replied. "I want you to go back," said the professor, "and listen to that man preach again and again, until you can say, 'Come to Jesus,' as he did, and people come."

It is our prayer that those of us who are here will go back to our churches, our ministries, our evangelism, to the corner of the vineyard where God has called us, having listened to Peter, Paul, Joshua, and Jesus again and again, until we can so speak of Christ from the Scriptures in such a way that when we say, "Come to Jesus," men will respond.

All of us here may not have all the gifts that would make us great preachers, but we can all learn how to give a strong invitation. For it is at the moment of invitation that most of us have felt a great sense of inadequacy. Keep in mind also, that no one person knows it all when dealing with this subject. Perhaps that explains the devastating dearth of printed material in this area. Nevertheless, let us learn from one another, from those who have written something about it, from our personal experiences, and from our discussions with one another later on in the seminar hour.

Let us begin by focusing our attention on these main thoughts: *the powerful mandate* that is given to us; some *practical methods* that can be used; several *popular misunderstandings* that might confront some of us; and, finally, the *prayerful manner* that ought to be involved when extending a good invitation. Later, we will have a time for your input, questions, and helpful discussion.

First then, from the Scriptures, the Old Testament and the New, we consider the powerful mandate that is given to us to extend an invitation.

## 1. *The powerful mandate*

a. *The Old Testament.* The giving of an invitation is not new. Joshua and Jeremiah did it. Peter and Paul, John and Jesus did it. In the Old Testament in Genesis 3:9, you will remember, God called Adam saying, "Adam, where art thou?" God was calling Adam to Himself.

When Moses came down from Mt. Sinai, he discovered the people giving themselves over to idolatry and worshipping the golden calf. Exodus 32:26 declares that he thundered, "Who is on the Lord's side? Let him come to me." That was a clear call to his people to make a public decision and to take a public stand for the Lord.

After Moses' death, when Joshua was commanded to lead the nation of Israel, the people had again lapsed into idolatry. You will recall that it was toward the end of Joshua's life. He therefore called all the tribes together in 24:15 and said, "Choose this day whom you will serve: whether the gods which your fathers served that were on the side of the flood, or the gods of the Amorites in whose land you dwell: but as for me and my house, we will serve the Lord." That, too, was a call for public commitment of loyalty to Jehovah.

Centuries later, idolatry again was the issue. This time, Elijah is the man of the hour. Standing on Mt. Carmel, he asked the question, and in doing so, called for a decision. "How long halt ye between two opinions? If the Lord be God, follow him; but if Baal, then follow him" (1 Kings 18:21).

In Ezra 10:5, this great scribe and man of God called upon his contemporaries to swear publicly that they would carry out the principles of his reforms.

Nehemiah's book also indicates that the Jewish leaders were called on to sign on the dotted line, a covenant of loyalty to the Lord after their revival (Nehemiah 9:38).

   b.   *New Testament.* Notice the termination of Peter's sermon on the day of Pentecost. It called for an immediate and definite response. Acts 2:38 reads, "And Peter said to them, Repent and be baptized every one of you in the name of Jesus Christ for the forgiveness of your sins; and you shall receive the gift of the Holy Spirit." Chapter 2:40 reads, "And with many other words did he testify and exhort saying, Save yourselves from this untoward (crooked) generation." The word "exhort" is *parakeleõ*, and Thayer suggests that it means, "to call to oneself." Thus, can you see Simon Peter calling to himself those who were willing to obey his invitation to repent? It is clearly a New Testament basis for a public invitation, and we know from the text that 3,000 responded that day.

   In addition, numerous New Testament texts support the invitation. I will briefly mention a few for your further study. Our Lord invited people to follow (Matthew 4:19), and to come to Him (Matthew 11:28,29). Philip encountered the Ethiopian eunuch and preached to him Jesus, leading to his conversion (Acts 8:26-39).

   Paul the Apostle sets forth our salvation, proclamation, and invitation, saying, "We beg you on behalf of Christ, be reconciled to God" (2 Corinthians 5:18-20). Again, "Knowing the terror of the Lord, we persuade men" (2 Corinthians 5:11). And, John the beloved sets forth the crystal clear invitation of the Holy Spirit for the spiritually thirsty to come and drink of the water of life (Revelation 22:17).

   Thus we have ample evidence for a powerful mandate to give an invitation. The biblical basis is clear and concise in both the Old and New Testaments.

   Since we are now on a firm foundation, let us move on to some practical methods that can be employed in extending an invitation.

2.   *Practical methods*

   a.   *The public invitation.* This is the kind of invitation you see take place in most Billy Graham Crusades and in many churches. The advantage of this kind of invitation is that it is clear-cut and decisive when done properly. All through the message, it is assumed that you have been preaching for a verdict. If that is true, then you are building toward this moment of decision. The invitation is not something that you tack on to the end of the message as a kind of afterthought. Rather, it should be explained ahead of time or during your message. Many times, in my introductory remarks to the people, I lay the ground work for the invitation. I might say something like this: "We have come to your city, (church or village) for the purpose of proclaiming the Gospel and extending an invitation to you to invite Christ into your life. At the conclusion of the service, I am going to invite you to leave your place and come and stand before this pulpit (platform, etc.) as an indication of your decision to follow Christ from this moment on." One of the dangers of a public invitation, especially in a local church, is that the pastor or evangelist does not make clear the distinction between those who come forward as inquirers, and those who come to join the church. There is a desperate need for more than a handshake with the minister and the filling out of a card. Thus, individual counseling must be combined with the invitation.

   I have found it helpful to speak of the symbolism involved in the invitation. For example, I often begin by saying, "Why do I ask you to come publicly? Because Jesus said, 'If you will confess me before men, I will confess you before my Father.' The symbolism comes in at this point: coming forward can be compared to a soldier who salutes a flag. That outward physical sign of saluting the flag indicates in the soldier's heart that he is saying, 'I am loyal to my country.' Or when two business-men shake hands on a deal, that outward physical act of shaking hands is an indication that they are saying in their hearts, 'I am going to keep my part of the bargain.' So when you walk down to the front in a physical way with your feet, you are saying with your heart, 'I am coming to Jesus.' In other words, your action becomes an out-ward sign of an inward reality." You might also like to explain it as a means of *obey-ing Christ's commands to confess Him*. That will help to make the decision definite and clear-cut.

b. Inquiry room. A second type of invitation which is advantageous is to invite people to come to an inquiry room. Asahel Nettleton, a Congregational evangelist, employed a similar method. In his day, it was called the "anxious room."

Charles Finney spoke rather of anxious benches or seats where people who were spiritually troubled could be helped.

Dwight Moody is really the founder of the inquiry room. And this probably rep-resents the most effective combination of public response and private counsel of any invitation in the history of mass evangelism.

Mr. Graham's invitation is similar, but because of the large stadiums and huge response, counseling must be done on the grass where privacy is not afforded.

The inquiry room allows well-trained counselors to deal with particular problems without haste and in privacy. It gives time for people to think and shy folks to re-spond, a distinct advantage indeed.

c. *Invitation to sign a card*. Sometimes cards are placed in the back of pews. A clear statement might be printed on it indicating a desire to accept Christ. The pastor or evangelist then follows up these people with a personal call at their home.

Or it could be utilized in other ways. Some time ago, I was at a church in a cer-tain city speaking at a series of banquets. One was a youth banquet, two others were men and women's banquets. In each case, the believers were required to bring an unbeliever. Cards were placed at each table with a clear statement about accepting Christ or knowing more about Him. These cards were then followed up by the believ-ers who had invited them.

d. *The raising of a hand*. This kind of invitation was popular in years gone by. When employed with tact and discretion, it can be of real spiritual benefit to those who are seeking. Charles Fuller used it with great success, tact, and power. It assists the pastor or evangelist in knowing who is indicating their desire for help and need for further counseling. This kind of invitation is used often in prisons, where men some-times are not allowed to be called forward.

e. *The invitation to remain behind*. This type of invitation can take on many forms. An opportunity is given to those who are interested to remain behind. With this invitation, it is good to state what you are going to do, how long the meeting will last, and give assurance that they will not be embarrassed in any way.

One Lutheran pastor, at the conclusion of his message, had his deacons explain the various types of decisions the Holy Spirit leads men to make—both Christians and non-Christians. Then an invitation is given to anyone to come to the altar and pray and meet God or to remain behind. Hundreds of Lutheran churches are doing this and many are finding Christ while others are rededicating themselves to Him (Conrad Thompson, Lutheran Secretary of Evangelism).

Remember, the invitation is not cut-and-dried. No one method fits every situa-tion. A variety of methods can be used. Suppose the two blind men that Jesus healed met each other. One asks the other, "How did it happen to you?" He replies, "All Jesus said was, 'Be healed.'" The first man who was blind says, "You mean He didn't put mud on your eyes? Man, you are still blind—you are not healed at all."

You see, our trust is not in *methods*, but in the *Lord.*

3. *Popular misunderstandings*

a. *Theological.* There have been some preachers, such as the late Dr. Donald Grey Barnhouse and Dr. Martyn Lloyd-Jones, who refused to give any kind of public invitation.

Their objection was not to a spiritual decision, of course, but to the conflict they felt with the whole question of God's sovereignty and man's responsibility.

Leighton Ford in his book, *The Christian Persuader*, tells the story of a young seminarian who came to the Scottish preacher, John McNeill. The young man was deeply concerned that in preaching he might offer free grace to some who were not of the elect.

Mr. McNeill, with a twinkle in his eye, said to the student, *"Laddie, don't be worried. If you should get the wrong man saved, the Lord will forgive you."* McNeill's good humor may be of more help than all the theological arguing that has divided Calvinists and Arminians.

But according to J.I. Packer, there is a real incompatibility between these two doctrines. We cannot solve it. We must learn to live with it. Matthew 11:27,28, holds the two truths together. Paul in Romans 9:1-4 speaks of God's election but still has a strong burden and yearning for men.

Thus, if any here feel that they cannot give an invitation for a sinner to come to Christ because of man's inability, remember that Jesus invited a man whose hand was paralyzed to do what he could not do: He said, "Stretch out your hand" (Matthew 12:13).

Jesus commanded Lazarus to do what he could not do when He said, *"Lazarus, come forth"* (John 11:43).

To me, only the sovereignty of God is sufficient ground for preaching to a verdict. Otherwise, evangelism is a hopeless task. We are told that the natural man cannot receive the things of the Spirit of God because they are spiritually discerned (1 Corinthians 2:14), and that men are dead in trespasses and sins (Ephesians 2:1). Well, then how can a dead man live and a blind man see? With God, all things are possible.

In addition, confidence in God's sovereignty guards us from self-dependence. So many of us are faced with this *success status idea*—the pressure to produce results. This is heavy pressure on the evangelist and the pastor. If we play the game, then it means we have to have better programs, bigger attendance, etc. Soon we are depending on tricks, techniques, manipulation—which lead to abortive decisions.

You see, God holds us responsible for *faithful evangelism, not for success.* So in your ministry and especially in your invitation—*never coerce.* Jesus never did.

Remember the story of the rich young ruler in Luke 18:18-24. Here was a retreating figure filled with unutterable grief. But Jesus did not run after him. He did not twist his arm or lower His demands. Nor did He increase the pressure. So when you and I invite men to Christ, stay close to the biblical pattern. Depend much on the sovereignty of God.

b. *Emotional issue.* Many people react against pastors and evangelists who give an invitation without tact, taste, or dignity and who manipulate people emotionally. There is a difference, however, between emotionalism and emotion. Emotionalism is emotion isolated. It is emotion for emotion's sake. You can be overzealous and you can be overcautious.

Dr. Mackay says, "Something is wrong when emotion becomes legitimate in everything but religion." There is a place for emotion in preaching the Gospel.

Yet, we must recognize the dangers involved in a decision that is primarily emotional in character. Two things can happen: (1) The person involved attempts to reproduce the emotional state and this can lead to an unbalanced Christian life. (2) The person might feel betrayed and react against any religious experience at all.

How do we avoid this very real peril? One way might be to *speak to the whole man, the intellect, the conscience, and the will*. We are to "love the Lord with all your heart, soul, mind and strength" (Mark 12:30). The pastor and the evangelist must appeal to the intellect. Put a strong emphasis on teaching in your evangelistic ministry. "Obey the truth" is how Paul describes the response to the Gospel.

In Acts 9:29 . . . he disputed
In Acts 17:2 . . . he reasoned
In Acts 18:4 . . . he persuaded
In Acts 18:11 . . . he taught

The pastor and the evangelist must *appeal to the conscience*. Second Corinthians 4:2 declares, "Commending ourselves to every man's conscience." Through the avenue of the intellect, conscience, and emotion, we seek to reach the citadel where a man in his total personality says "yes" to the yes of God.

Now the invitation is not only theologically correct—it is emotionally sound. People need an opportunity for expression. One psychiatrist has said, "What many people need today is an experience at an old-fashioned Methodists' mourners' bench." In other words, people need the experience of repentance. When a man makes a decision or responds to the invitation, it is like driving a nail through a board. Professor William James says, "When once the judgment is decided, let a man commit himself; let him lay on himself the necessity of doing more, let him lay on himself the necessity of doing all. Let him take a public pledge if the case allows. Let him envelop his resolution with all the aids possible" (quoted by Leighton Ford, *The Christian Persuader*, 1966, p. 124).

Always be aware of the fact that some people will respond to supercharged atmospheres, to pathetic stories. Therefore, you must plan your evangelistic presentation and invitation so that the *Truth of the Word of God* stands central and supreme and is the focus of attention. *Warn people* that the Christian life does not move on *moods and thrills*, but by *faith and obedience*.

There will be some neurotic and disturbed people who will respond. These will need sensitive and expert counseling. But the bottom line is this: recognize the problems, preach the Word; and you will discover that the blessings of evangelism, and the invitation that confronts men to decide for Christ, far outweigh the perils.

Well, we have looked at the mandate and reviewed the methods. We have talked about the popular misunderstandings. Now, let us consider the prayerful manner in which the invitation ought to be extended.

4. *The prayerful manner*

a. *Spiritual preparation*. Eternal issues are involved whenever the Gospel is presented. The responsibility is an awesome one. Many lives are lonely, broken, fragmented and guilt-ridden. Thus, the mind of the person extending the invitation should be spiritually prepared. Dr. W.E. Sangster says that is the basic thing at the last. Let a man be sure of that, and keep his certitude by obedience, and he will have the answer to all the doubts which dog the steps of a preacher regarding his vocation.

Commissioned of God to teach the Word, a herald of the great King, a witness of the eternal—could any work be more high and holy? To this supreme task God sent His only begotten Son. In all the frustration and confusion of the times, is it possible to imagine a work comparable in importance with that of proclaiming the will of God to wayward men?

Only a divine commission can justify it. Lacking that, it is a gross impertinence. No humble man would take upon himself the task of talking to others in a public place about the most intimate things of the soul. With that kind of responsibility, we need to be bathed in prayer long before we ever get to the invitation . . . Amen?

b. *Be kind and loving.* Don't embarrass people. The Holy Spirit is always a gentleman—and we must also be prepared to risk embarrassing failure. Even if no one responds, don't get angry in your spirit. Continue to be kind and loving. It is still good to have given the invitation even if you have no response, because it emphasizes the decisiveness involved in following Christ.

Some time ago, I was preaching in a city called Alice Springs in Northern Australia, among the Aborigine people. It was extremely hot that day and we were inside under a corrugated tin roof. Suddenly it began to rain. The noise from the rain falling on the tin roof became louder and louder. I was not sure if anyone could hear what I was saying. I moved into the invitation, but on one moved. Then from the very back, and old mangy mutt (skinny dog), slowly walked down the aisle and sat down right in front of the pulpit and began to scratch himself. That was my only convert that day.

c. *Be clear.* Tell people exactly what you want them to do. If you want them to make a public open decision, tell them that. Do not try to be profound, professional, and polished. Just be clear, simple, and concise.

d. *Be honest.* If you say you are going to sing one more verse of a hymn, then do not continue with two or three more. Deception must by all means be avoided.

I feel there is danger in asking people to go through several steps. For example: "Raise your hand . . . then stand up . . . now come forward." Some people would raise their hands but would have no intention of going forward. They might feel that they have been tricked or betrayed. It is better to explain clearly and ask people to take just one step.

Tell them what will happen when they come. For example: "I want to talk to you, answer any questions you might have. A counselor will be coming to show you the way. I want to give you some literature that will help explain the decision you are making. If you have come with friends, they will wait for you. Then we will have a prayer together." Be honest.

e. *Be patient.* Do not try to rush people. Give them plenty of time to think and the Spirit to work. He is the great communicator. Let Him do His work.

Perhaps you may want to take time between verses to express some of their questions, hesitations, fears, and longings of those who are deciding. Give brief answers to their questions.

f. *Be authoritative.* There is no reason for apology in the extending of the invitation. You are inviting people to accept a quality of life they can never find anywhere else.

Watch Mr. Graham as he gives the invitation. He has all the authority of heaven behind him. *"God commands all men everywhere to repent"* . . . and if we are preaching His Word, in His Name, then we have that same authority.

Lack of authority is one of our worst failures in giving an invitation. Do not be wishy-washy. Do not say, "If there is anyone here who might want to come, you could come, or you could wait and see me afterward."

Rather, let it be, *"God is calling. Come now. Don't delay."* Give the invitation with expectancy. "According to your faith, be it unto you," Jesus said. If you do not believe anything is going to happen, nothing will.

One author says, "Set your invitation on fire and people will come and watch it burn." I do not know exactly what that means, but I do know that with authority and without apology, the invitation should be given.

g. *Sense of urgency.* It may be the last time you will preach or have the opportunity to give an invitation, and it might be the last time someone will hear the message. Remember the Scriptures, "Knowing the terror of the Lord, we persuade men."

People should not be encouraged to leave the service without being brought face to face with their responsibility of responding to Christ.

The classic story is told of D.L. Moody who gave his hearers the opportunity of leaving the service to meditate on the question, "What will you do with Jesus?"

Sankey, Mr. Moody's song leader, came to sing the closing hymn:

"Today the Savior calls
For refuge, now draw nigh
The storm of justice falls
And death is nigh."

The next morning, much of the city of Chicago lay in ashes, for it was that fateful Sunday of October 8, 1871. Mrs. O'Leary's cow had kicked over the lantern and the great Chicago fire began. To his dying day, Moody regretted that he had told the people to wait. He said this: "I have never dared to give an audience a week to think of their salvation since. If they were lost, they might rise up in judgment against me. I have never seen that congregation since. I will never meet those people until I meet them in another world. But I want to tell of one lesson I learned that night which I have never forgotten; and that is, when I preach, to press Christ upon the people then and there, and try to bring them to a decision on the spot. I would rather that my right hand be cut off than to give an audience a week now to decide what to do with Jesus" (Clarence E. MacCartney, *The Greatest Questions of the Bible and Life*, 1948).

God, bless you, my brothers and sisters, as you preach the Word boldly and graciously, and invite people to the Savior.

# DEVELOPING A SERMON DIRECTLY FROM SCRIPTURE
## Robert P. Evans

1. *Prepartion of the messenger*
    a. *Prayer*—Confession of personal sin, intercession for listeners, prayer about message. Choice of the *right* one will bring peace. You will know when you find it.
    b. *Scripture*—Regular daily Bible study will suggest many evangelistic outlines.
    c. *Observation*—Study of people and their reactions; study of events and their significance.
    d. *Reading*—Read and study evangelistic sermons, books on evangelism.
    e. *Anointing*—Only the Holy Spirit can raise the dead. Only Spirit-filled evangelists can bear fruit.

2. *Preparation of the message*
    a. *Unity*—Must hang together, have total meaning and impact.
    b. *Order*—Must progress *logically* from one point to another, so listeners can easily follow.
    c. *Movement*—Must develop *rapidly*, without devoting too much time to any one point.
    d. *Content*—Must contain the following four elements:
    (i)   *Sin and judgment*, eternal punishment
    (ii)  *Hope* through the redemptive work of Christ
    (iii) *Belief* and the assurance of eternal life
    (iv)  *Urgency* to act now while there is time
    e. *Structure*—*Easiest* method is to retell a Bible story based on a single short passage, using specific points easily remembered. (Used by Moody, Sunday, Graham, Palau, etc.)
    *Hardest* method is to refer to many verses throughout the Bible (difficult for listeners to follow)
    No one structure to follow
    f. *Style*—Many styles used, but we must:
    —Be sincere, logical, clear, persuasive, compassionate.
    —Most evangelists move around freely, use some gestures.
    —Style is a personal thing, an expression of individual personality.
    g. *Language*—Avoid academic expressions. Use the language of the man-on-the-street. Some say, "Preach to the 12-year-old level." Always choose short, expressive words, brief sentences.
    h. *Illustrations*—Almost all evangelists use vivid ones. The best are from real life or events. Jesus illustrated from farming, animals, the weather, current events, family life, etc.
    i. *Humor*—Do not use if not natural to you. Use sparingly, especially at start for audience contact.
    j. *Beginning and ending*—Special attention should be paid to these, with careful preparation. Don't be hesitant, apologetic, but "start running," not walking.

3. *Preparation of the meeting*
    a. *Prayer*—Evangelist should try to make sure there is special prayer for conversions if he has any control over meeting. Results may be proportionate to burden and intercession of local believers.

   b.   *Place*—If evangelist is in charge, he should influence choice of central, attractive location with adequate features.

   c.   *Publicity*—Two basic kinds: invitations by believers, paid-for publicity. If possible, use both.

   d.   *Sound and lights*—Good control is essential.

   e.   *Music*—Is it fitting? Will it be dominant or subordinate to the message? Try to influence this important feature.

   f.   *Counselors*—If possible have some help after invitation, making sure they are trained properly and seated conveniently. Brief them on what you expect of them.

   g.   *Literature*—Have Bibles, Testaments, tracts, and booklets available, with people to distribute or sell.

   h.   *Follow-up*—In a single meeting, or a series of meetings, it is wise to have individuals and churches ready to do follow-up.

**4.   *Preparation of the invitation***

   —Evangelistic preaching pushes for a verdict—maybe a public one, maybe not—but always a response.

   —In one sense, the whole message is an invitation.

   —Types of invitation

   a.   *Unspoken*—Under certain circumstances one does not feel led to give a public call for response, or is forbidden to do so. But the "come unto me" of Christ can still be powerfully present (but constant recourse to this can be a cop-out).

   b.   *Show of hands* (with heads bowed)—*Advantage*: Leads listener to act physically to demonstrate his inner desire to believe. *Disadvantage*: Not open or public in full sense, is semi-secret. Sometimes difficult to get further action to bring seeker in contact with counselor.

   c.   *Come forward*—*Advantage*: completely public, with physical action tending to coincide with spiritual decision. Easy to connect seeker with counselor. *Disadvantage*: difficult to do in some cultures (Note: seekers can be prayed with as a group, dealt with standing or kneeling, taken to another room, finally instructed from pulpit.)

   d.   *Tarrying*—Request everyone to leave front area, and seekers to be seated in first rows. *Advantage*: Instruction and prayer easy from pulpit, or with individual counselors right there or in another room. *Disadvantage*: Sometimes public does not cooperate, is noisy, does not leave front rows free, interrupts proceedings.

   —Are public invitations biblical? *Billy Graham*: "Everyone whom Jesus Christ called to follow Him, He called publicly." He often asked people if they believed, and expected a response.

   —No message or communication is complete until it is understood and acknowledged by the hearer. Something must be done with God's offer of eternal life as a free gift. Will the sinner accept it—yes or no?

   —The lostness of man places him in great jeopardy. If he dies without Christ, he is eternally lost. Often the question, "Will you accept Christ now?" will trigger a "yes."

   —Psychologist *William James*: "The performance of a physical act, which is under direct control of the will, makes a mental decision easier." Example: I do not want to vacuum the floor, but if I can force myself to get the cleaner out and plug it in, I will probably consent to vacuum the floor.

# TRENDS IN THEOLOGY: EVANGELISTS BEWARE!

*Arthur P. Johnston*

Kingdom theology is a recent development of the last half of this century. It is a theological phenomenon that developed in non-evangelical circles during the last thirty years and has come to prominence in the last twenty years. The fullest expression of Kingdom theology was developed by the World Council of Churches at its 1980 Melbourne meeting of the Committee of World Mission and World Evangelism. This theology has an unwritten foundation in a universalism which sees all people redeemed by Christ's birth or death or the love of God in eternity. Kingdom theology is a view that the Kingdom arrived with the incarnation of Christ the King and, for many, was initiated at Pentecost. The focus is upon the continuity of the theocratic kingdom of the Old Testament as transferred first to the Apostles and to the Church as the "Community of the King." Its emphasis is upon the presence of the Kingdom *upon the earth* (D. T. Niles) now. It understands the Gospel as practical changing of society by the Church.

The Church is given for the present transformation of the world. The Church is not an end in itself. While some expressions of Kingdom theology are more alien to the Bible than others, in general, it has a low view of the inspiration of Scripture and bases its interpretation of Scripture upon higher-critical methods which undermine the authority view of the Bible.

Kingdom theology may take many forms and represent many shades in evangelical beliefs. Many good, biblical evangelicals are caught up in some aspects of it, and other non-evangelicals follow it to the extremes of liberation theology. In this brief study, five elements common to most "kingdom theologies" are identified and will be considered. They are: (1) The world is under God's control. (2) God is renewing and changing the world in this present age. (3) The Church is a means to establish social and economic justice. (4) Justice is part of the Good News. (5) The Gospel is authenticated by churches visibly united to achieve justice.

Because evangelicals can agree with some of these elements on the *surface*, some evangelicals have been led to accept "Kingdom theology." But while there is truth to some of these elements, when they are interpreted by "Kingdom" theologians and integrated into systems of "Kingdom theology," they may become dangerously misleading and often become instruments for the suppression of true, biblical evangelism there. These, then, are the five major elements and a consideration of each.

*The world is under God's control.* Kingdom theology is based upon the premise that the world now is God's and that He is working in it. This is true inasmuch as God *is* working in the world by His Spirit to gather a people out of this world system to His spiritual body, the Church, and its visible body, the local church. God's Spirit certainly works to restrain humans in the full accomplishment of their evil. God is also working providentially in the world toward the accomplishment of His eternal purposes. But Kingdom theology is erroneous in that Satan, the prince of this world, is either ignored or declared to be a symbol of the evil structures in society. He is considered either as a personality rendered helpless at the resurrection, or as a symbol of the evil economic-political structures of an unjust society.

*God is now renewing and changing the world in this present age.* Kingdom theology proposes that God is renewing and changing the world in this present age. And it is true that the Gospel changes the lives of those who are born again and, in a measure, transforms the society in which they live—at home, at work, and in their own communal relationships. Kingdom theology errs, however, in asserting that the renewal of society is a major focus of God's concern upon the earth before the return of the King. Rather, personal renewal by evangelism and the regeneration of people may lead to societal improvements. The real renewal is the growth of the Church. When people trust in Christ, His vicarious death is vindicated by believers joined to Christ and the local visible church awaiting His second coming.

*The Church is a means to establish social and economic justice.* Kingdom theology teaches that the concern of the Gospel accounts is the kingdom of God and that this concern is a continuity of Old Testament teaching. That is, because of the failure of the Jewish theocracy initiated under Moses by God and culminating in the exiles of Israel and Judah to Babylon and Egypt, God's design and plan is to reestablish the rule of Christ upon the earth through the Church. The Church can accomplish on earth that which Israel failed to do. The Church is the New Jerusalem or the "new humanity" of believing Jews and Gentiles. The Good News is the proclamation and implementation of social, political, economic, and racial justice for the poor. The Kingdom is not a "pie in the sky" event, but it is a present reality upon the earth. The heart of the Church's mission, then, is to help the oppressed poor of the world. The Gospel is a relevant, socio-political "good news."

The truth of this viewpoint is that the King has come, He is gathering a people for His name in all the earth who do, in fact, become citizens of God's Kingdom now. Christ *reigns* in the hearts of believers now and He reigns sovereignly over world history. Furthermore, there will be a time *in human history* when the Lord Jesus will *rule* as well as reign upon the earth. The error is, first, in understanding the present manifestation of all God's people as a political power for the earthly imposition of "social justice" upon unregenerate peoples and upon non-Christian nations and ideologies. Scripture clearly teaches, however, that until Jesus Christ returns the second time to rule, as was promised (Acts 1:11), the commission given His followers was to be witnesses of Jesus from Jerusalem to the ends of the earth. The people "born again" into His kingdom were to be gathered into His Church, to await His return and to be delivered from the wrath of God coming upon a rebellious and sinful humanity (1 Thessalonians 1:1,10). Between the time of the ascension of Christ Jesus and His return in glory, God is calling out citizens of the Kingdom who are being prepared in the fellowship of His Church to rule gloriously with Christ upon the earth (Romans 8:17; Revelation 5:9,10).

*Justice is part of the Good News.* Kingdom theology believes that "justice is an essential and integral part of the Good News" (Raymond Fung, *A Monthly Letter on Evangelism*, WCC; CWME, No. 4, April, 1985, p. 1). The truth in this view is that the Good News speaks clearly concerning justice or righteousness, the righteousness of God in judging sin and sinners or the righteousness or justice of God imputed to the believing sinner (Romans 1:17; 5:1; 2 Corinthians 5:21). The error of Fung and others, at this point, is that this justice as seen as "the opportunity to participate in the building of a more just society in this imperfect world of ours . . ." For some, the righteousness of Christ has already been imputed to the entire human race and for others it will be imputed later on in eternity (universalism). They fail to recognize the righteous judgment of God on man's sin, man's hopelessness without Christ and man's helplessness to transform a world of unregenerate people.

Biblical evangelism, on the other hand, touches society at the level of the unregenerate heart and "new creatures" in Christ possess transformed lives which change families, communities and even nations. We must acknowledge that regenerate believers have civic and social responsibilities *as Christian citizens* though not as churches. As they fulfill their responsibilities, people, families, communities and even nations are helped. Nevertheless, the kingdom of God will never come in the promised messianic glory until the King Himself returns to rule with divine authority and power upon the earth.

*The Gospel is authenticated by churches visibly united to achieve justice.* Evangelism is, according to many proponents of Kingdom theology, authenticated by the visible, organizational unity of churches which are united to achieve the transformation of society by the exercise of their combined influence upon unjust political structures. In many ways, Kingdom theology is a reincarnation of the "social gospel" of the early part of this century—except that one is able to mix in it the traditional evangelical evangelism in varying degrees. That is, one can insist upon the regenerating experience of the new birth as well as the necessity of social transformation as the message of the Gospel. But some, on the other hand, consider the "new birth" to be simply the arousing of social consciousness in a person who "accepts" Christ as Lord and becomes involved in socio-political revolution for the justice of the oppressed.

The truth of this teaching is that the believer is delivered from his personal sin and sins. Naturally, this will have implications on the people around him. The converted alcoholic, for example, is delivered from a personal slavery to drink; his family life is transformed, he may no longer be a charge and fiscal responsibility to the community or state. He is transformed into a productive and responsible citizen. But the error of this view is the belief that society may be changed *without* individual regeneration. This is like camouflaging a polluted body of water instead of removing the source of pollution and decontaminating the water. Christ alone can make a person new from the inside out. Then social change may follow.

Another error of Kingdom theology is the contention that a transformed society, often conceived as a socialistic government of one form or another, authenticates the evangelistic message. This error neglects the power of the Word of God, the Bible, and the accompanying ministry of the Holy Spirit to convict sinners, convert the believer, and produce a new way of living according to Scripture. The Holy Spirit is the authenticator of the evangelistic message founded upon Scripture. God's Word is living and powerful and will accomplish God's intended purpose (Hebrews 4:12; Isaiah 55:10,11). While visible unity of true believers is important, organizational unity of biblical and heretical churches has no intrinsic power to authenticate the evangelist's message. Unity can, at best, only attract attention to Christianity. The authenticity of the evangelistic message is not demonstrated by a church or combination of churches, but by the testimony of the Holy Spirit. The evangelist must say, "Thus says the Lord" not, "Thus says the Church." He must say, "Jesus says" not, "My pastor says." And he must say, "The Bible says" not, "The consensus of all historical Christian churches says."

*Conclusion.* It has been shown, then, that while there is some truth to the elements of Kingdom theology, the overall effect of their combination is an unbiblical understanding of the Church, of the Gospel, and of salvation. But the great and tragic *consequence* of Kingdom theology, is that it hinders, distracts from, and even destroys biblical evangelism. It *hinders* evangelism because the pastor or evangelist cannot proclaim the Gospel in full dependence upon the proclamation of Jesus Christ and the power of Scripture as accompanied by the Holy Spirit. It *distracts* from evangelism because the focus is upon the fruits of Christianity in society, rather than upon the dynamic roots of the tree which will produce such fruit, namely, regenerate people in the society. Kingdom theology destroys evangelism when the goal of evangelism becomes societal transformation as a focus of the kingdom, rather than the goal of personal regeneration for the spiritual and numerical growth of the visible local church.

Kingdom theology also *destroys* evangelism because sin is seen as societal and the product of an oppressor society, rather than endemic to the heart of man himself. Consequently, salvation becomes societal, for it is society collectively that has sinned against people. People as sinners in society are the victims of their societal structure rather than being responsible for their own sins. Where there is no personal responsibility for sin, there is no need for personal repentance and regeneration, and hence, no need for an individual to respond *personally* to the Gospel. Thus the need for evangelism is destroyed.

There is room for different evangelical interpretations of the Kingdom, but in many cases this new Kingdom theology is an instrument of the enemy to sow tares among the wheat. As evangelicals, we must not deny or denigrate the personal and public social responsibility of believers. But we must recognize that the fulfillment of such responsibilities begins in personal regeneration through the Word and the Spirit. God *is* in the world. His Kingdom *is* in us who believe. But the kingdom of God will not begin to be established in secular society upon the earth. Every historical effort to do so has failed. While believers may reflect the fruits of God's Spirit in society, this Kingdom does not consist in earthly social justice. It is not now a socio-economic-political body. God's Kingdom is His spiritual rule in the hearts of all believers in the body of Christ, and it will be established on the earth *only* when Christ, the head, returns in glory as its King.

# A CRITIQUE OF LIBERATION THEOLOGY FOR THE EVANGELIST

## Jose D. Camacho

The perspective from which we propose to treat the subject is definitely biblio-theological. Although we cannot ignore the philosophical, sociological, and psychological trends that surround the theme under discussion, those emphases are not here the object of our attention. Our contribution aims to begin a reflection on this contemporary theme that confronts the Christian believer from different religious perspectives, creating confusion and unrest, within and outside the Church.

What does God's Word have to say about this issue that claims not only our attention, but also our acceptance and our compromise?

### 1. The so-called Liberation Theology

We begin in a South American university. For five nights the auditorium of this institution of learning and revolutionary unrest was totally filled for a series of lectures on *"The Place of Biblical Christianity Confronted by Historic Materialism,"* which they had invited me to offer. After each lecture we met with a considerable number of persons interested about that evening's talk. Naturally, most of the questions were directed to me. But at one point, a young man began to expound his own ideas. Now it is I who am asking and stimulating him to continue. He is a political activist. He speaks without mincing words, but with respect and dignity. He seems to be convinced of the value of his position. He knows well the condition of his country, its history, its proletarian struggles, the clamor of the oppressed masses. And he also knows, and states publicly, the participation of the Official Church in intimate connection with the governing powers of his country in the exploitation of the poor and the perpetuation of the ignorance of the vast majority of the people. It requires courage to express oneself as he is doing. His words sound grave, existential, as he concludes with this challenge: "What does Christianity have to offer us? We have embraced a cause to which we are committed. We have something to live for and something to die for, if it be necessary."

The answer from one sector of Roman Catholic thought to the challenge of this youthful voice, representing a continent inflamed by a revolutionary unrest, fanned by diverse ideological trends, was what we know today as the liberation theology. This trend of thought is incubated in the guilty conscience of a clergy in contact with the oppressed masses, not only by tyrannical and corrupt governments, but also by the Official Church to which they belong. The incubation period took all of the decade of the 60s; and appears in definite form, although not completely coherent, at the beginning of the decade of the 70s.

We are facing a revolutionary-type Roman Catholic thought that responds to a socio-political problem, that of exploitation and slavery, for which one sector of the church feels guilty. We are not here before a genuine theological idea that tries to enlighten a socio-political problem, but before a growing revolutionary unrest looking for a backing, and for a theological explanation that appraises and gives authentic character. From here, precisely, comes the name: liberation theology.

### 2. Is it a question of a theology of liberation or a theory of revolution?

Samuel Silva Gotay, a scholar and ideologist of the so-called liberation theology, affirms: "My book is on the theoretical crisis that imply the political options of the

Latin American revolutionary Christianity and the way in which its militants resolve the crisis to make possible the theoretical integration of the Christian faith with the Latin American thought that postulates the revolutionary and socialistic change as the only option for the creation of a just society'' (El Pensamiento Cristiano Revoluciona-rio, 1983, p. 17).

It is necessary to recognize the writer's honesty—not shared by many of his revolutionary colleagues who operate from within the Evangelical churches in Latin America—in offering us in his book an explanation of the surging of a revolutionary Christianity, its theoretical expression in liberation theology, and its organizational expression in movements such as Christians For Socialism.

On the other hand, he echoes the affirmation of the Latin American theologians, who do not elaborate a theory of revolution starting from theology. They immediately affirm that liberation theology tends to respect the autonomy of its own theory of revolution that surges from a scientific socio-economic analysis for which theology admits having no scientific influence (p. 29).

**3. *Are we facing a theological thought, or a socio-political speculation of religious thought?***

The theologians of the so-called liberation theology try to form a theology in a sociological context. This position would merit more respect if instead of pretending to form a theology (or theologies) they would admit that it really deals with socio-political speculation of religious thought. This diminishes revolutionary thought into innumerable ideological blends—the politicizing of religious thought, the intimate relationship with Marxist socialism, the armed revolutionary struggle, the terrorist atrocities, the utopian idea of an earthly kingdom of God (temporary, historical) brought about by man himself, in his own image and likeness.

A sound Christian theology must reject such theological speculation. On the other hand, we cannot ignore the fact that we are dealing with a theory of revolution which is making a considerable impact in our ranks. This explains the revolutionary uprising, called Christian, that has plagued Latin America—in the university setting, Evangelical and Catholic seminaries, and even in the pulpits. This explains the prevailing tension and uncertainty within the Evangelical denominational leadership, especially in the United States and Latin America. The effects of the ''liberation theologies'' have been sad for the unity of the Church and its ministry, causing wounds difficult to cure and barriers difficult to overcome.

This theory maintains that:

a. It is possible to be both Christian and revolutionary. A revolutionary here is understood as a political activist of the left wing with a revolution that alters the capitalist socio-economic order and proposes a takeover by the working masses and peasants for the creation of a socialistic state.

b. Christian faith and theology has to be unconditionally at the service of the ''liberation theology,'' in a total identification with the purposes and the process of the social revolution. It is understood that Christian thought possesses its own resources to express the revolutionary concept.

c. The Christian revolutionaries can enter into a strategic alliance with the Marxist revolutionaries.

**4. *Where is the theological base for this religious thought?***

The great problem of liberation theologies is their biblical hermeneutics. They not only break away totally from the classic orthodox theology, but also sustain a ''particular'' scriptural interpretation, with the purpose of adapting its theory of revolution from a religious perspective.

Here we are facing a ''theological'' endeavor where revelation is superfluous and where the saving history of the Bible is manipulated to conform to a predetermined end: the establishment of a socio-political order of socialist and universal character, in place of the theological concept of the kingdom of Heaven.

In an attempt to categorize theologically the revolutionary theory, the theologians of liberation theology reinterpret two great biblical events: the historical liberation of the children of Israel from Egyptian slavery; and the proclamation of the kingdom of God, for the liberation of man, from the lips of our Lord Jesus Christ.

On this reinterpretation hang the theological platform and the materialistic and historical world vision of the ''illuminated'' theologians of the liberation. Nevertheless, for some of them this speculation results in a serious attempt to confront problems that have shamefully been put aside by the official churches, and by religious leaders protected by absolutist, corrupt, and exploiting governments not only in Latin America, but in different parts of the world throughout history.

The liberation theologies tend to reduce the essence of man to a purely historical entity, within the secular context of history—where his only fulfillment is in his ''liberation'' from exploitation, oppression, material poverty, and economic misery. Such a theology puts God only on the side of the poor and against the rich. So limited and prejudiced a God is not capable of transcending the problem of classes, political systems, or ideological positions.

This theological reinterpretation of the salvation of man and the kingdom of God, according to the thinking of liberation theology, is expressed clearly in the following affirmation: ''Salvation in biblical thought is articulated in the historical sense of the liberation of all those who impede the realization of justice, as a necessary condition for the development of the new man of the kingdom of God. Biblically this kingdom has a revolutionary character by origin and definition: it is a kingdom for men, oppressed, rejected and exploited, and does not tolerate any social order which generates the relation of rich and poor'' (Silva Gotay, p. 98).

The theological absurdity arrives at its climax in the reinterpretation of the kingdom of God as a ''political symbol'' no more no less. ''The preaching of the kingdom of God is, then, in Latin America today, the promise of God that this unjust society will be judged and an invitation to solidarity with Him in the construction of a just society. Contrary to the apocalyptists (and to Jesus), we cannot simply await the arrival of the kingdom, but must analyze the present reality to discover the way toward the kingdom. The preaching of the kingdom is not the promise of a panacea, but the invitation to a sacrificial and solidarity struggle'' (Jorge Pixley, quoted by Silva Gotay, p. 120).

Says Lucio Gera, another liberation theologian: ''When Christ seeks to express what God is, the formula He uses is the 'kingdom of God.' He proclaims God speaking of the kingdom of God, the kingdom of God arrives, the kingdom of God comes, God comes. The concept of the kingdom is a political concept, that of the kingdom, the living kingdom within man; not a territory, but a people'' (quoted by Silva Gotay, p. 121).

Even more absurdly, Silva Gotay explains to us with all candor: ''As a result of the historical comprehension of the kingdom and understanding the 'knowledge of God' in terms 'doing justice' to man, the essential importance of the active participation of man in the construction of the kingdom is redeemed. The Christian hope is converted into a hope actively political and subversive that must be realized through man's work for justice starting from the present conditions'' (p. 121).

Hebrew prophecy, particularly the minor prophets, exponents of the message of social justice for their historic times, is exploited in the theory of revolution. Here the saving perspective is lost behind the purely historic happening. All is reduced to divine intervention to accomplish the liberation of the exploited, the prophets being the town criers of this intervention throughout the history of Israel.

We have offered a sketch of the synthesis of the "theological" thought advanced by the ideologies of the so-called liberation theology or theologies because it deals with a train of thought that applies independently to each particular situation: the Central America situation, the Brazilian, the Argentinian, the Caribbean, or more particularly the Puerto Rican situation. Yet all have a common denominator: a theory of the revolution, forcibly framed in Christian thought.

### 5. *The God of Evangelical Theology*

Facing liberation theology, our responsibility is to reinvestigate and affirm our Evangelical Theology. Our religious leaders, seminary and institute professors, denominational executives, missionaries, ministers, pastors, evangelists, and laymen have now before them the challenge to take seriously the profound and systematic study of the Word of God and the theological reflection of biblical doctrines.

We start from the classical orthodox interpretation of theology—the knowledge of God in His relationship to man throughout history. The objective of Evangelical Theology is to know, apprehend, and listen to God who speaks in virtue of His own initiative of revelation, acting and manifesting Himself in history, provoking an encounter with man. This God of evangelical revelation is the God committed to the salvation of all men: good and bad, white, black, yellow, and all other colors, of all races; rich and poor, exploited and exploiters, governors and governed, slaves and free men, the moral and the immoral, males and females, the God that is no respecter of persons (Acts 10:34; Galatians 2:6).

He is the imminent God, present in history in the person of our Lord Jesus Christ, God in us: Emmanuel (Isaiah 7:14; Matthew 1:23). At the same time He is the transcendent, trans-historical God, Creator and Lord of the universe, whom no one can manipulate (Romans 1:18-20; 11:32-36; Isaiah 42:1, 8; 57:15).

The Swiss theologian Karl Barth masterly expresses this concept when he says: "The God of the gospel, therefore, is not a thing, an item, an object like any other, is not an idea, a principal, a truth, or a sum of truths. The being of God, His truth, is in the event of His own revelation, the splendor of His glory as the Lord of Lords, the sanctification of His name, the coming of His kingdom, the fulfillment of His will in all His work" (*Evangelical Theology*, 1963, p. 9).

### 6. *The biblical concept of revelation*

Let us look at the two favorite events of the liberation theologies. First, the liberation of the "children of Israel" from the land of Egypt (Exodus 12:37-51). The emphasis on this particular historical incident may cause us to lose its real and global perspective and the resulting significance.

The departure is not an isolated, accidental act, improvised by God. It is really the nucleus or center of a series of historical acts within the divine plan and purpose. It does not deal with liberation for liberation's sake. So many incidents and historical acts happen (within the saving history of God) in order to complete the event, of which the departure (liberation) is only a part.

a. God tells Abram, "I will make of thee a great nation . . . and I will bless them that bless thee, and curse him that curseth thee: and in thee shall all families of the earth be blessed" (Genesis 12:1-3).

b. God reveals to Abram that his descendants (the children of Israel) "shall be a stranger in the land that is not theirs, and shall serve them; and they shall afflict them four hundred years" (Genesis 15:13).

    c.  God promises Abram that He (God) will judge the oppressing nation, liberating the children of Israel (descendants of Abram): "And afterward shall they come out with great substance" (Genesis 15:14; Exodus 12:40, 41).

    d.  God makes a covenant with Abram and promises him the land of Canaan for his descendants (Genesis 12:6, 7; 15:18-21).

    e.  God shows that His purpose in liberating the children of Israel (the descendants of Abram) is to make a people for himself: "Now therefore, if ye will obey my voice indeed, and keep my covenant, then ye shall be a peculiar treasure unto me above all people; for all the earth is mine: and ye shall be unto me a kingdom of priests, and an holy nation" (Exodus 19:5,6; Deuteronomy 4:20, 7:6, 14:2, 26:18; Titus 2:14).

    The departure or liberation of the children of Israel from the hands of the Egyptians is not just a liberation from the oppressing hand and from poverty (after all, the children came out "with great substance"). The liberation is a part of a historical process in the formation of a people that God is creating with a special purpose. The liberation of the children of Israel from Egypt is an episode within the saving history of God for all the nations of the earth.

    Second, let us glance at the concept of the kingdom of God within evangelical theology. We have already seen how the will of God is made manifest to us in the biblical concept of history. God is Lord of history. Everything that happens in history is, in it last analysis, divine activity in process. That is why history has to be seen as a unit, and not in isolated events. History, however, neither limits nor determines God, since He is the very subject of history. That is why we talk about "salvation history," and of Christian faith as "historical faith," and of the Christian Church as an "historical church." And we talk about the historical fact of the event of incarnation-crucifixion-resurrection-and-ascension of our Lord Jesus Christ.

    The salvation history, by nature and definition, needs a Savior: God (*subject-liberator*), and an oppressed subject to be saved (man-sinner-mankind). History, temporary reality, turns into a stage where the saving history shows us the divine will committed to God's liberation plan, in the struggle with the human will (man oppressed) that refuses to be liberated by God. It is within this historical drama that the glorious proclamation of the kingdom of God comes and is given. Writes Emil Brunner: "God wishes to have His people, His mankind, His kingdom. For this reason the final realization of His will is the coming of His kingdom, the coming of that which brings mankind and history to their consummation" (*The Christian Doctrine of the Church,* 1960, p. 362).

    The concept of the kingdom of God is fundamental in evangelical theology because it occupies a prominent place in the expression of the message of Jesus who identifies Himself with the kingdom and makes it the central theme of His proclamation (Mark 1:14, 15; Matthew 4:12-17).

    Of primary significance to the concept of the kingdom of God is the sovereignty of God, the rule of God, the will of God. The kingdom is not a symbol but an experience; not a utopia, but a reality; just as God is real. Here we face the reality of the "new order of God," in the expression of another great evangelical theologian, Dr. John A. Mackay. But the sovereignty of God, His will and order, is not made known in a vacuum, but is a reality made known in history.

    The sovereignty of God (the kingdom of God) becomes present in the person of Jesus Christ. In Him we have the present, actual dimension of the kingdom, the here and now of the kingdom. And Jesus Christ is no symbol, no utopia, no fabrication of the mind, but a reality. Our faith, the Gospel, preaching, the Church, and God's order have no meaning if we deny the present and actual reality of the Lord Jesus Christ. Therefore, the kingdom of God has a present dimension in history. He is the eternal contemporary of man (Luke 17:20,21; Matthew 12:28; Luke 10:9; 11:20).

The sphere or dominion in which the sovereignty of God operates and manifests itself is the Church of Jesus Christ, the community of the believers who respect and live within the will of God. The new man within the new order of God. It is a question of the people of God in history, a people on a pilgrimage toward the consummation of the divine will, but at the same time announcing the sovereignty of God for all humanity.

The Church identifies itself with the present—temporal—dimension of the kingdom. In the meantime it submits itself to the sovereignty of God and to His saving plan, but it is not the kingdom. It is rather the antechamber of the kingdom, the earnest, the advance that gives testimony and at the same time proclaims the other dimension of the kingdom: the eschatological dimension.

The actual presence of the Lord Jesus Christ—His sovereignty in the Church, the body of the believers, the children of God—manifests itself in the work of the Holy Spirit in the believer. The dynamics of the Holy Spirit produces the knowledge of the divine will and the ability to obey it. It is He who reveals "all truth" from the Father and the Son, and who makes the believer aware of his new and real humanity, the new creature that is converted into a child of God (John 1:12,13; 16:4-15; 1 Corinthians 6:19).

But the kingdom has another transcendental, trans-historical dimension that goes beyond even the eschatological phase to become finally a culmination. The kingdom of God is what gives sense and finality to history. Evangelical theology holds that the Christian faith is based on the promise of the consummation of human history and the social reality as we know it now, to give place to the final coming of what we now "see only through a glass darkly": The peak of the dimension of the kingdom of God. That's why the Lord taught us to pray: "Thy kingdom come. Thy will be done in earth, as it is in heaven" (Matthew 6:10).

The plan of God to exercise His sovereignty gives sense to history in the fact that the expectation of His Church—His people—will be fulfilled in the second coming of our Lord Jesus Christ, the parousia, when finally the glorious promise in 1 Corinthians 15:22-26, will be fulfilled. It is in this culmination that the final expression of the model prayer receives meaning: "For thine is the kingdom, and the power, and the glory, forever. Amen" (Matthew 6:13).

A so-called theology that does not consider the ultimate dimension of the kingdom, the power, and the glory of God; and that glorifies poverty in itself, as a condition to participate in a political, social and economic order as the result of a revolution fed by hate and vengeance, cannot deserve the respect and the serious consideration of the Christian evangelical people of Latin America, nor of the rest of the world!

I want to leave with you a note of challenge and of real optimism, despite the fact that the world, and even the Church, has so much evil and confusion in the theological arena. We have been called to witness—to evangelize—to this world that God continues to love, and in order to redeem it offered His only begotten Son on the Cross of Calvary. Let us respond to the challenge of this hour, remembering that "where sin abounded, grace did much more abound: that as sin hath reigned unto death, even so might grace reign through righteousness unto eternal life by Jesus Christ our Lord (Romans 5:20-21).

"Watch ye, stand fast in the faith, quit you like men, be strong" (1 Corinthians 16:13).

# III

# VARIOUS METHODS
# OF EVANGELISM

# THE EVANGELIST'S COMMITMENT
# TO THE CHURCH

*Nilson Fanini*

*Text: Ephesians 4:11-13.* "It was he who gave some to be apostles, some to be prophets, some to be *evangelists*, and some to be pastors and teachers—to prepare God's people for works of service, so that the body of Christ (the Church) may be built up until we all reach unity in the faith and in the knowledge of the Son of God and become mature, attaining to the whole measure of the fullness of Christ."

It is a great honor to be here speaking to you, and I am grateful to my Lord and to Dr. Billy Graham for the invitation to speak to this great Conference. I believe, in the first place, this may be one of the most strategic conferences of this century. With the help of the Holy Spirit and prayer support from each of you, we will look together at the topic assigned to me. Let us study it from three aspects.

1. *The Church of Jesus Christ*
   "In the beginning God created the heavens and the earth. He created man in His own image and likeness. Afterwards He saw that man was lonely. So, He made man fall into a deep sleep and took from him a rib and from it made a bride, Eve. When Adam saw her, he said, "This is now bone of my bones and flesh of my flesh . . ." (Genesis 2:20-23).
   In the same manner thousands of years later, the same God made the Second Adam fall asleep for three days. Jesus died on the Cross, spilled His blood, was buried, and after three days was resurrected—and His bride was created. Jesus said when seeing that bride, the Church—"This blood of my blood will be called the Church; she was made and bought with my blood." And Jesus affirmed after the admission of Peter in Matthew 16:16-18, ". . . *I will build my church.*"
   The Church actually has two addresses—one geographic, the other spiritual. For an example, look at 1 Corinthians 1:2—"To the church of God *in Corinth (geographic)*, to those sanctified *in Jesus Christ (spiritual).*"
   The Church everywhere around the world calls on the name of the same Lord, your Lord and my Lord, Jesus Christ.
   *"The Church everywhere"—"The body of Christ."*
   The Church is of great importance because she is located in all places. For example, we have evangelists from 170 countries of the world in this congress. We are not the same outwardly—we dress differently, have different habits, eat different foods, speak different languages. Yet each still belongs to the same family, God's family in Christ, which meets in different addresses around the world.
   I preached once on an Asiatic island and afterwards they took me to a restaurant. The waiter picked up a snake right in front of me, cut off its head and its tail, then asked me, "Pr. Fanini, how would you prefer it—stewed or fried?" I responded, "I'm not really hungry any more."
   We're brothers in the Church of our Lord.
   I spoke in another country, and later they served the Lord's Supper. I looked into the cup and saw a greenish liquid. When I drank it, it had a strong, unidentifiable taste. I asked about the color and taste and was told, "We have no grapes in this area, so we make coconut wine."
   Those brothers belong to Christ, to His Church everywhere.

I preached in a crusade which united 16 tribes. I spoke through three interpreters. In the middle of the sermon in that mass of over 10,000 people, someone stood up and began to sing. (Now that's a good suggestion for helping out a weak sermon!) Everyone joined in and began to sing and to cry. I asked my interpreter, "What's going on?" He said, "They are praising God for sending you." Alleluia! When they finished I continued my sermon.

They are my brothers in the Church around the world.

I preached in Angola, in Luanda, the capital. It was one of the most blest meetings of my entire life. The last service was on a Sunday; and at noon people began to arrive and the singing began in the various languages. At 8 P.M. they were still praising and singing to God. They don't use a watch in their services; they use a calendar!

They, too, are the Lord's bride, my brothers.

I preached a crusade in Latin America. The soccer stadium held more than 50,000 people. Do you know what they do? Whoever has a musical instrument brings it with him to use in the time of praise in the stadium—drums, trumpets, bass guitars, violins, guitars. Everyone sings, everyone plays his instrument wherever he might be sitting, and everyone claps hands. In the midst of the preaching someone stood and hollered, "Who saves?" All hollered back, "Jesus!!!" "Who's coming again?!?" All respond together with increasing enthusiasm, "Jesus! Jesus!! Jesus!!!"

They also are the Church, my brothers . . .

When I preach in the U.S.A., in Canada, or in Europe, I preach and preach and preach and everyone quietly sits, mutely—almost as though they were asleep.

They are my brothers, part of the Church everywhere!

*The Church is everywhere.*

2. *The evangelist*

Ephesians 4:11 says, "It was he who gave some to be apostles, some to be prophets, *some to be evangelists*, and some to be pastors and teachers."

We must make a distinction between "spiritual gifts" and natural abilities. When you were born into this world God gave you certain natural abilities, perhaps in mechanics, or in art, in athletics, or in music, or in communicating ideas with facility. In this regard, all men are not created equal, because some are smarter, or stronger, or more talented than others. But, in the spiritual realm, each believer has at least one spiritual gift, no matter what natural abilities he may or may not possess. A spiritual gift is a God-given ability to serve God, and other Christians, in such a way that Christ is glorified and believers are edified.

How does the believer discover and develop his gifts? By fellowshipping with other Christians *in the local assembly*. Gifts are not toys to play with. They are rather tools to build with. And, if they are not used with love, they become weapons to fight with, which is what happened in the Corinthian church.

There are three lists of spiritual gifts given in the New Testament: 1 Corinthians 12:4-11,27-31; Romans 12:3-8; and our reference in Ephesians 4:11, all composed by the Apostle Paul.

Paul mentioned not so much the "gifts" as the person gifted by God and placed within the Church. There are four categories: *apostles, prophets, evangelists, pastor-teachers.* It is the *evangelists who are literally the "bearers of the Good News."* These men traveled from place to place to preach the Gospel and win the lost.

An example appears in Acts 8:26-40. "Now an angel of the Lord said to Philip, 'Go south to the road—the desert road—that goes down from Jerusalem to Gaza.' So Philip started out, and on his way he met an Ethiopian eunuch, an important official in charge of all the treasury of Candace, queen of the Ethiopians. This man had gone to

Jerusalem to worship, and on his way home was sitting in his chariot reading the book of Isaiah the prophet. The Spirit told Philip, 'Go to that chariot and stay near it.'

"Then Philip ran up to the chariot and heard the man reading Isaiah the prophet. 'Do you understand what you are reading?' Philip asked.

"'How can I,' he said, 'unless someone explains it to me?' So he invited Philip to come up and sit with him.

"The eunuch was reading this passage of Scripture—'He was led like a sheep to the slaughter, and as a lamb before the shearer is silent, so he did not open his mouth. In his humiliation he was deprived of justice. Who can speak of his descendants? For his life was taken from the earth.'

"The eunuch asked Philip, 'Tell me, please, who is the prophet talking about, himself or someone else?' Then Philip began with that very passage of Scripture and told him the good news about Jesus.

"As they traveled along the road, they came to some water and the eunuch said, 'Look, here is water. Why shouldn't I be baptized?' And he ordered the chariot to stop. Then both Philip and the eunuch went down into the water and Philip baptized him. When they came up out of the water, the Spirit of the Lord suddenly took Philip away, and the eunuch did not see him again, but went on his way rejoicing. Philip, however, appeared at Azotus and traveled about, preaching the gospel in all the towns until he reached Caesarea."

Or Paul's famous encounter that took him to Macedonia. In Acts 21:28, "Men of Israel, help us! This is the man who *teaches all men everywhere* against our people and our law and this place. And besides, he has brought Greeks into the temple area and defiled this holy place."

Paul said to Timothy in 2 Timothy 4:5, "But keep your head in all situations, endure hardship,, *do the work of an evangelist,* discharge all the duties of your ministry."

The apostles and prophets laid the foundation of the Church, and the evangelist built upon it by winning the lost to Christ and adding to the Church. Paul himself was an apostle, pastor, *and* itinerant evangelist!

### 3. *The evangelist's commitment*

The Apostle Paul points out that the purpose of the gifts of apostle, prophet, teacher and *evangelist* is "for the edifying of the body of Christ" (Ephesians 4:12). And he adds, ". . . from him the whole body, joined and held together by every supporting ligament, grows and builds itself up in love, as each part does its work."

The proclamation of who Jesus is and the building of His Church are clearly linked. Pentecost launched the apostles into a ministry of proclamation that began to build Christ's Church. In the book of Acts we read references to the numerical, structural, and geographical exposition of the Church.

*Acts 2:41*—"Those who accepted his message were baptized, and about three thousand were added to their number that day."

*Acts 5:14*—"Nevertheless, more and more men and women believed in the Lord and were added to their number."

*Acts 6:7*—"So the word of God spread. The number of disciples in Jerusalem increased rapidly, and a large number of priests became obedient to the faith."

*Acts 11:26*—"For a whole year Barnabas and Saul met with the church [in Antioch] and taught great numbers of people. The disciples were first called Christians there at Antioch."

(Confirming Affirmation XII of *A Biblical Standard for Evangelists*, Amsterdam 1983.)

Paul wrote, "Christ also loved the church, and gave himself for it" (Ephesians 5:25). It should be the norm, therefore, for the evangelist to love the Church that Jesus loves.

For the evangelist, responsibility to the Church begins in fellowship with the local church. This may be the church that first recognized and encouraged his evangelistic gift. It certainly should be a church which gives him prayerful and practical support. Ideally, it would also provide a caring spiritual home for his wife and family, particularly when he is away.

The responsibility of the evangelist to the church continues in his preparation for an evangelistic campaign. Such preparation is done through the local church. Each evangelistic endeavor must both begin and end in the local church to be effective and lasting!

To do God's work, three types of power are necessary—God's power, man power, and money power. Often the work is made difficult by a lack of necessary resources. We, the evangelists of the Third World, have a greater obstacle in financing travel and the actual crusade meetings. Thus, we are obligated to act as "pastor-evangelists," which requires a redoubled effort on the part of the evangelist. But I personally am grateful for the increased insight into the life of the local church which this dual role has offered me.

Many years ago, Walter Vivian of CBS was checking the equipment which had been installed to carry the message of King George to the British troops throughout the world. In the last-minute inspection a break in the wires was discovered. There was no time at all for a repair. With one of his hands on the end of each of the two segments of wire, Walter Vivian allowed 250 volts of electrical current to pass through his body, so that the King's message could go through. He came out of the experience with burned hands, but the words of the King did go through.

So may it be with us as we transmit the message of the King of Heaven to the lost of the world. We must pay a price. But whatever the cost, however difficult the circumstances, let us be about the business of using the God-given gift of bringing souls to Jesus Christ before the night settles in!

*Conclusion*

Demographers tell us that the world population by the end of the 20th century will be more than six billion persons. In 25 years, the estimated world population is to be 10.5 billion!

Missiologists report that the Christian population presently grows at the daily rate of 78,000. Now—before we pat ourselves on the back and begin to celebrate, we are forced to look at other figures. How many persons are daily added to the total world population?

By the year 2000 the population will be increasing at the rate of 228,000 per day! Summarizing, the Christian population will increase by 28.5 million per year, while the world population explodes at four times that rate, 93 million per year, more or less.

The numbers speak clearly to each of us. Let us each commit ourselves and all we are as evangelists to multiply our efforts in the worldwide Church.

And—let us never become so busy, so overcommitted in our schedules that we fail to see the Lord and let Him work in us. Bailey Smith, a Southern Baptist pastor and evangelist, in his book, *Real Evangelism* (1978), says "We get so busy working *for* Jesus that we often don't pause and submit to the work He wants to do *in* us." He further says, "Our vessel is so tired, we can't clearly appreciate the treasure (we hold in it)."

Jess Moody, pastor to the Hollywood culture, in contrasting his fast-moving, "fabulous" ministry there to his humble beginning in a small-town Texas church says, "I miss the sound of sandaled feet," the quiet coming of the Master into our lives. Doctrine and desire for souls saved are wonderful, but are worth little—if we, the evangelists of the world, don't know the Man.

The story is told of a man who for 20 years rang the huge bells of a French cathedral twice each day. His ability was such that people by the hundreds would stop across the miles to listen to the beautiful melodies of inspiration as they were carried on the breeze. Those hearing the melodies said that they actually gave them strength to meet the day's demands. It seems that the man, the bellringer, had become deaf from the tremendously sonorous bells, and for four years continued to bring joy to others though he himself never heard a note. Beware, fellow evangelists, lest we get so close to the bells that we miss the Music! It is in the hearing of the Music that we are empowered to fight for the faith and eventually win the crown.

It has been said of Charles Taylor, former president of Wake Forest College in North Carolina, that "the Good News he preaches to others was *first of all* the *best of all* news to his own soul." May it be said of us as well, and may we then ring the bell—ring the bell—ring the bell till *all* the nations, all the lands, all the islands, all peoples, all the earth can hear the Good News of Jesus Christ. Amen.

# THE EVANGELIST'S GOAL: MAKING DISCIPLES
*Kassoum Keita*

I would like to invite you to reflect on the evangelist and discipleship. The goal of the evangelist: Making Disciples.

1. *The evangelist's great responsibility towards his new converts*
    As a sick person has placed his trust in his doctor, so the new convert has confidence in the evangelist who showed him the way of salvation in Christ. This confidence involves his responsibility.
    The great evangelist Paul was concerned by the state of his new converts. Paul said: "Let us return and visit the brethren in every city in which we proclaimed the word of the Lord, and see how they are" (Acts 15:36). The evangelist must be concerned with the state of all those who have responded favorably to his call to repentance. Their walk with the Lord must be at the center of his concern. He will do his best to create a favorable setting for their spiritual growth. This growth must necessarily affect their maturity.
    Paul and Barnabas were concerned to faithfully proclaim the Good News. But they also felt their responsibility toward all who had believed their message and had turned to the Lord. They not only had the concern to establish the new converts in their faith, but they were determined to give structure to their lives. Thus, they left behind them stable and dynamic churches. It is in this way that they created a powerful movement for the evangelization of the world.
    When Paul expressed his desire to return to see "the brothers in every city," it was because the apostle sensed that the new converts in these cities needed encouragement and instruction. Evangelism which does not make disciples does not conform to the New Testament model. Conversion must lead to service. The new birth must lead to a new life of communion *with* Christ and of service *to* Christ.
    The evangelist has also the great responsibility to help the new convert to become strong in his faith and active in a local church. In Colossians 1:28,29, the Apostle Paul shows us his great concern with this subject: "And we proclaim him, admonishing every man and teaching every man with all wisdom, that we may present every man complete in Christ. And for this purpose also I labor striving according to his power, which mightily works within me." Paul's objective is clear: to present to God every man perfect in Christ.
    The role of the evangelist does not stop at conversion. Confidence in God, faith in God—in its origin and development—results from a heart knowledge and from an intellectual knowledge. This knowledge must continue to grow in order for the Christian to move from the state of infancy to that of an adult.
    Though through repentance the heart of the new convert is washed by the blood of Jesus, he needs to be built up in his faith. His knowledge of Christ and of His Word must be constantly renewed. He must learn to have confidence in his Savior and to love Him. One must help him develop habits which will cause him to continue to grow spiritually. He must learn to speak about Christ to others. One must see to it that he feels at ease in the fellowship of a local church. Finally, he must become a mature disciple of Christ. All these things underline the responsibility of the evangelist.
    To better conserve his results, the evangelist must fight against the idea that his responsibility ends the moment he has delivered his message. This very idea leads one to believe that the follow-up of a campaign is the responsibility of others. Many itin-

erant evangelists think that God has called them only to proclaim the Good News for the salvation of men. They do not believe that it is up to them to make disciples of the new converts by teaching them to follow all that Jesus commanded.

Paul and Barnabas retraced their steps to visit the churches and follow up the new converts. They did not consider the fact of proclaiming the Gospel sufficient. They were evangelists of great courage.

2. *What must the evangelist do to assure that a ministry of discipling will follow his campaign?*

First of all he must break with the old habits. There must therefore be a change in his attitude and in his understanding of his role as evangelist. What is your attitude and your understanding of your ministry as an evangelist? There are two possible concepts:

    a.   The concept of addition which consists of preaching to the maximum number of people, hoping that the Lord will save many.

    b.   The concept of multiplication which consists also of preaching to the maximum number of people, but with the desire to train and mobilize other Christians in order to lead them to do what one is doing oneself. All will certainly not be great preachers, but all can make witnessing a way of life.

*Characteristics of the man who believes in addition*

(i)     He tries to do everything himself.

(ii)   He does not take into account the gifts of others.

(iii)  He does not know how to share his vision with others.

  (iv)  He does not know that his gift of evangelism must also permit him to prepare others to do what he is doing himself according to Ephesians 4:11,12.

(v)    He does not give much time to the follow-up and training of others.

(vi)   He does not have the concern to reproduce workers through training (Matthew 9:37,38).

(vii)  He feels threatened and in competition with the ministry of others.

*Characteristics of the man who believes in multiplication*

(i)     He loves to work on a team.

(ii)   He desires to share his know-how with others.

(iii)  He knows how to share his vision.

(iv)   He recognizes that his gift of evangelism is there to prepare others to do what he is doing.

  (v)    He takes time to follow up and train others.

(vi)   He has a fervent desire to reproduce other workers through training and prayer.

(vii)  He does not feel threatened or in competition with the gifts or the ministries of others.

To which category do you belong?

The evangelist must make every attempt to leave a real spiritual movement after his campaign—that is to say a movement which will ensure that after the campaign new conversions continue to be registered. This will happen because training will have become a way of life leading to continuous evangelism. A strategy and a plan are required for this to take place. The plan must include at least three basic points:

1.   Before the campaign (the pre-campaign)
2.   The campaign
3.   After the campaign (the post-campaign)

It is not enough to send the new converts into the churches without assuring oneself that they will be followed up effectively. The evangelist must remember that Jesus said, "You did not choose me, but I chose you and appointed you, that you should go and bear fruit, and that your fruit should remain, that whatever you ask of the Father in my name, he may give it to you" (John 15:16).

The preaching is not, therefore, an end in itself. The end that must be kept in mind is the outcome. The outcome must be given all of the conditions favoring its development and both its numerical and qualitative multiplication. That is to say that one of the emphases of an evangelist should be training—a training enabling the new convert to follow Jesus and to learn from Him.

It is necessary to confess Christ. It is necessary to be a member of the family of God. But it is also important to be directed and used by the Lord. The Great Commission includes discipleship. Good collaboration of the evangelist with the local churches allows him to train counselors. This training can even extend to his own fellow-workers. It must, on the one hand, permit him to gather new converts and teach them all the basic elements of the Christian faith. It must, on the other hand, initiate them into personal evangelism. The new convert will therefore grow by learning how to share his faith with others. In this manner the ministry of the evangelist will result in multiplication. From the beginning, the training of counselors must take into account that the objective is multiplication. When teaching counselors to communicate simply the contents of the Gospel, we must do it in a transmittable way. In other words, we must do it so simply that they can repeat it to others.

The evangelist calls people to make a decision for Christ. The person who responds favorably to this call is still capable of making other important decisions; such as making the decision to be trained in order to be more committed to the Lord, His Word and His people. He can even decide to commit himself to train others by simply repeating to them the teaching and training he has received.

The training of disciples has great implications. Paul told Timothy to do the work of an evangelist (2 Timothy 4:5). He also said to him: "And the things which you have heard from me in the presence of many witnesses, these entrust to faithful men, who will be able to teach others also" (2 Timothy 2:2). Proclamation has always been easily accepted. But the making of disciples does not appeal to many evangelists. They feel a great deal more at ease with a crowd than with a small group of disciples.

Throughout the life of the great evangelist Paul, it is evident that he was preoccupied with the training of disciples. He understood that God is concerned with men and that God's plan for men is realized by men themselves. What kind of men? Disciples who every day follow the word of the Master, the Lord. Disciples who are being conformed to His image and who commit themselves to participate in the accomplishment of the Great Commission, reconciling the world with God in dependence on the Holy Spirit.

The strategy and the plan of Paul were inspired by what Jesus did. The plan that Jesus conceived was to create spiritual movements. With Matthew 28:19,20, one can summarize the Great Commission in three words: *win, build* and *send*. That is exactly what constitutes the training of disciples: disciples who are themselves not only conformed to the image of Christ, but who are capable of teaching others to be disciples and of training others to form disciples.

The model that the New Testament gives us is represented by four generations: Paul, Timothy, faithful men, others. Taking this as a model, and equipping himself with dynamic material, the evangelist will leave behind him one or several action groups. These groups which are being conformed to the image of Christ commit themselves to share their faith with others. In this way, and thanks to the training of disciples, the evangelist will leave behind him spiritual movements which will permit real growth of the local churches. The fact of training disciples always implies multiplication, a multiplication of our ministry.

In Matthew 28:18-20 Jesus also said, "All power has been given to me in heaven and on earth . . . and lo, I am with you always." In the gospel of John 14:16,17, and 16:7, Jesus tells us that He will send the Holy Spirit to be with us always. He also said that the Holy Spirit will glorify Christ and that the Father is glorified when we bear much fruit. John 15:8 tells us, "By this is my Father glorified, that you bear much fruit, and so prove to be my disciples." These passages advise us that the remaining fruit of our ministry is in reality the work of the Holy Spirit through us.

The Holy Spirit is the one who produces in us permanent fruit and who also makes of us disciples. The Holy Spirit must therefore remain as the foundation of our training of disciples. Our plans and our methods are useless if it were not for the power of God. This power is the Holy Spirit manifesting the life of Christ in us and through us. Everything in the Christian life must be based on this understanding: that is, the necessity of being directed by the Holy Spirit in everyday life. God does not tell us to produce, but to bear fruit.

To ensure that a ministry of discipling follows his campaign, the evangelist must include in his plan the training of counselors according to 2 Timothy 2:2. He must insist on the ministry of the Holy Spirit. He must also create the spirit of prayer. That is to say that his program of follow-up will have as its objective the creation of spiritual movements from spiritually growing action groups.

3.   *How can the evangelist communicate the ministry of discipling as a way of life for the believer?*

There are three basic biblical principles that Jesus and Paul used for the multiplication of disciples. These principles are not only biblical, but experience shows that they are fundamental to the growth of the Church and of every other Christian work. If one of these is missing, multiplication will not develop as the Lord would have wanted. And if there is no multiplication, there will be no spiritual movements and our campaigns will only be events.

a.   *Biblical teaching.* We all understand this necessity. In the history of the Church, this has been sufficiently emphasized. Unfortunately, men are often taught what they must do and what they must be, but the means of accomplishing it in dependence on the Holy Spirit are rarely taught. There must be a balance between exhortation and practical instruction. A good training of disciples must include a clear teaching on how to live a Christian life, and then on how to communicate it to others.

A servant of God, an evangelist like each of us, gave this testimony: "When I was young, in my church I heard a great deal of exhortation, but there was little practical teaching. This resulted in a feeling of guilt and frustration. For example, we were exhorted to witness, but no one showed us how to do it effectively. The more I was exhorted, the more I was frustrated and felt guilty." The least one can say of this testimony is that exhortation without explanation ends in frustration. There must be a balance between teaching and its practical application.

b.   *Evangelism.* This is the element of action. Paul, following Jesus' example, trained disciples by continual person-to-person evangelism. Most of the time, one who knows how to evangelize person-to-person can also be effective with a group. Evangelism is, therefore, a means of training disciples. Jesus demonstrated this in John 4:31-38. In verse 34 Jesus says, "My food is to do the will of him who sent me, and to accomplish his work." The point I want to make is that evangelism is not only what we do to lead others to Christ. It is also required for the spiritual growth of Christians. Evangelism is fundamental to our spiritual health. One often says that "impression without expression leads to depression." People forget easily that which they do not have the habit of using. Truth without practice is dead.

In our day, it is not rare to meet stagnant Christians, bitter and spiritually bound. Many have been saturated with good biblical theory without using it in their lives. The involvement of Christians, even new believers, in action is necessary for their own health and growth. We reap that which we sow, Galatians 6:7-10 tells us. If, therefore, the evangelist enlists new converts to bring spiritual aid to others, he will see them grow rapidly. It will be a matter of involving them in action, for it is in doing that one learns.

c. *The context for multiplication.* It is the relational element. It is also a demonstration. We come back to 2 Timothy 2:2. Paul's objective was to train Timothy so that he would be able to train other faithful men, who in their turn would be able to train others. We know that everyone is better trained in the context of personal relationships and by example.

Drawing again our inspiration from the example of Paul, we notice several important points:

(i)    Paul taught Timothy the basic truths, but he also gave him precise instructions about his life and ministry (1 Timothy 5:23; 2 Timothy 1:8; 1 Timothy 5:1,2; 1 Timothy 1:18,19).

(ii)    Paul supported Timothy in prayer and Timothy could observe the life of Paul as he was very close to him (2 Timothy 1:3; 1 Timothy 5:5; 2 Timothy 3:10,11).

(iii)    Paul expressed his confidence in Timothy and often delegated to him certain aspects of his ministry (Acts 17:14,15; 1 Timothy 1:3).

Paul asked Timothy to follow his example and to find faithful men. I assume that all who respond to the call of the evangelist will not have direct permanent contact with him. However, well-trained counselors and the evangelist himself can find faithful men. The question that remains is, "How does one recognize these faithful men?" Among all of the characteristics of the faithful man, I will mention three which seem to be fundamental:

(i)    A desire to please God. The Lord says, "You shall love the Lord your God with all your heart, and with all your soul, and with all your mind" (Matthew 22:37).

(ii)    A teachable spirit. This was the difference between the Jews of Berea and those of Thessalonica (Acts 17:11).

(iii)    A dependence on God, that is to say, the fullness of the Holy Spirit (Acts 1:8).

What did Paul mean when he said, "Being capable to teach others also"? According to what we read in Philippians 3:7, and 4:9, it did not have to do with being a professor of theology. Paul spoke of teaching others by example. He said, "That which you have learned and received and heard and seen in me, practice these things." For Timothy, it meant training disciples in the same way that he himself had been trained. That is, by example.

This was also the practice of Jesus. Jesus took His disciples with Him during all His ministry. He showed them how to live and minister spiritually to others. Jesus and Paul trained disciples in small groups. They favored personal relationships. They asked their disciples to do the same thing with faithful men. In imitating the same method, the evangelist will communicate the ministry of discipling as a way of life. Multiplication will happen to the extent that faithful men commit themselves to transmit to other faithful men what they are learning. These faithful men will simply repeat the same process, generation after generation.

Many evangelists do not have room in their ministries for any Timothys or faithful men. There are only themselves and the others.

Why is it that many evangelists and pastors are not ready to do this? Perhaps it is because they have not had the example of their leaders. Some are rather hostile to any change in their own ways. Others still have confidence in the methods of addition. Others ask themselves, "Whom can I make into a disciple?"

The disciples of the itinerant evangelist can come from several groups: counselors, other evangelists younger or with less experience, Christians from his circle of friends or even those who have received Jesus Christ through his ministry.

(i)     Whom are you training to do what you are doing now?

(ii)    How is your gift of evangelism serving to train and involve others in evangelism?

(iii)   How are you serving as an example in training and mobilization for evangelism?

(iv)    Are you sure that your experience is serving effectively to raise up qualified workers for the harvest?

The training of disciples permits the evangelist to go beyond his own limitations in evangelism and firming up of new converts. What are you going to do after Amsterdam 86? Are you going to continue a ministry of addition, or are you going to become a man or a woman of multiplication? Evangelists, let us commit ourselves to the training of disciples.

# THE MINISTRY OF MULTIPLICATION
*Ajith Fernando*

My talk is on multiplication, on the need for evangelists to multiply their ministries by helping to raise a new generation of evangelists.

There was a great need for laborers in Christ's time. That need still exists. Matthew says that when Jesus saw that the crowds were harassed and helpless like sheep without a shepherd, He was deeply moved. His response was a call to prayer. But it was not for prayer that people would be saved, though certainly that was important. Instead Jesus says, "Ask the Lord of the harvest, therefore, to send out workers into his harvest field" (Matthew 9:38). In Jesus' ministry we see His contribution toward answering that prayer. He trained His disciples to reap the harvest fields of the world.

The point I want to make today is that evangelists have both a great calling and a great responsibility to multiply themselves by helping develop younger evangelists. We will look at the way Paul multiplied himself by developing Timothy, and we will use 1 Timothy 1:18 as a base for our study. This verse says: "Timothy, my son, I give you this instruction in keeping with the prophecies once made about you, so that by following them you may fight the good fight."

We note first that Paul calls Timothy his "son." He had *a father-son relationship with Timothy*. In biblical times this was a way to describe the relationship between a master and his disciple. Elisha, for example, called Elijah "my father" (2 Kings 2:12).

The basic idea behind the use of this parenthood metaphor is that of *concern and affection*. In fact the word translated "son" is not the usual word for son, but a more tender and affectionate term. The ties of affection between Paul and Timothy are seen in 2 Timothy 1:4: "Recalling your tears, I long to see you, so that I may be filled with joy." Today we may be embarrassed by such an expression of affection. But it was quite natural for Paul.

The parenthood metaphor also carries the idea of *a responsibility to nurture, to teach and to help develop to maturity and usefulness*. Paul fulfilled this responsibility so well with Timothy that he could send him to Corinth as one who fully represents him. He says, "I am sending to you Timothy, my son . . . He will remind you of my way of life in Christ Jesus, which agrees with what I teach everywhere in every church" (1 Corinthians 4:17). Dr. Ralph Martin has said that Paul regarded Timothy "as almost an extension of his own personality" (*Colossians and Philemon*, 1973, p. 44). When Paul left this earth, not only did he leave behind a legacy of souls he brought to Christ and churches he founded, he also left evangelists who carried on his good work, men like Timothy, Titus, Epaphras, Tychicus and Trophimus. Paul had multiplied his ministry.

How did a busy man like Paul carry out this ministry of multiplication? Paul, like Jesus and Peter, almost never traveled alone. He always took young assistants with him on his journeys. Some of these traveling companions, like Timothy, Titus, and Tychicus, are mentioned later in the epistles as holding positions of high responsibility in the churches. As they traveled and ministered together Paul obviously invested himself in their lives.

A native of Lystra, Timothy was probably converted during Paul's first missionary journey. When Paul came there on his second visit he found Timothy highly esteemed by the Christian community. So he took him on as an apprentice in his travels (Acts 16:1-4).

During these years of intimate contact with Paul, *Timothy was able to observe Paul's life at close quarters.* That life became an example for Timothy to follow. In 2 Timothy 3:10,11, Paul says, "You, however, know all about my teaching, my way of life, my purpose, faith, patience, love, endurance, persecutions, sufferings." Commentators have pointed out that the word translated here as "know" carries the idea of "tracing out as an example" of "carefully noting with a view to reproducing"; and is "a technical term defining the relation of a disciple to his master." Timothy knew exactly how Paul believed and taught, acted and reacted. This was only possible because they had lived together, prayed together, studied the Word together, ministered together, and suffered together. During these experiences together, Paul had opened up his life to Timothy. Paul had adopted an open-hearted approach to ministry. This approach is described well in 2 Corinthians 6:11,12, where Paul says, "We have spoken freely to you, Corinthians, and opened wide our hearts to you. We are not withholding our affection from you" (also cf. 1 Corinthians 4:9; 1 Thessalonians 1:4-8).

This open-hearted approach to ministry is not common today. Professionalism has so invaded contemporary approaches to ministry that ministers are encouraged to keep their personal, private lives and their ministry lives separate. They are taught not to expose their personal lives to those to whom they minister. Only in formal, prearranged meetings like small groups do they open up and share about their personal lives. Contact with people is limited to meetings and occasional personal appointments. By guarding their private lives, they would save themselves a lot of pain and trouble, they are told. But the pain of exposure is the price of a deep ministry. Paul was willing to risk hurting himself by exposing himself to people like Timothy. And indeed we know that because of such a close link with his spiritual children he was hurt very often. But in the process he was able to multiply his ministry.

In my youth, I had the privilege of coming under the influence of two great disciplers—our leader in Youth For Christ, and a seminary professor. Their personalities and methods of discipling were different. But in many areas, the way they ministered to me were similar. I had regular times of prayer and Bible study with them, usually along with a few others. They both had me over to their homes, again often along with a few others, to spend time with them and their families. We would often eat together and sometimes join in the work around the house. We would laugh together, discuss current affairs, sometimes argue about issues facing us, and often talk about the things of the Lord.

Both these men took me with them when they went out on ministry assignments. I observed them witnessing, counseling, conducting meetings, preaching, and responding to crises. Sometimes I was also given a small part in the program. Some of the best times we had were when we traveled to or from a place of ministry by train, bus, motorcycle, or car. The conversations we had then imparted truths that went deep into my soul. Only in heaven will I know how much I learned from being with these two men of God. So, through concern and prolonged contact with Timothy, Paul became a father to him.

First Timothy 1:18 gives a second key to the ministry of multiplication when it goes on to say, "Timothy, my son, *I give you this instruction.*" The word instruction is representative of an activity Paul carried out comprehensively in Timothy's life. Paul's Epistles to him are loaded with instructions on a wide variety of topics. While they traveled together on their evangelistic tours, Paul not only preached the Gospel to the lost, he also instructed his young colleagues. Our verse says that the instruction was aimed at helping Timothy "fight the good fight." It was given to help him be an effective Christian warrior. Paul did not have his young assistants simply to help him in his evangelistic ministry. Paul had a sense of responsibility for their personal welfare. So he taught them about the faith and instructed them about their lives.

Paul's teaching ministry is well described in the famous text on the discipling ministry, 2 Timothy 2:2: "The things you have heard me say in the presence of many witnesses entrust to reliable men, who will also be qualified to teach others." Here it is a body of truth that is said to be passed down along four generations of Christians. During their times together Paul had given Timothy a complete theological education. He had conducted a traveling Bible college. This is the way a lot of the ministerial training took place in the Bible—not in the formal team. This is how Jesus trained His disciples. I believe this is still the most effective way to train evangelists. Formal theological education is indeed God's calling for some. But I believe we are dumping on seminaries some of the work that we should be doing. We should be discipling leaders to maturity. And one of the most effective environments for doing this is a ministering team where vital body life is being experienced and active ministry, careful supervision, and regular teaching are being done. Here, soldiers are trained for battle in the battlefield itself. Such soldiers are best able to handle the warfare.

Some of the most effective evangelists I have met have had no formal theological training. Strangely, all of them seem to wish that they had taken some such training. But their ministry did not indicate the need for it. They were people of the Word, with a passion for Christ, a burden for the lost, and a gift for preaching. They had learned to study the Word carefully and apply it relevantly to life. Significantly, all of them spoke of an older evangelist who had taught them the Bible, and how to handle it and how to proclaim it. They had been trained in the biblical way by men who believed in the ministry of multiplication. One thing they lacked was a certain type of recognition in certain circles. But the recognition we seek most is in heaven. And there we are recognized not for the quantity of our academic qualifications but for the quality of our life and ministry.

The next thing Paul says in 1 Timothy 1:18 is that he gives his instructions "in keeping with the prophecies once made about" Timothy. Paul knew of a message given through prophetic utterance which indicated that Timothy had a bright future ahead of him. These prophecies became the basis of *Paul's ambitions for Timothy*. He wanted to do all he could to help Timothy to achieve all that God intended for him. What a beautiful thought this is! We have ambitions not only for ourselves but also for others. We dream not only for ourselves but also for others.

It has been said that individualism and self-centeredness are occupational hazards of public evangelism. So much attention is focused on the preacher that the self can easily be encouraged in an unhealthy way. Here is a good remedy for selfish individualism—developing ambitions for others! By pushing others forward you develop an attitude and life-style which helps you to avoid pushing yourself forward in an unhealthy way.

Now we see that Paul did everything he could to help Timothy to fulfill these ambitions he had for him. We know that *Paul regularly prayed for Timothy*. In 2 Timothy 1:3 he says, "Night and day I constantly remember you in my prayers." In 1 Timothy 5:5 Paul says that widows who separate themselves for God's work should continue to pray night and day. We all would say a hearty "Amen" to that. The specialist prayer warriors on their knees keep those on the front lines on their feet. Yet the Bible is clear that the evangelist is also a specialist in prayer. And so that same demand that Paul made of the widows, he fulfilled in his own life. If we were to analyze all of Paul's references to his prayer life and take note of the great details he went into in his intercessory prayers and the number of people he prayed for, we would have to conclude that he spent a significant amount of time in prayer. This is also true of Peter, the other prominent evangelist of the early church. He made sure that he and his colleagues were released to give their attention to prayer and the ministry of the Word (Acts 6:4).

One of the main topics of prayer for a person involved in the ministry of multiplication is the young ministers whom he is discipling. And so it is not surprising that Timothy figured prominently in the prayer life of Paul. It is interesting to note that the only record of Jesus' speaking about His own prayer life was concerning His prayer for His evangelist-in-training, Peter. Luke 22:32 says, "I have prayed for you, Simon, that your faith may not fail."

We also see that in helping Timothy fulfill his ambitions for Timothy, *Paul gradually handed over some of his ministry to Timothy.* The first record we have of this is during the first journey Timothy took with Paul. In Berea, Jews from Thessalonica stirred up the people so much that Paul had to leave the city. He left Timothy behind with the more senior man, Silas, to complete what needed to be done there (Acts 17:14,15). Later on Timothy was sent out on numerous missions as Paul's representative. Many of Paul's letters have Timothy's name along with his in the opening identification. This shows that Paul was seeking to have the churches recognize Timothy as a key leader. It was the case of the senior man acting as the public relations officer of the junior man! Here is another example of how having ambitions for junior people helps the evangelist to overcome the dangers of individualism. By the time the letters to Timothy were written, he was in charge of the large church in Ephesus. This was such a big responsibility for a person his age that he seemed reluctant to stick with it. So Paul had to urge him to continue in it (1 Timothy 1:3).

Paul could never have done such an amazing amount of lasting work for the Kingdom if he had not multiplied his ministry in people like Timothy. There is, of course, a price to pay in handing over ministries to younger assistants. They would not, at first, do the same high-quality work as the leader. In fact, they may make some big mistakes that could jeopardize the reputation of the leader. Some may, on the other hand, end up overtaking the leader as far as prominence is concerned. This happened to the veteran Barnabas, who was outshone by his young assistant, Paul, after some years. But the Gospel moved out. A lasting work was accomplished. Churches were established. Capable men were left behind to lead them. And is not this what any evangelist would like to see accomplished from his ministry?

So when an evangelist takes a few younger believers with him as a team, he may first give them assignments that don't carry much responsibility, such as sharing a testimony or a counseling opportunity. Gradually larger responsibilities are handed over to them until finally they launch out on their own, perhaps with their own team of younger assistants.

Let me close by urging you to look for someone to pour yourself into. You may be surprised to find out that someone may just be waiting to be asked. Spend time with him. Pray for him. Develop ambitions for him. Take him with you on your ministry assignments. Teach him what you know. Find opportunities for him to develop his ministry gifts. Soon you will find that you have multiplied your ministry. You would have done your part in helping answer the prayer of Jesus about sending laborers into the harvest field.

NOTES:
1. All Bible quotations are from the New International Version.
2. Much of this material appeared in *The Work of an Evangelist*, pp. 203-207.

# THE EVANGELIST AND
# THE GREAT COMMISSION
*Gottfried Osei-Mensah*

The New Testament clearly shows that the Great Commission was given to the disciples by our risen Lord in different forms, on different occasions, and at different places. Each has a special emphasis. In this paper we shall try to answer two questions:
1. What is the special emphasis for the evangelist in each statement?
2. How does the special ministry of the evangelist fit into the strategy of the Church to fulfill the Great Commission?

*Matthew 28:18-20. Make disciples*

What does the Lord Jesus mean by a disciple? Earlier in Matthew (10:37,38; 16:24), we see that a disciple is someone who is totally committed to the Lord Jesus Christ. The Lord clearly claims the first place in His disciples' thinking, desires, choices, ambitions and relationships. Although discipleship is a life-long commitment to the Lord Jesus Christ, it has its decisive beginning in the act of baptism.

How do we "make disciples"? The evangelist's role is vital in making such committed followers of Christ. By our preaching we must encourage our hearers to think very carefully what it will mean in practice for them to submit to Jesus Christ as Savior and Lord (Luke 14:27-30).

*Mark 16:15,16. Preaching for a response*

The preaching of the Gospel is an awesome responsibility. The eternal destiny of the hearers is at stake. Mark emphasizes the response of men and women to the Gospel. Wherever it is faithfully preached, the Gospel always divides mankind into two groups. Those who believe in the Savior and submit to Him in baptism are saved. Those who disbelieve and reject His offer of forgiveness and new life must ultimately face His judgment and condemnation.

Nevertheless, the Gospel is "Good News" and we must always preach for decision, earnestly seeking to persuade our hearers to turn to the Savior in personal faith and repentance (2 Corinthians 2:15,16).

*Luke 24:46,47. Repentance and forgiveness*

The Great Commission in Luke's Gospel highlights the proclamation of repentance for the forgiveness of sins, in Christ's name, to all nations.

How should we proclaim repentance? We need to emphasize that it was on account of my sins that Jesus died. My sins crucified Him. God commands me as a sinner to repent. Christ forgives each repentant sinner, but He will judge the unrepentant. Christ has broken sin's power for me, so I can live in righteousness for Him.

How should we encourage the assurance of forgiveness? By emphasizing that God lifts the crushing load of guilt from those He forgives. He washes away the stain of sin. He restores the repentant sinner to His favor because of Christ's death on the Cross. God's forgiveness brings inner joy and peace, and a fresh desire to love and serve Him. Blessed is the man whose sin is forgiven.

Evangelists are at the cutting edge of fulfilling the Great Commission. We present Christ's royal offers and His claims to people as individuals. We have the authority of the One whom "God has exalted at His right hand as Leader and Savior, to give repentance to Israel, and forgiveness of sins'' (Acts 5:31), to proclaim God's free forgiveness, because Christ died.

### John 20:21.   *Sent into the world*

The Lord saw the disciples' mission in the world to be like His. "As the Father sent Me, even so send I you."

To whom was Jesus sent? He was sent by the Father to a lost humanity; to men and women spiritually dead in sin (John 3:16). Jesus identified completely with those to whom He was sent. To them He brought God's message of salvation and the offer of eternal life to all who would believe in Him (John 17:2,3). The world did not receive Him kindly. It was openly hostile.

What then is our mission as those whom He sends? To borrow the words of John Stott, we must resist the temptation to "shout the Gospel to people from a distance." Instead we must try to "involve ourselves deeply in their lives, think ourselves into their culture, identify with them in their problems and feel with them in their pains" (*Christian Mission in the Modern World*, p. 25).

We have the same Gospel to share, which we have received ourselves (1 Corinthians 15:3-5). The Lord has already warned us that the world will be hostile to us, as it was to Him (John 17:14,15). Nevertheless we should seek to love and care for those to whom we are sent, without losing our Christian identity.

### Acts 1:8.   *Power for witness*

The work of bringing the Gospel to the people of all the nations is beyond man's power to fulfill. Therefore the Lord Jesus promised the disciples the supernatural power of the Holy Spirit. Since the day of Pentecost, the Holy Spirit is available to help the Church obey Christ.

How do we receive the Holy Spirit's power for our work? First we must be sure that we are ourselves born again. The Holy Spirit is available only to those who belong to Christ (Romans 8:9). The Lord Jesus said that we should ask the Father specifically for the Holy Spirit (Luke 11:13). The Spirit is holy, therefore we must take care not to grieve Him with unconfessed sin or quench Him through unbelief. Instead, we must open our hearts to be filled by Him every day. We do so by seeking to know God better through His Word, and by bringing our wills in line with His (Ephesians 5:17,18). When I make it my purpose to do the will of Jesus Christ, I can trust Him in prayer for the Holy Spirit's help.

Who is a witness? A witness is so sure about what he has seen or heard that no one can silence him. When the Jewish leaders commanded the disciples not to preach the Gospel, they answered, "We cannot stop speaking of what we have seen and heard" (Acts 4:20). They were witnesses and prepared to suffer for truth. We must walk closely with the Lord Jesus every day, so that our witness for Him is fresh and powerful. When we know His presence and power in our lives through the Holy Spirit, then we are ready to go anywhere for Him.

### Acts 26:18.   *Deliverance from darkness*

When the Lord Jesus commissioned Paul on the Damascus road, He emphasized another important aspect of our task. The unbelievers to whom we are sent are spiritually blinded by Satan and held captive by him (2 Corinthians 4:4). Our preaching must therefore be accompanied by the Spirit's power to open their blind eyes and break their chains, before they can turn to the Lord for forgiveness (1 Thessalonians 1:5; Colossians 1:13).

The strength of Satan's control varies from one unreached people group to another. In those communities where evil spirits are very active, the need for effective prayer to break the power of darkness is vital. Evangelists are at the front line of the spiritual warfare. We must mobilize active prayer support in the local churches and Christian fellowships, if our Gospel is to capture enemy territory for Christ.

The whole church is called to witness to its risen Lord by its distinctive life-style of purity, and caring love for its members and neighbors (see John 13:34,35; Matthew 5:13-16). It is the special call of evangelists to pioneer the spread of the Good News into new territory. As we clearly present the message of salvation to unbelievers, and call for faith in the Lord Jesus Christ, we lay the solid foundation on which committed discipleship can be built (see Acts 2:41,42).

# THE EVANGELIST'S MINISTRY AMONG SITUATIONS OF HUMAN NEED

*Franklin Graham*

Today I have been asked by the Program Committee to make a presentation on the topic of human needs and evangelism. Assisting me in giving first-hand personal examples will be Reverend A. Qalo, Reverend Ezra Sargunam, and Reverend Sami Dagher.

In times past, evangelists have been accused, many times rightly so, of ignoring human need. The world makes a lot of "to-do" over social action. We have the Red Cross, the Red Crescent, and thousands of humanitarian agencies throughout the world, Christian and non-Christian. All of these piled together will not open one door to the eternal city of Heaven, and will not last one minute in the fires of everlasting hell.

What are we to do as evangelists when strife, poverty, war, and famine strike? How are we to implement the Gospel of Jesus Christ in action in the face of these great human needs?

A careful study of Jesus' ministry in the New Testament reveals that He brought both spiritual and physical healings to those He ministered to. He showed compassion to the physically disadvantaged, the unattractive, the diseased, the unsanitary, and the unsaved. From the very outset, Jesus demonstrated His care by meeting their personal needs—those who came to Him or met Him wherever they were. He willingly and visibly identified Himself with the lowly, the least, the last, and the lost.

This was the pattern of Jesus' ministry—meeting physical human needs to draw men to Himself. This must be the model of our evangelistic ministry today.

Our evangelistic ministry must cover the *whole life* of a person. Jesus said in John 10:10, "I have come that they may have life and have it more abundantly." The *total being* of a person is God's concern, and must be our concern as well.

My text this morning is Luke 16:1-13—a passage of Scripture that many people have never fully understood. The employer commended his dishonest manager because he had acted shrewdly—this is not Christ commending him, but his master. In this story, Christ is rebuking His disciples by saying, "This world is more shrewd in their dealings with one another than those who follow me—my disciples—those who call upon my Name."

Friends, this is so true today. Jesus Christ is rebuking us. The world is shrewd in its business dealings and in all of its affairs, but many times we waste valuable opportunities. We evangelists need to be shrewd in using every opportunity, as our Lord Jesus Christ did, to meet the total need of our world. I believe wars, I believe famines, I believe earthquakes, illiteracy—all of these—can be stepping stones, a platform, from which to preach Christ. None of us is too poor to help somebody. When you help somebody who has fallen in a ditch along the road of life, give a cup of cold water to the thirsty, food to the hungry, a shirt for the naked, that person will listen to you. You have earned the right to be heard. We evangelists need to be shrewd, and seize and hold on to every opportunity so that we can preach Christ and Him crucified.

Does this really work? Does this result in evangelism? Let me take you to three areas of our world—places I have been and experienced God at work. Listen to these exciting reports.

Papua New Guinea is a land of great contrast. Jet airplanes land at the International Airport in Port Moresby, and less than 100 miles away people live in a stone-age culture where today battles are still fought with bow and arrow. There is much famine and much disease. Twenty years ago a man was sent from his home country of Fiji as a missionary-evangelist to be a church planter in the Highlands of Papua New Guinea. I would like my friend, Reverend A. Qalo, to come and share with you some examples of how God used the meeting of human needs to draw men to Himself.

*A. Qalo:*

During the last 20 years, I lived and worked among the mountain people of Papua New Guinea, who were once known as "Headhunters." A country of three million with 700 languages spoken; a place where animism was their religion, where tribal fightings seemed to be a weekly event; a place where half of the population are still illiterate, and where the standard of living can be classified as "semi-primitive."

With these problems and needs I, with many others, shared the Gospel as practically as we could, following Jesus' model of ministry.

The people of Papua New Guinea responded well to the Gospel—a Gospel of faith in action. Remember—actions speak louder than words! Whether it be on *Health Care, Education, Village Projects, Personal or Family Needs,* or *Economic Development,* meeting these human needs are all vital to our evangelistic ministry among the people.

Let me just share with you a couple of very simple but effective examples of meeting human needs that led two families to accept the Lord Jesus Christ.

A Christian youth group heard of a family who had very little in their home. The father was a sorcerer and an evil-spirit worshiper. He was wounded in a tribal fight. He could not do any work and could not support his family any longer. Their house was in bad shape and was leaking. There was not enough in their garden to live on.

The young people were filled with compassion and wanted to help. They went to the family to repair their house and plant their garden with sweet potatoes, sugarcane, and vegetables.

That sorcerer and his family were deeply moved when they saw the action demonstrated by those young people. It was through this visible evangelistic witnessing and the Gospel message that the family accepted Christ as their Savior and Lord. Jesus said, "Truly, I say to you, as you did it to one of the least of these my brethren, you did it to me" (Matthew 25:40).

Years ago, when my daughter was just four years old, she was playing with some village children near our home. She noticed a small girl of her age sitting under a tree shivering from the cold. This girl did not have any clothes other than her native bush dress. My daughter was sad to see the girl in that condition and came running home pleading with her mother to give one of her sweaters and a dress to that little girl. She called the girl into the house and helped her to put the clothes on to keep her warm and comfortable. Late in the afternoon on that same day, we saw this little girl with her mother beside her. They had come to thank my daughter and ask if it would be okay for them to attend our prayer meeting that evening. This led them into church and, later on, the father came; and they as a family eventually became Christians as a result of the Gospel message.

Although my daughter acted with a childlike love and compassion, she did not know that her action would lead that family to the Lord Jesus Christ.

These are just two examples of many where immediate human needs were met which led the recipients to the Lord.

Yes, this is evangelism in action!

*F. Graham:*

Thank you, Brother Qalo. My dear friends, this man's daughter shared an article of clothing and because of this a family came to know Christ. A simple sweater brought the warmth of Christ to a cold heart. These young people had compassion on a witch doctor filled with evil, controlled by the power of Satan; yet the love of Christ in these young people was more powerful. Little is much when God is in it.

Over 20 years thousands have come to Christ and hundreds of churches have been planted. Friend, you can do the same.

Many thousands of miles away from Papua New Guinea is the great nation of India. How do you evangelize a nation caught in the grip of poverty and despair? Ezra Sargunam, pastor and vice president of the Evangelical Church of India, faced this problem a few years ago and is evangelizing in a unique way. I want him to come and tell you how his church is meeting human needs and drawing men and women to Christ.

*E. Sargunam:*

As an Indian evangelist and church leader, I have always been concerned and burdened about how to reach the poor families throughout all of India. By God's grace and His leading we put together a program of love and sharing, where we would provide every family around the churches with a coconut plant. The family plants this young tree and within five years the coconut tree produces coconuts. In India, no part of the coconut is wasted. Within ten years, the coconut tree can double the family's income. Remember these are very poor people whose average annual income would be less than 50 U.S. dollars. Giving these people coconut trees demonstrates our love and provides an opportunity for the pastor and evangelist to follow up and check on the family with the coconut tree to see how it is growing. This builds a bridge of friendship and understanding, and gives the evangelist or pastor an opportunity to win their trust and share Christ. It is our prayer that thousands will come to Christ.

In a small village near Madras there was an old lady 75 years old who received a coconut plant from the church after standing in the hot sun for more than an hour. When the pastor visited the home of this lady, he found she was living with her only daughter and two grandchildren whose daddy had left them several years before. The daughter of the lady had to work hard in the fields and in house construction as a laborer. After several visits, the pastor was able to explain the way of salvation and lead the whole family to Christ. They gave up their worship and became followers of Christ, and now regularly worship the Lord in the little church.

Today, the coconut plant is growing and so are the members of this family—growing in the grace and knowledge of the Lord.

Of all of our programs, the well project has been most successful. Wells were drying up in India. We, the church, decided to dig our own. We call them "Jesus wells." Through the generous gifts made available from Samaritan's Purse we have so far drilled 100 wells and we have a goal of 1,000 wells for 1,000 churches. These wells are placed on church property. We have heard from the non-Christians in the localities that have "Jesus wells" that they never go dry. They say, "We get the best water in this whole area."

Water is an essential commodity in life. Without water we cannot survive. In India, much of village life is centered around a community well. From washing clothes to bathing, for drinking, cooking, for agriculture, a village well plays a vital role. In providing a well right in front of the church we are also trying to provide the community with the "living water" that they may never thirst again. The results are overwhelming. In a number of villages where there had been so much opposition to the

Gospel, we found after we dug a well, all the tensions vanished immediately.

In the month of January we had organized mass baptisms in Aurangabed, near Bombay. And in a matter of two weeks we baptized 2,062 converts drawn from 14 villages. One of the factors behind these mass conversions is the ''Jesus wells.''

Many people are throwing away their idols and sinful habits to follow Christ. It is a new day for India. Our Lord and Savior, who was once sitting by the well in Samaria waiting for His prospects, is still waiting today at these ''Jesus wells'' in India . . . calling the poor people of India, ''Ho, every one that thirsteth come to the waters, he that hath no money come . . .'' (Isaiah 55:1). Let us not be weary in doing good for we shall reap if we faint not.

*F. Graham:*

Thank you, Dr. Ezra Sargunam. Meeting human need in a land of great need—the hope is to draw millions to drink from the well that takes away thirst forever. Imagine, a simple thing like a well bringing men and women to Christ! A coconut plant given in the Name of Jesus Christ gives an evangelist years of opportunity to go and check on that family, to see how that gift is producing. It's a witness for Jesus Christ. Friends, when you get home you pray that God will give you opportunities like this. All of us can give, and all of us should be meeting needs of men and women to draw them to Christ.

Let me take you now a few thousand miles away to a land ravaged by war—Lebanon—a word that we all know. The Bible has a lot to say about Lebanon. It is mentioned many times throughout the Scriptures. The prophets spoke of Lebanon. Today, it seems as though every demon in hell has been unleashed in Lebanon. Murders and killings are an everyday occurrence. The streets of Beirut literally flow with blood of men, women, and children. But in the midst of darkness there is light, in the midst of hatred there is love, in the midst of death there is life.

Reverend Sami Dagher, a pastor and evangelist from Beirut, has been used mightily of God over the last ten years to meet the needs of human suffering, and through it to draw men and women to Christ. Sami, come and tell us how God has used you.

*S. Dagher:*

In the fourth chapter of Amos we read these words: ''I sent you hunger, saith the Lord, but it did no good—you still would not return to me. I ruined your crops by holding back the rain—yet you would not return to me! I sent you plagues like those of Egypt long ago, I killed your men in war—and yet you refused to return to me. I destroyed some of your cities—and still you wouldn't return to me, saith the Lord.''

We learn from Amos that whatever happens to us—individually, or as a nation—in the mind of God He is using it to bring us to Himself. Knowing this fact, we should ask ourselves, ''How can we as believers and servants of the Lord Jesus Christ use the tragic situations of the world to bring people to Himself?''

Tragedies create needs for the people—both material and spiritual. And we as believers should be able to help and meet the needs of the people.

In my country of Lebanon we have been engaged in war for over 11 years. Half of our Christian community have been made refugees in their own country. They have lost their land, homes, businesses, and jobs. Overnight they have become poor.

In the beginning I did not know what to do. After seeking the Lord's will in prayer, I found that God expects us to help no matter what people will say. Because if we help, people will talk; and if we don't help, people will talk. We chose to help and be in the will of God.

For nearly ten years now we have been engaged in helping people—in the Name of the Lord—to find people houses, work to support themselves, food, and medical assistance. All of this has been done for the glory of Christ and in His Name.

This gave us the right and opened the door to personal witness. Jesus said, "Let them see your good works and glorify your Father in Heaven."

Not only have we helped our own people, but also our enemies. The Palestinians are the worst enemy for Lebanon. They have done much damage to our country—destroying our cities, killing our children, and spoiling the reputation of our country. But we as believers, after we heard of the massacres which took place in the Palestinian camps, were moved with compassion and reached out to help them.

For six months my team of seven men visited the camps from morning until afternoon giving them clothes, food, and medical assistance. By helping in this way, we had the opportunity to share the Gospel of Jesus Christ.

More than 30,000 New Testaments were given away and every man on our team had a chance to sit and talk with the families that he visited.

I cannot tell you of the results. We leave that to the Lord; as we know that it is the Holy Spirit who will convict people of their sins and draw them to the Savior.

What we have done was in obedience to the Lord's command to love our enemy and to go to all nations and preach the Gospel. For "the Gospel is the power of God unto salvation to everyone that believes."

*F. Graham:*

I wish you could go to Beirut and visit the church Sami Dagher pastors and the Bible school he has started—his ministry has grown. Why? Because he has shared Christ, made Him relevant to human needs.

Let me review just for a moment, before we close, what we have heard today. A simple sweater has brought warmth to a cold heart, a witch doctor was won through the concern of a youth group, coconut trees provide opportunities to witness. The wells bring the water of life, and even in the heat of war there is hope and healing through Jesus Christ. This is what we all can do. A cup of cold water given in Jesus' Name can be used to bring people to the Savior.

Remember what God asked Moses? "What do you have in your hands?" Are you willing to use what God has given you to reach people for Christ? What can you do in your community? Your country? What are the human needs that surround you? Will you meet them in Christ's Name? If you look around, you will see the need. Be shrewd. Remember we are the Body of Christ. We must see what He sees, hear what He hears, do what He has done. Do all you can do. This, too, is the work of the evangelist.

# PREPARING AN EVANGELISTIC EVENT
## *Sterling Huston*

### 1. *Preface*

The objective of this seminar is to communicate the principles and processes essential for effective preparation of an evangelistic event, so that the participants will be able to understand and apply them appropriately to their own ministry.

The assumption is made that each evangelist who chooses an evangelistic event or method has done so based on a clearly stated purpose, an evaluation of the target audience needs and receptivity, an inventory of the available resources within the Christian community seeking to reach that target audience, and a review of the evangelist's. own ministry gifts and resources.

For illustration purposes, we will assume that we are applying the principles of this lecture to a mass evangelistic meeting (Crusade) involving ten cooperating churches. You may or may not be involved in mass evangelism or inter-church evangelism, but it is necessary to define the event used in order to understand the application of the principles.

### 2. *Purpose*

The primary purpose of any evangelistic event is to "make disciples." Before His ascension, Jesus commissioned His followers to "Therefore go and make disciples of all nations . . ." (Matthew 28:19). The goal of evangelism is not "decisions," but "disciples." It is not collecting statistics, but accumulating servants who live out their commitment to Christ under His Lordship in a local body of believers.

A commitment to the purpose of making disciples affects both the message and the methods an evangelist uses. The methods will be geared both to reaping and discipling, and the message will include the cost of discipleship. An understanding of our Lord's standard of success in fulfilling the Great Commission (making disciples) will avoid the temptation to preach a message of "easy believism," or to manipulate the invitation to produce "decisions." It also will place greater responsibility on methods that prepare for discipleship, and especially for linking those who respond to a local body of believers.

Discipleship is not the evangelist's sole responsibility. It is essential that the local church become the primary instrument for the continuing work of discipleship after a commitment to Christ is made. However, the evangelist sets the tone and the priorities for the whole event. He must integrate his efforts so thoroughly with the whole body of Christ, and particularly with the local church, that discipleship is the natural flow of activity for the inquirer after he responds to the evangelist's invitation.

Two potential problems occur if this goal is not approached in a balanced way:

First, the evangelist who has always measured success by large numbers of decisions without concern or preparations for discipleship can often produce disillusionment: disillusionment on the part of those who respond but are not given adequate spiritual care, and who fall by the wayside; disillusionment on the part of the local churches and Christians who find that so little fruit remains; and disillusionment on the part of the evangelist who sees so little enduring results from his ministry.

A second problem involves those who are overly cautious about preparing every aspect of discipleship. Often this mentality prevents people from conducting evangelistic events until they feel their discipleship program is "fully prepared." This can place too much dependency on man's efforts and hinder generous sowing which is the key to generous reaping.

What are your goals as an evangelist? Do you measure success in terms of numbers of decisions? Where are those "decisions" five, ten, and fifteen years later? Ultimately, our service and ministry will be evaluated by Jesus Christ Himself, and anything less than reaching His goals will not please Him or pass the Judgment Seat of Christ. Jesus made His goals clear, "Therefore go and make disciples of all nations . . ."

### 3.  *Perspective*

A proper perspective on an evangelistic event reveals that there are three major stages: Preparation, Proclamation or Presentation, and Preservation. One way to illustrate this is by an iceberg. We are told that 90% of an iceberg is below the surface of the water and only 10% appears above. The larger the 90% portion, the larger the more visible 10% area.

Since proclamation is the area of his primary gift, an evangelist often puts most of his efforts into this stage. The proclamation stage is very important. However, effective evangelism, that implements biblical purposes and principles, requires substantial preparation and preservation efforts as well. Your percentages may vary from these, but all three stages need to be represented. It is appropriate to expect more effort and energy to go into the preparation and preservation stages than into the proclamation stage.

The law of the harvest mandates the necessity of good preparations. Paul reminds us, "A man reaps what he sows" (Galatians 6:7). This is an inescapable law of creation. If we sow well we will reap well, but the converse is also true. Conditions, cultures, and churches vary across the world; but, in the North American environment, no longer will "a prayer, a poster, a preacher and a place to meet" accomplish effective evangelism. We need to sow well in good preparations for the harvest as well as for preserving that harvest.

How do you plan your evangelistic ministry and events? What percentage of your time do you spend in the area of proclamation—90, 80, 70, 50 percent? What percentage of time is given to the preparation stage by those responsible for these events? What percentage of effort goes into the preservation stage of your ministry? In the natural realm, a farmer spends 80 to 90 percent of his time preparing for and caring for the harvest. Only about 10 percent is actually spent in harvesting. In God's economy of New Testament evangelization, these percentages also could generally apply.

### 4.  *Principles*

Effective preparation of evangelistic events needs to be done according to proven biblical principles. It has well been said: "Methods are many, principles are few. Methods often change, but principles never do."

The event that works for one evangelist may not work for another. The method that fits one culture may not fit another. The proper choice of a method should be made in light of some essential principles for evangelism. Understanding these principles will help each evangelist choose methods effective within the cultural context in which he works. There are seven important principles, among others, which are involved in effective preparations for an evangelistic event.

*The first principle: evangelism is the work of the Holy Spirit.*

Jesus made it clear that the power to witness to Him comes from the Holy Spirit (Acts 1:8). The harvest at Pentecost was obviously a direct result of a great movement of the Holy Spirit. He further emphasized that "it is the Spirit that quickeneth; the flesh profiteth nothing" (John 6:63).

We have discovered that effective Crusade evangelism is not built on persuasion, personality, or promotion. These may play a small part, but only the Holy Spirit can convict of sin, call to repentance and faith, and convert the soul (John 16:8). Although men, methods, and materials are important instruments in preparing for evangelism, we must not depend on them. God knows what we are actually trusting in. He will not bless faith in human instruments; but rather, faith in God to use and empower human instruments through the work of the Holy Spirit.

In light of this, prayer is the greatest priority in preparation for evangelism. James tells us that "the effectual fervent prayer of a righteous man availeth much" (James 5:16). Armin Gesswein, who led the prayer emphasis in many of Billy Graham's earlier Crusades says, "Without doubt this (prayer) is the master secret behind the Graham Crusades through the years. There is no other way to account for such a massive work of God." Luther battled his way through the Reformation by prayer and the Word of God. Finney increasingly stressed the primacy of prayer.

A.T. Pierson, the great leader of the Alliance Church, observed, "No revival has ever come about but by united supplicatory praying, as in the Acts; and no revival has ever continued beyond that same kind of praying." Moody remarked that "every work of God can be traced to some kneeling form." And Billy Graham has said, "The secret of each Crusade has been the power of God's Spirit moving in answer to the prayers of His people. I have often said that the three most important things we can do for a Crusade are to pray, to pray, and to pray."

As the Psalmist has said, "Except the Lord build the house, they labor in vain that build it" (Psalm 127:1). Everyone involved needs to understand that our resources are in God and we receive those resources as the people of God pray. Prayer should be emphasized for everybody involved.

You cannot organize prayer, but you can organize opportunities for prayer. That organization should make the opportunities both biblical and attainable. It should also make the opportunities convenient to people's daily life patterns, not adding unnecessary work to the already hard work of prayer.

One very workable and flexible model of this is the Prayer Triplet program, which was introduced to us through Mission England. The Prayer Triplet program is based on Matthew 18:19,20: "Again, I tell you that if two of you on earth agree about anything you ask for, it will be done for you by my Father in heaven. For where two or three come together in my name, there I am with them." The concept is for three people to meet once a week praying for three unreached people whom each one has identified. This means nine people are prayed for weekly. This has proven to be a highly effective and powerful way to encourage specific prayer.

*A second principle: reaping requires sowing*

Paul said, "I planted the seed, Apollos watered it, but God made it grow" (1 Corinthians 3:6). Sowing is indispensable in the preparations for evangelism if we expect to reap souls. The gift of an evangelist is effective only as other gifts of the church are exercised. Christians must sow the good seed of the Word through their witness, and water it with loving concern and prayer, to prepare the harvest for the work of an evangelist. An obstetrician cannot deliver physical life until there has been conception and a period of gestation. This is also true of the "spiritual obstetrician"—the evangelist.

In the great wheat fields of America's Midwest, the farmers plant and prepare the crop. Then harvesters come to help in the reaping. Both rejoice when the harvest is safely in. This is true also of the spiritual harvest. Jesus said, "He that reapeth . . . gathereth fruit unto life eternal: that both he that soweth and he that reapeth may rejoice together'' (John 4:36). A recent survey of Crusade inquirers revealed that 82 percent of those who responded to the invitation did so on the first night of attendance. This indicates that there had been sowing and watering in their lives that prepared them for the gift of an evangelist to reap.

It is important to emphasize the opportunity for, and responsibility of, every believer to sow and water. Just as in the natural realm, it takes time to prepare the harvest, so also in the spiritual realm. For that reason, preparations must begin well in advance, and every member of the church needs to be involved in the sowing and watering.

To attempt to reap without sowing will frustrate the reaper. Every evangelist has had the experience of finding only the gleanings and not the abundant harvest. On the other hand, to challenge Christians to sow generously, but not offer them a time of reaping, will frustrate the sowers. God expects both to occur in balance for His Church to fulfill the Great Commission.

An emphasis on sowing and watering begins with pastors preaching regularly about the responsibility of every Christian sharing his faith in loving ways to those around him. Some practical methods include the Prayer Triplet program, which asks for specific goals that lead to specific acts of witness. In addition, the Operation Andrew program of Crusade evangelism emphasizes not only praying specifically for others, but cultivating their friendship and seeking opportunities to share Christ with them. There are many other ways to sow and to water. Every believer can be involved in some way in preparing for the gift of an evangelist to be exercised.

*A third principle: evangelism is built on relationships*

The biblical illustration of this is Andrew, who brought his brother Simon to Jesus (John 1:40-42). This is the basic pattern for all evangelism: one person who has found life, meaning, forgiveness, and hope in Jesus Christ is motivated by love to bring others to encounter the same living Christ. D.T. Niles expressed it well in his classic definition, ''Evangelism is one beggar telling another where he found bread.'' He is no better than his fellow beggar, but is motivated by love to share where he found the answer to his need.

Each Christian has a web of relationships about his life involving family, friends, neighbors, and acquaintances where he works, shops, or goes to school. Church growth experts tell us that the greatest outreach is through our natural relationships. Surveys of Crusade inquirers in Billy Graham meetings reveal that at least 80 percent of the unchurched were brought personally by someone else, and that 75 percent of all inquirers, whether churched or unchurched, were given a ride to the meetings. Another survey reports that 85 percent of all evangelical Christians could point to at least one family member who would have prayed for their salvation. Individual Christians have a world of surrounding relationships to which they have both opportunity and responsibility to witness.

The Operation Andrew program in a Crusade emphasizes this principle by asking believers to pray specifically for unreached people, and to reach out to them. According to church growth expert, Peter Wagner, only about 10 percent of the members of an average evangelical church believe they have the gift of an evangelist. However, every member can be a witness to his or her world.

The Operation Andrew program emphasizes the need to cultivate the soil before attempting to plant the seed and harvest it. This cultivation can be done by an invitation to dinner, to a ball game, for a backyard picnic, for coffee or a concert, or just by being helpful whenever there is a need. Genuine acts of love can earn the right to be heard, and open hearts to receive the Good News of the Gospel.

After cultivation and sowing, the gift of an evangelist is needed to reap the results of personal witness. All involved Christians should be encouraged to sow and water through specific programs in order to effectively prepare the harvest.

*A fourth principle: involvement produces commitment*

Management experts tell us that involvement plus participation equals commitment. Jesus involved a band of twelve and an inner core of three. These men became committed to His goals and led the early church in obeying the Great Commission.

Involvement in the process, and participation in the decisions, yields commitment to the end goals of any project. This is a God-given principle for life. When a man is asked to usher, he makes a commitment that affects his praying, his family, his friends, his neighbors, and his attendance at the meetings. When a woman agrees to open her home for prayer or to sing in the choir, she makes a commitment that affects her praying, her family, her friends, her neighbors, and her attendance at the meetings. In light of this principle, one should seek to involve as many people as possible in advance of the meetings in at least one meaningful role. Spread the responsibilities around as much as is feasible to increase involvement.

As we have discussed earlier, around each life is a circle of relationships. The larger the number of people involved in some role in the preparations, the larger the number represented by their relationships who will be influenced by these involved people. This involvement has a direct effect on attendance, on witness, on invitation to the unchurched, and on prayer for needy people through every aspect of the preparations. Thus, specific plans need to be made to organize for recruitment down to, and within, the local church to assure maximum involvement in the event.

*A fifth principle: we must organize for effectiveness*

Moses received good advice from his father-in-law, Jethro, who told him he was wearing himself out by seeking to judge all the people, and that he should divide and delegate the responsibility (Exodus 18:13-26). That organizing is best accomplished by following the "3-D" Rule.

*First, divide into "bite-sized" tasks.* Moses used a one-to-five and one-to-ten ratio, asking one person to be responsible for the activities of five to ten others. The result was that he served the people and God's purposes far better than by trying to do it himself.

*Second, delegate the responsibility.* Good delegation occurs when we choose capable people who will commit themselves to a specific task that is equal to their talents. This requires defining the task and the responsibilities for that person, but it multiplies the leader's effectiveness and greatly increases involvement.

*Third, deadline its completion.* Whenever a specific task is given to a particular person, it is essential to specify when and how it must be completed. The assignment of realistic and meaningful time deadlines is imperative for good organization.

*A sixth principle: establish faith-sized goals.*

Establishing goals produces greater results. Goals determine our priorities, and priorities determine our schedule. It should be noted that "no goal" is also a goal and, if we aim at nothing, we are bound to hit it. It is essential, in a Christian context, to set goals too big to be reached by human resources alone, yet small enough so that you can believe—with God's help—they can be reached. Such goals need to be established prayerfully, with a realistic appraisal of the opportunities, the needs, and the resources—but always looking to God for His direction and assurance. Goals should be established for every level of leadership in an evangelistic event. Major goals need to be set for the event itself, such as attendance, choir, ushers, counselors, and prayer involvement. Further, each local congregation involved in the event should be challenged to set goals for its own involvement, attendance, and giving. Finally, every person who becomes involved should be challenged to set goals in two ways:

First, by committing themselves to a place of service, such as a choir member, usher, counselor, prayer group leader, or visitation worker.

Second, each believer can be expected to be involved in four general ways: by praying, by witnessing, by inviting others, and by attending.

Practical mechanisms should be provided to allow people to respond specifically in each of these areas, indicating their commitment to goals.

*A seventh principle: train for responsibilities*

Paul, in writing to Timothy, instructed him, "And the things you have heard me say in the presence of many witnesses entrust to reliable men who will also be qualified to teach others" (2 Timothy 2:2). Jethro admonished his son-in-law, Moses, to train the people in how they were to live, to make his responsibilities of judging easier. He said, "Teach them the decrees and laws, and show them the way to live, and the duties they are to perform" (Exodus 18:20).

All persons recruited for involvement in an evangelistic event should be trained for their specific task and for the general responsibilities that every Christian should carry. That specific task might be leading a prayer group, serving as a counselor, working in follow-up, singing in the choir, helping as an usher, visiting others, or raising finances for the event. In addition, the training program should include both the challenge and the methods of sharing their faith, praying with others, and inviting others to the meetings.

Training is as essential in the preparation of an evangelistic event as it is in any other arena of life. It is unfair to assume people know how to do what they have never been trained to do. It is unrealistic to expect them to perform effectively without the resources of training.

Each of these seven principles needs to be applied as thoroughly as possible in preparing an evangelistic event. Specific programs for them would be tailored to the type of event, the resources of the evangelist, the cultural context in which it is conducted, and other variables of the localized situation. However, each principle should be considered indispensable for effective evangelism preparations.

5. *Process*

The principles involved in preparing an evangelistic event are "fleshed out" in a process comprised of four general phases of activity: organization, recruitment, training, and function. Although these phases may overlap somewhat for specific committee tasks, they provide a sequential order for effective preparations.

a. *Organization.* The organizing phase includes defining the overall event by specific tasks, such as choir, ushers, arrangements and publicity, and choosing capable leadership for each responsibility. In Billy Graham Crusades the leadership model for the guiding policy-making committee, which carries out the specific tasks, is an Executive Committee.

Second, the outreach area needs to be organized for recruitment by maintaining a "leadership-to-contact" ratio of one-to-ten or less. This results in what we call the inverse pyramid model, whereby each person expands his or her recruitment to enlarge the base of involved people. Asking people to take a larger leadership-to-contact ratio, especially if distances or hindrances to communication are great, will limit organizational effectiveness.

Third, a time line for the preparation phases needs to be established. A sample time line for a Billy Graham Crusade covers a nine-month period. Your time line may be shorter or longer, but it should be planned in advance.

Fourth, each local church should be provided with an organizational model which will interface effectively with the organization for the overall event. In this case, a local church congregational committee is established and each recruited leader is contacted by the Crusade Executive Committee member who is chairman of his or her specific committee (i.e., local church choir leader by choir chairman).

Finally, every recruited person who accepts a leadership role in the organizational phase is challenged to pray with the understanding that organization is only an effective instrument when it is empowered by the Holy Spirit.

b. *Recruitment.* The recruitment phase permits the application of several principles. Goals need to be established for every level of the recruitment process. First, everyone recruited should understand that the ultimate goal of a Crusade is making disciples, and that each Christian can have a meaningful role in reaching that goal. Second, specific goals for the event, such as attendance, counselors, or choir members should be determined. Third, goals are set for the area organization of recruiting up to ten people. In the case of our model, that would be one person from each church to serve in the corresponding leadership role. Finally, every church is challenged to set faith-sized goals for recruitment for the various opportunities of involvement.

In addition to setting goals, the recruitment process involves briefing all recruited leaders for their task, providing them with the materials and resources needed, and establishing time deadlines for their completion. Most important, every recruited member is challenged to pray for the preparations and to witness to others in order to prepare a harvest.

c. *Training.* The third phase involves training. Once the recruitment goals have been attained, and the completion deadlines reached, recruited personnel need to be trained for their specific Christian responsibility. During the training sessions, they are provided with the necessary instruction, materials, and resources for carrying out their specific task. In addition, they are trained and challenged to pray specifically for others, to witness, to invite and bring others to the meetings, and to attend faithfully.

d. *Function.* The final phase is that of functioning. It is during this time that trained workers fulfill their responsibilities. Some of the tasks will start before the proclamation stage of a Crusade (i.e., prayer and visitation), and others continue after the meetings have been completed (i.e., counseling and discipleship). However, most workers will function during the period of the Crusade meetings. Throughout the function phase, all workers will continue to pray, to witness, to invite and bring, and to attend.

Each recruiting committee goes through this preparation cycle, though the cycle time lines do not necessarily coincide. It is essential in planning an evangelistic event that allowance be made for these phases to occur. Short-circuiting or eliminating any phase will hinder the effectiveness of reaching your evangelistic event goals.

Ultimately, evangelism must be a passion before it becomes a program. A Holy Spirit-inspired sense of mission precedes the choice of a method to fulfill that mission. The choice of a method to reach your evangelistic goals should be guided by biblical principles. Once chosen, that method can be effectively implemented only as these same principles are thoroughly and prayerfully applied in all phases of the preparations.

# COUNSELING
*Tom Phillips and Charles Riggs*

In the early history of the Church, little was said about counseling and the work of the counselor. Psychology is barely 100 years old. Seminaries have only in recent years started training pastors in the field of counseling. However, much is now being done by the church and para-church organizations to reach out to people in spiritual need and help them in their search for a meaning in life. To accomplish this task, multiplied thousands have been trained to share their faith, to counsel in-depth, and to help disciple individuals who have trusted Jesus Christ as Lord and Savior. Although the Bible doesn't say a lot about counseling, much is said about sharing what we have, as Christians, with others.

## 1. Biblical admonition

To lead a person, we need only be one step ahead. If I have made a commitment to Jesus Christ as my Lord and Savior, I can introduce others to Him. I can use John 3:16 to share my faith. Someone has called this passage "the Gospel in a nutshell." If the Holy Spirit is at work, there is enough Gospel in John 3:16 to lead a person to faith in Jesus Christ. In essence, the more spiritual truth that I know and have experienced in my life, the more I can share with others. The Bible says, "Personally I am satisfied about you, my brethren, that you yourselves are rich in goodness, amply filled with all (spiritual knowledge) and competent to admonish and counsel and instruct one another also" (Romans 15:14).

The Holy Spirit, who indwells every believer, gives the dynamic to share Christ with others. The Bible says, "But you will receive power when the Holy Spirit has come upon you; and you will be witnesses to me in Jerusalem, and in all Judea and Samaria, and to the end of the earth" (Acts 1:8).

One of the best illustrations of personal work is found in Chapter 8 of the book of Acts. The story concerns Philip the evangelist, an Ethiopian government official, the Word of God, and the work of the Holy Spirit. The Ethiopian official had journeyed several hundred miles to Jerusalem to worship, and was on his way back home but without Jesus Christ. The angel of the Lord sent Philip from Samaria to Gaza, where he met the Ethiopian riding in his chariot, reading Isaiah 53 (Acts 8:26-28). Philip was led of the Spirit to join the Ethiopian. When he found him reading Isaiah, he asked him if he understood what he was reading. The Ethiopian asked for help and Philip explained the passage and led him to faith in Christ (verses 29-39).

Not everyone has the gift of evangelism, but every believer can be used somewhere in God's service. In every congregation there are lay people who, with proper training, can be used of God. The Bible says, "It was he who gave some to be apostles, some to be prophets, some to be evangelists, and some to be pastors and teachers, to prepare God's people for works of service, so that the body of Christ may be built up" (Ephesians 4:11,12).

## 2. Counseling in an evangelistic campaign

a. *How it started: Billy Graham's burden.* Mr. Graham was privileged to hold a successful evangelistic Crusade in 1949 in the city of Los Angeles. This Crusade caught the eye of the nation; and in 1950 major Crusades were held in several large cities from coast to coast in America. During this time, Mr. Graham became greatly burdened for the masses of inquirers who were responding to his message. He wondered what was happening in follow-up and where these people would be a year later. Mr. Graham decided that he must do something to help in the follow-up. He contacted Dawson Trotman—founder of The Navigator organization—whom he knew to be a man of God with a discipleship vision. Mr. Trotman had developed Bible study material and was enjoying a successful ministry with multitudes of servicemen, helping them in their Christian walk and witness. In 1951, Dawson Trotman accepted Mr. Graham's invitation to help with Crusade work.

b. *Why counselors: clear commitments: start follow-up.* Mr. Trotman attended his first Crusade as an observer. After two weeks of listening to Mr. Graham's message, invitation, and prayer of commitment at the end of each service, he was challenged by the opportunity of helping, but sensed that something was missing. He felt that effective follow-up started with a clear commitment to Jesus Christ as Lord and Savior. If the inquirer wasn't clear, the results could be spurious. He wanted to know if the inquirer really understood what was happening. That, he felt, could be determined only by personal counseling. Inquirers could easily come under great conviction during the message, be moved to tears, say a prayer, and yet not fully understand the meaning of total commitment to Jesus Christ as Lord and Savior.

Mr. Trotman took the responsibility of follow-up with the agreement that he could personally train counselors in future Crusades. That was the beginning of counselor training in Billy Graham Crusades.

3. *Training counselors (Philosophy of Teaching)*

In our counselor training program, we have much more in mind than teaching people to witness and counsel in a Crusade. In the classes, life-changing investment principles are taught. Participants are challenged to: walk in the Spirit; live a disciplined life in Bible study and Scripture memory; make the Quiet Time a daily habit and preferably at the start of the day; share their faith as God gives opportunity; become involved in a discipleship ministry to help not only in bringing a person to Christ, but to help the new Christian grow and become established in the local church.

a. *Recruitment of counselors.* Prospective counselors are recruited from the participating churches. The more churches you have involved, the greater potential for counselors. Several weeks before the Crusade, dates should be set and locations confirmed for the training classes. A simple training schedule or brochure should be printed to be put in the hands of church leaders and prospective counselors. A letter should be sent to all pastors and church leaders inviting them to become involved and to encourage members of their congregation to attend the classes. Sufficient schedules or brochures should be printed for pastors who would like each of their members to have one. Everyone in the church, from their teens and upward, are welcome to attend the training without any obligation. Whom you recruit, and how, will depend on your locality. You may be in a very primitive area where local methods would be very different.

The number of class locations will depend on the size of the community, and how many churches are involved. If it is in a one-church Crusade, recruitment and training will be centered at that church. If more than one community is involved, you will want to have more than one class location, to make it easier for people to attend. For example, you could have a Monday class in one community, a Tuesday class in another community, and a Thursday class in another community.

b. *Training.* The Billy Graham counseling and follow-up training program consists of four different lessons. Each lesson or class session lasts approximately 1-1/2 hours. That means six hours of class material. The training program could be done in one day, but it would be like feeding people four large meals at one sitting. You can imagine what would happen to the digestive system. Our philosophy is to give the participants a little at a time—one class a week over a four-week period. At the end of each class session we ask participants to join together in twos or threes, and share with one another what they have learned from the lecture; and/or practice the use of some graphic tool that was shared in that particular class session. Then we have them pray together about their own life and witness. The practice session usually takes ten to fifteen minutes. Before dismissing the class, we make sure everyone understands the homework assignment, and give them a challenge to do their homework, to practice what they were taught in that particular lesson, and to return the following week.

Spacing the classes a week apart gives time to work on Bible study, Scripture memory, and to better assimilate the lesson material.

c. *Criteria for counseling.* We have found that approximately 50 percent of the people who attend the training classes become counselors. Many people attend simply for their own benefit, without any thought to counseling inquirers. Some participants may think they are qualified to counsel, but are not. A method of selection is necessary.

In the third week of training, a counselor application should be handed to each participant. The application should ask for the name, address, church, and pastor's signature. On another line of the application, the participant should state how many class sessions were attended. We normally expect counselors to attend a minimum of three classes. The application should determine to what degree the applicant understands the Gospel, and what steps he would take to lead a person to receive Jesus Christ. This can be determined by asking questions such as: "Why does a person need to be saved?" "What did Christ do to make salvation possible?" "How does a person become a Christian, a child of God?"

Incidentally, these questions can be answered from the Scripture the applicant has memorized, or from the homework Bible study which the applicant has completed.

Finally, the applicant should write out a brief testimony stating when he became a Christian, and how he knows he has eternal life. At the close of the testimony, space should be provided for the applicant's signature.

The counseling applications should be produced before the classes begin. This should be done by the individual responsible for the counselor training program and a select group of participating pastors. Applicants receive the application at the third session and return it at the fourth session. During the intervening week, all applicants should receive their pastor or church leader's signature. The applications can be handed in just prior to the last session, or following the class.

The ideal plan for selecting counselors would involve a small committee of pastors and church leaders. This committee would be responsible for receiving the applications at the fourth class, and conducting a brief interview with each applicant as the applications are handed in. This interview would take place just prior to, or following, the fourth class.

After all the applications are handed in, every committee member should carefully read each application he has received before making a final selection of counselors. The interview and the completed application should help confirm the applicant's grasp of the Gospel and ability to help a person receive Christ.

[This is part of the presentation given at the Counseling Seminar.]

# FOLLOW-UP SEMINAR
*Tom Phillips and Charles Riggs*

Follow-up has been defined as "the process of giving continual attention to a new Christian until he is integrated into the church, discovers his place of service, develops his full potential for Jesus Christ, and helps to build Christ's church." This is the ideal, but Jesus Christ can make it possible if we but surrender to Him and follow His example.

1.  *Biblical mandate*

    a.  *Matthew 28:19,20, Go make disciples.* Jesus lived about 33½ years. Of this time He spent approximately three years training His disciples. The Bible says, "And He appointed twelve, that they might be with Him, and that He might send them out to preach" (Mark 3:14). His disciples heard Him quote the Sermon on the Mount. They watched Him feed the multitudes many times. They watched Him walk on water and still the storm. They watched Him heal and perform other miracles. They watched Him suffer from day to day. The watched Him pray and learned much from His personal discipline and example.

    To give them further training and to see how much they had learned, Jesus would send them out to put into practice what they had been taught. The Bible says, "And the apostles gathered together to Jesus and told Him all things, both what they had done and what they had taught" (Mark 6:30).

    Knowing that His time was short, and there was much to be done to reach the world with the Gospel, Jesus left this mandate with His disciples. "All authority has been given to Me in heaven and on earth. Go therefore and make disciples of all nations, baptizing them in the name of the Father and of the Son and of the Holy Spirit, teaching them to observe all things whatever I have commanded you; and behold, I am with you always, even to the end of the age" (Matthew 28:18-20). The disciples were faithful to this commitment, and many of us are Christians today because of their faithfulness.

    b.  *Apostle Paul's precedent.* The Apostle Paul was another person who taught much by his own life and example. He wrote most of the New Testament, and from his writings we can learn so much about discipleship. He was a missionary with a vision of multiplying workers for the harvest.

    (i)   Acts 13:2,3, *First missionary journey.* Paul's first mission with Barnabas was launched from Antioch. The Bible says, "As they ministered to the Lord and fasted, the Holy Spirit said, 'Separate to Me Barnabas and Saul for the work to which I have called them.' And when they had fasted and prayed, and laid hands on them, they sent them away" (Acts 13:2,3). Before they returned again to Antioch, they visited many cities preaching Jesus Christ. On one occasion, ". . . almost the whole city came together to hear the Word of God" (Acts 13:44).

    (ii)  Acts 15:36, *Second mission—follow-up.* The prime objective of their second major trip was follow-up. The Bible says, "And after some days Paul said to Barnabas, 'Let us go back and visit our brethren in every city where we have preached the word of the Lord, and see how they are doing'" (Acts 15:36). Before Paul returned again to Antioch you will find him in many cities for weeks and months at a time confirming the disciples.

    (iii) Acts 18:23, *Third mission—follow-up.* The third trip was for the same purpose. "And after he had spent some time there, he departed and went over all the region of Galatia and Phrygia in order, strengthening all the disciples" (Acts 18:23). The precedent is clearly set. New Christians do need care for various reasons, and the care should be administered by *someone*. The Holy Spirit is able to minister to individuals, and the Scriptures provide the food necessary for growth; but the one who wins a person to Christ is logically the one who should help work with a new Christian. That means being available for further help and counsel, encouraging good devotional habits, and providing for regular church attendance where the new Christian will be nurtured and become active for Christ.

    c.  *Apostle Paul's methods.*

    (i)   Personal visits—Paul knew the value of personal contact. He liked to sit face to face with people and teach the Bible. He was willing not only to impart the Gospel to individuals, but to give freely of himself. The Bible says, "So, affectionately longing for you, we were well pleased to impart to you not only the gospel of God, but also our own lives, because you have become dear to us" (1 Thessalonians 2:8). On one occasion Paul was teaching the Bible in Troas and forgot what time it was. About midnight a young man by the name of Eutychus fell asleep, and fell from a loft where he had been seated. The Bible tells us that Paul ministered to the young man and after they had eaten a snack went to preaching again. Apparently, he taught the Word of God until the break of day (Acts 20:7-11).

    (ii)   Letters—2 Corinthians 2:9 (Most of the New Testament). In his letters Paul poured out his heart of concern to individuals and to churches. His letters brought assurance, comfort, direction, and strength to the early church. He shared what he was praying for them. Today we are blessed, inspired, and instructed by the letters of Paul.

    (iii)   Sent representatives—1 Thessalonians 3:1-3. Paul ministered to the then known world at that time. As the work grew, the more demands there were on his time. Eventually, he just could not attend personally to all those he had led to Christ. But Paul knew the value of personal contact, so he often sent some of his own trained workers to visit in his place. As you read the Scriptures, you will find Paul sending Timothy, Titus, or Tychicus to various cities to encourage the brethren and to assure them of Paul's love and concern.

    (iv)   Prayer—1 Thessalonians 3:10. Paul was a great prayer warrior. Not only did he pray for others, but he taught us a lot about the importance of prayer. The Bible says, "Night and day praying exceedingly that we may see your face and perfect what is lacking in your faith" (1 Thessalonians 3:10). Sometimes, distance may prevent personal visits. In cases like this, your letters and prayers can be very important to the new Christians.

## 2.  *Why follow-up?*

We do follow-up today in obedience to the Great Commission. We are under the same compulsion today as the early disciples, not only to win people to Christ, but to disciple them. High on the evangelist's priority list should be follow-up and working with the local churches in nurturing new Christians. Evangelism without follow-up could lead to simple addition. Evangelism with effective follow-up could result in multiplying disciples.

    A newborn baby is absolutely helpless and dependent on the mother and father for *feeding, protecting,* and *training.* This also is true with the new Christian. They need feeding to nurture the "inner man," protection from the "evil one," and training in discipleship.

    a.  *1 Peter 2:2—Feeding.* The Apostle Peter states, "As newborn babes, desire the pure milk of the word, that you may grow thereby, if indeed you have tasted that the Lord is gracious'' (1 Peter 2:2,3). The Bible is food for the new spiritual life, which needs to be nourished just as the physical body does. Special care must be given to help feed the new Christian, especially if the individual comes from a hostile environment with no encouragement from family or friends. Follow-up must be accomplished by someone, not some thing. You can have the best materials and methods, but without the loving touch of an individual, something will be missing. A new Christian should have someone with whom he can share burdens, from whom he can seek counsel, and who will help him over the rough spots in the early days of his pilgrimage. We must be willing not only to preach the Gospel, but to share our own lives. This takes vision, and calls for a sacrifice of time and effort, but it pays real dividends in the end.

b. *2 Corinthians 11:2,3—Protecting.* The new Christian needs protection. The ''evil one'' blinds the minds of the unbelievers and never stops attacking the saints. Probably the Apostle Paul's greatest concern was the attack of the enemy. The Bible says, ''For I am jealous for you with godly jealousy. For I have betrothed you to one husband, that I may present you as a chaste virgin to Christ. But I fear, lest somehow, as the serpent deceived Eve by his craftiness, so your minds may be corrupted from the simplicity that is in Christ'' (2 Corinthians 11:2,3). The enemy is winning the battle for the mind in many parts of the world, through the ministry of cults and false religions. These groups thrive, for the most part, by winning church members to their beliefs. Someone has said, ''Feed your dog at home, and he will stay at home. Neglect him, and he will go the neighbors, or to the garbage dump.'' We must prepare for the work of the ''evil one'' and fortify our efforts with prayer and sound teaching. ''That we should no longer be children, tossed to and fro and carried about with every wind of doctrine, by the trickery of men, in the cunning craftiness by which they lie in wait to deceive'' (Ephesians 4:14).

After the Galatians had trusted Christ, they were led astray by false teachers. They went back to the Law and rituals. Paul exhorted them to ''stand fast therefore in the liberty with which Christ has made us free, and do not be entangled again with a yoke of bondage'' (Galatians 5:1). Many Christians today are carrying burdens through ignorance of the truth that sets us free.

c. *Colossians 2:6,7—Training.* The Christian life is continually one of growth. We never stop growing and should ever press on to maturity and Christlikeness. The Bible says, ''As you have therefore receive Christ Jesus the Lord, so walk in Him, rooted and built up in Him and established in the faith, as you have been taught, abounding in it with thanksgiving'' (Colossians 2:6,7). The Word of God is food for the ''inner man,'' and prayer is our lifeline to God. One of the most important lessons that we can teach the new Christian is how to feed himself through daily fellowship with God through the Word and prayer.

3. *Who should do follow-up?*

a. *Evangelists and pastors/teachers (1 Thessalonians 1:5-9).* The Apostle Paul gives us a perfect pattern for discipleship. The Bible says, ''For when we brought you the Good News, it was not just meaningless chatter to you; no, you listened with great interest. What we told you produced a powerful effect upon you, for the Holy Spirit gave you great and full assurance that what we said was true. And you know how our very lives were further proof to you of the truth of our message. So you became our followers and the Lord's; for you received our message with joy from the Holy Spirit in spite of the trials and sorrows which it brought you. Then you yourselves became an example to all the other Christians in Greece. And now the Word of the Lord has spread out from you to others everywhere, far beyond your boundaries [Macedonia and Achaia], for wherever we go we find people telling us about your remarkable faith in God. We don't need to tell them about it, for they keep telling us about the wonderful welcome you gave us, and how you turned away from your idols to God so that now the living and true God only is your Master'' (1 Thessalonians 1:5-9).

The following is a good outline for this passage. Take note of how Paul multiplied his ministry.

   (i)     The Thessalonians received his message with open hearts.

   (ii)    They responded positively to his follow-up efforts.

   (iii)   They became active believers to the extent of sharing their faith throughout their whole country.

Wouldn't it be exciting to see something like that happen today? Could that happen in your community? We have the same Gospel, with the same power, today. We have the same Holy Spirit who spoke in and through Paul the Apostle. In our work, we keep praying for something like this to happen wherever we hold Crusades.

   b.   *Trained church leaders.* For the past several years now in our Crusades, we have trained the laity to lead Nurture Group Bible Studies. In every church, even in the small ones, there should be other people in addition to the pastor who could lead a Bible study. Most churches would have Sunday School teachers, church officers, or youth leaders that could be recruited to help with the nurture Bible study program. Depending on the number of inquirers, one or more of your leaders could be responsible for helping to nurture new Christians. This is good experience for the lay leaders. As they study and teach, they grow and become more useful to the local church.

   c.   *Counselors/personal workers—1 Thessalonians 2:7,8.* In our Crusades we ask our counselors to phone, write, or visit within 24 to 48 hours, everyone they counsel. The counselor cannot take the place of the pastor or the church, but the one who wins the person to Christ is logically the one who should help work with that new Christian. That means being available for further help and counsel, encouraging good devotional habits, and providing for regular church attendance where the new Christian will be nurtured and become active for Christ.

4.   *Who could do follow-up after your campaigns?*

Since the local church is the main organism that God uses to build His Kingdom and since evangelists are the arm of the Church, it is the privilege and responsibility of the evangelist to bring back to the local church those who have made commitments in and through his campaigns.

The evangelist himself can follow up individual inquirers, but often this is very difficult. However, in a situation where no church exists in the geographical area of the campaign, the evangelist is obligated to follow up personally. Using the Apostle Paul's methods, the evangelist could use one or more of the following procedures:

   a.   Stay in the area and disciple the new Christians until there are enough believers maturing in the faith to begin their own church.

   b.   Correspond with every person who has made a commitment.

   c.   Send someone else to see to the discipling of the new Christians.

Paul used all three methods as he built new churches throughout the Roman Empire.

Evangelists have historically been too independent of churches. Many have not asked the churches in the localities if they could come and preach as the evangelistic arm of the Church. Certainly, many have not been invited by the churches. They have simply gone. Billy Graham is an example to all of us in that he goes by the invitation of the Church and is a servant to the Church.

There are many within the local cooperating churches who can not only serve in the follow-up of the campaign but also give leadership to that follow-up: pastors; deacons; other church leaders, such as Sunday School teachers; experienced Christians with a knowledge of the Bible.

Turn to the evangelist next to you and discuss who could serve with you in the follow-up during and after your campaigns.

**5.** *Training follow-up leaders*

All you need for a Bible class is a Bible or the gospel of John. You provide the environment conducive to growth by inviting new Christians to a Bible study. Start with the gospel of John. The leader should make certain that everyone has a Bible or the gospel portion. A simple format could be used, for example:

    a.  Have prayer.

    b.  Start reading slowly verse by verse as the class follows in their Bibles.

    c.  The leader should take time to expand on certain passages like John 1:12,13.

    d.  Emphasize the new family relationship through receiving Jesus Christ (verse 12).

    e.  Explain what it means to be "born of God," born into God's family (verse 13).

    f.  On occasions, ask for questions. On other occasions, ask questions that would lead to discussion.

# THE EVANGELIST WORKING IN INNER CITIES
*Floyd McClung*

1. *Opportunities and disadvantages of inner city evangelism*
   a. *Opportunities.* Cities are exploding in size as never before in human history. During the time of Christ only about 3% of the world's population lived in cities, but today it is about 45% worldwide and much higher on some continents. By the year 2000 it is estimated that approximately 85% of all the people in the world will live in great cities.

The following scale gives an idea of how fast cities are growing in different geographical regions:

|            | 1980 | 2000 |
|------------|------|------|
| Africa     | 26%  | 45%  |
| Asia       | 25%  | 60%  |
| Australia  | 86%  | 85%  |
| L. America | 61%  | 73%  |
| Europe     | 69%  | 82%  |
| U.S.A.     | 74%  | 94%  |

There are people in the cities! Millions of them! To ignore the cities is to ignore humanity. You don't have to hunt for people in the cities; they are there, waiting for us. There are well over 400 cities in the world that have more than a million people. Every one of these cities should be targeted for evangelism. Cities with more than one million people or that have international influence are often referred to as "world class cities."

When this many people are crowded together in cities it creates many problems. This is especially true in geographical areas where there is high unemployment, poverty, and injustice. By their very nature, cities tend to be very impersonal. They also break down the strong ties of family and tradition. Combine this with the disillusionment that results when one does not find the proverbial pot of gold at the end of the rainbow, and it spells trouble.

The social problems that exist in cities are not only found in developing countries, but also in the West. Inner-city crime, drug addiction, high unemployment, divorce and high levels of sexual promiscuity lead to a very unstable social and economic environment.

These social problems are a mandate to the church of Jesus Christ to get involved. We must not ignore these problems. To do so is to leave a vacuum that others will fill, including religious cults and ideological political groups that will play on the bitterness of the poor and needy. The preaching of the Gospel, along with caring for the poor, is the only answer for the great cities of our world.

Not only are these social problems a mandate in themselves, but when people come to an end of themselves they are often more open to the Gospel. An evangelist sensitive to the felt needs (those needs that people are aware of because of their pain and suffering) can bring healing and hope to inner-city dwellers. His sensitivity, his compassion, his willingness to care and listen, will touch people's hearts with the love of God.

b. *Disadvantages.* There is a multitude of spiritual forces at work in the city. The evangelist who wishes to be used of God to reach people with the Gospel in the city has to compete with many forces that are at work to capture the attention and the hearts of the people.

City evangelism is not a game. Cities are complex; people are kept busy with many attractions and temptations. The lines that divide people are deep and well-defined. Cities throw people together from different tribes, colors, languages, clans, and cultures. New networks of relationships emerge to replace the old and familiar ones. Young people break the old taboos.

There are many competing spirits vying for the soul of the people. The evangelist working in the city must take seriously the nature of the spiritual battle he will be involved in. The enemy often uses cities as his stronghold. Some cities become a kind of spiritual capital for particular types of evil. To break through in the spiritual strongholds requires much prayer, righteous living, and humble dependence upon the Lord for breakthroughs that cannot come in our own strength.

There are also the emotional and psychological effects on people from living in the city. The busyness, the noise, and the crowded conditions all tend to either make a person withdraw and live in isolation, or find some form of escape. Sex, alcohol, drugs and violence are but few of the many avenues one may follow to deaden the pain of a meaningless and overwhelming life-style.

For many, the jump from a rural setting of well-defined cultural expectations to an environment where anything goes is too overwhelming. Life suddenly offers too many choices. In this setting an evangelist who understands the true heartache underneath the outward sinfulness and joviality of urban slum dwellers and inner-city residents can speak deeply into the hearts of city folk who are hurt, confused and trapped by sin.

Any evangelist who would make an impact on a city must develop an urban spirituality. One must learn to resist the busyness and draw close to the Lord. One must walk in peace in the midst of the hustle and bustle. One must stay free from the spirit of materialism and selfishness that is not only prevalent in the West but also grips the hearts of so many of our African, Asian, and Latin youth when they move to the big city.

2. *The role of the preaching evangelist in the inner city*

Jesus is our model. Look at His life, especially in the city. He went out among the people. He touched them, He listened to them, He healed them, He wept over them. One thing more than any other characterized His relationship with the sinner and the sinned against: *He cared.*

He took the little children in His arms. He forgave the woman caught in adultery. He went to the home of the greedy tax-collector. He talked to the Samaritan woman—and in public. He ate in cafes with street people. People. *People. He loved people.* People were more important to Him than programs.

And not only did Jesus love people, but He also called them to celebrate. He did this when He turned the water into wine at the wedding feast; He did it when He went to the homes of publicans and sinners to feast with them; in fact, it was Jesus who said there would be time enough for fasting after He was ascended into heaven. And it is the Lord Jesus who has gone before us and someday will call us to join Him at the great wedding feast of the Lamb at the end of history.

City life is filled with so much hurt and pain. Most people in the cities have got problems. They don't need a religion that gives them more. The preaching evangelist should surround himself with celebration: in music, in worship, in joyous praise, in drama, and in the demonstration of the power of God. He more than anyone else should be a person who celebrates, because he is the bearer of the "good news."

Lastly, the preaching evangelist must not be afraid of power encounters. When you invade the city, you step on the devil's territory. In the chaos of the city Satan seeks to pull men into his lair. He makes deals: he exchanges raw power for the souls of men. When the evangelist comes he challenges the right of Satan to deceive and to destroy with a greater power—the power of the Gospel.

The preaching evangelist must pray for and expect God to confirm the Gospel with miracles through the authority that is in the Cross of Jesus. This always happens when there is a conflict of Kingdoms: God's and Satan's. It is God's way of getting the attention of those who will listen.

3. *Principles for launching ministries in the inner city*

There are three foundational principles for launching a city-wide campaign or evangelistic outreach. The first is prayer. If Jesus, being the Son of God, needed to spend forty days in fasting and prayer at the beginning of His earthly ministry, why do we think we should do any less?

We must saturate our outreaches in prayer: prayer chains, prayer chairman, prayer groups, prayer walks, prayer conferences, prayer meetings. *Prayer, Prayer, Prayer.*

It should be organized and it should be spontaneous. It should be before, during, and after the outreach. God has offered us through prayer the opportunity to participate with Him in what He is doing in a particular city or nation. It is in prayer that we learn God's strategy for a city. It is through prayer that we hear the heartbeat of God for a city. And it is in prayer that we discover the traps of the enemy.

Another strategy for working in cities is unity. Cities by their very nature tend to divide. In an attempt to survive in a city environment, people become more independent. They withdraw from one another and work alone. The spirit of the city is the spirit of independence and pride. Man shakes his fist in the face of God and tries to go it alone.

But we as Christians must stand against this spirit. We must refuse to become isolated in our own little circle of Christians. We must reach out and include the whole body of Christ. If people draw a circle around us and exclude us, then we must draw a bigger circle around them, and include them! It is the spirit of unity and love that will release the anointing of God upon an outreach.

The last foundational principle to follow in launching new ministries in the inner city is righteousness. What we do must be done in a spirit of meekness and humility. We must rise above the spirit of greed and lust that rules the cities of our world and minister in the power of the Holy Spirit. We must be free from the pride and independence that is typical of so much of what happens in cities. We must flee the spirit of manipulation that so often creeps into our Christian works, and do our evangelism in a spirit of servanthood.

# CHURCH PLANTING AND THE EVANGELIST
*John Bueno*

Church planting is as old as the New Testament. Reading through the pages of the book of Acts, we discover that evangelism was not a hit and miss proposition. But it was planned under the guidance of the Holy Spirit, and men and women that God used to develop a solid, maturing church wherever the Gospel was preached. There are four major areas in Paul's missionary methodology to which I would draw our attention.

## TARGET NEW TERRITORIES
Paul deliberately went to the places where his ministry could have the most lasting benefits. Invariably he went to the large and important centers on his journeys where he could develop a local church. He didn't always look for the easiest place; rather he looked for the most strategic center where the Gospel then could reach out in the different areas and continue its influence even after he moved on to new locations. One of the most important things in his strategy was to find the appropriate place and settle down as long as it would take to establish a local body of believers.

In our work in Latin America we have discovered sometimes the opposite approach is taken. We look for the easy places where there are no major obstacles to setting up a campaign, regardless of the location and eventual feasibility of the area. For this reason many of our large cities in the world are virtually abandoned as far as the Gospel is concerned. I believe one of the main thrusts that challenges the Church today are the great metropolises of the world that desperately need the evangelist who will stay long enough to develop a thriving local church. Regardless of whether it is the large city or the village, proper planning must be made to establish the church. Several items need to be considered: population centers, availability of property, zoning laws, etc.

Another strategy in Paul's method of reaching new territory was looking for appropriate leadership. He never set out to do something in the area of evangelism without seeking out those people that he could disciple and who could eventually take over the leadership of that local body. We find that this is a pattern that he used over and over again in establishing churches in the New Testament. Again, in contemporary evangelism we see the opposite approach taken sometimes. An evangelistic crusade is started, and when it is in progress we begin to wonder about leaders from those who will take charge of the crusade when the evangelist leaves. I believe the proper approach is to look for the appropriate people that can be disciples and trained to take leadership in that local body before even starting the crusade.

## NEVER WENT ALONE
Paul was always part of a team. I believe the New Testament shows how the work of the church is a team effort. If he wasn't traveling with Barnabas he had Silas, and if it wasn't Silas it was Timothy or Titus. All through the pages of the book of Acts we discovered that he was always part of a team, so that in the process of his endeavors for the Kingdom he could disciple those with him. Just as soon as he arrived at the new location of ministry, he always gathered about himself the leaders who could be trained and discipled for future ministry. Perhaps due to the problems and costs of travel today, many times this very important aspect is overlooked. The fact is that

time and money can be saved if the evangelist takes advantage of this great means of developing future leaders for the church.

## FLEXIBILITY

The great apostle was flexible in those areas that required it. His formula changed from place to place so that he could adapt to each situation. One of the great needs of the church today is flexibility and sensitivity to the will of the Spirit in regard to church planting. Sometimes, he would stay two years in a place, other times it was just a few months. Whatever it required to get the job done, Paul was willing to adapt to the situation. Often we see evangelists with preconceived ideas and strategy set in concrete that will not adapt to the different situations. Adaptability is a must in the world in which we live. We see this even in areas of finance. At times Paul relied upon his tent-making to finance the beginning of a new church. Sometimes he relied on the offerings of friends from other churches and in the community itself to finance his endeavors. He was always willing to find the methods and the strategy most adequate for the location even if that meant the subordination of his own ideas and plans.

## FOLLOW-UP

Paul was a great example in the importance of follow-up. He just didn't abandon crusades and go on his business shaking the dust off his feet. He remained very concerned about those congregations, and even after he had put them in the hands of leaders he had trained, he was always in contact with them through letters and return visits. God give us evangelists with that kind of concern—a concern that not only emphasizes numbers and decisions at the altar, but that will remain interested in seeing these souls established in the faith. The evangelist who will be willing to prevail in prayer even after the meeting is over and new leadership has taken over that new congregation. Periodic visits and constant concern are requirements for the establishing of new churches after the crusades are over.

Having reviewed Paul's methodology in the New Testament and that of some of his first-century contemporaries, let us look at our world and see if some of these patterns can be imitated. Let us now discuss four major areas that will guide us as evangelists in church planting in the 20th century.

1. *Starting churches as a result of evangelistic campaigns*

Proper planning must be done previous to the outset of a crusade in order for this to be successful. This can be done by meeting with neighboring pastors (if such are available) and leaders in the area. If no church is in the immediate area, then one should seek out the counsel of those nearest by. A committee should be formed to find the appropriate location and the local leaders who will be involved. It is generally advisable that the property in which the crusade is held already be secured as a future location for the church. If this is not possible, a site nearby should be secured before the crusade starts.

In some cases great crusades have been carried on in locations of the city only to be frustrated in the end by unavailability of properties near by. Generally, if the property is already secured, it will also avoid difficulties that might arise through religious prejudices or things of this nature. Many times people in the community raise the price of property, because they feel the church has to purchase something there. On other occasions it gives fanatical groups an opportunity to organize resistance to church planting.

Other matters such as: rainy season, holidays, and local rules and regulations need to be considered. Great consultation should be taken to make sure that the time and place are in God's perfect order. We generally recommend that the location be where public transportation is readily available. It should be on a main street with easy accessibility. It should be close to the main population centers. Great care should be taken that P.A. systems don't disturb the neighbors and create a negative atmosphere for that local church. In some countries permits need to be secured from local authorities.

All these matters should be taken care of in plenty of time so as to avoid problems at the last minute. Since many funds will be spent in advertising in getting ready for the crusade, it obviously is the greater part of wisdom to make sure that everything will proceed in order at the appointed time. From the very first night of the crusade, people should be advised that this isn't just a one- or two-week crusade, but an effort to establish a new church. As people begin to make their decision for Christ, they need to begin feeling a part of this local body.

It is vitally important that they begin to recognize their responsibility as Christians to further that local body's cause. Discipleship principles should accompany the preaching of the Word. In some cases there is a vesper service to train the new Christians in the principles of the Lordship of Jesus Christ and discipleship. A positive approach should be taken right from the beginning in the preaching of the Gospel. Negative things about other religions and religious groups won't help in winning the hearts of the people. A positive exposition of the Gospel of Jesus Christ is always the best course.

2. *Principles of using mass evangelism to find potential disciples*

If from the very beginning the evangelist and those working with him realize that one of their most important tasks will be choosing those to be involved in leadership in that local church, great strides will be taken to make that a successful endeavor. Churches involve people, and there is no way we can avoid the responsibility of asking God's direction in choosing the right people. Gary W. Kuhne, in his book *The Dynamics of Discipleship Training,* states his list of criteria for faithful men: 1. Hunger for God's Word. 2. A thirst for holy living. 3. A desire for a greater knowledge of God. 4. A basic commitment to the Lordship of Christ. 5. A desire to be used by God. 6. A love for people. He defines a disciple as a person "who is growing in conformity to Christ, is achieving fruit in evangelism, and is working in follow-up to conserve his fruit." When a Christian is in his first love, it is the best opportunity to channel him into meaningful ministry. Those involved in the campaign should recognize that this is their primary responsibility: finding and training disciples who will take over the leadership of that church.

3. *Serving a beginning church before a pastor is recruited.*

In some cases the evangelist will stay three to six months in the one location to get the nucleus started. Other times it may be a more prolonged stay. Because of the evangelist's busy schedule, he may have to bring somebody to serve as interim pastor. If this is the case, great care should be taken by the interim pastor to state his position as being temporary. The process of discipling and training leaders should continue unabated. If this man has outside support, he should be sure he begins to share the responsibility of the church to support their future pastor.

Principles in stewardship should be taught from the very beginning. This will enable the new pastor to gain the support he needs to do a meaningful job in the church. Principles of discipleship and the Lordship of Jesus Christ should be a part of the program from the outset. People need to know of their responsibility in helping to make that effort a success. Christian commitment and responsibility are factors vitally important in the establishment of new Christians. Concerted effort should be made by all of those who have a part in the project to make this happen on a consistent basis.

4. *Examples of church planting patterns involving evangelists*

I am taking the liberty to share a plan that was developed in El Salvador to consolidate the results of evangelistic crusades. Almost all of these 25 churches have been started by evangelists in crusades organized for that purpose. I now list the guidelines that served this purpose in such a meaningful way in San Salvador.

## GUIDELINES FOR NEW CHURCHES

Sensing an urgent need to reach the city of San Salvador for Christ and conscious of the commission of our Lord to preach the Gospel to every creature, we have initiated the "Filial Church" plan that will enable us to fulfill this vision.

Because the fulfillment of this mission is so complex in our times, especially in large cities, and often our local churches lack the means to accomplish total evangelization, we have felt the need of this special plan to enable us to reach our objectives.

## OBJECTIVES

The "Filial Church" plan shall accomplish the following objectives:

a.   Provide physical and economic means to raise up new works in the city of San Salvador and surrounding areas.

b.   The Evangelistic Center shall provide a rented hall and eventually the property for the Filial Church. It will provide, when necessary, benches and pulpit to begin services.

c.   It shall provide the human element necessary for its development. A Filial pastor shall be named by the Church Board to guide the new church. It shall designate voluntary members that live in that area to assist the pastor in the various responsibilities of the Filial Church.

d.   It shall provide administrative assessment and spiritual guidance. Taking into account the accumulative experience of the mother church down through the years, the Evangelistic Center shall provide counsel and spiritual guidance in smoothing over the difficult problems that are involved in church planting.

e.   It shall provide the fellowship of a big church as a spiritual balm in the growth of the new church. This will avoid a feeling of being alone and forsaken in their difficult task.

## DEVELOPMENT

The Church Board shall choose strategic locations to establish "Filial Churches." To accomplish this it shall take into consideration population density, the lack of churches in the area, and the availability of preaching in rented halls. After selection of the site, the lay-pastor shall be named. The aforementioned shall be a person of spiritual maturity and be able to meet the requirements of 1 Timothy 3:1-7. He shall enjoy the respect and goodwill of the members of the Evangelistic Center and have a testimony worthy of his charge.

The lay-pastor shall oversee the spiritual and material progress of the new work, presenting monthly reports to the Church Board. He shall be in charge of the services in the Filial Church over which he presides and shall supervise all its activities under the direction of the Holy Spirit. He may name helpers who will aid him in the administration of the work, among these a treasurer who shall keep careful record of the financial movement.

The Filial Church shall have autonomy in the administration of its funds and must defray its own expenses after twelve months. (This with the exception of the property which shall be provided by the Evangelistic Center.) Once the new church is free of obligations locally, it shall contribute to the extension of other Filial Churches that the Board shall designate.

The lay-pastor and helpers shall be members of the Evangelistic Center, but designated to their respective Filial Church. The norms of conduct and membership requirements shall be the same as the other Assemblies of God churches and shall be guided by the Fundamental Doctrines and Practices of the Assemblies of God in El Salvador. The lay-pastor shall have the right to meet with the Church Board at least once a month. This shall make it possible for him to render his report and the interchange of ideas and plans. It shall also provide an opportunity for the pastor and Church Board to assess the progress of the new work. On these occasions plans will be made, new goals set, etc.

The Filial Church must maintain an evangelistic vision. It shall not forget the purpose of its conception—making disciples for the Kingdom of God. It must maintain fresh its passion for the souls in the vicinity, always conscious of the overall objective. It shall not allow tradition, routine, and rigid programs to interfere with its mission.

It may establish its own departments, such as: Sunday School, Christ's Ambassadors, Women's Missionary Council, Men's Fellowship, Missionettes, etc. This should not coincide with the weekly fellowship service on Sunday mornings.

Particularly to conserve the unity of purpose, communion, and loyalty to the mother church, it is recommended that the lay-pastor and his members attend the morning worship service on Sundays. This shall provide a time of spiritual renewal for the entire fellowship. The importance of this meeting should not be underestimated, as this is where the members will receive the greatest spiritual benefit—that is, communion with the entire congregation. This will help the Filial Church not to feel isolated and forsaken in its efforts.

The first Sunday of the month, communion will be served with the participation of all Filial Churches and their pastors. A spirit of isolation or division shall be avoided at all costs.

## GOALS

a. Saturate the metropolitan area with a testimony of the Gospel in every vicinity.

b. Provide outlets for Christian laymen who recognize the Lordship of Christ in their lives and who are willing to follow His order.

c. Speed up the fulfillment of the Divine Commission before His soon return for the Church. With the help of Almighty God we want to see San Salvador won to Christ.

d. We do not pretend the establishment of a new denomination. We promise loyalty to the norms and precepts of our beloved Conference, and we join with them in their ideals and purposes with all sincerity. We desire only to be sensitive to the Divine Call and faithfully fulfill His will.

The principles the Lord laid on our heart during 1970 were shared with our congregation which at that time numbered about 400 adults. For twelve or thirteen Sundays in succession, sermons were delivered on the Lordship of Jesus Christ and our responsibilities in the area of discipleship. To state it briefly, this brought revival to our church, and soon we didn't know what to do with all the people. Our auditorium seats approximately 2,000 people, and when it was filled to capacity we began thinking of ways to consolidate this fruit and permanently bless His Church.

Our Church Board went on an all-night retreat, where we spent the time in prayer and in considering what God would have us do in regard to this wonderful blessing He had sent our way. The Lord laid the Filial Church plan on our hearts, and it has proved to be a great blessing to His work here in San Salvador. Since the latter part of 1970, twenty-five churches have been started in the city of San Salvador. We have selected different areas of the city where there is no Christian witness and have seen how the Lord has raised up beautiful congregations in these areas. In some cases we have rented halls for a short time until property could be purchased and a building erected. Some of these Filial Churches now are running over 3,000 in their own Sunday School outreach. As soon as the churches are mature enough to be able to govern, support, and propagate themselves, they are turned over as sovereign assemblies of the Assemblies of God in El Salvador. Fifteen of these churches are now operating under the General Council of the Assemblies of God here, and have developed into strong and growing witnesses in the city. Ten of these Filial Churches are still being administered by the Evangelistic Center. We had a combined total of 18,359 the last Sunday in March 1983. We believe that this is just the beginning of great things that God is doing in the city through this witness.

In the beginning, all these churches are pastored by lay-workers. We have two leaders in each satellite who are called Pastor and Co-pastor of the Filial Church. This helps us develop leadership with on-the-job practical training. We also have training courses for them during the week, and they take turns coming to these courses so as not to leave the church without leadership. As they develop in their ministries, then they are taken to different areas of the city to develop new congregations and continue the discipleship process. It has been beautiful to see how the Lord has provided the finances and the personnel to develop these congregations throughout the city of San Salvador.

# THE EFFECTIVE STREET-PREACHING EVANGELIST
*Shad Williams*

There are two basic kinds of evangelism. First, there is the "they come to me" type such as an organized, advertised crusade, rally, church meeting, movie showing, etc. I am in a place and I am asking people to come to my place. This kind of evangelism is a large part of our work, but we realize it often passes over people who just will not come to an organized religious event. Thus the need of the kind of evangelism that says, "I go to them"—that is, preaching on the streets or places of public gathering.

To be truly effective as a public-place evangelist, a man must be able to do the following:
- Adjust his thinking, methods, manner, and message to suit the "I go to them" approach.
- Plan and organize a street-preaching event from start to finish.
- Attract and hold a crowd long enough to hear a complete Gospel message and invitation.
- Preach a simple, clear, relevant message that calls for a verdict that demands an immediate decision.
- Deal adequately with inquirers.

There are many different ways to approach street-preaching or, I prefer to say, "public place evangelism." Personnel can range from one lone evangelist to a large ministry team with singers, testimonies, counselors, etc. Equipment can range from the evangelist's voice and a box to stand on, all the way to a big platform, sound system, lights, etc. The location could have a potential audience of 10 to 20 or it could have 2,000. The size of the crowd does not determine how important the event is in the sight of God, but it does tell us what is needed in the way of team and tools. In order to be effective, the evangelist must have the right *attitude*, a workable *plan*, an attentive *crowd*, a simple *message*, an appealing *style*, a clear *invitation*, and a way to handle those who *respond*. Let us look at these areas.

1. *Our attitude*
   Keeping a few facts in focus will help us gain and keep the right attitude or outlook regarding our role as an evangelist to the public place.
   - This crowd will not be spiritually prepared like a church group.
   - They will be standing and will tire if you take too long, or if you are dull or boring.
   - They will be distracted by traffic, noise, vendors, weather conditions.
   - They are not obligated to listen or to stay.
   - They do not know you. There is no human reason why they should believe you. You have no credibility.
   - You do not have a pre-determined amount of time to speak—you may have to fight for time as you go along.
   - They may have never heard a Gospel message before and may possess a very conflicting religious belief, or no belief at all.

2. *Our plan*
   The most effective evangelist will have a plan and will be prepared in each area of the event. Do not just rush out. Know ahead of time what you are going to do and

how you are going to do it. Here are some simple, basic things to remember:

*Survey* the town or village and choose a location where there is a crowd or the potential of attracting a crowd. Be sure to get permission from local authorities.

*Determine* the best time of day to hold the meeting, the best place to preach from, what is needed to elevate the preacher above the crowd so he can be seen, what team members are needed, what sound equipment, lights, etc. are needed, and what tool or method will he use to attract attention.

*Get help* from local churches. Local pastors can provide church members to help in singing, testimonies, setting up a platform, providing prayer support, counseling, etc.

*Write a program* (a schedule) from start to finish and give a copy to each person participating in the event. Who is going to sing, play an instrument, draw a picture, give a testimony, preach, counsel, and when they are going to do it. Put a time limit on each portion—all the while, of course, being sensitive to the leading of the Holy Spirit.

*Do it.* Proceed by faith, believing God, and do not listen to Satan's objections and reasons why it will not work.

3.   *Our audience*

The most effective evangelist to the public place should:

*Know* his audience. Spend time in the area observing things in their life that can be drawn upon in preaching Jesus. Talk to them, get acquainted with their needs. Look for a common bond among them. Note their basic age, economic range, interests and so on. Where do they live, work, spend time, and how do they travel?

*Attract and hold* his audience. The crowd is there but how does he get them to listen to him? One of the things we use is music groups. They must be lively and good—not "churchy" and not a choir in robes. I can communicate Christ and yet be appealing. Try to use a platform, create an atmosphere of something about to happen. Use a sound system if available. If at night, use lights—whatever it takes to draw attention. Another idea is a sketch board, a puppet show, a drama, a well-known person giving his or her testimony, a movie, and so on.

The attention-getter is just that, and should last just long enough to accomplish its purpose with the promise to do more *after* the message. Show half of the film before and the second half after the message. Preachers, singers, and other believers present should be casual. Do not walk around with a tie on and holding a big Bible under your arm. You will scare people away. Many times I do not even pick up my Bible until I am into the message. Do not try to recreate a church service on the street with hymns, long prayers, etc. Introductions are not necessary—just begin and do it. The Bible tells us "not to spread the net in the sight of the bird" and to "be wise as a serpent and harmless as a dove."

After the crowd has been attracted they must be held. Interact with them. Ask questions. Promise more music, etc. Ask them to please listen to a short message. Mention short time segments as you preach—"five more minutes," "three more minutes."

*Relate* to the audience. Draw upon their everyday life experience and needs. Use such things as work, home, food, water, birth, marriage, life, and death. Do not be clerical, churchy, or theological. Be warm, friendly, interesting, caring; and above all, be real and be simple. Your objective is to be understood, so stick to the basics of the Gospel. Draw illustrations from their surroundings, their life and activities. At the ferry-boat landing, for example, I use the boats to illustrate Jesus taking us to the other side. At the bus station I use the bus—one must get on. On a street I use the "way to heaven—one way to my home." On a beach I use "solid rock—sinking sand." At the market I use "bread of life" or "a gift money can't buy" and so on. Adjust your preaching style to suit the situation. Do not be stiff—move around, using broad gestures.

**4.** *The message*

At this point in the program a transition takes place. *It is a critical moment.* Whatever has been used to attract the crowd is stopping. So how will I continue to hold them? It usually is not a problem if an adequate job is done in the first part. Sometimes the crowd even grows as the preaching begins. The preacher should begin by just talking to the crowd. How you begin will directly affect the way you end. Here are some suggested opening comments:

"We really want to thank you for stopping and listening to us today" (shows gratitude and humility). "I know you are busy and many of you are tired from working all day" (shows care and understanding), "but I want to take a moment and explain what the group was singing about and why we are here" (stirs curiosity). "You are probably wondering what these crazy people are doing out here on the street" (makes light of self and disarms critics). "Well, we are not here for money, we are not here to get you to join anything, we are not here to promote any particular church or to condemn anyone" (answers at least some questions). "We are here for one reason—because of the love of Jesus. He has given me eternal life; I know I am going to heaven and I want you to go also (states purpose).

*Introduction to message.* Mold crowd together, initiate a sense of agreement between the audience and yourself. Something like this:

"Every one of us here today is exactly the same in many ways. We were all born into this world the same way. We all need the same things for life—air, food, water, love, security. We all have the same basic desires—home, job, education, family, success, future, peace, joy, happiness. We are all going to live somewhere after we die—heaven or hell. If there is a heaven and hell, then everyone here wants to go to heaven, if we really get honest. God loves everyone of us here today, no matter how bad, good, rich or poor we are. And He wants everyone of us to spend eternity with Him in His perfect heaven. Jesus said in the Bible in John 14:6, 'I am the way, the truth, and the life—no man comes to the father but by me.' There are three simple steps to heaven, to eternal life: (1) Face the truth about yourself, (2) Face the truth about Jesus, (3) Face the truth about eternity."

As you preach include the following information:

a. *Man is a sinner and separated from God* (Psalms 14, Romans 3:12-18,23). He is a sinner for two reasons.

(i)   By birth—God created man (Adam and Eve) with a clean heart, free of sin. He gave them a choice of how to live and they chose to turn from Him and go their own way (Romans 5:12). Sin did not stop there but continued on from generation to generation, to you and to me. We all have the same great-grandparents and have all inherited sin.

(ii)  By choice—All men choose to sin (Romans 3:23) and all are separated from God.

b. *God wants us to go to heaven* (2 Peter 3:9; John 3:16-18). But how? Heaven is a perfect place where no sin is allowed. How can a man with sin in his heart go to a heaven where there is no sin?

c. *God provided the way—Jesus* (1 Peter 2:24, Romans 5:8). God said sin must be paid for by death, the shedding of perfect innocent blood. But the one who dies must be perfect, free from sin. Who can qualify? No one. So God sent Jesus from heaven to become a human being, live a perfect life, and go to the Cross to die, to shed innocent blood for the payment of our sins. Only Jesus satisfied the demands of God. Only Jesus died on the Cross—not the church, not good works, not some other religious leader, no one.

d. *You must make a choice, a decision to receive Christ* (Romans 10:13, John 1:12). How can a person receive Christ? How can he be born into God's family? (John 3:1-7) He must do three things—three easy steps.

(i) *Admit* to God he is a sinner, he is guilty and separated from God.

(ii) *Believe* on Jesus. Make a choice to believe that Jesus is God in the flesh, He died on the Cross and shed His blood in payment for our sins. Believe He died, was buried, and rose again.

(iii) *Call on him.* Ask (Romans 10:13) Him to come into your heart. Receive Christ as your personal Lord and Savior.

e. *How can you receive Christ? Through prayer.* Now is the time which everything has built toward—the invitation. You have preached a message including the above information. It has been clear. You used illustrations drawn from the audience's life experience. Now they know what they must do and now you must carefully, methodically, step-by-step, help them do it. Have counselors intensify prayer support and resisting Satan at this point. Have some men who do not bow for prayer discreetly keep a lookout for disturbances. Now—this is how I conduct the invitation regardless of what kind of meeting I am in.

5. *The invitation*

I want to thank you all for listening and now I am going to ask everyone here to receive Christ in their heart, to become a new person, to become a child of God, to know for sure you are going to heaven. Would you like to have that assurance, that guarantee? You can right now. How? Admit you are a sinner, believe on Jesus, and ask Him into your heart. How? Through prayer. That is what we are going to do right now. Talk to God, tell Him those three things. He is waiting to hear from you right now. I am going to help you talk to Him, and He is going to answer and come into your heart.

- "Everyone bow your head and close your eyes—everyone—out of respect to God—thank you very much.
- (I am going to pray)—'Dear God, please open the hearts of everyone here to receive your Son Jesus as their Lord and Savior' (don't say "amen"—if you do they will look up and you will have to ask them to bow again and it breaks the flow).
- "Now—with your heads bowed and eyes closed I am going to pray another prayer. I will pray out loud but you pray silently in your heart, just between you and God. We are going to tell God three things—we are a sinner, we believe on Jesus and we ask Him into our heart. Are you ready? Here is the prayer—repeat after me, silently in your heart . . . 'Dear God (allow time for repeating after each phrase), I am a sinner—I am separated from you . . . but I want to go to heaven . . . I choose to believe on Jesus . . . He is your Son . . . He died for me . . . Lord Jesus . . . come into my heart . . . I receive you right now . . . I turn from the devil and turn to you . . . Thank you for hearing my prayer . . . and receiving me into your family today . . . I now belong to you forever . . . (do not say "amen").'

- "Now, with your heads bowed and eyes closed, you just prayed that prayer and God just kept His promise to you. Jesus is now in your heart. I want to pray a prayer of thanksgiving for the decision you just made. So—I am going to ask those of you that just prayed that prayer to quietly lift your hand (now pray the prayer). 'Dear God, thank you for these raised hands . . .' (do not say "amen").
- "Now, with heads bowed, I want to ask those of you who raised your hand to step out of the crowd and come and stand here in front with me. I want to be the first to welcome you to the family of God. After everyone has come, we are going to have a special prayer of commitment together, then a counselor is going to talk to you personally for a few moments and then you can go. Do not be timid, just come now. Jesus died for you publicly and you should take a public stand for Him. Come right now" (soft music and singing, but not distracting).

Now is the time for counselors to come from the crowd slowly, bringing people with them—others will follow. *Note:* If it is dark, people are slower to respond. Get some light on the crowd at least during the invitation. As people come, thank them for coming and continue to call them. Speak to segments of the audience. "Those of you on the right side, those of you in the back, those of you here in front, you come. You fathers need to come. You teenagers need to come," and so on.

6. *The conclusion*

The event is not complete until all those who have come forward are properly dealt with. A counselor should stand with each person who comes. After everyone has come who is going to come, I pray with the entire group having them repeat aloud a prayer of thanksgiving and commitment. Now the counselors go to work. Collect names and addresses on cards. Go through a simple tract to make sure each inquirer has a clear understanding and assurance. Have prayer with the person, give him available literature, answer questions. Turn cards over to the participating churches. An evangelist to the public place has not been totally effective until his converts are channeled into the care of a local church. If there is no church he should attempt to start one.

If you do not have counselors, then you will need to deal with inquirers en masse. Or if you have only a few helpers, divide the inquirers into groups. The more personal the better.

# THE EVANGELIST WORKING IN SITUATIONS OF NATURAL CRISIS
*John M. Bate*

An evangelist is a "Gospel bearer," however he may do it, and so our theme today is "How does the 'Gospel bearer' react and work in situations of natural crisis?"

How many have lived through a disaster? How many have endeavored to minister in a disaster? You are here, then, either to help us with some answers, or present some very practical and relevant questions.

a.   Shock and grief are the two most immediate responses to a natural crisis. You see, we're all the same—we normal people. We never think it is going to happen to us, a "natural crisis." And by some mystery, it does! Here are for the evangelist the two most prominent human reactions, and unless we understand them we will be of little use to either God or man.

No matter what the disaster is—national, local, or personal—the grief process is the same, for grief is the vehicle with which we deal with any kind of loss. It is necessary to face up to the reality of the loss, and to rebuild life again after the loss. When a person who has suffered any kind of loss or trauma does not successfully process his grief, then there can be serious results affecting his physical and emotional health, to say nothing of his spiritual experience.

Disaster victims are grievers. Depending on the kind of disaster, they may have lost one or more of the following: the security they previously enjoyed; a member of the family; a home or other property; their livelihood. And in all this their religious faith and security may well have taken a beating.

We have to acknowledge that disaster is no respecter of persons. So often our Gospel in these circumstances is for not only the poor and destitute. The greatest grief and shock can be experienced by those who were very secure and most self-sufficient. They are now forced to depend on others.

It is vital that the evangelist be aware of the nature of the loss experience, that he be aware of how he can facilitate the important task of processing grief, and spiritually aware of how he can introduce Christ who is there in the middle of man's suffering, perplexity, and confusion.

b.   It is the experience of many who have worked in crisis situations that there often appears to be no reaction. The people are dazed or stunned—unemotional. Just as physical shock needs treatment, so does emotional shock. Sensitivity, understanding, and above all empathy (not sympathy)—that is, "not knowing how you feel, but feeling how you feel," and this can bring the victim from stoic shock to various degrees of weeping, and sometimes great waves of emotion. The person can be totally caught up in his loss. Often the living of life is halted to enable the person to become totally caught up in that loss.

In a study of bereaved persons the following grief reactions were recorded: depression, 87%; sleeping disturbance, 85%; crying, 79%; difficulty in concentrating, 47%; loss of interest, 42%; anxiety attacks, 36%; irritability, 36%; tiredness, 29%.

It is important for the evangelist to recognize that the vast majority of disaster victims are suffering from depression and sleeping disturbances—*which are both very spiritual problems*!

Normally these reactions subside and usually within a couple of months normality returns, particularly with good counseling and spiritual care. It is vital for the evangelist to know the facts and timing of the crisis to enable him to recognize the process of healing and its development.

    c. Can the Christian legitimately grieve? I think so. I know Paul did, and I feel if it was recognized and experienced by this great man of God it is hardly likely that I am going to escape it.

    He wrote on one occasion that he had "great heaviness and continual sorrow" in his heart (Romans 9:2). To the Corinthians (2 Corinthians 6) he wrote urging us as workers together and proving ourselves as ministers of God "as sorrowful, yet always rejoicing—as poor yet making many rich" (verse 10).

    To the Philippians he wrote thankfully that God had been close to him "lest he should have sorrow upon sorrow" (2:27). The difference for Paul and for all Christians is that in his grief he does not grieve as those without hope. And perhaps Romans 12:15 could be our text for this workshop—"Rejoice with them that do rejoice, and weep with them that weep."

    Here, then, is our role in ministering, in "bearing the gospel," to disaster victims in their grief:

    (i)    Accept the grief. Do not deny it or pretend it isn't there.
    (ii)    Help the grieving process.
    (iii)    Give hope for the future.
    (iv)    Be God's representative!

    d. *The ministry—to the grieving.* The evangelist in natural crisis must be aware that he is God's man! If he knows it, he does not need to shout it! His ministry must be person-to-person even if he is preaching to 10,000 or to one. "Thus and thus saith the Lord" is not generally the way to start the text in time of crisis!

    The ministry is always assisted by a listening ear. Discernment comes through listening, not talking. He must listen to the story. And when all the listening is done and the impact of the suffering has come upon him, and he has sought God's guidance, he can start to rebuild—with the help of the Holy Spirit—new lives, new hopes and very often a new world.

    We must be aware of guilt feelings of those involved—"If only I had . . ." As in no other circumstance the evangelist is recognized as the man of God, and as His representative he is in a position to give assurance.

    And let the man of God always be identified. If he wants to be lost in the crowd when walking the street he should never be so in times of disaster. The people are looking for God's representative as at no other time.

    Of course there are some vital issues to be dealt with.

    (i)    What is your theological perspective on natural disasters? Who or what causes them? Isn't nature God's domain? Is He punishing us?

    How would you react to the lady in Santiago that morning after our March 1985 earthquake? While inspecting one of our heavily damaged properties I questioned a passer-by how she had fared in the "terremoto." "Oh, we were safe," she replied. "God protected us for we love Him." And one-tenth of the population of that country in less than four minutes was left homeless!

    (ii)    Is every crisis a turning point? What is God trying to say in the midst of it all, whether He caused it or not?

    (iii)    How is God's love available in the aftermath of this tragedy?

    e. *The ministry—to disaster victims.* It is important to repeat that we represent God to most victims, and that's why it is so necessary to understand all that has been said previously. We should not underestimate the assistance given, whether it be food or clothing. These can be sacramental acts of service. Do it with care and sensitivity.

Forgive my referring yet again to Chile and our recent earthquakes, but the memories are still very vivid. We received very quickly a shipment of clothing from Sweden and were distributing garments and food when a small child said to the officer handing her a sweater, "Did you make this?" "No," he replied. "This came from a long way away." Came the immediate response, "Oh! It must be a big world!"

A caring world brings hope and consolation to those in need, and while it may seem little or nothing to us, how often has the response by the world to tragedy been the very evidence of the presence of God to those in need. And this truth should remind us never to give the smallest aid without an accompanying prayer that in some way God will display His healing presence.

Do not be thrown by expressions of anger against God. Don't feel you have to defend God for what has taken place—and don't try to calm the outrage. You don't have the answers! Only God does, and He may not give them for a long time. Simply try to be a good listener, an ambassador of hope for the future and a mediator of God's compassionate presence, remembering that times of crisis are the most potent moments for personal change.

f. *Prayer.* We should always take the opportunity to pray with those afflicted in disasters and crises but we must always be honest! Honest in prayer? What do I mean? We must never deny the reality of what has happened nor the results, nor should we disregard in prayer the strong feelings which persist (especially negative ones) of the victim. Rather, acknowledge God's presence in the midst of suffering and honestly try to express the victims' feelings.

We all know that the Bible is well illustrated with pain, suffering, grief and loss, and one of its greatest and strongest themes is God's involvement in it all. And this involvement finds its fulfillment in the Cross.

The evangelist's message in natural crisis must not differ from his message on other occasions in that he should call for action—in this case, action to give the victim or victims some sense of worth and value, no matter how small. The evangelist needs assistance in his task. In any crisis those most affected can so often be of greater use and purpose both to themselves and others when they are quickly involved in practical propagation of purpose and service.

The past is tragedy, the present may be confusion; but for the evangelist the task is to project the victims into the future in the light of God's will for them.

The world will judge a tragedy by the number of deaths. And, of course, deaths are always tragic in disasters. But do not let deaths fog our vision of reality. The dead must be respected but (forgive the frank expression) the "dead are dead"! Our ministry of counsel—our ministry of hope and comfort is for the living—the families and loved ones—and the homeless.

The real tragedy is with the living, not the dead; and this will tax the spirit, energy, and dedication of any evangelist.

# THE EVANGELIST AND THE NURTURE OF NEW CHRISTIANS

*John Mallison*

Paul took seriously his nurturing of new disciples: "You are our witnesses, and so is God, that our conduct towards you who believe was pure, right, and without fault. You know that we treated each one of you just as a father treats his own children. We encouraged you, we comforted you, and we kept urging you to live the kind of life that pleases God, who calls you to share in his own Kingdom and glory" (1 Thessalonians 2:10-12). "Watch, then, and remember that with many tears, day and night, I taught every one of you for three years" (Acts 20:31).

Many sections of the Church need to rediscover the importance of caring for new Christians and how to go about it.

1. *Enable them to have a good experience of Christian fellowship*

One of the first steps to helping a new Christian is to ensure that they have a good experience of Christian fellowship. It is important for them to feel accepted and loved within their new "family."

Human behavior is adversely affected psychologically by lack of love in the first months following birth. I believe it is similar in the spiritual realm. People who don't experience being loved, cared for, and being made to feel welcome in those early months after becoming a Christian usually have long-term problems.

Christianity is a relational religion. "God is love." Love can only function within the framework of relationships. We have a relational God, who woos us into a relationship with Himself through Jesus Christ. This is the prime relationship which is meant to affect all other relationships. Jesus taught that we are to love God with all our mind and soul, and our neighbor as ourselves.

New Christians need to feel that other Christians are pleased they have joined them.

2. *Clarify the step they have taken in becoming a Christian disciple*

The next step is to clarify the step taken in becoming a Christian. After an intensive evangelistic event, most who respond to the invitation are usually very emotional. Very little that is shared by the counselor is understood or retained. Joe Blinco, at one time a revered member of Billy Graham's team, frequently explained the role of the counselor at a Crusade meeting as essentially "being an extension of the Everlasting Arms." Making a commitment to Christ, for many people, is little more than a step in the right direction toward God. There is a realization they are not right with God; they grasp in some way that Jesus Christ is the answer to their spiritual needs, and then respond with a very simple step of faith. Usually they are more receptive later on to what the counselor may have endeavored to explain to them at the Crusade. It is important that the new disciple is helped to clarify the step he or she has taken in becoming a Christian disciple.

3. *Help them understand that conversion should result in a changed way of living*

Conversion should result in a changed way of life. "If anyone is in Christ he [or she] is a new creation; the old is gone, the new has come" (2 Corinthians 5:17). It takes a whole lifetime to learn what is involved in Christian life-style, and even then we haven't got it all together.

Paul makes it clear that we are called to be positively different: "I beg you to lead a life worthy of the calling to which you have been called'' (Ephesians 4:1). The Christian seeks to develop a new life-style worthy of God's grace. Each needs to be free to develop his or her own style of living with Christ as our model, but that has to be interpreted by believers into their own respective situations. There is no one blue-print—no single homogeneous pattern. Each must be allowed the freedom to be guided by the Holy Spirit in growing to become more like Jesus Christ.

**4.  *Teach them the "1, 2, 3's" of the Christian life***

   a.  *One body.* It is not an optional extra to belong to the fellowship comprised of those who have faith in Christ. We are not saved to an individualistic Christian experience. By faith we are born into the family of God. We can't be truly Christian alone, we need each other. In becoming like Christ we need each other's ministry—each other's love, care, counsel and prayers (Ephesians 4:25) ''. . . we are members one of another.'' When we gather with other believers in worship, fellowship, and service we both receive and give.

   We need to be involved in the local expression of the ''Body''—our church—and also in a small group of disciples who are eager to grow and serve. The small group is a microcosm or smaller expression of the larger community of faith.

   b.  *Two natures.* Many become confused when they experience the continuing evil potential within them after their commitment to Christ.

   Within each follower of Christ there is a potential for evil and a potential for good. The ''old nature'' is that self-centered, rebellious spirit which dictated our former way of life. These old ways have to be abandoned (Ephesians 4:22). But this is no negative appeal to merely abandon evil ways. Such would result in a vacuum which would quickly revert back to former ways. The new God-like nature has to be put on (Ephesians 4:24).

   In Galatians 5:16-25, Paul develops this concept further, calling the two natures ''the flesh'' and ''the spirit.'' They are opposed to each other, the old nature seeking to draw us away from God and the new nature, created by the Spirit, restoring the image of God (''in true righteousness and holiness'' Ephesians 4:24) and strengthening our relationship with God.

   Many new Christians would have been saved much inner agony if this had been explained early in their pilgrimage. Christians are not all good. The potential for evil regularly surfaces in un-Christlike attitudes and behavior. But the balancing force of the Spirit is present to set us free to be pleasing to God.

   c.  *Three aspects of salvation.* Our salvation in Christ is not solely a past experience of being set free from the penalty of sin. It is a continuing process. God frees us from the power of sin as we continue to live by faith. There is a present experience of salvation. Part of the Christian's hope is the future aspect of salvation when we shall be set free from the presence of sin. Appreciation of this process of salvation is important for spiritual growth.

**5.  *Present the Christian life as a growing experience***

   Conformity to the image of Jesus Christ is a process which is never completed in this life. ''God who began a good work within you will keep right on helping you grow in grace until his task within you is finished on that last day when Jesus returns'' (Philippians 1:6). ''Grow up in every way into him'' (Ephesians 4:15).

   It is an encouragement to new disciples when they realize that they are not expected to be perfect the day after they are converted! A Christian is a saint in the making—saints without halos, people on a journey. The word ''disciple'' literally means ''learner.'' All learners make mistakes—indeed they grow significantly by reflecting on these mistakes.

It helps when those of us who minister to new Christians share the growing edges of our own lives, and feel free to admit that we are still in the process of becoming ourselves. Paul gives us a good example in this regard in his letter to the Philippians (3:12-16).

**6.  *Explain Christian maturity as essentially deepening one's relationship to Christ and others***

An essential aspect of our objective as Christians is to progressively become more and more like Jesus Christ. Indeed our name "Christ-ians" emphasizes this. Christ is the "secret center" of our lives to which we need to relate all our attitudes, behavior and values. Paul was Christo-centric: "So that it is no longer I who live, but it is Christ who lives in me. This life that I now live, I live by faith in the Son of God, who loved me and gave his life for me" (Galatians 2:20).

In His parable of the vine, Christ clearly emphasizes the need to "abide in Him"—to maintain an intimate living relationship with Him—"remain united to me . . . for you can do nothing without me" (John 15:4,5).

**7.  *Make clear they are not on their own—the Holy Spirit indwells them***

Christians have the Holy Spirit as their divine traveling companion. They are never on their own. He is always with them to convict of sin, point to Christ, stimulate faith, restore the image of God in us, guide, help, comfort, gift and empower for ministry, give understanding of the Word, impart divine love in and through them, give peace and joy, make prayer and worship effective, and plead at the Throne of Grace as their Advocate. He is our lifeline! How essential that Christians understand the supernatural resources available to them through the Holy Spirit. Every day they should open their lives for a fresh anointing of the Holy Spirit.

**8.  *Help them develop Christian certainty***

How can a person be sure that their spiritual experience is really from God and not purely emotional?

In "He Touched Me" (1974), John Powell shares his belief that when God touches a human being, the experience will survive three tests:

"1. *The Time Test:* "The person touched by God will never be the same again. Even if the change is not dramatic, the experience will leave a permanent work." This is a long-term test. Only time will prove that it was not a "flash in the pan" (Philippians 1:6). "I am sure he is able to do a good work in you and bring it to completion."

2. *The Reality Test:* A proof that a person has had a genuine experience of God's grace is that it puts him or her in touch with the world as never before. It doesn't leave him or her living "on cloud nine" in an unreal world, but deepens awareness of the world around. People should be lifted out of their selfish little world and come alive to both the beauty and sorrow of the wider world, as never before.

3. *The Charity Test.* When people are touched by God they mirror this God of love in their behavior. They become more loving. They love in the way Christ loved—aloofness from others' needs gives way to identification; and selfishness fades into self-giving. The love of God floods into their hearts by the Holy Spirit producing a new love for God and humankind. "We know that we have passed out of death into life, because we love the brethren" (1 John 3:14).

Powell's "reality test" and "charity test" are included in what is often referred to as the *"outer witness"* or evidence of a changed life. The indwelling Holy Spirit produces a new quality of life within, which is evidenced in new attitudes and behavior as we saw in the notes on Ephesians 4. The new disciple will not always be aware of this change. Christian friends play an important role in recognizing and affirming this outward evidence of the new inner creation.

Christian certainty is not based on feelings. There will be times of joy and elation, but these will fluctuate according to circumstances. The Holy Spirit who indwells the Christian disciple will produce an inner certainty, what John Wesley referred to as *"the inner witness."* "When we cry, Abba! Father! it is the Spirit himself bearing witness with our spirit that we are children of God . . ." (Romans 8:16). "We know that he abides in us, by the Spirit which he has given us" (1 John 3:24; cf. 4:13, 5:10).

Assurance rests heavily upon an understanding of *the Scriptures* and an acceptance by faith of the promises they contain. As we read the Scriptures and become more aware of the breadth and depth of His grace in Christ, and respond in faith, this certainty grows (1 John 5:13).

It is not presumptuous to have a humble certainty that we are forgiven and accepted into a right relationship with God. The promises of the new covenant are for us to claim by faith (1 John 5:11,12; John 1:12, 6:37, 5:24). To say a Christian believer can never be sure is to cast serious doubts on God's integrity (1 John 5:10).

9. *Give opportunities to share their faith story within the acceptance of Christian fellowship*

They will gain confidence by beginning to witness in an accepting, caring fellowship. This brings joy to those listening as well as strengthening the beginning in the faith. A small group of fellow believers provides a good setting for sharing what Christ means. Sometimes it is best to interview the person using such questions as:

—Can you think of one word to describe how you *felt* when you made your commitment to Christ?

—What impressed you most about the meeting where you made your commitment to Christ?

—What helped you make this step?

—How is it working out for you now?

Most times it will be best to have all present in the small gathering share as these questions are addressed to the group as a whole.

10. *Give help in how to use their survival/growth resources (means of grace)*

God's grace is channeled to us in a number of ways, through prayer, Bible study, fellowship, obedience, worship, the sacraments. All of these help us develop spiritually. These "means of grace," used effectively, facilitate spiritual growth. The "how" rather than the "ought" needs to be emphasized here.

Avoid burdening newcomers to the faith with too much too soon. In *What's Gone Wrong with the Harvest?* Engel and Norton suggest that some well-meaning Christians might say, "Now that you are a Christian here are some things you will want to do:

1. Have a daily quiet time. It's best to do this in the morning. Try to read at least one chapter of the Bible.

2. Keep a prayer list for your unsaved friends. Pray for them daily.

3. Make witnessing a way of life. Every time you are with a person five minutes, consider this a divine appointment and seek ways to share Christ with him.

4. You should be in Sunday School, Sunday morning service, Sunday evening service, Wednesday evening prayer service, and Saturday morning men's prayer group. And of course, that's just the beginning of the good things going on at church.

5. And be sure you get into Scripture memory. Five verses a week is a good start for a young Christian like you.''

And on it goes. Here is a job description that becomes an impossibility! Obviously all of these things are good and will probably be present in one form or another in the life of most mature believers. But these good works emerge slowly through maturity and should never be imposed artificially. All too often, this becomes just another form of legalism, which can squeeze the very joy out of the Christian life.

So here we have it—a kind of assembly line that produces one standard model of "good, orthodox, properly-behaving, Bible-believing Christians." But somehow that first joy evaporates. Instead of the new-found freedom the new Christian is forced into another mold, characterized mostly by an innocuous blandness.

11. *Help them to get a correct perspective on temptation and sin*

Many new Christians have faulted here. How crucial to learn early in one's Christian journey that temptation is not sin. All are tempted—even Christ was tempted (1 Corinthians 10:12,13).

Faith in Christ's victory over sin is the key (Hebrews 4:15,16; 1 John 5:4,5). Overconfidence in one's own resourcefulness rather than the divine resources leads to inevitable failure. Trust in God's faithfulness and His completed work in Christ must always be encouraged.

Confession and acceptance of forgiveness immediately when one fails keeps one's relationship to God open and close (1 John 1:9).

12. *Encourage them to share their faith with others from within the Christian fellowship.*

All Christians do not have the gift of evangelism but all are called to be witnesses. Sharing our faith experience of Christ is the responsibility of every one of Christ's followers. "You shall be my witnesses" might be the theme of the whole book of Acts but few find this easy—indeed the Greek word for "witness" is the same one from which the English word "martyr" is derived.

Help given in how to witness will emphasize dependence on the Holy Spirit, the divine witness (John 15:26) for the opportunities, the wisdom, and the grace and love to communicate effectively.

Vital Christian fellowships will provide varied opportunities for witnessing. However, the witnessing of a style of life rather than words without works will always need to be stressed.

13. *Help them discover and equip themselves for ministry*

The continuing ministry of Jesus Christ is shared by all the *"laos"*—the people of God. Each and every Christian is gifted by the Spirit for ministry. Discovery, development and use of gifts is a vital function of the Christian Church, best done in small groups.

Understanding the New Testament teaching on spiritual gifts is the first step. Training needs to be linked with field work and continuing opportunities for ministry, built-in support, accountability, and encouragement.

14. *Provide opportunities for informal socializing with other Christians*

Time for doing some fun things together and meeting informally develop relationships and provide for restoration—usually much neglected in the Christian fellowship, especially among the more deeply committed. New Christians need to be guided away from a life-style which is too intense and lacks an opportunity for relaxation. Usually such imbalance is associated with an inadequate commitment to development of meaningful relationships.

15. *Begin to introduce them to some basic Christian beliefs and help them to relate these to daily living*

"What you heard from me . . . entrust to faithful men who will be able to lead others also" (2 Timothy 2:2).

Biblical illiteracy is one of the curses from which most sections of the Christian Church suffer. Education of new Christians, as with all Christian education, needs to address itself to the needs of the recipients and opens up the Scriptures so that the relevance of life's situations can be explored. Educational methods will be used appropriate to the age, abilities, and commitment of the participants. Participatory learning, small group work, relational Bible study, action planning, support and accountability are all part of an educational package which will help people grow. Variety, fun, and the unexpected are further ingredients of good learning. The importance of modeling by the teacher is crucial. Paul must have been an amazing person to be able to say, "What you have learned, and received, and heard, and seen in me, do" (Philippians 4:9). Christianity is both taught and caught. People who are sensitive are clearly indwelt by Christ and empowered by the Spirit to give a living demonstration of the faith and make it easier for people to understand and act.

Acknowledgments:
*What's Gone Wrong with the Harvest?*,
Engel & Norton, Zondervan, p. 105

# THE EVANGELIST PREACHING IN PRISONS
*David Stillman*

It is of great significance to those of us involved in a prison ministry to discover that Jesus Himself was identified with prisoners both at the beginning and at the end of His earthly ministry. Luke tells us (Luke 4:16-21) how in the early days of His ministry Jesus preached in the synagogue at Nazareth. He read from the book of Isaiah: "The Spirit of the Lord God is upon me, because the Lord has anointed me to bring good news to the afflicted; He has sent me to bind up the brokenhearted to proclaim liberty to captives and freedom to prisoners; To proclaim the favorable year of the Lord, and the day of vengeance of our God; to comfort all who mourn" (61:1,2).

If ever there was a body of people who need to hear of "the Lord's favor" it is men and women in prison. They know material and spiritual poverty. In addition to physical imprisonment, many are in bondage to drugs and alcohol and are oppressed by demons, perversions, hatred, bitterness, and rejection.

Then, as far as we know, the last human being Jesus spoke to before He died was a criminal on the cross next to Him (Luke 23:42-43). If we are to be truly like Christ we must minister to prisoners.

"Remember those in prison as if you were their fellow prisoners, and those who are ill-treated as if you yourselves were suffering" (Hebrews 13:3).

1. *Ministry development*

While he was at Oxford University, John Wesley regularly made time to minister to the inmates of Oxford Prison. I had the privilege to begin my prison ministry 18 years ago in that very same prison when I visited to show a Billy Graham film at an evangelistic meeting. In those early days as an itinerant evangelist I discovered that Christian films were a very effective tool for evangelism in prisons. Wherever I had the opportunity I would show Christian films in prisons. Sometimes it was included as part of the general entertainment program in the prison. Other times I would show the film in the prison chapel as part of the ongoing religious program in the prison organized by the chaplain. (In England every prison has a chaplain from the State Church, the Church of England.)

From those early film showings a wide-ranging, ongoing ministry of evangelism in prisons has been developed. First, there are activities designed to bring the evangelist into contact with as many prisoners in the prison as possible. This can include the showing of Christian films and videos, Gospel concerts, chapel services and other preaching meetings, discussion groups, and Bible study classes. They are a point of initial contact with prisoners and present good opportunities for sowing the seed of the Gospel.

From these initial contacts there are obviously prisoners who express interest in coming to Christ. The second point of contact is to provide these men and women with Christian books to read and ensure that they have a Bible in a translation/version that they can read and understand. They are also encouraged to enroll in a Bible study correspondence course which we provide for them. The one thing that prisoners always have plenty of is time on their hands. Because of the boredom that results from being locked away for long periods, prisoners will read anything to fill their time. This means that men and women who would not bother to read the Bible or consider the claims of Christ if they were free to go about their normal life will often do so in prison.

As the prisoners progress with their correspondence courses or request further literature, we can discover those in whom the Holy Spirit is working. We then correspond with them by letter, beginning to apply the Gospel to their individual situation. Our third point of contact is then to visit the prisoners individually—to spend time with them counseling in a one-to-one situation and to lead them to Christ.

There is an additional point of contact that I would like to add. It relates to the practical needs of prisoners. I make it an addition not because it is of secondary importance or insignificant, but because in my own country generally there is not the need for us to be providing food parcels, clothing, toiletries, etc. Prisoners are adequately clothed and fed. I know from my travels that this is not the case in many countries. Some of you will have to consider meeting these practical needs of prisoners as an important part of your outreach.

2. *Follow through*

It is one thing to see a prisoner professing faith in Christ as Savior and Lord, but quite another to see that same prisoner going on in the Christian faith to live a life of obedience to Christ. It is so easy to feel that our work is done when a prisoner comes to Christ. Conversion to Christ is not the last step in a person's spiritual experience. It is only the first step in a walk with Him. This means that when a prisoner comes to Christ our work and our responsibility has only just started. As far as preaching the Gospel in prison is concerned, *if we fail to follow through we fail!*

Obviously, as one individual you will not be able to meet all the needs of all the prisoners who come to Christ through your ministry. You will need to mobilize others in the church to help. In our prison ministry in Britain we seek to ensure early on in a prisoner's Christian experience that he/she is linked with another Christian outside prison who will accept responsibility to help in the caring process. Letters are exchanged, visits are made, the prisoner is prayed for by name at the church prayer meeting, etc.

As time passes the prisoner receives visits from other members of the local church family and receives regular news about the church activities. The intention is that if and when the prisoner is released there is a church into which he will be welcomed, where he will not be a total stranger.

To have an effective ministry to prisoners takes time and is time-consuming. You must be available. You must resist the pressure to accept a world view which often says, "Do it quickly," rather than do it properly; because so-called efficiency is more important than effectiveness. This means you must be prepared to give a lot of time to an individual without necessarily seeing any progress in the short term, in order to be effective in the long term.

You must be open about your ministry. Your reasons for wanting to minister to prisoners will have considerable influence on the effectiveness of your ministry. Do you want them to come to Christ because you love them? Or do you say that you love them because you want them to come to Christ to prove your ministry? Is your love for prisoners conditional upon their cooperation, or do you love them even if they never respond? Do you want them to conform to the acceptable "norms" in your society, or do you want them to become completely new people in Christ? Do you represent the establishment or the kingdom of God? Despite all of the problems their life-style has brought them, prisoners have a knack of knowing "where you are coming from." To help prisoners you must be genuine and trustworthy. Treat a prisoner as you treat your friends, and he will want to become your friend too!

You will need to be firm in your dealings with prisoners. Firmness in relationships helps build security into the lives of prisoners. One of the reasons why divorce and the breakup of the family unit contribute so much to juvenile delinquency in Western society is because of the insecurity it brings into the lives of the children involved.

Some years ago I was involved, with the headmaster of a school, in counseling one of his pupils. In school the boy was a model student, but outside school his parents could not control him and the police were regular visitors to his home on account of his misbehavior. We discovered that his family environment was so bad that the only place he felt secure was at school. It was the only place that he was treated with any degree of firmness.

It is not enough to talk about the love of God to prisoners. You must *be* the love of God to them and demonstrate the characteristics to them. This requires the long-term commitment to follow through.

## 3. Conclusion

If there is one place where the Gospel of Christ is particularly relevant it is in prison. The failure syndrome is prevalent in the lives of most prisoners. This places the minister of the Gospel in a unique and privileged position. Jesus came into the world specifically for failures.

*Matthew 9:13*—"But go and learn what this means: 'I desire mercy, not sacrifice.' For I have not come to call the righteous, but sinners."

*1 Timothy 1:15*—"Here is a trustworthy saying that deserves full acceptance: Christ Jesus came into the world to save sinners."

Many people in prison found themselves "write-offs" at an early age. Written off by parents, teachers, social workers, employers, as being helpless and hopeless. They have known failure all their lives. Failure at home through divorce and family breakdown. Failure at school through bad family environment or laziness on their own part. Failure at work through lack of ability and motivation. They are even a failure at crime, otherwise they would not be in prison.

*Romans 3:23*—"For all have sinned and fall short of the glory of God."

*Romans 6:23*—"For the wages of sin is death, but the gift of God is eternal life through Christ Jesus our Lord."

Recently I took part in a communion service in a prison chapel. As I shared the bread and wine in remembrance of Christ with the prisoners, I realized I was kneeling alongside murderers, rapists, men serving time for armed robbery, and other crimes of violence. I was keenly aware that I had to come to God the same way as all of these prisoners—through the sacrifice of Calvary.

When you go to prison with the Good News of Christ you go as failures to other failures with a message of hope for the future.

*All Scriptures quoted from New American Standard Bible*

# PLANNING FOR CRUSADES IN SINGLE CHURCHES
*Richard H. Harris and Tom McEachin*

The burden of any crusade effort is to get the church members to be the church of the living Lord and unbelievers to receive the Good News of Jesus Christ. The church is the called-out family of God, the local body of believers who continue the activities and work of Christ. Biblical revival is the reawakening of faith. Revival is the sovereign work of God, on behalf of His people, where He restores them to the fullness of His blessings. Revival is the new beginning of obedience to God. The goal of any crusade is to help the church experience revival.

"Crusade preparation is the various activities and events utilized to get the local church ready for the crusade. Various aspects of human involvement in the planned activities and events will be necessary for thorough crusade preparation.

"A distinction needs to be made between a single church crusade and revival. A single church crusade is a series of evangelistic worship services for the purpose of reawakening Christian faith, a calling of God's people to renewed obedience and a sharing of our Christian faith. A revival is the actual experience of spiritual renewal. A crusade is the means to reach a desired result. The revival is the desired result. Ideally, all crusades will result in revival, but experience would teach otherwise.

"The greatest guarantee that a crusade will result in heaven-sent revival is thorough preparation. A definite connection exists between the amount and type of preparation and the spiritual renewal that actually occurs. This does not suggest God is not sovereign—He certainly is. But God has given in the Bible certain principles He honors. People have the responsibility to abide by those principles if spiritual blessings are to be experienced.

"Perhaps you are thinking, if crusades do have great spiritual potential and crusade preparation is so important, why are many Christians skeptical toward crusades? No doubt the answer lies in the fact that crusades and revival have been equated. Some people have concluded that a series of evangelistic services and an excited emotionalism in religion would always result in changed lives. But when little to no lasting change occurs in the lives of the church members, apathy, complacency, and skepticism inevitably come. Because of this, some people feel little need to give an all-out effort to prepare adequately for the next crusade.

"Adequate preparation is an absolute necessity. God's sovereignty and people's responsibility never clash in the Word of God. God, in His wisdom, has chosen to do His work through His people. God has so bound up His purposes with people that He limits His workings to their obedience.

"Revival is nothing more than the right use of the appropriate means. Although churches cannot make revival, they can prepare for it and be ready to make the most of it when it comes. Paradoxical as it may seem, the churches which are fully prepared for revival are already in revival. Revival means you have a successful crusade. Revival will then issue in effective evangelism" (Richard H. Harris Member's Booklet/Individual Study Guide, 1983, (item 7749-03), pages 2,3).

Preparation involves people. Meaningful involvement of large numbers of your people will be a key to the success of your crusade. Encourage personal involvement from all church members. Actively involve choirs, ushers and personal counselors to deal with people at the altar. Get a large number of persons committed to come to the altar each evening for special prayer for the crusades. More involvement of people results in more lost people reached. Church leaders must have a real commitment to the crusade.


## STEPS IN PREPARING FOR REVIVAL

A great crusade involves visiting, witnessing, and attending, as well as prayer, confession, and repentance.

1. *Set the date*

Schedule the crusade so that it will affect the most people, in and out of the church. Use the organizations in the church which will involve the greatest number of all ages in the church. Make the crusade the only major activity for that period of time.

2. *Select and invite evangelistic help*

a.  An evangelistic team could consist of a preacher and musician, or just a preacher, or a preacher and others who are responsible for helping prepare for and conduct your crusade. Use evangelistic leaders who are moral, cooperative, and effective preachers; and musicians with sound doctrine, and wise methods.

b.  Guide the church to pray for selection of the right persons to lead your crusade. The invitation should be extended to the persons whom the pastor and church believe to be God's leaders for this meeting. This invitation should be made at least one year, preferably two years, before the date of the crusade.

c.  Be specific about exact dates of the meeting. Confirm the dates (specify days, month and year) in writing with the evangelistic team. Give evangelistic helpers as much pertinent information as you can about your church and community.

d.  Request from the evangelistic team any plans or materials they want to use in preparation for the crusade. Try to lead the church to follow the suggestions as far as possible.

e.  In the invitation make plain who is responsible for paying the travel expenses, food, and lodging. If they are to receive an honorarium (a specified amount provided by the church) inform them of the amount they will receive. If they are to receive a love offering (monetary contributions given by those attending the crusade as an expression of Christian love), indicate this and assure them they will receive all that is given for this purpose.

f.  Keep the evangelistic team informed during all steps of crusade preparation before they arrive on the field. During the six months preceding the crusade write them at least monthly to share the details of crusade preparation.

3. *Create expectancy*

The pastor is the key to creating expectancy for a successful crusade. The church begins to expect a great crusade when they feel excitement from the pulpit. Be a witness! When the pastor is concerned, so is the church. Lead people to believe that God is going to do something great.

4. *Organizing for crusade*

Name committees or individuals (chairpersons) who will assume certain areas of responsibility (e.g., prayer, publicity, music, ushers, visitation, counselors). Large churches want committees, smaller churches may use a steering committee with one person responsible for each area of preparation. A steering committee is made up of each crusade committee chairperson, pastor, church staff, and anyone else the pastor wishes to invite. The steering committee coordinates all details of plans for the crusade. Committee members must be totally committed to revival. *Priority should be given to involve a large number of people with small but meaningful assignments.*

5. *Set goals*

Set specific goals for the crusade. Goals will allow you to evaluate more effectively the results of the crusade.

a. Goals are specific actions we can and intend to do. They state our specific purposes and intentions.

b. Goals are measurable. When the crusade is over you should know if you have accomplished what you set out to do.

c. Goals are related to a definite time period. Goals are intended to accomplish specific results within a specific time frame. Examples of goals could be:

| | |
|---|---|
| Sunday School attendance | Number of counselors trained |
| Number in crusade choir | Number of people trained as |
| Number of people in prayer meetings | personal witnesses |
| Number of ushers | Number of prospects located |
| Additions to church | Total members involved in setting |
| Average nightly attendance | these goals |

Involve leaders of the church in setting the goals.

6. *Program a calendar*

Start from the crusade week, then move backward and place each event and committee responsibility on a calendar. Crusade success depends on the crusade having priority. Crusade plans are only dreams until they are scheduled. Plan your work and effectively work your plans.

7. *Follow-up*

Be prepared to follow up on all who respond publicly during the crusade. Put materials in their hands at once. Immediately involve the new convert in the total church program. Encourage another Christian to disciple the new convert.

8. *Evaluate the crusade*

Do this within a month after the revival. Note strengths and weaknesses of planning. Send a report to the evangelistic team. Establish a file for future crusade preparation.

## BENEFITS OF SINGLE CHURCH CRUSADES

Benefits of conducting single church crusades are:

1. It reminds us to keep our priorities in proper order. Individuals or a church easily forget that our priority is to share Christ with a lost world. In crusades God refreshes our spirit and renews our vision so that we will recommit ourselves to "seeking and saving that which is lost."

2. It is a retreat with God from the ordinary. A church should commit itself to attendance and prayer expecting God to do something unusual. Every church needs a period of time to isolate itself from worldly cares and pleasures. In this setting it can hear the voice of God clearly. A crusade can be a spiritual retreat.

3. It is the unified voice of the church declaring to a community Christ's concern for the lost. The community knows that normally the church shows extra concern for its spiritual welfare during a period of crusade. This should not be the only way a church shows Christ's concern, but it should be one way.

4. It focuses on special spiritual needs of a church. Crusades can help strengthen spiritual areas of need. Some focal points could be the family, witnessing, loving

Christian fellowship, inactive members, stewardship, evangelistic music and preaching. Not all crusades will be specifically focused on the lost; *however,* real revival in any area of life should result in winning the lost.

5.  It intensifies and develops prayer life. There is usually more planned prayer for crusades than for any other type of religious service. We expect God to do something unusual, so we pray more. Prayer is a method of evangelism in a crusade more than any other time.

6.  It sets a spiritual atmosphere that ripens the harvest. The intensified atmosphere of concern and proclamation makes it easier to achieve a harvest of souls. Adequate planting and watering guarantees such a harvest. Without proper planning, praying, and preparation, crusade efforts are fruitless.

### THE PASTOR AS LEADER IN AN EVANGELISTIC CRUSADE

Every pastor is called to "do the work of an evangelist" and to "equip the saints for the work of the ministry." The "called" pastor of a local church is to be a personal soul winner and an equipper for life-style evangelism. The evangelistic pastor will set the spiritual tone for the crusade.

Witnessing is a spiritual ministry and can only be done effectively by spiritual people. Prayer is absolutely essential. Pray alone, pray with your staff, pray with your deacons, pray as you work. Work as though everything depends on you. Pray as though everything depends on God.

### THE PASTOR MUST FOLLOW JESUS

Jesus said, "Follow me and I will make you fishers of men." If you are not fishing for men you are not following Jesus. Our Lord set the example in equipping His disciples for witnessing.

Jesus' method was to select ordinary men. They were impulsive, temperamental, prejudiced and easily offended. Jesus understood small group dynamics. Most of His public ministry was devoted to 12 disciples upon whom He staked His entire ministry. He kept them close to Him. He required them to obey Him. He gave Himself to them. He showed them how to live. He sent them out to witness. He checked up on them. He expected them to reproduce. He kept them going.

### THE PASTOR MUST MOTIVATE PEOPLE

People need information to enable them to know what to do. Motivated people want to witness. Most Christians know enough to witness, but lack motivation to share Christ with others.

1.  Enthusiasm comes from the Greek word *enthusiasmos,* itself from *entheos,* "inspired" (*en,* "in," plus *Theos,* "a god"). Excite people to witness by being enthusiastic about sharing Christ.

2.  Repetition. Keep before people the urgency of outreach and the imperatives of evangelism. At every committee meeting, every assembly and in every sermon talk about witnessing for Jesus.

3.  Demonstration. Show people how to witness. Set the pace. Lead the way. Determine each week to have somebody ready to make a public commitment to Christ in each Sunday worship service and crusade service.

The way to build a witnessing church for Jesus Christ is to *keep it simple; say it often; make it burn.*

# THE MUSICIAN: AN AMBASSADOR ON THE EVANGELIST'S TEAM
*Bernie Smith*

Today I want to do two things: to talk with you about the role of the song leader in evangelism, and to show you helpful hand signals for leading singing so that you will feel confident to lead people in any audience where you might be conducting an evening—or several evenings—of evangelism. After I have finished sharing these thoughts, we will take the remainder of the time for as many of you as time permits to come forward and lead the rest of us in songs in 2/4, 3/4, and 4/4 times.

1.  *Why the song leader is a key person in evangelism*
    a.  He's (usually) the first person to appear on platform nightly.
    b.  He's the person to establish rapport—good feeling with audience.
    c.  He's the person to relax audience and establish the mood.
    d.  He leads in the only thing all can do together.
    e.  He helps create a feeling of fellowship as he leads in praise and worship.

2.  *What makes a good song leader?*
    a.  A person who is *friendly* and *sincere*.
    b.  A person who "loves" music, and enjoys leading singing.
    c.  A person who has good rhythm.
    d.  A person who likes people.
    e.  One who knows what he wants from his audience.
    f.  A person whose "hand signals" are clear.

3.  *Choice of hymns and other songs*
    a.  Always *begin* with a hymn or chorus that is simple and well known. Try to find a song that will become "yours," one that is so good—or that you do so well—it makes your audience want to sing.
    b.  Choose songs that move toward the theme or purpose of the evening meeting, songs that fit the topic of the speaker in question.
    c.  Choose hymns or choruses that are scripturally sound. Avoid the choruses lacking significant theological or biblical meaning.
    d.  Make an attempt to use variety of song choices—especially when the audience is mixed in ages.

4.  *Leading the audience*
    a.  If you are the song leader—*lead*! That is to say, don't *be* led by the pianist, organist or guitar player. The song leader must take humble but definite authority, and lead.
    b.  If you want loudness or softness—either say so—or show by your hand signals that you want a bigger or smaller sound at any given point.
    c.  If leading with no accompaniment—announce the song, give the pitch, then start with a vigorous downbeat, strongly singing the song in question. If your announcements, vocal entry, or hand signals are weak the singing will be weak too.
    d.  Remember all songs do not start on the downbeat. When they do not, then more than ever your *preparatory* beat must be clear, and such as to make no mistake that you are wanting them to start.
    e.  There are three basic times that all the songs ever written tend to fall into.

They are 2/4, 3/4 and 4/4. What this means is that in every bar of music there are so many beats. And the second number tells us what note gets a beat.

# THE EVANGELIST'S USE OF RADIO AND TELEVISION
*Howard O. Jones*

Today we witness an incredible phenomenon—the international explosion of various kinds of information and knowledge around the world through sophisticated means of communication. What a tremendous challenge to all evangelists who desire to preach the Gospel to the world, a global village of more than 4.5 billion people, most of whom have no saving knowledge of Jesus Christ.

I will endeavor to show why evangelists should consider the use of radio and television, and discuss other vital matters regarding the ministry of Christian broadcasting in today's world.

1. *Radio and television have great potential.*

Before His ascension, Jesus Christ challenged the disciples to continue His global program of evangelism and missions. They were told to depend on the Holy Spirit's presence and power and adopt His methods as models for Christian service. Note His instructions:

"And this Gospel of the kingdom shall be preached in all the world for a witness unto all nations; and then shall the end come" (Matthew 24:14).

"And He said unto them, Go ye into all the world, and preach the Gospel to every creature" (Mark 16:15).

When the Church has obeyed these divine orders it has been blessed and effective in its outreach ministry for Christ. But when it has forsaken them, dark ages have settled on it like a cloud.

The fact that the Great Commission was practically the closing message of our Lord emphasizes its importance. In those closing hours, He concentrated on the work to which the Father had commissioned Him. Now that He was leaving, His disciples were to finish that work.

What did Jesus consider to be the supreme task of the Church? It was the evangelization of the world through the preaching of the Gospel. In this corrupt, confused and changing society, the Great Commission still stands, and we are under orders to obey it.

We have a biblical mandate for using radio and television in our ministry of evangelism. Did not our Lord also say to His disciples, "Greater works shall ye do than I have done." I am convinced that the "greater works" Jesus predicted almost 2,000 years ago apply to the unlimited opportunities Christian broadcasting affords us today.

Billy Graham, one of the pioneer Christian broadcasters, delivered a dynamic speech entitled, "The Bible and the Technological Age" at the annual NRB Convention and Exposition in 1983.

"Perhaps more than any other group of people in the world," Graham said, "broadcasters have a weighty responsibility on their shoulders: the capacity to effect positive changes in our nation and our world—even changes that could give the next generation hope, which it has little of now.

"The Gospel of Jesus Christ is still the answer for a world aflame. The Bible is still God's Word reaching out to rescue and renew the world. For religious broadcasters it is a time of decision—hard and demanding decisions—decisions that will shape forever our future and the future of those who look to us for spiritual leadership," he challenged.

2.   *Popular radio and television program formats.*

First, on the *evangelistic* radio or television program the evangelist delivers a Bible message which is produced in a recording studio or at the scene of an evangelistic crusade. The program is targeted primarily for evangelizing the unconverted, unchurched people who listen to religious radio and television programs.

On a *Bible teaching* program, the evangelist excels in expository preaching, expounding the great themes and doctrines of the Bible to feed and nourish Christians, to help them grow in grace and in knowledge of the Lord.

*Interview Format*

On an *interview* program the evangelist profiles various guests and discusses with them their ministry and ideas on issues affecting the church and society.

The *question and answer* program is another favorite program style. Years ago when our family lived at radio station ELWA in Monrovia, Liberia, my wife, Wanda, and I conducted a 15-minute program called *The Question Box*, which was one of the most popular broadcasts on the station. Our radio listeners sent in questions dealing with the Bible, the church, the family, and other matters.

The *special emphasis* program allows the broadcast evangelist to deal with certain pressing issues and problems which concern people. The topics might include marriage, the family, youth problems, world missions, or Bible prophecy. *Focus on the Family* radio broadcast is one among many broadcasts today that excels in special emphasis programming.

*Musical* programs with gifted singers and musicians reach people with sermons in song, followed by a closing message from the evangelist.

Finally, with *educational* or *documentary* programs evangelists can effectively reach people with the Gospel. One could cite Billy Graham's TV programs, which present his evangelistic crusades and give the viewing audience valuable insights regarding the culture of distant people. Graham's spectacular, NRB award-winning television program of his 1984 crusade tour of Russia is a good example.

Each evangelist must prayerfully seek God's will for the radio or television program format that will enable him to develop his God-given gifts and abilities as a broadcaster.

3.   *Preparation of a Christian radio or television program.*

The spiritual preparedness of the broadcast evangelist is essential. He must be soundly converted and called by God to the ministry and live a consistent, consecrated and holy life before God, his family, the church, and his community.

In this permissive, perverted, and polluted world the broadcast evangelist must also guard against these major, subtle temptations which Satan uses to destroy a ministry:

1. Pride
2. Jealousy
3. Love of money
4. Lust
5. Alcohol
6. Bitterness/unforgiving spirit
7. Departure from Gospel truths

*Preparation required*

To keep spiritually fit the evangelist needs to maintain a warm and meaningful relationship each day with the Lord. This calls for determination, the discipline of time, established place for prayer, the study of and obedience to the Word of God, the anointing and empowering of the Holy Spirit, and submission to the will of God.

The evangelist also needs a preparation of mind, keeping fresh and alert intellectually. He must also be informed regarding current events in today's world. Above all, he needs to love people; to know their joys, hurts, and sorrows.

Good programs don't just happen!

The evangelist must pray and strive for excellence in his preparation. This demands careful planning, designing, development and the writing of a broadcast script that complements the music and message of the broadcast. Many Christian broadcasts fail to attract the listening audience because they are poorly prepared.

In his preparation, the evangelist must always use good quality recorders and other technical equipment. An excellent program is ruined if recorded on inferior equipment or in studios not properly constructed.

*Promotion of a radio or television program.*

An evangelist should send out a monthly or quarterly newsletter that reports on God's blessing, along with the concerns, plans and future goals for a more effective soul-winning ministry. Always produce a well-written and attractive newsletter, since it reflects upon you and your ministry.

*Two-Way communication*

Listener letters are invaluable and inspirational. Encourage people to write by offering them free books, tracts, printed copies of sermons, and other Christian literature. People often write for information on how they might obtain sermons on cassette tapes. Because listener responses help to build a broadcast mailing list, answer all radio mail and provide spiritual counseling for people requesting it. Once people detect your sincerity and love for them, they will support you with prayers and, if possible, financial gifts.

Christian magazines play a major role in promoting religious programs. The evangelist pays for advertising the broadcasts, affording him good visibility with the reading public. Religious magazine editors and other writers feature stories on various evangelists and ministries.

Paid advertising in the secular press is often expensive, but the cost actually appears minimal when compared with the tremendous publicity newspapers can provide for evangelists in reaching thousands in a city and surrounding areas.

In promoting their broadcast ministries, many pastors and evangelists hold special radio and TV rallies or banquets in large churches or hotel ballrooms.

*Financial integrity*

Guidelines are needed to help broadcast evangelists maintain a standard of integrity, credibility, and accountability regarding the raising of funds to support the broadcasts. Be brief and to the point in handling this matter. Do not talk too much about yourself or your accomplishments. Always keep a low, humble profile before God and the people. Be honest and sincere in your presentation.

When raising money, the radio or TV evangelist should never, under any circumstances whatsoever, unduly plead, beg or use questionable pressure tactics in influencing people to give. I believe this practice dishonors God, disgraces the ministry, and disgusts many people who will turn off the program. Others who continue to listen may suffer spiritually because they have been conditioned to reflect more on money and other material things than about Jesus Christ and the Word of God.

Financial needs will always arise in a broadcast ministry. But when it happens let us not lose faith, be discouraged, or panic as though God suddenly declared Himself bankrupt, and is financially incapable of supporting His work and workers, and now looks to us for help. He owns all the wealth in the world.

As Hudson Taylor once said, ''God's work done in God's way will never lack God's supply.'' In view of this we should handle financial matters on the broadcast in such a way that it bears a good Christian testimony before our broadcast family.

Some of the best-known Christian broadcasters have a policy not to make any financial appeals on their radio or television programs. Instead, they raise finances by contacting people on the mailing list or presenting the matter to individuals who attend their public meetings.

God honors such faith and the ministry continues to grow. Whatever method is used in fund-raising, be sure that it honors the Lord. When we trust Him, He never fails us. Note His precious promise in Philippians, chapter 4 and verse 19: ''But my God shall supply all your needs according to his riches in glory by Christ Jesus.''

The National Religious Broadcasters organization has published a book, entitled: ''NRB Financial Guidelines for Religious Organizations.*'' This is a very helpful document that you might want to secure for further study on this matter.

*Response to Christian broadcasting.*

Whenever I read our radio mail from various races and nationalities of people who listen to the *Hour of Freedom* broadcast, I discover that Christians are blessed and helped, while the unconverted find salvation and joy in Jesus Christ.

Some pastors and other Christian leaders believe that the increase of radio and television programs today seriously threatens local churches. Generally, the majority of surveys and polls taken reveal that radio and television programs complement local church ministries rather than competing or conflicting with them.

*Extended ministry*

Some of the largest churches in the United States have national and international radio and television programs that reach many unsaved and unchurched people, without inhibiting the church's growth and expansion. Individuals who find Christ through these church broadcasts usually join evangelical churches in their communities or help in planting new churches.

Great numbers of people converted in years past through Billy Graham's evangelistic crusades and radio and television programs are now pastors, evangelists, missionaries and Christian workers, serving in various segments of society.

The evangelist's ministry on radio and television also extends and enhances his public ministry. For instance, during my 1983 evangelistic tour of six African countries, radio and television programs prepared the way for our city-wide crusades.

Christian radio and television programs are an encouragement to missionaries in foreign countries, who, along with national pastors and Third World evangelists, often send letters testifying of this. They gather people together around the radio in church or in a home each Sunday to hear the Word of God. Others record sermons in English and preach them by translation to their own tribal people.

*Prospects for Christian broadcasting.*

I foresee a promising future for evangelists who preach the Word of God today via the electronic media.

NRB's Ben Armstrong states, ''The missionary call continues to propel the electric church. Today more than 60 Christian organizations operate international radio stations, and hundreds of organizations on every continent produce programs. International stations, operating 128 transmitters, place enormous power at the service of those willing to accept the challenge and the financial responsibility of transmitting the Gospel worldwide.''

*Spiritual conflicts*

Encouraging reports, however, should never allow us to forget that Christian broadcasting always conflicts with Satan and the forces of evil.

Many times we broadcasters have felt Satan's presence, power, and attacks against us as we began to prepare a radio or television program. There might be an electrical power failure, a breakdown of equipment for no valid reason, and other strange distractions and interruptions. Why? Because Satan wants to hinder and discourage us from getting God's Word out to the people.

As broadcasters, therefore, we dare not trust in ourselves, our education, gifts, talents and abilities, or in the power made available to us through the media.

Instead, we must undergird every phase of our ministry with fervent and earnest prayer, energized by the Holy Spirit who indwells us.

Broadcasters, redeem the time for the days are evil. May we use radio, television, the printed page, and every other means possible to reach as many people as possible with the Word of God, to complete the unfinished task of evangelism and world missions, and to hasten the return of Jesus Christ.

*See Ben Armstrong, *The Electric Church*, page 180.

# THE EVANGELIST'S USE OF SCRIPTURE DISTRIBUTION

*Lars B. Dunberg*

We are living in a world that is experiencing a population explosion unprecedented in history, with more and more people settling in the urban centers. By year 2000 Mexico City will have a population of over 31 million, Cairo 16 million and Calcutta 19.7 million.

When Christ walked here on earth the population was 250 million people. The evangelism challenge facing the apostle Paul and the early Church was to win these people for the kingdom of God.

It took until Martin Luther's day before the world's population had doubled. Today we add the population in Paul's days to our own within three years.

If this exploding world ever will hear about Jesus Christ, one of the key components has to be God's Word—whether it is communicated in printed, oral or audio-visual form. In this session we will deal more with the printed form.

Many people have been aware of the power of the printed medium. It was Benjamin Franklin who said: "Give me twenty-six lead soldiers and I will conquer the world." With those he meant the letters in the English alphabet.

Today, leaders of different political persuasions and people in various cults are using the printed medium most effectively to communicate their message to the remotest parts of our world.

Thank God for groups that are working to translate and distribute the Scriptures around the world. Although they work hard, large areas are neglected because of lack of distributors. Quantities produced are often small, compared to the speakers of the language, and in some areas Scriptures are available but not used.

Around the world illiteracy is on the decline. UNESCO is teaching 350 million people to read. Young nations are putting literacy programs at the forefront in their budgets. But what will they read? What will the Church, you and I, give them to read?

## 1. Scripture distribution means communication

God is closer to people when He speaks their language. All Bible translations deal with communications—to accurately communicate what God is saying in His Word. The aim of both the Scriptures and the evangelists is to communicate the message of the Gospel so effectively that people understand it and can respond to it.

If people do not understand what they read, they will not understand what the message is all about. That is why it is so important to have a Scripture version available that speaks the language of today, avoiding confusion among non-Christians by religious phrases or an archaic church language.

## 2. Scripture distribution has a great history

In early church history, the regular way to become a convinced Christian was to read the Holy Scriptures.

Therefore, the Church wanted the Scriptures to be open and available, not only for Christians but for non-Christians also. Translation work started in many languages as the Church spread its message. The translators were not out to create literary masterpieces, although that sometimes became a by-product, but their aim was to spread the Gospel. Their motive was purely evangelistic, as they wanted people in language group after language group to read the Scriptures for themselves, and come into a living relationship with their Lord.

Men like Wycliffe, Luther, Tyndale, and others had the same longing. Erasmus said: "I totally dissent from those who are unwilling that the sacred Scriptures, translated into the vulgar tongue, should be ready to the unlearned. I would wish even all women to read the gospels and the epistles of Saint Paul. I wish they were translated into all languages . . ."

The revival in the days of Wesley, Whitefield, and others was not only rooted in the Bible, but it gave the Bible a central place. Everyone needed to learn to read the Bible to grow in their newfound faith. Wesley's traveling evangelists went through the land with the Bible in their pockets and the flame of evangelism in their hearts.

It seems that biblical renewal and evangelistic advance have gone hand in hand through church history. Where the Bible is discovered afresh as God's saving Word to men, evangelism seems to develop. Many of the leading Bible translation and distribution movements started out of fervor to evangelize with the Scriptures.

The Bible Society Movement started in Great Britain in 1804 and spread like wildfire across the world, as people moved by God's Word wanted to share it with the world's millions.

Hudson Taylor in China wanted to see a Chinese translation available that could be distributed for evangelistic purposes. For years he worked on a vernacular translation that the ordinary Chinese in the marketplace could understand.

Charles Alexander, songleader for R.A. Torrey, became the leader for the Pocket Testament League. In one of their evangelistic campaigns in Britain, he met a lady who loved the Bible so much that she sewed a special pocket on her dress to carry a small New Testament with her all the time, and she encouraged all her friends to do the same.

Charles Alexander fell in love with the lady, married her, and together they launched the Pocket Testament League. They would challenge anyone they met—on trains, in the street and just about everywhere—to read the Bible. Anyone who signed a pledge, promising to read the Bible every day, was given a New Testament.

In one city, one of the Pocket Testament League workers went out on the street to try the "new" method. The first man he encountered was a policeman. "Officer, do you know what this is?" "It looks like a Bible to me!" "Promise that you will read it every day and it will be yours!"

A month later, Alexander was conducting a crusade in the same town. The first man to come forward at the invitation was a tall man. Alexander asked him: "What led you to Christ?" "It was this New Testament that someone gave me that led me to Christ." In five months eight policemen at the station had received Christ as a result of this man's testimony.

The same eagerness in this century led Cameron Townsend to create Wycliffe Bible Translators, William Chapman to start the World Home Bible League, Rochunga Pudaite to begin Bibles for the World, and Kenneth Taylor to launch Living Bibles International.

The Lord may give you a vision today for distributing His Word that will have a lasting impact on thousands for eternity.

3.   *Scripture distribution is a tool for evangelism today*

The Bible does not just contain the Gospel, it *is* the Gospel. Through the Bible, God Himself is evangelizing, communicating the Good News to the world.

According to Michael Green, the Word of God is the second greatest medium for evangelism, the first being the Holy Spirit. He asserts rightly that the Word of God is the very sword that the Spirit uses.

How can evangelism take place without using the book that is the only source of the Good News? Without the Bible, evangelism is impossible.

Lord Donald Coggan, former Archbishop of Canterbury, has said: "Books can often go where persons cannot. When you sell a man a book, you do not sell him just twelve ounces of paper, ink, and glue. You sell him a whole new life. This is supremely true about the Bible."

All down the centuries, the Church has gone to the world with a book in its hand, translated into the languages of the nations which it has sought to evangelize in response to the Master's command. That book is its indispensable tool.

Bishop Charles Gore once said: "There is no surer way of getting men and women of whatever religious tradition again into the presence of Jesus of Nazareth than by giving them the Gospel in their own language."

The Bible is the best evangelistic tool there is. As a Christian worker in Asia once said: "We would be absolutely lost without the Bible. We go into the bazaars, hold it up and say: "Here is the Book!"

### 4. *Scripture distribution focuses on God's power*

There is power in God's Word. Sometimes we wonder how we will win the battles over the enemy. Martin Luther, who fought many such battles, pointed to the power in the Word of God. "One little word will knock him down!"

As Scriptures are being used in distribution, we see God's Spirit take that Word and work through it. Most often its impact rarely stops with the person receiving it, because when someone finds life, he shares it with others.

Let me give you a few examples of the power of God's Word:

a. *South America.* A few years ago, a distribution program brought Spanish Living New Testaments to all school children of Bolivia. A few months ago, I met a missionary who had gone to northern Bolivia to start a pioneer work in a village. When she arrived, she found that over half of the villagers were already believers. They told her how the children had come home from school with the New Testaments. The parents read them as well and accepted Christ.

A similar project is now going on in Brazil where several organizations are supplying 25 million Portuguese New Testaments to school children. One high school boy in Brazil received a copy and committed his life to Christ. As he read more of the Scriptures, he realized that other things needed to be cleared up in his life. Before the books arrived, he had made his girlfriend pregnant. She had to leave school and was now living out in one of the villages. He went out to find her, married her, and provided a Christian home for his daughter and wife.

b. *Middle East.* It is interesting to see how many Muslims have found Christ by reading God's Word rather than listening to or observing the life of Christians.

One of our associates has a daily radio program in the Middle East and many people write requesting Scriptures. One day he received a letter from a country which is rather closed to the Gospel. A man wrote and said: "Thank you for the book (a New Testament) you sent. I read it and accepted Christ. Can you come and baptize me?" It was impossible to travel to that country, but my friend suggested to him in a letter to find a Christian who then would be able to baptize him. After several months the man wrote back: "I looked everywhere, but I found no Christians. But I gave the book to my brother, and he accepted Christ. Last Sunday we went for a drive in the countryside and there I baptized him and he baptized me."

c. *Asia.* In Thailand, many Christians have had a burden for the people living on the canals of Bangkok. Since the summer of 1985, a special distribution program has been going on, taking a certain Scripture portion by small boats to the 150,000 homes on the canals. Many have accepted the Lord, because Christians cared about these "forgotten" people. In one instance, a whole family dedicated their lives to Christ.

In India over 40% of the population cannot read, but they all have ears and need to hear the Gospel. Every day, a dramatized family situation, discussing everyday problems with Bible solutions, is broadcast in six different languages by medium wave radio. Many respond by saying: "I have accepted Christ" . . . "I want to know more about Jesus."

In one city, a Hindu temple keeper wrote to us, saying: "I was sitting in the temple playing cards while the radio was blaring. I heard your program and slowly I could see that all my worshiping to different gods and the way I was spending my time were all in vain. I wrote letters to you and got some literature. Then you invited me to a conference and it became the turning point in my life. There I accepted Jesus as my Savior."

In Japan, animated Bible stories have portrayed the message to thousands of secular Japanese homes. Before, during, and after the program, it is announced that the Bible can change your life and how you can obtain a copy locally. One Japanese girl wrote and said: "If you are considerate enough to interrupt my favorite program to talk about a book, I need to be considerate and go and get a copy. I did, I read it, and committed my life to the Person in the book."

One of the things that has made the church in Korea such an outreaching, missions-minded church, is the thousands of Bible study groups, focusing on the Word of God and how to share it most effectively.

God's Book—His Word—is indeed a powerful tool in evangelism.

5.  *Scripture distribution takes people*
Only the Church that has been touched by the flames from the Scriptures will ever be distributing Scriptures. Before any person will take part in Scripture distribution, he must have a burning desire to share what God has done for him through the Word of God. The greatest problem in Scripture distribution today is not lack of material, although that is at times a factor, but in the dedication of the distributor.

The best way of getting Scriptures into the hands of non-Christians is to take it to them. Paul's methods were not so much: "Come and hear me" as "I will come to you."

Satan is a master strategist. Eyeball-to-eyeball contact with the unconverted is something Satan will do everything to prevent. The enemy delights in tying God's people into organizational knots, which keep production as the end in view, and hides from view the distribution of the product. You as an evangelist need to become a Scripture distributor and encourage believers everywhere to join you.

6.  *Scripture distribution must have its target*
Few people would be happy to give someone a Bible and say: "Read it and you will become a Christian." Just reading the Bible does not necessarily produce Christians. Karl Marx wrote a commentary of the gospel of John at 15 years of age, but as far as we know it did not have a life-changing impact upon his life.

Many people we give Scriptures to give up, totally discouraged. "The Bible has too much information," they say, or, "I started to read but I did not get anywhere."

In many parts of the world over half of the people do not read the Bible because they simply cannot read. Sometimes our eagerness to quickly distribute Scriptures through the mail or put portions in letter boxes has not been very effective, because just to have something to read does not always mean that you will read it.

In some cultures people feel they must be willing and able to read to become a

Christian, because the Word of God is only distributed in written form.

You must know whom you are distributing to. Just as Matthew, Mark, Luke, and John wrote the Gospel story for different audiences, so you need to choose the best communicating Scripture tool for the kind of target audience you are concentrating your distribution to.

For people who cannot read, it may be parts of the New Testament dramatized on cassettes. For others it may be the Gospel on film, such as the JESUS film, where select portions of the Scriptures are portrayed. For yet others, songs, music, drama, and mime are ways to get the Scripture message across to them.

Among literates, there are various target groups. While some cultures prefer booklets with colorful illustrations, others want a whole New Testament or a Bible with no illustrations at all. Even different titles for "the Gospel of John" or "the New Testament," such as "the Offer of Life," "the Book of Life," "the Contemporary Gospel," can be used to break down other barriers to the Scriptures.

7. *Scripture distribution—how not to do it!*

Sometimes we think that the more portions we have distributed in a short time span, the more effective we are. That is often not the case, as the time-consuming personal contact often makes the piece of literature so much more valid to people. Do not dump tons of Scripture over villages from helicopters!

Never hand Scriptures out to strangers without any explanations. Often, people want to know who you are and what you hand out. In some cultures it is of utmost importance to explain that the literature is not evil spirited.

Do not force Scripture portions on people who refuse to accept them. Never be rude or give the impression that "you know it all." By our love and courteous behavior will the world know that we are His disciples.

To place 100 New Testaments in each church you visit is not distribution but relocation of warehouse space. Distribution takes place when the Scriptures are in the hands of the people they were intended for.

8. *Scripture distribution—some practical steps*

Now we will deal with some practical steps in Scripture distribution, whether in large quantities or on a one-on-one basis.

a. *Prepare yourself.* Before you begin doing any Scripture distribution you need to be prepared.

First of all, bathe the Scripture portions in prayer. The Word is the sword of the Spirit, so pray for the right person to talk to; and for receptivity, so that God's Spirit can open the truth.

Bring a pen and a small notebook. You will meet people with special needs, and you may want to write them down. They may also want to have further contact so you need to write down names and addresses.

Bring some money with you. If you happen to sell Scripture portions, you need some change.

Bring along a plastic bag or a sheet of plastic. This will shield the books from rain or dust.

As a practical rule—wear comfortable shoes!

b. *This New Testament is free, or . . .* Sometimes it becomes necessary to charge for the Scripture portions you are distributing. Because in some countries only propaganda is free, and often propaganda is one of the most unwanted materials in the country.

In some countries people only appreciate things that have cost them something. It is possible that a stranger is more likely to read the Scripture portion if he has paid something for it than if he just received a free copy.

In some areas you cannot sell literature without government permission or license, but you may be allowed to receive donations for the Scriptures you hand out.

Charging something for the Scriptures also makes it possible for you to have an ongoing Scripture distribution program, as many suppliers of Scriptures have to charge you for the material. As your financial resources are limited, this will create more funds for you to purchase further Scriptures for distribution.

c.  *Scripture distribution on a one-on-one basis.* This is how Scriptures can be distributed in individual work:

Trains and buses are excellent places to share the Gospel and give people a Scripture portion, as they have time to read and are not in a hurry.

Family gatherings of all kinds create a good atmosphere to hand out portions of God's Word.

Any places where people are gathered or linger, such as marketplaces and outside temples, cinemas, and large shops, provide excellent distribution spots.

d.  *Scripture distribution in concerted efforts.* One effective method of visitation linked to Scripture distribution is where a village or city is canvassed by church members visiting every house, inviting people to services and offering Scripture portions. Such a Scripture campaign can often be a starting point of an evangelistic crusade.

In follow-up work of all those that came to know the Lord in an evangelistic campaign, Scripture portions should be distributed to all new converts. Sometimes, a Gospel can be distributed in the crusade meetings to everyone who attends. Make sure that the messages are taken from the Gospel that is distributed.

e.  *Scripture distribution in cities.* Cities provide great opportunities for Scripture distribution. There are people all around you and many are "hanging around" idle because of lack of work or nothing to do in their free time.

A simple book table is effective in areas where people gather. It does not need to be anything fancy. A plank on two carpenter horses can do and you can place your Scripture portions on it. Such tables are useful at markets, cinemas, parks, fairs, circuses, political meetings, and university campuses, to name a few.

Sometimes it is effective to distribute Scriptures in "newspaper boy" style. While you call out: "Here is a book about life . . . most powerful in the world." You will draw a crowd!

f.  *Scripture distribution in villages.* To distribute Scriptures in villages is often quite different. Usually you do not need to draw attention to yourself, as your very presence as a stranger will do that. Make sure you give a positive and good impression as you visit the village, as in most cases every move you make is being observed.

Some of the best distribution spots in a village are in the central square, the market, at public wells or fountains, at the door of the local cinema, in the market, or at factories and construction sites.

g.  *How to present the Scriptures.* Many people have only a vague idea of what the Bible is. Some do not even know that the four gospels are in the Bible. This provides an excellent opportunity to introduce them to the Scriptures. A simple questionnaire can open the conversation and help you get started.

When you distribute a whole Bible, you may want to say: "This is a copy of the Bible. It is not just an ordinary book, but a book that was inspired by God Himself. The book shows how you can know Him personally."

"Have you a Bible in your home? If not, I am sure you will be interested in one. This is a book that has helped many families to stay closer together."

When distributing the whole Bible, you need to hand out a simple guide on how to read the Bible, or at least instruct them in what books of the Bible to read first. This will vary from culture to culture, as Buddhists, for example, would be more interested in Psalms, John, and Acts; while many cultures in Africa would be more interested in Genesis, Hebrews, and Matthew.

Generally it is not difficult to distribute the New Testament. When you do it, you can say: "This is the New Testament, the second part of the Bible. It gives the life and the teachings of Jesus."

"This little book has changed more lives than any other book in history. I read it every day and find help to live through its message. I recommend that you start reading the book of John (or Mark or Luke) and then read the book of Acts."

When you make a presentation of the Gospel to a person, it is good to give that person something to refer back to. A Gospel or another Scripture compilation is an excellent tool. You may want to refer to several verses in the Scripture portion as you present the truth to the person, and then hand him the book to keep.

Gospel distribution is especially important in poor areas, as the cost is minimal. People may not be able to afford to buy Scriptures at all, so it will be an even greater opportunity to hand out free copies. You can say: "Would you like a copy of the world's most-read book?"

"Have you ever read this little book? It contains the most important message ever given to man and it only costs . . . (and I want you to have this free copy)."

Always give people some practical helps in how to read the material and, as much as possible, give people an address where they can contact you, a Christian organization, or church for further help; or where they can write in for a Bible correspondence course.

Finally, God's Word is not chained! It is God's powerful tool—but it needs your and my hands to be put into the hands of people from every nation and people group so they also may hear and respond to Him, who is the Living Word.

## BIBLIOGRAPHY

Books

Brown, Andrew, *The Word of God Among All Nations*, Trinitarian Bible Society, 1981.

Bryant, David, *In the Gap*, 1979.

Chirgwin, A.M., *The Bible in World Evangelism*, 1954.

Dunberg, Lars, *Handbook for Living Translations*, 1982.

Taylor, Robert, *Wings for the Word*, 1978.

Svard, Arvid, *Bibelns vag till folken*, 1971.

Verwer, George, *Literature Evangelism*, 1977.

Wagner, Peter, *On the Crest of the Wave*, 1983.

# THE EVANGELIST'S USE OF MUSIC
*Irv Chambers*

It is obvious in the study of Scripture that music has played an important role from the early Old Testament days on down to our present day. It has been the medium of expressing adoration, praise, supplication; and it is used today, perhaps more than ever, as a tool for evangelism.

D.T. Niles defined evangelism as "one beggar telling another beggar where to find bread." Another has described evangelism as "bringing the whole Gospel to the whole person." Don Hustad, in his book *Jubilate! Church Music in the Evangelical Tradition* (1981), points out that "in a narrower, more typical use of the word, it denotes the initial, significant confrontation of the individual with his need of God and with the salvation provided through Christ; the objective is the individual's acknowledgment of need, acceptance of God's provision, and personal faith in and commitment to Jesus Christ as Savior and Lord." There are many vehicles for evangelism—including poetry, art, drama, film—not the least of which is music, to which we are addressing ourselves today.

As musicians our special challenge is, "Speak to one another with psalms, hymns and spiritual songs. Sing and make music in your heart to the Lord, always giving thanks to God the Father for everything, in the name of our Lord Jesus Christ" (Ephesians 5:19,20).

## 1. Music—a medium for worship and communication

In the books of First and Second Chronicles, we are told of both leaders in music and singers or choirs. In Ezra 2:64,65, we read of a congregation of over 42,000 "and there were among them 200 singing men and singing women." Again and again throughout the Psalms is the exhortation to "sing unto the Lord" or to "make a joyful noise to the rock of our salvation. Let us come before his presence with thanksgiving, and make a joyful noise unto him with psalms" (Psalm 95:1,2).

Psalm 150 reminds us to praise the Lord using many different kinds of instruments, and concludes by saying, "Let everything that hath breath praise the Lord. Praise ye the Lord." Scriptures clearly indicate that part of this music of praise and thanksgiving was done not only by a "professional" musician, but by the congregation. Christianity is not a spectator religion, but one that calls for the participation and involvement of its entire constituency.

Religious "awakenings" or "revivals" have been accompanied by a strong musical program. Frequently, the leaders used a contemporary musical sound of that era. The Wesley brothers were accused of adopting the popular street or drinking song melodies for their own lyrics. The charge is apparently true, for we find the basis of many of our older hymns to be "folk melodies" or popular songs of another generation. The gospel songs of the Fanny Crosby period and those of Ira D. Sankey, D.L. Moody's songleader-soloist, were written in the popular ballad style of that time.

Further, Dr. Hustad points out that "invariably these revival periods have been graced and supported by a flowering of new hymns which quickly became very popular. . . . The music of the new hymns has ignored traditional sacred symbols, taking on the characteristics of secular forms of the day. Generally speaking, these new 'secular' forms and sounds have remained in the church and have become part of a new 'sacred' worship language."

To minister effectively to an audience we must:
a.   *Know our audience.*
b.   *Know our (musician's) role.*

2.   *Music—preparing the audience*

The message we have to convey can be communicated musically through congregational singing, vocal solos, duets, small ensembles, and large or mass choirs, as well as with various instrumental presentations.

a.   *Congregational singing.* This is perhaps one of the best ways of communicating, since it involves audience participation, and they are actually verbalizing the words of the message you are trying to convey to them. Also, congregational singing often has the added benefit of repeating certain aspects of its message over and over, thus drumming the message into the conscious or subconscious of the participants. Singing not only involves people but also effectively teaches the doctrines and principles of the Christian faith.

One of the frequent urgings that we receive in our crusade efforts is that we have more congregational singing. Cliff Barrows in the Billy Graham crusades and others before him have adopted theme songs, like "How Great Thou Art," which have been used night after night in the crusades. Hundreds could be heard on subways, buses, and trains singing these songs on their way home from the evening services.

b.   *The choir.* This is another part of the "ministering team." The music should be carefully selected to reflect both the emphasis of the evening and the message of the evangelist.

c.   *The soloist.* A good soloist can ably set the stage and change the mood of an entire service by selecting an appropriate song, and by the way he or she presents it. The wrong approach at this crucial time could completely destroy the atmosphere and make it extremely difficult for the evangelist to regain the audience.

On one occasion, we had a visiting choir whose great talent and ability was overshadowed by an extreme lack of wisdom. The audience was whipped into such a frenzy that it was difficult to bring the audience back to a state where they could listen to a message. In show business terminology "it stopped the show," but at the same time it also seemed to quench the Spirit. It was one of those situations where everything after that seemed anticlimactic.

d.   *The music.* While the music should appeal basically to the masses, its message should not be abstract or lost in the lyrics or the music. Bill Winter, the program director for African Enterprise, notes that in selecting music the content needs to fit both the theme of the message and the audience who will hear it. He also notes that it is often difficult to monitor the people in the audience and to know which type of music will appeal to them. He suggests that it is important to evaluate the various types of music which should be considered for the audience, including traditional, renewal types, and ethnic or cultural styles. In all of this, he calls for high standards and a quality presentation.

3.   *Musicians—selecting and recruiting team musicians*
a.   *Basic considerations.* It is naturally ideal if you can have your own musicians with you for each of your evangelistic efforts.

Several primary considerations should be given to choosing a team member with whom a long-term (as opposed to a one-night guest appearance) relationship is anticipated. The musician should share the evangelistic burden for evangelism. A theological compatibility also is essential to a good relationship between the musician and the evangelist. The musician needs to be a communicator, one who can ably convey the message of Christ and His love.

Reliability, punctuality, the musician's temperament, and a compatibility of musical tastes between the musician and the evangelist all need to be considered for a lasting relationship.

b. *A preliminary understanding.* It is important in establishing a relationship that each team member in the agreement has a thorough understanding of what is expected of the musician, both on and off the platform. What are the musician's responsibilities at supplemental meetings during the day, such as breakfasts, prisons, retirement centers, universities, and businessmen's luncheons?

Finance is another area where there is often misunderstanding, usually due to a failure to give adequate consideration to it at the beginning of the relationship.

c. *Guest musicians/testimonials*—one day only. The use of nationally known musicians, professional sports personalities, in the evangelistic crusade program has served as an added incentive for the Christian community to bring their non-Christian friends to the services. A person whom the secular community looks upon as a "star" will often help to attract people from both the secular and the Christian communities.

d. *Communicating with your team members.* It is essential that the evangelist and musicians have a good understanding with each other. More than an "I'm the boss—you're the employee," there needs to be a mutual understanding and sympathy for the God-given gifts and talents of the other.

Agreement on the basic program format for the services, the amount of time given to music, when the evangelist is to begin, how the invitation is to be handled, should all be worked out in advance.

4. *Music—using it to attract large crowds*

a. *Name musicians.* There are several ways of increasing attendance through the use of music. First, by the selection and use of well-known artists who will, by their name and reputation, attract either the Christian or the secular community, or both.

b. *Choir.* There is another way of using music to increase attendance. It doesn't take a mathematical genius to realize that if you have a choir of 100 and increase that choir from 100 to 200, you have increased your overall attendance by 100 people. It should also be noted that increasing the size of your choir from 100 to 200 does not necessarily mean that you will increase the quality of their presentation; however, you will reap several other benefits which can help to create a chain reaction for bringing other people.

A friend of mine, who organized a one-day religious rally with an attendance approaching 100,000, told me of his "one-in-five" theory. For the occasion, he recruited a 2,000-voice choir. He also planned a massive pageant involving 5,000 people, and he recruited thousands of ushers. His theory was that for every individual involved, there was a potential for them to bring four other people with them—a spouse, children, parents, neighbors, or business associates—people who would come to see him or her perform. I believe that there is validity to this theory, though I cannot vouch for the number equation. We all know that when the little children sing in our church services, suddenly parents who never come at any other time are there to see and hear their children perform.

There is another factor to be considered in thinking of the mass choir. I can't tell you how many people have told me in glowing terms of an experience that they had five, ten, or twenty years ago when they sang with 3,000 or 4,000 others in a Billy Graham Crusade choir under Cliff Barrows. The experience is one that they will never forget, and they look back on it as a highlight in their spiritual pilgrimage.

In recruiting singers for a mass choir, it is important that recruitment not be limited to those who are already actively involved in a church choir. Choir members can be recruited from school choirs, service clubs, the community choirs, youth choirs (we limit participation to those 13 and older), people who have sung in choirs previously, or others who "have always wanted to sing in a choir."

    c. *On the campus.* Bill Winter, of African Enterprise, said, "Music is an excellent communication form in its own right, and it provides a platform for preaching." The right contemporary group who sets up at the crossroads of a college campus (with permission), and who performs a mini-concert, is an ideal way to attract students. The group's contemporary sound attracts the students who are then introduced to the evangelist.

    d. *Publicity.* Once you have agreed to use the individual or group, it is essential that you determine how you will get the word out to the community at large. You would want to promote them through your regular campaign publicity, but you also may want to consider using them on local radio and television shows. For show business personalities, you may want to place an ad in the entertainment page and also try to get an interview with one of the entertainment editors.

    Maximize the use of your musicians' talents by involving them before every appropriate secular audience possible, and where there would be a natural appeal.

    e. *In the marketplace.* Frequently, permission can be obtained to have a musical group performing in a shopping mall or an arcade or a park on a day when there are many shoppers and spectators. Again, care should be used in the selection of the music, and the approach thought of as "pre-evangelism."

5. *Musicians—what evangelists want*

    Evangelists want musicians who are godly, loving, available, caring, flexible, sensitive, discerning, relevant, personable, and understanding.

6. *Musicians—what they hope to find in their evangelist*

7. *Conclusion*

    Many people have contributed to the thoughts included here. Points 5 and 6 came as a result of conversations with a number of musicians and evangelists.

    But the greatest help has come by example and association. It has been my privilege to work with Leighton Ford, who is a living example of what he preaches. He prays as though everything depends on prayer, and preaches as though everything depends on preaching. He is a brother, a friend who loves not only me, but my family. He is a constant encouragement as well as a challenge. He loves music and is as interested in the musical part of our crusades as he is in the preaching, and he is one who loves to "come before His presence with singing."

# FRIENDSHIP EVANGELISM AS A BASIS FOR INVITING PEOPLE TO AN EVANGELISTIC CAMPAIGN

## T.E. Koshy

The purpose of this workshop is to better equip the participants on the subject of friendship evangelism so that they may become more effective and efficient in their task. As evangelists, God has called us to represent Him here on earth in different parts of the world among people of various backgrounds. This means those who see us and hear us may see and hear Christ and be attracted to Him through our lives and actions. For Jesus said, "Let your light so shine before men that they see your good works, and glorify your Father which is in heaven" (Matthew 5:16).

Paul points out, "Now then we are ambassadors for Christ" (2 Corinthians 5:20). "For we are unto God a sweet savor of Christ, in them that are saved, and in them that perish" (2 Corinthians 2:15). How then can we, who are limited by our own weaknesses and human frailties, ever measure up to God's expectation and represent Christ to a needy and dying world around us? As Paul asks, "Who is sufficient for all these?" (2 Corinthians 2:16).

Indeed, our sufficiency is of God. We can do all things through Christ who strengthens us, including world evangelism through friendship evangelism.

*What is evangelism?* Evangelism means proclaiming or communicating the Gospel (Good News of the Lord Jesus Christ) to those who have not heard it before.

*What is friendship evangelism?* Evangelism is a process. Friendship evangelism is where friendship precedes evangelism. It is sharing Christ with others out of relationship and friendship in a language and cultural background in which they can understand and appreciate it best. Christ-like love is the motivating force behind friendship evangelism. It is evangelism that cares. It is evangelism out of love and not out of duty. It is evangelism where we treat human beings as people rather than "targets." In short, friendship evangelism is the by-product of our love for the unsaved. We evangelize because we love people. We love because He first loved us. "God so loved the world that He gave His only begotten Son, that whosoever believeth on Him should not perish, but have everlasting life" (John 3:16).

*When is a person evangelized?* A person is evangelized when the Gospel of Christ is shared with that person in love and in a language and cultural background in which the person can understand and appreciate it best. So that he or she shall know: (a) what God has done for their redemption (Salvation) through Christ; (b) the consequences of their acceptance or rejection of Christ.

*What is the goal of evangelism?* The goal of evangelism is the conversion of sinners. "Whosoever shall call upon the name of the Lord shall be saved. How then shall they call on him in whom they have not believed? and how shall they believe in him of whom they have not heard? and how shall they hear without a preacher?" (Romans 10:13,14). Those who are converted through the Holy Spirit and by the Word may be discipled, equipped so that they may be conformed to the image of Christ as His Bride to reign with Him forever and ever.

1. *Why is there a need for friendship evangelism?*

a. Biblical evangelism is friendship evangelism and applicable throughout the world. Christ and His followers practiced friendship evangelism. Friendship evangelism is the most effective evangelism to bring men and women to Christ, particularly in this complex and technological world.

b.   Christ expects all the believers to be His witnesses. While many Christians may have difficulty in following various kinds of evangelistic strategies and methods, most of them can practice friendship evangelism with better and lasting results. This approach is more natural and effective. It enables us not only to lead many to Christ but to discipleship and Christian maturity. While this approach may be more difficult and involves more time and effort, it is better received—with lasting results.

c.   The traditional evangelistic method of direct preaching to strangers will not be effective in this generation in many parts of the world as it was until the Second World War. Since then, with the advancement in travel, communication, and various anti-Christian world views, people have negative notions about Christian preachers and Christianity.

d.   Much of our modern evangelism depends too much on our technique and strategy; and less on the Holy Spirit, love, and relationship. In our enthusiasm for world evangelism, we seem to forget the fact that God's work (evangelism) must be done in His way rather than our way. God's way is service beyond self. Our words must find the practical demonstration in our life-style to make evangelism credible, effective, productive, and lasting. For evangelism to be authentic and effective, it must be incarnational. Those who see and hear us must see and hear Christ in us.

e.   There are many barriers to evangelism, such as color, caste, religions, traditions, nationality, politics, secular humanism, materialism, communism, misunderstanding, prejudices, to mention a few. Most people in Asia and Africa still think that Christianity is a white man's religion. They feel that by becoming a Christian one has to follow the cultural and dietary ways of the West along with the faith. Some think that by becoming a Christian a person may lose his or her national or ethnic identity. Others equate Christianity with Westernization and all its permissive and immoral life-styles. Therefore they look down on Christianity as good only for Westerners. In the Western countries, many have turned their backs on the God of the Bible and the Gospel. Because of the decline in the belief in and the practice of the Judeo-Christian morals and ethics, coupled with the appalling spiritual condition in the West, many non-Christians and nominal Christians are of the opinion that Christianity and Christ are not relevant to the problems of the world. Their minds are closed for the Gospel of Christ.

Therefore, we have to earn the right to be heard by building bridges of friendship and trust. As Arthur G. McPhee points out, "The best evangelism takes place in a relationship of trust. Your greatest witness is your deepest relationship (*Friendship Evangelism*). As Paul says, "When I am with the heathen, I agree with them too . . . Whatever a person is like, I try to find common ground with them so that he will let me tell him or her about Christ and let Christ save them" (cf. 1 Corinthians 9:21,22, The Living Bible).

### 2.   *What are the principles for friendship evangelism?*

In order to do anything effective, we have to follow certain fundamental principles. The more efficient the principles are, the more effective the results are. The principles for friendship evangelism are love, compassion/caring, identification, service, friendship, relationship, trust/confidence.

a.   *Love.* Love is a universal language. It transcends all the barriers. The secret of true friendship is Christ-like love—love that seeks to do the best for others. Love is the driving force behind friendship evangelism. Love was central to the Person and work of Jesus Christ. "Greater love has no man, than to lay down his life for his friends" (John 15:13). True love is self-sacrificial. It enables us to serve people without any "strings attached" and helps us to treat people as "precious" as Jesus treats them, even when they disagree with us and refuse to respond to what we have to say. As Paul says, "The love of Christ must be the motivating force causes us to serve others" (The Living Bible, 2 Corinthians 5:14). This love was the secret of the effective evangelism of the early Church.

Many people are engaged in evangelism out of duty rather than love. That's why we are not making a real impact upon the lives of the people whom we try to reach.

A well-known Western missionary veteran told me, "Koshy, I went to such and such a country as a missionary out of duty. I never loved the natives and my life was a failure." No communication is effective unless it is communicated with love.

b. *Compassion/caring.* This is the by-product of Christ-like self-sacrificial love. Compassion is action-oriented. Compassion compels us to do something positive to help the person who is in need without asking questions and without prejudice or prejudgment. Compassion gives us passion for souls beyond measure; and that burdens us to pray for sinners, without ceasing. That was true of Christ. When He saw the multitude, He was moved with compassion on them. His heart went out for them. He prayed for them and served them without any strings attached. Compassionate people, like Christ, try to be open, free and friendly to others and available to serve them at any cost. They give themselves freely to others.

c. *Identification* (empathy). Identification is the by-product of compassion. Compassion constrains us to sit with others where they sit, and to take time to listen and get to know them. As we understand their needs as human beings, *we try to accept them as they are and for what they are.* Identifying with people, we try to experience and minister to their felt needs. In short, our aim will be to "scratch where it itches." As McPhee points out, "We have to earn a hearing, which necessitates building relationships. And to build relationships, you must associate and identify." As Paul points out we must become "all things to all people." "To the weak became I as weak, that I might gain the weak: I am made all things to all men so that I might by all means save some" (1 Corinthians 9:22). It costs us to identify with others—it costs us time, money, comfort, convenience, and even life itself. Look at the example of Christ. To identify with humanity, Christ the Eternal Son of God was made sin for us. He humbled Himself and became a man. He took upon Him the nature of man. Though He was rich, for ourselves He became poor. Jesus told His disciples, "As the Father hath sent me even so send I you." Unless we are willing to identify ourselves like Christ with those whom we are trying to reach, our communication will not be effective and our results will not be lasting.

d. *Service.* Genuine service to others is the by-product of our identification with their felt needs in love. Serving others in love is the hallmark of true Christianity. The Lord Jesus Christ set an example for us to follow by stooping down to serve others irrespective of their position, possessions and prestige. The ultimate purpose of the incarnation of the Eternal Son of God as a man was to serve the fallen humanity in a practical way by giving Himself in service to others. In His service to others He gave Himself totally, completely, and unconditionally. "Any one wanting to be a leader among you must be your servant. And if you want to be right at the top, you must serve like a slave. Your attitude must be like my own for the Messiah did not come to be served but to serve and to give his life as a ransom for many" (Matthew 20:26-28). The greatest love is shown when a person lays down his life for his friends (John 15:13). When we serve others with a sacrificial love like Christ, people accept us as their friend indeed.

e. *Friendship.* This is real when we identify ourselves with others and minister to their needs. Then they will accept us as their friends to whom they can turn at any time. Jesus identified Himself with the sinners and publicans. He was known as the friend of sinners and publicans. Because Jesus was the friend of people, they were free to turn to Jesus at any time for help and He never turned anyone away empty.

f. *Relationship.* Man is a rational being. Our happiness is based on the kind of relationship we have. In the absence of relationship, the very life itself becomes meaningless and empty. Genuine friendship leads to genuine relationship. In order to enter into a relationship with a sinful man, the holy God had to take upon Himself the form of a sinful man. As the Scripture says, ''For he hath made him to be sin for us, who knew no sin . . .'' (2 Corinthians 5:21). In order to enter into meaningful relationship with sinful man, the Eternal Son associated Himself with man to help him understand how much God loves and cares. Similarly, we can communicate Christ to others only when we enter into a meaningful relationship with them. Before we share the Gospel we must take time to develop a meaningful relationship with people whom we are trying to reach. Arthur G. McPhee points out, ''Such an approach may take longer, but almost invariably it is better received, and its results are more lasting.''

g. *Trust and Confidence.* Trust and confidence are developed as we are genuine friends. As people accept the fact that we are here to help rather than to hurt them, barriers of many kinds—racial, national, religious, and so on—will be overcome. Then the initial suspicion will be removed and new trust will pave the way for building bridges of relationship and understanding.

Communicating Christ can happen after we have gained a person's confidence. Then he/she may speak for Christ and people will be ready and open to listen to what we have to say. After they have seen the love of Christ demonstrated in our lives, they will more readily listen as we verbalize about that love. Our hope is that they will realize that our words are an extension of our lives and that our lives are an extension of the life of Christ. As Paul said in Colossians 1:27, ''Christ in you, the hope of glory.'' At this juncture in our relationship, any communication about Christ would be more credible and effective. Over the years, we have had the joy of seeing many people from various backgrounds and nationalities responding to the love of Christ positively. Let me briefly give two examples.

A Muslim student was attending our weekly meal for internationals. When he first came, he was very suspicious of our motives but he kept coming week after week. We helped him in practical ways like providing transportation to pick up his groceries, and in other ways. One day after our regular weekly friendship meal, he came over to me and said, ''Dr. Koshy, in Islam we do not have the dimensions of love. You and your friends have been loving and caring for me ever since I came here as a student. Will you please help me to understand the secret of this love? Please tell me more about your Jesus.'' That gave me an opening to share the Gospel with him. Because we had won his confidence through our love, compassion, and identification by ministering to his felt needs, he was ready to accept what we had to say. Moreover, he had seen the reality of Christ in our lives. After I explained to him the way of salvation from the Scriptures, I welcomed him to receive the Lord Jesus Christ as his Savior and Lord. He accepted Christ and then joined our discipleship group and grew in the Lord. After completion of his studies, before returning to his country, he witnessed to the Lord in the waters of baptism.

One day an educated Hindu told me angrily that I should not speak to him anything about Christ. I agreed. In the days and months that followed, I tried my best to be of service to him whenever and wherever possible. I also prayed for him. About two years later, he called me and asked me whether I would teach him Bible as he was deeply interested in learning more about Christ. I was glad to help him. Then one day he came to me and said that he wanted to apologize to me for misunderstanding me. He said, "When you invited me and other non-Christian friends to your home for meals and made yourself available to serve people, I thought you were doing all that to convert people from their religion to yours (Christianity), but watching you over the years I realized you serve people because you love them and because you love them, you wish the best for them and that best is Jesus Christ." Then tears rolling down his cheeks he said, "Please forgive me . . . Please do not ever stop what you are doing . . . Please continue to pray for me."

Men are still God's method. As Robert E. Coleman says, "When will we realize that evangelism is not done by something, but by someone? It is an expression of God's love, and God is a Person. His nature, being personal, is only expressed through personality, first revealed fully in Christ, and now expressed through His Spirit in the lives of those yielded to Him. Committees may help to organize and direct it; and to that end they certainly are needed, but the work itself is done by men reaching other men for Christ" (*The Master Plan of Evangelism*).

The Lord has never told us to go and convert any human being. He told us to be His witnesses through our lives and our words. "Let your light so shine before men, that they may see your good works, and glorify your Father who is in heaven" (Matthew 5:16). May the Lord enable us to be His instruments of life, love, light, and liberty so that those around us may know that Jesus loves and saves.

# NATIONAL STRATEGIES AND THE EVANGELISTS
## Gaetano Sottile

I am thankful to God for this unique opportunity to lead you in this study. Our only guide will be God the Father who always talks to us through His Word, infallible and inerrant, translated in our hearts by the Holy Spirit. Therefore, I will not try to communicate my ideas or opinions but the biblical principles on evangelism and how they can be applied in our national ministries.

1. *Importance of evangelism* (Matthew 28:19; Acts 1:8)

When I left Sicily (Italy) to go to Bible College in the U.S.A., my parents took me to the airport. Before takeoff I remember my mother shouting these words, "Guy, my prayers and Jesus will be with you!" She could have said a lot of other things, but she expressed the main concern of her heart. Also, when my grandmother was dying, before departing she called all of her children and told them to love one another. She too expressed the main concern of her heart.

When people leave or depart for a short or a longer time they tend to express the main burden or desire lying on their heart. By the same token, before Jesus left to ascend to heaven He expressed His main desire—that is, "Go and make disciples of all nations" (Matthew 28:19). *This is the foundation and purpose of evangelism.* "You shall receive power when the Holy Spirit has come upon you; and you shall be my witnesses" (Acts 1:8). *This is the primary consequence of the filling of the Spirit.* "For the Son of man has come to seek and save that which was lost." Matthew 28:19 and Acts 1:8, together with Luke 19:10, bring out the indisputable importance of the ministry of evangelism.

2. *Importance of identification* (1 Corinthians 9:19-22)

The most important principle of evangelism according to the Scriptures and my own experience is the principle of *identification.* Let us look for it in the ministry of Jesus, Peter, and Paul.

a. *Jesus*

(i) John 1:14: "And the Word became flesh . . ." In order to communicate His plan of salvation, God became one of us in the person of Jesus. Jesus lived a common life identifying Himself with His people, their culture and their backgrounds. His first priority was to win their trust through sympathizing with their deepest needs. Let us see how He did it.

(ii) John 3:1-7: ". . . you must be born again." Nicodemus here represents the religious people who do their best to follow God in order to deserve eternal life. Today many religions teach that works (that is, obeying religious laws) lead to salvation. Jesus doesn't condemn Nicodemus for doing good works, rather He wants to make sure that they follow the birth of man into the Kingdom of God. It is like adding zeros after zeros, rather than starting with a one and then adding zeros. Number one is the moment of conversion whose agent is not works but the Holy Spirit (John 3:8).

(iii) John 4:1-28. Jesus' approach to the Samaritan woman is radically different. Our Lord first sympathizes, breaking all the walls of culture and tradition, talking directly to a Samaritan woman, thus starting His identification approach. After He wins her trust, Jesus uses her physical need of water to show her spiritual need for living water.

b. *Peter* (Acts 2:14-36). Here, Peter, knowing his audience, starts his evangelistic message with quotations from the Old Testament, well known by the same audience. This represents his identification.

In my ministry in Italy, among Roman Catholic people, I often use this approach. Many times I use Mary's words to support the plan of salvation (e.g., John 2:5).

c. *Paul* (Acts 17:22,23). Here the Apostle Paul commends the religiosity of the people of Athens, thus identifying himself with them. Then, in love, he shows their ignorance, and points them to Jesus.

These are *some* examples of evangelistic approaches. The underlying principle is *identification.* However, identification does not mean compromising, but rather finds the positive points of contact that help us build the bridge on which we'll send God's plan of salvation.

3. *Identification characterized by compassion and prayer*

Evangelism can be both individual, that is on a one-to-one basis, or corporate, that is, done by the church(es).

In Matthew 13:3 the task of the evangelist is compared to the task of a sower. The sower must work hard and pays a big price in order to sow and thus expect a harvest. Life, however, cannot be given by the sower—only God is the giver of life. In our evangelistic ministries we must bring people to the point of accepting or rejecting salvation in Christ. This is our responsibility. In John 2:7, it is stated that the servant's responsibility was to fill the waterpots, but it was Jesus' responsibility to turn the water into wine. We cannot change or give life, we can only sow with faithfulness and expectation. If this is true, our sowing must be characterized by *compassion* and *prayer.*

a. *Compassion.* In many places in the New Testament before approaching needy lives, Jesus was moved with compassion. Paul's compassion came to the point that he declared, "I have great sorrow and unceasing grief in my heart. For I could wish that I myself were accursed, separated from Christ for the sake of my brethren . . ." (Romans 9:2,3).

In the Latin language *compatire* means *patire*-suffer and *com*-with, or suffer with. This is the root word for the English word compassion. It means to enter into the skin of another; in other words, identify with his grief and pain. Our listeners are taken not as much by what we say but rather how we say it. Is there urgency, compassion, love in our ministry? Is vision for lost souls the motivating factor in our ministry? In Lamentations 3:51 we read, "My eyes bring pain to my soul . . ."

The day I accepted Jesus as my personal Savior and Lord, Dr. Stephen Olford was preaching in Messina, Sicily. At the time (1974) I did not know any English. However, I was touched by the urgency and compassion—even before paying attention to the interpreter's translation. Many people who have accepted the Lord through my ministry have said the same thing to me. Our evangelistic message must be born out of our heart and characterized by compassion and nothing else.

b. *Prayer.* Since God is the giver of life, we must ask Him to draw people to Himself and that must be done through prayer. The best function of prayer in evangelism has been stated by Oswald J. Smith in his book *The Passion for Souls* (p. 108). He says, "When we learn how to travail in prayer there will be revival. Isaiah 66:8 tells us that as soon as Zion travailed, she brought forth her children. Can a baby be born without pain? . . . So it is with newborn babes in the family of God. Somebody has suffered; someone has travailed. There has been soul agony. It is because there is so little travail today that there are so few souls saved. My friend, we will have to get back to the days of soul travail if we are to pray effectively. Once again there will have to be half nights of prayer and those who pray will have to learn to take hold of the horns of the altar and travail in prayer if souls are to be born into the kingdom and revival is to come.''

4. *Importance of identification together with the local churches*

Since the purpose of evangelism is to make disciples, the evangelist must make sure to work together with the local churches. In Italy the ministry of evangelism has not been very fruitful in the past years because of very little involvement by the local churches. Some independent evangelists have come and have independently developed evangelistic ministries. Through my experience and the results obtained, particularly in Naples, I believe that not only must the local churches be involved in the evangelistic efforts but they have to continue such a ministry after the evangelist is gone. I know that the evangelistic effort has persevered when the messenger is forgotten and the message remains.

I feel it is very important for an evangelist to work interdenominationally. Unity produces strength and power. The evangelist can bring about unity because every believer agrees on the terms of salvation. I remember having a crusade in Naples with one church and having good results. The same happened in Rome with a church of a different denomination. When the opportunity arose I got the leaders of both churches together sharing all the good results of their evangelistic crusades and suddenly they discovered how close they were. It is not easy, it is a painful process, but it is worth it. The secret is to be willing to work with all the Christian denominations and to be willing to wait patiently for their confidence and trust.

The story is told of two sailors fighting on the deck of their ship, but when they heard the cry, "MAN OVERBOARD," their struggles quickly turned to working together in the rescue. Evangelism can be the uniting factor as we try to rescue a lost world for Christ.

5. *How to involve the local churches*

Before the evangelistic effort starts there must be a time to develop a theology on evangelism and its importance with the local church. It must be communicated by the evangelist that evangelism is not optional but mandatory, and that *all* Christians have been called to be witnesses. A witness is one who bears testimony to a fact. As Christians we testify to the power of the resurrected Christ working in us to effect salvation. An evangelist is a preacher of the Gospel. All Christians are witnesses, some are evangelists.

During this time the church(es) must give birth to a vision for lost souls and to the urgency of evangelism. Priority must be given to prayer and unsaved ones must be prayed for regularly.

Also, it must be decided when and where to have the evangelistic crusade. This is a very important issue. For instance, in Italy the best time is summer or early fall, and the place is a tent. Roman Catholics will never enter into an evangelistic church. A theater might be too expensive. A tent is ideal. It is a neutral place and can be put up in a crucial part of the city where everyone can notice it. Last fall in Naples, we unknowingly put up the tent in front of the building where the president of the Mormons for the city lived. By God's grace he, his family, and many Mormons came to know the free gift of salvation in Jesus.

During this time of evangelistic outreach, gifted ones from the congregations must be encouraged to be part of the crusade program. Through the evangelistic crusades we train local leaders and members how to lead and develop an evangelistic crusade. The churches know that we do not represent a professionally trained team, but we provide only guidelines and the evangelist—they must provide the rest. This is a sound involvement of the local churches. They know by deeds what it means to be a vital part of the crusade.

The importance of the church(es)' involvement increases when the new converts must be followed up, trained and incorporated in the local church. It is indispensable to communicate that after salvation comes sanctification, and it happens only in the corporate life of the church. The Christian believer cannot be an island.

Therefore, the follow-up programs and the incorporation of the new converts in the local churches must be the target of evangelistic efforts. Let us try now to think of this without the involvement of the local churches. Someone might say, "How about places without local churches?" In this case the evangelist must be working together with a church-planting team that represents, though small, a local church.

As I said before, working with the local churches is a very painful and humbling experience. Nevertheless it represents the biblical norm for evangelism. Paul was willing to work with the synagogues first, better explained as "dead" churches. So, how much more should we strive to work with the already existing local churches? My experience has been both positive and negative.

I was invited by a very important church in Florence, and after sharing my vision and gift of evangelism, several Christians were stirred up for a lost world and there was one conversion. Yet the church did not feel at peace to support my ministry. It was a painful and humbling experience for me.

I did the same in Naples and in two years, through two evangelistic crusades, 350 converts and many more as an indirect result of the crusade, echoed the ministry throughout Italy. During the first year only one church sponsored the crusade; now the same church has grown from thirty to over 200. During the second year five churches were cooperating, thus making a bigger impact on the city.

God could not have seen all of this without the support of the local churches. Italy would not have heard these results without the backing of the local churches.

**6. Conclusion**

Let me share again the principles I have tried to communicate through this study.

a. The importance of evangelism
b. The importance of identification
c. The importance of identification together with the local churches.

Also, let me share that the circumstances will not always be encouraging. During this time it is of vital importance to know that our faith is not on circumstances but on the Almighty God for whom nothing is impossible! (Numbers 13:30, 14:11; Deuteronomy 28:13).

One of my involvements while in Bible college was a prison ministry. There I sought to put into practice the principles of identification in evangelism. Being from Sicily, which is well known for the Mafia, one day I went dressed up as one of them. Speaking in heavily accented English, I told the group of prisoners gathered that I was sent to them by my boss with a message. Because the Mafia is a cause which they understand and respect, I immediately had their attention. That opened up the opportunity to explain that my boss was Jesus Christ and the message was one of salvation and liberty. Mubrok, a towering Negro and a ringleader in the prison, sobbingly came to know Christ as Savior. The common ground established had let the seed of the Gospel be planted.

# WRITING FOR PUBLICATION BY THE EVANGELIST
*Sherwood E. Wirt*

There are four keys which, if the evangelist grasps them and uses them, will make him a successful published author. He may not have a polished education or a high intelligence quotient; he may be poor, and live far from the marts of trade and the centers of learning, but I guarantee that he can be published and that people will read what he writes.

1. *Motivation:*
We begin by returning to our personal spiritual commitment. Christians who write believe that Jesus Christ, who gives meaning to everything in life, gives meaning and purpose to their writing. From Him we receive the Spirit of the Lord. What then is our motive? It is to spread the blessings of the Christian message. Rather than proclaim the Gospel from the housetops, which seems a singularly ineffective medium in our day, we prefer the printed page. We believe that in the teachings of Jesus Christ—and even more in His life, death and resurrection—our Lord was unfolding to the human race the mystery of our existence and the key to our survival.

So in the nuclear age we are bearers of a life-and-death message. No matter what the literary genre, the message remains the same: Jesus Christ died to save sinners. And while this message is also being channeled through other media, we remain committed to the written word because we are convinced of its power. Many major changes in recorded history have been brought about through literature.

The very existence of the Christian Church is dependent on the writings that were first penned, then preserved in a way that no other has been kept. In an age when so much emphasis is being placed on evangelism over the air waves, we need to remind ourselves of the permanence of the printed page. Simply to walk into a local library is to communicate with the great thinkers of history whose words have come down to us. A hundred years from now Billy Graham may be remembered not by his films, cassettes, videotapes, newspaper columns or tracts, but by his books. They'll be there till Jesus comes.

Our motive, then, is to produce Christian writing that is action literature. We want to see things happen, to watch the Spirit of God sway opinion and change people's lives by turning them around. We want to warn, to inform, to encourage, by precept and admonition and parable and poem and every known literary device. It's true we are enthusiasts. The Marxists invade the literary forms to propagandize for their own ends; we do so for the kingdom of God.

Much of our motive is wrapped up in the poor quality of much current reading material. Words can save, but words can also corrupt. The pornography market is mushrooming. Christian bookstore owners tell of people with no interest in spiritual things coming into their stores and asking, "In God's name, have you anything decent to read?"

We are commissioned not just to write evil down, but to write God up. We are instructed to teach, to train, to interpret, to inform, to edify, to kindle the imagination, to narrate stories as Jesus did, and even to entertain. We are to provide milk for children, solid foods for full-grown men and women, and the elixir of poetry to express our love for our Creator. We are to write about frustration and victory, justice and mercy, sin and redemption, joy and adversity, and always grace and glory. We are to give people a handle to grasp as they seek to attain a worthwhile and productive existence under Christ.

So we draw our motivation not only from divine mandate but also from human yearning. A taste gap exists in much of the literature that is being produced today. We Christian writers wish we were better qualified to fill it; but fill it we shall, for as long as there is language, there will be readers. Many of these people will never come to church; they will never be touched by preaching or music, by radio or television or cassettes. They are waiting for us to write the word and make it plain, that they may read and know the truth.

## 2.   Contacts:

As you are drawn deeper into writing, you will learn that the writer lives by encouragement. He is essentially in a lonely profession, and when the rejections pile up and the interest flags, he slides easily into the blues. To all such writers I have one suggestion: cover your machine, walk out the door, and go calling. Either that, or pick up the telephone. If possible, talk to an editor or a fellow writer.

I have often said that getting into print is like getting into Heaven: it's not what we do but whom we know. In today's world most business is carried on by personal contact. Someone knows someone. To be in touch with the right person at the right time with the right ability and skill to meet a need is to be a success in the writing field, as in many another profession.

Thousands, even millions of aspiring writers, are eating their hearts out because they spent hundreds of hours on a manuscript and can't find anyone to publish it. Every week people come to me and say, "I've written a book, now what do I do? I've sent it here and there and it comes back." I shake my head, and sometimes I say, "Let's put that manuscript on the shelf and just talk about your idea."

Or I might say, "Have you visited the editor of your local paper? He may not be a Christian, but you should get acquainted with him." Believe me, that is an exciting prospect. I can tell you many stories of Christian writers who have taken that tip, and are now writing columns once or twice a week, and being paid for them. It took time to cultivate the editor, but eventually it paid off.

Go to a writers' conference and meet the editors. Visit them in their offices and take them to lunch. Get on a first-name basis with them, if it seems appropriate. Then broach your article idea, or your book idea, and if they don't shoot it down in flames, they may publish it. That's the way it's done—through friendship. Sending a query letter to an editor is good; but getting to know him and then calling him up and sounding him out is better. When it comes to being accepted for publication, so often the contact is the key.

You will find that editors are not ogres, not impersonal people who delight in sending rejection notices. They like writers, and want to help them. They don't like being inundated with unsolicited manuscripts, but they are always looking for fresh ideas. My friend Norman Rohrer tells writers, "Sell it, then write it." That is good advice.

It's amazing what an editor's interest will do for a writer. Rarely does an editor buy a manuscript before he sees it completed—but he will often give the writer hope. He will read early chapters and often lend advice. He will encourage the writer to submit his work "on speculation." That does wonders for the writer's morale. No longer is he shooting in the dark, trying to break into print as an unknown, facing a hostile market.

I am not suggesting that because you live next door to an editor, or marry a publisher, that guarantees your access to authorship. But it certainly doesn't hurt! Meanwhile, you can make friends with people you meet in writers' groups and attend editors' workshops and visit the publisher of your national paper—not to try to unload your writing, but to learn what people in the publishing world are looking for, and then try in a modest way to meet some of their needs.

Once you have broken the ice, once your piece has been accepted, then it is vitally important to follow up. Keep the editorial contact warm! Use letters, use the telephone, use visits. Make it clear you are willing and available, in case he has an assignment. Your writing career is cumulative; the more you appear in print, the more you will be used. It may not be the thing you want to write, but that can wait. After you are established, and you have given the editor what he wants, you will have earned the right to suggest a topic close to your heart, and the editor will listen.

3. *Discipline:*

Logically, discipline is the natural outflow of motivation. What we want badly enough, we are usually willing to work for. The difficulty is that we want so many things, and our schedule becomes crowded. All of the great preachers of the past hundred years made their reputations not through their pulpit oratory but through their writing. Not even television has changed this fact. Every great movement in the history of the world that has brought change, has been accomplished through writing—at least since the alphabet came into use. And yet all this will not sway you and cause you to become a writer. There simply isn't time!

That is where discipline comes in. If, for example, a writer swings into the habit of writing something every day, his literary output will increase markedly. Some authors rise early to write; others prefer the evening. Dostoevsky's custom was to write all night, beginning at midnight. The hour is not important; the discipline is. The temptations that beset a writer are infinite. A free-lance writer I know says that when he is composing on the typewriter he often paces about the house and usually finds himself meditating either in front of the refrigerator or the bed. But books are not written in beds or around iceboxes.

Discipline is especially vital in establishing the accuracy of what you write. To get up from your chair and check a source or a fact is not easy, but it is better than relying on memory. Shortcuts in research mean that we are relying on guesswork, and while preachers can get away with it, writers cannot. Thus your writing research will make you a better preacher! It will also make you respected for the truth of your writing.

The most important application of discipline to the writing profession is in rewriting. You may recall that when King Jehoiakim of Israel burned the scroll that contained the words of the prophet Jeremiah, the prophet dictated another scroll that contained all the words that had been destroyed, *and added many similar words,* according to the record. In other words, the second draft was an improvement on the first. To go over what you have written inevitably means to make it better. Very few writers can turn out clean copy at the first writing. To rewrite is the first law of the profession.

The word processor has made it easy to insert corrections in one's copy, but it has not noticeably improved the general quality of writing. To begin again, to use the first typing simply as a basis for a thorough revision is to guarantee a superior product. It's true that we may have a suspense date; that we don't have time to polish; that we must crank it out and let it go. That may bring some quick cash, but it will not produce literature. Good writing calls for discipline. Sentences need to be changed. Adjectives need to be taken out. More precise language, or more exciting language, needs to be substituted. You can do all kinds of things on the rewrite to make your copy better, but it means work.

Suppose you have an idea, and jot it down on the back of an envelope. You take the idea to your machine and bang it out in a few paragraphs. That is nothing! Leave it overnight and the next day, use a fresh sheet and rephrase it, expanding as you go. Do that three or four times, and you might have something fit to read to someone else. Then after it has been critiqued, go over it again. Now your discipline is beginning to pay off. You have found a key to eventual success.

4.  *Tools:*

No professional can do his best work without sharp tools. A scalpel with a razor edge, clean lumber, quality paints, a well-oiled machine can make all the difference.

It's true that some authors have turned out masterpieces in prison; others have written in rooms filled with relatives and crying babies; millions of manuscripts have been turned out in longhand. I admire all such, but have no desire to imitate. My output comes hard enough without making it more difficult. At some pains I have collected what I consider the proper tools and equipment for a Christian writer. When I come into my study and sit down to work, it is a pleasurable experience. Some years ago I wrote, "Give me food and sleep and exercise, and put me in a room by myself with an electric typewriter, a Bible, some dictionaries, a synonym finder, and an idea, and for three hours I wouldn't trade places with anyone on earth."

Let me expand on that. I'd also like a good light over my shoulder. I'd like a reliable Bible commentary, a book of quotations, an atlas, a concordance, and a good encyclopedia. I'd want some good bond paper, a filing cabinet, a book of markets, an address file, a copying machine, a manual of style—the list goes on and on. The freelance writer needs sharp tools to turn out salable work.

Tools will not, of course, substitute for ideas. Tools will not inspire. C.S. Lewis wrote better with a nib pen than I ever will with the latest Xerox Memorywriter. But I can do better on my machine than I could with a nib pen, and I'd feel much more like doing it. The craftsman equips himself for his craft.

Motivation alone, contacts alone, discipline alone and tools alone will not make the successful writer, but *together they will*. I guarantee it. Of course we must then ask, what is success? For the Christian the quintessential element in writing is the message itself—its content, its significance. The Creator has given His children the gift of language, and has told us to use it to spread the truth of His salvation. The same God gave us the Bible in written form, and kept it through the centuries that we might use it to rescue a lost humanity from its own bent on self-destruction. Now, if God used writing, why shouldn't we?

People come to our meetings, they hear our sermons, and often they leave unmoved. But on their way out the door they may pick up a tract, a testimony, or even a book, and read it quietly in solitude. As they read, the Spirit of God speaks to them. They may return to church with a fresh outlook, perhaps even a new heart. It happens all the time. Kenneth Strachan, the late founder of "Evangelism in Depth," told me that nine out of ten Latin Americans come to Christ through the reading of some form of Christian literature.

A popular Anglican divine of the 17th century, Thomas Fuller, relates a story about a "devout but ignorant Papist" who lived in Spain and faithfully said each day his Paternoster and Ave Maria. The man knew he was also supposed to add his own prayers to God, but he didn't know how. Instead, each morning he would get on his knees and lift his eyes and hands to Heaven and *solemnly repeat the alphabet*. Then he would say, "Now, O good God, put these letters together to spell syllables and

words that make such sense as may be most to Your glory and my good.''
    May the Lord in His mercy do as much for all of us.

# WORK OF THE EVANGELIST AMONG UNREACHED PEOPLE
*Joanne Shetler*

I cannot teach *you* how to evangelize—but let me share what I first learned from my adopted Balangao father. At his house we ate rice with our fingers, sitting on the floor. He had never been to high school. But wisdom doesn't have any connection with school. I suspect that you also have learned much from wise men in your areas— men who know how to communicate and reason in culturally acceptable and powerful ways. Therefore, I am here to encourage you to *do* what you know is effective; it is already deep in your heart. *Follow* what God has taught you by virtue of your very culture.

We *long* to reach people with the Gospel: *but . . . our witnessing doesn't always work.*

Tony is my Balangao brother. He moved away from Balangao, partly to have land to farm, and partly to do missionary work. A tribal man who himself had sacrificed to spirits, now he believed. He was an elder in our little church. He came home to Balangao to report about his year-and-a-half of missionary work. And he wept, brokenhearted. For those one-and-one-half years he'd walked four hours each Sunday, in an unsafe area, often in the dark on the way home; he *never* missed. He'd gather the people together to study each Sunday, telling them about sin, forgiveness, and everlasting life in Jesus Christ. He knew the people well; he'd visit in their homes. He stood in front of them and told them the Gospel and even had them read it from their own newly translated Scriptures. But after one-and-one-half years they *still* didn't believe! Perhaps the biggest problem was that the people whom Tony taught just couldn't apply this information to their lives. And they misunderstood why he was standing in front of them instead of sitting beside them. *That's why this way didn't work!*

*Our witnessing does produce fruit at other times.* It was different with Ilat. He'd go and sit in their homes—but no formal church service. At night he'd sit and listen to their problems. Almost always the problem was sickness and the need for pigs, chickens and even carabao to sacrifice to the spirits that caused sickness. Spirits cause sickness because that's how they ask for more animals for themselves. First Ilat listens and then he tells them about the God who created these animals—how He doesn't need to ask for sacrifices because He made them. And that this God has power to defeat sickness; and one day He will destroy those spirits. Ilat also tells them how much this God loves them. After some hours of questions and answers, he asks if they would like him to pray for the sick one in Jesus' name. It's putting God "on the spot," but God responds, and He heals them. And often the whole village turns out to ask myriads of questions about this God who has power to heal. Dozens of churches have sprung up in village after village, although it doesn't happen in just one night.

*Why did this approach work and the first one didn't?* It works because this Good News we bring *meets the needs* of the people we take it to! Ilat connected the Gospel to their needs; Tony was teaching truth from a book, but the people couldn't understand how they needed that information.

A key: When God helps you where you are with your problems, you are interested in the Gospel!

There are four important aspects involved in our introducing God to people for the first time. Let's look at each one as it has happened in the Scriptures and then see how each has also worked out in the Philippines:

1. *God is most powerfully introduced to people when they see Him meet the needs they feel.*

Ever since I started preparing for this workshop, the book of Acts has amazed me. Acts is a book about Jesus Christ being introduced to many people who have never heard before. Jesus Christ is brought not only to the Jews who knew God well, but also to those who worshiped other gods.

When Peter went to Lydda in Acts 9, he went to visit fellow believers. There (v. 34) he sees a man who was bedridden for eight years, and he demonstrates the power of Jesus Christ by healing him. Consequently, the whole town came out to hear and ask questions, and in the end they turned to the Lord! When God meets the real-life needs of people, they *want* to hear more.

God uses healing to gain their attention so they would ask questions. Of course, some come just for the healing, but others start to ask questions and then believe.

Later in Joppa in Acts 9 Peter actually raise to life one godly woman; when it became known in the city (v. 42), many came with questions and then they also believed.

Now, I had never prayed for the sick until I went to Balangao; and frankly, I wasn't comfortable doing it. But we didn't have a hospital there, and I didn't know what else to do! So in desperation, we prayed for the sick and God heard us. And then, when people *saw* God's power, they wanted to know about Him.

Ilat still finds that when God heals the sick, that is the most powerful proof of who God is in his evangelism. For if God doesn't help sick people *who* will help them? When God does the seemingly impossible for people, their ears become open to hear about His plan and His Son.

That's how it was with me and two old women in Balangao. Old Forsan and Cha-linggay were spirit mediums, and they never could understand what I was talking about when I talked about God. But when I started talking about God's power to de-feat evil spirits, they understood just fine, because it was evil spirits that bothered them.

"Look what they do to you!" I cried out. "You're crippled; all your children are dead; you can't sleep at night . . . they do all that to you; why do you serve them! They're without mercy!" The old woman with fear shouted back at me, "They make me do it!" I was just as loud: "You don't have to obey them; you can just ask God to send them away, and you don't have to obey what they say." The two old women couldn't understand what I explained to them about the Gospel. But they could under-stand this! Hope mixed with fear . . . "Could a person live and not obey the spirits?" they wondered. The spirits literally tried to kill these two old women when they be-lieved; they risked their lives to turn to the living God, but that is how badly they wanted to be free. When the spirits couldn't kill them, that's when the whole valley came to inquire about this God who has more power than the spirits! They asked me, "Now what is it I tell God when I want to become a child of God?" and, "Is it OK if we go tell this to other people?"

I asked myself, "Why did I wait so many years with this good news about God defeating the evil spirits?" Of course, the reason is because I was an outsider; I had to discover what it was that bothered these people. You will too, unless you already know. Ilat introduced his Good News at the point where people felt their greatest need. Tony also had Good News, but the people couldn't understand how it would affect them.

Key: Our message becomes *good news* when it meets people's real needs. That is when they become interested enough to listen! When we know God only by explaining Him, that is good for the mind. But for people who already know the force of unseen powers, they need to see God deal with the needs of their lives. That persuades our hearts and gives us hope to live!

Peter met a very real need in Acts 3. To the man begging he said, "I don't have what you're asking for—money; but I'll give you what I do have; in Jesus' name, stand up and walk." And he did! He jumped and ran and shouted. That man was impressed by Jesus' name and he immediately wanted to follow Him from then on!

*Something special speaks to each person: our job—find it!*

We all have different needs to which God speaks as an introduction to Himself. For example:

*Americans* need: *Love and care.* They have money, but their families are broken apart. No one cares about them. They aren't worried about sickness because they have hospitals; the spirits don't bother them—but who will love them? And who cares about what happens to them?

*Balangaos* need: *Power that conquers the spirits.* They are loved; their families are a source of strength and take care of them . . . but oh, if only they could be freed from the power of the evil spirits!

*Negritos* need: *One who can help them find food.* The translator working there has many stories about God helping them find daily food.

My younger brother Doming went to teach at a Bible conference in a neighboring language group. I asked him what he was going to teach. With wisdom beyond his years, he answered, "How can I know what to teach them . . . I haven't heard their problems yet." He went and sat through the night with them, heard their problems and God helped him be very relevant in what he taught.

People become hungry for the Good News about God, when God meets the need they feel. We must find out what these needs are and be brave to ask God for help for them!

2. *We must win the right to be heard.*

Even if we have learned what people's real-life needs are, if they do not listen to us, what good is our teaching?

Can you effectively witness to just anyone? You who are young, can you tell an old man how to believe? You who are lowly, can you witness successfully to a high person? You who are strange to that village you want to reach, will people just listen to you? However, there is a way to reach those who are older, higher than we!

In our place the young people never teach the old. However, it was my young Balangao brother, Doming who told me that it was still possible for the young to teach the old. "But you have to follow the acceptable way," he said. "You just need the high person to give you the authority to speak—then, when he asks you questions you can teach!"

But I didn't know that when I first went to Balangao. I'd been witnessing to my Balangao father for over five years—daily I explained to him how to believe! I couldn't figure out why he wouldn't believe. I didn't realize it was because "children don't teach their fathers." But one day I gave him a typewritten copy of the translated book of 1 John to correct. Now fathers can correct their child's translation. And so it was when he read the Scriptures that he began to understand and believe. Then he told me others would believe if only they could hear; and since he didn't fully understand it all yet, he asked me to be the one to teach them! That was how he gave me the authority to speak. Then it was appropriate for people to listen, and many have believed.

Conclusion:

So, how can we win right to be heard? My Balangao father advised me thus:

a.   Go to the leader of the village and visit with him and win his friendship. Ask questions and learn what their problems are and how they handle them.

b.   Ask if they'd like to hear how God handles those same problems, and ask if you could also explain this to the people.

c.   Share your commission from God to tell everybody about Him, and how you didn't want them left out.

d.   Always respect and follow their customs of respect. Be humble.

**3.   *In presenting Christ to people we need to make it clear they're turning to God and not just following a form***

Even though we understand what the *real needs* are that people have, and have gained the *right to be heard* as we show them how God can help them in their needs, we must know what kind of a change we expect in the people we are evangelizing. And that means understanding what people treasure in their hearts.

There was a time when I thought if we could just get people to be born again, that's all that really mattered. Now of course, that is what matters! But I thought it was getting them to raise their hands; pray a prayer after me; believe certain aspects of what I told them, and then be baptized. But why didn't their lives change?

Then I look at how Jesus dealt with people. His primary concern was a relationship with God. Each person had something unique that prevented that relationship, so Jesus dealt specifically with that issue. Conversion is "turning around," And salvation is beginning a new relationship with a new Master (1 Thessalonians 1:9,10).

Old Forsan wouldn't know much. If you had asked her how she knew she was saved, I don't think she would have been able to give you a satisfactory Bible school answer. But she knew how to respond to evil spirits when they tried to persuade her to take a gift from them. "No! God will be angry if I have anything to do with you. I'm following Him now."

Bontoc: They're talking about following God, but it's hard to believe there, for they must defy their spirits and stop sacrificing. What will the spirits do to them?

Even if we explain and explain the Gospel, so that we get people to believe certain things and then do and say certain things, is it enough? Must we not go further and deal with the deep problems they face (like evil spirits, charms and magic, omens, sources of power, ancestors, etc.), so that they make a new and different allegiance in their life with a new center and a new Master?

I found it totally impossible to present the Gospel in Balangao without knowing first what they believed and what they feared, what they valued—what the treasure of their hearts was. I could then see how they would interpret what I was telling them. For I found that people interpret the Gospel according to what they already understand of God. It must be clear in our presentation that all of life now has a new master, and they are responsible to Him in every part of life.

So therefore let us be sure people are turning in their *inner* being to the living God, and not just following a form of religion.

**4.   *People understand best about God when we present Him in the framework of their traditional understanding***

I had read Acts 17; I knew about Paul preaching in Athens. But I didn't realize how important it was that he had walked around first; he did a lot of looking, he talked with people, and understood how they thought. He noticed that these people were very concerned about worshiping all the gods. So when Paul saw among all the worshiping places one for the unknown god, he used that as his bridge into their minds. Paul went from the known to the unknown. He took them from where they were on to God. Of course, you must know their language to do this, and also you must know how they think! Our explanation of the Gospel has to "fit" how the people understand life; we need to explain it properly.

There are 100,000 Tboli in the Southern Philippines. They understand that one must cross a bridge after death to get to the "other world"—but it's a shaky bridge, and it's very dark. And wicked powers try to shake one off into the bottomless black pit below. That's why people at a young age endure having their arms and legs burned—to make shiny scars—to hopefully reflect some light, so they might be able to see as they cross that bridge in death. But very few ever make it, they say. Can you imagine how their hearts leapt in hope when they heard that there was Someone who had crossed that bridge and that He was the Light of the world; and that He would take anyone across . . . all you had to do was commit your life to Him. Thousands believe in Tboli country now. The Gospel made so much sense to them—it came to them on bridges of their understanding!

The people of Babuyan needed a door into heaven! They'd always known there was a way to heaven, but it had been lost. And now the way was so treacherous that few would ever dare to try. Snakes lined it and none knew where the entrance was. The Gospel brought indescribable hope to the people of Babuyan when they heard that there was a door they could enter! The Gospel made sense to them; it answered their traditional problem of no doorway!

I remember when my Balangao father and other men went to Pasil to witness. The Balangaos and Kalingas are both headhunting tribes and were enemies before. Only the peace agreements, called peace pacts, have maintained peace. And now, even though the peace pacts were expired, the Balangaos went there anyway to witness. They arrived very early in the morning. All day long my old father and the oldest man among them, all they talked about was who held the peace pacts of the past! All the others kept silent; everyone just enjoyed listening to what the two old men said. At last the old Pasil man said, "Friend, we should renew the peace pact between you of Balangao and us of Pasil." "Yes," my dad said, "that's why we've come here. Only this peace pact that we bring includes not only you of Pasil and us of Balangao, but this one includes the High God in heaven."

Suddenly this new topic of "High God in Heaven" captured all their interests. For two days and three nights that's all they talked about, asking questions about this new "peace pact" and believing in God. They were ready to believe when the Gospel came over the bridge of their understanding.

Notice also how Jesus always answered people according to their interests (John 4). The lady was getting water and Jesus offered her better "water." She evaded Jesus with a technicality on "worship," so Jesus spoke to her about true worship. He answered every topic she brought up!

One of the secrets of relevant witness is to see life through the eyes of the people. In *Balangao: geneaologies validated the Scriptures*. My old father said, "I didn't know this was true!" And as he reasoned with others, he asked them, "Where'd we ever have the very names written down?"

The Apostle Paul tells us how to do it: "Be all things to all people . . ." We need to watch the old men to see how to do it.

When we gain the right to speak and be heard, and even when we take advantage of traditional understanding to make our message fit into their thinking, we still need to use the language they use and the terms they speak in. We need to say it their way. For example, in Balangao a person can't "receive/accept" Christ; the lower can never receive the higher. (Christ can accept us, though.)

5. *Conclusion*

We won't just only tell them what we want them to know. We'll listen to their problems, their life, and then explain how Jesus Christ meets those needs!

Think of the people you want to reach:

a.   Do you know the language? Are you willing to learn it? The national language doesn't have "teeth" in it; the spirits might not respond in that one.

b.   Willing to learn their beliefs, values?

c.   Are you willing to spend the time—this takes time. Paul spent a year in Antioch, 1-1/2 years in Corinth, 2 years in Ephesus!

d.   Do they have the Scriptures in their language? Maybe you should ask someone to come translate them.

God has chosen you to do this job, and He's given you all the qualifications! You understand the "bridges" into people's lives, their needs, values, and their "point of view."

You can make the message meaningful to them; Billy Graham can't; I can't. You have special ability to clothe the message in its proper clothes. It doesn't come naked; it comes clothed properly. It comes in a G-string for Balangao; it wears a fez for some; robes and veils for some. *Know your village.*

a.   New places must see God meet their needs; the sick, spirit-possessed, whatever.

b.   We must win our right to speak and be heard.

c.   Remember, we give the whole Gospel, but different parts are sharpest to different people . . . start with that.

d.   Use traditional beliefs as a vehicle on which to bring the Gospel.

# THE WORK OF AN EVANGELIST AMONG CULTS
*Jeff Y. Amano*

1. *Defining the terms*
    a.  By *"evangelism"* we mean the presentation of the message that if we only trust in the saving work of Jesus Christ, we will be forgiven our sins and have an everlasting life with the true God.
    b.  By *"cult"* we do not mean a non-Christian religious group, for this would not distinguish a cult from a world religion. We mean a religious group which has these five common structural elements:
    (i)     Authoritarian leader
    (ii)    Highly structured, strictly disciplined
    (iii)   Deems group as sole possessors of truth
    (iv)    Often apocalyptic (concerned with the end of the world)
    (v)     Ends justify the means (e.g., unethical business practices in order to bring in finances for "the good" of the cause).
    Examples of such religious groups: Children of God; Hare Krishna Movement (ISKCON); Latter-Day Saints (Mormons); the Unification Church (Moonies); The Way International
    c.  *The problem:* How do we present the message of Jesus Christ to someone who is a member of a cult?

2. *Discovering the background of cult members*
    a.  *Paul at Athens* (Acts 17:16-34):
    (i)     Paul knew the religious and cultural background of his audience (vv. 16,21-23).
    (ii)    He found a common ground as a basis for evangelism (vv. 22,23,28).
    (iii)   He did not fail to preach the saving message of Christ (vv. 30,31).
    b.  *Psychological characteristics* of people who join the cults in American culture (However, many common characteristics are helpful for all cultures because of the nature of cult groups):
    (i)     Above average intelligence
    (ii)    Between 18-25 years old
    (iii)   Difficult time assuming adult responsibilities
    (iv)    Idealistic
    (v)     Recently experienced profound sense of loss; lost enthusiasm for career; recently broke up with lover/companion; future unsure and foreboding
    (vi)    Low self-esteem, or at point of low-esteem
    (vii)   Religious background
    (viii)  Have a domineering and self-centered parent with submissive spouse
    (ix)    Major communication dysfunction with family members
    (x)     Conclusion: the best candidate for cult membership is someone who is authority-dependent.
    c.  *Benefits* to such individuals by joining a cult group:
    (i)     Provides sense of identity and direction
    (ii)    Provides outlet for enthusiasm, discipline, and dedication
    (iii)   Escapes self-dissatisfaction, loneliness, and boredom
    (iv)    Projects ideal qualities on the leader
    (v)     Becomes de-individualized

(vi)   Conclusion: when an authority-dependent person has had his authority structure shaken, he is eager to replace it.

d.   One should keep in mind that although technical forms of "brainwashing" have never been documented or proven of most cult groups, a kind of "mind-bending" often takes place in the cult group's method of evangelism/indoctrination:

(i)   Move individual to very controlled, secluded environments (e.g., retreats).

(ii)   Consciousness-altering practices like chanting, speaking in tongues, ecstaticism, continual recitation.

(iii)   Cut off communications with family members and friends.

(iv)   Only the group leader makes important decisions.

(v)   Leader is entitled to special honors.

(vi)   Instant intimacy and hierarchy: offering comfort, encouraging acting silly and childish to regress to state of dependence.

(vii)   Depersonalization: appeal to "we"-ness.

(viii)   Guilt induction: exaggerating negative aspects of life and encouraging confession of failures.

(ix)   Sensory overload: bombardment with activities, singing, exercising, waking up early, sharing, participating, taking notes, working at chores; deprivation of privacy.

(x)   Indoctrination: repeated presentations of apparently consistent and coherent body of new data.

(xi)   Appeal to higher authorities.

(xii)   Personal testimonies of other converts.

(xiii)   Patterns of behavior: behavior is changed so that attitudes, beliefs, and feelings will change as well.

(xiv)   Stress on conformity.

(xv)   Commitment by default: not encouraged to make conscious decision to stay, but made convenient to stay and difficult to leave.

(xvi)   Contrast of good and evil; "us" and "them."

(xvii)   Avoidance of independent thought; avoid negative aspects of group.

(xviii)Isolate potential recruits from each other and surround individual recruit with cult members.

(xix)   Encouragement of group's positive aspects.

(xx)   Actionizing: put newfound faith into immediate action.

(xxi)   Redescription of the familiar: redefining vocabulary and introducing new terminology.

(xxii)   Conclusion: The point of all of these techniques is to replace the authority structure of authority-dependent people by destroying their former authority.

3.   *"Deprogramming" techniques*

a.   *Forced deprogramming:* this method involves actions such as kidnapping, confinement, and forced counseling. It has come under attack by both secular and evangelical critics because of its often illegal, ethically debatable, techniques and a real question about its lasting effects.

b.   *"Exit counseling"* is based on the willingness of the cult member to listen to the counselor. Such a form of counseling would go something like this:

(i)   Win the cult member's attention by listening to personal account of his religious quest.

(ii)   Indicate respect for personal gains achieved.

(iii)   Analyze these gains and demonstrate how they already knew, or could know, these truths without their group (and the structure, dishonesty, etc.).

(iv)    Provide an alternative explanation of his experience.

(v)    Explain the process of obedience to authority and conformity.

c.    *Principles* to keep in mind when counseling a cult member:

(i)    Most conversions of this kind do not last.

(ii)    Do not confrontationally debate the subject. Remain neutral while expressing interest in knowing more about the cult.

(iii)    Note "floating" symptoms after deconversion: they express mourning phenomena (denial, anger, guilt, bargaining, depression, and finally acceptance).

(iv)    Do not substitute dependencies (authority structure), encourage them to think independently.

**4.    *Declaring the Gospel of Jesus Christ to a cult member***

a.    *Prerequisites:* Strong sense and conviction of salvation; biblical world view; biblical support for important doctrines; active prayer life.

b.    *"Pre-evangelism"* (where the believer is concerned with *preparing* the unbeliever for the Gospel) often entails being able to intellectually reason about our faith (cf. 1 Peter 3:15), as well as refuting those who contradict it (Titus 1:9). Of course, this assumes that we are familiar with the beliefs and structure of the particular cult group that our cultist friend is a part of, and know how to effectively refute them logically and biblically.

(i)    Ask them *why* they believe *what* they believe. This will not only expose their basis of authority but place the conversation in an atmosphere conducive for discussing how and why something is true or not.

(ii)    Remember that it's not necessary to memorize all of the details and theological fine points of these cult groups. All you really need to know (the minimum requirement) are the four basic elements of any and every religious system: their view of God; their view of man; their view of man's problem; and their view of man's solution. Learn these basic categories and the particular cult's terms and concepts in accordance with them.

(iii)    Sometimes, people are so dependent upon their authority structure of leader (e.g., a cult group like Bhagwan Rajneesh, TM, the Unity Church, etc.) that this source must be shaken up. Usually criticism of their leader's morals is ineffective. But documented evidence of lies, plagiarism, false prophecy, or cover-ups can be devastating to their group's leadership who are supposedly the sole possessors of truth. Many competent critiques of various cults and religious organizations can be found for specific information of this type.

(iv)    It is important here that we make use of the common ground that we believe God provides in every belief system (e.g., Paul at Athens; see also Don Richardson's *Eternity in Their Hearts*). With Mormons, for example, one can appreciate their stress on morality, family emphasis, and their regard for the Bible—without accepting their doctrines of salvation by works, evolution into godhood, or reigning over other planets.

(v)    Explain the Christian position in plain language. Christian "lingo" is natural for us, just as lawyers, printers, brokers, and others in specialized fields have their own vocabulary. Now when we have to sign a contract we rightly demand to understand the terms of the document. Likewise, unbelievers have every right to understand the terms of Christianity before they commit themselves to the biblical world view.

c.    Present the message that Jesus sacrificed His life for us that we might be forgiven our sins and have personal relationship with God forever.

**5.  *Conclusion.***
     The key to witnessing to people involved in the cults is to understand that they are basically authority-dependent people who did not really learn to think for themselves. If they grew up in the Church, they were not taught why they should believe the doctrines of the faith. In order to effectively witness to these people, we must understand that authority structure, get familiar with their doctrines, and be able to prove through sound reason and Scripture that their group is false and Christianity is true. The best way to practice witnessing to the cults is to do it! Prepare yourself with the facts, pray about the situation, get out there and spread it around!

Selected Resources:
Appel, Willa, *Cults in America: Programmed for Paradise*. NY: Holt, Rinehart and Winston, 1983.
Bussell, Harold, *Unholy Devotion: Why Cults Lure Christians*. Grand Rapids, Michigan: Zondervan, 1983.
Enroth, Ronald, *Youth, Brainwashing and the Extremist Cults*. Grand Rapids, Michigan: Zondervan, 1977.
Enroth, Ronald, ed., *A Guide to Cults and New Religions*. Downers Grove, Ill.: InterVarsity Press, 1983.
Hesselgrave, David J., ed., *Dynamic Religious Movements: Case Studies of Rapidly Growing Religious Movements Around the World*. Grand Rapids, Michigan: Baker Book House, 1978.
Larson, Bob, *Larson's Book of Cults*. Wheaton, Ill.: Tyndale House Pub., 1983.
Martin, Walter R., *The Kingdom of the Cults*. Revised and expanded version. Minneapolis, Minnesota: Bethany Fellowship, Inc., 1985.
Mead, Frank S., *Handbook of Denominations in the United States*. 7th ed. Nashville: Abingdom Press, 1980.
Pement, Eric, "Witnessing to Cults." *Spiritual Counterfeits Project* Newsletter 9:5(Nov.-Dec. 1983):9-10.
Streiker, Lowell D., *Mind-Bending: Brainwashing, Cults, and Deprogramming in the '80s*. NY: Doubleday & Co., 1984.

# THE EVANGELIST WORKING CROSS CULTURALLY

*Panya Baba*

*"But how can they call to Him for help if they have not believed? And how can they believe if they have not heard the message? And how can they hear if the message is not proclaimed? And how can the message be proclaimed if the messengers are not sent out?" Romans 10:14,15.*

## INTRODUCTION

The number of unreached people today is a great challenge to our generation. The 2/3 of the non-Christians in the world who live separated from Christians and any existing churches indicates the urgent need for more evangelists who will work cross culturally in order to accomplish total world evangelization. If the Gospel is to reach out to the most unreached people, it has to be done by cross cultural evangelists. For example, in the continent of Africa there are about 1,600 tribes who speak different languages. Most of these do not have their language written down. Many do not have the Scriptures written down. Some areas have no evangelist or missionary working among them to share the Gospel with them. Other continents have a similar need. Therefore one of the greatest needs in evangelism today is for evangelists who will work cross culturally.

## A.   Biblical Principles for Cross-Cultural Work
### Historical Background: Why there are differences in Cultures.

The history of cultural differences goes back to the time of the building of the tower of Babel not very long after the flood. Cultural differences were well met by God. God used languages as an obstacle to stop the pride of mankind so that they could not understand one another and had to give up the work and be scattered over the face of the earth, Genesis 11:7,8. Today, different cultures cause misunderstanding between persons, groups of people, tribal people and ethnic people, or between speaker and the listener. Cultural differences cause much misunderstanding, mistrust, confusion, and even fighting. When one pastor did some research he found that in his local church there were about twenty different languages spoken by the members, and many of these members had different practices as a result of their culture. For example, he discovered that some members do not greet women, or shake hands between a man and a woman; while other groups do shake hands between a man and a woman. To others, to greet without shaking hands will not be very effective. Because of this an evangelist must be very sensitive and concerned as to how he should communicate his message cross culturally.

Hausas have a saying, "Rijiya ta bada ruwa amma guga ta hana." That means the well has given the water, but the container prevents it taking effect. An evangelist must be very careful not to become a container which cannot hold water and satisfy the people. Let us have a closer look at this problem. There are several reasons why a container prevents the water from giving refreshment:

1.   No rope long enough to reach the water in the well is attached to the container. Although there is water in the well your hand will not reach it.

Therefore enough rope must be available to reach the water and give satisfaction.
2.   The container may have a large hole in it, so that when the bucket is brought to the surface all the water has escaped.
3.   The container is too dirty. Even if the water is brought to the surface safely, nobody would want to drink the water because it is dirty.
4.   It could be that the container is not heavy enough to sink and take water. No matter how long you work at it nothing will come out of the well.

There may be other reasons why the container prevents water getting to the people. Likewise, there are other cultural differences and problems where, if an evangelist is not careful or considerate, he could lose contact with his audience. We believe in the power of the Word of God and the Holy Spirit, but the evangelist can be an obstacle to his own message to the hearer. That means he can become the container which prevents any impact of the power of the Word of God to take effect. Paul instructed Timothy to be an example. How? By his lifestyle, his words, his appearance, his behavior, etc.

**B.   *Learning Attitudes***

The evangelist should be willing to be a learner. Although he is gifted by the Holy Spirit he needs to learn how he can use his gifts more effectively. He needs to learn how to communicate the message a better way.

1.   *Learn from Jesus* (Matthew 11:29)
Jesus was the founder and initiator of the Gospel and the first missionary and evangelist. He so identified with us that the Gospel message of salvation might get across to us. Jesus is the last method that God used to speak to the world in these last days. How?

—The Word was made flesh and dwelt among us (John 1:14).

—Being in the form of God . . . but made Himself of no reputation, and took upon Him the form of a servant, and was made in the likeness of men (Philippians 2:6,7).

2.   *Learn from the Apostles* (Older ones)
Paul said, Learn from me or follow me (1 Corinthians 11:1). How can we learn and follow him?

In 1 Corinthians 9:19-22, Paul said that though he was free from all men, yet he made himself a servant unto all, that he might gain more. He also said that "unto the Jews I became as a Jew, that I might gain the Jews; to them that are under the law, as under the law, that I might gain them that are under the law. To the weak became I as weak, that I might gain the weak: I am made all things to all men, that I might by all means save some." In 1 Timothy 3:10, Paul points out the importance that a deacon prove by his life that he is blameless.

3.   *Learn from the people to whom you are sent.* Try to know their standard and knowledge of God, in order to have a starting point.
a.   *With Jews.* Paul went to the synagogue and sat down (Acts 13:14). Notice the time they were asked to speak. Notice the kind of message

which Paul preached (vs. 15-43). Paul started with their knowledge of the law. (Think of Muslims as an example.)

b. *With Gentiles.* He preached about creation, providence and protection of God (Acts 14:15-18; 17:22-32).

What I am saying is that the evangelist should not appear to be too big or too low for his audience. His message must not be above or below his hearers.

C. *Practical Principles of Cross Culture*

1. *Methods of communication*

   a. *Non-Verbal communication* (1 Corinthians 9:26,27)
      1. Physical appearance of the evangelist.
         —clothes—what and how he wears them.
         —cleanness of his body, and place of worship.
      2. His respect for and obedience to the Word of God.
      3. His family life.
      4. His behavior with other people. In everything he should try to be an example (1 Thessalonians 1:6,7).

2. *Verbal communication*

   a. Using the language which is most understood by the audience.
   b. Using clear simple words which the hearer will understand, instead of big words which might bring confusion. Remember, misusing one word or even one letter can change the meaning of the whole sentence. For example: In the hausa language the words Ubangiji, Allah mean ''God the Lord'' but when it says Ubangij*in* Allah, it means the Lord of God. The Muslims in Nigeria will close their ears when they hear you saying there is another Lord above God!
   c. He must be very kind in his talking. Colossians 4:6, ''Let your speech be always with grace, seasoned with salt, that you may know how you should answer every man.''

3 *Testing the soil*

   The parable of our Lord Jesus indicates that there are four kinds of soil for sowing (Matthew 13:1-9).
   a. At the roadside
   b. On the stony ground
   c. In the thorny areas
   d. On the fertile soil.

   We are commanded to witness for Him in Jerusalem, Judea, Samaria, and the uttermost parts of the world (Acts 1:8) at the same time. However, we should be wise enough to test the soil to find out where the Holy Spirit has prepared the soil for the sowing of the seed. The prepared soil should be the evangelist's priority ground for sowing the seed, unless a clear message is given to him (as Ezekiel received) to go to an unresponsive area (Ezekiel 2:3-5). The fertile soil could be in a city or a town somewhere else. The evangelist must be flexible to follow the directions of the Holy Spirit, the Lord of the Harvest.

4. *Building the Bridges*

   An evangelist must be wise in his work (Matthew 10:16). When an evangelist is out doing the work of an evangelist, he must realize some of the cultural problems which new converts may have to face if they openly confess their faith in Jesus Christ. This happens particularly among the Muslims who have accepted Christ as Savior. Some are persecuted. They are put out of their homes, they are mocked and isolated. Sometimes their wives are taken from them along with their children. They face a lot of problems.

The evangelist needs to build bridges through friendly relationships in preparation for their open confession. He should continue building the bridges of the same relationship after their conversion. Building bridges helps to prepare the parents, friends, and other relatives of the new converts to accept them in their homes even if they have changed their religion. Sometimes it hurts the parents or relatives more if they see an evangelist isolating their brother or child who is a new convert to live in his house. Building bridges is most needful so that the new convert will not suffer alone. This will mean some sacrifice on the part of the evangelist.

*Here are several examples for building bridges for relationships:*
1.  The Evangelical Missionary Society (E.M.S.) in Nigeria discovered the Koma people who live in the mountains along the border between Nigeria and the Cameroons. They were afraid of anyone outside of their tribe. They would run away and hide if anyone tried to visit with them. They spent their time farming, and they could see no need of the Gospel message that the missionaries brought to them. They were completely devoted to farming.

    One day some of us demonstrated our concern for their occupation of farming. As we were passing through the farm of a village head, we stopped and borrowed his hoe and did some farming for him. When we gave back the hoe, he was amazed that we would be willing to help him. That action changed his attitude, and that of his family, toward the missionaries and their message. The following day, the village head asked for someone to come and live among them so that they could learn more about the Word of God.

2.  In Nigeria we sent a missionary couple to Katarma district to evangelize and teach new converts the Word of God. The following day, after their arrival, the district head, who is a very aggressive Muslim came and asked the missionaries to leave his district. "I don't like your people or the mission. You have come to spoil my people. I hate you. You must go back, or else be blamed for anything that might happen to you," he said to the missionaries.

    Our missionaries did not know what to do. But after prayer, asking the Lord to give them wisdom, they discovered that the Muslim district head was not denying the truth of the Gospel, but rather confirming the truth of the Gospel which he knew would be an eye opener to his subjects. And it would make it impossible for him to continue cheating his people or manipulating them. Then the missionary took steps to building a relationship with the Muslim district head. He wrote a letter to the head, asking him to set apart a day when he and the new converts could go and assist him at his farm. He also requested the type of instruments he would need for farming.

The district head was very amazed and could hardly believe what he read in the letter from the missionary—that he and other Christians wanted voluntarily to come and farm for him. The district head set up a day when they should meet at the farm. When the day came the missionary and the converts worked very hard until noon. In the afternoon the district head came to visit them on the farm and found that almost the whole of the field had been farmed. He was so surprised that he went to the missionary and bent down before him and said, "Please forgive me for the way I talked to you. I am sorry for what I said. I did not know that you were such a good man and God-fearing. Never before has anyone ever volunteered to help me farm. I always have to force my subjects to work for me. But you and the other Christians have done this work gladly. From now on, I permit you to go anywhere in my district to preach and teach my people about God. I even want you to come and teach my children too!"

Since that time, many people in the area have become Christians because they are no longer afraid of the village head who might have persecuted them for believing. Everywhere people in the area are responding, because they know the missionaries have been accepted by the village head.

3. Waziri was sent as a missionary to work among the Kagoma people. He spent a year in the district but there was no response to the Gospel. Rather, the people hated him and even poisoned his child so that she died. Instead of being discouraged, Waziri and his wife kept praying for wisdom and patience to communicate the Gospel to these people.

When the rainy season came Waziri took notice that the villagers did not care to take the grass away from the roads and widen their paths to their neighboring compounds. One day Waziri decided to do it himself. It seemed like a small sacrifice to make for the Lord. He started at his neighbors' compound and then moved from compound to compound clearing away the grass. Lastly he did his own path. When everyone returned they found all the paths had been cleared. When they walked along the paths the grass no longer touched them. They began to ask who had cleared the paths. When they discovered that it had been done by Waziri many of them came to Waziri in tears and asked for forgiveness for killing his daughter by poisoning her. They said they were even ready to receive court punishment. But Waziri refused to take court action. He forgave them. As a result, many people came to know the Lord and a church was planted in the following three months.

From these examples we see again how important it is for the evangelist to build bridges. Until the parents, friends, and relatives know what kind of person the evangelist is—whether he is a good or bad person, or a wicked or God-fearing person, or whether he is kind or rude to the people—they will have reservations about allowing anyone to accept the Gospel and practice Christianity.

5. *Training others for discipleship*
One of the important things for an evangelist to do is discipleship, to train

others who will participate in the ministry (2 Timothy 1:13,14; 2:2).

The converts will communicate the Gospel better and easier among their tribal people if they are trained on how to do it. Sometimes when the converts are illiterate, the evangelist can start a class immediately where the new converts will learn how to read and write. The Bible stories and memory verses will be taught at the same time. For further follow up, a home Bible study or Vacation Bible School should be prepared, where the converts will be grounded in their faith and the truth. This training doesn't necessarily need many converts before it can begin. The evangelist needs to take the converts with him, and give them opportunities to participate in witnessing to others. When they make mistakes, he should correct them later.

6.   *Evaluation*
Some clear objectives should be set up by the evangelist right from the beginning of his work, so that from time to time he can evaluate his work to see how much success or failure he has. He will also find out some of the reasons for some of the failures, and make sure to correct them in the future.

## D.   *The Role of The Holy Spirit*

An evangelist should remember the most important thing in his work is the role of the Holy Spirit. The Holy Spirit is the Lord of the harvest. The labor of the planters and those who watered would be unprofitable or useless unless God, the Holy Spirit gives the fruit (1 Corinthians 3:7). "For without me, you can do nothing" (John 15:5). Therefore, the Holy Spirit is the master planner of every evangelist who works cross culturally. He is the doer of the work, and uses the evangelist as an instrument to accomplish His purpose and plan.

The evangelist needs only to depend on the Holy Spirit and submit himself to Him totally for His guidance, wisdom, and instruction in all that he does and wherever he goes.

# EVANGELISTIC STRATEGIES FOR THE EVANGELIST

*John Robb*

In the famous children's classic, *Alice in Wonderland*, the main character finds herself lost in the forest and seeks directions from the Cheshire cat. She asks, "Cheshire puss . . . would you please tell me which way I ought to go from here?" "That depends on where you want to get to," said the cat. "I don't much care where . . ." said Alice. "Then it doesn't matter which way you go," said the cat.

What is the point of this story? As the cat perceptively saw, Alice needed a clear idea of where she was going, where she wanted to get to, before she could determine the way to get there.

If you sometimes feel like Alice—not exactly sure where you want to go or how to get there—this workshop is for you! Developing a strategy for our life and ministry is a way of ensuring that we will stay on course and ultimately accomplish what we set out to do. This workshop is about strategy. We will discuss what strategy is, and its importance in evangelism. We will discuss the elements of developing an effective strategy and particularly concentrate on how we can devise a strategy for reaching an unreached group we are burdened for.

## 1. *The meaning of strategy*

What is strategy? The dictionary defines it as a careful plan, more specifically, the art of devising or employing plans to reach a goal. Originally the word comes from a Greek term meaning "generalship," that is the science and art of military command exercised to meet an enemy in combat. We could sum up the military idea of the word as the careful planning necessary to fight a war in order to attain the ultimate goal of victory.

Most of you have seen war movies in which the general or admiral pictured was studying a chart on the wall and considering how the whole operation ought to be conducted. Failure to carefully plan maneuvers—foreseeing dangers, and above all, keeping the final objective in view—will result in disaster and ultimate defeat. Even though he may be successful in winning some smaller skirmishes, the commander will lose the war. Good strategy, therefore, is related to long-range planning and foresight.

We practice strategic planning not only in war but in all areas of life. If you are married, when you got married, you or your parents (depending on which part of the world you come from) employed strategy in finding the right partner for you. In such a consequential matter we cannot afford not to exercise foresight and plan properly. At one stage in my premarital days, I became infatuated with a young lady without thinking clearly ahead what marriage with her would be like, particularly since I had felt God's call into missions. My wise old pastor took me aside one day and said, "John, there are worse things than being single!" With his cooler, calmer perspective he could see my pursuing her would be a bad marriage strategy.

We utilize strategy, whether consciously or not, in deciding the career we will pursue, how many children we will have (unless the Lord sends you more than you anticipated!) and how they will be educated. We want to make wise decisions because of the long-range effects they will have upon us and our families, so we think and plan carefully beforehand the best way of accomplishing life goals. This is strategy.

## 2.   *The value of strategy in evangelism*

Having said all this, when we come to evangelism it is strange that we often don't adopt a clear strategy for our ministry. Many of us do not employ long-range planning, foreseeing where we want to be, what we want to have accomplished one year, five years or ten years down the road. We are busy preaching the Gospel, carrying out evangelistic activities of one sort or another; and this is good, but we are like Alice. We don't know where it is, besides heaven, that we ultimately want to get to in our work.

Many of us are pursuing evangelism with its related activities of preaching, teaching and healing as if they were ends in themselves, although evangelism is actually a means to an end. For example, in the Great Commission of Matthew 28:19,20 Jesus commands us to "Go and make disciples of all nations, baptizing them in the name of the Father, and of the Son and of the Holy Spirit, and teaching them to obey everything I have commanded you." In the Greek of the passage, of the four action verbs "go," "make disciples," "baptize," and "teach" only one is an imperative— "make disciples." The three others are participles and describe the means by which the end of making disciples is to be achieved. Many of us, including myself, have been involved in evangelistic activities that, while good in themselves, did not result in actual disciples made. If we had thought through a clear strategy of disciple-making beforehand, it is doubtful we would have spent our time in activities which seemed worthwhile but were ineffectual in terms of achieving the overall objective.

Several years ago, I gave my time and involvement, along with other Christian leaders, to a mass media evangelistic campaign in Kuala Lumpur, Malaysia, where I was serving as a missionary. It was known as the "I Found It" campaign. Perhaps some of you have heard of it. It was reported to have been highly successful in other cities, so we decided to lend it our support. Many of the pastors and churches were involved and gave heavily of their time, energy, and money. To make a long story short, the campaign appealed to a certain segment of the population—English-educated young people—and there were many "decisions" from among this group. However, as far as we know, very few became disciples and were integrated into the churches. On top of that, 50% of the population, the Muslims, were incensed by this culturally insensitive approach. If we pastors and missionaries had thought strategically and exercised foresight in visualizing the probable impact of the campaign as far as the likely number of disciples that would be made and the adverse reaction by Malay Muslims, we would not have employed this standard prepackaged approach to our unique culturally diverse city. We would have developed long-range evangelistic strategies for each of the distinct social and cultural groups, that took into account their uniqueness as groups.

When we busy ourselves with evangelistic activities without taking the time to do long-range planning, we are applying tactics without strategy. Tactics is another military term. It is defined as a method of employing forces in combat, such as when infantry movements are deployed to secure a particular section of the battlefield. Good tactics are important. No war could be won without them. However, they need the overall direction that a strategy supplies. Otherwise, they form a chain of unrelated, uncoordinated events that do not contribute to that one supreme purpose we are trying to achieve. Strategy informs and guides tactics so that each tactical action counts. The Apostle Paul was talking about the relationship of strategy and tactics when he affirmed that he didn't "run like a man running aimlessly" or "fight like a man beating the air" (1 Corinthians 9:26). Each tactical activity—whether it was preaching, teaching, or healing—he applied as part of a larger strategy to bring the peoples, the Gentiles of the Roman Empire, to faith in Jesus Christ. Tactics were important, but they fit into a long-range plan.

Today, most of us evangelists are good tacticians, but we are generally weak as strategists. We may be gifted in sharing the Gospel with individuals or from a platform. We may be effective at arranging and holding evangelistic campaigns in churches or stadiums. We may be good at mobilizing and leading others to participate in communicating their faith. We may have the anointing to pray for the sick and see miraculous healing. But have we ever sat down and in prayerful dependence on the Holy Spirit drawn up a long-term strategy for our ministry? Up until just a few years ago, my ministry had no such concept of strategy other than a vague notion of serving Christ and being His instrument to reach others for Him. It wasn't until I began thinking and praying about what I would like to see accomplished in the future that a clear strategy of ministry began to crystallize.

Strategy is concerned about the future and what it ought to look like according to God's revealed purposes for mankind. One evangelistic strategist put it this way: "Strategy is an attempt to anticipate the future. [It is] our statement of faith as to what we believe the future should be like, and how we should go about reaching that future" (E.R. Dayton and D.A. Fraser, *Planned Strategies for World Evangelization*, 1980, p. 16).

Strategizing about the future is an act of faith. Perhaps you are like me. For many years as a member of a pietistic faith mission, I felt it was presumptuous and unspiritual for me to carefully plan for the future. That was God's business. But it is clear from Scripture that both God and man have a part in bringing about the future. Proverbs 16:9 says, "The mind of a man plans his way, but the Lord directs his steps." God expects us to use our minds to plan our way in accordance with His revealed word. That's strategy. As we implement our strategy, He promises to direct the outworking of that strategy, maybe even modifying it as we go, just as He did with Paul in his Macedonian vision experience. But the important thing is that a strategy provides us with direction as we travel towards the future. It is like a road map or a compass. Those of us who came to Amsterdam from other parts of the world flew on planes with precision maps and compasses enabling them to fly half way around the world across vast expanses of ocean and to land right on target at Schiphol airport. An evangelistic strategy will do the same for your ministry of evangelism.

Strategizing about the future enables the building of new vision. From time to time, we need to use our imaginations to envision the limitless possibilities of God's working through us. Ephesians 3:20 says: "God is able to do far more abundantly than all we can ask or think, according to the power at work within us." I like the saying of Cho Yonggi, pastor of the world's largest church. In his book, *The Fourth Dimension*, he said: "God's people need to allow themselves to dream, that is to imagine what is the greatest thing God could do through me, then ask Him to do it and He will." Strategizing in faith about the future opens the doors to new possibilities we have never dreamed of before.

Another form of direction a strategy provides is help in deciding what we will *not* do. There are a host of good activities that can soak up our time and divert us from that one, most strategic, objective. A strategy enables us to concentrate all our resources on what we have determined as the essential task we need to perform. Paul said, "This one thing I do." What is that one thing you ought to concentrate your whole being on attaining? Clausewitz, the great Prussian military strategist, said something that is as true in evangelistic ministry as in war. He said, "The best strategy is always to be very strong . . . *at the decisive point.* . . . There is no more imperative and no simpler law for strategy than to *keep the forces concentrated.* No portion is to be separated from the main body unless called away by some urgent necessity . . . all forces which are available and destined for a strategic object should be *simultaneously applied* to it . . . *compressed into one act and one movement"* (emphasis mine) (A. Rapoport, ed., *Clausewitz on War*, 1968, p. 83). In the sense that evangelism is war of a different kind, we would do well to heed this admonition. We need to concentrate all our energies and efforts on what we have determined is the strategic, decisive object.

3.   *The elements of an effective evangelistic strategy*
      Then how do we determine that one overarching objective? What are the elements of an effective evangelistic strategy? Many missionaries and evangelists have a general, hazy purpose in mind, e.g., "To bring God's Word to this nation" or "To reach this city for Christ."
      But unless a purpose is operationalized, it remains nothing more than a pious wish, a noble intention, an incomplete strategy. If we are to put teeth into our strategy and hold ourselves and others accountable for its accomplishment, we must add to our purpose measurable supporting goals and action plans detailing exactly how we will achieve those goals. An effective strategy is, therefore, composed of a clearly defined purpose, measurable goals marking progress toward fulfillment of that purpose, and action plans as to how we will go about attaining those necessary goals to make accomplishment of the overall purpose possible.
      If our purpose is "to establish a cell of believers among the Muslim Tuareg people of the Sahara region in North Africa," our measurable goals might look something like this:
      a.   Have learned to ride a camel! (August 1)
      b.   Speak the Tuaregs' language (April 1987)
      c.   Have developed friendships with one nomadic group (June 1987)
      d.   Understand their way of looking at the world and felt needs (December 1987)
      e.   Have shared the Gospel message with ten families (January 1988)
      f.   Have established a Bible study group (March 1988)
      g.   A cell of 20 believers is meeting regularly for worship and fellowship (June 1988)
      Our action plans would concern the details of how we plan to accomplish our goals by the proposed date, for example:
      a.   Hire Ahmad the camel driver to give me riding lessons twice a week for the next six weeks.
      b.   Buy Tuareg tapes and listen to them 2 hours daily. Enroll in the North African Language Institute for classes three times per week.
      This kind of strategic thinking and planning works. A close friend and national colleague in Malaysia set out to reach the unreached in a large district. He gave himself ten years to establish groups of believers in every town in the district. In only six years he has already met his goal and has trained up leaders to take over so he can go to another area of the country to repeat the process. When we formulate clear measurable goals and devise concrete plans to reach them, we are no longer wandering in the forest like Alice. We know where we're going and are determined to get there, because measurable goals are a powerful motivating force. They will keep us on the track and prevent us from being deflected by lesser concerns and distractions.

4.   *The people group approach to strategic evangelization*
      One of the most important aspects of developing an effective evangelistic strategy

is that it be people-centered rather than evangelist-centered. That is to say, our strategy for reaching an unreached group of people, whether it be an ethnic group like the Tuareg or Mali or an occupational group like the taxi drivers of Taipei, needs to arise from an understanding of their unique characteristics as a group rather than be imposed upon them from the outside. Too often we don't take time to understand the way a people are, to listen to them describe life as they see it with the needs and problems they face. We are too eager to preach before adequate listening and understanding, so that our preaching misses the mark; it does not scratch where they itch.

It is estimated that 80% of the world's non-Christians are across cultural and language barriers from existing forces of evangelism. The great majority of the over 15,000 unreached people groups will have to be reached by evangelists who are willing to adapt themselves to a different culture and learn another dialect or language. How imperative it is for us to include careful study of the people group we are trying to reach as part of our strategy for reaching them.

In the Great Commission of Matthew 28, Jesus laid out a grand strategy into which all our personal strategies ought to fit. He said, "Make disciples of all nations." The word used for "nations" is very significant. It's the Greek term, *Ta ethne*, from which we get the English word "ethnic." Instead of the political nations of today such as China, India, or Nigeria, Jesus was thinking of ethnic groups, the peoples that make up those political nations. He was thinking of the 3,000 caste groups of India, the 494 distinct ethnic groups of Nigeria, the many different occupational groups of China's cities. His strategy calls for our making disciples of all the diverse people groups that make up our society. In order to do this effectively, we may need to select one group and concentrate all our efforts on that particular group to whom we feel God is calling us to devote ourselves. This is really the most strategic thing to do in the long run, because as the Gospel takes firm root in the lives of some members of the group, they will be able to spread it more effectively to the rest of their group. I know it is difficult for an itinerant evangelist to contemplate concentrating on one people group, but ultimately this in-depth evangelism and disciple-making will bear the most fruit. We cannot reach everyone in a country, but there is one people group that we are specially suited and gifted to reach.

5. *Conclusion*

In summary, we have talked about strategy: what it is, its value in evangelism. We have also identified the main components of an effective evangelistic strategy: a clearly defined purpose, measurable goals and action plans. Finally, we dealt with the unreached people approach to evangelization and steps to develop a strategy for any unreached group.

It has been a delight to be with you and may the Lord, that greatest strategist of all, guide and empower you to strategize and evangelize effectively for Him.

# BUILDING AN EVANGELISTIC TEAM
*Barry Moore*

The crying need of the hour is for the Christian Church to get back to Apostolic evangelism. The Church in its first 25 years of existence accomplished more than any other time in the history of Christianity.

"The period covered by the Acts is approximately 33 years (B.C. 4-A.D. 30), and thus showing how intense is the activity of this first generation of church history. Had the later generations of the church followed the example of the first, the world would have been evangelized 50 times by now." (Dr. Graham Scroggie)

As we consider building an *evangelistic team* for today, we will do well to understand the *milieu* in which the early church worked, the *means* they utilized, the *mitigation* they faced, the *miracles* they enjoyed, before looking at the *method of team construction* that they used.

## I. APOSTOLIC EVANGELISM

The evangelism of the early Christians appears as:

### 1. *A COMBUSTION That Was Spontaneous*

Pentecost was the initial day of a new order. It was the first page of a new book entitled, "The Acts of the Holy Spirit" or "The Autobiography of the Holy Ghost." It was a new beginning of a new spiritual life, a new relationship, a new fellowship, a new authority, and a new power.

So great was the enthusiasm and aggressiveness of the early Church that when the enemy heard them unhesitatingly speak "the things which we have seen and heard" (Acts 4:20), they called a council meeting whose theme was, "How Can We Stop This Gospel Epidemic" . . . "that it spread no farther" (Acts 4:15-17). The more they were assaulted or insulted, the more dynamic they became, until they were accused of being "these that have turned the world upside down" (Acts 17:6).

### 2. *In A COMMUNITY That Was Hostile*

The Church lived among enemies. Her message was in direct opposition to the Jewish religion and to the laws of Imperial Rome. Paul was accused by Tertullus before Ananias the High Priest, that he was "a mover of sedition among all the Jews throughout the world" and "profaned the religion of the Jews" (Acts 24:5,6).

When he managed to escape to Berea from a riot in Thessalonica, they brought Jason, who had given him hospitality, to the Roman rulers of the city and accused him and Paul of preaching in opposition to the decrees of Caesar (Acts 16:21). They faced bitter foes.

### 3. *With A CHARACTER That Was Unprestigious*

The early Church had none of the elements which we would believe were necessary for success in the contemporary church today. They had no numerical prestige for they were a little flock. They had no financial prestige for they were not wealthy and had a common treasury. They had little social or educational prestige, for aside from Luke, who was a physician, and Paul, who sat at the feet of Gamaliel, they were basically unlettered and untutored men.

They had no theological or ecclesiastical prestige, for they were "un-degreed, and unschooled." They had no real estate holdings or church buildings. When they preached the Gospel, it was in the synagogue to the Jews; and when they worshiped with communion, it was in a private home.

4.   *They Enjoyed A CONQUEST That Was Unforgettable* because they

(i)   *Challenged the Powers of Darkness*

Peter seems to defy the whole nation of Israel and the religious leaders when he says fearlessly in Acts 2:32,33, "This Jesus hath God raised up, whereof we all are witnesses. Therefore, being by the right hand of God exalted, and having received of the Father the promise of the Holy Ghost, He hath shed forth this, which ye now see and hear." The early Church did not back down, neither compromise the Lordship of Jesus Christ.

(ii)   *Believed in the Personal Presence of Christ*

They did not worship or serve an historical Christ but rather a Liv-ing Lord. They believed He was in their midst (Matthew 18:20). Even their enemies realized the vitality of their witness because "when they saw the boldness of Peter and John, and perceived that they were unlearned and ignorant men, they marvelled; and they took knowledge of them, that they had been with Jesus" (Acts 4:13).

(iii)   *Were in One Accord*

Not less than seven times in the early chapters of Acts, this phrase or its parallel is used (Acts 1:14; 2:1,44,46; 4:24,32; 5:12).

(iv)   *Holy Living Was Their Standard*

They had not only beheld who Jesus Christ was and believed on Him, but they behaved like Him (1 Peter 4:1,2).

Robert Murray McCheyne said, "A holy minister is an awful weapon in the hand of the Living God."

(v)   *Persecution Was Severe but Valuable*

The circumstances under which Paul evangelized were severe. There was no New Testament assembly of evangelical believers; no one could quote a verse of the Bible apart from the Orthodox Jew; no one could sing a Christian hymn, and the city was totally given over to idolatry.

It was into this pagan city, steeped in superstition and sin, that

Paul went with his feet shod with the preparation of the Gospel of peace (Ephesians 6:15).

The early Church was persecuted daily and had only an occasional rest from the onslaught of the enemy. Acts 9:31 says, "Then had the churches rest throughout all Judaea and Galilee and Samaria, and were edified; and walking in the fear of the Lord, and in the comfort of the Holy Ghost, were multiplied." This is an illuminating verse because after the persecution, God now gives the churches rest and edification. They walked in the fear of the Lord and in the comfort of the Holy Spirit and grew in great numbers. There is value in persecution.

(vi) *Atmosphere of Prayer Was Vital*

Acts 1:14 — These all continued with one accord in prayer and supplication, with the women, and Mary the mother of Jesus, and with His brethren.

Acts 2:42 — And they continued steadfastly in the apostles' doctrine and fellowship, and in breaking of bread, and in prayers.

Acts 3:1 — Now Peter and John went up together into the temple at the hour of prayer, being the ninth hour.

Acts 4:24 — And when they heard that, they lifted up their voice to God with one accord, and said, Lord, thou art God, which has made heaven, and earth, and the sea, and all that in them is.

Acts 4:31 — And when they had prayed, the place was shaken where they were assembled together; and they were all filled with the Holy Ghost, and they spake the Word of God with boldness.

Acts 6:4 — But we will give ourselves continually to prayer, and to the ministry of the Word.

Acts 12:5 — Peter therefore was kept in prison: but prayer was made without ceasing of the church unto God for him.

Acts 13:3 — And when they had fasted and prayed, and laid their hands on them, they sent them away.

Acts 14:23 — And when they had ordained them elders in every church, and had prayed with fasting, they commended them to the Lord, on whom they believed.

Acts 16:25 — And at midnight Paul and Silas prayed, and sang praises unto God: and the prisoners heard them.

(vii) *Preaching the Word Was Foremost*

A noted preacher and author asks, "What is the subject matter of the apostles' preaching?'' And the answer: ''Throughout the book of the Acts, there is one word that recurs again and again. It is the word, 'WORD'.''

Acts 2:41    On the day of Pentecost, ''they that gladly received the WORD were baptized.''

Acts 4:4    When Peter spoke after the lame man had been healed, ''many of them which heard the WORD believed.''

Acts 4:29    After the disciples had been threatened by the council and forbidden to speak Jesus' name, they besought the Lord ''that with all boldness they may speak thy WORD.''

Acts 4:31    The Lord answered their prayer for they ''spoke the WORD of God with boldness.''

Acts 6:4    The seven deacons were chosen that the apostles might ''give ourselves continually to prayer, and the ministry of the WORD.''

Acts 8:4    When the great persecution arose, the disciples ''went every where preaching the WORD.''

Acts 8:14    ''Now when the apostles which were at Jerusalem heard that Samaria had received the WORD of God, they sent unto them Peter and John.''

Acts 8:25    Of their last visit we read, ''And they, when they had testified and preached the WORD of the Lord.''

Acts 8:35    When Philip found the eunuch reading the Scriptures, he ''began at the same SCRIPTURE, and preached unto him Jesus.''

Acts 10:44    In the house of Cornelius, ''while Peter yet spake these words, the Holy Ghost fell on all them which heard the WORD.''

Acts 11:1    ''And the apostles and brethren that were in Judaea heard that the Gentiles had also received the WORD of God.''

Acts 13:5    Of Paul and Barnabas, ''And when they were at Salamis, they preached the WORD of God.''

Acts 13:26    When Paul was preaching at Antioch, we find him saying to the Jews, ''To you is the WORD of this salvation sent.''

Acts 13:44    ''And the next Sabbath day came almost the whole city together to hear the WORD of God.''

Acts 14:3    At Iconium, Paul and Barnabas ''gave testimony unto the WORD of His grace.''

Acts 14:25   ''And when they had preached the WORD in Perga . . .''

Acts 15:7   Peter, in speaking of his mission before the apostles and elders at Jerusalem, when the matter of circumcision in relation to the Gentiles was under consideration says, ''Men and brethren ye know that a good while ago God made the choice among us, that the Gentiles by my mouth should hear the WORD of the Gospel and believe.''

Acts 15:35   In Paul's second missionary journey, he ''and Barnabas continued in Antioch, teaching and preaching the WORD of the Lord.''

Acts 15:36   And in referring to the places already visited by the apostles, ''Paul said unto Barnabas, let us go again and visit our brethren in every city where we have preached the WORD of the Lord.''

Acts 16:6   ''And were forbidden of the Holy Ghost to preach the WORD in Asia.''

Acts 16:32   To the jailer and his household, ''they spoke unto him the WORD of the Lord.''

Acts 17:11   Of the Berean Jews we read, ''that they received the WORD with all readiness of mind.''

Acts 18:11   Paul remained at Corinth ''a year and six months, teaching the WORD of God among them.''

Acts 19:10   Of his ministry in the neighborhood of Ephesus, we are told, ''This continued by the space of two years; so that all they which dwelt in Asia heard the WORD of the Lord Jesus.''

Acts 20:32   And Paul's departing commendation to the elders was, ''And now, brethren, I commend you to God, and to the WORD of His grace.''

When Paul said to Timothy, ''PREACH THE WORD,'' he had apostolic history and fruitfulness with which to back him up.

(viii)   *They Believed the Only Hope for Mankind Was in the Gospel*

It was this conviction that led them on a holy crusade, day and night, in season and out of season, to fearlessly and sacrificially enter the enemy's territory with the message of the Evangel. The early Christians were born of the Holy Spirit (John 3:5); filled with the Holy Spirit (Ephesians 5:18); and sent by the Holy Spirit into the world (Acts 1:8).

(ix)   *There Was No Distinction between Clergy and Laity*

It was the truth of a royal priesthood, and that every believer was a witness, that was the dynamic force in the early Church. So much so, that there were saints even in Caesar's household. The distinction between clergy and laity is a relic that has been brought over from Romanism. John Huss died in Czechoslovakia for the doctrine of the priesthood of all believers. The Hussite symbol to this present day is the communion cup standing over the open Bible.

(x)   *There Was No Room for an Idle or Selfish Individual*

Every believer was a Worker (1 Corinthians 15:58), a Warrior (Ephesians 6:10-12), and a Witness (Acts 1:8). He came into the Church just as soon as he believed and was subsequently baptized. He became a member of the body where everyone had an office and must needs fulfill his function in order to maintain the health of the whole Church.

Then, as a worker, historian Edward McGibbon says, "It became the sacred duty of a new convert to diffuse among his friends and relations the inestimable blessings he had received."

(xi)   *They Were Unconventional in Their Witness*

The late Bishop Ryle, commenting on the Christian leaders in the 18th century said, "They preached everywhere. If the pulpit of the parish church was open, they gladly availed themselves of it. If it could not be obtained, they were ready to preach in a barn. No place came amiss to them. In the field or by a roadside, in a village green or in a marketplace, in lanes or alleys, in cellars or in garrets, on a tub or on a table, on a bench or on horseback, wherever hearers could be gathered, the Spiritual Reformers of the last century were ready to speak to people about their eternal souls. They were instant in season and out of season in doing the fishermen's work which encompassed sea and land carrying forth their Master's business."

(xii)   *Preaching Was Done Everywhere*

The places that the Gospel was preached by apostolic Christians were:

| | |
|---|---|
| Acts 2:14 | . . . On the streets of Jerusalem |
| Acts 3:10 | . . . At the gate of the temple |
| Acts 5:27,29 | . . . In the council chamber |
| Acts 8:28-30 | . . . In a chariot in the desert |
| Acts 9:20; 13:14 | . . . In the synagogue |
| Acts 10:24 | . . . In the house of Cornelius |
| Acts 16:13 | . . . At a river side in Philippi |
| Acts 16:24,31 | . . . In an inner prison |
| Acts 16:32 | . . . In a jailer's house |
| Acts 17:22 | . . . On Mar's hill at Athens |
| Acts 19:9 | . . . In the school of Tyrannus |
| Acts 20:20 | . . . From house to house |

Acts 24:24 ... Before Felix the governor
Acts 26:1 ... Before King Agrippa
Acts 28:30 ... In a hired house

(xiii) *Spiritual Results Were in Evidence*
Pliny, the Roman historian, gives witness to the results of apostolic preaching when he says to Emperor Trajan, in A.D. 110, "The number of the accused is so great as to call for serious consultation. Many persons are informed against—every age and rank of both sexes—and many more will be accused. Nor has the contagion of the superstition (Christianity) seized cities only, but the lesser towns also and the open country. The temples are almost forsaken and the sacred rites abandoned."

Not only that, but the Scripture, in the book of the Acts, states:

Acts 2:41 ... 3,000 saved
Acts 4:4 ... 5,000 believed
Acts 6:7 ... disciples multiplied—great company of priests obedient to faith
Acts 8:6 ... multitudes gave heed to Gospel
Acts 9:35 ... "all" that dwelt in Lydda and Saron turned to the Lord
Acts 10:44 ... all Cornelius' house
Acts 11:21 ... great number believed
Acts 13:44 ... whole city gathered to hear Word of God
Acts 14:1 ... great multitude believed
Acts 14:21 ... many disciples made
Acts 16:5 ... churches increased in number
Acts 17:6 ... world turned upside down by Paul and Silas preaching
Acts 18:8 ... numbers of important people converted (Crispus; key Corinthians)
Acts 19:18 ... revival at Ephesus because Word of God prevailed

## II.    INSTRUCTION FOR TEAM BUILDING

The two-fold source of instruction for building an evangelistic team is first, experiential; and second, scriptural.

I have been allowed by God to establish teams in three areas: namely, with Youth for Christ, whose target was YOUTH; with Greater Europe Mission, whose aim was MISSIONS; and Crusade Evangelism International, which is singularly EVANGELISTIC.

However, biblical guidance surpasses personal experience and, therefore, I immediately point to the *four* examples of evangelistic teams mentioned in the Scriptures.

1. Twelve Disciples   —CALLED and sent out to PREACH
   Luke 9:1-6        "Then He called His twelve disciples together and gave them power and authority over all devils, and to cure diseases."

2. Seventy       —APPOINTED and sent to PRECEDE Him

    Luke 10:1-11      "After these things the Lord appointed other seventy also, and sent them two and two before His face into every city and place, whither He Himself would come."

3. Every believer   —SCATTERED but PREACHED every where

    Acts 8:1-4       "Therefore they that were scattered abroad went every where preaching the Word."

The saintly F.B. Meyer said, "Antioch will be famous in Christian annals, because a number of *unordained* and *unnamed* disciples, fleeing from Jerusalem in the face of Saul's persecution, dared to preach the Gospel to Greeks and to gather the converts into a church in entire disregard of the initial rite of Judaism."

Someone else has well said, "The final responsibility for the testimony of the church falls upon the whole congregation and is shared equally by every member, man, woman, young and old. The ministry of the Word or the gifts of the Spirit are the responsibility of *every member*." The above text indicates that all the rank and file of the church preached; that they preached every where; and that their ministry inevitably ended in personal evangelism.

4. Special Teams — SEPARATED and SENT OUT

| Acts 13:2 | . . Separation | 13:42,43 | . . Persuasion |
|---|---|---|---|
| 13:3 | . . Commission | 13:45 | . . Opposition |
| 13:5 | . . Association | 13:48 | . . Elation |
| 13:6-11 | . . Opposition | 13:49 | . . Proclamation |
| 13:12 | . . Perception | 13:50 | . . Persecution |
| 13:13 | . . Desertion | 13:50,51 | . . Expulsion |
| 13:14 | . . Exhortation | 13:52 | . . Jubilation |
| 13:15-41 | . . Explanation | | |
| Acts 14:22 | . . Confirmation | 15:22 | . . Selection—Paul & |
| 14:27 | . . Recitation | | Barnabas joined by Judas & Silas |
| | | 15:32 | —Judas & Silas |
| | | 15:39 | . . Contention |
| | | 15:40 | —Paul & Silas |
| 16:1-3 | . . Addition—Paul & Timothy | | |

III.  FORMATION OF AN EVANGELISTIC TEAM

Four questions will help define pertinent team characteristics.

1. *What is its Primary Goal?*

Every fruitful evangelistic team must be built upon and feature strong, faithful biblical preaching. God's Word clearly states "that it pleased God by the foolishness of preaching to save them that believe" (1 Corinthians 1:21). The Roman epistle declares, "How shall they hear without a preacher?" (Romans 10:14).

Music, testimonies, drama, films which might be considered worthy to be used in a given service must all prepare the heart of the listener for the "borning-again" Word of God. Each of these is in a sense subsidiary or secondary to the preached Word.

2.   *Who may be Involved?*

Each team must comprise those who may be experienced and those who are not; those who assume major roles and those who have minor ones; those who are in full-time service with those who are not.

No one is inadequate, even the most inexperienced. Each may play a significant part to point men to Christ. It should be remembered that *eleven* different people were involved to see Naaman, the Syrian general, obey God. *Seven* of the *eleven* were unnamed servants! They may be considered unimportant by some, but each was a link in the chain to induce Naaman to obey God (2 Kings 5).

God uses the foolish (moronic), weak (sickly, anemic), base (ignoble, of low birth), despised (scorned), "are-nots" (nobodies), of this world to serve Him (1 Corinthians 1:26-29). Peter and John were classed as ignorant and unlearned men but they reflected Christ Jesus (Acts 4:13).

3.   *Where will it Minister?*

Big cities and large population centers are great challenges and, in fact, were targets of the itinerant evangelism of the Apostle Paul. But we must never forget the small, out-of-the-way places whose people are ofttimes more ready to listen to visitors expound the Gospel, because their tiny hamlets receive very little of a special nature such as a visiting team.

Work with the existing evangelical churches is vital because the evangelist is a part of the Church and is gifted of God to build the Church (Ephesians 4:11,12). If there is no evangelical witness in the area, then prayerful attention to the conserving of results must be given and perchance the establishment of a church may follow.

4.   *Who is its Leader?*

Every team must be responsible to a capable leader. The qualities of a God-reared, God-directed, Spirit-filled leader will be easily recognizable. His ability to preach the Word of God, his warmth with people, and his commitment or dedication will be in evidence. Since the Scriptures indicate that there is "safety in a multitude of counsellors" (Proverbs 24:6), there will be a goodly number who will agree as to the leadership qualities of this specific individual.

The leader should then fit the following description:

1.   Gifted of God.

2.   Acknowledged by the majority.

3.   Lead by example.

4.   Recognized as a man of prayer. He would be one to call team members to pray over a problem before he would seek to plan to

circumvent the problem.

5.  Untarnished in his personal and family life relationship.

6.  Explicitly honest in business dealings relative to the functioning of the team.

7.  Characterized by vision and a commitment to the mission of reaching the lost.

8.  Exhibit ability to:

   (i)   Establish principles and a plan agreed upon by team members.
   (ii)  Delegate responsibility and then permit the individual to do the job without intruding upon it. If principles are agreed upon by which the job should be done, casual counsel afterwards, where errors might have happened, is better than intruding upon the job when it is being accomplished.
   (iii) Be careful not to demand of his team something that he would not attempt himself.
   (iv)  Watch for talent in others.
   (v)   Encourage the hesitant team member.
   (vi)  Give opportunity to the untrained team member to increasingly become more trained.
   (vii) Be available and approachable by his team members with suggestions, ideas, and input.
   (viii) Utilize as many of these suggestions as are adequate.
   (ix)  Involve as many team members and/or individuals as possible in the presentation of the message.
   (x)   Have high interest in personal counseling among those who respond to his invitations to trust Christ as Savior.

IV.   FRUSTRATIONS TO BE ENCOUNTERED IN EVANGELISM

1.  Persecution      (1 Peter 4:4,12,16)
                     (Philippians 1:12-14)

2.  Opposition       (Nehemiah 4:1-3,10)    •
                     (Nehemiah 4:1-4 — ridicule)
                     (Nehemiah 4:10-12 — discouragement)
                     (Nehemiah 5:1-5 — greed)
                     (Nehemiah 6:1-8 — craftiness)

3.  Unfaithful team members who may be critical, contentious, inconsistent.

4.  Disagreements in policy (Philippians 2:1-4; 14,15).

5.  Disinterest of other Christians, both leaders and laity.

6.      It should be noted that it is easier to start something than it is to maintain it.
        Don't begin unless there is a commitment to follow through.

7.      Lack of evident results could be highly discouraging but one is reminded to
        remain faithful (1 Corinthians 15:58).

8.      Good success (that is, large crowds and many results) can negatively affect
        the ego of the evangelist should he consider "largeness" to be equal with
        blessing.

# THE EVANGELIST AS A "TENTMAKER"
*M. Ezra Sargunam*

The scope of this paper is to seek and find ways and means by which itinerant evangelists may "earn" their living while preaching; and thereby provide resources, food, clothing, shelter for themselves and for their families. Many of them work in non-Christian organizations in order to have enough money to survive. These evangelists may not necessarily be full-time traveling evangelists.

We shall examine "tentmaking evangelism" from the standpoint of Scripture, its spontaneity, and its practice from the early Church to the present.

My presentation is based on my studies made from literature available in this field, such as *Today's Tentmakers* by J. Christy Wilson Jr., and *Laymen in World Mission* by Paul Loeffer. I owe a great deal to my good friend, a tentmaker evangelist Dr. B. D. Vijayam, Senior Professor of Geology, Osmania University, South India, whose thought and materials I am using quite extensively. A good deal of resource is drawn *from our own experience* in planting self-supporting indigenous churches through tentmakers in the villages of India.

## 1. Two class of tentmakers

Tentmakers may fall into two classes:

a. The evangelists from advanced countries live on salaries of, let us say, $1,000 a month. Unable to get visas for specifically Christian ministry, they enter other countries as businessmen, manufacturers, professors in secular subjects, and the like. This class of tentmaking is currently being promoted by quite a few organizations such as the U.S. Center for World Missions.

b. The second kind of tentmaker is the Third World village evangelist-pastor who is paid nothing from foreign sources. He goes around preaching and planting congregations and shepherding them, while continuing to earn his living as he did before he became a Christian. His members may be encouraged to give him a handful of rice daily or harvest gifts at times of harvest. But from a half to nine-tenths of his income comes from his own labors.

In a gathering like this here in Amsterdam, where 70% of the participants are from the Third World countries, it will not serve much of a purpose to get into a detailed discussion on the tentmakers of the affluent West. I shall try to deal with the second class of tentmakers, in no way the inferior class, though a brief mention may be made of the former.

## 2. The scriptural model

In the beginning when God created the world and all the things thereof, He declared about His creation that "it was good." God also made man to have dominion over all creation. Because God is the chief architect of this universe and hence of its history, man has no right to segregate part of God's creation as sacred and the rest as secular. In the Old Testament the Levites and scribes were full-time ministers of those days without any earthly inheritance. For them, "God was their portion."

However, the Prophets, the counterparts of the evangelists of our time, were men who were mostly tentmakers. In fact, they were the real messengers of God with a great following. So we find God using men and women from diverse backgrounds and occupations. Thus Adam was a gardener and cultivator, Abel a sheep farmer. Abraham was a cattle raiser, Hagar a domestic worker, Isaac a farmer, and Rebekah a water carrier. Jacob was a roving rancher, Rachel a sheepherder, Joseph a premier. The young girl Miriam was a reliable and resourceful baby-sitter! Moses was a prince and a flock grazer, and Joshua a military commander. Bezaleel was a skilled artisan, Rahab an innkeeper, Deborah a national deliverer, Gideon a military leader, Samson a champion fighter, Ruth a gleaner, and Boaz a grain grower. David was a shepherd boy turned ruler, Asaph a composer, Solomon an emperor, the Queen of Sheba an administrator. Baruch was a writer, Job a gentleman farmer, Amos a sharecropper. Daniel was a prime minister, while Shadrach, Meshach and Abednego were provincial administrators. Queen Esther was a ruler, and Nehemiah a governor. Many God-fearing kings, government officials and military leaders are mentioned in the Old Testament.

In the New Testament our Lord's stepfather, Joseph, was a carpenter. Martha was a housekeeper, Zacchaeus a tax collector. Nicodemus and Joseph of Arimathea were supreme court councillors.

Barnabas was a landowner, Cornelius an officer, Luke a doctor. Priscilla, Aquila, and Paul were tentmakers. Lydia was a purple-dye seller, Zenas a lawyer, and Erastus a city treasurer. Even our Lord, though He was Creator of the universe, humbled Himself to become a self-supporting carpenter.

Some of these tentmakers of the Bible eventually received the call for full-time ministry. At times they had even to quit their professions to give priority to the high calling. Nevertheless the kind of distinction we make today between the "secular" and "sacred" was quite foreign to the men of the Bible, though they were set apart for God's service.

The concept of secular and sacred has a recent origin from European history as a consequence of severe conflict between church and State. A genuine Back to the Bible movement and spiritual awakenings have always caused the men of God to recognize and come to grips with the realities of God's eternal truth—the priesthood of all believers.

### 3.   The Pauline model

As we read in Acts, chapter 18, Paul, Barnabas, Aquila and Priscilla were tentmakers. From here we derive the traditional terminology "tentmaker evangelist." Writing about his experience in 1 Corinthians, Paul says that although they had a right to be supported by the church they had never claimed the right (1 Corinthians 9:12, 19-24,27; 10:23,24,33; 1 Thessalonians 2:9; 2 Thessalonians 3:8,9; Acts 20:34-36). Here are some of the reasons he gives for this practice.

a.   To avoid any possible hindrance to the spread of the Gospel. Compare his reason for refusing to be "a burden" to the Corinthian church, but rather depending on the Macedonians' contributions. His purpose was to cut the ground from under the feet of detractors and opponents of his Gospel (2 Corinthians 11:12). (Compare also the concern of Paul that none should bring a bad name to the Gospel in anything: Titus 1:7; 2:4,5,7,9,10; 3:8,14; 1 Timothy 6:1; 2 Corinthians 6:3).

b.   Because it was his privilege or "reward" to preach the Gospel free of charge (1 Corinthians 9:18).

Preaching the Gospel is a matter of absolute obligation for him ("necessity is laid on me"). He does it as if under compulsion. But to preach it free of charge is a matter of special satisfaction—"my reward" (1 Corinthians 9:16-18).

c.   In order to win as many as possible: to win some people somehow (1 Corinthians 9:18,19,22).

d.   To set a good example to fellow-Christians who are not evangelists (2 Thessalonians 3:7-10).

    e.    To set an example to fellow-elders and evangelists (Acts 20:35).

    f.    To be able to help ungrudgingly those who are less gifted than himself, and to illustrate by his life the Lord's teaching that it is more blessed to give than to receive (Acts 20:34,35; cf., 2 Corinthians 8:1,2).

    g.    So that he himself should not be disqualified after preaching to others. Hence his harshness in imposing the hard discipline of manual labor on his body, as on a slave (1 Corinthians 9:27).

In short, the Pauline model was the best for the Gospel, for the edification of Christians, for his own blessedness, and for the glory of God.

## 4.   *The Carey model*

Next to the Apostle Paul, William Carey (1761-1834) was probably the greatest self-supporting missionary who ever lived. He said, "My business is to witness for Christ. I make shoes just to pay my expenses." This statement summed up his life principles as he continued to support himself and those working with him on the mission field as a tentmaker in India. When the East India Company threatened to deport him for being "unfaithful" to his official position with the company, he took his family into the interior of the country, worked at an Indigo plantation, and went forward with his vision as a tentmaker. It was he who clearly brought out that the Great Commission applied to every Christian. He said if the command of Christ to teach all nations were limited only to the apostles, then doubtless the promise of the divine presence in this work must be so limited. But Matthew 28:19 is worded in such a manner that it explicitly precludes such an idea. "Lo, I am with you always, to the end of the world." Thus our Lord gave the Great Commission to every Christian, whether he or she is a fully-supported or a self-supporting missionary.

## 5.   *The Third World model*

As the Gospel went forth from the more affluent countries to the underdeveloped parts of the world, the missionaries were not always sensitive to the local cultural, social, and economic conditions. Wherever mission agencies have poured in money without any thoughtful plans for the future, wherever the entire program was stage-managed by funding agencies with top-heavy administration, the projects simply collapsed. However, where wise and cautious planning, evangelism, and church planning activities have been carried out within the cultural and socio-economic context, and have been coupled with indigenous leadership, there have been amazing and lasting results.

The Church Missionary Society (Anglican), the London Missionary Society, and the Society for the Propagation of the Gospel have all carried out extensive missionary activities in the rural areas of South India during the 19th and early part of the 20th centuries. Quite spontaneously they encouraged the village school teachers to be evangelists as well as catechists in young congregations too poor to support full-time paid pastors. Interestingly enough, this pattern is very much in practice even today. These village teacher-catechists, though they have their salaries paid by the Indian government, are still in charge of congregations as well as of the ongoing evangelistic ministry.

Let me narrate briefly how we were led into tentmaker evangelism in our evangelism and church-planting ministry. I belong to the Evangelical Church of India which was founded by the OMS International, one of the modern faith missionary organizations. During the last thirty years, starting from nothing, we have planted 350 churches with well over 30,000 membership. A large percentage of the members are first-generation Christians. Of late we were quite overwhelmed by the unprecedented growth of churches as a result of people movements among a number of responsive groups. We were challenged with the task of shepherding the congregations as we were short of seminary-trained pastors. The only answer was to allow the key leaders from these groups to step in and fill the gap. It was also quite natural, for these key men were to take care of the follow up because in the first place the Gospel had been preached to the new believers by these "unbaptized hidden missionaries" of these areas.

To give an example, in the villages around Aurangabad near Bombay, a man named Balarao was a notorious decoit. When Balarao found Christ several years ago, he completely changed from his past wicked and terrible life, and went around the same villages which he had previously looted, on the back of the same horse, but now preaching the love of Jesus Christ. Hundreds of thousands of people were astonished and turned to Christ. Balarao is now called "Guruji" (a religious teacher). He also used unbaptized key leaders to help him in the cause. We discovered that these hidden missionaries, more particularly the bandit-turned-itinerant-evangelist Guruji Balarao, had strategized organized evangelism and people movement. As a result 2,062 converts have gone through the waters of baptism and been brought openly into the household of God in the month of January 1986. The fourteen churches planted are shepherded fully by the leaders from among these congregations, for whom we are having a series of leadership training programs. From our side, there is not such heavy recurring expenses involved in hiring pastors. Our only expense is about $20 a month as an honorarium paid to Guruji Balarao to feed his horse. He is not even on our payroll; neither is his horse! Balarao and his men continue to be tentmaker evangelists and pastors spreading the movement to the neighboring villages and districts.

## 6. Opportunities and challenges

The need is enormous. Sometimes it is recognized, but often even unrecognized by the most spiritually needy. Many of these will never normally cross the path of a trained evangelist or a pastor.

Millions of people have never once heard the name of Christ. Millions more are totally ignorant concerning His person and His saving work. In many areas there is no church, no recognized Christian worker. But millions of needy, untouched people do meet ordinary Christian lay people in the course of their normal day-to-day people-contact, their travel, their dealings with health workers, teachers, agricultural trainers, government officials. All Christians need to be effectively mobilized for evangelization on a world basis.

Homes of believers—baptized or unbaptized—may become the focal points of nurture and of ministry, especially in regions where there is no church meeting place. Indeed, Priscilla and Aquila present a husband-wife open home model. How needful for world evangelization is the available Christian home, with the tentmaker host and hostess able to receive and counsel the present-day Apollos! Husband and wife complement each other as evangelists, Bible teachers, counselors, even church planters—without leaving their own four walls, or neglecting their family responsibilities. Perhaps we are guilty of neglecting the potential not only of the Christian laymen, but also of the other 50% of the church called lay-women! (Our previously considered scriptural model included twelve ladies to thirty-seven men. Quite a healthy sprinkling!)

The opportunities and challenges are extensive. By and large, the Third World countries are open for the preaching of the Gospel. The labor of thousands of missionaries from the West has met with great success, though not without opposition. Their contribution to the fields of education, industry, science and technology, social development, etc., is well recognized and has created a lasting impact on the society wherever they had been called to serve. Though there might have been apprehension about accepting their message, people could not resist the social and economic betterment that came through their way. Not all who heard the Gospel changed their religion, but the majority have to admit, if not verbally, that they are the beneficiaries of the missionary enterprise.

More than ever before, it has become obvious that evangelization cannot be done effectively and extensively just by the trained full-time evangelists alone. The time has come for the church leaders to rethink the pattern of the early church and engage lay people in the ministry while they are continuing their secular jobs. It is the responsibility of church leaders to encourage and create avenues for these tentmakers to serve the Lord wherever they may be. I am fully convinced that the work of evangelism is not the monopoly of the hierarchy of the church but the duty of every believer. The scriptural teaching of the priesthood of all believers must be understood and practiced in every church.

In some quarters there is an unnecessary fear on the part of the clergy concerning the promotion of lay-evangelism. There is a definite need for a proper understanding of Christian ministry by the clergy and the laity. William Kerr writes, "Without lay people involved in world evangelism the task will never be completed." One can see how this is true today, especially with mainland China opening up to Christian tentmakers. The tragedy is, the Church has the vision and the burden for evangelism, but has miserably failed to make use of the hidden talent lying within itself. The frozen asset of unused talents in the church must be released and exploited to the fullest extent.

### 7. *Problems to be counteracted*

Tentmakers do have certain problems. Some men who are in secular jobs, out of their earnest zeal for evangelism, involve themselves in evangelistic work and continue to function in both contexts effectively. At the same time, there are others who get into evangelism with wrong motivation. They consider tentmaking ministry a source of additional income! Such people in course of time are tempted to give up tentmaking and become full-time evangelists since they get enough support from the ministry. Sometimes ministry becomes an easy-going profession, with greater respect attached to it than to their old secular jobs.

On the other hand those who are in full-time ministry, for want of support, sometimes resort to tentmaking. These tend to lose their original zeal and direction because of their entanglement in secular jobs. Tentmakers by and large do not make ideal pastors/evangelists. Since they are employed elsewhere they cannot spend enough time with the people to get to know them and to minister to their needs.

Moreover, tentmakers are mostly untrained and hence considered inferior to the full-time ministers. Their teaching may not be so sound and systematic as that of a trained worker. The pastoral concept of most of the Eastern countries makes it hard for the tentmakers to command respect from the congregations as they are not full-time, trained, set apart for the ministry with a specific call like that of Aaron. This ethos must change. God has given different gifts to different people. All have some gifts, and no one has all the gifts. Therefore, everyone must utilize his gift in the total ministry of world evangelization. God has called some to be apostles, some evangelists, some pastors and teachers. Likewise there are elders and deacons in the church to take care of the various ministries of the church. This being the case, there is certainly no need for any superiority or inferiority complex: because as members of the body of Christ they all fulfill the Great Commission of our Lord.

Yet another problem of the tentmakers is this: as God blesses them and their ministry both spiritually and materially, there comes the subtle danger of losing their faith in their mother church. Gradually they drift away and go independent to start another church under some fanciful name. Such tentmakers no longer feel that they can still be part of the church and work with and under the existing leadership of the church. As they allow the desire for independence to grow stronger, a church split becomes inevitable. This creates strife and tensions among the congregation. With division, weakness sets in. The fervor for evangelism is lost.

It seems that at times God uses a split as a means to the furtherance of the Gospel. For example, when there was difference of opinion between Paul and Barnabas with regard to taking John Mark in the missionary journey they could not help parting ways. But the Gospel went forth in two different directions. However, I don't believe that this is the pattern for every-day ministry. A tentmaker should not start a new group just for the sake of starting one. Unless God gives him a definite leading, he should not venture to divide a church. The motivation for starting a new group must be pure and honest. It is very essential that tentmakers always maintain their membership with a particular local church and establish credibility with all other churches. In other words, tentmakers must be churchmen.

### 8. *What Amsterdam 86 can do*

We are privileged to participate in the historic Amsterdam 86—said to be the biggest ever in the annals of the Church. Besides learning new methods in evolving strategies, refining of skills and sharpening of tools in evangelistic efforts, God has bestowed upon us abundant spiritual blessings through His dear servants. Many of us have been really moved in our spirit emotionally, and feel that we can hardly wait till the end of the conference but would like to go back right away to be on the Master's business. I thank God for the challenge we have received. But the question is—is that enough?

We have already considered the advantages of tentmaking evangelism and have identified certain problems connected with it. Opportunities and challenges have also been brought to light. It is time we chalked out a clear-cut strategy and suitable plan for tentmaking evangelism. As we have already said, the harvest is plentiful but the laborers are few. As we pray for the Lord of the harvest to send more laborers, we need to be ready to train and equip them to become tentmakers. I suggest the following for consideration.

a. *Set up tentmaking training centers.* These centers have a two-fold purpose. First, they provide training for those who are unemployed but have a desire to preach the Gospel. These centers must recruit such unemployed persons and train them in a trade of their choice.

In this way we not only take care of the unemployment problems but also produce tentmaking evangelists. Second, invite the evangelists who do not get enough financial support to these centers and train them in productive trades, so that they will be able to make some extra money for their livelihood. By doing this, we could relieve the evangelists of their financial burden to a great extent, thus helping them to preach the Gospel boldly and with their chins up. Here I would like to mention a very viable program in this respect conducted by my good friend Dr. Vijayam of Hyderabad, India. His program is known as "Training for Evangelism Needs Technology" (TENT) with a list of trades which can be adopted by the tentmakers.

b. *Set up a revolving fund.* Many Third-World evangelists suffer from lack of financial support. They do not have the means even to join a trade training center.

Therefore, it would be helpful if Amsterdam 86 would set up a revolving fund in various countries to be used to help such evangelists to start their own tentmaking trades, such as bakery, secretarial work, radio and watch repairing, making of pickles, toy making, fish breeding, poultry farming, lace work, carpentry, and dairy. These trades could be started with a small investment but would bring a steady income to the evangelists. Some of the evangelists may already know the skills needed in some of the trades, but be unable to use their skills in a tentmaking sense on account of lack of finances to establish the project. The evangelists could draw enough money from this revolving fund to start the trades of their choice, and repay the capital by installments. The fund could then be made available to other evangelists to help start their tentmaking. "Farms-India" is a small-scale agricultural project already experimenting along these lines.

   c. *Organize fellowship meetings.* Organize such meetings for tentmaking evangelists at regional and national levels according to the convenience of the tentmakers. Valuable suggestions and experiences could be shared and learned in these meetings, and tentmaker evangelists encouraged by one another to pursue this approach and to help others get involved in this type of ministry.

   d. *Introducing tentmaking in seminaries.* Negotiate with the existing Bible seminaries and institutions which are majoring only on the imparting of theological studies, to explore the possibilities of offering courses on tentmaking side by side. This would certainly help the graduates go out with great confidence to face the world.

   e. *Popularize tentmaking evangelism as widely as possible.* Produce literature on tentmaking evangelism to remove wrong notions about tentmaking. We need to educate our members that tentmaking evangelism is not sinful or inferior; it is not something new but it is as old as Adam, practiced by the men and women of the Bible and by the saints of God down the centuries.

   Let us honor the tentmakers. Let tentmaking evangelism flourish. Let us make the task of evangelizing the world simpler and less expensive by producing numerous tentmakers—the twentieth century Pauls, Aquilas and Priscillas, Careys, and Balaraos.

# THE EVANGELIST IN HOSPITAL EVANGELISM
*Francis Grim*

Hospital evangelism is one of the most important—if not *the* most important—methods of evangelism, for the following reasons:

1.  More people pass through the hospitals of the world each year than through the churches. While in hospital they are usually more receptive to the Gospel message than when they are healthy, self-assured, and prospering. Here they are conscious of their need of a Comforter and a Savior.

2.  Our Lord Jesus Christ devoted a large proportion of the three-and-a-half years of His public ministry to the sick. "Follow me," He commanded. "As my Father has sent me, even so send I you."

3.  Whereas churches are closed and public preaching silenced in countries where a tyrannizing ideology or religion dominates, hospitals are seldom closed.

To do hospital evangelism in a competent manner does not require great learning, but certainly great love and gentleness are essential. The problem of suffering has bewildered and distressed mankind throughout the ages. You will confront men and women who are not only face to face with this mystery, but who tangibly experience its discomfort. Remember that the shadow of death rests upon some of them and that the hospital may be their last stop before eternity. According to the Bible they will spend this unending period either in Heaven or in Hell. Your task requires all the compassion, concern and solicitude possible. Ask God to give you His own love for the lost (unbelievers). Try to discover their deep needs, especially the spiritual ones. Develop the art of making good human contact—eyes, voice, touch, etc.

A terminal cancer patient nervously asked a doctor: "Please tell me, am I going to die?" Quietly and deliberately he replied, "Can you tell me of anyone who is not going to die? I am well and you are ill—but it may be that I will die before you. The question is not, 'When will I die?' but, 'Where will I go when I die?'" This provided an excellent opportunity to explain the way of salvation and the atoning work of Christ.

## Practical Proposals

Because evangelism in hospitals is so significant and sensitive and can produce such a considerable harvest, it is most important that it be carried out in an effective manner. The following are some practical recommendations:

Go prayerfully and carefully. The people you are about to visit have been weakened by illness and pain. To a greater or lesser degree they are afraid and anxious. You are required to be both serious and yet cheerfully hopeful. Tenderness of spirit must characterize your bearing. Do not go till you have prayed earnestly, thoughtfully, and compassionately. "Blood and thunder, fire and brimstone" preaching will be out of order on this occasion.

All healing institutions, whether they are large or small, have certain rules which govern them. Acquaint yourself with these and abide by them. You are not about to enter a church or an evangelistic hall, but a place far different and whose function aims to provide physical or mental healing for patients.

Those in control of hospitals are sometimes strongly opposed to evangelism being carried on in their institutions. Perhaps in the past they have had unfortunate and unpleasant experiences with unwise or over-zealous evangelists, or may even consider your visit as an unwelcome intrusion into the lives and treatment of those committed to their care. As a wise visitor, however, you may become a valuable member of the healing team that surrounds the patient.

Always ask for permission to see the patient if your visit is out of visiting hours; do not interrupt ward routine. Patients should not be visited just after surgery and during a doctor's ward round. Introduce yourself to the person in charge of the ward (station) and say you have permission from the director/manager/matron. Ask her whether she knows of patients who do not have visitors and tell her whom you plan to visit.

*Important do's and don'ts.*

- Unless you are already known to the patient, introduce yourself and explain that you are from a certain church/organization and so put him or her at ease.
- Ask for the patient's name—and use it.
- Begin by asking casual questions: "How are you?" "How long have you been in hospital?"
- Sit down while talking—it is easier for them to see you at their own level and indicates that you are not in a hurry.
- Never sit on the bed—especially if the patient is in pain.
- Don't stay too long; avoid looking around at other patients or paging through magazines. Give your undivided attention to the one you are visiting.
- Bring the conversation round to the spiritual as soon as possible. Trust the Lord to lead you.
- Talk about fear, depression, anxiety, and the Bible's answers to these.
- Observe whether there is a Bible or Christian book, ash tray and cigarettes, or rosary on the locker.
- Always speak kindly and gently—never too loudly.
- Never argue to prove your point.
- Patients do not require sermons—just simple facts. Use "Four Steps to God" by the International Hospital Christian Fellowship.
- Always speak about the person of Jesus Christ.
- Keep to the great and fundamental truths of salvation.
- Be patient if they do not understand.
- Remember that the person you visit probably has more than physical illness.
- Be willing to be an attentive listener. Share your own experience and give the patient the opportunity to share his. Help him to understand how God often allows physical illness to bring spiritual blessing.
- Aim to speak to the patient alone and be careful not to embarrass him if someone else is present.
- Avoid being too personal and the "if you die" approach. Rather speak of eternal life.
- Be respectful.
- The very ill patients need shorter and more frequent visits.
- Pray in a sensitive way. When you pray for physical healing and pray for the soul of the patient, include a request for divine blessing on all the treatment being given.
- Do not talk to others about what the patient has shared with you in confidence.
- Offer practical help, for example to deliver a message, make a phone call, etc. Be extremely sensitive to the patient's needs.
- Be available. Leave a phone number or address.
- Be faithful in visiting. The patient will eventually look forward to your coming.
- Be prepared, after you have led patients to Christ, to follow them up by encouragement, teaching and edification.

- Encourage Christian patients to keep on trusting the Lord and to seek for a deeper relationship with Him.
- Spend much time in personal prayer for them, and ask the Lord to give you the right words "in season" for each particular patient.
- Include the staff in your ministrations. Remember they spend most of their time with the patients. Some may be Christians; get to know them.. They too can help the patient spiritually. Aim to make them your collaborators and an extension of your evangelism. In countries where hospital evangelism is not permitted, seek to train the hospital staff in evangelism, prayer, and discipleship.

*Singing groups and ward services*

Hospital evangelism may be done by singing groups (confine the number to seven persons) from churches. When permitted, they could include a brief message, personal talks with the patients, and the distribution of suitable booklets. Singing groups are especially welcome at Christmastime and Easter.

*Your message*

Simply stated, the Gospel message is that we are all sinners and deserve eternal punishment. But God so loved us that He sent His only Son to bear our guilt on Calvary's Cross. Encourage the patient to ask for forgiveness and believe that God grants it for Christ's sake. Keep the message simple and clear. Witness to what God has done for you personally—that you are not simply a professional Christian worker, but that you have yourself experienced what you are talking about.

Learn when and how to ask the most important question—"Would you like to open your heart and receive Jesus as your Savior?"

Offer to pray *with* them—especially the very ill patients—to help them to verbalize a prayer with you. "Even unconscious (comatose) patients can be led to Christ by praying with them, even if they themselves cannot respond verbally," says Professor Gerry Landry, former associate professor in Internal Medicine. Look for any response they may give—a move of the hand, or eyelid, or head. Use Scripture as much as possible, for though the mind may be inactive, the spirit can respond to the Word (Hebrews 4:12).

*Arguments against hospital evangelism*

Many and varied are the arguments raised against Hospital Evangelism. Be encouraged though, that your Lord Himself freely dispensed the Gospel message while He healed the physical diseases of men and women. The case of the paralyzed man who was let down through the broken-open roof at Capernaum is a good example. The Lord Jesus first forgave his sins and then He healed his body.

Hospital evangelism is sometimes opposed on the assumption—

1. That we are taking advantage of a person's weakness to constrain him to believe what he would not fully accept when sound in body and mind. The answer to this is that we are, in fact, bringing comfort and a message of hope, peace, and love which can only have a positive and healing effect. Salvation brings calm and immense joy. Also, we are commissioned to preach the Gospel to every creature. God often uses a sick-bed to arrest a person's careless and headlong dash toward a Christless eternity. Many are in hospital due to sinful living. Look upon every patient as someone in whom the Lord is expressing a particular interest. When sickness strikes, backsliders, too, are frequently brought to realize that they have strayed from the Lord.
2. That we make patients nervous when we speak to them about religion, since it gives them the impression they are about to die. Actually many people who are

laid aside by sickness come under a severe and depressing sense of guilt, and are only too glad to be able to speak to someone who can help them find relief. "I was brought low, and He helped me," wrote the Psalmist (Psalm 116:6). In reality, we are not bringing "religion" to the patients, but are telling them about Jesus Christ, whose kindness and help to the sick and suffering is acknowledged by Christians and non-Christians alike.

*The use of literature*

Patients.often have time to read, and a well-selected book or booklet could be of lasting value to them. Remember they are in hospital because they are unwell and consequently not able to give their full quota of concentration to whatever they may read.

A "heavy" book—whether it is so physically or in its content matter—is not the best choice. A paperback or tract with large print and containing a message to cheer and enlighten the patient would be the most acceptable. Some tracts and books which are calculated to arouse, shock, awaken, and thus bless an unbeliever when he is well, could prove to be detrimental when he is in hospital. Attractively printed booklets containing Scripture portions such as those published by the Bible Societies and the Scripture Gift Mission are often very acceptable to patients. These are obtainable in many languages.

*Conclusion and summary*

Do not look upon hospital evangelism as of secondary value in your ministry. The New Testament records several instances of private and personal interviews the Lord Jesus and His apostles held with individuals. These meetings had important and far-reaching results and are recounted for our encouragement and enlightenment. God's love for the sick is your guarantee that He will enable you to reach them.

May the Lord anoint and use you in this vital service!

# TEACHING AND TRAINING LAY EVANGELISTS
*Gideon Mahlanthini Makhanya*

*Text: 2 Timothy 4:5b*

My task in this brief workshop is to simply state the undebatable fact that to "do the work of an evangelist" is to do the work between apostles and prophets, or pastor-teachers. This is not a job needing the gift of the Spirit. Timothy had been trained in doing this kind of work by the apostle Paul and was, naturally, expected to perform it and, in doing so, train others also—2 Timothy 2:2: "And the things that thou hast heard of me among many witnesses, the same commit thou to faithful men, who shall be able to teach others also."

If the term "do the work of an evangelist" was used to Timothy who may have had no prominent gift of evangelism, then the instruction is aimed at all other Christian workers. To the individual this means more than just preaching; more than living a life-style fit for Christians; more than embodying the ("Evangel") good news. It means living the Gospel, not just so that sinners can see Christ in and through you, but so that new believers can learn through your evangelistic example the way to follow the same life-style!

To make this clearer and simpler, let me borrow Dr. D. James Kennedy's language—"It is even more important to equip a trainer than merely to win one soul." He goes on to say, "It is even more important to equip a trainer of soul winners than merely to train a soul winner." To "do the work of an evangelist" is to proclaim the good news to unbelievers in front of new Christians so that they themselves may learn how to share the Gospel effectively.

1. *The principles of teaching and training lay evangelists*
    When Jesus Christ was on this earth He modeled and inaugurated principles for evangelism for which no replacement or supplement has, or ever will be, found. Let us give these principles a name at this workshop. Let us call them "The Ten Commandments for Teaching and Training Lay Evangelists." They are:
    a. *Invitation.* Jesus invited men to learn from Him how to evangelize the world—"Come and see" (John 1:39). The lay evangelist can best be taught through the example of his teacher. Knowing Jesus' willingness to accommodate learners into His private and public life, the first disciples invited others to join them. At the end of it all John could say: "That which was from the beginning, which we have heard, which we have seen with our eyes, which we have looked upon, and our hands have handled, of the Word of life. . . . That which we have seen and heard declare we unto you, that ye also may have fellowship with us . . ." (1 John 1:1, 3).
    *Exercise:*
    (i)    How many times does "see" and its synonyms appear in this text?
    (ii)    What are your impressions of this text?
    (iii)    Would the principle of Christ's invitation be practical and transformable to your ministry?
    (iv)    What would be your plan of action to implement this major principle in your ministry?
    b. *Association.* Jesus, having invited His men to see His home and witness His life, employed the best possible means of training. He walked with them daily and taught by example. Yet this is the weakest corner in the structure of the modern

Christian church. I believe the program and structure of today's organized church is the reason for so few baptisms in our time. Jesus did not need highly scholastic books and curricula to train evangelists—*He* was, *He* is and *He* will always remain the curriculum for the building of His church: "Upon this rock I will build my church and the gates of hell shall not prevail against it" (Matthew 16:18). And Christ's association with mankind didn't end on the day of the Ascension. No! Remember the words, "Lo, I am with you always, even unto the end of the world." And, furthermore, people can recognize those who have an association with the living Christ: "Now when they saw the boldness of Peter and John, and perceived that they were unlearned and ignorant men, they marvelled; and they took knowledge of them, that they had been with Jesus" (Acts 4:13).

*Exercise:*

(i)   What could stop people being critical of our ministry? (Acts 4:10-14)

(ii)   Do you see your ministry influencing people associated with you? Your wife? Your children? Your co-workers? If you answer "No" to these, seek help from someone.

c.   *Instruction.* Jesus' method of instruction has not been, and never will be, equaled by the modern world. His was the Rolls Royce of education. As Ray Rozell says, "There is no teaching where there is no learning." "I have glorified thee on the earth: I have finished the work which thou gavest me to do. . . . For I have given unto them the words which thou gavest me; and they have RECEIVED them, and have known surely that I came out from thee, and they have believed that thou didst send me (John 17:4, 8). If we would study the methods Christ used to instruct His lay evangelists, we would want to imitate Him. By studying the life of Jesus we can see clearly that His methods are the best ever!

*Exercise:*

Below are listed some of the methods Jesus used. Would they be applicable to your ministry?

(i)   Lecture method: Matthew 5:2

(ii)   Answer questions method: Matthew 9:14-17

(iii)   Summarize and enrich method: Matthew 15:10-20, Matthew 18:1-14

(iv)   Story method: Luke 10:29-37

(v)   Discussion method: Matthew 16:13-20

(vi)   Visual method: Matthew 6:28

(vii)   Project method: Matthew 10:5-11.

d.   *Demonstration.* The youth of this era are said to be saying to the older generation, "What you do makes so much noise, we can hardly hear what you are saying!" In Acts 1:1 we read, "The former treatise have I made, O Theophilus, of all that Jesus began both to *do* and *teach.*" How practical is this part of our life's sermon to our audience? "For Ezra had prepared his heart to seek the law of the Lord, and to do it, and to *teach* in Israel statutes and judgements " (Ezra 7:10). Jesus gave His pupils many good examples, e.g., the knowledge of the Scriptures as was seen in His life and His speech. He, therefore, challenged His hearers to do likewise: "If ye abide in me, and my words abide in you, ye shall ask what ye will, and it shall be done unto you " (John 15:7). A further example is His soul-winning and the way He expected His disciples to handle the problems of seekers. The disciples in John 4 saw Jesus winning a soul which *immediately* blossomed into a glowing witness.

*Exercise:*

From this example, what do you visualize (dream of) for your own local ministry?

e. *Consecration.* Discipling/teaching and training is not a cheap involvement and the would-be disciple must not be given false hope, i.e., being told, "Just join our group, and you will have everything going for you." This is a deceitful way of recruiting disciples, and a dangerous way. When the Master clarified the cost of discipleship He said, "Foxes have holes, and the birds of the air have nests; but the Son of man hath no where to lay His head." And to the one already involved, He explained that once you start on the discipleship road there is no turning back, "Follow me; and let the dead bury their dead" (Matthew 8:20,22). Jesus demanded "No servant can serve two masters; for either he will hate the one and love the other; or else he will hold to one and despise the other. Ye cannot serve God and mammon" (Luke 16:13). This was strong teaching and not many could take it. Actually, when Jesus had made the point clear concerning His ministry and the Kingdom of God, many turned away from following Him (John 6:25-66). Their exact words were John 6:60, "This is a hard saying: who can hear it?" And Jesus did not go on His knees to beg them to increase His membership roll! Training and teaching lay evangelists needs similar character.

*Exercise*

What do you think is the best method to use for the selection and assuring dedication of the would-be trainees in lay evangelism?

f. *Explanation.* Jesus' method of teaching and training lay evangelists wasn't complicated, yet He took pains to explain how the lay evangelists were to go about His work:

Power: the Holy Spirit was fully explained to the disciples

(i)    As the agent of new birth (John 3:3-9)

(ii)    As the agent of growth (John 4:14; 7:38,39)

(iii)    As the agent of service (John 15:3, 17:17; cf. Ephesians 5:26)

(iv)    As the agent of evangelism (Luke 4:18; Matthew 12:28)

(v)    As the agent of communication (Matthew 10:19,20; Mark 13:11; Luke 12:12)

(vi)    As the agent of conviction to sinners (John 16:9)

(vii)    As the agent of illumination to sinners (John 16:14)

(viii)    As the agent of miracles to the evangelist (John 14:12; cf. Hebrews 2:3,4)

Jesus also explained the content and intent of the message. Let us together study Matthew chapter 10 and observe the order in which the Master wanted the evangelization of the world done:

Verse 1: "He gave them power"

Verse 5: "Sent them to church goers/religious"—a very important principle. Never give your first-time students a tough first-time experience—they may be put off forever.

Verse 7: "As ye go, preach, saying, 'The Kingdom of Heaven is at hand'." Note carefully, Jesus was very explicit and clear as to the manner in which the Gospel was to be preached. "As they went ". . . in their ordinary day-to-day life, as they do . . . in their unprofessional life-style. Also evident was the Good News that God's Kingdom is at hand! What else does our world, whether First or Third, need to hear better than that God's Kingdom is at hand?—an old phrase relevant today in the space age! Not only did Jesus instruct the people to go and preach, He actually verbalized the message.

Verse 8: The most important principle lost in the carrying out of the Great Commission; the principle we from Third World countries cannot afford to be without in our ministries—"Heal the sick." Any Gospel that is preached without bringing healing to both soul and body is done in disobedience to the Holy Spirit. If we would only give God the Holy Spirit a chance to convict the world of sin by proclamation, equally so we should give God the Holy Spirit the opportunity to deliver the world from sickness of all kind. "How shall we escape, if we neglect so great [a] salvation; which at first began to be spoken by the Lord, and was confirmed unto us by them that heard Him; God also bearing them witness, both with signs and wonders, and with diverse miracles, and gifts of the Holy Ghost, according to His own will?" (Hebrews 2:3,4). This two-verse sentence to me passes judgment on us who claim to be doing the work of an evangelist, if we only care to do the work halfway.

Verses 9,10: "For the workman is worthy of his meat." These words summarize the end results of evangelism. Their witness had to be so obvious that it would be recognized by the people they were preaching to—who knew their responsibility to priests according to Old Testament Law.

Verses 11 and 13: "And if the house is worthy." Here Jesus is telling you to select your target. Don't shoot wildly—don't waste ammunition.

Verse 12: "Salute." They were to use a natural way of approach.

Verses 13-20: "But beware of men . . ." Jesus warned them about the hardness of man, and prepared His students for it, ensuring that His disciples were shockproof.

If this is the pattern of teaching/explaining evangelization used by Jesus, what better can we use than this?

g. *Supervision.* If Jesus wanted to do the work by remote control, He would not have come to the world. Since His principle was that of using man to save man, He made sure that He supervised the work. It is commonly reported in our modern world that people don't do what they are expected to do, but what they know is going to be inspected. This was true of Jesus. "And the apostles gathered themselves together unto Jesus, and told Him all things, both what they had *done* and what they had *taught*" (Mark 6:30; Luke 9:10).

*Exercise:*
Evaluate your ministry against this principle.

h. *Mobilization.* Jesus gave His lay evangelists a chance to test His principles. We may say He gave them exercises. Jesus taught about what He expected to be done—His lessons were practical. Another good example is when He sent the seventy (Luke 10:1). Like a mighty army He mobilized His lay evangelists. Thus, the early church could be as dynamic as it was. Peter the great revivalist had to explain and follow lay evangelists on the day of Pentecost who were mobilized by the Holy Spirit. "We do hear them speak in our tongues the wonderful *works* of *God*" (Acts 2:11).

*Exercise:*
Visualize lay evangelists going before your crusade/campaign.

i. *Examination.* When the disciples had learned the work of an evangelist, they always brought their homework to Jesus for evaluation and examination. There are a good number of such examples which would make an excellent study (e.g., Matthew 17:14-21; Mark 4:38-41; Luke 9:13,14; Matthew 14:25-31).

j. *Delegation.* The apostles were being constantly reminded that they were going to assume full responsibility for the evangelization of their world. Jesus, therefore, kept a constant practice of delegating tasks to them. In Matthew 10:40 Jesus made it very clear that His method of delegation was somehow different to the systems of man: "He that receiveth you receiveth me, and he that receiveth me receiveth Him that sent me." John 13:20 puts it a little stronger: "Verily, verily, I say unto you, He that receiveth whomsoever I send receiveth me, and he that receiveth me receiveth him that sent me." As far as Jesus was concerned His disciples were going to be His ambassadors and representatives.

In John 20:21 Jesus makes the authority of His delegation even stronger by completely vesting the same authority the Father gave Him onto the apostles, "Peace be unto you: as the Father hath sent me, even so send I you." My temptation at this point is to belabor the Great Commission (Matthew 28:18-20). I am so sorry that this has become the great omission instead of the Great Commission!

Jesus made sure that this delegation message was clear and as He was about to ascend back into Heaven He repeated the injunction in Luke 24:47,48: "And that repentance and remission of sins should be preached in His name among all nations, beginning at Jerusalem. And ye are witnesses of these things." I am so glad that I can testify to the fact that I have seen many come to know the saving power of Jesus in my lifetime and through my testimony to what He has done for me. I have been involved with two great movements in my ministry whose aims are closest to the Great Commission. These are "Go Teach Ministries" whose theme is "His Last Command is Our First Concern," and "Evangelism Explosion III" whose slogan is "It is even more important to equip a trainer of soul winners than merely to train a soul winner."

*Exercise:*
(i)     Are you delegated to "Go Make Disciples"?
(ii)    How do you make disciples?

## 2.    *The potential of lay evangelists in evangelism*

The next question that has to be asked is surely, "Why should we teach and train lay evangelists?" We realize that Jesus made it His aim to use men to reach men. As John puts it in words immortal, "And the Word was made flesh and dwelt among us (and we beheld His glory, the glory as of the only begotten of the Father) full of grace and truth." God, the greatest soul winner of all time, came among us in our human form so that we can see that it takes a life of God embodied in human flesh and environment to set free those that are bound in sin. Therefore, the first potential of enlisting lay evangelists in evangelism is that God saw man as the only form of example to solve man's plight. Man was to live among man a godly life, and thus prove to the lost that it is possible to live a heavenly life on earth.

The second reason why lay evangelists are a potential is that they live and work with the lost. They speak the same language of the lost. Day and night they rub shoulders with the lost. The lay evangelists are found among all classes of our society. Thus they have more contact with the lost world.

The third reason is that the lay evangelists have the same struggles and background as the man in the street, and their testimony is relevant to the man in the street. This point is illustrated in the selection of the disciples, their contrasting backgrounds and characters.

Dr. D. James Kennedy has a valuable statement about the potential of lay evangelists in his book *Evangelism Explosion* under the heading "Let the Generals Fight the War." "Right away we say, 'That is ridiculous! Such a ludicrous idea could never be put over on any people.' Yet in the church this, in essence, is exactly what Satan has done! I am certain that for the vast majority of Christian church members the idea firmly taken root in their minds is that it is primarily the task of the minister to fight the battles of Christ—especially for the souls of men. In the minds of most, the work of evangelism is the work of professionally trained men. 'After all,' they say, 'I'm just a butcher, or baker, or candlestick maker, and what do I know about theology? I've never been to seminary; leave it to the trained ecclesiastical generals!'" This, I believe, has been the greatest tragedy that has befallen the Church of Jesus Christ. Its results are so far-reaching, so vast in scope, that we have little concept of what damage has been done. But it wasn't this way in the early church! This is how the Church of Jesus Christ in 300 years accomplished the most amazing results. The whole pagan Roman Empire was undercut and overthrown by the power of the Gospel of Jesus Christ which, on the lips of Christ-conquered disciples, crossed seas and deserts, pierced the darkest jungles, seeped into every city and town, and finally into the senate and the throne. How? Because everyone was evangelizing.

The Christian Church was burgeoning with such rapidity that by the middle of the second century one of the great apologists could say, "We are everywhere. We are in your towns and in your cities; we are in your country; we are in your army and navy; we are in your palaces; we are in the senate; we are more numerous than anyone." Constantine knew very well that he had no chance of unifying the Roman Empire or holding power in that empire without the help of the Christians.

3. *Problems of teaching and training lay evangelists*

The number one problem is the underrated excitement of the Good News of Jesus Christ. If all Christians were as excited about this Gospel of grace as the early church, our world would have been covered by a generation of new creatures. This enthusiasm would outweigh the lack of a vision of a perishing world. We would not be preaching the Gospel as a hell solution only. While burdened by the fact of the awesome results of unbelief, we will be motivated by what God has done, and is doing, through Christ. We have a small vision of so great a salvation.

The second problem is the unfortunate misunderstanding of the role of ministers in teaching and training lay evangelists and the equipping of the saints for the work of the ministry (Ephesians 4:11,12). Are we aware of the fact that over ninety-nine percent of the Church is made up of lay evangelists who are spectating less than one percent ministers, many of whom are not involved in evangelism?

The third problem is the inbuilt resistance of the professional clerics to train lay evangelists for the ministry for fear of loss of status. The other fear is not having a clear-cut message. Many Christians I have discipled have a similar testimony, namely, that they don't know what to say to unbelievers. As soon as lay evangelists have a concise message to share with the hungry world they go and tell! The last excuse is sheer laziness! Evangelism is a process and we are instructed to make disciples and not decisions. This, then, involves begetting children, bringing them up and nurturing them into the family of God and teaching and training them to "commit to faithful men, who shall be able to teach others also" (2 Timothy 2:2).

4. *Proposals for teaching and training lay evangelists*

a. *Books.* The book I found most useful is the unchangeable Holy Bible. Study the life and ministry of our Lord Jesus Christ. Other books recommended include D. James Kennedy, *Evangelism Explosion;* Robert E. Coleman, *The Master Plan of Evangelism,* and *The Heartbeat of Evangelism;* and Stephen F. Olford, *The Secret of Soul Winning.*

There are many more books on this subject, but these could make a good start and I have found them helpful in my own ministry.

b. *Programs.* There are a number of good programs on the market today. Allow me to be selfish and suggest one, and give my reasons for recommending it: *Evangelism Explosion III International.* This ministry has been very helpful to me as I have ministered in Soweto, Johannesburg, these past two years. God called me to a church, known in the denomination as a spiritual mortuary. The known membership was 100, of whom ten were regular at Sunday worship. These ten never prayed, never studied the Bible, never confessed Christ, and gave little thought to what church work they could do.

After attending an EE III clinic, I started doing what the Bible teaches: to "do the work of an evangelist." First of all, I taught and trained my wife and two leaders for a period of seventeen weeks, and during this time the number of believers increased from 30 to 100 committed members. These three trained evangelists each trained two others and during this training term our membership became so big that we had to extend our church building by demolishing the vestries. When the third group of lay evangelists was being trained we had an average weekly church attendance of 450 people, young and old. I thought, "This is it!" From there, we started to invite other pastors to our church to be trained, and I am pleased to report that 107 pastors have been trained at that church.

I am proud to say that I have now been released to go around Africa to share how it can be done. God has enabled me to be instrumental in producing "The Condensed Version of the Evangelism Explosion," a simple teaching method employing the use of a blackboard. Having attended an EE III clinic, the pastor is instructed in this method, which doesn't call for expensive materials, complex administration, and great literary skills.

Lay evangelists needn't be educated or rich; they needn't possess great administration skills or be able to master complicated methods; they need only have the desire and be willing to spread the Good News. The pastor needs nothing other than a set of basic clinic notes and a blackboard, plus dedicated disciples. With this Condensed Version the student is not asked to write an examination; the pastor need only know that his disciple is a discipler.

# MANAGEMENT SKILLS FOR THE EVANGELIST
*Lloyd Olson*

Your ministry as an itinerant evangelist will grow as you learn the skills of management and use them in your work. It is a wonderful thing to realize that you have been given a very special spiritual gift from our wonderful Lord. The gift of evangelism is a wonderful gift.

You, as evangelists, are often called "natural leaders." You, in the situations in which you are exercising your gift of evangelism, are able to gather around you others who share your vision for reaching people for Jesus Christ and your enthusiasm for this most important work.

We also call you entrepreneurs. You are the pioneers. You are the ones who go forth into the territory of the enemy. You are on the front lines. You are at your best when you are presenting the Gospel of Jesus Christ to people who are lost and destined for an eternity apart from Jesus Christ.

## 1. *What is leadership?*

For years, people have worked on defining who is "a leader." Are leaders born or made? Do they have some specific attributes? These questions have been debated for years and we have little to offer on the subject. Leaders operate in many different ways. They have many different personalities. Some are loud. Others are quiet. Some are big. Others are small. About the best that has been done in defining the term is: "Leaders are people who have followers in a given situation." There are people who will follow you, but in almost every case they will follow you only in some situations.

If we think for a moment, we can see how true this is. How often we discuss the fact that you are a well-known leader as an evangelist; but you often have little to say about what goes on in the home, or in other situations.

## 2. *Leaders need to become managers*

Your leadership ability is restricted to various situations. You have probably found that while you are using your gift of evangelism, you have great leadership power. What may happen is that as you work in other situations, you will see that that same dynamic does not exist.

As your ministry grows and develops, you begin to have new situations in which you have difficulty leading. You are not always sharing the Gospel with others. You find it necessary to make arrangements, or to counsel others. It is part of your work to write letters and articles. It is necessary for you to arrange programs. It is sometimes difficult for you to get others to help with your evangelistic meetings. You sometimes wonder why there are not more people at your meetings and services. Perhaps in doing administrative work or counseling you notice that you seem to be less effective. What we begin to see is that your spiritual gift of evangelism may not allow you to be the best manager of your time and ministry.

In addition to your spiritual gift of evangelism, you need to learn some management skills. Another way of saying this is that the gift of evangelism and your use of that gift tend to happen naturally. The Holy Spirit seems to give you maximum results with minimum effort. You may have had little training in being an evangelist. It is a gift to you.

By contrast, managers are trained. Management is a profession. It has specific skills which it uses, skills which can be explained and learned. In order for you to grow and to have your gift of evangelism be used to reach more and more people for Him, you need to learn these management skills, or find those people who have them.

Dr. Billy Graham is a good example. We all know that he has the gift of evangelism. Most of you identify with him in this special gift. God has given him a world-wide impact. We are all here as a result of his special gift, *and* the management skills necessary to maximize his effectiveness. It is my prayer that you will gain knowledge here about management skills. It is my prayer that you will go back to your country and learn and practice the necessary skills of management to allow your ministry to be greatly increased in the days ahead.

We all know that it is not the gift of evangelism that made this conference possible for us. There has been an incredible use of other gifts and management skills to bring this conference about. The planning for this conference began in 1983. The organization to make it happen has been developed since that time, as well. Dr. Graham, Dr. Smyth, and the Reverend Werner Burklin have been providing leadership to the hundreds and thousands of people who are working here to serve you. All of this work has been controlled by various standards, dates, and budgets. We can say that Dr. Billy Graham knows how to find people with the necessary management skills to serve him. Among them is Mr. George Wilson, executive vice-president of the Billy Graham Evangelistic Association, who has the spiritual gift of administration.

3.  *What are these management skills?*

There are many ways to look at management skills. They seem to fit into four categories. There are various other ways of summarizing the work of management, but we will use a four-function definition of the work of management: planning, organizing, leading, and controlling.

In each of these functions we find natural leaders. There are some people who do well in planning. There are others, such as those who like to work with people, who are very good at organizing. There are people who like to work in a step-by-step way, who are naturally skilled in the controlling function. Probably most natural leaders are those who enjoy leading. It is quite likely that many of you do your best work through leading. Many of the natural skills that you possess are probably within the function of leading. Yet, not all of the management work of leading may be easy for you.

For example, you may be very good at communicating and motivating people. You may be good at developing people. Yet you might not do as well in selecting people to work with you. Or you might prefer not to make decisions. All of these— communicating, motivating people, selecting people, developing people, and decision making—are activities within the management function of leading.

4.  *Management is work*

When you are planning, organizing, leading, or controlling, you are "managing." This contrasts with your doing the work of preaching or teaching. These are your "doing" work. We use this word "doing" as a contrast to "managing" in order to have you become more aware when you are using management skills.

For example, if you write a list of things that need to be done to make arrangements for a meeting, you are "managing." When you go and visit someone, make a call, or telephone ahead to "do" some of the things on your list, you are "doing." It is important to know when you are *doing* and when you are *managing*.

5. *A definition of management*

A good definition for our purpose is "Managing is getting things done through other people."

Managing is *not* doing everything yourself. That is not to suggest that you should never do things yourself. But when you are doing things yourself, you are not getting them done through other people; therefore, you are not managing. Most of you find that you do some managing work, and you do some things yourselves. It is very important to understand the difference.

You may be breaking out in a cold sweat at the thought that you are a manager. You fear that this will keep you from having personal relationships with people and that you will just sit behind your desk. If you want to be good at your job of managing, you cannot let that happen. You must be an example to the people who are doing work for you. Often you must show them how to do things they are to do. You must learn how to work well with people, because you are responsible to get things done *through people*.

Another fear you may have is that you will be sitting around in meetings trying to agree on things. But remember, a manager is responsible for *getting things done*. He must be dynamic, willing to get out and lead his people, if that is needed. Do you think Jesus would have gone to Jerusalem that final time before His death if He had relied on the disciples to make up His mind for Him? No. He had to lead them.

6. *A brief summary*

First, we have seen that your spiritual gift of evangelism does not necessarily allow your ministry to grow.

Second, we have seen the need for us to learn and use management skills, and to have people do more of the work.

Third, we have heard that "managing is getting things done through other people."

Fourth, we have begun to look at some of the activities of management: planning, organizing, leading, and controlling.

In order for us to grow and serve our Lord better, we need to learn management skills.

# RELIEF AND DEVELOPMENT IN EVANGELISM
*Jun Vencer*

1. *A marriage relationship*

The inclusion of this topic in ICIE 86 is a welcome and significant contribution to the urgent task of world evangelization. As in the Lausanne Covenant, it is "the whole gospel to the whole man." Our total mandate, Dr. Graham says, "encompasses every effort to declare the good news" to all mankind.

The open recognition of the dual mandate of evangelism and social responsibility will result in a more responsive Gospel to the needs of a suffering world. We begin with a general framework on the relationship between the two. The Consultation at Grand Rapids on the Relationship of Evangelism and Social Responsibility gives us three basic relationships.

a. *Social concern is the consequence of evangelism.* The reality of God's love in us enables us to act out in compassion. Our faith in Christ is demonstrated by our works in His name. Evangelism has inescapable social implications (Galatians 5:6; James 2:14-18; 1 John 3:16-18; Ephesians 2:10). Scripture informs us about the naturalness with which the early disciples did what we call "holistic ministry." They were even surprised that the final judgment has reference to feeding the hungry, water for the thirsty, hospitality for the strangers or refugees, clothes for the naked, or shelter for the homeless, care for the sick, visitation for the prisoners. These deeds to the needy, we are told, were done to Jesus Himself (Matthew 25:31-46).

b. *Social concern is a bridge to evangelism.* Undeniably, social services to the needy many times lead to a favorable hearing of the Gospel. It may be out of gratitude, or the desire to understand the reason for an act of love, or the realization of the varying levels of human needs—from the physical and social to the spiritual. People have seen a glimpse of the hereafter visualized in the here and now. Perhaps it is for this reason that Jesus gave His disciples "authority over unclean spirits, to cast them out, and to heal every kind of disease and every sickness" (Matthew 10:1). These were to be signs of the kingdom of God that has come and is still coming (Luke 17:21).

c. *Social concern is the partner of evangelism.* Evangelism and social responsibility are distinct from one another but are integrally related to each other in our obedience to the Gospel. Time and time again, the ministry of Jesus is described best by the phrase "proclaiming the gospel of the kingdom and healing every kind of disease" (Matthew 4:23; 9:35). Notice the conjunction "and." This compels the evangelist to recognize that the Christianity founded by Christ is a conjunctive religion. Carl F. Henry said that ours is the gospel of justification and justice. They are the two things we do. They are married.

While the Grand Rapids Consultation, the Lausanne Covenant, and the Amsterdam Affirmations recognize the primacy of evangelism, they do not deny that the emphasis and response of the evangelist is determined by the felt need of the situation. Thus at times, the response may be to proclaim the Gospel, and at other times simply to give a cup of cold water to the thirsty. Nevertheless, there is always that desire that in the appropriate time the Lord would open the door for a Gospel witness. This desire is what some refer to as "prayer evangelism."

Some may find problematic the term "relief and development in evangelism." It can obscure the distinction between the two, and put relief and development as part of evangelism. For our workshop, let me simply say that it is a tacit admission that an evangelist cannot divorce his preaching for the conversion of souls from his correlative duty to touch needy bodies as well.

2. *A conceptual framework*

   a. *Relief.* This is brought about primarily by a natural (e.g., typhoon, flood, fire, earthquake, drought, epidemic, pestilence) or man-made (e.g., war, nuclear leakage, arson) disaster resulting generally in hunger, sicknesses, dislocations, and lack of shelter. Necessarily, the response is a relief ministry to provide food or potable water, medical services and medicines, and temporary shelter as well as clothing. The main thrust is to prevent death or the aggravation of sicknesses that may lead to death. Thus, the deterioration of the situation is arrested.

   b. *Rehabilitation (or recovery).* From the initial relief work, the attempt now is to restore the people's life-style to its original state before the disaster struck. The basic response would be short-term or one-time grants to help people help themselves. Mostly small-scale loans to farmers in terms of seeds and fertilizers, or small boats to fishermen, capital for a small business, and construction materials for their destroyed homes. The need of people determines the appropriate response so that people can have the means to survive, the strength to labor, and the basic structures of their houses.

   c. *Development.* The program now is an attempt to further improve the people's quality of life above and beyond their former levels of existence. This integrates literacy and leadership programs, health education, income-generation, and discipleship. The focus is on long-term changes so that people are enabled to become dynamic participants in the dynamic process of becoming all that God wants them to be.

   The word "development" encompasses all these phases. I am using these distinctions to simplify the activities as background for our workshop without denying their overlapping relationships. Given all these, let us now deal with the ministry of evangelism in these programs.

3. *The evangelistic dimension*

   In all these phases of activity, the proclamation of the Gospel must be done. The evangelist, however, must be sensitive to the prompting of the Holy Spirit as to when he should proclaim.

   a. *In relief ministry.* In a relief program, after the people have gathered in a place to receive their relief assistance, the evangelist "explains" why the assistance is given. The love of God in Christ is expounded. This ultimately leads to the appeal to receive the Bread of Life because man shall not live by bread alone (Matthew 4:4). For this reason, whenever possible, include a Gospel tract or portion, or a New Testament in your relief assistance. Then the relief distribution takes place. As the situation allows, I would suggest that the proclamation takes place after the distribution, to diminish the pressure of making "belly Christians."

   b. *In development (rehabilitation) ministry.* The evangelism component is integrated in the project. This may come in under a literacy program (using Bible stories), home Bible studies, or through the local church in the area. The life-style and personal witness of the project coordinators and church members themselves would be important. Their lives should incarnate the Gospel in their community. Paul wrote to the Thessalonian Christians saying, "We were well pleased to impart to you not only the gospel of God but also our own lives . . ." (1 Thessalonians 2:8).

4. *The operational structure*

   The basic consideration is whether the itinerant evangelist should do relief and development evangelism directly. It is easy for the evangelist to get sidetracked and become a relief worker rather than an evangelist.

The example of the early apostles reminds us that they created a body to serve tables so that they could "devote [themselves] to prayer, and to the ministry of the word" (Acts 6:4). They saw the need and necessity of serving tables (Acts 6:2) but they refrained from doing the ministry directly. The evangelist should listen to Paul's exhortation "not to neglect the spiritual gift within you" (1 Timothy 4:14).

My conviction is that, whenever possible, the itinerant evangelist should do relief and development through the local church(es). Every church can be a relief center reaching out to suffering people. It is the most concrete manifestation of God's kingdom—to be light and salt in a given locality. Most are already located in poverty-stricken and depressed communities. They are central to God's redemptive and transforming plan for man-in-community.

There are many advantages to this procedure:

a. *The local church knows the needy in the community better.* The local people know who would truly be in need. This is a valuable requirement to good stewardship, to maximize impact with limited resources. Moreover it will give them visibility and credibility in the community.

b. *The local church is the logical structure for discipleship.* She can effectively follow up those who professed Christ or who have shown interest. In many cases the growth of the local churches has been most rapid because they followed up individually and by families those who have received help. Bible studies took place and the Gospel was understood and accepted. The incorporation of believers to the local church can take place at various times later.

c. *The local church could experience transformation itself.* The incarnation of divine love has found expression in good deeds. This makes the church a compassionate church. Eventually, helping the needy becomes a way of life for them.

It is one thing to make an altar call. It is another thing to follow up and encourage new believers to be part of a local church. As normally is the case, after the relief ministry, the question of nurturing professing believers remains. The evangelist will be gone, but the need for a continuing witness remains.

For this reason, a vital partnership with the local church is of crucial importance. Work through the local church. All structures and systems will pass. Only the church will last. Jesus said, "I will build my church and the gates of hades shall not overpower it" (Matthew 16:18; cf. Matthew 18:17).

Certainly, an itinerant evangelist can operate alone and directly. But in the same way that he works with local churches in evangelism, I believe that he should do the same in relief and development.

We have a rule in PHILRADS (the relief and development arm of the Philippine council of Evangelical Churches) on relief and development programs. If the general secretary is more known to the people in the community than the pastor, then we have failed.

5. *Some warning signals*

There are dangers that an evangelist must be aware of. Let me give you a general idea of the most basic issues.

a. *The dignity of man.* When the Gospel is preached during a relief operation, many would probably respond to the invitation to receive Christ as Savior and Lord. How are we to view these responses?

To be sure, some would be genuine conversions. But some others may not be. It is argued that they were pressured to favorably respond, otherwise they may not receive relief assistance. In such a case, a hungry stomach and not a broken heart determines one's decision. The resultant product is what many call "rice Christians."

b. *The motive of the evangelist.* He must examine his motive for doing relief and development evangelism. Is he using relief goods as "baits" to catch souls from the pond of poverty? If he is, then the method is ethically questionable if not morally culpable. Even the poor are entitled to dignity. That may be all he has left of value to him. Moreover, the free exercise of the will is a necessary element to true faith.

The evangelist, as often is done, gets pictures of the operation. One can enter into "relief pornography," i.e., he can unduly expose for sensationalism's sake the nakedness of people in poverty. This is more reprehensible if the design is to evoke a strong emotional reaction for people to give.

Obviously, fund raising for legitimate causes is not sinful. It is a ministry. It enables people to respond to genuine need. But it must not be an end in itself. It must have respect for human dignity and be culturally sensitive in its presentation.

c. *The scope of the operation.* The other danger area would be in the coverage of the operation. Who should be given the relief assistance? How does one determine the balance between the shortage of funds and the excess of need? Such a concern can lead to favoritism, i.e., giving only to Christians. This can be viewed with disfavor by the non-believers and eventually create resistance to the Gospel itself.

The problem can be carried to the area of church relationship in places where more than one evangelical church exists. To work through one or a few to the exclusion of others would create division, a situation which the evangelist could not do in the light of John 17.

The evangelist, then, is faced with many situational problems which he needs to resolve. He must constantly seek what Scripture is saying and consult with the local body of believers to help him. His idealism is constantly challenged by pragmatism. Even the injunction "Let us do good to all men, and especially to those who are of the household of faith" (Galatians 6:10) would not be so easy when operationalized in an actual relief situation. Our experience, however, on church relationship is to help mobilize them to jointly respond to the crisis. Ultimately we need to allow the Holy Spirit to work creatively, knowing that ultimately "to his master he stands or falls . . ." (Romans 14:4).

d. *The proselytism debate.* One of development's "thorns in the flesh" is the issue of proselytism, or "sheep stealing." People leave their churches to join the one that offers relief and development assistance. In fact, some insist that relief and development programs are potentially proselytizing activities.

There is no easy light on this. Proselytism as used in the New Testament simply means change of faith, change of conduct, and change of community. The ethical problem is recognized. In some cases, government legislation explicitly forbids it. Yet we must also allow for the working of the Holy Spirit in the lives of believers as to where they should worship God in spirit and in truth.

e. *The dependency syndrome.* Relief and development assistance can make parasites of the recipients. If the evangelist is not careful, instead of making people self-reliant they can become dependent on him for their living. In fact, if this takes place, it can be a good sign that no genuine faith exists, or that the discipleship program is not effective.

The relief evangelist must help people to recover their self-respect as creatures created in God's image. They must be taught the dignity of labor and to harness their potential, not only for themselves but also for others. They must be encouraged to contribute and to be productive.

6. *Suggestions for starting relief evangelism*
Ministering to the poor can be one of the most difficult ministries a person can undertake. An evangelist can prepare himself for it.

a. *Study God's Word concerning the ministry.* Examine the commands and the warnings. Do some reading on the subject and learn from whatever studies have been done by some of God's people. Two brief but helpful starters are John Stott's "Commentary on the Lausanne Covenant" and "Grand Rapids Report—Evangelism and Social Responsibility." Ronald Sider's "Cry Justice" is a good biblical anthology. A contemporary cross section of evangelical thinking on the subject is "In Word and Deed, Evangelism and Social Responsibility" edited by Bruce Nicholls.

b. *Examine the different expressions of evangelical social concerns* from past to present to get the feel of the pulse of the Church. I find Shumacher's "Small is Beautiful" excellent. David O. Moberg's "The Great Reversal" provides a good historical perspective. Readings on the subject from evangelical scholars such as Carl Henry would be most useful. Continue the discipleship of study.

c. *Learn from practitioners.* Inquire from practitioners more about the operational side of the ministry and how evangelism actually is integrated in the program. From these the evangelist can design his own policy or guidelines as to how he will be involved.

d. *Preach the whole Gospel to the whole man.* This is a vital contribution of the evangelist. In his messages, he should balance the claims and commands of the Gospel. Encourage people to look around them and see people in need. Challenge them to respond to them in the name of Christ. Matthew 25 enumerates some of these areas of ministry.

e. *Give to relief and development ministry.* Do not go into this ministry just because you may feel that there is money in it. But should there be extra funds for your ministry, consider supporting relief ministries, particularly, through local churches. As the Lord leads, make an appeal for special relief and development needs.

f. *Get involved in a meaningful way.* Be with the people. Be God's instrument in meeting their needs—physically and spiritually. Give yourself to them as you touch them in the name of Jesus.

# DEVELOPING PRAYER SUPPORT FOR THE EVANGELIST AND HIS MINISTRY
*Millie Dienert*

Are miracles happening today? We have seen God perform miracles as a result of prayer in many places in the world.

Dr. Billy Graham had been invited for evangelistic meetings in North India in an area called Kohima. Before the meetings were to take place, civil war and guerrilla warfare broke out with intensity, so much so that the government officials were going to cancel the visit of Dr. Graham to their country.

However, God's people went from village to village telling the Christians to join together in prayer for the situation, so that the doors of the country would not be closed for this evangelistic effort. God answered their prayers, and the meetings were held and thousands were born into God's family.

The Christians of that area refer to those days as the Kohima Miracle. What made the difference? The intense prayer support. Prayer always makes the difference, especially between a meeting and a miracle.

More than 100 years ago in England there was a community of Christians called Moravians who saw the need for spiritual renewal and revival among their own people. One hundred of them formed a 24-hour prayer chain effort. They divided one hour into 15-minute periods of time so that 8-10 people were praying through every hour. At the end of 12 hours, which was from 12 noon to 12 midnight, 96-100 people had prayed. Then from 12 midnight to 12 noon they prayed again.

They continued that for 100 years. When anyone of their number died, that particular period of time in which they had been praying was passed on to someone else to take their place.

What was the result of that prayer effort? First, there was a tremendous spiritual revival among the Christians; second, the beginning of the greatest worldwide missionary effort in history. Prayer and evangelism must go together.

Now, we are going to be talking about one particular area of prayer. There are three main areas of prayer. The first is request praying or petition praying. It is this type of praying that we do daily and constantly, such as, "Lord, help me," "Lord, lead me," "Lord, work out this situation." As God's children we are making known to our Heavenly Father our specific needs.

The second area of prayer is intercessory prayer. That is what we're going to be talking about today. Prayer on behalf of others. When we move into that area of prayer which deals with petitions, it generally includes our own person and our problems or our situations in life. And, of course, it can include others and their situations, but the majority of times when we are praying with petitions, we are praying our own petitions concerning ourselves. But intercessory prayer deals with praying for others and their needs.

The third area of prayer is praise. We do not often take time to just praise the Lord wherein we do not ask anything, we do not intercede on behalf of anyone, but we're praising Him in all the different areas of our lives in which He has participated and in which He has granted requests in the past or in the immediate present.

Basically, prayer should not be the way to get God to change things, but prayer is the way God will change us. There is no place as life-changing as the place of prayer.

We note in Luke 9:29 that as Jesus prayed, His facial expression was changed. That is very significant. The renewing work of the Holy Spirit, which is absolutely necessary, is accomplished through prayer.

Of course, there are numerous examples of Jesus and His prayer life. Also, Jesus taught basic principles on prayer in Matthew 6:5-8. Beginning in verse 9, Jesus gave His disciples a formula for prayer, which in Christian communities all over the world Christians do pray—beginning with, "Our Father, which art in heaven."

Before Jesus performed the miracle of resurrection in the life of Lazarus, He commanded them to roll away the stone, and then we read, "After they took away the stone from the place where the dead was laid, Jesus lifted up his eyes, and said, Father I thank you that you have heard me. And I know that you hearest me always: but because of the people which stand by I said it, that they may believe that you have sent me. And when he had thus spoken, he cried with a loud voice, Lazarus, come forth" (John 11:41-43).

Again we see that Jesus taught by example the necessity of prayer. In Mark 9 Jesus healed the child, which was being tormented by the evil spirit, and took the child "by the hand and lifted him up; and he arose. And when he was come into the house, his disciples said unto him, Why could not we cast the demon out of that child? And he said unto them, This kind [of miracle] can come forth by nothing, but by prayer and fasting" (Mark 9:26-29).

These are a few instances where we see not only that our Lord performed miracles, but how He did them. First, He was in direct contact and communication with the Father, which is prayer.

Having those examples before us, it was no surprise that Jesus sent His disciples to a prayer meeting when He left them to return to His Father. Furthermore, the early church which came out of a prayer meeting continued steadfastly with prayer (Acts 2:42). Paul exhorted the church to pray for the ministry of spreading the Gospel. Second Thessalonians 3:1, "Finally, brethren, pray for us, that the word of the Lord may have free course, and be glorified even as it is with you: And that we may be delivered from unreasonable and violent men: for all men do not have the faith."

Notice the exhortation that Paul gives here. "Pray that the word of the Lord will have free course." That is necessary in the Christian community.

Consequently, renewal in the individual, revival in the church, and the success of evangelism are the results of prayer. We need to encourage the Christian community to be an active part of evangelism by means of prayer. Now we do this in three ways:

Suggest that Christians have a prayer partner. Two people meeting together to pray. Jesus promised in Matthew 18:20 that He would be the silent one meeting together with two people who are praying together.

Thus, two people plus one, who is the Lord Jesus, equals three. What did Jesus say in Matthew 18:20? "Where two or three are gathered together in my name, there am I in the midst of them." This is a powerful prayer fellowship and togetherness.

The special needs of the evangelist and his family should be given as prayer requests to those who are praying in groups of two.

These two people will meet with each other to pray for the spiritual needs of people and the needs of the Christian community as well.

It is very important that these prayer partners know what God is doing in the ministry of the evangelist because of their faithfulness in prayer.

Also, they are to pray for the ministry of the evangelist and the needs related to his ministry. Ephesians 6:19 tells us to pray that words may be given so that the one ministering the Gospel will be fearless in making the Gospel known.

It is always best to put into action what we teach. And so gather together in groups of twos. Select one—either on your left or on your right—and pray together. Pray for the needs that you have as an evangelist, for the needs of your family, for the needs of the Christian community wherein you are ministering.

*Prayer action with two people praying together*

You note that Jesus also mentioned in Matthew 18:20 that where three people are praying together He is in the midst of them.

In England before Dr. Billy Graham arrived for evangelistic meetings in 1984, the Christians prayed in groups of three for nine unconverted people. This they did for months before Dr. Graham arrived. God richly blessed that prayer effort.

And so, we have three people praying for nine unconverted people. Each one of those three have three names of the ones they want to see born into the family of God.

It is a special joy to pray for people who need the Lord, even if you do not know them. When you get together with two others, you are praying for six other people whom you do not know, and that is very exciting.

Therefore, the three Christians are praying together for nine people. Now these three Christians must meet together to pray at least once a week if possible.

Again we remember in Ephesians 6:18 that we are told to pray consistently and frequently, and on all occasions. Each one in the group of three prays for the other six names, who may be strangers to them, in their personal prayer time when they are apart from each other.

When they meet to pray, they need to pray for God's guidance and wisdom to be given each one, relative to what can be done to put their prayers into action. For example, definite ways and means to touch the lives for whom they are praying—with some act of kindness and love.

When God through His Holy Spirit works in the lives of those for whom the three Christians are praying, there must be a time of praise and thanksgiving to the Lord for answers to prayer.

*Prayer action with three people praying for nine unconverted people*

Now last but not least, we see the early church meeting together in homes consistently in Acts 2:42, and we read, "They continued steadfastly, not only in fellowship with each other or in teaching of doctrine to each other, but in prayer."

And so we come to the area of group praying wherein we suggest that Christians get together at a special time to pray together. As we read in Acts 12:5, "Prayer was made by the church without ceasing," which means earnestly unto God. There is power in united prayer for the cause of evangelism and for the evangelist.

Prayer is an absolute necessity to the carrying on of God's Word. In the early church it was a decision of those in leadership that they would give themselves continually to prayer and the ministry of the Word.

There should be an appointed day of the week or a special time during the day for group togetherness in prayer. At that time, the group prays that the Gospel will be unhindered by the attacks of Satan. This is very important because we know that Satan wants to hinder the Gospel message in every way possible, and that Satan is increasing his activities against the Gospel.

Paul reminded the church in Colosse in Colossians 4:2-4 to "devote themselves to prayer so that there will be an open door for the gospel message and also that it will be proclaimed clearly."

In addition, the group needs to pray for the Christians—that they may be like Andrew who brought his brother to Jesus. We need to encourage them to pray for an

Andrew vision and ministry among the saints.

They need to pray that the Christians will be willing to disciple the new Christians, and by so doing help them grow up in the Lord.

And, we need to consistently pray that the Christian community will be experiencing spiritual renewal and revival in every individual life and family (2 Chronicles 7:14).

Also, we must pray for an attitude of unity among the believers. Now these are the areas that we need to submit to the groups who are going to be meeting at a special time praying on behalf of evangelism. That group can be a group of four, five, ten, twelve; it does not matter how many there are just as long as there is a concentrated prayer effort on behalf of God's people meeting together at a specific time for specific needs relative to evangelism and outreach.

*Prayer action with groups of four, five or six*

Now in conclusion you are being given four pamphlets. Each one of these will explain to you what we have talked about and what we have done today. It will explain once again prayer partners, prayer triplets (or three people praying together for nine unconverted people) and the Christian community praying together in groups of any number, it does not matter, but at a specific time. Also, praying in prayer chain routine.

The ministry of the Word of God will only be blessed and enriched and increased as God's people go to their knees. So encourage the family of God to be active in prayer. May God richly bless you and your ministry for the glory of the Lord. Thank you.

# COMMUNICATION SKILLS FOR THE EVANGELIST

*Abraham Philip*

Suppose we are seated at the dinner table. I find that the soup doesn't have enough salt. I tell the man sitting next to me, "Pass the salt, please." When I tell him this, I am communicating. What I am communicating may be something trivial and of no lasting value. Nevertheless, I am communicating. I am sending a message. And the receiver of the message understands me. He has no difficulty in understanding me because the message is so simple. Communication in this case is very easy.

Now let us imagine that we are standing on a street corner conducting an evangelistic service. I stand up to preach. A small crowd of curious listeners is in front of me. I attempt to communicate to them the message of John 3:3. "You must be born again." Now the problems of communication begin. Our Lord Himself made this attempt one night. He had one of the greatest Bible scholars of His day as His listener. But His message was grossly misunderstood. Nicodemus thought our Lord was speaking about the natural birth. "How can a man be born when he is old?" he asked. "Can he enter the second time into his mother's womb, and be born?" Our Lord had to use a series of illustrations and explanations to drive home the point of this message to Nicodemus. Most probably John gives only a summary of our Lord's words to Nicodemus. Still it takes up some 20 words. Communication in this case is very difficult.

These two illustrations show that the greater the importance of the message, the greater the difficulties of communication. We must note that as evangelists our task is to communicate the most important message in the world to all of our fellowmen. The eternal destinies of countless millions depend on our fulfilling this task faithfully. This consideration should drive us to desperate earnestness in sharpening our communication skills.

In communication one person sends a message and another receives it. Speaking and writing are the most common methods of sending the message. Listening and reading are the most common methods of receiving the message. As evangelists we may have occasion to listen, to preach, to counsel, and to write. All of us will be preaching to gathered audiences or in street corners. Many of us will also be writing for publications of limited circulation. But there are the mass media—the press, the film, the radio and the TV. These media have immense possibilities for evangelizing the unreached and unreachable regions and peoples of the world. It should be the desire of every evangelist to use them whenever and wherever possible. But to use any of the media effectively it is necessary that we should master the basics of effective communication.

These basics are more or less the same for writing and the use of the media as for preaching to live audiences. Once the basics of effective preaching are mastered it will be easy to adapt them to writing and to the use of the media. To preach effectively we should prepare our sermons properly. The purpose of this workshop is to acquaint you with the principles of sermon construction and to get you to construct an outline for a sermon on your favorite sermon topic. In the construction of the outline I would like you to follow the format as closely as you can.

A sermon should have an immediate impact upon the listeners. In order to secure this impact, the sermon must be free from ambiguity. It should contain no extraneous material which is foreign to its main theme. On the other hand, it must have a distinct form or pattern. The ideas in the sermon should indicate continuity of thought. And the whole discourse should move toward a definite goal or climax. The message must be clearly presented from beginning to end so that the hearers follow, point by point, the truths you seek to unfold from the Word of God.

This is possible only if your sermon has a homiletical structure. The basis of this structure is a proper outline. The outline should be in a proper format. The purpose of the format is to make the outline obvious. When the outline is put in this form it serves as a visual aid. It enables you to see the entire message at a glance. In the format, the introduction and the conclusion are given headings and the points under them are numbered, so that each item in the introduction and conclusion stands out clearly, and the progression of thought can be easily seen. Main divisions are placed to the left of the paper. By the use of indentation the subdivisions are clearly seen to be subordinate to the main divisions.

Of course, the number of main divisions and subdivisions is not limited to the number contained in this format. The same is true of the number of items under the introduction and the conclusion.

But an outline should be brief. The introduction and conclusion, as well as the main divisions, should be expressed in as few words as possible. In like manner the items contained in the discussion must be stated concisely.

1.  *The title*

In the construction of a sermon the title is usually the last item to be prepared. The general procedure is to formulate the proposition and the main outline first. But we shall discuss the items in the order in which they appear in the format.

We must know clearly the meaning of the words, "subject," "theme" and "title." These terms are often confused. But they do not have the same meaning. The "subject" gives the general idea, but the "theme" or "topic" is a specific or particular aspect of the subject, stated clearly and briefly. For example, you may select "grace" as a subject. But "grace" covers a broad range of ideas. You won't be able to speak about all aspects of grace in one sermon. So you should limit your theme to a particular aspect of grace, such as "facts about God's abundant grace," "the effects of grace," or "conditions for growth in grace."

The title is an expression of the specific feature to be presented in the sermon. It should be stated in a manner suitable for advertising the sermon. Thus the title is an embellishment of the theme. For example, if your theme is "conditions for growth in grace," the title can be "How to Grow in Grace" or "Maturing in Spiritual Stature."

If the "theme" or "subject" is sufficiently interesting in itself it can be used as the title.

The following principles should be observed in the preparation of sermon titles.
a.  The title should be pertinent to the text or to the message.
b.  The title should be interesting.
c.  The title should be in keeping with the dignity of the pulpit.
d.  The title should generally be brief.
e.  The title may be stated in the form of an affirmation, interrogation, or exclamation.

2.  *The text*

Some preachers base their sermons on too many different verses of Scripture. When you do that, you can seldom achieve unity in your message. So try to use one passage of Scripture as your text. Other passages may be cited to support your explanation of the text.

3. *The introduction*

In actual practice the introduction, like the title, is usually one of the last parts of the sermon to be prepared. The reason is that you cannot introduce something that doesn't exist. If the sermon does not exist in concrete form you cannot introduce it. When you begin the introduction you should know what you are introducing. But we consider it here to follow the order of the format.

The introduction is the process by which the preacher endeavors to prepare the minds and secure the interest of his hearers in the message he has to proclaim.

The success of the entire message often depends on the introduction. In the introduction you should secure the good will of your hearers. You should also arouse their interest in the theme of your sermon.

The following principles should be observed in the preparation of the introduction.
a. It should generally be brief (1/5 or 1/6 of the total preaching time)
b. It should be interesting
   —arouse curiosity
   —use variety
   —state the title or quote the text
   —relate the sermon to life situations
c. It should lead to the dominant idea or central thought of the message. To accomplish this, the statements in the introduction should consist of a series of progressive ideas culminating in the one main idea of the discourse. Any quotations, explanations, illustrations, or incidents that are told should have this one purpose in mind. Repetition must be avoided.

Consider the model outline in which the introduction consists of a series of progressive ideas leading to the theme of the sermon.

4. *The proposition*

The proposition is a simple declaration of the subject which the preacher proposes to discuss, develop, prove, or explain in the discourse. In other words, it is the sermon reduced to one sentence.

The proposition is the most essential feature in the organization of a sermon. There are two main reasons for this.
a. The proposition is the foundation of the entire structure of the sermon. When it is stated correctly, it enables the preacher to organize his material around the dominant idea which he has planned.
b. It clearly indicates to the congregation the course of the sermon. If the message is without a clearly stated objective, it cannot be easily followed and will often make for inattention on the part of the audience. But if the direction of the discourse is clear the hearers can follow the message intelligently and with ease.

The following principles should be observed while formulating the proposition:
a. The proposition should contain one main idea. If more than one idea is introduced in the proposition, the unity of the entire sermon is at once destroyed. An example of such a statement with two ideas is: "We should live holy lives and be faithful in church attendance." These are really two propositions, making it impossible to maintain unity in the sermon.
b. The proposition should generally be expressed in the form of a timeless truth stated simply and clearly. As a rule, it is a declarative sentence and contains a gener-

alization or truth which is always valid. But a truth cannot be fully expressed by a mere phrase or fragment of a sentence. It must be stated in a complete sentence. For example, such an expression as "the need for Christians to be witnesses" is not a sentence, and does not contain a truth. It is merely the fragment of a sentence. If used as a proposition it will result in ambiguity and disunity.

    c.  The proposition should be stated as concisely as possible, consistent with clarity. There may be occasions when it is necessary to use a complex sentence. But as far as possible the proposition should be a simple sentence.

    d.  The proposition should often be stated to suggest the idea of obligation, worthiness, or desirability. Note the subject sentence in the outline below:

> Title          : Triumphant Living.
> Text           : Philippians 1:12-21.
> Proposition    : Christians can be triumphant in Christ.
>
>   i. In the face of adversity, as Paul was, verses 12-14.
>   ii. In the face of opposition, as Paul was, verses 15-19.
>   iii. In the face of death, as Paul was, verses 20,21.

    e.  The main divisions of the sermon should not be stated in the proposition. For example, in the outline under the preceding rule, you cannot say in the proposition, "Christians can be triumphant in the face of adversity, opposition, and death."

**5.  *Interrogative***

    The interrogative is the first of the two links usually used to connect the proposition to the sermon.

    Any one of the five interrogative adverbs is commonly used in connecting the proposition to the main points of the discourse. These interrogatives are: "Why?" "How?" "What?" "When?" and "Where?" For example, if the proposition is "You should pray always," the interrogative can be, "How can you pray always?" or, "Why should you pray always?"

**6.  *The transitional sentence***

    The interrogative leads to the transitional sentence. This sentence ties the proposition and the main points of the sermon together. It also provides a smooth passage from the proposition to the main divisions. Besides, it contains a key word which classifies or delineates the character of the main headings of the outline. If the interrogative is, "Why should you pray always?" the transitional sentence may be stated as, "There are several reasons why you should pray always." Obviously, the word "reasons" is the key word which now characterizes the main divisions, and relates the proposition to the main points of the discourse.

    The key word is a useful device by which it is possible to characterize or classify the main divisions in the transitional sentence. But a key word is possible only when there is structural unity in the outline. When there is structural unity, the same key word can be applied to each of the main divisions.

    This can be illustrated by the following outline on Luke 15:25-32. If we take "The character of the elder brother" as the theme, we may outline the message as follows:

    a.  *Proposition:* The character of the elder brother reflects the character of the Pharisee of yesterday and today.

    b.  *Interrogative:* What features of the elder brother's character resemble those of the Pharisees of yesterday and today?

    c.  *Transitional sentence:* As we examine the text we observe four features regarding the elder brother's character which are like those of the Pharisee of yesterday and today.

    i.   He was a self-righteous man, verses 29,30.
    ii.  He was an unloving man, verses 28-30.
   iii.  He was a fault-finding man, verses 25-30.
   iv.  He was a stubborn man, verses 28-32.

The word "features" becomes the key word in the transitional sentence. Suppose we have "The elder brother's father, verses 29-32," as the fourth item. In that case the word "features" in relation to the character of the elder brother can no longer be applied to all the main divisions.

The proposition should always be written out in the preacher's sermon notes. But in the course of delivery it will not always be necessary to make a formal declaration of the thesis.

The proper place for the proposition is generally at the end of the introduction. But sometimes the preacher may want to withhold the aim of his sermon until the very end. He may use the main points to bring the message to a forceful conclusion in the statement of the proposition. The following example shows how this is done.

    Title: "How To Be Saved."
      i.   Can church membership save us?
      ii.  Can baptism save us?
     iii.  Can good works save us?
     iv.  Can good intentions save us?

*Conclusion and proposition:* The work of Jesus Christ on the Cross alone can save us from sin (Ephesians 2:8,9, Acts 4:12).

A smooth transition from the proposition to the main divisions is of special importance to the thought structure of a sermon. An awkward or faulty transition can be misleading and weaken the effectiveness of a discourse. Because the key word is a vital part of the transitional sentence it is also necessary that great care should be taken in the choice of the correct key word. The word "things" is too general a term to be employed as a key word. Instead you should aim to use the specific word which accurately characterizes the main divisions.

## 7. *The divisions*

The divisions follow the transitional sentence in the format. They are the main sections of an orderly discourse. They promote clarity and unity of thought. They assist the preacher in the proper treatment of a subject. They also enable him to remember the main points of his sermon. They enable his listeners too to understand the sermon and recall its main features.

The following principles should be observed in the preparation of the main divisions.

a.  The main divisions should grow out of the proposition. Each main division should be essential to the development of the proposition. Each successive division should in turn expand a further aspect of the subject sentence.

b.  There must be no overlapping of the divisions. Each must be entirely distinct. Otherwise the preacher will merely be repeating himself. The following is an example of overlapping divisions.

| Title | : | "The Christian's Ideal" |
|---|---|---|
| Text | : | 1 Corinthians 13:1-13. |
| Proposition | : | We may learn much on the subject of love by a consideration of 1 Corinthians, chapter 13, the great "Love Chapter" of the Bible. |
| Interrogative | : | What may we learn about the subject from this chapter? |
| Transitional sentence | : | There are four main facts about love which we may learn from this chapter. |

   i.   The preeminence of love, verses 1-3.
   ii.   The characteristics of love, verses 4-7.
   iii.   The continuity of love, verses 8-12.
   iv.   The duration of love, verse 13.

It is obvious that the third and fourth divisions overlap because duration of love is included in continuity. It would be preferable to form from verses 8-13 one division: "The permanence of love."

c.  The main divisions should be arranged in some form of progression. The preacher may treat the items in the order of any one of the following:

   i.   According to time sequence.
   ii.   In the order of space or geographical location.
   iii.   In the order of importance.
   iv.   From cause to effect.
   v.   From effect to cause.
   vi.   In the order of comparison and contrast.
   vii.   In the order of contrast and comparison.

d.  The main divisions as a whole should exhaust or completely develop the proposition. Failure to complete the discussions of the proposition leaves the sermon unfinished. It may disappoint the audience. It is important, therefore, that all the divisions necessary to the development of the proposition be included in the outline.
*Proposition:* The principal bases for world missions are clearly set forth in the Scriptures.

   i.   All men need the Savior: Romans 5:12.
   ii.   God has provided salvation for all men: John 3:16.

If we omit the Great Commission (Matthew 28:19,20 or Mark 16:15) we fail to exhaust the proposition, because it is certainly one of the principal bases for world missions.

e.  The main divisions should be stated clearly, with each division expressing a single idea.

f.  The main divisions should be in parallel structure. The main headings should be in symmetrical form and follow a uniform pattern. If, for instance, the first main heading is a phrase, all the main headings should be phrases and not sentences or single words.

Words in positions of emphasis also should be uniform. When the first division begins with a certain part of speech the other divisions also should, as a general rule, begin with the same part of speech.

8. *Subdivisions*

The construction of the subdivision closely follows the same principles governing that of the main divisions. But there are some differences in the application of these principles to the subdivisions. So the following distinctive principles should be kept in mind.

a.   Subdivisions are derived from their respective main divisions and should be a logical development of them.

b.   Subdivisions should be in parallel structure.

9. *Conclusion*

The conclusion is the climax of the whole sermon. In the conclusion, the preacher's one constant aim reaches its goal in the form of a forceful impression.

No new idea should be introduced in the conclusion. Its purpose is solely to emphasize, reaffirm, establish, or finalize that which has already been declared in the sermon.

The conclusion can be in the form of a summary, illustration, application, or appeal.

The conclusion should be reasonably brief and simple. The final words of the conclusion should be carefully and thoughtfully chosen.

# RESOURCES FOR EVANGELISTIC PREACHING
*John Wesley White*

*TEXT: "Without a parable spake He not unto them" (Matthew 13:34).*

When Jesus was here on earth, He set the precedent for evangelistic preaching for all time. He looked around, and pointed His hearers to a current event, drew an illustration of the Gospel from it, substantiating His teaching by quoting from the Scriptures, and then proceeded to apply that Kingdom truth, calling His hearers to repentance, belief, and discipleship. Not only does an observant student see this pattern in the gospels, it is also to be noted that the apostles followed our Lord's precedent.

Jesus, in Luke 13, had heard the prime-time news of "those 18, upon whom the tower of Siloam fell, and slew them, think ye that they were sinners above all men that dwell in Jerusalem? I tell you, nay: but except ye repent, ye shall all likewise perish" (vss. 4,5). So Paul, when he felt it on his heart in the Athenian Areopagus to preach that God "commandeth all men everywhere to repent" did so by pointing to the current events around him—to the publicly-displayed inscription, "To the Unknown God."

While the evangelist must "preach the Word" to "do the work of an evangelist," he or she must bridge-build into the minds and consciousness of the hearers with illustrations drawn from current events which occupy the thinking and understanding of those whom he or she seeks to win to Christ.

The Good News of the Gospel shines out in sharpest relief from the backdrop of the bad news with which most people are inundated. Sin is an ugly fact of life. People spend a great deal of time indulging evil, and even more time gloating over the wrongdoing of others. In that no one can come to Christ without acknowledging his sin, it is a simple thing to allude to the evils of drunkenness, drug-taking, immorality, and illegal crimes being highlighted in the newspapers and on radio and television. It is also very easily demonstrated from the news the terrible price in the life here—let alone the life hereafter—of the consequences of sin.

From the same sources there are also constantly to be found love stories of sacrifice: a mother giving her life in a fire to save her child; a father for his son; etc., etc.: illustrative of the fact that Christ loved us and gave Himself for us.

So we want to see people come to a decision for Christ. Whether you're in a community in the jungle or the rain forests, or whether in a steaming ghetto or on a sprawling farm, there are always current events in the conversations of the villagers, on the television screen or radio, or recorded in the newspapers and magazines—accounts of the rewards for those who make the right decisions, or the perils of neglecting to make the correct decision. So it is with Christ's call to us to come to Him. You call your dog, your cat, your sheep, your donkeys, your horses, or cattle. They come. That means they're fed and they get shelter. So it is when Christ calls. You must respond. You simply can't be too simple when you preach the Gospel. And you can't be too plain and vivid. This you can only do when you express yourself in the coin, the vernacular, the picture language of those you are seeking to reach. And this can only happen when you're constantly on the lookout for vehicles upon which the Prince of Life can ride—veins through which His blood can flow, voices through which He can speak. This you get by vigilant and constant attention to what's happening in contemporary society as recorded in magazines, newspapers, and on radio and TV.

# CREATING AN EVANGELISTIC TRACT
## Doug Salser

How effective is a tract at telling the Gospel? Here is what a young man in England says:
"I thank you sincerely and from the bottom of my heart for printing the tract *'How to Be Sure.'* I picked it up second-hand from a friend. I then read it at a Christian youth group that met at my house. As a result the whole group of five realized that we had never really understood the Christian message at its most basic level and as a direct result made a commitment to Christ. It was a most marvellous occasion—five newly, truly committed Christians (myself included). I'd been in and out of all religions for years and knocking around the local church for about eight years. Now, for the first time, I can say 'I am saved' and with full conviction." (Quoted from a letter to American Tract.)

If it were my goal today to convince you about the effectiveness of gospel tracts, I would draw from the more than 1,000 individuals who, like these five young men, come to know Christ every year through the tracts we publish. As an evangelist I know you would rejoice to hear them all. But your presence at this workshop tells me you are already aware of the power of the printed page.

Evangelists Billy Graham and Luis Palau are two men who will tell you that without question tracts are great evangelistic tools. *As Luis Palau says of the tracts he has authored, "We have gotten testimonies of people converted in the most unusual manners by reading tracts"* (quoted from a personal letter to Doug Salser). Long after the words of a crusade sermon have drifted away, the gospel message can continue indefinitely if you use a tract to reinforce and to supplement your words. Tracts last for weeks, months, even years, always ready to present the Gospel.

So, my goal is to convince you that *YOU CAN WRITE A TRACT.*

### GETTING READY TO CREATE A TRACT
Realize that a tract is within your abilities. *If you can write a sermon you can write a tract.* "Not that we are competent to claim anything for ourselves, but *our competence comes from God"* (2 Corinthians 3:5).

*Plan to multiply your evangelistic ministry through tracts.* Depend upon the Holy Spirit to help you accomplish *in print* the work of planting the Word for a future harvest just as He helps you in preaching. "So neither he who *plants* nor he who waters is anything, but *only God, who makes things grow"* (1 Corinthians 3:7).

### CREATING AN EVANGELISTIC TRACT
### STEP ONE: CHOOSE YOUR READER
Who do you most want to read your tract? If you could only write for one person (your "target" reader), who would that person be? Only after you have chosen the "target" reader can you most successfully write a tract. Ask yourself these two questions as you decide.

*WHO?* Who is the reader you have in mind—a college student, a child, a businessman, a farmer? The answer will help you write with that particular kind of person in mind. A subject that may be very interesting to a farmer may be boring to a businessman. A tract written for children would probably have little appeal to a college student.

*WHY?* Why do you want to write to that particular reader instead of another? What is it about your hoped-for ("target") reader or his present situation that urges you to try to reach him at this time? Your tract writing will be more convincing when you have a sincere concern and a specific burden for your reader (Mark 6:34).

IMPORTANT: It is also necessary to ask yourself *who will distribute* this tract. Others who work with you during crusades? Local church members? The Christians you hope will help distribute the tracts will probably use only tracts that they appreciate. While you must write for the reader, also write so that other Christians will use the tract. It will increase your ministry and theirs if you stay with the *essentials* of the salvation message.

## STEP TWO: SELECT A SUBJECT LIKELY TO INTEREST YOUR READER

Once you know WHOM you are trying to reach with the message of your tract, you are ready to choose a *subject*. Narrow your choices by describing your reader.

*WHAT?* What is the reader thinking about? When he reads your tract will he be thinking of a major national event, famine, the uncertainty of war, disaster, political unrest, or economic problems? What problems face the reader normally each day? What are his interests?

What is his level of literacy? Is he college educated? Or is he able to read only simple words that might accompany drawings or photographs? These kinds of questions will help you write on a subject that the reader is either already thinking about, or will more readily think about.

*WHERE?* Where will the reader be when he receives the tract? In the marketplace? At a crusade you will be holding? At a sporting event? On a college campus? Where does the reader live? Will he relate to the illustrations you use to explain the Gospel?

*HOW?* How can you best relate the Gospel of Christ to the reader's needs? It will be much easier if you know to whom you are writing, where that person spends his life, and what occupies much of his thinking. Remember, your goal is to make the Gospel clear. *Stay with a single, evangelistic emphasis.* A tract does its best work when aimed at one target. If you aim your tract at both Christians and non-Christians, you may not reach either one!

## BIBLICAL ILLUSTRATIONS: MATCHING THE APPROACH TO THE HEARER

| Passage | 2 Samuel 12# | Matthew 4:18,19# | Acts 7* | Acts 17* |
|---|---|---|---|---|
| Speaker | Nathan | Jesus | Stephen | Paul |
| Hearer | David (godly king who had sinned) | Fishermen | Religious leaders | Philosophers |
| Hearer's Interest | Justice, as a good king | Catching fish | Tradition | New ideas |
| Where received | Palace | Lakeside | Council hall | Athens, Mars Hill |
| How the Message Reached Hearer | Touching story about injustice | Easily understood illustration | Familiar history of the nation | Related to their search for truth |

#General illustrations    *Evangelistic illustrations

*STEP THREE: ORGANIZE YOUR IDEAS*

Just like preaching, writing is work. One good starting place for your tract may well be a sermon you have *already* preached. Choose one that God has especially blessed to bring people to salvation. If you will write down the main points of your message, *you can use those points for the main ideas of your tract.* But whatever the subject you have chosen, here is the important first step.

1. Write down the main things you want to say about your chosen subject. Make these brief, noting the basic thoughts and the application of Christian truth you plan to make. Don't worry about all the details yet. You can add those later. Just get your first ideas on paper so you can begin to work with them.

2. Write down Scripture references that come to mind as you think about your subject. You may not use them all and you may think of others later, but make a note of them anyway.

3. Make a note of what you would hope the reader's response will be when he has finished reading the tract (for example—"I want him to turn from his sins and trust Jesus Christ for salvation."). This will keep you from losing sight of your goal for writing a tract in the first place, and will strengthen your conclusion.

*STEP FOUR: FILL IN THE DETAILS*

Using your outline as a guide, now you can fill in more details and actually write the tract manuscript.

1. Start with a sentence that will capture the reader's interest.

   You've worked hard to figure out who your reader will be and what he is like. Still, you have no way to know exactly what is on the reader's mind when he receives your tract. That means that *this first sentence and the paragraph that follows it are very important.* They must interest the reader if there is any hope of getting him to read the entire message.

   Write out as many first sentences as you can think of. Do not include in them any words that have little or no meaning to non-believers.

   ILLUSTRATION OF A STRONG FIRST SENTENCE:
   "Knowing safety facts isn't enough."

2. Develop the subject in terms the reader can follow.

   Talk in terms the reader understands about things with which the reader is familiar. The idea begun with a good first sentence deserves to be developed in the next paragraphs to explore the subject you have chosen. Your goal is to build a bridge from the *reader's thoughts to your thoughts.*

   ILLUSTRATION OF INITIAL DEVELOPMENT:
   "To really be safe you must act on the facts. For example—fire. In the United States there are over 300 fires each hour, or 2½ million a year. 300,000 people will be injured this year in fires. . . ."

3. Tell how God and His message (in the Bible) relate to the subject you're discussing.

   ILLUSTRATION OF A PROPER TRANSITION:
   "Are you prepared? Do you have a home fire extinguisher and an escape plan? Do you buckle up? ("Buckle up" refers to wearing seat belts when riding in a car.) Make the best use of your knowledge by acting upon it. Only then will you

really be safe. Actually, spiritual safety is even more important than physical safety. Are you prepared if you should become one of those fatal statistics? The Bible says we can be prepared.''

4. Tell how God offers help to those who realize their need for Him (through the reading of your tract message).

This is the place to make the way of salvation very clear. When you explain how a person becomes a Christian through faith in Christ alone, back up your explanation with well-chosen Scripture verses. Don't be afraid to say, *"God's book, the Bible, says . . .".*

ILLUSTRATION OF A SALVATION EXPLANATION:
*"First,* recognize that you are a sinner. We all gossip; we lie; we hate. The Bible declares, 'All have sinned' (Romans 3:23). *Second,* realize that there is a penalty for sin. The Bible says, 'The wages of sin is death' (Romans 6:23). And physical death leads to total separation from God for all eternity. *Third,* remember that you are bankrupt spiritually and cannot pay the penalty for your sin. Romans 5:8 says, 'While we were still sinners, Christ died for us.' Jesus Christ was our substitute. He took our place. And He rose again from the dead, proving that He paid the complete penalty for our sin.''

5. Write a strong conclusion that ties the entire tract together.

The conclusion will reflect your purpose in writing a tract in the first place. If you want the reader to trust Christ as Savior, don't be afraid to encourage him or her to do it. "Since, then, we know what it is to fear the Lord, we try to persuade men. . . . be reconciled to God" (2 Corinthians 5:11,20).

Make the invitation personal by including your name at the end of the tract. And if you want the reader to write you for helpful Christian literature, include your mailing address on the back.

ILLUSTRATION OF A GOOD CONCLUSION:
"But knowing these facts is not enough. We must believe in the Lord Jesus. 'Believe in the Lord Jesus, and you will be saved' (Acts 16:31). What does it mean to believe? When you use the fire extinguisher you are relying on it for safety. When you buckle up the seat belt you are trusting it to save you. You must make a decision to benefit from seat belts or fire extinguishers, and so it is with trusting Jesus as your Savior. What's keeping you from making that decision now?''

6. Now go back through your manuscript and make it better!

Rewrite, rewrite, rewrite! Don't be afraid to shorten your manuscript. It usually makes the message stronger. Have Christians who will give their honest opinions read your manuscript *after* you have rewritten it.

Have a non-Christian friend read your tract and give his opinion. Tell him, "I'm trying to explain the Gospel to (your "target" reader). Do you think I've made it clear?" This is a great way to *pre-test your tract . . .* and you will help your friend come closer to salvation!

*STEP FIVE: WORK HARD TO GET AN ATTENTION-GETTING TITLE*
A title that catches a person's attention as soon as he sees it is what you want. If the title doesn't interest the potential reader, all your hard work is for nothing.

So, write down as many possible titles as you can think of. Some ideas will probably come from wording in the tract itself. Perhaps a few words will capture the overall emphasis of the tract. Try titles that ask a question or that make a thought-provoking statement (like, ''When What You Know Isn't Enough''). Maybe a special saying in your country could be used with a spiritual application. Whatever you choose, choose wisely.

*STEP SIX: MAKE THE PRINTED TRACT AS NICE AS POSSIBLE*

By now you have done lots of hard work. All that remains is putting your tract into a suitable setting for your culture.

A good place to start is at a print shop in your area. The printer can tell you what would be the most economical way to print your tract. He can give you help in finding a typesetter (he may also have this service) and local artists if you want an illustration on the cover. He can probably also help you find a photograph if you need one.

Be sure the print is readable and that any pictures, illustrations, and colors you use are *fitting for your culture*. What works in another country may not work for you at all. Decide carefully, but don't be afraid to have a tract ''fail.'' If that happens, learn why it wasn't well received, and correct the mistakes when you write your next tract.

By the way, after your tract is prepared for printing, recheck every word and sentence again to discover any accidental errors that may have happened in the preparation process. To avoid disappointments, never print your tract without this final review.

Many people will judge a tract by its cover. That's why it's so important for tracts to look inviting. As you write new tracts, develop both a variety of covers and subjects.

*A REVIEW OF THE SIX STEPS TO CREATING AN EVANGELISTIC TRACT*

STEP ONE:   Choose your reader
STEP TWO:   Select a subject likely to interest your reader
STEP THREE:   Organize your ideas
STEP FOUR:   Fill in the details
STEP FIVE:   Work hard to get an attention-getting title
STEP SIX:   Make the printed tract as nice as possible

Now the challenge is yours to CREATE A TRACT! Continue to spread the Gospel through literature! You can do it by God's grace.

# HOLISTIC EVANGELISM: ITS SIGNIFICANCE IN THE SOCIO-ECONOMIC AND CULTURAL CONTEXT TODAY

*M. Ezra Sargunam*

William Carey's book, *An Enquiry Into the Obligations of Christians to Use Means for the Conversion of Heathens,* (1792), has been considered the Magna Carta of the modern missionary movement. The book has changed the life of the Church and the world in a manner Carey had never dreamed of. From the YMCA's triangular emphasis on body, soul, and spirit, to the Salvation Army's soap, soup, and salvation philosophy, almost all mission agencies have stressed *the total ministry of the total man.*

Since World War I, there has been a great shift in mission thinking on life values. It has often been said that a sick body can go to heaven, but not a sick soul. Missions in the past have concentrated on souls that are eternal instead of bodies that perish in Hades. School and hospital approaches have been frowned upon by "modern missionary zealots." It has also been alleged that "crazy" missionaries wasted their time producing educated pagans in Christian schools.

We now seem to be back where we started two hundred years ago. The only difference is that the oldtime missionary was so busy making history that he had no time to write about it. He planted churches while we plan churches. We talk about cross-cultures while he crossed cultures. He was an evangelist while we are evangelicals. He had the methodologies while we have the terminologies. The latest addition to the dictionary of missiology is the term "Holistic Evangelism."

*A scriptural mandate*

In behavioral science, the study of the whole personality of man is called "Holistic Psychology." The word "holistic," a derivative of wholistic, encompasses the total concept of what Christ's mission is all about—salvation of the entire man, both physical and spiritual.

In the Old Testament, salvation was primarily Yahweh's mighty act of deliverance for His children from political oppression, natural calamities, disease and death. Only during the time of the prophets did the inward transformation underlined in man's wrongdoing lead to the foretelling of an apocalyptic, messianic salvation (Isaiah 45:17; Daniel 7:13,14). The Old Testament doctrine of salvation is best described in the portrayal of the suffering servant (Isaiah 53). The Old Testament sets the scene for, and outlines, New Testament salvation.

Even the mission of the "Anointed One" was not to be confined to the preaching of good tidings alone. His mission also included binding up the brokenhearted, proclaiming liberty to the captives, and opening prisons for those who were bound (Isaiah 61:1-3; Luke 4:17-21). It is apparent that Old Testament salvation has celestial, terrestrial, physical, and spiritual aspects. Interestingly enough, Yahweh is invoked more often for physical deliverance than for spiritual deliverance. In Jonah's mission to the heathens, the Ninevites were asked to repent—not only for their personal salvation, but also for the salvation of their great walled city from total annihilation.

In the New Testament, the verbs *"sōzō"* and *"diasōzō"* both cover aspects of salvation in a wider spectrum. The words literally translated, mean saving from peril, injury or suffering (Matthew 8:25; Mark 13:20; Luke 23:35); and healing, restoring to health and being made whole (Matthew 9:22; Mark 5:34). The words also mean salvation from spiritual disease and death, whether it be past, present, or future (Romans 8:24; Acts 2:47; Matthew 10:22).

The Son of man inaugurated His ministry at a wedding by saving the master of the feast from embarrassment: He promptly produced wine from water. "This beginning of miracles did Jesus in Cana of Galilee," says John, "and manifested forth His glory and His disciples believed on Him" (John 2:11).

The question before us is whether we could also manifest the glory of God today by providing food for the hungry. Civil supply departments are at a quandary to try to handle the situation. Throughout His life and ministry, our Lord constantly made efforts to fulfill the spiritual and physical needs of the people around Him. After Jesus' preaching and teaching, the natural tendency of the disciples was to send the multitude away; but Christ's attitude was different. He wanted to make sure they were satisfied physically as well. It should be pointed out that feeding had always been preceded by solid preaching.

In India, we are always overwhelmed by poverty and hunger. But our Lord has taught us that we should begin with what we have. In Jesus' time, physical healings were often followed by spiritual admonitions, like "sin no more." It may be safer to conclude that the ministry of Christ's salvation is completed only when both the spiritual and physical needs are perceived and met. He has safeguarded against the danger of overplaying one, or of placing one against the other. At the same time, Jesus hated people staying around Him simply for a bowl of rice and free healing. He has refused to heal the sick just for the sake of healing, or feeding people just for the sake of satisfying hunger.

When Jesus reached the pinnacle of His popularity, He never decided to go one step further and restore the kingdom back to Israel, with the possibility of becoming king. Instead, He used that time to take the whip and cleanse the temple to restore the House of God, the seat of the spiritual kingdom. Since the road to justice, righteousness and truth was so rough and rugged, our Master encouraged His disciples to take a sword with them—not for perpetual use, but for the sense of security that they might derive from carrying them. Christ had ruled out the possibility of His followers using force in fighting for truth and justice. The supreme way of establishing love, truth, and righteousness was through suffering—and, if need be, laying down one's life for the cause.

*Should we drive wedges or build bridges between evangelism and social action?*

Why is the Church of Jesus Christ unable to make a noticeable impact on world evangelization? We have the vision, resources, personnel, and facilities at our disposal. In spite of them, we are making little progress. Our achievements amount to precious little in the form of souls brought into the Kingdom. Why?

We used to think sectarian quarrels and denominational and theological barriers were the causes for the polarization in Christian witness. But there are other causes, too. Specialized ministries, whether evangelistic or comprised of social action, were placed against each other. There is a total distinction between these two Christian responsibilities. Even worse is the fact that liberation from political, socio-economic oppression and suppression is at times called "salvation."

In recent conferences, at Melbourne ("Your Kingdom Come") and Pattaya ("How Shall They Hear?") the World Council of Churches and Lausanne Committee for World Evangelization were both concerned with the Church's mission to the world. There had perhaps been a distinction between the two conferences; while one focused its attention on the "poor," the other focused on the "lost."

Dr. John R.W. Stott feels that the Melbourne documents pulsate with indignation over human injustice and long to liberate the oppressed; whereas their call for world evangelization lacks a comparable passion. As for COWE, it was almost preoccupied with evangelism. This led to the issue of "Statement of Concerns," that was quickly signed by about 200 participants, mostly from the Third World. The "Statement of Concerns" criticized the conference for having backed down from the Lausanne Covenant's commitment to both evangelism and socio-political involvement.

However, I still feel that Pattaya came out with a well-balanced statement that both the church and the para-church organizations around the world should seriously consider putting into action: "Although evangelism and social action are not identical, we gladly reaffirm our commitment to both, and we endorse the Lausanne Covenant in its entirety. It remains the basis of our common activity, and nothing it contains is beyond our concern so long as it is clearly related to world evangelization."

We should not dissipate our God-given energy and the gifts of the Holy Spirit by driving wedges between evangelism and social action and other related ministries. Instead, we should strive wholeheartedly to build bridges between these two specialized ministries. This would result in the planting of strong indigenous churches among the unreached people of our generation. Let us desist from pulling in different directions. Let us take heed to John Stott's call for cooperative evangelism in fulfilling Christ's mission to the world: "My personal belief is that we should develop many more mission teams, so that evangelists, teachers, doctors, agriculturalists, social workers, and relief and development experts can work together in the name of Jesus Christ, offering a humble, holistic service to the whole neighborhood to which they have been called."

Although the primary concern of Amsterdam 83 was the training and equipping of itinerant evangelists, the conference did lay an emphasis on evangelism through relief and development. An information office was open throughout the conference, counseling and encouraging evangelists from all over the world to submit their applications for consideration in areas of social concern. The Billy Graham Evangelistic Association, which sponsored Amsterdam 83, funded the projects which met its carefully defined criteria. A number of projects in relief and development were funded by the Tear Fund U.K. and by the Dutch agency I.C.C.O., as referred to them by the Amsterdam 83 Follow-Up department. Rev. Franklin Graham, the president of Samaritan's Purse, undertook to fund some of the more than 600 project requests received.

During an Amsterdam 83 workshop conducted by Rev. Franklin Graham and Pastor Davidson, the founder of Grace Community Church at Tempe, Arizona, U.S.A., the need for a balanced holistic ministry was stressed: "We must also recognize that we must see the whole man and his total need. Underline the fact that if you see only his physical need, you will become a humanitarian. If you see only his mental need, you will become an educator. If you see only his political oppression, you will become a politician or a revolutionary. And if you see only his spiritual need, you will become a religionist. It is in seeing the whole man with the strongest emphasis on the spiritual that you become a Christian witness, a missionary, an evangelist, a communicator of God's Word" (*The Work of An Evangelist*, p. 855).

*Applied strategies on holistic evangelism*

Christian philanthropic organizations like Samaritan's Purse, Food for the Hungry, Tear Fund, and a great number of both Protestant and Catholic institutions have all engaged themselves in holistic evangelism in one form or another. For our pur-

pose, let us consider briefly a few strategies found to be effective along this line.
    Let us take a case study from the early part of the 17th century in South India.

1.   *Holistic evangelism through social reforms*
    Socially depressed groups, dominated by an oppressive force, whether economic, political, religious, or racial, are looking for better answers to life. They are often ready to accept the Christian solution. Those living in peace and security are satisfied with the answers. They are not seeking new ones.
    Those Christian missions who identify themselves with such groups and bring about social liberation through the Gospel of Jesus Christ, have added large numbers to the Christian faith.
    We remind ourselves of the example of the Old Trivancore Cochin State. The people belonging to the Nadar community were liberated from the suppression of the high caste Nairs by the London Missionary Society.
    There was a time in the Trivancore State of South India when the women of the low caste communities like Nadars (to which I belong) were not permitted to wear anything above their waist. When Christian women covered their breasts with loose, plain jackets, it was heavily objected to by the Nairs. It was considered an insult to them.
    From 1822 until 1856, great revolutions broke out. In all, there were three major "upper cloth" revolts. The men belonging to the high caste went around raping the women belonging to the lower caste. The missionaries and the young Christians gave their full support to the socially suppressed Nadar community. A dressmaking cottage industry known as the Dorcas Society was formed, and clothes were provided for the poor Christian women. As more blouses were ripped and torn by the high caste men and women, more clothes were made and supplied to the Nadar women. Even the Maharaja of Trivancore punished the Nairs and set the Nadars free. The missionaries and the native Christians continued their fight.
    Ultimately, the British Government passed an ordinance. A proclamation was issued on July 26, 1856, which allowed the Nadar women to cover themselves. In 1850, before this proclamation, there were 16,839 Christians and 210 churches with well-trained national pastors and teachers.
    Christian evangelists, missionaries, and churches should make every effort to put an end to social injustice and suppression. Many times, great motives for conversion are social and not necessarily theological.

2.   *Pre-evangelism efforts through rural development*
    Dr. Dhyanchand Carr, of the Tamilnadu Theological Seminary at Madurai in South India, reported at the first consultation of the Association for Evangelical Theological Education in India (AETEI) how his Rural Theological Institute (RTI) has been involved in various aspects of rural development, community health, economic development and self-employment programs in South India.
    In a few of the villages, the members of the Institute have very successfully trained and have organized basket weavers who were able to earn their living by making baskets out of palm leaves for packing jaggeries, fruits, and other perishables. Dr. Carr is now working on a project for this work to become more profitable to the basket weavers. He is organizing a cooperative society, enabling these poor, hard-working laborers to by-pass the rich middlemen to whom these baskets are being sold.
    The RTI community proclaims Christ to these poor villagers by explaining the reasons for their involvement in the village's welfare. In addition to these explana-

tions, the RTI seeks to celebrate Christmas and Easter by inviting the people to join in their joy. Dr. Carr concludes: "Increasingly, I am beginning to understand the nature of our work as a preparation for the Gospel rather than preaching the Gospel itself."

In the next case study, I shall attempt to show how the Evangelical Church of India (ECI) has capitalized in a number of areas where pre-evangelism efforts have already been started.

3. *Church planting through relief and development*

The Evangelical Church of India (ECI) was founded by OMS International about thirty years ago with the specific commitment for direct evangelism and church planting. ECI has grown to 300 churches with a membership of about 30,000. OMS, at the home base as well as in the fields, has already associated with the Holiness groups. Even pastors' wives were not allowed to hold secular jobs. We were neither trained nor engaged in social work. Then and now there were no budget allotments for relief of development ministries. Our philosophy has been primarily soul winning and not bread winning. However, the Lord has clearly led us into situations where we have reaped a bumper harvest of souls in places where other groups had been involved in social action.

To cite an example: about ten years ago, we had entered into the Jolarpet-Tirupathur area (150 miles northwest of Madras). We baptized 1,000 converts and planted more than twenty churches. The villages of the Jolarpet-Tirupathur region were very receptive because of the selfless medical service rendered for over fifty years by Dr. Patton and Dr. Savarirayan Jesudasan of Christukula Ashram. The harvest is being reaped today because these two stalwarts of the Indian Church had literally sown their lives in the good soil around Tirupathur.

Recently, we have opened a department with ECI for Relief and Development ministries with a small full-time staff. As much as possible, our strategy has been to work in full cooperation with our local churches. Subsequently, we have been encouraging relief and development projects throughout our local churches for the benefit of the poor, young converts who are otherwise deprived of job opportunities in the government as well as in private sectors. Our projects have also been a means to impress the message of the Gospel upon the hearts of thousands of non-Christians. As a result of seeing our ability to deliver goods, relief agencies such as World Vision of India and Samaritan's Purse came forward to assist us with a number of our projects.

Our relief programs also included flood and fire victims and others who suffer through national calamities. We are also involved in the Family Helper Program serving Christian and non-Christian orphan children, through Compassion of India.

Our relief programs normally included providing food, shelter, and clothing on a temporary basis. The program also included rehabilitation of the victims through our assistance. Local believers and seminary students were undoubtedly able to impress the love of Jesus Christ upon thousands of suffering people. In a few situations, we planted a few churches in the areas of our relief activities.

At the time of the flood and the cyclone in the city of Madras in October 1984, ECI had focused its relief efforts in North Madras through aid received from Samaritan's Purse. We further concentrated our efforts in one of the worst-hit pockets of this area by establishing a few families from a low-lying area to a higher level. We built a few thatched-roof houses and provided a well for them. We also supplied free clothing and food that lasted for several days. A place of worship was built, and an evangelist was appointed for follow-up efforts. Several families gave their hearts to Christ without any pressure or coercion from our side. A few families were baptized and became the nucleus of believers there.

The same day these converts were baptized, the new settlement was christened as FRANKLIN NAGAR (Colony) after Franklin Graham, the president of Samaritan's Purse. A church was born as a result of genuine loving and caring relief ministries.

Our development projects were geared to assist men and women in and around our churches. They were used to find employment through sewing, stitching, rope-making and similar cottage industries. Some of these projects were initially financed by the Grace Community Church of Tempe, Arizona.

Unlike some other evangelical groups, ECI has not rejected the good old "school and hospital approach" to evangelism. But there is a difference; our schools are connected with our local churches. I personally learned this principle from Accelerated Christian Education. Our church building facilities are put into good use during the week for running schools and in addition, for sewing, knitting, and other development programs. Undoubtedly, the local churches make a better impact with the message of the Gospel in the cities we seek to serve.

*Proposals for well-balanced holistic evangelism*

Let me outline a few practical suggestions for well-balanced holistic evangelism.

1. As true imitators of Christ, the church should find ways and means by which we relive the life of Christ. We should have a compassionate ministry to the total personality of man in meeting both his physical and spiritual needs.

2. In our attempt to present the total Gospel to the total man, let us in no way create an imbalance by over-emphasizing one or the other.

3. At the same time, we realize that our primary concern is the regeneration and reconciling of man to God. The church needs to listen to Dr. Donald McGavran who warns the church of leaning too heavily toward service missions and neglecting the preaching of the Word. Therefore, let us minimize social action and maximize Gospel action.

4. Relief work is only a means to an end. Service agencies need to come to grips with this awesome reality.

5. Where necessary, the church should not hesitate to identify with the suppressed and the oppressed. The church should take direct and indirect action to put an end to corruption, social injustice, and exploitation of all kinds. But this must be done with a clear understanding that political liberation is not spiritual salvation.

6. Churches in affluent countries must realize their moral responsibilities to the struggling churches in impoverished and under-privileged nations. The churches must come forward to do something other than merely sharing their leftovers. On the other hand, developing countries should not depend entirely on relief received from outside agencies. They should realize their own responsibilities in sharing what they have with their neighbors. Dr. Elmer Kilbourne of OMS International reports that the Korean churches were taught and trained to help each other and solve their own problems. This is one of the reasons why Korea has moved very rapidly toward self-reliance. This has resulted in the emergence in South Korea of some of the world's largest evangelical churches.

7. Relief organizations should constantly bear in mind that their foremost concern is to their fellow believers. They must minister to the widows and orphans and to the poor and needy in the household of faith (Acts 6:1-7; Galatians 6:10; 1 Corinthians 16:1; 2 Corinthians 8:9). In a broader perspective, we should not forget our obligation to the poor and the sick, in order that spiritual needs may be met and imperishable souls may be won.

8. Relief and development ministries must be implemented in and through the local churches. There is no better method of communicating the Gospel other than through relief operations of local Christians. Christian service agencies should try to avoid joining hands with government and other non-Christian agencies in relieving the sufferings of the people.

9. In our effort to meet physical needs, we should guard ourselves from the dangers of being accused of exploiting the exploited, and making "rice Christians" through inducement. Let us remember that we are going to be criticized at all times under all circumstances. Let us not become weary in doing good.

10. The relief activities, the submitting of reports and statistics and the financial transactions must be handled with the utmost care and caution. God expects both the giver and receiver to be good stewards of His money. Newspapers and periodicals in India often flash out scandalous statements about men and organizations who are involved in relief and social work. Thank God there are other organizations who maintain an excellent record of their finances and are above suspicion in all matters. They are in a position to be able to say with Paul:

> "We want to avoid any criticism of the way we administer this liberal gift. For we are taking pains to do what is right, not only in the eyes of the Lord, but also in the eyes of men" (2 Corinthians 8:20,21).

# IV

# CONTRIBUTORS

# CONTRIBUTORS

**Dr. Tokunboh Adeyemo** has been the General Secretary of the Association of Evangel-icals of Africa and Madagascar (A.E.A.M.) since 1978. Before working with A.E.A.M., he was a pastor and teacher in the United States. From 1970 to 1973, he was a traveling evangelist in Nigeria. Dr. Adeyemo has earned a bachelor's degree, master of divinity degree, and a doctor of philosophy degree. He has also published several books. He is chairman of the World Evangelical Fellowship Executive Council and an associate of the Lausanne Committee for World Evangelization. He and his wife, Ireti, have two children. His favorite Bible verse is Philippians 1:21.

**Mr. Jeff Y. Amano** works for Probe Ministries, Richardson, Texas, as a research asso-ciate, a position in which he analyzes new religious movements and evaluates them from a biblical perspective. A central part of his work at Probe is to lecture in classes on university and college campuses. This has given him many opportunities to demon-strate the uniqueness and superiority of Christianity in contrast to other belief systems, and has brought many into the body of Christ. A graduate of Northern Arizona Univer-sity, he received a master of theology degree at Dallas Theological Seminary. He and his wife, Debbie, have three children. His favorite Bible verse is 2 Corinthians 10:5.

**Reverend Panya Baba** is the director of the Evangelical Missionary Society in Jos, Nigeria. He coordinates sending out cross-cultural missionaries for evangelism and church planting. Reverend Baba conducts the seminars and orientations for missionaries in personal evangelism and for participation in city campaigns. Before working for EMS, he was a pastor for eight years and a missionary for four years. He earned a diploma from All Nations Christian College (U.K.), and also from the School of World Mission. He and his wife have eleven children and twelve grandchildren. His favorite Bible verse is 1 Corinthians 15:10.

**The Reverend Cliff Barrows** is vice chairman of the Board of Directors for the Billy Graham Evangelistic Association. He serves as radio and television program director, and has been the music director since Billy Graham's first crusade in 1949. Since 1950, he has been program director for the "Hour of Decision" radio broadcast. From 1965-1970, he was president of World Wide Pictures. Rev. Barrows studied sacred music at Bob Jones University in Greenville, South Carolina. He and his wife, Billie, have five children and twelve grandchildren, and live in Greenville, South Carolina. His favorite Bible verse is Isaiah 40:31.

**Lieutenant-Colonel John Bate** is a Salvation Army officer serving as chief secretary for the South America West Territory. He was a pastor in New Zealand for two years and has served with the Salvation Army in South America, Rhodesia, New Zealand, and Jamaica. In 1975 the Colonel was appointed to Great Britain as information officer; and in 1979 was appointed private secretary and A.D.C. to the international leader of the Salvation Army in which capacity he was able to visit every territory in which the Army works. Colonel Bate attended Victoria University, Wellington, New Zealand. He and his wife, Valda, have two children. His favorite Bible verse is John 10:10.

**Bishop Michael Baughen** is the Bishop of Chester (Church of England). Ordained in 1956, he has ministered in Nottingham, Reigate, and Manchester. He was Vicar, then

Rector of All Souls, Langham Place, in London. Bishop Baughen is particularly involved in music for congregational worship. He has edited several songbooks. Bishop Baughen has also published several books. He is a requested speaker at many conferences throughout Australia, the United States, Canada, England, and Europe. He has also been in the broadcasting field for many years. Briefly in accounting, he was then called into the ministry. He received his bachelor of divinity from the University of London. He and his wife, Myrtle, have three children. His favorite Bible verse is 2 Timothy 4:7.

**The Reverend Ralph S. Bell** is an associate evangelist with the Billy Graham Evangelistic Association in Minneapolis, Minnesota, a position he has held since 1965. Prior to that, he was pastor of West Washington Community Church in Los Angeles, California. Reverend Bell attended Moody Bible Institute in Chicago, Illinois; earned a bachelor of arts degree in history from Taylor University in Indiana; and a master of divinity degree from Fuller Theological Seminary in Pasadena, California. He and his wife, Jean, have two sons and live in Bellevue, Colorado, U.S.A. His favorite Bible verses are Jeremiah 29:11-13.

**Dr. Howard E. Brant** is the outreach coordinator for the international headquarters of SIM International. Since 1971, he has been preaching the Gospel in both east and west Africa with a special ministry among animistic tribes and Muslims. Today there are hundreds of believers and numerous churches as a result of his ministry. Dr. Brant attended Prairie Bible Institute, Canada; Seattle Pacific University; and Trinity Evangelical Seminary, U.S.A. He has also done correspondence studies through Fuller School of World Mission and is a graduate of the Nairobi Institute of Cross-Cultural Communication. His favorite Bible verse is Acts 26:18.

**Dr. Bill Bright** is founder and president of Campus Crusade for Christ International. Founded in 1951, Campus Crusade has a full-time and associate staff of over 16,000 working in more than 150 countries and protectorates. Dr. Bright is a graduate of Northeastern Bible College in Oklahoma, U.S.A. After teaching at Oklahoma State University, he completed graduate work at Princeton and Fuller Theological Seminaries. He is the author of numerous books, and has received many awards for his worldwide ministry to youth. Dr. Bright has received honorary doctorates from John Brown University, Los Angeles Bible College and Seminary, Joenbug National University of Korea, and Houghton College.

**Dr. L. John Bueno** is pastor of the Evangelistic Center in San Salvador, El Salvador, which has an average attendance of 20,000 persons each Sunday. It is a "filial church" program, in which individuals from the central church pastor other congregations in other parts of the city. Presently, Dr. Bueno is the sub-director of CELAD, the Executive Council of the Assemblies of God. Dr. Bueno earned a bachelor of arts degree from Bethany Bible College and was awarded an honorary doctor of law degree from the same school. He and his wife, Lois, have four sons and reside in San Salvador, El Salvador. His favorite Bible verse is 1 Corinthians 1:15.

**Reverend Irv Chambers** is the director of programs with Leighton Ford Ministries. From 1955-1962, he was the executive director of Sacandaga Bible Conferences, a Christian conference and camping ministry in Broadalbin, New York, U.S.A., and he has been associated with the Billy Graham Evangelistic Association since 1962. In his ministry, he has traveled to Australia, Europe, Asia, and South America. Reverend Chambers attended Moody Bible Institute and King's College. He and his wife, Marilyn, have two daughters, Shari and Susan. His favorite Bible verses are Joshua 1:8,9.

**Dr. Robert E. Coleman** is a professor of Evangelism as well as director of the School of World Mission and Evangelism and chairman of the Department of Mission and Evangelism at Trinity Evangelical Divinity School. He serves as chairman of the North American Lausanne Committee for World Evangelization. He also holds membership in the Evangelical Theological Society, National Association of Evangelicals, and the World Evangelical Fellowship. He is a graduate of Southwestern University, Asbury Theological Seminary, Princeton Theological Seminary; and the University of Iowa, U.S.A. He and his wife have three children and reside in Deerfield, Illinois, U.S.A.

**Mrs. Fred (Millie) Dienert** works with prayer ministry for the Billy Graham Evangelistic Association and is also an international consultant for International Christian Women's Clubs, based in Kansas City, Missouri. She was prayer director for Amsterdam 83 as well as Amsterdam 86. She was prayer coordinator for the Lausanne Congress on World Evangelization and has served on the board of directors for the International Christian Women's Clubs. She is a graduate of the Philadelphia College of Bible and also attended the University of Pennsylvania. She is a popular author and lecturer. She and her husband, Fred, have three children and nine grandchildren. Her favorite Bible verse is Ephesians 3:20.

**Dr. Robert P. Evans** is a special representative of the Billy Graham Evangelistic Association. In 1949, he founded Greater Europe Mission and continued as the mission's director until 1985. A pastor and evangelist for many years in the U.S.A., he has served as executive director and vice-president of Youth for Christ International, and has worked with Billy Graham crusades in various capacities. Dr. Evans received a bachelor of arts degree from Wheaton College, a master of divinity degree from Eastern Baptist Theological Seminary, a doctor of philosophy degree from the University of Manchester, and honorary doctorates from Wheaton College and Eastern College. He and his wife, Veanette, have one daughter. His favorite Bible verse is 2 Corinthians 8:9.

**Dr. Nilson Fanini** is pastor of the First Baptist Church in Niteroi, R.J. Brazil; and also the director and producer of REENCONTRO, a television program heard weekly throughout Brazil. He is a member of the Lausanne Committee for World Evangelization, president of the Baptist Theological Seminary of Niteroi, and has served as president of several Billy Graham Crusades in Brazil. He earned his bachelor's degree in law at the Universidad Federal Fluminese in Brazil, and his master's degree in theology at Southwestern Baptist Theological Seminary in Texas. He and his wife, Helga, have three children and live in Brazil. His favorite Bible verses are Job 42:1,2.

**Ajith Fernando** is national director for Youth For Christ in Sri Lanka. His ministry includes discipling youth workers, preaching, and Bible teaching. Mr. Fernando is a member of the Executive Committee of the Lausanne Committee for World Evangelization, and also a member of the Lausanne Younger Leaders Committee. He has published several books. Mr. Fernando earned a bachelor of science degree at the University of Ceylon, a master of divinity degree from Asbury Theological Seminary, and a master of theology degree from Fuller Theological Seminary. He and his wife, Nelun, have two children and live in Sri Lanka.

**Dr. Leighton S. Ford** was an associate evangelist of Dr. Billy Graham from 1955 through 1985 and spoke to audiences totaling more than three million, on every continent of the world. He has recently begun a new phase of his ministry with the formation of a new organization, Leighton Ford Ministries. He was Program Chairman for Amsterdam 83 and also for Amsterdam 86. He currently is Chairman of the Lausanne Committee for World Evangelization. He is a graduate of Wheaton College, Wheaton, Illinois; and of Columbia Theological Seminary, Decatur, Georgia. He has been awarded a doctor of divinity degree by Houghton College, Houghton, New York; and a doctor of literature and letters degree from Gordon College, Wenham, Massachusetts. He and his wife, Jean, live in Charlotte, North Carolina.

**William (Billy) F. Graham,** evangelist, lives in Montreat, North Carolina, U.S.A., and is the founder and president of the Billy Graham Evangelistic Association, based in Minneapolis, Minnesota, U.S.A. He is a graduate of Florida Bible Institute and Wheaton College. He was ordained as a Southern Baptist minister in 1940; and was pastor of First Baptist Church, Western Springs, Illinois, from 1943-1945. From 1947-1952, he was president of Northwestern Schools, Minneapolis. In 1950, he founded the Billy Graham Evangelistic Association. He has preached around the world, and has written more than ten books. He and his wife, Ruth (married in 1943), have five children: Virginia (Mrs. Stephen Tchividjian), Anne Morrow (Mrs. Dan Lotz), Ruth Bell (Mrs. Ted Dienert), William Franklin, and Nelson Edman.

**Dr. William Franklin Graham, III,** is president of Samaritan's Purse, an interdenominational relief organization working in remote areas of the world to provide assistance to missionaries, national pastors, and individuals in times of immediate need. Dr. Graham is also president of World Medical Mission, a companion organization of Samaritan's Purse, which was founded in 1977 to recruit physicians for short-term mission service around the world. A graduate of Montreat-Anderson College and Appalachian State University, Dr. Graham lives with his wife, Jane, and four children, in Boone, North Carolina, U.S.A. He is the son of Billy and Ruth Graham. His favorite Bible verses are Proverbs 3:5,6.

**Mr. Francis Grim** is the founder and president of the International Hospital Christian Fellowship, Voorthuizen, The Netherlands. For the past fifty years, he has traveled extensively and worked in the spiritual interest of those serving in the health field, a ministry that has taken him to over 100 countries. His current involvement in evangelism includes holding evangelistic meetings, as well as encouraging Christians worldwide to become involved in evangelism. The author of several books and articles, he is the president of South African Action for World Evangelization and is a member of the Action Moral Standards and Intercessors for South Africa. He and his wife, Erasmia, live in Kempton Park, South Africa. His favorite Bible verse is 2 Corinthians 9:8.

**Dr. Richard H. Harris** is the director of the Mass Evangelism Department of the Home Mission Board, Southern Baptist Convention, Atlanta, Georgia, U.S.A. He was a pastor from 1973-1981, and has served as a part-time evangelism consultant to the Baptist General Convention of Texas and the Kentucky Baptist Convention. He is a graduate of Cumberland College, Williamsburg, Kentucky; Eastern Kentucky State University; and Southwestern Baptist Theological Seminary, Fort Worth, Texas. He and his wife, Nancy, have two children. His favorite Bible verses are Proverbs 3:5,6.

**Dr. E.V. Hill** is pastor of Mount Zion Missionary Baptist Church in Los Angeles, California, U.S.A.

**Dr. Sterling W. Huston** is director of North American crusades for the Billy Graham Evangelistic Association. He was director of associate crusades from 1972 to 1973; personnel assistant, associate crusades, from 1969 to 1971; and crusade coordinator from 1966 to 1969. From 1961 to 1966 he was executive director for Rochester Youth for Christ, Rochester, New York, U.S.A. He is a graduate of the University of Maine, Maine, U.S.A., and the University of Rochester, Rochester, New York, U.S.A. In 1984, he received his Doctor of Divinity degree from Roberts Wesleyan College, Rochester, New York, U.S.A. He has also authored two books. He and his wife, Esther, have two children, and live in Rochester, New York, U.S.A.

**Dr. Arthur Johnston** is the first president of Tyndale Theological Seminary. For twenty years, he was the field chairman and missionary with TEAM in France, was president of St. Paul Bible College in Minnesota for one year, and was a professor of missions and evangelism at Trinity Evangelical Divinity School for eleven years. Ordained by the Christian and Missionary Alliance, he has written several books on evangelism. Dr. Johnston received a bachelor of arts and master of arts degree from Wheaton College, Illinois, U.S.A.; and a doctor of philosophy degree from the University of Strasbourg, France. He and his wife, Muriel, have five children. His favorite Bible verse is Psalm 84:11.

**Dr. Howard O. Jones** has been an associate evangelist on the Billy Graham team since 1958. He studied music at the Oberlin Conservatory of Music; but, following a deep conversion experience, he felt called to the ministry. Upon graduation from Nyack Bible College in New York, he pastored churches in New York City and Cleveland, Ohio. Dr. Jones has an international weekly radio broadcast entitled "The Hour of Freedom." He serves as a board member of the National Religious Broadcasters, and Baseball Chapel, Inc. He is active in evangelistic crusades, Bible conferences and missionary conventions. Dr. Jones has also authored three books. He and his wife, Wanda, have five children and live in Oberlin, Ohio, U.S.A.

**The Reverend Kassoum Keita** is the pastor of the Evangelical Church in Bomako. He was formerly president of the Evangelical Protestant Church in Mali, and president of the Evangelical Association of Churches in Mali. He was the director of the Here's Life campaign in Mali, and was the director of New Life For All campaigns in Mali from 1967-1970. He is the Regional Director for French-speaking West Africa for Campus Crusade for Christ. He studied at the Bible Institute in Mali, and has authored two books in French and five books in Bambara. He and his wife, Keritan, have nine children and live in Bomako, Mali. His favorite Bible verses are Ephesians 3:20,21.

**Dr. Jang Hwan (Billy) Kim** is the deputy vice chairman of Youth for Christ International and is the director of the Far East Broadcasting Company, Korea. Elected as vice chairman of Baptist World Alliance in 1985, he has also served as president of Youth for Christ in Korea, and has been active in city-wide crusades, conferences, and youth work. In 1982, he was recognized by the president of Korea for his contribution in the area of mass media. Dr. Kim is a graduate of Bob Jones University, South Carolina; and has received honorary doctorates from Trinity College and Southwestern Baptist University. He and his wife, Gertrude (Trudy) have three children and live in Seoul, Korea. His favorite Bible verses are Proverbs 3:5 6.

**Dr. T. E. Koshy** is evangelist and executive director of International Friendship Evangelism, Inc., Syracuse, New York, U.S.A. During his 34 years as an evangelist, he has had the opportunity of ministering among people from more than 100 countries. He and his wife, Dr. Indira Koshy, share in a hospitality ministry to international students. Born and raised in India, Dr. Koshy attended Bombay University, Moorlands Bible College, England, and has received a master of arts degree in journalism and a doctorate in mass communication from Syracuse University, U.S.A. He and his wife, Indira, have one son. His favorite Bible verse is 1 Corinthians 9:22.

**Richard Kriese** is a German Baptist evangelist. He participates in evangelistic crusades in Germany, Switzerland, and Austria. Mr. Kriese also works as a radio evangelist with Trans World Radio in German and Polish broadcasts. He was previously a Baptist pastor. Mr. Kriese is the author of twelve evangelical and Christian books. He is affiliated with the Lausanne Movement of Evangelism and Trans World Radio. First trained as an engineer, he was then called into the ministry. He completed his studies at the German Baptist Theological Seminary. He and his wife, Berti, have two daughters and one son. His favorite Bible verse is 2 Corinthians 12:9.

**Rev. Samuel O. Libert** is the president of the Evangelical Baptist Convention of Argentina. In addition to his pastoral ministry, he is a member of both the Latin American Theological Fraternity and the World Evangelism Strategy Group of the Baptist World Alliance. He has served for ten years as a member of the Lausanne Committee for World Evangelization, was the Southern Coordinator for the Baptist Crusade of the Americas, and has been active in itinerant evangelism in many countries of the world. Rev. Libert is the author of numerous evangelistic books, articles, and tracts. He and his wife, Rosa, have one daughter. His favorite Bible verse is Philippians 4:13.

**Mrs. Anne Graham Lotz,** daughter of Billy and Ruth Graham, is a noted Bible teacher in Raleigh, North Carolina, U.S.A. Mrs. Lotz started a Bible Study Fellowship Class in Raleigh that now involves thousands of men and women in weekly classes.

**Rev. Gideon Mahlathimi Makhanya** is the associate director of Evangelism Explosion III, South Africa (Pretoria) and general secretary of the Baptist Convention of Southern Africa. He was a pastor for ten years, was the traveling secretary of the Student Christian Movement for four years; and is currently teaching and training pastors and Christian leaders in Evangelism Explosion in South Africa, Zimbabwe, and Zambia. Rev. Makhanya received a diploma in theology and has earned certificates in Evangelism Explosion III as an international teacher and senior teacher. He and his wife, Dorothy, have three children. His favorite Bible verse is John 3:16.

**Reverend John Mallison** of John Mallison Ministries, works with the Uniting Church in Australia, where he is the director and minister for leadership development. He was a parish minister for 17 years and was involved in full-time Christian education for 14 years. He is now a consultant and trainer in the area of nurturing new Christians, life-style evangelism and the role of small groups in evangelism. Reverend Mallison earned a degree in theology from Sydney School of Theology at Sydney University. He and his wife, June, have four children. His favorite Bible verse is Revelation 3:8.

**Floyd McClung, Jr.** is the director of Youth With A Mission for Europe, the Middle East and Africa. He also serves on the International Council of Youth With A Mission.

With his wife Sally, he has ministered in the West Indies, the South Pacific, and in Afghanistan. The second coup when the Communists took over Afghanistan in 1979 caused the closing down of their ministry there. Floyd and his family are now based in Holland, specifically working with "Urban Missions" in Amsterdam. He earned a degree from Southern California College in 1964. The author of four books, he is also a popular speaker at universities and conferences. He and his wife, Sally, have two children.

**Dr. Barry Moore** is the president and evangelist of Barry Moore Ministries, London, Ontario, Canada. For the past 25 years he has ministered in city-wide crusades throughout Canada and in 39 other countries. Dr. Moore received a bachelor of arts degree from the University of Western Ontario, a master of arts degree from Columbia Bible College, and a doctor of divinity degree from Winnipeg Bible Seminary. He is a board member of Greater Europe Mission and Gospel Missionary Union. The parents of three children, he and his wife, Audrey, reside in London, Ontario. His favorite Bible verse is Psalm 84:11.

**Reverend Stephen Mung'oma** works with African Evangelistic Enterprise, an interdenominational Christian organization in Nairobi, Kenya. He is an evangelist involved in many facets of preaching, teaching and training.

**Dr. Stephen F. Olford** is president of Encounter Ministries, Incorporated. Dr. Billy Graham calls him "the man who most influenced my ministry." From Great Britain, he has been a broadcaster for 25 years and is presently heard in the U.S. and around the world on the program, ENCOUNTER. In 1970, Dr. Olford launched Encounter Ministries, Incorporated, an interdenominational organization, dedicated to the fulfilling of the Great Commission. He is also the Editor/Writer/Producer of a sermon preparation service in the United States. Dr. Olford is recognized all over the world for his expository preaching and pastoral leadership. He and his wife, Heather, have two sons and live in Wheaton, Illinois, U.S.A. His favorite Bible verse is Galatians 2:20.

**Lloyd W. Olson** is currently working with Campus Crusade for Christ in Arrowhead Springs, California, U.S.A., in the area of special strategies and projects. He served as a coordinator for Explo 85, has worked with Christian leaders in 37 countries, and co-authored a book on accounting for missionary organizations. He is a member of the Evangelical Foreign Mission Association, Evangelical Council for Financial Accountability, and Christian Ministries Management Association. Mr. Olson has earned a bachelor of science degree in business from the University of California in Los Angeles and is a certified public accountant. He and his wife, Johanna, have five children. His favorite Bible verse is Philippians 3:10.

**The Reverend Gottfried Osei-Mensah** works with the Billy Graham Evangelistic Association in special ministry to pastors, churches, and students. Previously, he was the executive secretary of the Lausanne Committee for World Evangelization; and also the pastor of the Nairobi Baptist Church in Kenya. Before he entered the ministry, he was a sales engineer for Mobil Oil, Ghana, Ltd. Rev. Osei-Mensah is also the vice-president of the International Fellowship of Evangelical Students (IFES). He graduated with a bachelor of science degree in chemical engineering from Birmingham University (U.K.). He and his wife, Audrey, have two children. His favorite Bible verse is Galatians 2:20.

**Dr. Luis Palau** is president of the Luis Palau Evangelistic Team, based in Portland, Oregon. Dr. Palau has spoken before more than six million people in 39 nations, plus millions more through worldwide radio and television broadcasts. His team has held more than 100 crusades and rallies throughout the United States, Latin America, and Europe. He has written fifteen books that have been translated into many different languages. Dr. Palau is a graduate of St. Albans College, Buenos Aires, Argentina; and received an honorary doctor of divinity degree from Talbot Theological Seminary, La Mirada, California. He and his wife, Pat, have four sons. His favorite Bible verse is Galatians 2:20.

**Dr. Abraham Philip** is the founder and director of New India Evangelistic Association. He has been serving the Lord as an evangelist for the last ten years, and was principal of the New India Bible College. A citizen of India, he taught in schools and colleges in Ethiopia and Nigeria from 1964-74. Ordained in the New India Bible Church, he has trained young people for evangelistic and pastoral ministry and has been involved in church planting. Dr. Philip earned a doctorate in missions from School of World Mission, Pasadena, California. He and his wife, Ann, have three children. His favorite Bible verses are Matthew 28:19,20.

**Dr. Tom Phillips** is director of counseling and follow-up administration—and is also a crusade director—for the Billy Graham Evangelistic Association. He has been with the Billy Graham Evangelistic Association since 1974. Dr. Phillips has served in crusades in the U.S.A. and all over the world, and as an instructor at the School of Evangelism for Billy Graham Crusades. He formerly pastored churches in Indiana and Mississippi, U.S.A. Dr. Phillips received a degree from the University of Mississippi, a master of divinity degree from Southern Baptist Theological Seminary, and a doctor of ministry degree from Southern Baptist Theological Seminary. He and his wife, Ouida, have three children and reside in Tacoma, Washington, U.S.A. His favorite Bible verse is Psalm 67:2.

**Charlie Riggs** is a crusade director and Director of Counseling and Follow-up for the Billy Graham Evangelistic Association based in Minneapolis, Minnesota, U.S.A.

**Mr. John D. Robb** is the senior research associate for unreached peoples, with MARC (Missions Advanced Research and Communication) World Vision International, a ministry working with national leaders to stimulate evangelization of unreached peoples. From 1966-1970, he was involved in campus evangelism; worked the next three years in a coffeehouse ministry; and served as a missionary in Malaysia before joining MARC in 1985. Mr. Robb received bachelor and master of arts degrees from Yale University and a master of divinity degree from Trinity Evangelical Divinity School. He and his wife, Lori, have three children. His favorite Bible verse is Philippians 4:13.

**Douglas D. Salser** is the director of publications for the American Tract Society in Garland, Texas, U.S.A. He is involved in selecting topics, editing and supervising publications, and follow-up with new converts. He has served as a pastor; and was executive director for Youth for Christ in Vancouver, Washington, for four years. He is a member of the Christian Ministries Management Association, Christian Booksellers Association, and the Evangelical Christian Publishers Association. Mr. Salser is a graduate of Dallas Bible College and has earned a master of theology degree from Dallas Theological Seminary. He and his wife, Linda, have two sons. His favorite Bible verses are Hebrews 12:1,2.

**Dr. M. Ezra Sargunum** is the vice president for Evangelism and Outreach for the Evangelical Church of India (ECI). He served as president of the ECI for nine years ECI has 311 churches located all over the country of India. Dr. Sargunum has ministered in the U.S.A., Great Britain, South Korea, Japan, and several other Far Eastern countries. He has earned a bachelor's degree, a master of divinity degree, master of arts degree; has received an honorary doctorate, and is currently working on his doctor of philosophy degree from William Carey International University. He and his wife have two daughters. His favorite Bible verse is Acts 20:24.

**Mr. Glen L. Sheppard** serves on the staff of the Home Mission Board, Atlanta, Georgia, as special assistant in spiritual awakening with the Evangelism Section. Before assuming his present position, he pastored churches in Georgia and Kentucky and has spoken extensively in the United States and abroad. He has written articles for several Southern Baptist Convention publications and is the author of a seminar on prayer. Mr. Sheppard is a graduate of Valdosta State College, Valdosta, Georgia; and Southern Baptist Theological Seminary, Louisville, Kentucky. He and his wife, Jacquelyn, have three children and live in Atlanta, Georgia, U.S.A. His favorite Bible verse is Philippians 1:6.

**Joanne J. Shetler** works for Wycliffe Bible Translators doing Bible translations in the Philippines. She currently heads the anthropology department of the Philippine branch and works as a consultant for "Scriptures-In-Use." For the past 25 years, she has been establishing and encouraging tribal people to reach out to their own families and beyond their own borders in evangelism and discipling. In 1982, twenty years after its inception, she and her fellow workers dedicated their finished translation of the New Testament in the language of Balangao. Joanne Shetler has a bachelor of arts degree from Biola University. She is currently working on her master's degree at Fuller School of World Mission. Her favorite Bible verse is John 15:16.

**Mr. Bernie Smith** works with "Bridging the Gap" located in Calgary, Alberta, Canada, primarily a youth ministry. For seven years he worked with Inter Varsity Christian Fellowship; and has spent the last nine years in faith ministry including freelance preaching, conference speaking, song leading, and ministering among young people. While serving with Venture Teams in Kenya, he saw several hundred come to Christ, and has also had an effective ministry among Koreans in Calgary. The author of numerous Bible studies and follow-up materials, Mr. Smith is a graduate of Kent State University, Kent, Ohio, U.S.A. He and his wife, Margaret, have two children. His favorite Bible verse is Psalm 40:3.

**Dr. Paul B. Smith** is the senior minister of the Peoples Church, Toronto, Canada. He worked ten years as an itinerant evangelist, has written 15 books, and has held evangelistic crusades in over eighty countries and territories. His Bible-teaching ministry has been featured on many of the outstanding Bible conference platforms of the world. In 1983 he made four films on world missions and faith promise offerings, and currently appears on a weekly television broadcast. Dr. Smith has earned doctorates of divinity, literature, and humanities. He and his wife, Anita, have three children. His favorite Bible verse is 1 Corinthians 13:7.

**Gaetano (Guy) Sottile** is the founder and president of Harvest Ministries, based in Seattle, Washington, and Messina, Italy. He was previously involved in church planting.

Mr. Sottile has participated in crusades in the United States and throughout Italy. He has also ministered in Canada. Mr. Sottile received a bachelor of arts degree from Columbia Bible College in 1979. His wife, Sondra, was formerly a professional studio singer and now accompanies him in his ministry. His favorite Bible verse is Galatians 2:20.

**Reverend David Stillman** is the founder of the David Stillman Evangelistic Association in Reading, England. Previously, he was a board member of the British Youth for Christ. He has also served as the minister of evangelism at Calvary Baptist Church in Virginia Beach, Virginia. He is currently involved in the development of prison ministry in Great Britain. In addition to England, he has ministered in countries all over the world. He was educated at King Alfred's School in Wantage, England, and the Reading School of Technology. He and his wife, Theresa, have two children. His favorite Bible verses are John 12:24,25.

**Dr. George Sweeting** is the president of Moody Bible Institute, Chicago, Illinois, U.S.A. He is the editor-in-chief of *Moody Monthly* magazine, a weekly speaker on the international radio broadcast "Moody Presents," and has been featured in a number of Moody Institute of Science films. From 1951-1961, he traveled worldwide as an evangelist, and has served as a pastor for over ten years. Dr. Sweeting has received an honorary doctor of divinity degree from Gordon-Conwell Theological Seminary, an honorary doctor of humanities degree from Azusa Pacific College, an honorary doctor of laws degree from Tennessee Temple College, and an honorary doctor of letters degree from John Brown University. He and his wife, Margaret, have four sons.

**Dr. Stephan Tchividjian** holds a Ph.D. in Psychology from Marquette University, and has a busy practice in South Florida. Born and raised in Switzerland, he completed studies in Humanities at Lausanne and spent several years in the family investment business before making the move to his current career. Dr. Tchividjian's other responsibilities include the training of lay counselors, an active teaching and speaking schedule around the U.S., and involvement with Youth for Christ, Samaritan's Purse, and World Medical Missions. He and his wife, Gigi Graham Tchividjian, have seven children.

**Reverend Agustin B. Vencer, Jr.,** works with the Philippine Council of Evangelical Churches, World Relief Corporation, Phils. Relief and Development Services (PHILRADS), and Alliance Fellowship Church. Active in evangelism, he has ministered in the Philippines, Central African Republic, Singapore, Hong Kong, Seoul, Japan, the Netherlands, U.S.A., and the United Kingdom. he is the author of several books and is a member of the Integrated Bar of the Philippines. Rev. Vencer received a bachelor of science degree in pre-medicine and a bachelor of laws degree. He and his wife, Annabella, have four children. His favorite Bible verses are Philippians 3:13,14.

**John Wesley White** is an Associate Evangelist with the Billy Graham Evangelistic Association and the author of 17 books, including his latest works: *The Survivors, Arming For Armageddon,* and *The Man From Krypton.*

**Robert L. Williams** is the Associate Director, International Conference For Itinerant Evangelists, Amsterdam, The Netherlands, and a Crusade Associate with the Billy Graham Evangelistic Association.

**Evangelist Shad Williams** is the president of Shad Williams Evangelistic Association, Memphis, Tennessee, U.S.A., and is the international director of Global Field Evangelism. His ministry has included one year with Memphis Union Mission, two years with the Scarlet Thread (a youth evangelism ministry), three years as a youth evangelist in the Southern Baptist Convention, four years as youth minister at Briarcrest Baptist Church, and nine years as international evangelist in Africa, South America, Central America, the Caribbean, and the Orient. Mr. Williams received a bachelor of arts degree from Union University, Tennessee. He and his wife, Sheila, have two children. His favorite Bible verse is Psalm 57:2.

**Dr. T. W. Wilson** is an association evangelist for the Billy Graham Evangelistic Association and executive assistant to Dr. Billy Graham. A pastor from 1942-1945, he was vice-president for Youth for Christ International from 1946-1948, and was an independent itinerant evangelist for four years. He has served as Chairman of the Board of the Christian Broadcasting Company and president of Blue Ridge Broadcasting Corporation. He graduated from Bob Jones University, U.S.A.; attended the University of Alabama and Faith Theological Seminary; earned doctor's degrees from Bob Jones University and Trinity College; and received an honorary doctorate from Gordon-Conwell Theological Seminary. He and his wife, Mary, have two children. His favorite Bible verse is Romans 8:28.

**Dr. Sherwood E. Wirt** is the founder of the Christian Writers' Guild of San Diego County, California, U.S.A. A pastor from 1951-1959, he became the founding editor of DECISION magazine in 1959, a position he held until his retirement in 1976. He has served with the Billy Graham Team ministries as both an evangelist and a writer. The author of 18 books, Dr. Wirt earned a bachelor of arts degree from the University of California, a bachelor of divinity degree from Pacific School of Religion, and a doctor of philosophy degree from the University of Edinburgh, Scotland. He and his wife, Winola, have one son. His favorite Bible verse is Romans 5:5.

**Dr. Ravi K. Zacharias** is the president of Ravi Zacharias International Ministries, based in Atlanta, Georgia, U.S.A. From 1981-1984, he held the Chair of Evangelism and Contemporary Thought at Alliance Theological Seminary. He conducts evangelistic meetings, conferences, and seminars around the world. He is well-versed in comparative religions, cults, and secular philosophies. Dr. Zacharias graduated with a bachelor's degree from Ontario Bible College in Toronto, Canada. He graduated summa cum laude from Trinity Evangelical School in Deerfield, Illinois; and was also awarded an honorary doctor of divinity degree from Houghton College in New York. He and his wife, Margaret, have three children. His favorite Bible verses are Romans 1:16, and Psalm 37:5.

# V

# THE AMSTERDAM
# AFFIRMATIONS

## I

We confess Jesus Christ as God, our Lord and Savior, who is revealed in the Bible, which is the infallible Word of God.

## II

We affirm our commitment to the Great Commission of our Lord, and we declare our willingness to go anywhere, do anything, and sacrifice anything God requires of us in the fulfillment of that Commission.

## III

We respond to God's call to the biblical ministry of the evangelist, and accept our solemn responsibility to preach the Word to all peoples as God gives opportunity.

## IV

God loves every human being, who, apart from faith in Christ, is under God's judgment and destined for hell.

## V

The heart of the biblical message is the good news of God's salvation, which comes by grace alone through faith in the risen Lord Jesus Christ and His atoning death on the cross for our sins.

## VI

In our proclamation of the Gospel we recognize the urgency of calling all to decision to follow Jesus Christ as Lord and Savior, and to do so lovingly and without coercion or manipulation.

## VII

We need and desire to be filled and controlled by the Holy Spirit as we bear witness to the Gospel of Jesus Christ, because God alone can turn sinners from their sin and bring them to everlasting life.

## VIII

We acknowledge our obligation, as servants of God, to lead lives of holiness and moral purity, knowing that we exemplify Christ to the church and to the world.

## IX

A life of regular and faithful prayer and Bible study is essential to our personal spiritual growth, and to our power for ministry.

## X

We will be faithful stewards of all that God gives us, and will be accountable to others in the finances of our ministry, and honest in reporting our statistics.

## XI

Our families are a responsibility given to us by God, and are a sacred trust to be kept as faithfully as our call to minister to others.

## XII

We are responsible to the church, and will endeavor always to conduct our ministries so as to build up the local Body of believers and serve the church at large.

## XIII

We are responsible to arrange for the spiritual care of those who come to faith under our ministry, to encourage them to identify with the local Body of believers, and seek to provide for the instruction of believers in witnessing to the Gospel.

## XIV

We share Christ's deep concern for the personal and social sufferings of humanity, and we accept our responsibility as Christians and as evangelists to do our utmost to alleviate human need.

## XV

We beseech the Body of Christ to join with us in prayer and work for peace in our world, for revival and a renewed dedication to the biblical priority of evangelism in the church, and for the oneness of believers in Christ for the fulfillment of the Great Commission, until Christ returns.